1992
YEAR BOOK OF
PEDIATRICS®

The 1992 Year Book® Series

Year Book of Anesthesia and Pain Management: Drs. Miller, Kirby, Ostheimer, Roizen, and Stoelting

Year Book of Cardiology®: Drs. Schlant, Collins, Engle, Frye, Kaplan, and O'Rourke

Year Book of Critical Care Medicine®: Drs. Rogers and Parrillo

Year Book of Dentistry®: Drs. Meskin, Currier, Kennedy, Leinfelder, Matukas, and Rovin

Year Book of Dermatologic Surgery: Drs. Swanson, Salasche, and Glogau

Year Book of Dermatology®: Drs. Sober and Fitzpatrick

Year Book of Diagnostic Radiology®: Drs. Federle, Clark, Gross, Madewell, Maynard, Sackett, and Young

Year Book of Digestive Diseases®: Drs. Greenberger and Moody

Year Book of Drug Therapy®: Drs. Lasagna and Weintraub

Year Book of Emergency Medicine®: Drs. Wagner, Burdick, Davidson, Roberts, and Spivey

Year Book of Endocrinology®: Drs. Bagdade, Braverman, Horton, Kannan, Landsberg, Molitch, Morley, Odell, Rogol, Ryan, and Sherwin

Year Book of Family Practice®: Drs. Berg, Bowman, Davidson, Dietrich, and Scherger

Year Book of Geriatrics and Gerontology®: Drs. Beck, Abrass, Burton, Cummings, Makinodan, and Small

Year Book of Hand Surgery®: Drs. Amadio and Hentz

Year Book of Health Care Management: Drs. Heyssel, Brock, King, and Steinberg, Ms. Avakian, and Messrs. Berman, Kues, and Rosenberg

Year Book of Hematology®: Drs. Spivak, Bell, Ness, Quesenberry, and Wiernik

Year Book of Infectious Diseases®: Drs. Wolff, Barza, Keusch, Klempner, and Snydman

Year Book of Infertility: Drs. Mishell, Paulsen, and Lobo

Year Book of Medicine®: Drs. Rogers, Bone, Cline, Braunwald, Greenberger, Utiger, Epstein, and Malawista

Year Book of Neonatal and Perinatal Medicine®: Drs. Klaus and Fanaroff

Year Book of Nephrology®: Drs. Coe, Favus, Henderson, Kashgarian, Luke, Myers, and Strom

Year Book of Neurology and Neurosurgery: Drs. Currier and Crowell

Year Book of Neuroradiology: Drs. Osborn, Harnsberger, Halbach, and Grossman

Year Book of Nuclear Medicine®: Drs. Hoffer, Gore, Gottschalk, Sostman, Zaret, and Zubal

Year Book of Obstetrics and Gynecology®: Drs. Mishell, Kirschbaum, and Morrow

Year Book of Occupational and Environmental Medicine: Drs. Emmett, Brooks, Harris, and Schenker

Year Book of Oncology: Drs. Young, Longo, Ozols, Simone, Steele, and Weichselbaum

Year Book of Ophthalmology®: Drs. Laibson, Adams, Augsberger, Benson, Cohen, Eagle, Flanagan, Nelson, Reinecke, Sergott, and Wilson

Year Book of Orthopedics®: Drs. Sledge, Poss, Cofield, Frymoyer, Griffin, Hansen, Johnson, Simmons, and Springfield

Year Book of Otolaryngology–Head and Neck Surgery®: Drs. Bailey and Paparella

Year Book of Pathology and Clinical Pathology®: Drs. Gardner, Bennett, Cousar, Garvin, and Worsham

Year Book of Pediatrics®: Dr. Stockman

Year Book of Plastic, Reconstructive, and Aesthetic Surgery: Drs. Miller, Cohen, McKinney, Robson, Ruberg, and Whitaker

Year Book of Psychiatry and Applied Mental Health®: Drs. Talbott, Franes, Freedman, Meltzer, Perry, Schowalter, and Yudofsky

Year Book of Pulmonary Disease®: Drs. Bone and Petty

Year Book of Podiatric Medicine and Surgery®: Dr. La Porta

Year Book of Psychiatry and Applied Mental Health®: Drs. Talbott, Frances, Freedman, Meltzer, Perry, Schowalter, and Yudofsky

Year Book of Pulmonary Disease®: Drs. Bone and Petty

Year Book of Speech, Language, and Hearing: Drs. Bernthal, Hall, and Tomblin

Year Book of Sports Medicine®: Drs. Shephard, Eichner, Sutton, and Torg, Col. Anderson, and Mr. George

Year Book of Surgery®: Drs. Schwartz, Jonasson, Robson, Shires, Spencer, and Thompson

Year Book of Transplantation: Drs. Ascher, Hansen, and Strom

Year Book of Ultrasound: Drs. Merritt, Mittelstaedt, Carroll, and Nyberg

Year Book of Urology®: Drs. Gillenwater and Howards

Year Book of Vascular Surgery®: Dr. Bergan

Roundsmanship '92–'93: A Year Book® Guide to Clinical Medicine: Drs. Dan, Feigin, Quilligan, Schrock, Stein, and Talbot

1992

The Year Book of PEDIATRICS®

Editor

James A. Stockman, III, M.D.

Professor and Chairman, Department of Pediatrics, and Associate Dean for Hospital Academic Affairs, Northwestern University Medical School; Physician-in-Chief, The Children's Memorial Hospital, Chicago

Mosby Year Book

St. Louis   Baltimore   Boston   Chicago   London   Philadelphia   Sydney   Toronto

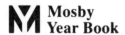
Mosby
Year Book

Dedicated to Publishing Excellence

Editor-in-Chief, Year Book Publishing: Kenneth H. Killion
Sponsoring Editor: Kelly Blossfeld
Manager, Medical Information Services: Edith M. Podrazik
Senior Medical Information Specialist: Terri Strorigl
Senior Medical Writer: David A. Cramer, M.D.
Assistant Director, Manuscript Services: Frances M. Perveiler
Assistant Managing Editor, Year Book Editing Services: Connie Murray
Production Coordinator: Max F. Perez
Proofroom Manager: Barbara M. Kelly

Editorial Office:
Mosby-Year Book, Inc.
200 North LaSalle St.
Chicago, IL 60601

International Standard Serial Number: 1041-1909
International Standard Book Number: 0-8151-6587-0

Table of Contents

The material covered in this volume represents literature reviewed through May 1990.

Journals Represented

Mosby–Year Book subscribes to and surveys nearly 850 U.S. and foreign medical and allied health journals. From these journals, the Editors select the articles to be abstracted. Journals represented in this YEAR BOOK are listed below.

Acta Psychiatrica Scandinavica
American Heart Journal
American Journal of Diseases of Children
American Journal of Emergency Medicine
American Journal of Hematology
American Journal of Human Genetics
American Journal of Medicine
American Journal of Obstetrics and Gynecology
American Journal of Ophthalmology
American Journal of Orthopsychiatry
American Journal of Pediatric Hematology/Oncology
American Journal of Preventive Medicine
American Journal of Public Health
American Journal of Roentgenology
Anesthesia and Analgesia
Annals of Emergency Medicine
Annals of Neurology
Annals of Surgery
Archives of Dermatolgy
Archives of Disease in Childhood
Archives of Ophthalmology
Archives of Surgery
Arthritis and Rheumatism
Blood
British Journal of Cancer
British Journal of Ophthalmology
Canadian Journal of Psychiatry
Canadian Journal of Public Health
Cancer
Child Development
Clinical Genetics
Clinical Orthopaedics and Related Research
Clinical Pediatrics
Clinical and Experimental Allergy
Clinical and Experimental Dermatology
Contact Dermatitis
Critical Care Medicine
Developmental Medicine and Child Neurology
European Journal of Pediatrics
International Journal of Epidemiology
International Journal of Radiation, Oncology, Biology, and Physics
Journal of Acquired Immune Deficiency Syndromes
Journal of Adolescent Health Care
Journal of Allergy and Clinical Immunology
Journal of Applied Behavioral Analysis
Journal of Applied Physiology
Journal of Bone and Joint Surgery (American Volume)
Journal of Burn Care and Rehabilitation

Journal of Clinical Endocrinology and Metabolism
Journal of Clinical Microbiology
Journal of Clinical Oncology
Journal of Dental Research
Journal of Developmental and Behavioral Pediatrics
Journal of Infectious Diseases
Journal of Medical Genetics
Journal of Paediatrics and Child Health
Journal of Pediatric Gastroenterology and Nutrition
Journal of Pediatric Ophthalmology and Strabismus
Journal of Pediatric Orthopedics
Journal of Pediatric Surgery
Journal of Pediatrics
Journal of Perinatology
Journal of Rheumatology
Journal of Trauma
Journal of Urology
Journal of the American Academy of Child and Adolescent Psychiatry
Journal of the American College of Cardiology
Journal of the American Medical Association
Kidney International
Lancet
Medicine and Science in Sports and Exercise
Nature
New England Journal of Medicine
Obstetrics and Gynecology
Ophthalmology
Otolaryngology—Head and Neck Surgery
PACE
Pediatric Cardiology
Pediatric Dermatology
Pediatric Emergency Care
Pediatric Infectious Disease Journal
Pediatric Pulmonology
Pediatric Radiology
Pediatrics
Prenatal Diagnosis
Respiratory Medicine
Reviews of Infectious Diseases
Southern Medical Journal
Spine
Transplantation

The following terms are abbreviated in this edition: acquired immunodeficiency syndrome (AIDS), the central nervous system (CNS), cerebrospinal fluid (CSF), computed tomography (CT), electrocardiography (ECG), human immunodeficiency virus (HIV), and magnetic resonance (MR) imaging (MRI).

Publisher's Preface

The 1992 volume of YEAR BOOK OF PEDIATRICS marks the first volume to be edited solely by James A. Stockman, III, M.D., following a 13-volume collaboration between Frank A. Oski, M.D., and Dr. Stockman. Dr. Stockman has applied his formidable energy and intelligence to his expanded responsibilities, and we believe the quality of his work will speak for itself.

Introduction

As I remarked in the Introduction to the 1991 YEAR BOOK, it was going to be difficult for me alone to maintain the tradition of quality that spanned more than a decade of co-editorship with Dr. Oski. This is the first edition of the YEAR BOOK in 14 years that does not have the name "Oski" on the cover. The readers probably did not realize it, but during that period, one of us edited the first half of the book and the other edited the remainder. We continued to edit the same chapters all that time, never switching. Imagine what it was like feeling that you probably knew only half of the pediatric literature. Eyes, ears, hearts, lungs, the gastrointestinal tract, blood, tumors, thyroids, muscles, and kidneys became sort of my forte. Food, newborns, skin, neurology, adolescents, toxins, and infectious diseases—well, they tended to be in the "other half" of the YEAR BOOK. As the only editor, I must now review not just half but the "whole" of the literature. Not surprisingly, the "whole" seems much greater than the sum of its parts. Keeping up with the rapid progress that is occurring in the field of pediatrics is not an easy task. That, of course, is why the YEAR BOOK exists.

There are approximately 280 articles abstracted from last year's literature within these pages and commentaries on most of these subjects, with frequent digression into topic areas including the following:

- Medicaid and the poor
- Malpractice experiences in pediatric emergency room
- Mercury and our teeth
- New information on inherited disorders such as phenylketonuria and biotinidase deficiency
- Current concepts in vaccine administration
- Recombinant drugs and the athlete (the impact of Epogen, recombinant erythropoietin)
- Extracorporeal membrane oxygenation
- The latest in heart, lung, kidney, liver, and bone marrow transplantation
- Old standbys such as otitis media and congenital dislocation of the hips

We trust that you will enjoy reading about these and many other fascinating developments in our chosen field of pediatrics. Above all, remember that the task of learning is best characterized by the ancient Latin words: "Nullum obesa cantavit"—It ain't over till the fat lady sings.

James A. Stockman, III, M.D.

1   The Newborn

Early Postnatal Dexamethasone Therapy in Premature Infants With Severe Respiratory Distress Syndrome: A Double-Blind, Controlled Study
Yeh TF, Torre JA, Rastogi A, Anyebuno MA, Pildes RS (Cook County Hosp, Chicago; Univ of Illinois, Chicago; Hektoen Inst of Med Research, Chicago)
J Pediatr 117:273–282, 1990   1–1

Oxygen toxic effects and barotrauma occur very early in the course of respiratory distress syndrome; hence, any therapy, to be effective in reducing lung injury, must be administered shortly after birth, during this early period of highest risk. In a double-blind, placebo-controlled study, the effect of early (≤12 hours) postnatal dexamethasone therapy in facilitating removal of the endotracheal tube and improving outcome was investigated in 57 premature infants with birth weights <2,000 g and severe respiratory distress syndrome. Twenty-eight infants were treated with intravenous dexamethasone in a dose of 1 mg/kg/day for 3 days, with the dose reduced progressively for 12 days; the other 29 infants received placebo. The groups were comparable in birth weight, gestational age, postnatal age, and pulmonary function at the start of the study.

Infants treated with dexamethasone had significantly higher pulmonary compliance, tidal volume, and minute ventilation, and they required lower mean airway pressure for ventilation than infants treated with placebo. The proportion of infants whose endotracheal tube was removed successfully was significantly higher in the group that received dexamethasone (57%) than in the group that received placebo (28%). The number of infants with lung injuries was significantly lower in the group that received dexamethasone (39%) than in the group that received placebo (66%). In addition, infants who received placebo required significantly longer duration of high oxygen therapy than infants who received dexamethasome. Mortality rates did not differ between groups because of the small sample size. Compared with the placebo group, the dexamethasone group had significantly higher temporary increases in blood pressure and plasma glucose concentrations and in delayed somatic growth.

The administration of dexamethasone shortly after birth and during the first 12 postnatal days improves pulmonary compliance, facilitates weaning from mechanical ventilation, and minimizes lung injuries in premature infants with severe respiratory distress syndrome.

▶ This is the first commentary in the Newborn chapter. Before getting into the commentary itself, it would seem appropriate to begin the Newborn chapter with a useful suggestion for those who joyfully provide words of wisdom to

1

new parents. The paternal side is in need of the most help, and the best advice to give such fathers is never to change a diaper in midstream.

Now, on to the subject of steroid therapy as part of the prevention and management of respiratory distress syndrome.

Glucocorticoids have been shown to be effective in increasing surfactant synthesis and in reducing oxygen toxicity in lung inflammation. Previous studies using dexamethasone in infants with bronchopulmonary dysplasia have shown the short-term benefits of improved lung compliance and easier removal of the endotracheal tube. These studies, however, were of infants who had well-established pulmonary abnormalities. Before the study by Yeh et al., no studies had been done early in the course of respiratory distress syndrome, when the infant has the highest risk of oxygen toxicity and barotrauma. Exactly how dexamethasone might work for this purpose is, at best, speculative. It could increase surfacant synthesis, stabilize cell and intracellular membranes, decrease neutrophil migration to areas of injury, alter the synthesis of prostaglandins and leukotrienes, and possibly even reduce pulmonary edema. It has also been shown that steroids decrease the activity of lung elastase, an enzyme associated with lung injury and the development of bronchopulmonary dysplasia (1). Whatever their modes of action, steroids remain part of the post-delivery management of respiratory distress syndrome.

Did you know that this year is the 20th anniversary of the now famous Liggins and Howie report on the first prenatal use of betamethasone for the rapid induction of lung maturation (2)? Now, in virtually every premature delivery in which there is time, glucocorticoid drugs are given to the mother. The only exception to this is in cases where there has been prolonged rupture of membranes (3). Continuing data suggest that glucocorticoid drugs are not needed for these patients because the simple stress of prolonged premature rupture of membranes produces enough endogenous steroid synthesis in the mother and fetus to induce surfactant production.—J.A. Stockman, III, M.D.

References

1. Gerdes JS, et al: *Pediatr Res* 23:506A, 1988.
2. Liggins GC: *Pediatrics* 50:515, 1972.
3. Suidin JS, et al: *Int J Gynecol Obstet* 32:237, 1990.

Maternal Glucocorticoid Therapy and Reduced Risk of Bronchopulmonary Dysplasia
Van Marter LJ, Leviton A, Kuban KCK, Pagano M, Allred EN (The Children's Hosp, Boston; Harvard School of Public Health, Boston)
Pediatrics 86:331–336, 1990   1–2

Antenatal maternal glucocorticoid (GLC) therapy is associated with a reduced incidence of neonatal respiratory distress syndrome in premature infants. Maternal antenatal GLC therapy also may reduce the risk of bronchopulmonary dysplasia (BPD). This hypothesis was evaluated in a sample of 223 intubated infants with birth weights <1,751 g. Of these,

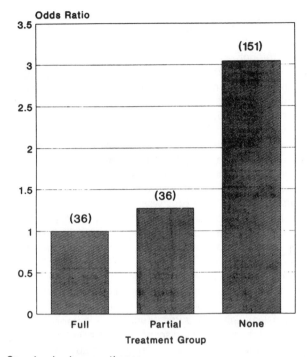

Fig 1-1.—Odds ratios for risk of bronchopulmonary dysplasia in glucocorticoid treatment groups adjusted for the effects of gender and birth weight in the logistic regression analysis. (Courtesy of Van Marter LJ, Leviton A, Kuban KCK, et al: *Pediatrics* 86:331–336, 1990.)

76 met diagnostic criteria for BPD as defined by both oxygen requirement and compatible chest radiograph, and 147 had no BPD by day 28 of life. Glucocorticoids were given only to enhance fetal lung maturation.

Infants whose mothers received a partial course of GLC were 1.3 times more likely to have BPD, and infants born to mothers who received no GLC were 3 times more likely to have BPD than infants whose mothers received a complete number of doses of GLC and who were born between 24 hours and 7 days after the last dose of GLC was given (Fig 1–1). When stratified by gender and birth weight at 1 kg, all subgroups except male infants with birth weight at or less than 1 kg showed a benefit of therapy.

A complete course of antenatal maternal GLC therapy is associated with a lower rate of BPD in very low–birth-weight infants.

▶ What's good for the goose may be good for the gander. What's good is steroids. The goose is respiratory distress syndrome; the gander is BPD. There has been a lot written about the administration of steroids to the infant after birth as part of the management of BPD. This report looks at what part maternal steroid administration might play in terms of its effect on BPD.

The apparent benefit of antenatal steroid therapy in the prevention of BPD, as noted in this article, is consistent with previous studies that demonstrated beneficial effects of steroid therapy in the prevention of respiratory distress syndrome. Glucocorticoids administered to the mother may exhibit an anti-BPD effect directly through anti-inflammatory mechanisms or by alteration of membrane and/or capillary permeability or, indirectly, by reducing the rate of patent ductus arteriosus (1). As you can tell from Figure 1–1, there is something special about little girls, because they seem to derive the greatest benefit from steroids given to their mother before they are born.

Steroids given to the infant after birth do not seem to be very helpful as part of the management of the acute phase of respiratory distress syndrome. Several studies, however, have reported both the usefulness and the complications of dexamethasone therapy in infants with BPD. One report noted significant improvement in pulmonary function, although amelioration of the overall hospital course of infants with BPD was found to be marginal (2). Perhaps Dr. Mildred Stahlman said it all in a commentary in Dr. Gellis's *Pediatric Notes* (3). She cautioned against the use of dexamethasone in the treatment of BPD because of the possibility of complications, and she suggested the need for a multicenter trial.

Two other reports have proved Dr. Stahlman's warnings to be correct. One is the study by Alkalay et al. (4), who documented that when steroids were given to very low–birth-weight infants for any significant length of time, they suppressed hypothalamic-pituitary-adrenal function. We had better start testing for this complication before abruptly discontinuing steroid therapy in our nurseries.

An even more important report is a landmark study from The *New England Journal of Medicine* by Northway et al. (5). In 1967, Northway et al. first described BPD. Twenty-three years later, they have reported on the long-term harvest of the seeds planted when we first began to ventilate premature infants in the 1960s. The harvest is a group of surviving adults who have mean values for all tests of airway function that are reduced by 25% to 50%, and who have more than a 50/50 chance of having physiologic evidence of airway obstruction. The majority of these young adults face the rest of their lives with mild-to-moderate abnormalities in airway function and a long history of increased respiratory morbidity that started when they were born, carried through childhood, and has continued into adulthood.

It is easy to sit back and ignore the outcome of individuals who were treated 23 or more years ago. Techniques of ventilation have improved. We do not let alveoli collapse as much these days. We give antenatal steroids. Right or wrong, we give steroids to the infant after birth, and we shove surfactant into the lungs. Most neonatologist friends of mine claim that data on respiratory morbidity and lung function of persons born in the 1960s, 1970s, and 1980s cannot be used to predict the future respiratory morbidity and physiologic function of children born in the 1990s. They are probably correct, but it doesn't take a fortune teller to add the missing variable to the argument: that we are routinally "salvaging" infants who have birth weights of 400–500 g to 900 g, which was unheard of in the 1960s.

Some have questioned whether what we are doing for the extremely tiny neonate is correct. There is an old saying: "Wrongs aren't wrong if they are done by nice people, like ourselves." Perhaps we should take the advice of individuals like Dr. Stahlman, and step back and examine the bigger picture as often as we have time to.—J.A. Stockman, III, M.D.

References

1. Waffarn F, et al: *Am J Dis Child* 137:336, 1983.
2. Kazzi NJ, et al: *Pediatrics* 86:722, 1990.
3. Stahlman M: *Pediatric Notes* 13:98, 1990.
4. Alkalay AL, et al: *Pediatrics* 86:204, 1990.
5. Northway WH, et al: *N Engl J Med* 323:1793, 1990.

Hydration During the First Days of Life and the Risk of Bronchopulmonary Dysplasia in Low Birth Weight Infants
Van Marter LJ, Leviton A, Allred EN, Pagano M, Kuban KCK (Children's Hosp, Boston; Harvard School of Public Health, Boston)
J Pediatr 116:942–949, 1990   1–3

Medical care practices in the neonatal intensive care unit may affect the risk of bronchopulmonary dysplasia (BPD). A case-control study of antecedents of BPD was done in a large group of infants enrolled in a prospective, randomized clinical trial of phenobarbital prophylaxis for intracranial hemorrhage.

Two hundred twenty-three infants who were patients in 1 of 3 neonatal intensive care units between 1981 and 1984 were studied. Radiographic evidence of BPD was found in 76 infants. These infants required oxygen treatment for at least 28 days. The remaining 147 infants served as controls. All of these infants survived until the 28th day of life without meeting either of the criteria for BPD. Infants with BPD received higher quantities of total, crystalloid, and colloid fluids per kilogram per day in the first 4 days of life than the control infants. Infants who had BPD generally had a net weight gain in the first 4 days of life, whereas the control infants had a pattern of weight loss. Patent ductus arteriosus was diagnosed significantly more often in infants with BPD on the third and fourth days of life. Infants who later had BPD were more likely to have been given furosemide on each of the first 4 days of life than controls. According to a multivariate model that included covariates, the administration of phenobarbital did not increase the risk of BPD.

Phenobarbital prophylaxis apparently does not contribute to the risk of BPD. Early postnatal phenomena such as excessive fluid treatment may play an important role in the pathogenesis of BPD, however.

▶ Dr. T. Allen Merritt, Professor and Chief, Division of Neonatology, University of California, Davis, comments:

▶ Van Marter and coworkers make several important observations. Excessive administration of fluids (both crystalloid and colloid) during the first 96 hours after birth are strongly associated with radiographic evidence of BPD and supplemental oxygen dependency at 28 days of life among premature infants. After adjusting for severity of illness, these associations persist, and the occurrence of patent ductus arteriosus and use of furosemide are strong predictors of eventual BPD. Use of pancuronium, but not phenobarbital, is also a predictor of PBD. Why would fluid intakes differing by only 20–30 mL/kg/day be a significant predictor of BPD? Undoubtedly, excessive fluid therapy in "leaky" lungs worsens pulmonary edema, inhibits surfactant function, and increases both the need for assisted ventilation and oxygen therapy and the duration of therapy. Infants with increased fluid administration were found to require more peak inspiratory pressure, positive end expiratory pressure, and higher rates. These findings remind me of the report of Hallman (1), who found that magnitude of fluid therapy was associated with severity of respiratory failure, and Kraybill et al (2), who found that modest increases in ventilation to maintain $PaCO_2$ at 38.5 ± 8.9 mm Hg vs. 43.4 ± 15.6 mm Hg at 48 to 96 hours after birth were strongly associated with the development of chronic lung disease.

Left to right shunting through the patent ductus arteriosus has been related to BPD for more than a decade. The present study confirms this previous observation and also found that diuretic drugs were less useful in the treatment of BPD than treatment with fluid restriction and indomethacin.

Fluid therapy in infants at risk for BPD should include a careful and frequent assessment of net fluid intake and fluid loss. Efforts should be made to maintain these infants in a neutral thermal environment with a moderate water loss. A weight loss of 10% during the first 72 hours of life is evidence of excessive fluid loss. Excessive fluid administration during this critical interval may have life-long adverse consequences.—T.A. Merritt, M.D.

References

1. Hallman M: *Acta Paediatr Scand Suppl* 360:93, 1989.
2. Kraybill EN, et al: *J Pediatr* 115:115, 1989.

Late Pulmonary Sequelae of Bronchopulmonary Dysplasia
Northway WH Jr, Moss RB, Carlisle KB, Parker BR, Popp RL, Pitlick PT, Eichler I, Lamm RL, Brown BW Jr (Stanford Univ Med Ctr; Children's Hosp at Stanford)
N Engl J Med 323:1793–1799, 1990   1–4

About 40% of infants with bronchopulmonary dysplasia (BPD) die, and those who survive have morbidity from respiratory disease more often than unaffected infants. Lung function was estimated in 26 adolescents and young adults who had BPD as infants. These patients, aged 14–23 years, were compared both with 26 age-matched controls who had not undergone mechanical ventilation and 53 normal controls. The age-matched controls were matched with the patients for birth weight and gestational age.

Seventeen of 25 patients tested had airway obstruction, and 24% had fixed airway obstruction. About half of these individuals had reactive airway disease (Fig 1–2). Hyperinflation was more frequent in those who

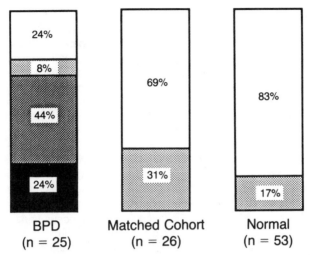

Fig 1–2.—Reactive airway disease in the subjects with BPD in infancy, the matched cohort controls, and the normal controls. The majority of the subjects with BPD (52%) had reactive airway disease ($P = .001$ for the comparison between subjects with BPD and normal controls). The *open areas* indicate the absence of reactive airway disease, the *lightly shaded areas* indicate a positive response to methacholine provocation, the *heavily shaded areas* indicate reversible airway obstruction, and the *filled areas* indicate fixed airway obstruction. (Courtesy of Northway WH Jr, Moss RB, Carlisle KB, et al: *N Engl J Med* 323:1793–1799, 1990.)

had BPD in infancy than in either control group. Six patients had severe pulmonary dysfunction or symptoms of respiratory difficulty at the time of assessment.

Pulmonary dysfunction is the rule in adolescents and young adults with a history of BPD in infancy, but symptoms usually are absent. Although most of these individuals lead normal lives, there is concern over vulnerability to progressive obstructive lung disease with advancing age. They should be strongly discouraged from smoking.

▶ Philip Farrell, M.D., Professor and Chairman of Pediatrics, University of Wisconsin Medical School, comments:

▶ In the 25 years since the classic description of BPD by Northway et al. (1), this disease has become one of the most important and challenging problems in pediatrics. Indeed, issues related to BPD have become a predominant concern in both neonatology and pediatric pulmonology. A review of abstracts submitted to meetings of the American Pediatric Society/Society for Pediatric Research indicates that BPD is the disease that receives the most attention at these national conferences.

This investigation of "late pulmonary sequelae" by Northway and associates extends our knowledge about the consequences of lung injury in the neonatal period. This follow-up study was carefully performed, and the authors are to be congratulated for completing a difficult longitudinal assessment. It is to their credit that they included comparison groups and examined potentially confounding variables such as smoking. The results of this investigation indicate that individuals recovering from BPD do not fully recover but have long-standing chronic obstructive pulmonary disease. Certain indices of pulmonary function such as the ratio of residual volume to total lung capacity provide a precise indication of functional disturbances. The correlation of lung function abnormalities with the duration of endotracheal intubation and the duration of mechanical ventilation provide more support for current attempts to limit the severity of lung injury by shortening the period of assisted ventilation. This study also provides encouraging information because Northway and associates found that "most such persons are leading normal lives" despite their abnormalities in pulmonary function.

The limitations of this study must be recognized and addressed by future research. Of greatest concern is the limited number of BPD survivors investigated and the lack of systematic follow-up to gather complete information on subsequent risk factors such as viral respiratory illnesses. In addition, it should be pointed out that 5 of the 26 subjects had complicating neurologic abnormalities with "some degree of cerebral palsy . . . hearing loss . . . and retrolental fibroplasia," which were not present in any of the matched cohort controls. These variables can affect pulmonary function indirectly, but it should be emphasized that neurologic injury is not necessarily a consequence of BPD per se. In fact, it is likely that cerebral palsy accompanying BPD can be related to perinatal or early neonatal events that cause hypoxic-ischemic brain injury or intracranial hemorrhage.

That only 26 appropriate subjects were available from the population born at the Stanford University Medical Center between 1964 and 1973 illustrates one of the major barriers in clinical research on BPD—the relatively small numbers of BPD patients being discharged from each neonatal intensive care unit. It should be emphasized that overcoming this limitation probably will require a network of BPD centers similar to multicenter programs devoted to other diseases such as cystic fibrosis and leukemia (e.g., the Children's Cancer Study Group). Establishing a BPD-focused network will be more difficult, however, for at least 2 reasons: there is no foundation, lay group, or national agency to assume responsibility for promoting and funding BPD centers; and BPD is an exceedingly complex disease that involves numerous pediatric subspecialists and care-delivery settings (e.g., neonatology, pulmonology, cardiology, developmental pediatrics). Nevertheless, the great need for more information on the epidemiology of BPD will make it necessary to establish such centers if we are to achieve optimal progress in the future.

The article by Northway and associates should stimulate future research on the sequelae of BPD. The number of patients included in follow-up studies should not only be increased, but mild cases of BPD also should be investigated. It is important to recognize that the study by Northway and associates included only patients with moderately severe or severe BPD.

Future studies also need to address growth and nutritional status in further detail. Appropriate comparison groups are needed to reach statistically valid conclusions. Despite their observation suggesting "significant differences in both height and weight between the subjects with bronchopulmonary dysplasia and the normal controls," Northway and associates emphasized that "the relation of reduced height and weight in the adolescents and young adults with bronchopulmonary dysplasia in infancy to the late pulmonary dysfunction is not clear." Indeed, it is simply not possible with such a small group of patients to reach any conclusion about long-term growth.

Finally, readers must be aware of the current perspective that major advances related to BPD are likely to come primarily from basic research rather than from longitudinal clinical studies or clinical trials. In the opinion of most pulmonologists, prevention or amelioration of lung injury will pay the greatest dividends in the future. Lessons learned during the past decade from clinical trials involving high-frequency ventilation techniques and other modalities have underscored the importance of learning more about fundamental aspects of lung injury before we embark on therapeutic misadventures.—P. Farrell, M.D.

Reference

1. Northway WH Jr, et al: *N Engl J Med* 276:357, 1967.

Health and Developmental Outcomes of a Surfactant Controlled Trial: Follow-Up at 2 Years
Ware J, Taeusch HW, Soll RF, McCormick MC (Harvard Med School, Boston; King/Drew Med Ctr, Los Angeles; Univ of Vermont, Burlington)
Pediatrics 85:1103–1107, 1990   1–5

Despite the early beneficial effects of surfactant replacement therapy in respiratory distress syndrome, little is known about its potential long-term risks or benefits. To determine the health and developmental consequences of surfactant therapy, 32 survivors of an initial 41 infants enrolled in a randomized, controlled trial of exogenous bovine-based surfactant therapy were reexamined at ages 1 and 2 years. Assessments of cognitive and motor skills were done using the Bayley Scales of Infant Development.

The frequency of abnormal physical findings at ages 1 and 2 years did not differ significantly between the surfactant-treated infants and controls, although there was a trend toward an increased frequency of allergic manifestations in the controls. Likewise, there were no differences in physical growth or in assessments of cognitive and motor skills between the groups. These data and those of 4 other follow-up studies of infants treated with surfactant provide encouraging evidence that surfactant therapy has no adverse effect on health and developmental outcomes.

▶ Mikko Hallman, M.D., and Feizal Waffarn, M.D., Division of Neonatal Medicine, University of California, Irvine, comments:

▶ The article by Ware and associates addresses an important concern— whether survival in surfactant-treated low–birth-weight infants is accompanied by an increased frequency of handicapping conditions. Although several thousand babies have been studied in randomzied surfactant therapy trials, to date only a few follow-up reports have appeared in the literature. However, according to many studies, surfactant supplementation has been associated with a decrease in neonatal deaths, and thus an increase in the population of infants who have a high risk of neurodevelopmental handicap. Surfactant substitution has not decreased the incidence of severe intraventricular hemorrhage (known to be associated with neurodevelopmental handicap), although this therapy clearly improves pulmonary gas exchange and decreases the incidence of lung ruptures, which are significantly associated with intraventricular hemorrhage.

In addition to the 30 infants in their present study, Ware and associates evaluated the follow-up studies on 170 other infants reported thus far and the authors inferred that surfactant therapy generally may not affect neurodevelopmental outcome adversely. It is also particularly encouraging to find that the infants in the present study who received bovine surfactant have had no increased incidence of allergic manifestations, despite exposure to bovine-based material at birth.

Although the present follow-up data favors the new therapy, it does not exclude the possibility that surfactant supplementation is associated with some increase in the number of small, premature infants who have neurodevelopmental handicaps. The hemodynamic instability, documented in association with surfactant supplementation, is of concern with respect to long-term sequelae. There is a compelling need to define and improve the treatment practices associated with surfactant substitution. Evaluations are pending on whether those infants who do not respond to exogenous surfactant or infants who develop chronic lung disease despite surfactant therapy constitute particular risk groups in follow-up studies; whether administration of surfactant at birth has any neurodevelopmental risks or benefits compared with the administration of surfactant in established respiratory distress syndrome, or vice versa; and whether therapeutic practices can be improved in favor of intact neurodevelopment.—M. Hallman, M.D., and F. Waffarn, M.D.

A Comparison of Surfactant as Immediate Prophylaxis and as Rescue Therapy in Newborns of Less Than 30 Weeks' Gestation
Kendig JW, Notter RH, Cox C, Reubens LJ, Davis JM, Maniscalco WM, Sinkin RA, Bartoletti A, Dweck HS, Horgan MJ, Risemberg H, Phelps DL, Shapiro DL (Univ of Rochester, NY; Albany Med College, Albany, NY; New York Med College, Valhalla, NY)
N Engl J Med 324:865–871, 1991   1–6

Intratracheal exogenous pulmonary surfactants are used to prevent or treat respiratory distress syndrome in premature infants. The results of surfactant treatment given prophylactically were compared with those of rescue therapy with surfactant.

In this multicenter trial, 479 fetuses of an estimated gestational age of less than 30 weeks were randomly assigned to received surfactant as prophylaxis or rescue therapy. There were 235 infants in the first group and 244 in the second. Those in the first group were given a 90-mg intratracheal dose of an exogenous calf-lung surfactant extract at the time of delivery. Those in the rescue-therapy group received 90 mg of the surfac-

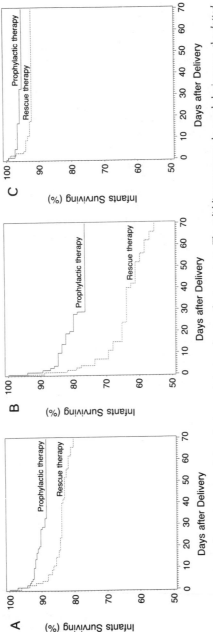

Fig 1-3.— Survival over time among infants in the prophylaxis and rescue-therapy groups. The *solid lines* represent the prophylaxis group, the *dotted lines* represent the rescue-therapy group. The 3 panels show Kaplan-Meier survival plots for all infants (A) and for 2 gestational age subgroups: the infants delivered at 26 weeks of gestation or earlier (B), and those delivered after 26 weeks of gestation (C). (Courtesy of Kendig JW, Notter RH, Cox C, et al: N Engl J Med 324:865–871, 1991.)

tant several hours after delivery if they had a fractional inspiratory oxygen concentration at least .4 or if they have a mean airway pressure of at least .686 kilopascal or both. Infants in both groups were given additional doses of surfactant at 12—24-hour intervals if these criteria were met.

A significantly higher proportion of infants in the prophylaxis group survived to discharge (88%) compared with those in the rescue-therapy group (80%). The difference was explained mainly by the longer survival of infants in the prophylaxis group who were born at 26 weeks or less of gestation. Seventy-five percent of these very premature infants in the prophylaxis group survived, compared with 54% in the rescue-therapy group. Proportional-hazards regression analysis showed that the distribution of survival times was better for all infants in the prophylaxis group and for the very premature subgroup in the prophylaxis group. Very premature infants treated prophylactically had a lower incidence of pneumothorax than very premature infants treated later (Fig 1–3).

Both prophylactic and rescue surfactant therapy can be used. In this series, survival was higher among infants treated prophylactically, especially those delivered at 26 weeks of gestation or earlier. This increase in survival rate was not accompanied by a rise in early morbidity. However, the long-term outcome of these infants is still unknown.

▶ You've never been as sick as just before you stop breathing. Thus, the rationale for surfactant, the "WD-40" of the lung.

I vote that H.G. Wells be reincarnated. I'd ask him to invent a workable time machine so that those of us who want to skip into the future can do so. This would avoid the pain and agony associated with having to live through the period that is producing so much interesting, non-interesting, confusing, conflicting, and otherwise obfuscatory information concerning surfactant replacement therapy for respiratory distress syndrome. In the last year alone, I have accumulated 87 articles on this topic, only 2 of which were selected for inclusion in the YEAR BOOK.

For example, after reviewing all of those articles, I thought I was beginning to get a handle on the various pros and cons regarding surfactant replacement. I finally concluded that surfactant replacement therapy does work (I tend to be a yes or no man; gray is not my favorite color). Then there appeared an article by members of the Departments of Pediatrics, Biostatistics, and Clinical Epidemiology of the Medical College of Wisconsin, who did a meta-analysis of previously reported clinical trials of surfactant extracts. What did they conclude? They concluded that ". . . further clinical trials are needed to evaluate other aspects of surfactant replacement therapy in premature infants because inconsistent results were observed among the several analyzed studies." Translation: you can bet we're going to be seeing more studies.

Summarized below are the highlights of the literature on surfactant therapy from the last year or so:

- "It was concluded that a single dose of surfactant given shortly after birth resulted in a decreased severity of chest radiographic findings 24 hours after treatment, but did not improve other acute measures of disease severity or clinical status later in the neonatal period." A report of a multicenter trial of single dose modified bovine surfactant reported by Soll et al. (1).

- "We conclude that improvements in respiratory physiology after a single prophylactic dose of Exosurf result in an increased likelihood of neonatal survival without bronchopulmonary dysplasia." (These are the results of investigations from the University of North Carolina.) (2).
- "These findings suggest that surfactant supplementation may provide therapeutic benefits for newborns with respiratory failure due to pneumonia or meconium aspiration and that expanded clinical trials of this therapy are indicated." (3).
- "There appears to be no clinical justification for routinely using a prophylactic approach to surfactant replacement therapy." (As opposed to using it only as a defined treatment in established situations). (4).
- "It is concluded that treatment with the single dose surfactant regimen used in this study reduces the severity of respiratory distress during the 48 hours after treatment and decreases the major pulmonary morbidity and intracranial hemorrhage in premature infants with RDS." (5).
- "We conclude that surfactant treatment at two to four hours after birth (but after the onset of severe RDS) is as efficacious as treatment at birth." (6).

I could go on and on, but you get the flavor of what is being said in literature. Surfactant-replacement therapy for premature infants seems to be here to stay. H.G. Wells is not coming back. We will have to live through the period in which the following practical questions about surfactant replacement will be studied: Is one form of surfactant better than another? What is the best timing for the first dose? What about the question of prophylaxis vs. rescue? What is the optimal dose? What are the indications for repeated doses? Is synthethic surfactant better than natural surfactant? Why do some infants not respond at all?

In conclusion, there is still much to be learned about surfactant. Lord, grant us the patience to survive the experience of reading the literature of the next decade.—J.A. Stockman, III, M.D.

References

1. Soll RF, et al: *Pediatrics* 85:1092, 1990.
2. Bose C, et al: *J Pediatr* 117:947, 1990.
3. Auten RL, et al: *Pediatrics* 87:101, 1991.
4. Dunn MS, et al: *Pediatrics* 87:377, 1991.
5. Fujiwara T, et al: *Pediatrics* 86:753, 1990.
6. Merritt TA, et al: *J Pediatr* 118:581, 1991.

High-Frequency Oscillatory Ventilation Compared With Conventional Intermittent Mechanical Ventilation in the Treatment of Respiratory Failure in Preterm Infants: Neurodevelopmental Status at 16 to 24 Months of Postterm Age

HIFI Study Group (Natl Heart, Lung, and Blood Inst, Bethesda, Md; and cooperating medical centers)

J Pediatr 117:939–946, 1990

1–7

Ten centers participated in a controlled clinical trial to compare the efficacy and safety of high-frequency oscillatory ventilation (HFO) with the efficacy and safety of intermittent mechanical ventilation (IMV) in low–birth-weight premature infants. Infants were assigned randomly to 1 of 2 groups; 327 infants received HFO, and 346 infants received IMV.

Psychometric evaluations using the Bayley Scales of Infant Development and a detailed neurologic examination were performed at 16 and 24 months of postterm age. At follow-up, the proportion of infants with a normal neurodevelopmental status was significantly lower in the HFO group than in the IMV group. There was no difference in growth or respiratory status between the 2 groups at follow-up. Cerebral palsy was diagnosed in 10% of the HFO-treated infants and 11% of the IMV-treated infants. The incidence of hydrocephalus was significantly higher (12% vs. 6%) in the HFO group. Both groups showed a strong association between the presence of grade 3 or 4 intraventricular hemorrhage and the development of major CNS or cognitive defects.

There were no significant long-term effects with the use of HFO rather than IMV for the treatment of respiratory failure in low–birth-weight premature infants. Because the HFO group had a higher proportion of survivors who had intraventricular hemorrhage, there were more neurologic deficits in this group.

▶ It is fascinating and, at the same time, curious to see ourselves getting into such high tech areas as high-frequency ventilation when we also still see new reports about locating the ends of endotracheal tubes (1). Nonetheless, high-frequency oscillatory ventilation is beginning to find its niche in our therapeutic armamentarium for infants who need respiratory assistance.

The High-Frequency Intervention Trial (HIFI) was a collaborative clinical trial designed not only to assess the potential effectiveness of this new technology in the management of respiratory failure in preterm infants but also to determine the extent of long-term pulmonary and neurodevelopmental morbidity (2). The original HIFI study reported an increased incidence of major intracranial hemorrhage for those infants whose lungs were ventilated in the high-frequency mode. This finding, along with reports suggesting an increased incidence of audiologic and visual problems, raised concerns. Thus, the rationale for the present study: to determine the risk-benefit ratio of this new form of ventilation. The results seem fairly clear-cut from this multicenter clinical trial. There was neither a beneficial nor a deleterious effect of high-frequency oscillatory ventilation on the neurologic outcome of the infants studied. These are not earth-shaking results, but they are a necessary piece to the puzzle in terms of understanding what is good, and what is not so good, in our nursery setting.

By now you are probably trying to guess what is the new method for location of the ends of endotracheal tubes. The new method (Trach Mate) is based on a highly scientific principle of magnetic field interactions (1). "Scientists" have been looking for noninvasive ways to find the ends of the endotracheal tubes for the last 30 years. Ultrasound doesn't work very well. You may recall the report of Heller et al. (3) that demonstrated the value of a fiber-optic strand incorporated into the length of an endotracheal tube. A high-intensity light source was shined into the end of the tube. In a darkened nursery, the glow could be seen in the infant's chest, and the tube could be located. Unfortunately, fiber-optic endotracheal tubes have caught on about as well as Prohibition.

On the other hand, Trach Mate is as hot as *Terminator 2* was last summer. The Trach Mate intubation system uses a metallic ring embedded in the wall of the endotracheal tube; the position of the metallic ring can then be located within the trachea with a portable, battery-powered magnetic sensing instrument.

Trach Mate may sound like such a simple idea that you wonder why you didn't think of it yourself. Indeed, I wish to take credit for the concept. In 1983, I was challenged by a dilemma presented by a neighbor's child who had stepped on a small nail. As the local friendly neighborhood doctor, I was asked to tell whether the nail was still embedded in the child's foot. It didn't take a rocket scientist to conclude that the easiest way to find out was to go into the garage and rummage through the carpentry box to find the stud detector (a device that finds nails in wall studs). Applied to the child's foot, it verified the presence of a nail. I would be willing to bet that my stud detector ($9.95 at your local hardware store) would be as efficient, and certainly more nifty, than the several-hundred dollar, portable, battery-powered magnetic sensing instrument that goes along with the Trach Mate.

There are many useful principles from the field of carpentry that can be applied to medicine. Orthopedists would be wise to remember the number 1 rule of woodworking: "Measure twice, saw once."—J.A. Stockman, III, M.D.

References

1. Blayney M, et al: *Pediatrics* 87:44, 1991.
2. The HIFI Study Group: *N Engl J Med* 320:88, 1989.
3. Heller RM, et al: *Pediatrics* 75:664, 1985.

Liquid Ventilation of Human Preterm Neonates
Greenspan JS, Wolfson MR, Rubenstein SD, Shaffer TH (Temple Univ; St Christopher's Hosp for Children, Philadelphia)
J Pediatr 117:106–111, 1990   1–8

The survival rates of preterm infants have improved with recent advances in respiratory support, but this support is frequently associated with serious complications of barotrauma. Animal studies have shown that insufflation of the premature lung with an oxygenated perfluorochemical (PF) liquid can eliminate interfacial surface tension, improve distribution of pulmonary blood flow, and support physiologic gas exchange at lower and safer alveolar inflation pressures. Liquid ventilation was used in 3 preterm infants in whom conventional therapies for severe respiratory distress had failed.

All 3 infants had marked cardiovascular instability that required resuscitative measures, and all 3 were considered to be at the point of death. Heated, oxygenated liquid PF was suspended in a reservoir above the su-

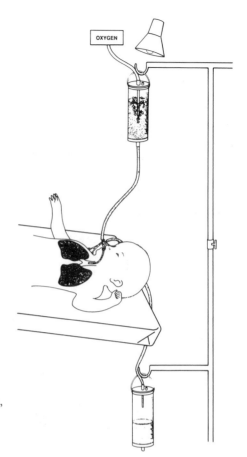

Fig 1–4.—Liquid ventilation system.
(Courtesy of Greenspan JS, Wolfson MR,
Rubenstein SD, et al: *J Pediatr* 117:106–111,
1990.)

pine infants and attached by a Y piece to the endotracheal tube (Fig
1–4). Liquid ventilation was performed without difficulty for two 3- to
5-minute cycles in the sedated infants. Skeletal muscle paralysis with pancuronium bromide was continued during the procedure. Conventional
ventilation and neonatal management were then resumed.

In all 3 infants, liquid ventilation lung distensibility improved markedly, but there was no change in cardiovascular status. Oxygenation improved in 2 infants. All 3 infants died within 19 hours of the procedure,
probably because of the underlying severity of lung disease. Two neonates had exhibited sustained improvement for up to 2 hours, but the
other died 30 minutes after liquid ventilation.

Despite the outcome in these infants, liquid ventilation shows promise
as a therapy for neonatal respiratory failure. No evidence of retained PF
fluid was seen in the lungs or pleural space. The effectiveness of the procedure might be improved by alternative liquids, a modified delivery system, or a longer period of treatment.

▶ When I first read this report, I was reminded of the story of the 2 insects that impaled themselves against the windshield of an automobile traveling on the New Jersey turnpike. One bug looked over to the other one and said, "It took a lot of guts to do that." The other replied, "I bet you don't have enough guts to do it again."

Well, it did take a lot of guts (courage) to do what these investigators did, but in view of the outcome (all infants died), it will take a lot of guts (real courage) to do this study again. I hope that this first human trial of perfluorocarbon liquid breathing will not be the last human trial. Although all 3 infants ultimately died of their underlying disease, this experience does suggest that liquid breathing can be used to support gas exchange, even in severely premature infants with advanced barotrauma resulting from prior ventilation.

As a hematologist, I have been interested in perfluorocarbons for the better part of 2 decades. Perfluorocarbons have been tested as a potential blood substitute, and under the right circumstances (battlefield use, etc.), they demonstrate some very interesting physical properties. In 1 atmosphere of pure oxygen, perfluorocarbons can carry 45–55 mL of dissolved oxygen per 100 mL of solution. If you put this into someone's lungs, the alveolar lining comes into direct contact with the solvent, and gases can be inhaled and exhaled just like the person was breathing air. There is already a body of literature on animal studies showing that perfluorocarbon liquid ventilation can be done safely with no adverse effects.

Perfluorocarbon liquid ventilation does not seem unusually farfetched to me. It is said that man evolved from the oceans. Each of us has spent at least 9 months of our lives in a totally liquid environment. Why not give Greenspan et al. the benefit of the doubt and encourage them and others to undertake further clinical trials. Pouring oxygenated liquid perfluorocarbon into the trachea and then draining it out, if successful, is a lot simpler than extracorporeal membrane oxygenation, which is the only other current alternative for these desperately ill infants.—J.A. Stockman, III, M.D.

Amniotic Fluid Glucose Concentration: A Rapid and Simple Method for the Detection of Intraamniotic Infection in Preterm Labor

Romero R, Jimenez C, Lohda AK, Nores J, Hanaoka S, Avila C, Callahan R, Mazor M, Hobbins JC, Diamond MP (Yale Univ)

Am J Obstet Gynecol 163:968–974, 1990   1–9

Intra-amniotic infection appears to be associated with preterm labor and delivery. Early diagnosis is desirable. To determine whether glucose concentrations in amniotic fluid are of value in the rapid diagnosis of intra-amniotic infection, 168 patients with preterm labor and intact membranes underwent amniocenteses. Amniotic fluid was cultured for aerobic and anaerobic bacteria and *Mycoplasma* species.

Amniotic fluid cultures were positive in 13.6% of the 168 cultures. Women with positive amniotic fluid cultures for microorganisms had significantly lower median levels of glucose in amniotic fluid than those with negative amniotic fluid cultures. Glucose levels in amniotic fluid below 14 mg/dL had a sensitivity of 86.9%, a specificity of 91.7%, a positive predictive value of 62.5%, and a negative predictive value of 97.8% in detecting positive amniotic fluid culture.

Determination of the concentration of glucose in amniotic fluid is a sensitive test for detecting intra amniotic infection in women with preterm labor and intact membranes. Determination of the glucose concentration amniotic fluid is also fast, simple, and inexpensive.

A Controlled Trial Comparing Vidarabine With Acyclovir in Neonatal Herpes Simplex Virus Infection
Whitley R, Arvin A, Prober C, Burchett S, Corey L, Powell D, Plotkin S, Starr S, Alford C, Connor J, Jacobs R, Nahmias A, Soong S-J, Natl Inst of Allergy and Infectious Diseases Collaborative Antiviral Study Group (Univ of Alabama, Birmingham; Stanford Univ; Univ of Washington; Ohio State Univ; Univ of Pennsylvania; et al)
N Engl J Med 324:444–449, 1991   1–10

Ninety-five infants less than 1 month of age with confirmed herpes simplex virus (HSV) infection were randomly and blindly assigned to receive vidarabine, and 107 infants were assigned to receive acyclovir. Actuarial rates of morbidity and mortality after 1 year were compared according to extent of disease at the time of entry into the trial. Disease categories were HSV infection limited to the skin, eyes, or mouth; encephalitis; or disseminated disease. None of the 85 children with disease confined to the skin, eyes, or mouth died, and 90% of them were developing normally at the time of follow-up. Mortality was lower in infants with brain infection than in those with disseminated disease, but the proportion of children functioning normally in these 2 disease categories was similar.

Acyclovir and vidarabine therapy appear to be equally effective in the management of neonatal HSV infection, although a higher proportion of vidarabine recipients than acyclovir recipients continued to shed virus during treatment (Fig 1–5). For both drugs, a dose of 30 mg/kg/day for 10 days is recommended for its ease of administration. Outcome varied significantly according to the extent of the disease, but no comparison of treatments within disease categories was statistically significant. Increased knowledge of HSV natural history, mortality, and morbidity will aid future therapeutic strategies; however, future efforts also should emphasize disease prevention.

▶ Dr. Laura T. Gutman, Associate Professor of Pediatrics and Pharmacology, Duke University Medical Center, comments:

▶ Between 1981 and 1987, 27 collaborating institutions participated in studies of the treatment of neonatal HSV disease that were directed through the Na-

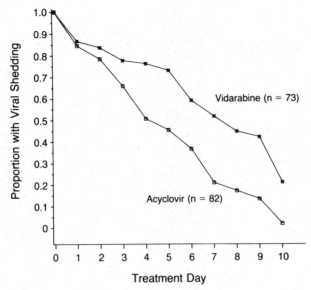

Fig 1–5.—Cessation of viral shedding at any site during treatment of neonatal HSV infection. The difference between groups was significant (*P* < .001). (Courtesy of Whitley R, Arvin A, Prober C, et al: *N Engl J Med* 324:444–449, 1991.)

tional Institute of Allergy and Infectious Diseases Collaborative Study Group. For this report, the collaborating institutions enrolled 210 infants into a comparative study of the efficacy of acyclovir and vidarabine. The infants were characterized according to the extent of their infection as skin-eye-mouth, CNS, or disseminated disease, and therapy was administered intravenously for 10 days. Part of the data from this meticulous and elegant study have already been released, and this report summarizes the current progress in the treatment of these difficult infections.

The study makes several points that are of particular interest to the clinician. Of the 71 infants with initially recognized CNS disease, 30 (42%) were dead or severely disabled at 12 months, confirming that neonatal HSV disease of the CNS commonly has long-term sequelae. Second, in an accompanying paper (1) the authors documented that children who had been classified as having disease limited to skin-eye-mouth had progressively worsening neurologic deterioration if they had dermal recurrences, and the disability was most severe in children who had had 3 or more dermal recurrences. In addition, 7 of 87 (8%) infants had episodes that appeared to be CNS recurrences of disease within 1 month after completion of therapy. There were no differences in outcomes between infants treated with the 2 comparative drugs, and the report concluded with the recommendation that the duration of treatment of neonatal HSV disease be unchanged (10 days), and that the drug of choice be acyclovir.

These reports have provided a very firm basis for understanding the prognosis of various forms of HSV disease and the responses of infants to currently recommended therapy. Of even greater interest will be the results of future studies that examine the outcomes of a longer initial course of therapy, increased doses, and the effects of suppressive therapy after completion of the parenteral course.

There are several reasons to examine the effect of lengthening the course of therapy. This study demonstrated that HSV can be recovered by culture of infected sites of some treated patients almost until the 10th day of therapy. In addition, case reports of relapsing CNS disease that occurred shortly after cessation of standard courses of therapy have included the demonstration of replicating HSV from brain biopsy (2). Perhaps the currently recommended course of therapy is not long enough to ensure control of replicating viral foci, either peripherally or centrally.

Another possible explanation for the poor outcomes of some children is that some may be experiencing a subclinical, relapsing subacute encephalitis (3). Reports of children who progressively lost previously attained developmental milestones months after the acute illness had subsided and had abnormal CSF parameters have raised this possibility (4). Other indications that the process may be recurrent have come from other reviews of patient courses (5), the recognition of persistent cognitive sequelae even in adults who were treated at a very early stage of illness (6), reports of persistently abnormal CSF alterations over long periods of time in survivors (4, 7), and the documentation of the relation between recognizable cutaneous recurrences and cognitive deterioration as demonstrated in the present studies (1).

What are the choices open to a clinician? For those children who can be admitted to a center that participates in the collaborative studies, expert care will be available. For the treatment of children outside the study centers, there are several decisions to be made. In an attempt to improve on the outcome, which parameters of therapy could the individual clinician elect to modify, and how? Adherence to the currently recommended regimen is certainly justified. Also justified by the considerations that have been mentioned is the decision to provide a longer initial course of therapy. It has been my personal decision to assign infants with neonatal HSV disease to a 21-day course of parenteral therapy, which brings it into the range of treatment of many other severe neonatal CNS infections. Future reports from the collaborative study should provide the answer to whether or not this therapeutic decision has been helpful or excessive. A more controversial question is whether a child would benefit from a prolonged course of suppressive therapy with acyclovir following the initial intensive treatment. Again, there are no curreht maps to this wilderness, and the clinician must act without completed studies for guidance. It is my opinion that suppressive treatment may improve the lives of children with neonatal HSV disease, in part because dermal recurrences can be an embarrassment and in part because of an optimistic hope that these children might be spared some of the disabilities that characterize the CNS sequelae of many cases of neonatal herpes. Data are urgently needed.—L.T. Gutman, M.D.

References

1. Whitley R, et al: *N Engl J Med* 324:450, 1991.
2. VanLandingham KE, et al: *JAMA* 259:1051, 1988.

3. Kohl S: *Pediatr Infect Dis J* 9:307, 1990.
4. Gutman LT, et al: *J Infect Dis* 154:415, 1986.
5. Malm G, et al: *Acta Paediatr Scand* 80:226, 1991.
6. Gordon B, et al: *Arch Neurol* 47:646, 1990.
7. Koskiniemi M, et al: *Rev Infect Dis* 6:608, 1984.

Absence of Need for Amniocentesis in Patients With Elevated Levels of Maternal Serum Alpha-Fetoprotein and Normal Ultrasonographic Examinations

Nadel AS, Green JK, Holmes LB, Frigoletto FD Jr, Benacerraf BR (Brigham and Women's Hosp and Harvard Med School, Boston)
N Engl J Med 323:557–561, 1990   1–11

At present, routine obstetric care includes screening for raised levels of maternal serum α-fetoprotein (AFP) between 15 and 18 weeks after the last menstrual period. If the levels are elevated in 2 samples and ultrasound examinations do not suggest an explanation, amniocentesis for measurement of AFP and acetylcholinesterase in amniotic fluid is routinely recommended.

The findings in 51 fetuses with spina bifida, encephalocele, gastroschisis or omphalocele that were delivered consecutively or aborted at 1 hospital were reviewed to evaluate the diagnostic accuracy of ultrasonography. In all instances, the mothers had undergone sonography at 1 facility between 16 and 24 weeks after the last menstrual period. This information was used to evaluate the probability of an affected fetus in a woman with a given level of maternal serum AFP and normal sonographic results.

Data were collected on 87,584 pregnancies during a 12-year period in women who intended to give birth at Brigham and Women's Hospital. Data were included on liveborn or stillborn infants and fetuses aborted in the second trimester. The total prevalence of spina bifida, encephalocele, omphalocele, and gastroschisis was .11%. The probability of these defects in fetuses of mothers with different maternal serum AFP values was calculated.

The congenital anomalies identified by an AFP screening program are unusual. Because there is considerable overlap between maternal serum AFP values in normal pregnancies and in those complicated by an anomaly, the probability is low that a patient with a raised maternal serum AFP level is carrying an affected fetus. In the present study, there was a 1.1% probability that the fetus of a woman with a maternal serum AFP level of 3 times the median was affected by a malformation associated with elevated AFP other than anencephaly.

Women with raised maternal serum AFP levels should be referred to institutions that are capable of carrying out level 2 ultrasonography. If the level 2 scan identifies an abnormal fetus, appropriate counseling should be provided.

▶ Do you believe that "The meek shall inherit the earth?" No matter what Psalms 37:11 says, it seems incontrovertible that the ultrasonographer will fill that role.

What this article is telling us is that ultrasonographic techniques have become so good that a woman who has an elevated serum AFP can now pass "go" and have only an ultrasound to determine whether there is a problem with her pregnancy.

Routine obstetric care has included screening for elevated levels of maternal serum AFP between 15 and 18 weeks after the last menstrual period. All women should have this done. If the levels are elevated in 2 samples, and ultrasounds do not suggest an explanation (such as incorrect estimation of gestational age, multiple gestation, fetal death, or a definite congenital anomaly), amniocentesis to measure AFP and acetylcholinesterase has been recommended routinely to exclude anomalies that might have been missed by sonography. The latter include neural-tube defects such as anencephaly, encephalocele, and spina bifida, as were as open ventral-wall defects, such as omphalocele and gastroschisis. Other causes of elevated AFP in maternal serum, to round out the list, include sacrococcygeal teratoma, bladder and cloacal exstrophy, cystic hygroma, obstruction of the upper gastrointestinal tract, renal agenesis, obstructive uropathy, fetal skin abnormalities, and congenital nephrosis.

With current high-technology ultrasound, a woman who has an elevated AFP level but who has negative ultrasound study, has only a .01% to .15% chance of having an affected fetus. The chance of having an affected fetus is therefore significantly less than the reported risk of abortion caused by confirmatory amniocentesis. What is the point being made? The point is that this low level of risk of having an affected fetus may lead some women with elevated AFP levels and a negative ultrasound to decide not to proceed with the hazards of amniocentesis.

The Nadel study is an important one. You are going to get questions on this topic from couples who call you to ask about your opinions on this subject. Have you read the article?—J.A. Stockman, III, M.D.

Antenatal Phenobarbital for the Prevention of Periventricular and Intraventricular Hemorrhage: A Double-Blind, Randomized, Placebo-Controlled, Multihospital Trial

Kaemof JW, Porreco R, Molina R, Hale K, Pantoja AF, Rosenberg AA (Univ of Colorado, Denver; AMI St Luke's Hosp, Denver; St Joseph's Hosp, Denver)
J Pediatr 117:933–938, 1990   1–12

Because peripartum hypoxia and ischemia play major roles in the pathogenesis of periventricular-intraventricular hemorrhage (PVH-IVH) in premature infants, therapy given before birth agents might be most effective in reducing PVH-IVH. Two previous studies have suggested that antenatal administration of phenobarbital, an agent shown to be neuroprotective in animals after cerebral hypoxic-ischemic insults, significantly reduces the incidence and severity of PVH-IVH in premature infants. To investigate further, 110 women at less than 31 weeks of gestation who had premature labor, premature rupture of membranes, or maternal–fetal complications necessitating elective delivery were studied. The women were randomly assigned in a blinded fashion to receive 10 mg/kg of phenobarbital intravenously or 10 mg/kg of placebo intravenously for 30 minutes before delivery. Infants were studied within the first 4 days of life by real-time ultrasonography.

Maternal demographics, complications of pregnancy antenatal management, and route of delivery did not differ significantly between the phenobarbital and placebo groups. The overall incidence of PVH-IVH was 20.4% among the 54 phenobarbital-treated infants and 28.4% among the 67 placebo-treated infants; the difference was not significant. Likewise, the incidence of grade 1 or 2 PVH-IVH was similar for both groups. However, the frequency of grade 3 and grade 4 hemorrhages was significantly lower in the phenobarbital group (3.7%) than in the placebo group (15%). There were no differences in the severity of associated conditions in the infants to account for the difference in the incidence of severe hemorrhage. Antenatal administration of phenobarbital appears to be effective in reducing the severity of PVH-IVH in infants delivered before 31 weeks of gestation.

▶ Dr. Edward S. Ogata, Professor and Vice Chairman, Department of Pediatrics, Northwestern University Medical School and Head, Division of Neonatology, Children's Memorial Hospital, comments:

▶ More than 15 years have passed since noninvasive cranial radiologic techniques were first applied to identify the incidence and quantitate the severity of periventricular IVH in premature infants. Although much has been learned about the development of IVH and its consequences, a means to prevent IVH is still not available. This is in part because of the gap in knowledge about the mechanisms that cause IVH. It is known that IVH originates from the immature vascular bed of the subependymal germinal matrix. Rupture of the poorly supported vessels within the matrix results in extravasation of blood into the adjacent lateral ventricle. Posthemorrhagic hydrocephalus, one extreme consequence of IVH, is caused by the development of arachnoiditis and the resultant obstruction of the arachnoid villi. Many of the problems that plague the premature infant are thought to be stresses that can cause germinal matrix hemorrhage and IVH. These include respiratory distress syndrome, pneumothorax, altered blood pressure and cerebral perfusion, and trauma during labor and delivery. Intrinsic biologic immaturity is probably another important factor, because the risk of IVH is inversely proportional to the degree of prematurity.

These thoughts have resulted in the empiric application of a variety of methods to prevent IVH. Of note, the use of exogenous surfactant to treat respiratory distress syndrome has not to date greatly reduced the incidence of IVH. Other methods include early paralyzation of infants with respiratory distress syndrome to prevent fluctuation in cerebral perfusion and the administration of various drugs, including indomethacin, vitamin K, and phenobarbital.

The use of phenobarbital has an interesting evolution. A 1981 report indicated a striking reduction in the incidence of IVH in a small number of premature infants who weighed 1,500 g or less who received phenobarbital after birth. Subsequent studies have failed to corroborate this finding, and 1 report suggested that phenobarbital may actually increase the risk of IVH. However, phenobarbital continues to be assessed, and this study by Kaempf et al. is one of a series of studies to suggest that potential efficacy of antenatal phenobarbital administration to prevent IVH. These investigators found that antenatal phenobarbital did not affect the overall incidence of IVH; however, it appeared to be associated with a lower incidence of severe IVH.

These observations and the previous ones are intriguing; they do not at this point mandate the administration of this drug to every woman in premature labor. It is unclear why phenobarbital administered to the fetus should prevent hemorrhage, whereas administration to the neonate is ineffective. Because numerous factors probably contribute to the development of IVH, a prospective, randomized multicenter trial with consideration of confounding variables is necessary to clearly confirm phenobarbital's usefulness. Fortunately, such a trial is about to be initiated. The mechanisms by which phenobarbital acts remain to be delineated. Although some data suggest that barbituates are neuroprotective, how phenobarbital might actually prevent hemorrhage is unknown. And of course, as always, the potential long-term complications of such therapy remain to be identified.—E.S. Ogata, M.D.

The Risks of Early Cordocentesis (12–21 Weeks): Analysis of 500 Procedures
Orlandi F, Damiani G, Jakil C, Lauricella S, Bertolino O, Maggio A (Ospedale V. Cervello, Palermo, Italy)
Prenat Diagn 10:425–428, 1990   1–13

The intravascular route has created many possibilities for direct treatment of the fetus. However, cordocentesis generally has been limited to relatively advanced gestational ages, although it can be done from week 12 with good results. The safety of early cordocentesis was examined in a series of 500 procedures done at 12–21 weeks of gestation, all by the same physician. Exclusion of therapeutic abortions left 370 concluded pregnancies available for follow-up.

The rate of fetal loss was 4.3% in this series, and the rate of preterm delivery was 5.9%. No fetal deaths preceded therapeutic abortion. Cord bleeding occurred in 13% of the cases with a normal outcome and in 5 of the 16 intrauterine fetal deaths. The procedure lasted considerably longer in cases of fetal loss.

Cord bleeding, fetal bradycardia, and a prolonged procedure time all are associated with an adverse outcome after early cordocentesis. Fetal blood sampling should be discontinued after 10 minutes.

▶ I don't think that there is a person in the world who would undertake tapping into the umbilical cord in utero unless it was absolutely necessary. The really timely issue, however, has not so much to do with cordocentesis but rather with chorionic villus sampling (CVS).

Is CVS a valuable addition or a dangerous alternative? It was introduced for first-trimester prenatal diagnosis of genetic disease more than 20 years ago. Using this technique, a sample of chorion can be taken, either through transabdominal or the transcervical route. The procedure may be done from 8 weeks of gestation to about 13 weeks of gestation. By contrast, second-trimester amniocentesis usually is not done before the 15th week of gestation. Depending on the techniques used, the results of cytogenetic analysis after CVS will be available anywhere from 24 hours to 2 weeks after obtaining the specimen, vs. 2–4 weeks for results after amniocentesis. Because of these positive attributes, CVS has caught on in the United States like wildfire. But what are the risks? First, European study showed that there was a 4.6% less chance of a successful pregnancy outcome with CVS compared with a second trimester amniocentesis (1). There are also several reports of congenital anomalies in infants after CVS. Firth et al. (2) reported on 4 infants with severe limb anomalies among 289 pregnancies in which CVS was done between 56 and 66 days of gestation. Mahoney, et al (3) reported the results of a follow-up of 9,588 pregnancies in the CVS arm of a large US study. In 1,025 procedures done at less than 66 days of gestation, significant limb reduction defects were observed in 6 infants, and 1 infant had minor defects. Apparently, performing CVS early in gestation can produce some vascular disruption, leading to malformations that include absence of the radius, ulna, fingers, toes, and fusion of bones.

All of this might be worth it if the ultimate accuracy of cytogenetic results obtained by CVS were better than by amniocentesis. They are not. Thus, the only significant value of CVS is the ability to obtain specimens early enough so that a woman does not have to undergo an abortion after 15 to 18 weeks of gestation. If a pregnancy must be terminated late in the second trimester, there is a higher risk to the mother of both physical and psychological complications. Any current counseling of women contemplating CVS must define the risks and the benefits of both procedures.

Is there any solution to the dilemma between the relative values of early CVS vs. late amniocentesis? The answer is yes. Once again, the ultrasonographer steps forth with a solution. With the advent of high-resolution ultrasonographic imaging, it is now becoming possible to safely sample amniotic fluid in the first trimester. When this hope becomes better realized, and if safety is demonstrated, CVS will be out of business.

Three cheers for the ultrasonographers who are inheriting the earth.—J.A. Stockman, III, M.D.

References

1. Editorial: *Lancet* 337:1513, 1991.
2. Firth HV, et al: *Lancet* 337:762, 1991.
3. Mahoney MJ, et al: *Lancet* 337:1422, 1991.

Infant Mortality in Sweden and Finland: Implications for the United States
Wallace HM, Ericsson A, Bolander AM, Vienonen M (San Diego State Univ; Natl Board of Health and Welfare, Stockholm; Statistics Sweden, Stockholm; Natl Board of Health, Helsinki)
J Perinatol 10:3–11, 1990   1–14

Reported Infant Mortality Rates in 24 Countries for 1985

Country	Rate	Country	Rate
Japan	5.5	Singapore	9.3
Finland	6.3	United Kingdom	9.3
Sweden	6.8	Belgium	9.4
Switzerland	6.9	German Democratic	9.6
Hong Kong	7.5	Republic	
Canada	7.9	Australia	10.0
Denmark	7.9	Spain	10.5
Netherlands	7.9	United States	10.6
France	8.0	New Zealand	10.8
Norway	8.5	Italy	10.9
Federal Republic of	8.9	Austria	12.3
Germany		Greece	14.0
Ireland	8.9	Czechoslovakia	14.0

Note: Rates are per 1,000 live births.
(Courtesy of Wallace HM, Ericsson A, Bolander AM, et al: *J Perinatol* 10:3–11, 1990.)

From 1920 to 1980 Sweden's reported infant mortality (IM) rate was the lowest in the world. Since 1981 Sweden, Japan, and Finland have had the lowest rates. The United States ranks 18th in IM. In 1985 the reported IM rate was 5.5 per 1,000 live births in Japan, 6.3 in Finland, and 6.8 in Sweden. In the United States it was 10.6 per 1,000 live births (table). Neonatal mortality reflects preconceptional, prenatal, and perinatal care, whereas postnatal mortality (from day 28 of life to first birthday) reflects the environmental care of the infant.

The mortality rate among white infants in the United States is substantially higher than that in Sweden and Finland. In 1985 the District of Columbia had the highest IM rate in the United States, 20.8 per 1,000 live births, which was 2½ times higher than that of the state with the lowest IM rate, Rhode Island.

Both Sweden and Finland have had a consistently lower incidence of low–birth-weight infants than the United States, 4.2% in Sweden and Finland and 6.8% in the United States in 1985. The rate of decline of the reported incidence of low birth weight from 1970 through 1985 was much more pronounced in Finland than in the United States. The incidence of low birth weight among blacks in the United States has consistently been about twice that of whites. Finland and Sweden have a much lower maternal mortality rate than the United States.

In Sweden and Finland a network of maternal health clinics throughout the country provides prenatal care to all pregnant women free of charge. These clinics are part of the national health service. Pregnant women are monitored early and continuously for high risk. Sweden and Finland also have an organized system of parent education both before and after delivery. In these 2 countries, 95% to 99% of pregnant women register early for prenatal care. This figure was 76% in 1985 in the United States. Prenatal care needs to be made freely and readily available to pregnant women of all ages, ethnic groups, geographic locations, and socioeconomic levels in the United States.

▶ James W. Collins, Jr., M.D., M.P.H., Assistant Professor of Pediatrics, Northwestern University Medical School, and attending Neonatologist, Children's Memorial Hospital, comments:

▶ Infant mortality in the United States has 2 disturbing characteristics: it is extremely high compared with other developed countries, and the death rate for blacks is twice that of whites. If our IM rate equalled that achieved by Sweden, there would be approximately 8,000 fewer black and 10,000 fewer white deaths in this country—a sum greater than the total number of deaths among all children aged 1 to 15 years. Approximately 6,000 black infant deaths a year could be prevented if the IM rate in blacks was lowered to the level of whites. There are also significant medical and economic considerations with the surviving small infant. An estimated 16% of all very low–birth-weight (<1,500 g) infants are moderately or severely handicapped. Between 1978 and 1990, the United States spent an estimated $2.5 billion in the first-year cost alone for more than 330,000 low–birth-weight infants whose hardships could have been been prevented. For the same amount of money we could have provided 68.7 million food packages under the Supplemental Food Program for Women, Infants, and Children (WIC); provided comprehensive prenatal care to 3.5 million mothers; and immunized 33 million children. Although numerous studies have shown that prenatal care improves pregnancy outcome, the proportion of women obtaining adequate prenatal care has stagnated. Moreover, the percentage of black women who received no prenatal care increased disproportionately during the 1980s compared with the percentage of white women.

The disparity between white and black infant death rates has grown over the last 3 decades. During this time period, the infant death rate for whites in the United States also has deteriorated compared with the rate for whites in Sweden. Improvement in our persistently poor international ranking in infant mortality cannot be anticipated until the racial gap is closed. Improved outcomes for whites and blacks depends on our ability to eliminate disadvantages experienced by blacks. We should support social programs aimed at removing racial differences in the known determinants of low birth weight—urban poverty, inadequate prenatal care, and poor nutrition. Universal health insurance for pregnant women and infants is a mandatory first step.—J.W. Collins, Jr., M.D.

The Relationship of Unwed Status to Infant Mortality
Hein HA, Burmeister LF, Papke KR (Univ of Iowa)
Obstet Gynecol 76:763–768, 1990   1–15

To study potential factors associated with low birth weight and infant mortality, the incidence of infant deaths in offspring of unmarried women was compared with the incidence in their married counterparts during 10 years in Iowa (Fig 1–6).

Infant mortality was significantly higher in unwed mothers. The unwed women were generally poorly educated, younger, and did not seek prenatal care. The unwed population had relatively more women who were younger than age 18 years (Fig 1–7).

Although health care is accessible throughout Iowa, unwed women had significantly fewer prenatal visits than married women. Unwed women also had a higher incidence of postneonatal death in term and near-term infants most likely to survive. Because unwanted pregnancy has been associated with a poor pregnancy outcome, increased education

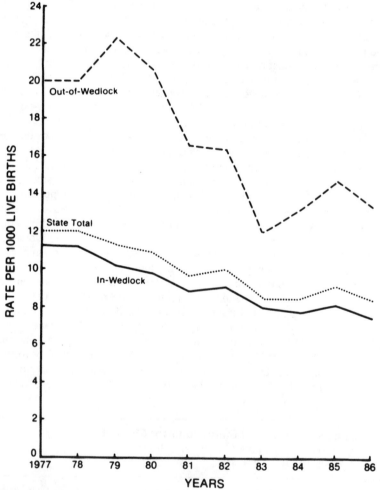

Fig 1–6.—Infant mortality rates for the state of Iowa, 1977–1986. $\chi^2 = 248.52$; $P < .001$. (Courtesy of Hein HA, Burmeister LF, Papke KR: *Obstet Gynecol* 76:763–768, 1990.)

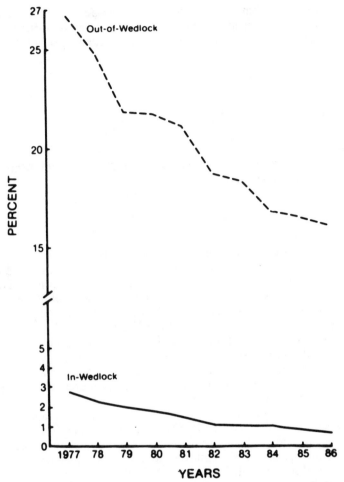

Fig 1–7.—Percent of births to women younger than age 18 years within the in-wedlock and out-of-wedlock groups. $\chi^2 = 26,712.88$; $P < .001$. (Courtesy of Hein HA, Burmeister LF, Papke KR: *Obstet Gynecol* 76:763–768, 1990.)

both in schools and for young adults to prevent unwanted pregnancy is advocated.

▶ The causes of infant mortality are so multifactorial that it seems a shame to pin them on 1 factor—whether or not the mother is married. The United States, probably the world's wealthiest nation other than Switzerland, has fallen from 6th to a tie for last place among the 20 industrialized nations with respect to infant mortality. This, of course, was a phenomenon that occurred in a 35-year period during which no other nation on earth was spending as much on health care as we were. Dr. Collins' commentary, immediately preceding this one, deals with infant mortality rates and says it all. There is a time for needed change, and that time is now. On every pediatric health care provider's reading list should be an article entitled, "Infant Mortality: A Practical Approach To The Analysis of The Leading Causes of Death and Risk Factors" (1).—J.A. Stockman, III, M.D.

Reference

1. Dollfus C, et al: *Pediatrics* 86:176, 1990.

Psychiatric Disorders at Five Years Among Children With Birthweights <1000 g: A Regional Perspective
Szatmari P, Saigal S, Rosenbaum P, Campbell D, King S (McMaster Univ, Hamilton, Ontario)
Dev Med Child Neurol 32:954–962, 1990   1–16

There have been conflicting studies on the association between pregnancy and birth complications and behavioral and learning problems in later childhood, possibly because of methodological limitations. The relationship between extremely low birth weight (ELBW) and psychiatric disorder was investigated in a cohort of children with birth weights of 500–1,000 g who were born between 1980 and 1982.

At 5 years of age, 82 of the 90 survivors were evaluated for a range of psychiatric disorders using instruments of known reliability and validity. Mean birth weight was 835 g, and mean gestational age was 27.4 weeks. The control group consisted of 208 5-year-old children from a stratified random sample in the community.

There were no significant differences in demographic, family, and developmental variables between ELBW children and controls, but developmental delay and problems with motor coordination were much more common among the ELBW children. In addition, the incidence of attention deficit disorder with hyperactivity (ADDH) was significantly higher in ELBW children (15.9%) than in control children (6.9%). The rates of conduct disorder and emotional disorder, however, were not increased, indicating that ELBW was a specific risk factor for ADDH. Multivariate analysis suggested that the relationship between ADDH and ELBW could be accounted for by a neurodevelopmental problem. Overall, only 24.2% of ELBW children had clinically significant psychiatric diagnoses at 5 years of age compared with 16.3% of the controls.

These results suggest that low birth weight leads to neurodevelopment problems, which in turn are associated with ADDH. However, if a child survives the neonatal period without major disabilities, such as cerebral palsy, the risk for these problems is low for ELBW infants.

▶ There are a lot of data now that very clearly describe the long-term outcome of infants of low birth weight. A large study from Australia that looked at the outcome of infants with birth weights of 500–999 g found that, at 8 years of age, 9% of these children had cerebral palsy, 7% were blind, 4% had poor vision, 6% required hearing aids, and 2% had seizures. In one quarter of the children, reading skills were at least 18 months behind those of a control group (1).

If you think the world down under is different, a study from Canada reported similar results (2). Also examining infants with birth weights of 500–999 g, these authors found that 12% had Weschler IQ tests that were more than 2 standard deviations below the mean. This weight group of premature infants did less well on reading, spelling, and mathematics testing. Approximately two thirds of these extremely low–birth-weight survivors were performing in a normal range.

Teplin et al. (3) provide the most recent update on neurodevelopmental health and growth outcome. They report on 28 extremely low–birth-weight infants (birth weight <1000 g) from Chapel Hill, North Carolina who are now 6 years old. Surprise: Chapel Hill is no different from Canada, Australia, and presumably the rest of the United States. At 6 years of age, the very low–birth-weight infants have grown up to be school-aged children with smaller head circumferences ($p = .015$) and with mild or moderate to severe neurologic problems (61% vs. 23% of controls).

Between this commentary and the one preceding it, you must think that I am extremely biased toward reporting only negative outcomes in the follow-up of children who were very low in birth weight. In fact, there is some heartening news. With a lot of help, these children can have a better outcome. The results of the Infant Health and Development Program have been reported. This is the first multisite, randomized clinical trial designed to evaluate the efficacy of combining early child development intervention and family support services with pediatric follow-up to reduce developmental, behavioral, and other health problems among low–birth-weight, premature infants (4). At 36 months of age, the intervention group had significantly higher mean IQ scores than the control follow-up group, by as much as 13.2 IQ points. Additionally, there were significantly fewer behavior problems reported by the mothers of these children. There was a small but statistically significant increase in minor illnesses reported by these mothers for the lighter–birth-weight group only, but there was no significant difference in serious health conditions.

Whatever else you believe about these weighty issues, improving the status of young children is the subject of policy debate currently and will be for the foreseeable future.—J.A. Stockman, III, M.D.

References

1. Victorian Infant Collaborative Study Group: *J Pediatr* 118:761, 1991.
2. Saigal S, et al: *J Pediatr* 118:751, 1991.
3. Teplin SW, et al: *J Pediatr* 118:768, 1991.
4. The Infant Health and Development Program: *JAMA* 263:3035, 1990.

28-Day Survival Rates of 6676 Neonates With Birth Weights of 1250 Grams or Less

Phelps DL, Brown DR, Tung B, Cassady G, McClead RE, Purohit DM, Palmer EA (Univ of Rochester; Univ of Pittsburgh; Univ of Texas School Health Science Ctr, Houston; Children's Hosp of San Francisco; Ohio State Univ; et al)
Pediatrics 87:7–17, 1991   1–17

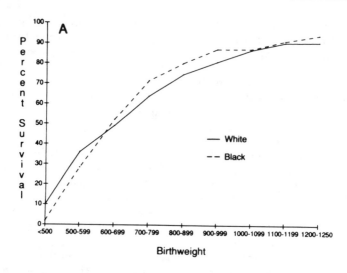

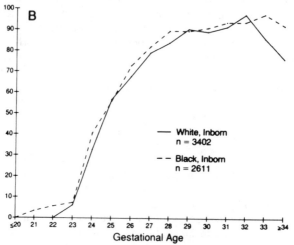

Fig 1–8.—Race-specific survival to 28 days for birth weight in 100-g categories (A) and gestational age (B). (Courtesy of Phelps DL, Brown DR, Tung B, et al: *Pediatrics* 87:7–17, 1991.)

Neonatal mortality in very-low–birth-weight (VLBW) neonates (<1,250 g) has improved steadily. Survival rates specific for birth weight, gestational age, sex, and race were calculated for 6,676 VLBW neonates delivered during 1986 and 1987.

Overall, 28-day survival increased with gestational age and birth weight. Survival rates increased from 36.5% at 24 weeks of gestation to 89.9% at 29 weeks of gestation and from 30% for neonates with a birth weight of 500–599 g to 91.3% for neonates with a birth weight of 1,200–1,250 g. Female neonates and black neonates fared better than their male and white counterparts, but the difference diminished after controlling for gestational age (Fig 1–8). Small-for-gestational-age neo-

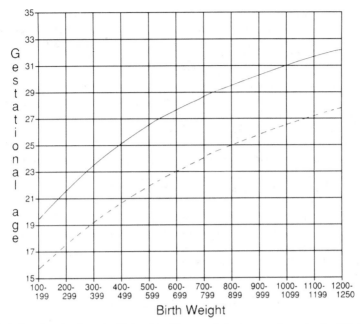

Fig 1–9.—Gestational age for birth weight. The smoothed curves are shown for the 10th *(broken line)* and 90th *(solid line)* percentile distributions of observed gestational ages for given birth weight categories in 7,371 neonates. (Courtesy of Phelps DL, Brown DR, Tung B, et al: *Pediatrics* 87:7–17, 1991.)

nates had lower survival rates than normal-sized neonates of the same gestational age. Multivariate regression analysis showed that, in order of descending significance, gestational age and birth weight, sex, race, single birth, and small-for-gestational-age status were independent predictors of survival. By plotting the 10th and 90th percentiles of the gestational ages for each birth weight, a curve was generated for estimating the gestational age of a neonate in the VLBW group (Fig 1–9). For example, 80% of 550-g neonates had a gestational age between 22 and 26 weeks.

Both gestational age and birth weight are strong predictors of neonatal survival in VLBW neonates. The importance of gestational age highlights the need for an accurate tool to assess the gestational age of VLBW neonates.

▶ The price to be paid for the fantastic improvement in survival rates reported by Phelps et al. is not insignificant. Reports from Stanford University (1) yielded the following statistics: the overall survival rate for infants born weighing between 500 and 750 g was 35%. For those infants who had been successfully resuscitated in the delivery room and were admitted to the intensive care nursery, the survival rate was 50%, 9% of these infants were severely handicapped, and 36% had remediable disabilities at 2 years of age. Good results, but at the same time somewhat disturbing.

In 1986, Hack and Fanaroff (2) presented data from 6 different centers dealing with the same birth-weight group. The mean survival rate was 33.5%. Of those infants who survived, 31% had significant neurodevelopmental handicaps. The cost of neonatal intensive care for these infants was obviously impressive. The average length of stay was 137 days, and the mean cost of care per infant was $158,800 (range, $72,110–$524,110). You could roughly increase the dollar amounts by about 50%, because these data were based on 1984-1985 dollars. The logical question to ask is the price–$150,000 to $750,000 (in 1992 dollars). Is this too much to pay to achieve the results that are being seen, given a society that has limited resources? Recently someone (3) had the courage(?) to suggest limiting treatment for extremely premature, low–birth-weight infants.

To date, we have never been in a situation where we have been forced to ask ourselves questions regarding allocation of medical care in the nursery. The issue here, however, is not really one of allocation of medical care. The issue is whether or not we are using the finite resources that we have in the most effective way to reduce infant mortality and morbidity. Might the $750,000 that it costs to save 1 neurologically impaired infant be better spent setting up a neighborhood program to facilitate maternity care for inner city unwed mothers? Would more infants be saved with this approach?

These are tough questions that can no longer be ignored. The inertia of the past cannot continue. Our society is characterized by the fact that apathy has become a major problem. But who cares?—J.A. Stockman, III, M.D.

References

1. Stevenson DK, et al: *J Perinatol* 8:82, 1988.
2. Hack M, et al: *N Engl J Med* 314:660, 1986.
3. Young EW, et al: *Am J Dis Child* 144:549, 1990.

A Study of the Relationship Between Bile Salts, Bile Salt-Stimulated Lipase, and Free Fatty Acids in Breast Milk: Normal Infants and Those With Breast Milk Jaundice

Forsyth JS, Donnet L, Ross PE (Ninewells Hosp and Med School, Dundee, Scotland)
J Pediatr Gastroenterol Nutr 11:205–210, 1990   1–18

The cause of breast-milk jaundice, which occurs in otherwise healthy breast-fed infants, remains uncertain. Previous research has suggested an association between breast-milk jaundice and increased lipase activity and elevated free fatty acid (FFA) concentrations in the milk. Other studies, however, found no differences in lipoprotein lipase or bile salt-stimulated lipase (BSSL) activity in mothers of infants with jaundice and control mothers.

The relationship of BSSL activity, FFA concentration, and bile salt concentrations in milk of normal infants and the milk of infants with breast-milk jaundice was examined. Mothers of healthy newborn infants were recruited to provide breast-milk samples. Forty-two provided samples at 2 weeks; 30 provided samples at 6 weeks; and 16 provided samples at 10 weeks, at 13 weeks and at 14 weeks. Twelve infants with breast-milk jaundice were included in the study.

There was a significant decline in both cholate and chenodeoxycholate levels with duration of lactation. Although BSSL activity fell significantly with duration of lactation, there was no correlation between BSSL activity and bile salt concentration. Free fatty acid concentrations, which were similar throughout lactation, were not related to either BSSL activity or bile salt concentration.

Compared with normal breast milks, the milk of infants with breast-milk jaundice had significantly increased concentrations of cholate and cholate-to-chenodeoxycholate ratio. Bile salt-stimulated lipase activity and FFA concentrations, however, were similar for the 2 groups.

▶ Dr. Richard Polin, Professor of Pediatrics, University of Pennsylvania Medical School, and Attending Neonatologist, The Children's Hospital of Philadelphia, comments:

▶ Considering the frequency with which breast milk is invoked as the cause of neonatal hyperbilirubinemia, it is somewhat surprising to me that the cause of the breast-milk jaundice syndrome still remains obscure. Breast-milk jaundice is probably the only "disease" where the number of theories regarding its cause greatly exceed the number of infants who have had adverse outcomes. Infants with the breast-milk jaundice syndrome have a progressive rise in the serum concentration of unconjugated bilirubin, which peaks by day 10 to 15 of life. This syndrome should be distinguished from the much more common "breast-feeding jaundice," which coincides temporally with the rise and fall of physiologic hyperbilirubinemia.

In the early 1960s Arias and Gartner (1) suggested that women whose infants had breast-milk jaundice syndrome had an inhibitor of bilirubin conjugation (3-α-20-β pregnanediol) in their breast milk. However, subsequent studies failed to identify this substance in breast milk samples fed to infants with presumed breast-milk jaundice (2). In the early 1970s, Bevan and Holton (3) demonstrated that nonesterified fatty acids inhibited the enzyme responsible for bilirubin conjugation in vitro. Although earlier studies suggested that breast milk from mothers of infants with this syndrome had increased lipase activity that was capable of digesting triglycerides to free fatty acids (4), more recent studies (5,6), including this report by Forsyth et al., have been unable to substantiate that finding. Moreover, free fatty acid levels have not been increased consistently in breast milk from mothers who have nursed infants with the breast-milk jaundice syndrome.

Most recently, a number of investigators have demonstrated that human milk contains significant amounts of β-glucuronidase (7,8). Beta-glucuronidase is an enzyme capable of converting bilirubin monoglucuronides (the predominant bilirubin glucuronide in neonatal bile) to unconjugated bilirubin, which can be easily reabsorbed. Gourley and Arend have shown that serum bilirubin levels in breast-fed infants are directly related to the concentration of β-glucuronidase in breast milk on days 3 and 21 of life and to levels of fecal β-glucuronidase on day 21 of life. Similarly, Takimoto et al. (9) have reported that β-glucuronidase concentrations in stool samples are higher in icteric infants than in nonicteric infants.

In summary, it is safe to say that the pathophysiology of breast-milk jaundice syndrome remains unclear. Although the presence of β-glucuronidase in some breast-milk specimens offers a plausible explanation, other past theories have seemed equally likely. It is important to remember that this syndrome is a diagnosis of exclusion, and other more common diseases must be considered first, before the breast is labeled as a villain.— R. Polin, M.D.

References

1. Arias et al: *J Clin Invest* 42:913, 1963.
2. Murphy JF, et al: *Arch Dis Child* 56:474, 1981.
3. Bevan BR, Holton JB: *Clin Chim Acta* 41:101, 1972.
4. Poland RL, et al: *Pediatr Res* 14:1328, 1980.
5. Odievre M, Luzeau R: *Acta Paediatr Scand* 67:49, 1978.
6. Constantopoulos A, et al: *Eur J Pediatr* 134:35, 1980.
7. Gourley GR, Arend RA: *Lancet* i:644, 1986.
8. Gaffney PT, et al: *Lancet* i:1161, 1986.
9. Takimoto MT, Matsuda I: *Biol Neonate* 18:66, 1971.

Phototherapy for Neonatal Hyperbilirubinemia: Six-Year Follow-up of the National Institute of Child Health and Human Development Clinical Trial
Scheidt PC, Bryla DA, Nelson KB, Hirtz DG, Hoffman JH, and Principal Investigators (Natl Inst of Child Health and Development; Natl Inst of Neurological Disorders and Stroke, Bethesda, Md)
Pediatrics 85:455–463, 1990   1–19

A multicenter, randomized, collaborative study was undertaken to assess whether phototherapy used to control serum bilirubin is safe and whether it is as effective in preventing brain injury as exchange transfusion. The neurosensory, neuromotor, and cognitive development of children at ages 1 and 6 years were reviewed.

Six neonatal care centers participated, and 1,339 newborn infants were randomly assigned to phototherapy or control groups by the following subgroups: (1) birth weight <2,000 g; (2) birth weight 2,000–2,499 g and bilirubin level >171 μmol/L (10 mg/dL); or (3) birth weight ≥2,500 g and bilirubin level >222 μmol/L (13 mg/dL). Phototherapy was administered for 96 hours, and exchange transfusion was administered to both groups when serum bilirubin levels reached predetermined levels.

At 1-year follow-up, 83% of patients returned for 6-year follow-up, 88% returned for examination. Mortality and diagnosed medical conditions did not differ significantly between phototherapy and control groups. At 6 years, the phototherapy and control groups had similar rates of cerebral palsy (5.8% vs. 5.9%), other motor abnormalities including clumsiness and hypotonia (11.1% vs. 11.4%), and sensorineural hearing loss (1.8% vs. 1.9%). The overall scores on the Wechsler Intelligence Scale for Children-Revised were not significantly different between groups. These findings were consistent for each of the birth-weight groups and ethnic groups, and for each of the 6 centers individually.

These data show that phototherapy can effectively control neonatal hyperbilirubinemia without evidence of adverse outcome at age 6 years and that phototherapy was at least as effective as management with exchange transfusion alone. Nonetheless, phototherapy should be used with the same concern for possible unknown adverse effects that is used for any therapeutic intervention in the newborn infant.

▶ When phototherapy became a widely used tool for the management of neonatal hyperbilirubinemia, the National Academy of Sciences Committee on Phototherapy in the Newborn expressed concern about the possible long-term effects of this treatment. There was a suggestion that photometabolic products might interfere with albumin binding of bilirubin. This raised the possibility that phototherapy might contribute to the neurotoxicity of bilirubin. There were even concerns about the possibility of delayed adverse effects on growth and development, vision, and skin.

The concerns were high enough that the National Academy of Sciences concluded that, because there was insufficient information about the safety of phototherapy, a large scale, long-term study should be conducted. The report abstracted above is the result of that recommendation. In this study, neonates were chosen at random for phototherapy or were placed into control groups if (1) birth weight was <2,000 g; (2) birth weight was 2,000–2,499 g, and serum bilirubin level reached 10 mg/dL within the first 96 hours after birth; or (3) the birth weight was ≥2,500 g, serum bilirubin reached 13 mg/dL within the first 96 hours after birth. Once the lights were turned on, they were left on for 96 hours. Exchange transfusion was performed in both the phototherapy and control group if serum bilirubin reached predetermined levels (10 mg/dL for infants weighing <1,250 g, 20 mg/dL for infants weighing >2,500 g).

The results are as noted in the abstract. The study vindicates what we have been doing for the last 20 years. Gosh knows what would have happened if one of our everyday practices of neonatology were shown to have some untoward long-term effect.

Let there be light!—J.A. Stockman, III, M.D.

Breast Milk Jaundice: Natural History, Familial Incidence and Late Neurodevelopmental Outcome of the Infant
Grunebaum E, Amir J, Merlob P, Mimouni M, Varsano I (Hasharon Hosp, Petah-Tiqva, Israel; Tel Aviv Univ, Israel)
Eur J Pediatr 150:267–270, 1991   1–20

Jaudice associated with breast-feeding is a common problem. Although much research has been done on breast-milk jaundice, its natural history, familial occurrence, and the late neurodevelopment of children with breast-milk jaundice are not clear.

Sixty consecutive infants admitted with clinical jaundice throughout the first 3 weeks of life or later were followed up. There were 2 bilirubin

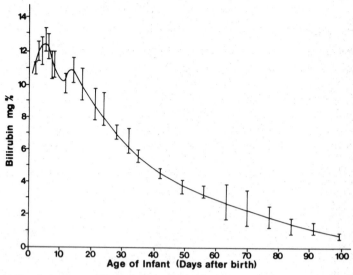

Fig 1–10.—Average mean bilirubin levels (mg%) in relation to postnatal age (in days) in 46 infants with breast-milk jaundice fed exclusively on breast milk. (Courtesy of Grunebaum E, Amir J, Merlob P, et al: *Eur J Pediatr* 150:267–270, 1991.)

level peaks, 1 on the 4th and 5th days and 1 on the 14th and 15th days of life (Fig 1–10). Among infants who were breast-fed continuously, hyperbilirubinemia disappeared slowly and was still detectable 12 weeks after birth. The familial incidence was 13.9%, suggesting that a unique genetic factor is expressed in some cases. There were no late neurodevelopment or hearing defects in these infants.

Breast-milk jaundice is not associated with sequelae. The protracted bilirubin burden observed in infants with breast-milk jaundice appears to be harmless, probably because the blood-brain barrier is strong enough in the first weeks of life and because there are no other endangering factors. Because breast-milk jaundice for up to 12 weeks is not associated with neurodevelopmental defects, the continuation of breast-feeding in such cases can be encouraged.

▶ The abstract says it all, so let's finish this Newborn chapter with a 3-part question quiz.

First question: A couple decides to have their first child. What is the average time from making such a decision to actually conceiving?

The answer here is pretty straightforward. A study of 2,817 women who planned for a pregnancy showed that the median time from trying to become pregnant to actually becoming pregnant was 2 months, with a mean of 4.5 months (1). Only 6% of women reported that it took longer than 12 months to conceive. This report is superb evidence that there is nothing better than an idea whose time has come. On the other hand, it is unequivocal proof that if you don't want to become pregnant, use birth control on every conceivable occasion.

Second question: What percent of fetuses suck their right thumb?

Would you believe that 95% of fetuses demonstrated on ultrasound to be sucking their thumb are sucking their right thumb. Some surprise? Actually, however, there is recent speculation that the reason why fetuses and their natural derivatives (us) are right-handed is that the right upper limb embryologically receives blood through a vessel that arises more proximately and earlier from the aorta than the supply to the left upper limb, resulting in earlier development of the right arm, hand, and thumb. The latter speculation appeared in a report from *Nature* (2) and could be a candidate article for *Ripley's Believe It or Not.*

Third question: After coffee consumption, frequency of intercourse, and age are controlled for, what is the effect of drinking 1 can of caffeinated soft drink per day on the monthly chance of conceiving?

The answer is an interesting one. It used to be said that an apple a day kept the doctor away. Well, 1 can of caffeinated soft drink per day is associated with a 50% reduction in the monthly chance of conceiving (3). This question has very practical implications. Although there may be a whole "Pepsi Generation" out there now, there very well may not be another one to follow, given all the oral contraceptives that are being drunk these days.

So closes the Newborn chapter of the 1992 YEAR BOOK OF PEDIATRICS. This has been my first opportunity to write the Newborn chapter. Frank Oski had the pleasure of doing that for the last 13 years. What have I learned after reviewing the entire world's neonatal literature for the last 12 months. I must conclude that given all the trevails of tiny tykes in nurseries, it is easy to see why infants don't have as much fun in infant'cy as adults do in adult'ry.—J.A. Stockman, III, M.D.

References

1. Joesoef MR, et al: *Lancet* 1:136, 1990.
2. Dryden R: *Nature* 350:27, 1991.
3. Wilcox AJ, et al: Lancet 115:9, 1991.

2 Infectious Disease and Immunology

Central Nervous System Tuberculosis in Children: A Review of 30 Cases
Waecker NJ Jr, Connor JD (Naval Hosp, San Diego; Univ of California, San Diego, La Jolla, Calif)
Pediatr Infect Dis J 9:539–543, 1990   2–1

Early diagnosis and specific antituberculous treatment are essential for prevention of permanent sequelae or fatal outcome in CNS tuberculosis.

The clinical symptoms of CNS tuberculosis may be similar to those of acute infantile and childhood infectious diseases (table). The definitive bacteriologic diagnosis is slowed by the usual low frequency of recovery from CSF and the slow growth of *Mycobacterium tuberculosis* in culture. Fifty percent or fewer of these patients have positive purified protein derivative test results. In a review of 30 pediatric patients with CNS tuberculosis, hydrocephalus (in 100% of the patients) demonstrated by cranial CT scan and active tuberculosis in the family were the most important findings. Communicating hydrocephalus in CNS tuberculosis is usually caused by blockage of the basilar cistern. Cranial CT with contrast medium is recommended as part of the initial work-up in a child suspected of having CNS tuberculosis.

Therapy should be initiated early when there is any increased index of suspicion, even in a patient who has both a negative purified protein de-

Preadmission Symptoms or Signs of 30 Patients With CNS Tuberculosis		
Symptoms or Signs	No.	%
Fever	29	97
Vomiting	22	73
Lethargy	22	73
Seizures	14	47
Anorexia	8	27
Stiff neck	8	27
Cough	7	23
Weight loss	7	23
Irritability	6	20
Changes in personality	3	10
Weakness/refusal to walk	3	10
Night sweats	2	7

(Courtesy of Waecker NJ Jr, Connor JD: *Pediatr Infect Dis J* 9:539–543, 1990.)

rivative test reaction and a normal chest radiograph. Initial therapy should include isoniazid, rifampin, and a third antituberculous drug. Pyrazinamide has been recommended over streptomycin as the third drug.

▶ As Ed Sullivan might have said, *the really big news* with tuberculous meningitis is its rapid diagnosis by the use of the polymerase chain reaction (PCR). Although this article gives us significant insights into the natural history of tuberculous meningitis and current treatment methods in children, we soon may be seeing a new era of a not-so-natural history with treatment. Specifically, whereas it used to take days to weeks to confirm a diagnosis of tuberculous meningitis, the diagnosis now can be made within hours with new DNA technologies that include the PCR (1,2). Use of the PCR is likely to improve the outcome of tuberculous meningitis.

Were you aware that about 10% of all tuberculous patients in developing countries have meningitis at the time of diagnosis, and that 1 in 4 patients who did not receive early treatment have severe neurologic sequelae? You can imagine, then, how welcome the PCR assays will be when they become widely available. In PCR-positive (for tuberculosis) meningitis, for example, long-term morbidity and mortality can be reduced by the early administration of dexamethasone along with routine antituberculous therapy (3).

The rapid diagnosis of herpes simplex encephalitis also can be made by use of PCR. Aurelius et al. (4) found that the PCR assay was positive in the CSF of 42 of 43 individuals with herpes simplex encephalitis proven by brain biopsy. Although the diagnosis of this life-threatening infection (particularly in newborns) can be made within a matter of hours, before you jump on the bandwagon, insisting that your local clinic or laboratory introduce PCR technology to amplify and identify DNA sequences from various pathogens, beware of the pitfalls with the PCR. The basic problem is with the diagnosis of herpes simplex encephalitis. Because the PCR is so sensitive, it will pick up even trivial contamination of samples in which there has been introduction of extraneous DNA into the specimen. Although CSF would seem to be the ideal starting sample for PCR amplification (because this fluid is normally free of herpes simplex virus DNA and is anatomically protected from external contamination), prevention of contamination with herpes simplex virus or its genome is especially difficult, because the virus is ubiquitous. Thus, attending physicians, nurses, and laboratory staff are all sources of a few "virons" here and there. With the PCR, these virons will be easily picked up, even though they would not be shown by culture.

We are going to be hearing a great deal more about the PCR's application for the rapid diagnosis of a variety of causes of meningitis and other infectious diseases as well. The PCR has been used to diagnose varicella zoster virus DNA from the airways of infected individuals (5). The technique can establish the definitive diagnosis of congenital toxoplasmosis in utero by means of amniotic fluid testing (6). This is an especially important application of PCR, because the majority of women who acquire *Toxoplasma* sp. infection during the first or second trimester of gestation will not transmit the infection to their offspring. Many uninfected fetuses could be unnecessarily aborted under current practices, because it usually takes weeks to establish the diagnosis by culture of amniotic fluid. The PCR permits rapid diagnosis of *Pneumocystis carinii* infection with an extraordinary degree of sensitivity and specificity (7). We all know how tricky the diagnosis of this infection can be. Lyme disease and even simple rotovirus diarrhea can be diagnosed within hours with the PCR (8).

If you think there is no end to the application of the PCR technology with respect to infectious diseases, you are probably right. As long as there is any DNA associated with an infection, sooner or later we will be able to diagnose it by the PCR. It is already being used to detect HIV in individuals in whom the diagnosis is not otherwise easily made. A classic example of the latter is the antibody-positive infant born to an HIV-positive mother. You don't know whether this antibody was passively transferred or whether the infant is, in fact, actively infected. Recently, the early detection of HIV infection by PCR in 1 dizygotic twin was reported. With the same technology, HIV infection was excluded in the other twin. Amazing!

Sorry to be so long winded about the PCR, but this technology is hotter than the core temperature of the Chernobyl nuclear reactor just before meltdown.— J.A. Stockman, III, M.D.

References

1. Kansko K, et al: *Neurology* 40:1617, 1990.
2. Shankar P, et al: *Lancet* 337:5, 1991.
3. Girgis NI, et al: *Pediatr Infect Dis J* 10:179, 1991.
4. Aurelius E, et al: *Lancet* 37:189, 1991.
5. Ozaki T, et al: *Arch Dis Child* 65:333, 1991.
6. Grover CM, et al: *J Clin Microbiol* 28:2297, 1990.
7. Wakefield AE, et al: *Lancet* 336:451, 1991.
8. Wilde J, et al: *Lancet* 337:323, 1991.

The Sequelae of *Haemophilus influenzae* Meningitis in School-Age Children

Taylor HG, Mills EL, Ciampi A, du Berger R, Watters GV, Gold R, MacDonald N, Michaels RH (Case Western Reserve Univ, Cleveland; McGill Univ, Montreal; Children's Hosp of Eastern Ontario, Ottawa, Canada; Hosp for Sick Children, Toronto; Children's Hosp of Pittsburgh)
N Engl J Med 323:1657–1663, 1990   2–2

Previous reports on the developmental sequelae of *Hemophilus influenzae* type b meningitis are inconsistent. Using a protocol for the comprehensive assessment of neuropsychological function, 97 school-aged children recruited from a sample of 519 children treated for *H. influenzae* type b meningitis between 1972 and 1984 were studied. Mean age of the patients was 17 months at the time of illness and 9.3 years at the time of testing. Cognitive, academic, and behavioral measures were compared between index children and their siblings nearest in age. Forty-one children had acute neurologic complications at the time of illness.

Only 14 (14%) children had persistent neurologic sequelae, including sensorineural hearing loss in 11, seizures in 2, and hemiplegia and mental retardation in 1. All these children had complications during the acute phase. As a whole, index children scored lower on reading ability and were more likely to be receiving special educational assistance than their siblings. However, the differences were small, and the differences on all measures were uniformly nonsignificant when the 58% of children without acute-phase complications were compared with their siblings. Behavioral problems were more common in index boys than in index girls and in those who were older at the time of testing, but sex or age were not related to cognitive or academic sequelae. Lower socioeconomic status and a lower ratio of glucose in cerebrospinal fluid to that in blood at the time of illness were also associated with sequelae. In contrast to previous reports, a favorable prognosis is suggested for most children treated for *H. influenzae* type b meningitis.

▶ Dr. Ralph D. Feigin, Distinguished Service Professor and the J.S. Abercrombie Professor of Pediatrics and Chairman, Department of Pediatrics, Baylor College of Medicine and Physician-in-Chief, Texas Children's Hospital, comments:

▶ The study by Taylor and associates is an attempt to gain additional insight into the sequelae of *Hemophilus infuenzae* meningitis with particular emphasis on neuropsychological function. Although the study was retrospective, it permitted a more detailed neuropsychological assessment made at an earlier age than was reported by investigators in previous studies. In addition, the index patients were compared with their closest-in-age and sex-matched siblings, and the study was controlled for occupational and educational status.

Only 14% of children who had been afflicted with *H. influenzae* meningitis had any residual neurologic sequelae. This figure is significantly lower than the 29% incidence of sequelae reported in 1972 by Sell and associates (1) and much lower than the incidence reported by Sell in 1983 (2) of 28% with significant handicaps, including 11% who were mentally retarded. In the 1983 report, Sell also compared children with meningitis with their closest-in-age sibling. It was noted that the IQ of the postmeningitic children was 86, whereas that of control children was 87 ($P > .05$). Comparison of results of individual pairs in Sell's study revealed that 29% of postmeningitic children scored 1 full standard deviation below their siblings and that no survivor had a score 1 standard deviation higher than his or her sibling. Feigin and Dodge have been following a group of children who had bacterial meningitis prospectively for 15–18 years. Five years after discharge, specific deficits were noted in only 10.1% of the total group. As a result of the onset of late seizures in some of these patients, however, the frequency of neurologic sequelae 15 years after discharge was 14%.

The most significant persistent neurologic sequela of bacterial meningitis in most studies following *H. influenzae* infection is that of sensorineural hearing loss. Although sensorineural hearing loss occurs in approximately 11% of all children with bacterial meningitis, it occurs in between 4% and 10% of children with *H. influenzae* meningitis. Hearing loss after pneumococcal meningitis is very prevalent, occurring in approximately 30% of cases.

Hemiparesis or quadriparesis after meningitis has been noted in as many as 15% to 20% of cases, but in 80% of those afflicted, the paresis clears completely by 1 year after discharge. In our own prospective studies of meningitis, patients were compared with their own siblings and with other control children. No significant difference in mean IQ was noted. A significantly greater proportion ($P < .01$) of children who recovered from meningitis had IQs less than 80 compared with children from control groups.

In an attempt to diminish the frequency of complications in patients with bacterial meningitis, the use of a short-term course of dexamethasone has been recommended. The studies performed to date have yielded variable results with regard to the impact of the administration of steroids on any specific neurologic handicap. Lebel and associates noted (3) that the administration of dexamethasone reduced the incidence of moderate to severe hearing loss significantly ($P < .001$) in children with *H. influenzae* meningitis. There were no significant differences between the steroid- and nonsteroid-treated groups with regard to other neurologic sequelae, the rapidity of resolution of clinical signs, or the duration of hospital stay. The incidence of hearing loss in children treated with steroids was 4%.

Using the same definition of moderate to severe bilateral hearing impairment used by Lebel and associates, Dodge and associates (4) reported that only 3% of children who did not receive steroids developed moderate to severe bilateral hearing impairment. Thus, the nonsteroid-treated patients in Dodge's study did not differ in their frequency of hearing impairment from those who received steroids in the studies performed by Lebel and associates. In the study by Schaad and associates (5), the incidence of hearing loss in patients who were treated with ceftriaxone but who did not receive steroids was also only 4%. An even more recent study by Odio and associates (6) describes the beneficial effects of early dexamethasone administration in children with bacterial meningitis, but in this study no difference with regard to the frequency of hearing loss was noted in steroid- vs. nonsteroid-treated patients. Nevertheless, the authors recommended early administration of dexamethasone, because the overall incidence of neurologic sequelae was significantly less ($P < .008$) in those who received steroids than in those who did not receive steroids. It should be noted that 38% of placebo recipients had one or more neurologic or audiologic sequelae at 5 to 25 months after discharge compared with 14% of the patients who received dexamethasone. A 14% incidence of sequelae in dexamethasone-treated patients is virtually identical to the incidence of sequelae noted by Dodge and associates and in the present study by Taylor and associates in nonsteroid treated patients.

The Infectious Diseases Committee of the American Academy of Pediatrics recently suggested that "Individual consideration of dexamethasone is recommended for bacterial meningitis in infants and children 2 months and older after the physician has weighed the benefits and possible risks." However, the Committee recognizes that some experts have decided not to use dexamethasone therapy until additional data are available. The effect of dexamethasone administration or lack thereof of neuropsychological function of children with meningitis has not been assessed.—R.D. Feigin, M.D.

References

1. Sell SH, et al: *Pediatrics* 43:206, 1972.
2. Sell SH: *Pediatr Infect Dis* 2:90, 1983.

3. Lebel MH, et al: *N Engl J Med* 319:964, 1988.
4. Dodge PR, et al: *N Engl J Med* 311:869, 1984.
5. Schaad VB, et al: *N Engl J Med* 322:141, 1990.
6. Odio CM, et al: *N Engl J Med* 324:1525, 1991.

Limited Efficacy of a *Haemophilus influenzae* Type b Conjugate Vaccine in Alaska Native Infants

Ward J, Brenneman G, Letson GW, Heyward WL, The Alaska *H. influenzae* Vaccine Study Group (Harbor-Univ of California Med Ctr, Los Angeles; Alaska Area Indian Health Service, Anchorage; Ctrs for Disease Control, Anchorage)
N Engl J Med 323:1393–1401, 1990   2–3

Several groups of Alaska natives, including Indians, Eskimos, and Aleuts, are at particularly high-risk of invasive *Hemophilus influenzae* type b disease. In a randomized, double-blind, placebo-controlled trial the protective efficacy of an *H. influenzae* type b polysaccharide-diphtheria toxoid conjugate vaccine (polyribosylribitol phosphate-diphtheria toxoid [PRP-D]) was studied during a 45-month period in which a total of 2,102 Alaska native infants received either the vaccine or saline placebo at approximately 2, 4, and 6 months of age.

During the 3,969 subject-years of follow-up, 32 episodes of *H. influenzae* type b disease occurred, and the overall incidence was not significantly reduced among the vaccinated subjects (6 cases per 1,000 patient-years), compared with the placebo group (9.6 cases per 1,000 patient-years) and a group of 3,880 other Alaska native infants who were not study subjects (6 cases per 1,000 patient-years).

There was no significant protective efficacy with the vaccine after 1, 2, or 3 doses. In fact, the efficacy was only 35% after 3 doses. This lack of efficacy was not related to the age at onset of disease, age at immunization, type of disease, degree of Alaska native heritage, time after immunization, or year of the study.

The levels of *H. influenzae* type b anticapsular antibody in the vaccine group were significantly higher than those in the placebo group only after the second and third doses. After 3 doses of vaccine, only 48% of vaccinated infants had antibody levels of greater than .1 µg/mL. Antibody responses did not correlate with the level of maternally acquired antibody, degree of Alaska native ancestry, or age at the time of first or second immunizations, but they increased significantly with increasing age at the third immunization.

In this study 3 doses of PRP-D conjugate vaccine in early infancy provided insufficient protection against invasive *H. influenzae* type b disease in Alaska native infants. The poor efficacy of PRP-D vaccine paralleled its limited immunogenicity.

▶ This report dealing with Alaskan native infants shows virtually identical data in terms of response to the *H. influenzae* type b polysaccharide vaccine was shown in a population of Apache Indian children in the same issue of *The New England Journal of Medicine*. Both groups of authors concluded that the higher incidence of systemic *H. influenzae* type b infections may be related to the lower natural antibody levels and reduced responsiveness to immunization with *H. influenzae* type b polysaccharide vaccines. This is probably because of adverse social and economic factors that result in greater crowding, lower nutritional status, and repeated infections. As yet, no data point to a genetic basis for this in Apache and Alaskan native children.

If you have been out of the country for the last year and a half, you have missed the whole revolution that has occurred with respect to immunization with the *H. influenzae* type b conjugate vaccines. Before October 1990, the American Academy of Pediatrics recommended that all children receive a dose of *H. influenzae* type b conjugate vaccine at 15 months of age (1). By the March 1991 issue of the *AAP News,* the current recommendations that immunizations should be initiated at 2 months of age were in place. There are all sorts of caveats, cautions, and red flags with respect to exactly how to go about immunization with *H. influenzae* type b conjugate vaccine, so if you are not familiar with the guidelines, look them up or read the package inserts carefully. The approved vaccines do have differences in immunogenicity, and the recommendations for the use of the vaccines differ. My apologies for even mentioning what just about everybody knows, but there are individuals who take sabbaticals, or take a year off here or there while in practice, and this past year has clearly marked a time of major change in vaccines.

One thing that has not changed is the beneficial effects of breast-feeding, which now include the demonstration of improved responses to *H. influenzae* conjugate vaccines in breast-fed infants (2). There is strong evidence that breast-feeding enhances the active immune response, and feeding methods should be taken into account in the evaluation of vaccine studies in infants.

Finally, as important as the information is about native American infants and Alaskan native Americans, the studies were done with the old type of vaccines. Thus, you can bet that within picoseconds of the introduction of the improved vaccines for use at 2 months, investigators were redoing these studies.

If you are not familiar with what a "picosecond" is, don't believe the dictionary, which usually defines it as a trillionth of a second. It is, in fact, that interval of time that occurs in Manhattan between the traffic signal turning green and the taxi driver behind you blowing his horn.—J.A. Stockman, III, M.D.

References

1. *AAP News* vol 6, July 1990.
2. Padst HF, et al: *Lancet* 336:269, 1990.

Safety Evaluation of PRP-D *Haemophilus influenzae* Type B Conjugate Vaccine in Children Immunized at 18 Months of Age and Older: Follow-Up Study of 30,000 Children

Vadheim CM, Greenberg DP, Marcy SM, Froeschle J, Ward JI (Harbor-Univ of California at Los Angeles Med Ctr, Torrance; Kaiser Found Hosp, Panorama City, Calif; Connaught Labs, Swiftwater, Pa)
Pediatr Infect Dis J 9:555–561, 1990   2–4

Infective immunization is extremely important to prevent invasive *Hemophilus influenzae* type b, the leading cause of morbidity and mortality in children younger than 5 years of age in the United States.

Approximately 30,000 children immunized between the ages of 18 and 60 months with polyribosylribitol phosphate-diphtheria toxoid (PRP–D) were evaluated prospectively for adverse reactions and hemophilus influence type b disease. Surveillance included postcard and telephone interviews with parents and data from laboratories, clinics, and physicians. Surveillance covered 2 periods after immunization: (1) the first 48 hours and (2) days 2 through 30.

Local and systemic reactions within 48 hours of vaccination with PRP-D were infrequent. Results suggest that minor reactions to PRP-D are not a significant problem. Hospitalization, seizures, and onset of disease were not significant.

Results indicate that PRP-D vaccine is safe when administered alone or with other vaccines; PRP-D does not increase the expected frequency of reactions when given in combination with measles/mumps/rubella, diphtheria/pertussis/tetanus, or oral polio vaccine.

▶ Dr. Trudy V. Murphy, Associate Professor of Pediatrics, University of Texas Southwest Medical Center at Dallas, comments:

▶ In general, infants have a poor immune response to bacterial polysaccharide, an important virulence factor for many of the agents causing invasive infection. The novel vaccine technology of covalently bonding, or "conjugating" a purified polysaccharide to an immunogenic protein was first explored in the 1920s. The effect of the conjugate is to elicit an enhanced immune response to the polysaccharide and to "prime" the immune system so that it quickly responds to rechallenge with the same antigen. This technology was further developed in the late 1970s and 1980s, culminating in licensure of several *H. influenzae* type b conjugate vaccines.

The first conjugate to be marketed in the United States was PRP-D *H. influenzae* type b vaccine. Because it was the first, it was very important to verify the excellent record of safety suggested in prelicensing immunogenicity trials. More than 150,000 doses of PRP-D had been given to Finnish infants, with few immediate or local reactions (1). The present study by Vadheim et al. extends that experience to older children in the United States. Their findings are reassuring. The rate of local reactions was low, and the reactions were generally mild. Fever and febrile seizures occurred in only a small percentage of those vaccinated. The frequency of reactions when PRP-D was given with diphtheria/pertussis/tetanus (DPT) was not substantially increased over the frequency associated with DPT vaccine alone. Anaphylactic or allergic reactions were rare in the Finnish study and also were infrequent in this study. No increase in invasive *H. influenzae* type b disease was detected after vaccination with PRP-D. Although extremely rare adverse events would not have been detected even in this large group of children, the results of this study continue to provide evidence that PRP-D conjugate is a remarkably safe vaccine.—T.V. Murphy, M.D.

Reference

1. Eskola J, et al: *N Engl J Med* 317:717, 1987.

Live Attenuated and Inactivated Influenza Vaccine in School-Age Children
Gruber WC, Taber LH, Glezen WP, Clover RD, Abell TD, Demmler RW, Couch RB (Baylor College of Medicine, Houston; Univ of Oklahoma, Oklahoma City)
Am J Dis Child 144:595–600, 1990   2–5

The high rate of influenza virus infection in children is significant not only as a cause of serious morbidity in this age group but also as a factor in the spread of influenza in the community. To determine the value of administering vaccine to children, 189 children, aged 3–18 years, were enrolled by family in a double-blind study of attenuated cold-recombinant influenza vaccine (CR) or trivalent inactivated vaccine (TIV) against natural influenza challenge.

All children in the 92 families received the same preparation; 30% of the families were assigned to each vaccine and 40% to placebo. Those given the vaccine received .5 mL CR by nose drops or .5 mL of TIV intramuscularly. Both were given a single dose. The children were treated in the fall of 1985 for protection against the 1985–1986 B/Ann Arbor epidemic.

In most (67%) of the children, a single dose of TIV produced fourfold or greater serologic increases to H1N1, H3N2, and influenza B. Heterotypic protection afforded by the influenza B/USSR component of TIV was 62% compared with placebo. Responses of fourfold or greater in hemagglutination-inhibition antibody titer was 60% to A/H1N1 and 21% to A/H3N2 after nose-drops vaccination; these responses with TIV were 73% to A/H1N1 and 83% to A/H3N2.

There was a particularly high risk of infection in the study population during the 1985–1986 B/Ann Arbor epidemic. The protection offered as a single dose of TIV was remarkable. These findings provide evidence that 2 doses of TIV may be unnecessary for protection against influenza B in school-aged children.

▶ Dr. W. Paul Glezen, Professor and Head, Preventive Medicine Section, Departments of Microbiology and Pediatrics, Baylor College of Medicine, comments:

▶ It is generally accepted that influenza virus infection rates in children are very high, but it may not be recognized that the consequences of these infections are serious. Although deaths associated with influenza virus infections are fortunately rare in children, illnesses severe enough to result in hospitalization are not. In fact, the rate of hospitalization of children <5 years of age is comparable to the rate for elderly adults ≥65 years of age. Whereas most of the elderly are burdened with chronic conditions that put them at special risk for complications of influenza virus infections, our studies have shown that only 13% of hospitalized children <5 years of age have a high-risk condition for which influenza vaccine is recommended. These observations have led us to the conclusion that protection against influenza is desirable for all children.

The study by Gruber et al. reinforces the value of inactivated vaccines for the protection of children from influenza. A study by Heikkinen and associates (1) added to the scope of the benefit of inactivated vaccine by showing a significant reduction in acute otitis media of children in day care who were vaccinated. These results are encouraging, but few have recommended routine annual immunization of young children with the inactivated vaccines. A more promising route might be intranasal immunization with CR vaccine, which is better accepted by young children and has significant advantages over the inactivated vaccines. The protection afforded young children appears to be broader (2) and more long lasting (3) with CR vaccine than with the inactivated vaccines. Serious consideration must be given for routine administration of CR vaccines to accessible populations of children in school and day care.—W.P. Glezen, M.D.

References

1. Heikkinen T, et al: *Am J Dis Child* 145:445, 1991.
2. Clover RD, et al: *J Infect Dis* 163:300, 1991.
3. Piedra PA, et al: *Semin Pediatr Infect Dis* 2:140, 1991.

Outpatient Management of Selected Infants Younger Than Two Months of Age Evaluated for Possible Sepsis

McCarthy CA, Powell KR, Jaskiewicz JA, Carbrey CL, Hylton JW, Monroe DJ, Meyer H (Univ of Rochester, NY)
Pediatr Infect Dis J 9:385–389, 1990   2–6

Eighty-six infants younger than 2 months of age were evaluated for sepsis. Fever was the primary reason for evaluation. The ability of the Rochester criteria, reported in 1985, to identify infants unlikely to have a serious bacterial infection and the safety of outpatient management for low-risk infants were assessed.

Infants meeting low-risk criteria were given ceftriaxone to cover the possibility of missing serious bacterial infections. There were no serious complications in the infants. Six required hospitalization for medical or social reasons.

The findings support the continued use of the low-risk Rochester criteria to distinguish infants unlikely to have a serious bacterial infection. In addition, good observational skills and follow-up are essential for outpatient management. The need for hospitalization for medical or social reasons must be continually reassessed.

▶ Dr. Kenneth B. Roberts, Professor and Vice Chairman, Department of Pediatrics, University of Massachusetts, comments:

▶ The notion that all febrile infants younger than a certain age need to be hospitalized and treated with antibiotics parenterally seems to offend us as diagnosticians. Multiple studies have demonstrated that the sensitivity of clinical judgment supplemented by laboratory results is not 100%; that is, not all infants with bacteremia are identified. Dr. Powell and his colleagues have been leaders in an alternative approach. They have asked whether it is possible to reduce the number of infants requiring hospitalization and treatment by identifying a group for whom the likelihood of sepsis is remote (preferably zero). The "Rochester criteria," proposed in 1985 and later modified as additional data were generated, specify the following characteristics as indicative of "low risk for serious bacterial infection": previously healthy; absence of otitis media, skin, soft tissue or musculoskeletal infection; white blood cell (WBC) count 5,000–15,000/mm^3; band form count ≤1,500/mm^3; urinalysis ≤10 WBC/high power microscopic field (HPF) (spun sediment); stool ≤5 WBC/HPF in infants with diarrhea. In the current study, 86 infants met these criteria; all were given ceftriaxone intramuscularly and sent home. Of the 86, 1 had bacteremia with *Neisseria meningitidis*. The authors combine their data with those from previous studies to suggest a rate of unsuspected bactermia of 1/356 (the infant in this study); the 95% confidence limit is <2%.

Before rushing to apply the Rochester criteria, a number of considerations should be raised. First, the screening criterion for urinary tract infection (UTI)—urinalysis ≤10 WBC/HPF—will miss babies with UTI, according to a study by Crain and Gershel (1). Even a less stringent criterion based on WBCs in the urine (5 WBC/HPF) fails to detect half of those with UTI. Because urine cultures were not done on all infants in the present study, it is not possible to determine whether UTIs were missed. Moreover, because all infants received ceftriaxone, it is likely that some UTIs would have been treated, postponing the identification of infants at risk for repeated infection or progressive renal damage. All babies in the study had lumbar puncture and blood culture performed; urine culture should not be omitted because of a lack of pyuria.

All infants in the study received antibiotic treatment. This was not a "treatment" vs. "no treatment" study, but a "treatment and hospitalization" vs. "treatment and no hospitalization" study. The availability of ceftriaxone has changed the question from "Do all febrile infants need to be treated?" to "Do all febrile infants need to be hospitalized to receive treatment?" Only if the answer to the latter question is "no" should we return to the former.

Combining studies and using 356 as the denominator to calculate the risk of unsuspected serious bacterial illness in the first 2 months of life presumes that the risk is evenly distributed during the first 2 months, which is not true. The rate of bacteremia in the first month of life is twice the rate in the second. In this study, only one third of the infants were in the first month of life; two thirds were in the lower risk second month. The overall rate, therefore, may well underestimate the risk for infants in the first month of life. This needs to be kept in mind by clinicians when applying the overall rate to a specific patient and by researchers designing their studies, so that sufficient numbers of patients are enrolled to permit age-specific rates to be estimated.

I continue to worry about my ability to assess the very young infant with fever—the infant who has not yet established a social smile. In studying older infants to construct the Yale Observation Scales, McCarthy found that no child with a serious bacterial illness smiled normally in response to a social overture (2). If I cannot elicit a social smile, I engage the parents' help. If the baby can smile, so do I; if the baby cannot smile, neither can I.—K.B. Roberts, M.D.

References

1. Crain EF, Gershel JC: *Pediatrics* 86:363, 1990.
2. McCarthy PL, et al: *Pediatrics* 70:802, 1982.

Strategies for Diagnosis and Treatment of Children at Risk for Occult Bacteremia: Clinical Effectiveness and Cost-Effectiveness
Lieu TA, Schwartz JS, Jaffe DM, Fleisher GR (Univ of Pennsylvania; Univ of Toronto; Harvard Med School)
J Pediatr 118:21–29, 1991   2–7

The optimal management of a febrile child without an obvious focus of bacterial infection remains controversial. Decision analysis was used to evaluate the probable health benefits, complications, and costs of 6 management strategies for febrile children at risk for occult bacteremia. The 6

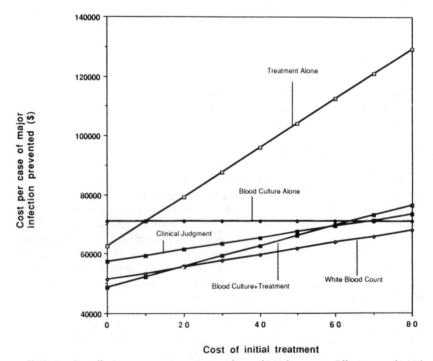

Cost of initial treatment

Fig 2–1.—Cost effectiveness at varying estimates of cost of initial treatment. Effectiveness of initial treatment is held constant at 20%. (Courtesy of Lieu TA, Schwartz JS, Jaffe DM, et al: *J Pediatr* 118:21–29, 1991.)

strategies included no intervention; treatment alone with a 2-day course of oral amoxicillin; blood culture alone; blood culture plus a 2-day oral course of amoxicillin; leukocyte count, with patients who had a count $\geq 10,000/mm^3$ receiving a 2-day oral course of amoxicillin; and clinical judgment. The decision model used data from the literature and from a 1987 prospective study of occult bacteremia in 955 children.

The strategy of blood culture plus treatment prevented the highest number of major infections and resulted in the lowest cost per major infection prevented (Fig 2–1). The leukocyte count strategy was as clinically effective and as cost effective as blood culture plus treatment, but it also averted many antibiotic complications. Blood culture alone was the third most clinically effective strategy but was the least cost effective. Of all interventions, treatment alone with a 2-day oral course of amoxicillin had the lowest average cost per febrile patient, but it was the least effective clinically. However, it was assumed that oral amoxicillin therapy was only 20% effective in preventing major infections after bacteremia. At higher estimates of effectiveness, treatment alone became a more viable strategy.

Management strategies that combine blood culture and empiric antibiotic treatment provided the most clinically effective and cost-effective treatment of febrile children at risk for occult bacteremia. Future gains in preventing complications may be made by finding ways to improve the effectiveness of initial treatment.

▶ Dr. Paul L. McCarthy, Professor of Pediatrics and Director, Division of General Pediatrics, Yale University School of Medicine, comments:

▶ In the past 2 years, 3 articles have been published that have used a decision-analysis methodology to address the topic of bacteremia in febrile children. The analysis of Lieu favors a blood culture followed by empiric oral antibiotics. That of Downs et al. (1) also favored blood culture and empiric oral antibiotic treatment. Lieu et al. found that a leukocyte count and blood culture followed by empiric antibiotics was nearly as effective; Downs et al. did not find this to be the case. Kramer et al. (2) found that no blood culture was the most effective strategy, whereas Downs and associates and Lieu and associates (the latter for cases of major infection prevented) found this approach to be the least effective.

A critical domain of decision analysis is the assumptions that are made to construct the decision model. For example, Lieu et al. list 18 assumptions that are made, and Downs et al. list 9. Also important are both the baseline status of the patients entered into the model and the outcomes that are studied. Because these parameters may vary from one study to another, it is not surprising that results may differ. Lieu et al., for example, note 2 important ways in which their study differed from that of Kramer et al: Kramer and associates did not have a "treat empirically" option at initial visit. In addition, Kramer et al. stated that children with pneumococcal bacteremia and fever at follow-up were hospitalized for 10 days instead of the 2 to 3 days suggested by Lieu et al. The effect that incorrect assumptions may have on results is only partially vitiated by varying the value of 1 specific assumption at a time as Lieu et al. and Downs et al. have done, because multiple assumptions are made, all of which interact simultaneously.

Although I do not believe that these studies have answered the issue definitively, the authors of each study are to be commended for making explicit the assumptions on which they base their analysis and for citing literature to support these assumptions. In this way, they have enriched the dialogue about bacteremia. Given the limitations I have outlined about decision analysis and the differing results of these analyses in the studies cited, I do not believe that an unequivocal case has been made to support treating all febrile children with antibiotics for the possibility of bacteremia.—P.L. McCarthy, M.D.

References

1. Downs SM, et al: *J Pediatr* 118:11, 1991.
2. Kramer MS, et al: *Pediatrics* 84:18, 1989.

Role of Bone Marrow Examination in the Child With Prolonged Fever
Hayani A, Mahoney DH, Fernbach DJ (Baylor College of Medicine, Houston; Texas Children's Hosp, Houston)
J Pediatr 116:919–920, 1990   2–8

Making a diagnosis in children with prolonged fever is problematic. Some investigators recommend a bone marrow examination to detect occult infection and malignancy. However, no one has estimated the yield

TABLE 1.—Final Diagnosis (Cause of Fever) in All 414 Febrile Episodes

Diagnosis	No. of episodes
Fever of unknown origin	120
Collagen vascular disease	51
Hematologic malignancy	48
Viral infection (culture-positive or presumed)*	46
Culture-negative infection†	43
Bacterial infection	32
Fungal infection	17
Mycobacterial infection	18
Solid tumor	3
Parasitic infection	5
Others	31
TOTAL	414

*Three culture-proven and 43 presumed viral infections on the basis of serologic or clinical findings.
†Patients who were presumed to have a nonviral infection on the basis of serologic or clinical findings despite negative cultures.
(Courtesy of Hayani A, Mahoney DH, Fernbach DJ: *J Pediatr* 116:919–920, 1990.)

TABLE 2.—Diagnosis in 34 Patients in Whom Histologic
Examination of Bone Marrow Uncovered
Noninfectious Conditions

Diagnosis	Patients	
	No.	%
Malignancy	28	6.7
Acute leukemia	21	5.0
Newly diagnosed	13	3.1
In relapse	8	1.9
Lymphoma	3	0.7
Solid tumor	3	0.7
Chronic myelocytic leukemia	1	0.2
Nonmalignancy	6	1.4
Virus-associated hemophagocytic syndrome	3	0.7
Disseminated histiocytosis	2	0.5
Hypoplastic anemia	1	0.2

(Courtesy of Hayani A, Mahoney DH, Fernbach DJ: *J Pediatr* 116:919–920, 1990.)

of bone marrow culture for evidence of occult infection in such cases. The incidence of diagnostic bone marrow findings by culture or histologic assessment in the febrile child for whom the diagnosis is otherwise unknown was determined.

The records of all patients from whom bone marrow specimens were obtained for assessment of prolonged fever were analyzed. Three hundred eighty-three children underwent 414 examinations. In 25% of the 414 febrile episodes, immunocompromising conditions were known to exist before marrow examination. Overall, infectious organisms presumed to be the cause of fever were isolated from 15, or 3.6%, of the 414 specimens obtained from 14 children. Bacterial organisms were isolated from the marrow of 8 patients. Nine of 15 febrile episodes associated with positive marrow culture occurred in children with an underlying immunocompromising condition (Table 1). Histologic assessment revealed a noninfectious condition in 8% of the 414 specimens (Table 2). In most cases, myelophthisis was suspected clinically before the bone marrow evaluation.

Bone marrow examination is indicated in children with prolonged fever and clinical or laboratory evidence suggesting malignancy. It may also be useful for establishing the diagnosis of opportunistic infection in immunocompromised children, especially those with AIDS. However, bone marrow examination is probably not warranted for detecting occult infection in children with prolonged fever who have no other findings suggestive of immunodeficiency or malignancy.

▶ Read the last sentence of the abstract. Performing a bone marrow aspirate for the purposes of simply culturing it in children who have prolonged fever but who do not appear to have a malignancy or immune compromise is unwarranted. Furthermore, if you do it often enough, you are going to get back some confusing and confounding false positive cultures.

One of the basic principles of clinical laboratory medicine is that if you do a silly test often enough, you are going to get a silly answer some of the time.—J.A. Stockman, III, M.D.

Distinguishing Sepsis From Blood Culture Contamination in Young Infants With Blood Cultures Growing Coagulase-Negative Staphylococci

St Geme JW III, Bell LM, Baumgart S, D'Angio CT, Harris MC (Children's Hosp of Philadelphia; Univ of Pennsylvania, Philadelphia)
Pediatrics 86:157–162, 1990

2–9

Coagulase-negative staphylococci now represent the most common cause of serious nosocomial infections in many intensive care nurseries. Because these organisms are also common blood culture contaminants, it has been difficult to distinguish culture contamination from sepsis. Whether quantitative blood cultures could make this distinction in young infants with peripheral blood cultures growing coagulase-negative staphylococci was determined.

In 3 years, 23 episodes of sepsis were identified in 21 infants, and 10 infants had blood culture contamination. These 2 groups of infants were similar in birth weight, gestational age, postnatal age, and presenting signs. Colony counts for the 2 study groups, however, were significantly different. In 9 episodes of sepsis, the initial peripheral blood culture grew >100 CFU/mL. In the remaining 14 episodes, initial peripheral blood

Clinical and Laboratory Characteristics of Infants With Sepsis vs. Infants With Blood Culture Contamination*				
Clinical Variable	All Sepsis (n = 23)	Low Colony-Count Sepsis (n = 14)	Blood Culture Contamination (n = 10)	Fisher Exact Test P Value†
Central catheter	17/23	10/14	2/10	.05
Abnormal WBC count‡§	7/23	6/14	1/10	NS
Abnormal I:T ratio‡§	12/19¶	7/11¶	2/9¶	NS
Abnormal platelet count	7/23	4/14	0/10	NS
≥1 abnormal hematologic value	19/23	12/14	3/10	.05
≥1 abnormal hematologic value or central catheter	22/23	13/14	5/10	.05
Multiple antibiotic resistance	10/22¶	6/13¶	6/10	NS
Staphylococcus epidermidis	15/18¶	8/10¶	7/8¶	NS

*Values are given as number of infants in whom the variable was present.
†All infants with sepsis and those with low colony-count sepsis vs. infants with blood culture contamination. *Abbreviation: NS*, not significant.
‡*Abbreviations: WBC*, white blood cell; *I:T*, immature neutrophil to total neutrophil ratio.
§Abnormal hematologic values: WBC < 5,000/mm³ or > 20,000/mm³; I:T > .12; platelet count < 150,000/mm³.
¶Information about this clinical variable was not available for all infants in this patient group.
(Courtesy of St Geme JW III, Bell LM, Baumgart S, et al: *Pediatrics* 86:157–162, 1990.)

cultures yielded ≤50 CFU/mL. All of the patients with blood culture contamination had colony counts of <50 CFU/mL.

Significant variables that distinguished infants with low colony-count sepsis from those with culture contamination included the presence of a central catheter and an abnormal hematologic value (table). Thirteen of the 14 infants with low colony-count sepsis had 1 or both of these variables.

Quantitative blood cultures help to distinguish sepsis from contamination in young infants whose peripheral blood cultures grow coagulase-negative staphylococci. Because many cases of sepsis may be associated with low colony-growth count, this finding should not be ignored as contamination. Other clinical and laboratory characteristics must be examined to rule out sepsis.

▶ Dr. Jeanne W. Ruderman, staff neonatologist, Cedars-Sinai Medical Center, Los Angeles, comments:

▶ The authors demonstrate the usefulness of the quantitative blood culture technique in differentiating sepsis from blood culture contamination caused by coagulase-negative staphylococci. Other studies also have found this method to be similarly useful. Comparison of the Isolator 1.5 microbial tube with the BACTEC radiometric system for bacteremia in children (1) revealed that most contaminated specimens were characterized by growth of only 1 colony on a single plate or growth occurring off the inoculum streak, and that specimens required 3 to 4 days of incubation to be considered positive. Another study using the quantitative technique to diagnose catheter-related sepsis in infants with indwelling central catheters (2) reported colony counts of ≤10 CFU/mL in 6 of 7 cases of blood culture contamination and 30 CFU/mL in the seventh case. These authors also noted a 3- to 4-day duration of incubation in these 7 cases. Coagulase-negative staphylococci were mostly responsible for blood culture contamination in both of these studies. Obviously, there is no absolute method to tell us whether a blood culture is positive because of infection or contamination, and we must practice the art of medicine in making such determinations. Combining the data of colony counts, duration of incubation, and pattern of microbial growth with a careful clinical assessment of each infant should increase the accuracy of our decisions.—J.W. Ruderman, M.D.

References

1. Carey RB: *J Clin Microbiol* 19:634, 1984.
2. Ruderman JW, et al: *J Pediatr* 112:748, 1988.

A Ten-Year Review of Neonatal Sepsis and Comparison With the Previous Fifty-Year Experience
Gladstone IM, Ehrenkranz RA, Edberg SC, Baltimore RS (Yale Univ)
Pediatr Infect Dis J 9:819–825, 1990   2–10

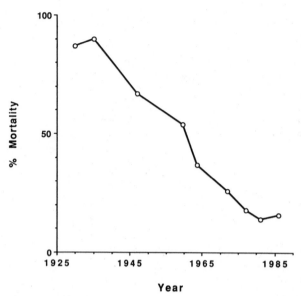

Fig 2–2.—Inborn neonatal mortality associated with sepsis at Yale-New Haven Hospital, 1928–1988, using the midpoints of each 5-year period, where available, or the midpoint of each study in the series. (Courtesy of Gladstone IM, Ehrenkranz RA, Edberg SC, et al: *Pediatr Infect Dis J* 9:819–825, 1990.)

At Yale-New Haven Hospital, records of all positive blood cultures in neonates have been kept prospectively since 1928. Prompted by recent reports that commensal species (CS) found in the skin and intestines of neonates may be significant causes of infections in the neonatal intensive care unit (NICU), a study was undertaken to determine the incidence of sepsis from CS in the NICU. Using a modification of the objective criteria of the Center for Disease Control to define sepsis, the records of all neonates with positive blood cultures in 1979–1988 were reviewed.

In this 10-year period, 270 episodes of sepsis occurred in 225 infants. Of 429 culture isolates of CS, 73 (17%) were considered to represent sepsis. For infants aged 30 days or younger, the sepsis rate was 2.7 cases per 1,000 live births, with a mortality rate of 15.9%. The neonatal mortality rate from sepsis declined during this decade, reaching a plateau near 15% (Fig 2–2). Group B β-hemolytic streptococci were the most prevalent cause of sepsis in neonates, followed by *Escherichia coli* (table). However, sepsis caused by CS increased significantly for neonates and dramatically for infants older than 30 days. The number of infants older than 30 days in whom sepsis developed also increased during the 10-year period. There appeared to be a link between low birth weight, sepsis with CS, and sepsis in older infants. For the 73 episodes of sepsis in which CS was isolated, the sepsis-associated mortality using the modified Centers for Disease Control criteria for bacteremia was 13.7%, whereas the mortality rate for CS isolates that did not fulfill the criteria was significantly lower at 4%.

Neonatal Inborn Sepsis, 1928–1989

% in each study

	1928–1932	1933–1943	1944–1957	1958–1965	1966–1978	1979–1988
Gram-positive aerobic bacteria						
Staphylococcus aureus	28	9	13	3	5	3
Coagulase-negative staphylococci				1	1	8
Beta-hemolytic streptococci						
Group B		5	6	1	32	37
Group D	38	36	2	10	4	8
Nongrouped and Other		2	10		1	3
Viridans streptococci		11	5		1	1
Streptococcus pneumoniae	5	2	2	3	1	1
Listeria monocytogenes				3		
Gram-negative aerobic bacteria						
Escherichia coli	26	25	37	45	32	20
Klebsiella-Enterobacter			21	11	12	3
Pseudomonas				15	2	3
Haemophilus				1	4	5
Salmonella			2		1	1
Gram-negative anaerobic bacteria					1	3
Fungi					2	1
Other	3	9	3	5	5	1
n =	39	44	62	73	239	147

*Percentages do not always add up to 100% because of rounding.
(Courtesy of Gladstone IM, Ehrenkranz RA, Edberg SC, et al: *Pediatr Infect Dis J* 9:819–825, 1990.)

These data show an objective increase in the incidence of CS sepsis in 1979–1988. This increase probably does not indicate a change in the virulence of infecting agents, but rather indicates a change in the population at risk (i.e., more premature infants).

Streptococcus pneumoniae Infections of the Female Genital Tract and in the Newborn Child

Westh H, Skibsted L, Korner B (Bispebjerg Hosp, Copenhagen)
Rev Infect Dis 12:416–422, 1990   2–11

Streptococcus pneumoniae is a rare pathogen of the female genital tract. *Streptococcus pneumoniae* infections of the female genital tract and in the newborn child reported between 1938 and 1988 were reviewed.

Thirty-six cases of pneumococcal infection of the female genital tract have been reported. Factors that predisposed to infection were the use of an intrauterine contraceptive device, a recent birth, and gynecologic surgery. All 24 patients with pneumococcal genital infection during the last 25 years survived, whereas 5 of 12 women seen between 1938 and 1952 died from their infection. Pneumococci were rarely isolated as the only pathogen in cases of bartholinitis.

Neonatal pneumococcal infections were rare, occurring in approximately 6% of all cases of bacterial neonatal meningitis and about 2% of all cases of septicemia. Neonatal *S. pneumoniae* disease with an early onset (less than 5 days) was associated with an intrapartum pathogenesis. The infections most often found were pneumonia, meningitis, and septicemia. Of the 23 cases of neonatal pneumococcal infection reported between 1980 and 1989, 11 (48%) of the infants died, and 3 (13%) of the survivors had severe neurologic sequelae.

Antibiotics and aggressive supportive therapy have reduced mortality among adults with pneumococcal genital infection to nil, but mortality among newborns with pneumococcal infection remains high. It appears that the prognosis for newborns has not improved during the last 10 years.

Invasive Disease Due to Multiply Resistant *Streptococcus pneumoniae* in a Houston, Tex, Day-Care Center

Rauch AM, O'Ryan M, Van R, Pickering LK (Univ of Texas Med School at Houston)
Am J Dis Child 144:923–927, 1990   2–12

Streptococcus pneumoniae has become increasingly resistant to penicillin and other antibiotics to which these organisms were previously susceptible. Data were reviewed on 2 children with invasive disease caused by *S. pneumoniae* contracted during an outbreak in a day-care center.

In July 1988, 2 toddlers, aged 12 and 14 months, respectively, who were attending the same day-care center, were hospitalized within 24 hours of each other. One had sepsis and the other had sepsis and meningitis caused by a multiply-resistant *S. pneumoniae*. Nasopharyngeal cultures were performed in 82 of 85 day-care center children, in 26 of 29 day-care center staff, and in 28 of 31 family members. *Streptococcus pneumoniae* grew from 29 (35%) cultures from day-care center children. Ten (34%) of these were resistant to sulfamethoxazole-trimethoprim, oxacillin, and tetracycline, and were relatively resistant to penicillin. Only 1 household contact and none of the staff members had positive cultures. All multiply-resistant isolates were serotype 14 and had the same pattern of antimicrobial susceptibility.

Rifampin, 10 mg/kg, was administered twice daily for 2 days to 97% of the day-care center children and staff members and household contacts who had positive cultures. Treatment resulted in a 70% reduction in positive nasopharyngeal cultures for *S. pneumoniae*. Despite treatment, 3 additional children and 1 family contact were identified by follow-up naso-pharyngeal cultures. No new patients with invasive disease caused by multiply-resistant *S. pneumoniae* were identified during a 9-month observation period.

This is the first report in the United States of an outbreak of invasive disease caused by multiply-resistant *S. pneumoniae*. Nasopharyngeal colonization is common among exposed children in day-care centers, but not among day-care staff or household contacts. Treatment with rifampin for 2 days only partially eradicates the organism from colonized individuals.

Immediate vs Delayed Treatment of Group A Beta-Hemolytic Streptococcal Pharyngitis With Penicillin V
El-Daher NT, Hijazi SS, Rawashdeh NM, Al-Khalil IA-H, Abu-Ektaish FM, Abdel-Latif DI (Jordan Univ of Science and Technology, Irbid, Jordan)
Pediatr Infect Dis J 10:126–130, 1991   2–13

The most common acute illnesses seen in pediatric practice are upper respiratory tract infection and acute pharyngitis. Whether treatment should be begun before or after results of throat cultures are obtained is debated. The effects of early and late treatment with penicillin V on the clinical course of acute group-A β-hemolytic streptococcal (GABHS) pharyngitis and subsequent episodes of GABHS pharyngitis were investigated in 306 children with probable GABHS pharyngitis. The study was randomized and double-blind.

Of the 229 culture-positive patients, 111 were given penicillin V immediately, and 118 were given a placebo for 48–52 hours, followed by penicillin V. The children were assessed clinically for 48–52 hours after treatment was begun. The acute to convalescent antibody titers were measured by the Streptozyme test.

Both early and late penicillin V treatment resulted in cure rates of greater than 92%. Children who received early treatment had significantly fewer and milder signs and symptoms on the third day and a significantly lower rise in antibody titer. However, the relapse rate in the early treatment group was 7%, and early and late recurrences were noted

Relapses and Recurrences in 2 Groups

	Early Treatment Group	Late Treatment Group	Chi Square
Relapse	8 (7)*	2 (2)*	4.2 (0.04) †
Early recurrence	18 (16)	6 (5)	7.6 (0.006)
Late recurrence	14 (13)	4 (3)	6.7 (0.009)

*Numbers in parentheses, percent.
†Numbers in parentheses, probability.
(Courtesy of El-Daher NT, Hijazi SS, Rawashdeh NM, et al: *Pediatr Infect Dis J* 10:126–130, 1991.)

in 16% and 13%, respectively. In the late treatment group, these rates were 2%, 5%, and 3%, respectively (table).

A throat culture should be done, and analgesic-antipyretic drugs should be administered to patients with signs and symptoms that suggest GABHS pharyngitis. Antibiotics should not be given if results of the culture are negative. When the culture is positive, oral penicillin is recommended. The dramatic impact of early penicillin V treatment should be considered when clinicians must decide on early or late treatment for individual patients.

▶ Dr. Robert Tanz, Assistant Professor of Pediatrics and Director of Continuity Clinics, Northwestern University Medical School and Children's Memorial Hospital, comments:

▶ Way back in '54 the Cleveland Indians won the American League pennant (111 wins—you can look it up) and Storm (1) suggested that early therapy with penicillin might prevent development of type-specific immunity to group A streptococci, which predisposes patients to the recurrence of streptococcal pharyngitis. Because throat culture results were generally not available for 48 hours, this concept met the same fate as the Indians in the World Series.

The advent of "rapid strep tests" now allows for immediate diagnosis and institution of therapy. Studies published in the last few years have demonstrated symptomatic benefit to early therapy. With this justification for rapid streptococcal testing, however, there have been second thoughts about the consequences of early therapy. Pichichero et al. (2) agree with Storm and El-Daher et al. that there may be an increased risk of recurrence of streptococcal pharyngitis among patients treated within the first 48 hours of onset of symptoms. Gerber et al. (3) have persuasively argued the opposite viewpoint, that type-specific antibodies may not be important in development of immunity to group A streptococci.

The real question is, "Why treat streptococcal pharyngitis?" The primary answer remains, as it has for about 40 years, to prevent acute rheumatic fever. All other reasons are secondary. Penicillin remains the drug of choice.

Penicillin should be started as soon as the diagnosis of streptococcal pharyngitis is secured. Because follow-up is never guaranteed, there should be no delay that might impede institution of therapy. There will be faster clinical improvement and decreased transmission if treatment is instituted as early as possible. Whatever the consequences of early treatment (if any), they will likely be less troublesome than rheumatic fever.—R. Tanz, M.D.

References

1. Storm J: *Acta Paediatr* 43:267, 1954.
2. Pichichero ME, et al: *Pediatr Infect Dis J* 6:635, 1987.
3. Gerber MA: *J Pediatr* 117:853, 1990.

Association of Group C β-Hemolytic Streptococci With Endemic Pharyngitis Among College Students

Turner JC, Hayden GF, Kiselica D, Lohr J, Fishburne CF, Murren D (Univ of
South Carolina, Columbia; Univ of Virginia, Charlottesville)
JAMA 264:2644–2647, 1990   2–14

A clear causative role for non–group-A β-hemolytic streptococci
(non–GABHS) in endemic pharyngitis has yet to be demonstrated. Previous studies failed to show consistent differences in isolation of non–GABHS among symptomatic and asymptomatic groups. An epidemiologic study was undertaken to determine whether non–GABHS could be detected more commonly in the throats of students with symptomatic pharyngitis than in healthy age-matched controls.

During 2 school years, throat cultures were obtained from 232 college students who had symptomatic pharyngitis and from 198 students who had come to the clinic for noninfectious problems. Duplicate throat swabs were inoculated onto plates that contained sheep's blood agar. One plate was incubated in a 5% CO_2 atmosphere and the other in an anaerobic environment.

Among the non–GABHS, only those from group C (GCBHS) were isolated significantly more often among patients (26%) than among controls (11%). Almost half (47%) of the GCBHS isolates from patients were detected in both the CO_2-enriched and anaerobic atmospheres. In contrast, 86% of the group GCBHS isolates from the controls were detected only in the anaerobic atmosphere. Quantitative colony counts of these isolates were generally higher among patients than among controls. Fever, exudative tonsillitis, and anterior cervical adenopathy were seen significantly more often in patients with group GCBHS than in patients whose throat cultures were negative for group GCBHS.

In this college student population, group GCBHS were epidemiologically associated with endemic pharyngitis. The rate of colonization in healthy controls (11%) suggests that some strains of group GCBHS may represent normal oropharyngeal flora.

Lack of Influence of Beta-Lactamase–Producing Flora on Recovery of Group A Streptococci After Treatment of Acute Pharyngitis

Tanz RR, Shulman ST, Stroka PA, Marubio S, Brook I, Yogev R (Children's Memorial Hosp, Chicago; Northwestern Univ; Naval Med Research Inst, Bethesda)
J Pediatr 117:859–863, 1990   2–15

Treatment failure occurs in 5%–19% of patients with acute streptococcal pharyngitis. Production of β-lactamase by normal pharyngeal flora has been suggested as the cause of penicillin treatment failure. The effect of anaerobic and aerobic β-lactamase–producing bacteria on bacteriologic outcome in acute group A β-hemolytic streptococcal (GABHS) pharyngitis was studied in a randomized, single-blind treatment protocol. Eighty-nine eligible patients, aged 2 to 16 years, with culture-proven acute GABHS pharyngitis received either phenoxymethyl penicillin or amoxicillin–clavulanic acid orally for 10 days.

After completion of therapy, throat cultures were positive for GABHS in 3 (6.5%) of 46 patients treated with amoxicillin–clavulanic acid and in 4 (9.3%) of 43 patients treated with penicillin. The initial GABHS T type persisted in all 3 patients given amoxicillin–clavulanic acid and in 1 penicillin-treated patient; the difference was not significant. Before therapy, β-lactamase–producing organisms were isolated in 63% of patients treated with amoxicillin–clavulanic acid and 67% of patients treated with penicillin. After treatment, they were found in 66% and 31%, respectively. Bacteriologic treatment failure, however, was not related to the recovery of β-lactamase–producing bacteria before or after treatment.

Penicillin treatment failure in patients with acute streptococcal pharyngitis evidently cannot be attributed to production of β-lactamase by pharyngeal organisms. Substituting an antibiotic effective against β-lactamase–producing bacteria will not eliminate the problem of bacteriologic treatment failure.

▶ As long as kids get sore throats, more articles will appear and trees will be felled as our knowledge and understanding of streptococci continue to burgeon.

The article by Tanz et al. (Abstract 2–15) demonstrates that the production of β-lactamase by pharyngeal organisms cannot be the only cause of treatment failure in patients with acute streptococcal pharyngitis. These authors found that therapy with an agent against β-lactamase–producing organisms was not associated with fewer treatment failures. Factors other than β-lactamase production must play a role in the clinical phenomenon of antibiotic failure. Possibilities for such failures include, but may not be limited to, noncompliance with therapy, infection with a new serotype shortly after completion of therapy, and a chronic carrier state. To say all of this differently, substituting an antibiotic effective against β-lactamase–producing bacteria for plain, old, simple penicillin may not eliminate the problem of treatment failure. The story is obviously much more complex than that.

The Turner article (Abstract 2–14) dealing with group C β-hemolytic streptococci as a cause of endemic pharyngitis among college students should come as no surprise to you. This organism has moved beyond the realm of simple small clusters of streptococcal pharyngitis. More recently, Gerber et al. (1) documented how common a problem GCBHS is in an office setting. During the winter and spring of 1986–1987, in a single private pediatric office setting in Danbury, Connecticut, 222 consecutive patients with clinical findings of pharyngitis were enrolled to determine the relative frequency of GCBHS compared with GABHS pharyngitis. In this series, GABHS was isolated from 41% of the patients, and GCBHS was isolated from 25%. The clinical presentation, unlike in the college student report abstracted above, was virtually identical, except that the GCBHS group was about 1½ to 2 years older.

So what is the importance of all of the above? The symptoms for GABHS and GCBHS are similar. Both respond adequately to the same antibiotics. The problem is that GCBHS may not be detected with routine screening tests or with standard culture techniques for GABHS. Read these articles in detail. You may wish to alter your office practice a bit when thinking about the older child who has what looks like a strep throat, particularly if you are accustomed to doing just cultures.

Birth, taxes, death, and strep will be with us forever. The latter is just like an old boomerang: It's impossible to throw away.—J.A. Stockman, III, M.D.

Reference

1. Gerber MA, et al: *Pediatrics* 87:598, 1991.

***Mycoplasma pneumoniae* Infections Associated With Severe Mucositis**
Alter SJ, Stringer B (Wright State Univ, Dayton, Ohio)
Clin Pediatr 29:602–604, 1990   2–16

Mycoplasma pneumoniae is primarily a pathogen of the respiratory tract, but extrapulmonary disease caused by this agent is not rare. Three boys aged 10–13 years were seen with respiratory infections and severe mucositis caused by *M. pneumoniae*. Signs included severe conjunctivitis, generalized ulcerative stomatitis and pharyngitis, urethritis, and fever.

All were seen within a 2-week period, but there was no obvious geographic, contact, or other epidemiologic link among them. All 3 had previously received 1 or more courses of antibiotics. None had exanthem; an acute *M. pneumoniae* complement fixation titer >256 was present. All patients improved after treatment with erythromycin.

This unusual temporal cluster of children had inflammation of several mucous membranes associated with *M. pneumoniae* respiratory infection. The findings may represent 1 type of clinical presentation within the spectrum of Stevens-Johnson syndrome, (e.g., without the presence of an exanthem), or it may suggest that *M. pneumoniae* directly causes mucosal disease.

▶ My, we've come a long way in our understanding about *Mycoplasma* sp. infection. At first, we thought that all *Mycoplasma* sp. did was to cause pneumonia. It is also a cause of sore throats. It can initiate an autoimmune hemolytic anemia. It can affect the central and peripheral nervous systems. It can cause disseminated intravascular coagulation, hepatitis, myocarditis, and pericarditis, and even the Stevens-Johnson syndrome. The next time you see a child who has what appears to be juvenile rheumatoid arthritis, but it doesn't seem quite right, think *Mycoplasma* sp. infection along with parvovirus B19. The next time you see a child with pneumonia and severe muscle aches, check the urine for myoglobin. *Mycoplasma* sp. infection causes myositis. Now we see that *Mycoplasma* sp. can cause an erythema multiforme rash with target lesions and severe mucositis. If that isn't enough, it is now suspected that *Mycoplasma* sp.

infection may hasten the time to the development of AIDS in someone who is HIV infected (1).

Mycoplasma sp. is an important organism, is an important organism, is an important organism. Generally, when you hear something 3 times, it's true.— J.A. Stockman, III, M.D.

Reference

1. Editorial: *Lancet* 337:20, 1991.

Risk Factors for Measles in a Previously Vaccinated Population and Cost-Effectiveness of Revaccination Strategies
Mast EE, Berg JL, Hanrahan LP, Wassell JT, Davis JP (Wisconsin Div of Health, Madison; Univ of Wisconsin, Madison; Ctrs for Disease Control, Atlanta)
JAMA 264:2529–2533, 1990   2–17

Large measles outbreaks continue to occur in schools, particularly among previously vaccinated children. In 1986 a total of 219 cases of measles were reported in Dane County, Wisconsin. Data from this outbreak were used to determine risk factors for vaccine failure and to assess the cost-effectiveness of 4 hypothetical school-based revaccination strategies. There were 170 patients and 144 controls.

Unconditional logistic regression analysis showed that vaccination before a change in the measles vaccine stabilizer in 1979 and vaccination before age 15 months were risk factors for vaccine failure (table). If measles-mumps-rubella vaccine were used, cost estimates for revaccination of all students were $3,444 per case prevented; for students vaccinated before 1980, the cost estimate was $3,166; and for students vaccinated before age 15 months, the cost estimate was $2,546. However, 43% to 53% of cases could not be prevented by using these strategies. The esti-

Risk of Measles in Relation to Age at Immunization and Date of Immunization

	No. (%) of Individuals		Odds Ratio	95% Confidence Interval	P
	Cases	Controls			
Age at vaccination, mo					
<12	21 (12)	3 (2)	21.2	5.6-116.2	<.001
12-14	120 (71)	53 (37)	6.9	3.9-12.1	<.001
≥15	29 (17)	88 (61)	1.0	Referent	...
Date of vaccination					
Before 3/1/79*	163 (96)	101 (70)	3.5†	1.5-8.5	<.02
After 9/30/80‡	7 (4)	43 (30)	1.0	Referent	...

Note: Dane County (Wis) measles outbreak, 1986.
*Distribution date for first lot of measles vaccine stabilized with buffered sorbitol gelatin medium.
†Adjusted for age at immunization, Mantel-Haenszel chi-square.
‡Expiration date for last of measles vaccine stabilized with sucrose, monopotassium phosphate, dipotassium phosphate, L-monosodium glutamate, and human albumin.
(Courtesy of Mast EE, Berg JL, Hanrahan LP, et al: *JAMA* 264:2529–2533, 1990.)

mated cost of revaccinating all students in the Dane County schools was $1,065,011, compared with $71,886 for revaccinating all students in schools in which students were exposed to case patients. Until a 2-dose vaccination schedule is implemented, revaccination of all students in schools assessed to be at risk for measles is recommended to prevent large outbreaks of measles in schools.

A Prefecture-Wide Survey of Mumps Meningitis Associated With Measles, Mumps and Rubella Vaccine
Fujinaga T, Motegi Y, Tamura H, Kuroume T (Gunma Univ School of Medicine, Maebashi, Gunma, Japan)
Pediatr Infect Dis J 10:204–209, 1991   2–18

In 1989, the Japan Ministry of Health and Welfare introduced measles, mumps, and rubella (MMR) vaccination into the routine vaccination program for children, aged 12–71 months. The vaccines used were the AIK-C strain for measles, To-336 strain for rubella, and Urabe AM-9 strain for mumps. Within 4 months of the introduction of the MMR vaccine, 4 children were hospitalized with signs of aseptic meningitis that developed 24 days or less after vaccination, and a prefecture-wide surveillance was begun on the possible complications of MMR vaccination.

Pediatricians affiliated with the 24 hospitals in Gunma Prefecture collaborated. An 8-month period beginning with the introduction of the MMR vaccine was studied. Within 2 months after vaccination, 35 children had meningitis, 6 had convulsive disorders, and 2 had parotitis. In

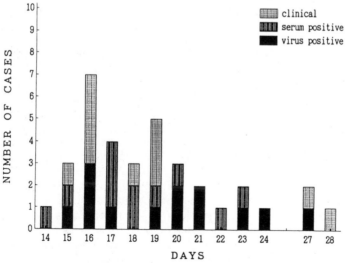

Fig 2–3.—Meningitis after measles, mumps, and rubella vaccination by day of onset after inoculation. The incubation period in the cases in which mumps vaccine virus was positive in the CSF ranged from 15 to 28 days. (Courtesy of Fujinaga T, Motegi Y, Tamura H, et al: *Pediatr Infect Dis J* 10:204–209, 1991.)

those with meningitis, the interval between MMR vaccination and the development of meningitis ranged from 14 to 28 days (Fig 2–3). Mumps virus was isolated from the CSF of 13 children with aseptic meningitis. The virus was characterized by determination of the nucleotide sequences of the P gene as mumps vaccine strain. The incidence of aseptic meningitis with positive mumps vaccine virus was calculated to be .11% during the study period. This incidence rose to .3% toward the end of that period.

Aseptic meningitis is apparently not a rare complication of MMR vaccination in Gunma Prefecture. The incidence of this complication seems to be higher than previously reported. Further research is needed to determine the safety of this vaccine.

▶ Whereas the strategy for immunization against measles, mumps, and rubella infection was introduced into the United States some 20 years ago, it was only in 1989 that similar policies were put into place in Japan. If you believe this report, aseptic meningitis is not a rare complication of MMR vaccination in Japan. In fact, McDonald et al. (1) reported an increase of mumps meningoencephalitis in Canada related to the introduction of a new mumps vaccine. The bad actor in the MMR is the middle M. Fortunately, however, the mumps meningoencephalitis that was seen was not terribly troublesome clinically.

The downside of not adequately immunizing with the MMR vaccine is so tremendous that we continue to accept the risks associated with it. Although the measles vaccine has been licensed for more than a quarter of a century, we have failed to eradicate the disease. It appeared as though we might be approaching that goal in 1983, when only 1,497 cases of measles were reported in the United States. Then came 1989. That year there were more than 17,000 cases clustering in miniepidemics. There appeared to be 2 groups that were most affected: preschoolers who had been largely unimmunized, and those 15–19 years of age, most of whom were immunized at a time when the vaccine was less than optimal. In 1989, the younger group had a higher attack rate and greater morbidity (69% of the deaths occurred in the young age group vs. none in the older age group).

Recognize that vaccine failures with MMR still are being reported because of improper handling. If you want to read one of the most useful articles of this past year, read the special article dealing with office practice of pediatrics by Casto et al. (2). This review explains all of the requirements for the safe handling of vaccines. Although most of us probably are familiar with the information contained therein, it never hurts to be reminded that the MMR vaccine must be kept at 2°–8° C, protected from light, and thrown away after 1–2 years from the data of manufacture or 8 hours after reconstitution. For those of you who are just entering training, learn as much about these vaccines as you can. A cloudy MMR is a no-no, a pink polio virus vaccine is OK, a turbid white DPT after reconstitution is exactly what you should suspect. Those are the ABCs of vaccine handling. For the XYZs, read the Casto article in detail.

Before moving off the topic of measles, please realize that measles still kills about 2 million children annually. Also realize that whenever you have a bad case of measles, the type that requires hospitalization, you should be giving the infected child vitamin A. The idea that vitamin A may have a protective effect in measles was first suggested more than 50 years ago. Recently, a double-blind trial involving 189 children showed that daily administration of 400,000 IU of vitamin A markedly reduced the morbidity and mortality of this disease (3).—J.A. Stockman, III, M.D.

References

1. McDonald J, et al: *Pediatr Infect Dis* 8:751, 1989.
2. Casto DT, et al: *Pediatrics* 87:108, 1991.
3. Hussey GD, et al: *N Engl J Med* 323:160, 1990.

Hypoglycemia During Diarrhea in Childhood: Prevalence, Pathophysiology, and Outcome

Bennish ML, Azad AK, Rahman O, Phillips RE (Internatl Ctr for Diarrhoeal Disease Research, Bangladesh, Dhaka; Harvard School of Public Health, Boston; Univ of Oxford, England)
N Engl J Med 322:1357–1363, 1990

2–19

Diarrhea is the major cause of death among children in some of the developing countries, even where oral rehydration therapy is widely used. The lethal complications of diarrhea other than dehydration remain poorly understood. Hypoglycemia is a known potentially fatal complication of infectious diarrhea in both well-nourished and poorly nourished children. A prospective study was performed to determine the frequency and outcome of hypoglycemia during diarrhea in children.

During an 8-month study period, 2,003 children younger than age 15 years were hospitalized with severe diarrhea at a special diarrhea treatment center in Dhaka, Bangladesh. Hypoglycemia was defined as a capillary blood glucose concentration of <2.2 mmol/L.

Of the 2,003 hospitalized children, 91 (4.5%) had hypoglycemia. Thirty-nine hypoglycemic children (43%) and 122 normoglycemic children (6%) died while hospitalized. Thus 39 (24%) of the 161 children who died had hypoglycemia. Plasma levels of glucoregulatory hormones and gluconeogenetic substrates were measured in 46 hypoglycemic children (mean age, 48 months) and in 25 age- and weight-matched normoglycemic children. Both groups had similar nutritional status at admission and similar pathogens identified in the stool.

Hypoglycemic children had been ill with diarrhea for a significantly shorter period than normoglycemic children. All hypoglycemic children had appropriately low plasma C-peptide levels and elevated plasma levels of glucagon and epinephrine that excluded failure of glucose counterregulation as a cause of hypoglycemia. Both groups had similar alanine and β-hydroxybutyrate concentrations.

A comparison of 18 severely malnourished hypoglycemic children and 26 better-nourished hypoglycemic children revealed that malnourished children had been ill longer, were less likely to have a fever, and had lower lactate and alanine plasma levels and higher plasma cortisol levels than better-nourished children with hypoglycemia, suggesting failure of gluconeogenesis as a causative mechanism.

In addition to dehydration, hypoglycemia is a major cause of death in children with diarrhea. Hypoglycemia in these patients occurs most often as a result of failure of gluconeogenesis rather than as failure of glucose counterregulation, which had been suggested in earlier studies.

▶ Dr. Boris Senior, Professor of Pediatrics at Tufts University, New England Medical Center Hospitals, comments:

▶ In this large-scale and meticulously executed study, the authors determined both the occurrence of hypoglycemia in children with diarrhea in Bangladesh (4.5%) and how many of these children died, (42.9%). They gathered a wealth of data in an effort to identify the precise factor(s) causing the hypoglycemia. It proved more elusive. They did determine that insulin levels were not increased and that the counterregulatory hormones were not depressed. They concluded that a deficiency of gluconeogenetic substrates was responsible for the hypoglycemia.

In anyone, fasting glucose levels are sustained by a precise balance between output of glucose by the liver and its use by the body, particularly by the brain. Once liver glycogen is depleted, glucose output continues through 2 distinct processes, recycling and gluconeogenesis. Recycling is the reconstitution of glucose from the 3 carbon products of glycolysis, lactate, pyruvate and alanine. This process of recycling conserves glucose but provides no additional glucose. Gluconeogenesis, by contrast, is the formation of *new* glucose from protein or fat. However, a critical examination of this process (1) found that negligible quantities of glucose are derived from protein, and only a small amount is derived from the glycerol or fat. Fatty acids, of course, provide none. Thus, of these 2 processes, it is recycling and not gluconeogenesis that provides the glucose leaving the liver. From this, the proposal that a shortage of substrate for gluconeogenesis is the cause of hypoglycemia in any situation seems very unlikely. However, recycling can only conserve glucose. Thus, for fasting levels to be sustained there must be, and is, a profound reduction in the use of glucose. This reduction in the use of glucose comes about by the provision of an alternative fuel for the brain—namely ketones. Any hindrance to the formation of ketones, from a deficiency of adipose stores causing a shortage of free fatty acids to an impediment to any one or more of the many complex steps needed to synthesize ketones, would result in hypoglycemia.

In the normal fasting child, ketone levels rise progressively with the duration of the fast and the fall in glucose. An inverse relationship exists between the concentration of glucose and of ketones. Furthermore the younger the child, the sooner ketones rise. To determine whether or not the provision of ketones is adequate, one needs to relate the levels to the ages and glucose levels of each individual subject. Unfortunately, only grouped values with ranges were presented in this paper. One ventures to postulate that in these patients, as in so many others with fasting hypoglycemia, the cause(s) will be found to reside in impairment of some aspect of the fat-to-ketone pathway.

Tragically, there will be ample opportunity to examine this and other hypotheses. As we read in our papers today, in Peru, in Kurdistan, and again in Bangladesh, diarrhea is widespread, and children continue to die.—B. Senior, M.D.

Reference

1. Senior B, Sadeghi-Nejad A: *Acta Paediatr Scand Suppl* 352:1, 1989.

Six-Year Retrospective Surveillance of Gastroenteritis Viruses Identified at Ten Electron Microscopy Centers in the United States and Canada
Lew JF, Glass RI, Petric M, Lebaron CW, Hammond GW, Miller SE, Robinson C, Boutilier J, Riepenhoff-Talty M, Payne CM, Franklin R, Oshiro LS, Jaqua M-J (Ctrs for Disease Control, Atlanta; Hosp for Sick Children, Toronto; Cadham Provencial Lab, Winnipeg, Manitoba; Duke Univ; The Children's Hosp of Denver)
Pediatr Infect Dis J 9:709–714, 1990   2–20

Except for rotaviruses and enteric adenoviruses, viruses associated with gastroenteritis cannot be detected by commercially available enzyme immunoassays and must be identified by electron microscopy (EM). Data from a 6-year retrospective surveillance of gastroenteritis viruses identified by EM in 10 centers in the United States and Canada were analyzed to define the prevalence, seasonality, and demographic characteristics of viral gastroenteritis.

From 1984 to 1989, 52,691 EM observations were made. The yearly

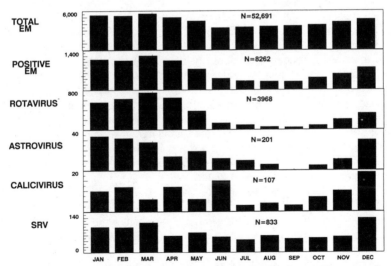

Fig 2–4.—Monthly number of EM examinations in comparison with the monthly number of specimens positive for any virus, rotavirus, astrovirus, calicivirus, and SRVs. (Courtesy of Lew JF, Glass RI, Petric M, et al: *Pediatr Infect Dis J* 9:709–714, 1990.)

positive detection rates among the 10 centers ranged from 8% to 34%, with a mean of 16%. Rotavirus was the most common agent identified (26–83%), followed by adenoviruses (8–27%), and small round viruses (SRVs) (0–40%). Overall, positive EM detections were lowest (8%) in the summer and highest (22%) in the winter. Rotavirus and astrovirus detections peaked in the winter, but no distinct seasonal trend was apparent for the other viruses (Fig 2–4). Of the astrovirus detections, 64% were in infants less than 1 year old, and SRVs were the only agents consistently detected in children 5 years of age and older. Among hospitalized patients, more than 50% of detections of astroviruses, caliciviruses, and SRVs occurred 7 days or more after admission, whereas rotaviruses and adenoviruses were detected earlier.

The data suggest that SRVs are common agents of gastroenteritis and may be important causes of nosocomial infection. Considering the relative insensitivity of direct EM as a screening method for SRVs, astroviruses, and caliciviruses, the detection rates in this study probably underestimate their true prevalence.

▶ Are you feeling as old as I am when you hear the terms "caliciviruses" and "astroviruses?" These are viruses that had not even been named when I was in medical school, and now we are seeing them as significant causes of diarrhea in children. Rotovirus remains the premier cause of the "poops," however. Rotovirus is thought to be responsible for 3.5 million cases of diarrhea in children each year in the United States, resulting in 70,000 hospitalizations and 125 deaths. It is certainly the most frequent cause of dehydrating diarrhea (1). Although we are ever so slowly inching toward an oral rotovirus vaccine, the inching has been at a snail's pace, with no perfect vaccine as yet (2).

The most fascinating advance, however, in our understanding of childhood diarrhea is our increasing knowledge of the astroviruses. Herrmann et al. (3) have shown that among 3,150 Thai children, astrovirus diarrhea was second only to rotovirus, occurring at about half the frequency. When I was growing up, the only "astro" that I knew was this little old lady down the street who had astro something or other after her name. She read palms. In 1975, things changed when, with the use of electron microscopy, someone discovered a new virus and named it astrovirus. The next time you see a child with what you think is rotovirus infection, but the roto test is negative, think astrovirus gastroenteritis. The clinical presentation is virtually identical.

Let's see whether you can answer 2 quiz questions on the subject of things that make our number 2 turn to water.

First, what time of the year are you likely to get rotovirus infection?

Well, the answer to this is, as with many things, it depends. It depends on where you live. The spread of this virus is one of the most interesting of any viral infection. LeBaron et al. (4) found something very unusual with this virus. Epidemics of it tend to spread regularly, occuring first in Mexico, then moving on to the southwest United States in late fall, spreading systematically across the continent in the winter and winding up in the northeast part of the country and in the Maritime provinces of Canada by spring. Obviously, we have no trade barriers with Mexico.

Second, in front of your eyes, a child who has been brought to the emergency room with diarrhea passes a blue-green stool. What is your diagnosis? The organism is likely to be *Pseudomonas aeruginosa*. There aren't many things that cause blue-green stools. Medications can do this (1 example is ametantrone, an anthracene derivative). Blue-containing dyes can do it as well. *Pseudomonas* organisms produce a phenazine pigment that can impart a brilliant blue-green discoloration to the stools. A corollary of this is that periungal infections caused by *Pseudomonas* sp. produce a similar telltale discoloration of the fingernails. The next time you observe a child who has diarrhea with blue-green stools, think, *P. aeruginosa* (5).

A concluding comment about this overall "stoolie" topic. Remember this editor's rule about experimentation: "Never step in anything soft."—J.A. Stockman, III, M.D.

References

1. *MMWR* 40:80, 1991.
2. Santosham M, et al: *J Infect Dis* 163:43, 1991.
3. Herrmann JE, et al: *N Engl J Med* 324:1757, 1991.
4. LeBaron CW, et al: *JAMA* 264:983, 1990.
5. Lee SK, et al: *Pediatr Infect Dis J* 9:371, 1990.

Bismuth Subsalicylate in the Treatment of Acute Diarrhea in Children: A Clinical Study
Soriano-Brücher H, Avendano P, O'Ryan M, Braun SD, Manhart MD, Balm TK, Soriano HA (Catholic Univ, Santiago, Chile; Procter and Gamble Co, Cincinnati)
Pediatrics 87:18–27, 1991   2–21

Despite substantial evidence that bismuth subsalicylate (BSS) is effective in the treatment of diarrhea, there have been no studies on the efficacy of BSS for acute diarrhea in children. In a double-blind, placebo-controlled, randomized study, 123 children aged 4–28 months, hospitalized with acute diarrhea, were treated with BSS and placebo for 5 days as an adjunct to rehydration therapy.

Treatment with BSS was associated with significant benefits within 24–48 hours, as evidenced by reductions in stool frequency and stool weights and improvement in stool consistency, significant improvement in clinical well-being, and shortening of the duration of disease. Patients treated with BSS had a significantly shorter hospital stay (mean, 6.9 days) compared with placebo-treated patients (mean, 8.5 days). Also, BSS reduced the use of intravenously administered fluid and hastened the switch to oral rehydration. Treatment with BSS effectively eliminated pathogenic *Escherichia coli* from the stools in 100% of the cases but was not different from placebo in rotavirus elimination. Therapy was well tolerated with no adverse side effects. Blood bismuth and serum salicylate levels were well below toxic levels. When used in combination with rehydration therapy, BSS is effective in the treatment of acute diarrhea in children.

▶ Pepto Bismol lovers take heart—not only does bismuth subsalicylate acid help prevent diarrhea (of the traveler's type), it can also be used to treat established diarrhea. Exactly how BSS works in the treatment of diarrhea is not well understood. It might prevent attachment of organisms to the gastrointestinal mucosa. It could have a direct antimicrobial effect. It is possible that it could inactivate toxins and because it is an anti-inflammatory, it might inhibit the effect on prostaglandins that control gastric and bowel motility.

There does not appear to be any question from the above study that adjunctive therapy with BSS can offer significant symptomatic improvement compared with rehydration therapies alone. If you believe the data, children treated with combination therapy get well sooner, have shorter hospital stays, and are able to resume normal oral intake faster. Forget not, however, that BSS is a salicylate, and if you still have any lingering doubts about the relationship between salicylates and disorders such as Reye's syndrome, think twice about having your patients swig down the "pink" stuff just because they have a little diarrhea.

It will be interesting to see whether we change our management of common diarrhea as a result of the above article. Chances are that we won't. As an example of our recalcitrance in terms of altering our therapeutic ways, a recent report examined how closely pediatricians have followed the 1985 American Academy of Pediatrics Committee on Nutrition recommendations on oral therapy for acute diarrhea (1). Only a third of us are using glucose-electrolyte solutions meeting the American Academy of Pediatrics recommended carbohydrate to sodium ratio of less than 2:1. Although the Academy's recommendation that feeding be reintroduced in the first 24 hours of a diarrheal episode, the majority of pediatricians still withhold feeding until the second day or later. Snyder et al. concluded that these findings indicate that educational programs on oral therapy during acute diarrhea are needed in the United States. One might alternatively think that the accumulative experience of more than 30,000 pediatricians would lead the majority to question the recommendations of the Academy. Who is right? Who is wrong? Is there truly a right way or a wrong way?

One could easily come to the conclusion that there is no liberal or conservative (left or right) to the rights and wrongs of refeeding in diarrheal states. In the final analysis, everything will turn out the same, given enough time. After all, 2 wrongs may not make a right, but 3 rights will make a left (sorry).

Do you know what the most useful telephone number is with respect to infectious disease these days? It is: (404) 332–4559. If you have a spirit of inquisitiveness, use Ma Bell and find out how helpful this number can be to you.—J.A. Stockman, III, M.D.

Reference

1. Snyder JD, et al: *Pediatrics* 87:28, 1991.

Clinical Features of Adenovirus Enteritis: A Review of 127 Cases

Krajden M, Brown M, Petrasek A, Middleton PJ (Hosp for Sick Children, Toronto; Univ of Toronto)

Pediatr Infect Dis J 9:636–641, 1990 2–22

Gastroenteritis may be a concurrent clinical feature in patients infected with certain adenovirus (Ad) serotypes associated with respiratory illness. However, case-controlled studies have suggested that Ad serotypes can be isolated as frequently from the feces of patients without gastroenteritis as from patients with diarrhea.

To assess the clinical features of infantile gastroenteritis associated with Ad, the hospital records of 127 patients were analyzed retrospectively. All patients had at least 1 fecal sample that was positive for Ad as detected by electron microscopy. The study included 69 males and 58 females. Ninety-four percent were less than 4 years old. The majority of the gastroenteritis cases (56%) were associated with Ad 40 and Ad 41, and Ad 31 was associated with 17% of cases. Of the 18 cases associated with Ad 31, 14 were nosocomial and associated with diarrhea. Clinical features of Ad 31, such as peak temperature, duration of fever and clinical illness, and the presence of respiratory illness, were indistinguishable from those of Ad 40 and Ad 41 (Figs 2–5 through 2–7).

In addition to Ad 40 and Ad 41, the nonfastidious Ad 31 can apparently be implicated in diarrhea. Therefore, rapid Ad detection systems should not exclude Ad 31. The role of Ad in nosocomial illness is also

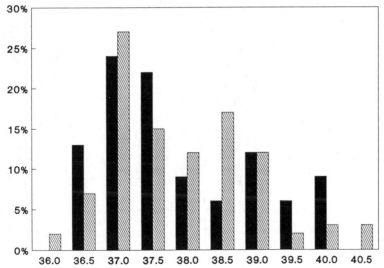

Fig 2–5.—Peak temperature, community-acquired *(filled square)* vs. nosocomial *(hatched square)*. *Abcissa,* temperature (°C) rounded to nearest .5°; *ordinate,* percent of cases within each category. (Courtesy of Krajden M, Brown M, Petrasek A, et al: *Pediatr Infect Dis J* 9:636–641, 1990.)

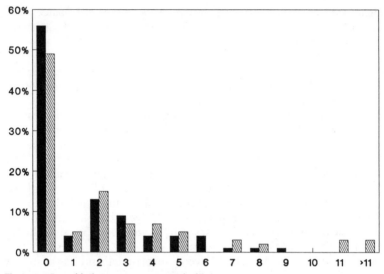

Fig 2–6.—Days febrile, community-acquired *(filled square)* vs. nosocomial *(hatched square)*. Ab*cissa,* days; *ordinate,* percent of cases within each category. (Courtesy of Krajden M, Brown M, Petrasek A, et al: *Pediatr Infect Dis J* 9:636–641, 1990.)

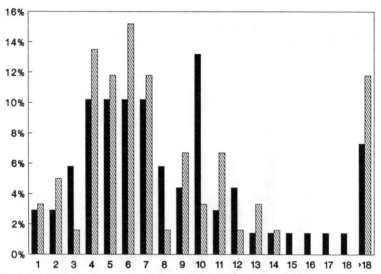

Fig 2–7.—Total duration of clinical illness, community-acquired *(filled square)* vs. nosocomial *(hatched square)*. Abcissa, days; *ordinate,* percent of cases within each category. (Courtesy of Krajden M, Brown M, Petrasek A, et al: *Pediatr Infect Dis J* 9:636–641, 1990.)

significant. The association of Ad 31 with enteritis should be confirmed in further controlled studies.

Perirectal Abscess in Infants and Children: Report of 52 Cases and Review of Literature
Arditi M, Yogev R (Northwestern Univ; Children's Mem Hosp, Chicago)
Pediatr Infect Dis J 9:411–415, 1990   2–23

Most data on perirectal abscess is derived from adult studies. Fifty-two cases of pediatric perirectal abscess were reviewed with emphasis on clinical presentation, predisposing conditions, bacteriology, therapy, and complications.

In adults this infection is associated with ulcerative colitis. In children, the most frequently observed predisposing factor is immunodeficiency, particularly neutropenia. In both adults and children, there is a strong male predominance (table).

Incision and drainage followed by appropriate antibiotic therapy and sitz baths is the recommended therapy for immunocompetent patients. For the patient who is severely immunocompromised or neutropenic, an initial trial of broad spectrum antibiotics followed by incision and drainage in selected cases is recommended. In all cases, management should include a search for the underlying condition.

▶ Dr. Itzhak Brook, Professor of Pediatrics, Uniformed Services Military School, Defense Nuclear Agency, Armed Forces Radiobiology Research Institute, comments:

▶ Perirectal abscess frequently is encountered in immunocompromised pediatric patients. The isolation of anaerobic and facultative bacteria of gastrointesti-

Predisposing Conditions in 50 Children With Perirectal Abscess

Condition	No. of Patients
Recent rectal surgery	8
Hirschsprung disease	4
Rectal biopsy or dilatation for imperforate anus	4
Neutropenia	8
Chemotherapy for malignancy	6
Aplastic anemia	1
Immune neutropenia	1
Human immunodeficiency virus infection	2
Crohn's disease	2
Diabetes/ketoacidosis	2
Ulcerative colitis	1
Severe combined immunodeficiency syndrome	1
Chronic granulomatous disease	1
Large dosage steroid therapy	1

(Courtesy of Arditi M, Yogev R: *Pediatr Infect Dis J* 9:411–415, 1990.)

nal origin organisms from the perirectal site is not surprising because anaerobes are the predominant organisms in the gastrointestinal tract, where they outnumber aerobes at a ratio of at least 1,000 to 1.

The bacteriology of perirectal abscess in children was evaluated in several other recent studies. *Staphylococcus aureus* and *Escherichia coli* were the bacterial agents most frequently isolated, and anaerobes were rarely recovered. However, anaerobic bacteriology was not used in these studies, suggesting that if proper procedures were used, many more anaerobes would be isolated from these types of specimens.

In contrast, whenever proper techniques for recovery of anaerobic bacteria were used, as was done in 83% of the patients studied by Arditi and Yogev, anaerobic bacteria were isolated in 58% of the patients. This is an important example of how improved methodology enhances the recovery of anaerobic bacteria from clinical specimens (1).

Surgery is the mainstay of therapy of perirectal abscess. The abscess should be incised as soon as possible, because attempts to allow it to localize further may lead to the spread of infection to deeper tissue planes. Simple drainage is insufficient. The infected crypt must be probed and unroofed. Fistulous tracks must be opened and excised, if necessary.

Early aspiration and Gram's stain for presumptive bacteriologic diagnosis may be helpful if antimicrobial agents are to be used before surgical intervention. Although surgical drainage is still the therapy of choice, administration of antimicrobial drugs is generally essential, is associated with less complication, and may be the only therapy needed (2). The predominance of anaerobic bacteria and enteric gram-negative rods in perirectal abscess requires the administration of appropriate antimicrobial therapy.

The presence of penicillin-resistant anaerobic bacteria such as *Bacteroides fragilis* group may warrant the use of one of the following antimicrobial agents: clindamycin, cefoxitin, chloramphenicol, or metronidazole. The administration of an aminoglycoside or a third-generation cephalosporin should provide adequate coverage from gram-negative enteric rods. Single-agent therapy with cefoxitin, imipenem, or the combination of a penicillin (such as ampicillin or ticarcillin) and a β-lactamase inhibitor (such as sulbactam or clavulanic acid), may be adequate.—I. Brook, M.D.

References

1. Brook I, Martin WJ: *Pediatrics* 66:282, 1980.
2. Glenn J, et al: *Rev Infect Dis* 10:42, 1988.

Congenital Syphilis Presenting in Infants After the Newborn Period
Dorfman DH, Glaser JH (Bronx Municipal Hosp Ctr, NY; Albert Einstein College of Medicine)
N Engl J Med 323:1299–1302, 1990   2–24

The incidence of congenital syphilis has increased dramatically, especially in urban areas. Congenital syphilis was diagnosed in 7 infants

Clinical and Laboratory Findings on Admission in Infants With No
Serologic Evidence of Syphilis at Birth

VARIABLE	PATIENT NO.						
	1	2	3	4	5	6	7
Sex	M	F	M	F	M	F	F
Age (wk)	7	12	3	4	7	5	14
Physical findings							
Rash	−	+	+	−	−	+	+
Rhinitis	−	+	−	+	+	−	+
Hepatomegaly	+	+	+	+	+	+	+
Splenomegaly	+	+	+	+	−	+	+
Lymphadenopathy	+	+	+	−	−	+	−
Laboratory findings							
Hematocrit	0.32	0.22	0.18	0.37	0.25	0.23	0.30
White cells ($\times 10^{-9}$/liter)	13	8	51	34	21	14	27
Monocytes (%)	11	8	23	15	19	15	13
Platelets ($\times 10^{-9}$/liter) *	314	381	155	NT	211	71	830
Blood-chemistry values							
Alkaline phosphatase (nmol · sec^{-1}/liter) †	>9990	5140	7475	NT	8660	11,620	7125
SGOT (nmol · sec^{-1}/liter) ‡	900	1970	9820	NT	8660	1,400	1350
SGPT (nmol · sec^{-1}/liter) §	315	900	5800	NT	3670	670	870
Cerebrospinal fluid test results							
VDRL test ¶	1:2	—	—	—	1:1	—	1:1
White cells ($\times 10^{-9}$/liter)	14	2	5	60	30	2	3
Protein (g/liter) ‖	0.72	0.37	NT	0.72	0.53	0.34	0.15
Radiologic changes	−	+	−	+	NT	−	+
Jarisch–Herxheimer reaction	+	+	+	+	+	+	+

Abbreviations: +, presence of finding; −, abscence of finding; *NT*, not tested; *SGOT*, serum aspartate aminotransferase; *SGPT*, serum alanine aminotransferase; *VDRL*, Veneral Disease Research Laboratory.
*Normal value, 150 to 350 × 10⁹ L.
†Normal value, 217–650 nmol/sec/L.
‡Normal value 117–450 nmol/sec/L.
§Normal value, 117–350 nmol/sec/L.
¶Results are given as negative or, if positive, as antibody titers.
‖ Normal value, .15 to .45 g/L.
(Courtesy of Dorfman DH, Glaser JH: *N Engl J Med* 323:1299–1302, 1990.)

when symptoms developed 3 to 14 weeks after birth. These infants were studied to determine why the diagnosis was not made at birth.

At delivery 4 infants and their mothers had negative qualitative rapid-plasma-reagin tests for syphilis. The remaining 3 mothers had been seronegative during pregnancy and were not tested again at delivery. Two of their infants were seronegative at birth; the third was not tested.

At age 3 to 14 weeks, when the infants became symptomatic, all 7 infants and the 5 available mothers tested seropositive for syphilis. Four infants had a characteristic diffuse rash. The remaining 3 had fever and aseptic meningitis on admission to the hospital (table). All 7 infants had multisystem disease, as evidenced by hepatomegaly, elevated levels of aminotransferase and alkaline phosphatase, anemia, and monocytosis. All the infants responded to treatment with parenteral penicillin.

Even when serologic tests are done for both mother and infant at birth, some infants will not be identified as having syphilis. This is probably because the infection is very recent and not enough time has passed for an antibody response to develop. Some infants with congenital syphilis of later onset do not have a typical rash, and serologic tests for syphilis should be included in the assessment of all febrile infants, at least in areas where the disease is prevalent.

▶ Dr. Jerome O. Klein, Professor of Pediatrics, Boston University School of Medicine, Director, Division of Pediatric Infectious Diseases, Boston City Hospital, Maxwell Finland Laboratory for Infectious Diseases, comments:

▶ Congenitally acquired syphilis continues to confuse pediatricians. The signs of disease are often subtle and nonspecific, and the serologic results are ambiguous. But pediatricians working in urban centers should relearn the lessons of the past because the recent increase in numbers of cases of congenital disease is likely to continue:

Lesson 1. All neonates in high-risk areas should be tested at birth. The Centers for Disease Control recommends testing for syphilis at the first prenatal visit and at delivery. The congenital disease is preventable and is readily treated with penicillin G, but cases will be missed unless there is universal testing in urban centers.

Lesson 2. If the diagnosis is suspected and the serology is negative, repeat the test. Mothers may be infected late in pregnancy after serology was performed or may be infected shortly before term and may not have developed an immune response when blood is obtained after delivery. Negative VDRL (or RPR) titers may occur because of the "prozone" effect that occurs when very high titers result in a negative test. Serial dilutions are necessary to identify the true positive, but the test must be requested from most laboratories.

Lesson 3. Remember to include syphilis in the differential diagnosis of the neonate and infant with unexplained rash, fever, or aseptic meningitis. Late onset disease may occur weeks to months after birth, and as is true of other congenital infections (including rubella, cytomegalovirus, and HIV), signs may not appear for years.

Lesson 4. Check the current treatment protocols. All strains of *Treponema pallidum* are highly susceptible to penicillin G, but recommendations for treatment schedules have changed over the years. Review the section on syphilis in the *1991 Red Book* before therapy.

Lesson 5. Be ready for surprises in women who are dually infected with HIV and *T. pallidum*. Among the concerns in patients with dual infection are relapse and progression of syphilis in spite of appropriate therapy and failure to serorevert following therapy. Some experts advise retreatment of the infant born to an HIV-infected mother who was treated for syphilis during pregnancy.

Lesson 6. When in doubt, treat. The risks of therapy are minimal (mainly the prolonged hospitalization), but the life-long sequelae of congenital syphilis will alter the quality of life of the infant.—J.O. Klein, M.D.

Reference

1. *1991 Red Book*, pp 457–459.

Children Born to Women With HIV-1 Infection: Natural History and Risk of Transmission

Ades AE, Newell ML, Peckham CS, European Collaborative Study (Inst of Child Health, London)

Lancet 337:253–260, 1991

2–25

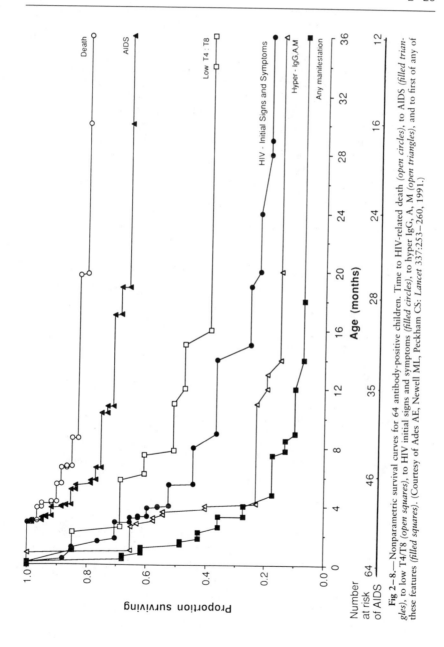

Fig 2–8.—Nonparametric survival curves for 64 antibody-positive children. Time to HIV-related death *(open circles)*, to AIDS *(filled triangles)*, to low T4/T8 *(open squares)*, to HIV initial signs and symptoms *(filled circles)*, to hyper IgG, A, M *(open triangles)*, and to first of any of these features *(filled squares)*. (Courtesy of Ades AE, Newell ML, Peckham CS: *Lancet* 337:253–260, 1991.)

Knowledge of the natural history of vertically acquired HIV-1 comes primarily from studies of children seen with symptoms at specialist centers. The results of the European Collaborative Study, a prospective investigation of children born to HIV-infected mothers, have now been reported.

Six hundred children born to infected mothers in 10 European centers were followed up every 3 months after birth to age 18 months and every 6 months thereafter. At the last follow-up 64 children were considered to have HIV infection. Nonparametric survival curves for these 64 are seen in Figure 2–8. Three hundred forty-three children had lost antibody and were presumed to be uninfected. In infected children the initial clinical feature was usually a combination of persistent lymphadenopathy, splenomegaly, and hepatomegaly. Thirty percent of the children, however, had AIDS or oral candidiasis rapidly followed by AIDS.

An estimated 83% of infected children had laboratory or clinical signs of HIV infection by age 6 months. By 12 months 26% had AIDs and 17% were dead of HIV-related disease. The disease subsequently progressed more slowly, with most children remaining stable or even improving in the second year.

Based on results in 372 children born at least 18 months before the analysis, the vertical transmission rate was 12.9%. Virus has been isolated repeatedly in an additional small percentage of children who lost maternal antibody and have remained normal clinically and immunologically. Without a definitive virologic diagnosis it was possible to identify HIV infection in 48% of affected children by age 6 months with a greater than 99% specificity by monitoring immunoglobulins, CD4/CD8 ratio, and clinical signs.

In the absence of a definitive diagnosis immunologic and clinical signs can serve as predictors of HIV infection in children younger than age 18 months. These findings have implications for management and the design of clinical trials.

Dideoxyinosine in Children With Symptomatic Human Immunodeficiency Virus Infection

Butler KM, Husson RN, Balis FM, Brouwers P, Eddy J, El-Amin D, Gress J, Hawkins M, Jarosinski P, Moss H, Poplack D, Santacroce S, Venzon D, Wiener L, Wolters P, Pizzo PA (Natl Cancer Inst, Bethesda, Md; Natl Inst of Health, Bethesda, Md; Medical Illness Counseling, Bethesda, Md)
N Engl J Med 324:137–144, 1991   2–26

The number of children infected with HIV is increasing. Zidovudine decreases morbidity and mortality from HIV infection in adults and children, but intolerance and toxicity, particularly myelosuppression, are common. Recent trials of dideoxyinosine (ddI) in adult patients with HIV infection have shown that it has antiretroviral activity with little hematologic toxicity. A phase I–II study was done to investigate the use of ddI in 43 children with symptomatic HIV infection.

Changes in Clinical, Immunologic, and Virologic Indexes in Response to
Treatment With ddI in Previously Treated and Untreated Patients*

INDEX	PATIENTS WITH RESPONSE		
	PREVIOUSLY UNTREATED (N = 27)	PREVIOUSLY TREATED (N = 16)	TOTAL (N = 43)
	percent		
>10% Weight gain	26	38†	30
Reduction in lymphadenopathy (n = 16)‡	62	67	63
Reduction in hepatosplenomegaly (n = 24)‡	94	57	83
Increase in CD4 cell count	33	25	30
Decline in p24 antigen level§	48	22	40

*Previously treated patients had received zidovudine and had either refractory disease of intolerance to zidovudine. One patient had toxic effects during an alternating schedule of zidovudine and dideoxycytidine.
†In 2 patients the increase coincided with the institution of hyperalimentation.
‡The number in parentheses is the number with the abnormality at entry.
§A decline from more than 100 pg/mL at entry to less than 50 pg/mL at each of the last 2 evaluations.
(Courtesy of Butler KM, Husson RN, Balis FM, et al: *N Engl J Med* 324:137–144, 1991.)

Sixteen patients (median age, 10.25 years) had refractory disease after zidovudine treatment or were intolerant to the drug, and 27 patients (median age, 2.6 years) were previously untreated. Dideoxyinosine was given orally in 3 divided doses for 24 weeks. Eight children did not complete the 24-week protocol: 6 died during treatment, 1 was withdrawn because of progressive disease, and 1 was withdrawn because of toxicity.

Both previously treated and untreated children gained weight and the degree of lymphadenopathy and hepatosplenomegaly was reduced at all dose levels (table). The median CD4 cell count was increased in 38 patients for whom paired cell counts were available. The response appeared to be more sustained than with zidovudine. In addition, there was a significant decline in the median p24 antigen level in 27 of 32 patients for whom paired values of p24 antigen levels were available. The plasma concentration of ddI correlated significantly with both the degree of decline in the p24 antigen and the degree of improvement in IQ scores.

Dideoxyinosine is well tolerated and shows promising antiretroviral activity in HIV-infected children. Because the clinical response correlates with plasma ddI levels, bioavailability should be an important consideration when using ddI to treat HIV infection.

► Philip A. Pizzo, M.D., Chief of Pediatrics, Head, Infectious Disease Section of the National Cancer Institute, and Professor of Pediatrics, Uniformed Services University for the Health Sciences, comments:

► On July 18-19, 1991 the Food and Drug Administration (FDA) Antiviral Advisory Committee reviewed the New Drug Application (NDA) for dideoxyinosine (ddI). It was a historical event, especially for pediatrics. This drug was the second antiretroviral agent to be reviewed by the FDA (the first being azidothymidine [AZT]). Unlike the prospective double-blind placebo-controlled trial that had led to the approval of AZT in 1987 for adults with AIDS, the data being reviewed on ddl consisted mainly of phase I–II clinical trials in adults and children. Also included were toxicity results from the expanded access program (also referred to as the "parallel tract") that had enrolled nearly 20,000 adults between 1989 and 1991. Thus the Advisory Panel was being asked to approve ddl based on presumptive activity rather than data from well controlled clinical trials long deemed essential by the FDA. Of course, much has changed since the initial experience with AZT. First, and most importantly, because of the demonstrable activity of AZT in reducing mortality and opportunistic infections, it is no longer ethical to design a placebo controlled trial. Although active controlled trials (e.g., AZT vs. ddl) are underway in adults (and are beginning in children), they were still in progress at the time of the ddl review, and the full results were unavailable. Second, many adults have become intolerant or refractory to AZT, making ddl one of their only therapeutic options. Although there is a clear need for new drugs against the AIDS virus, the ddl review underscored that new criteria may be necessary for their approval.

It was within this context that the pediatric study of ddl took center stage. Of course drug approvals for children often lag behind those for adults. Seventy percent of drugs in use have no specific pediatric indication. In line with this, AZT had not been approved for children until May 1990 (3 years after it was approved in adults) and even then its use required a special waiver. At the ddl review, however, an extension of the study reported by Butler et al. played a critical role in the Advisory Panel's recommendation to approve this drug. Not only did the study of 95 pediatric patients presented by the National Cancer Institute (NCI) investigators prove to be the largest single institution series in the world, irrespective of age, but the study design permitted important clinicopharmacological correlations that were viewed as important. Indeed, a number of the panelists commented that the pediatric data was the strongest being presented.

The agent ddl is not a cure for AIDS, but it does appear to offer an additional weapon to the antiretroviral armamentarium. This drug appears to be able to sustain the CD4 count, especially for children who start out with greater than 100 CD4 cells/mm^3. Butler et al. demonstrated that this lasted for 6 months, and the extended data from the same NCI investigators confirmed that CD4 counts could remain stable for more than a year when ddl was being administered. Virological activity was demonstrated by significant reductions in p24 antigen. As demonstrated by Butler et al., ddl has the unfortunate property of being acid labile, necessitating its co-administration with antacid. This can result in considerable interpatient variation in bioavailability, making it important to monitor drug levels. This is further underscored by the correlations of the area under the plasma concentration curve for ddl with improvements in IQ scores. Notably, detailed pharmacokinetic monitoring and correlations, often inherent to pediatric studies, were not as carefully addressed in the adult clinical trials of ddl.

The exact role for ddl remains to be determined. Its initial use will be for those who cannot tolerate AZT or who become refractory to it. Because ddl appears to be less myelosuppressive than AZT (although higher doses can cause pancreatitis or peripheral neuropathy), combination regimens are of interest and are ongoing in both adults and children. The proceedings surrounding the review of ddI mandate that all clinical investigators pause and reconsider the criteria that will be necessary to validate new drugs. But the central role that the pediatric data played in the approval recommendation, and the fact that ddI is a drug that was concomitantly approved for children and adults, represents a step forward for pediatric drug development—and for children with AIDS.

Neurologic Signs in Young Children With Human Immunodeficiency Virus Infection
Cogo P, Laverda AM, Ades AE, Newell ML, Peckham CS, European Collaborative Study (Inst of Child Health, London)
Pediatr Infect Dis J 9:402–406, 1990   2–27

The prevalence of neurologic involvement was studied in 39 children who had HIV infection and 164 other children who were born to HIV-positive women but were antibody-negative. All were followed up for up to 4 years after birth.

Five of 16 children (31%) who had AIDS or AIDS-related complex had serious neurologic manifestations, although in 2 children the signs were not likely related to HIV infection. None of 14 children with significant HIV-related symptoms or signs who did not have AIDS or AIDS-related complex and none of 9 who were asymptomatic had neurologic involvement. Two of 164 uninfected children had neurologic signs that were associated with drug withdrawal at birth and prematurity.

In contrast to previous reports, the prevalence of neurologic findings was not high in these HIV-infected children. Reports of more frequent neurologic involvement come from the United States. It is not clear whether this reflects methodological differences in patient recruitment, different viral strains, or different levels of social and health care.

▶ Dr. Ram Yogev, Professor of Pediatrics, Northwestern University Medical School, comments:

▶ Central nervous system involvement during HIV infection is well documented. Investigators have shown that HIV causes direct CNS infection as demonstrated by (1) HIV antigen in brain macrophages and endothelial cells; (2) HIV nucleotide sequences in brain tissue; and (3) increased CSF levels of anti-HIV antibody. Although HIV is found in the brain, its role in the neurologic deterioration of HIV-infected children is not fully understood, and little is known at the cellular level about the interaction between the virus and the immune system within the nervous system. Generally, neurologic deterioration follows the degree of immune deficiency. This is nicely reflected in the European Collaborative Study, which found that only patients with AIDS manifested neurologic impairment. Unfortunately, the true incidence of CNS disease in HIV-infected children is not yet known. Most reports from the United States regarding the incidence of CNS involvement include a large proportion of severely ill children and, therefore, probably overestimate the incidence of HIV-related CNS disease. In contrast, studies from Europe (including the current study) report lower incidences of CNS involvement, probably because they include many children with mild HIV-related disease and with relatively short (about 2 years) follow-up. It has been estimated that about 40% of patients who develop encephalopathy do so in the first 2 years of life, and the rest develop symptoms much later. Thus, short follow-up periods or a higher proportion of severely sick patients in the cohort studied affects the reported incidence. In addition, the term "HIV encephalopathy" has been defined differently in the various studies. For example, the current study includes only those with severe neurologic and neurodevelopmental manifestations, whereas the study by Belman et al. (1) included patients with cognitive deficits as well. These varied definitions of "neurologic syndromes" also affect the reported incidence.

The early manifestations of HIV encephalopathy have been documented only recently and only in a small number of patients. Poor head control, hypotonia, and hyperactive deep tendon reflexes are some of the earliest physical signs. Delay in development of a social smile or loss of previously acquired motor and social skills are also common early manifestations of CNS involvement. With the progression of CNS involvement, several clinical conditions have been observed. These can be divided into progressive encephalopathy and static encephalopathy. The predominant clinical findings of progressive encephalopathy include impaired brain growth, progressive motor dysfunction, and loss of neurodevelopmental milestones. In static encephalopathy the neurologic deficits do not progress. For example, the affected child manifests developmental (motor and/or cognitive) delay but does not regress. On occasion the distinction between progressive encephalopathy and static encephalopathy is difficult.

Treatment with antiretroviral agents such as zidovudine or ddl appears to improve the neurodevelopmental impairment. Thus, careful neurodevelopmental assessment of HIV-infected children must be an integral part of the routine care of these children.

Many questions are still unanswered. These include the following: What factors influence the progression of CNS manifestations? What early manifestations predict the outcome? When in the course of HIV disease does the CNS become involved? What are the interrelations between the local immune system and HIV? Only careful longitudinal studies will clarify these issues.— R. Yogev, M.D.

Reference

1. Belman AL, et al: *Am J Dis Child* 142:29, 1988.

Modeling the Impact of Breast-Feeding by HIV-Infected Women on Child Survival
Heymann SJ (Harvard School of Public Health)
Am J Public Health 80:1305–1309, 1990   2–28

Vertical transmission of HIV may occur prenatally, during birth, or postnatally. The former 2 routes account for infection in 24% to 46% of infants born to seropositive mothers. There has been concern whether infants who are uninfected at birth should be breast-fed. A decision analysis was performed to estimate the HIV transmission rate through breast milk above which HIV-positive mothers should be counseled not to breast-feed.

Given the relative risks of alternatives to maternal milk in developing countries, alternative feeding practices should be recommended only when warranted. The probability of HIV transmission through breast milk would need to be at least .12 in a community with an under-5 child mortality rate from non-HIV causes of 100 per 1,000 live births and at least .27 in a community with a rate of 200 per 1,000 live births. This critical transmission rate applies even to the known HIV-infected mother with an available feeding alternative and a relative risk of 2:1. Although the critical transmission rate does not vary significantly despite a 20% false positive rate for HIV screening in a high-risk population, it is very sensitive to the availability of HIV screening. An alternative feeding practice would probably not be recommended when maternal status is unknown. In communities in which the HIV prevalence among mothers reaches 40%, breast-feeding should still be recommended in the absence of HIV screening unless HIV transmission through breast milk exceeds 30%.

Apparent Vertical Transmission of Human Immunodeficiency Virus Type 1 by Breast-Feeding in Zambia
Hira SK, Mangrola UG, Mwale C, Chintu C, Tembo G, Brady WE, Perine PL (Univ Teaching Hosp, Lusaka, Zambia; Uniformed Services Univ of the Health Sciences, Bethesda, Md)
J Pediatr 117:421–424, 1990   2–29

The prevalence of HIV-1 infection in Lusaka is high, heterosexual intercourse being the primary means of transmission. In a previous study, the authors determined that the perinatal rate of transmission of HIV-1 in infants born to women who were seropositive for HIV-1 on admission to the labor ward was 38.5%. Some of the apparently perinatally infected infants may, however, have been infected after birth by human milk during breast-feeding.

Serodiagnostic tests for HIV were performed on 1,954 women admitted to labor wards. Tests were also performed on newborns and on the father in some cases. Of 634 HIV-seronegative women screened at 1-year follow-up, 19 had become seropositive, an annual incidence of 3%. Three incident cases of HIV occurred in the 19 children born to mothers who had seroconversion to HIV during follow-up. Maternal risks for HIV infection included blood transfusion, history of incident genital ulcers, and the practice of "dry sex." In dry sex, a cloth is used to remove vaginal secretions before or during intercourse.

Women at high risk of acquiring HIV, particularly those married to or having sexual relationships with HIV-infected men, should not breast-feed their children. Mothers at highest risk of postnatally infecting their infant with HIV appear to be those who were recently infected and have viremia. Although the risk of HIV transmission by breast-feeding is small, it does justify the use of formula for feeding. However, in Africa, the advantage of breast-feeding to prevent death from diarrheal disease usually outweighs the risk of HIV infection.

▶ The preceding 2 reports (Abstracts 2–28 and 2–29) look at the same question from different perspectives. When it comes to defining where the real culprit is in the transmission of HIV from mother to child, blaming breast milk is a violation of the principle: "The leak in the roof is never in the same location as the drip." To say it differently, although common sense may dictate that one would be crazy to expose an infant who may not yet have been infected by the mother to contaminated breast milk, the story is much more complex than that. The report from Zambia suggesting that there is apparent vertical transmission of HIV-1 by breast-feeding has not been substantiated in Haiti. There, the estimated mother-to-infant HIV-1 transmission rate in breast-fed infants was 25%, similar to the rates reported for non–breast-fed populations in the United States and Europe (1).

The modeling study of the impact of breast-feeding by Heymann (Abstract 2–28) compares the relative risks of alternatives to maternal milk in developing countries. What these authors are saying is that yes, there may be a risk of HIV transmission by breast milk, but if you are going to stop breast-feeding, the risk had darned well better be greater than the risk of not breast-feeding with all of its associated problems in underdeveloped countries. An interesting twist on a new and old problem: breast-feeding/HIV vs. non–breast-feeding/infection-malnutrition. I suppose the real question here is which is the lesser of 2 evils, because milk-borne transmission of HIV can occur in endemic cycles (2). The conclusion for us in the United States is pretty obvious, however. Because nutritional problems in this country are not nearly as high a risk as the vertical HIV transmission through breast milk, all infants of HIV-positive mothers should be bottle-fed.

If you are getting a sense that the issues related to HIV are species-specific to the countries in which the infection occurs (essentially everywhere now), you are quite correct. For example, how would you respond to the question: "How effective are condoms in the prevention of HIV infection in Ireland?"

The answer is pretty straightforward. They can't be very effective if you can't buy them. Ireland treats condoms the way other countries treat hard drugs for registered addicts—as products that can be obtained from a limited number of medical outlets with a doctor or pharmacist to control the release. Since 1988, the Irish Family Planning Association has been selling condoms in central Dublin. In May of 1990, the Association was convicted of selling 2 condoms for 80 pence and for that infraction was fined 4,000 pounds. On appeals, a certain Justice O'Hanarhan did change the outcome of the case. He raised the fine 500 pounds and indicated that for a second offense the fine would be 5,000 pounds. Pretty pricey condoms and some expensive fine for 1 act of commission. The Irish view of condoms easily documents that rational decisions do not always prove to be rational.—J.A. Stockman, III, M.D.

References

1. Halsey NA, et al: *JAMA* 264:2088, 1990.
2. Hino S, et al: *Acta Paediatr Jpn* 31:428, 1989.

3 Nutrition and Metabolism

Screening for Biotinidase Deficiency in Newborns: Worldwide Experience
Wolf B, Heard GS (Med College of Virginia of Virginia Commonwealth Univ, Richmond)
Pediatrics 85:512–517, 1990   3–1

The first neonatal screening program for biotinidase deficiency was initiated in 1984, and by 1988, 29 programs had been established in 12 countries, including Australia, Austria, Canada, Italy, Japan, Mexico, New Zealand, Scotland, Spain, Switzerland, the United States, and West Germany.

Of the 4,396,834 newborns screened, 32 had profound biotinidase deficiency, defined as an activity level of less than 10% of mean normal activity level, and 40 had partial deficiency, defined as 10% to 30% of mean normal activity level. The combined incidence of profound and partial deficiency was 1 per 61,067 live births. Profound deficiency occurred in 1 per 137,401 live births, and partial deficiency occurred in 1 per 109,921 live births. The estimated frequency of the recessive allele was .0040, and the estimated frequency of heterozygosity was 1 in 123.

Biotinidase deficiency was present in 1 black child, 1 Hispanic child, and 70 white children. The disorder did not occur in Oriental children. The incidence of biotinidase deficiency was highest among French Canadian children. The female to male ratio was .76. Most tested parents of children with profound and partial deficiency had biotinidase activity levels between 0 and mean normal activity levels; 6 children with profound deficiency were symptomatic at the time of diagnosis. None of the infants with partial deficiency had exhibited symptoms, but little is known about the natural history of infants with partial deficiency.

Although 8 pilot screening programs have terminated, 21 will continue either indefinitely or until predetermined targets are reached. The screening test for biotinidase deficiency is comparatively inexpensive, and with the incidence of low-level activity of 1 per 61,067 live births, the incidence of occurrence for this disorder is well within the range of other disorders for which newborns are tested. Each state, region, and nation must decide whether screening for biotinidase deficiency should be incorporated into its screening program for newborns based on the various advantages of screening, incidence of the disorder, availability of resources, and priorities.

▶ It is less than 10 years since biotinidase deficiency became part of newborn screening both here in the United States and elsewhere in the world. This report is important because it summarizes the screening data from 12 countries, including the United States. On balance, biotinidase screening has withstood the test of time. Although absence of this enzyme is relatively rare (1 in 100,000), if you have the disorder, symptoms that include seizures, skin rash, alopecia, hypotonia, ataxia, fungal infection, hearing loss, visual problems, developmental delay, and ketoacidosis can develop and are frequently fatal. Treatment with supplemental biotin does the trick. To say this differently, biotinidase deficiency is one of the very best examples of an inherited disorder that meets all of the criteria for successful newborn screening: affected children do not exhibit symptoms at birth, later in life they will, and the clinical consequences can be prevented. Enough said.

It is a shame that the same cannot be said of phenylketonuria (PKU). The same general guidelines and principles articulated above do apply to this disorder but in a more imprecise way.

Unlike biotinidase deficiency, there are problems with very early newborn screening for PKU. In the first 24 hours of life, negative tests may be seen. Unlike biotinidase deficiency, in which the treatment is to give something, with PKU the treatment is basically to withhold something—a more difficult challenge. In addition, there seems to be no age when you can stop a PKU diet. Smith et al. (1) reported that in 263 children born between 1964 and 1971, the mean IQ at 4 years of age rose with the year of birth from 24 points below revised IQ norms to 10 points below, presumably on the basis of improved management of these infants; in 545 children born between 1972 and 1980 there was no significant rise in IQ, and the mean remained 8 points below the norm. Intelligence quotient fell progressively by roughly 4 points for each 4 weeks' delay in starting treatment, for each 300 μmol/L rise in mean phenylalanine concentrations during treatment, and for each 5 months during the first 2 years during which the phenylalanine concentrations were too low. The most favorable treatment characteristics were shown in 46 children born between 1972 and 1980. Their mean IQ after standardizing for social class was 112. These data provide the background for the study by Thompson et al. showing neurologic deterioration in young adults with PKU who go off their diets (2).

Can you ever safely stop a PKU diet? Probably not. A report on 7 patients with PKU who stopped their diets after they reached adulthood stated that these patients had quadraparesis, ataxia, epilepsy, paralysis, hyperreflexia, dystonia, and tremors. Not all signs and symptoms were seen in every patient, but each patient had some of the above. On MRI, high signal abnormalities consistent with increased water content were shown in white matter. Going back on a PKU diet reversed some of the MRI and clinical findings.

To learn more about the long-term outcome relative to PKU, read the results of the Collaborative Study for Children Treated for Phenylketonuria, which reports the status of 95 children who have reached 12 years of age (3).

There are various epochs in every disease. Concerning PKU, the first began in 1934 when Folling identified a clinical entity that he called "imbecillitas phenylpyruvica" (4). The name was changed to phenylketonuria in 1946. The second era came with the successful exploration of dietary treatment. We are now into the third era, during which we have recognized the PKU gene on the long arm of chromosome 12. Unfortunately, at last count there were at least 44 haplotypes, 31 different PKU mutations, and many other modifiers that have been described on chromosome 12. To say it differently, PKU is not a simple single gene deletion. Thus its ultimate cure is likely to come from somebody smarter than you and me.—J.A. Stockman, III, M.D.

References

1. Smith I, et al: *Arch Dis Child* 65:472, 1990.
2. Thompson AJ, et al: *Lancet* 336:602, 1990.
3. Azen CG, et al: *Am J Dis Child* 145:35, 1991.
4. Guttler F, et al: *Acta Paediatr Scand* 73:705, 1984.

Valine, Isoleucine, and Leucine: A New Treatment for Phenylketonuria
Berry HK, Brunner RL, Hunt MM, White PP (Children's Hosp Med Ctr, Cincinnati; Univ of Cincinnati)
Am J Dis Child 144:539–543, 1990   3–2

The treatment of phenylketonuria (PKU) by dietary phenylalanine restriction during infancy and early childhood prevents irreversible brain damage. However, when the treatment diet is terminated and serum levels of phenylalanine increase, intellectual and neuropsychological functioning will deteriorate. When dietary restriction alone is not effective, the administration of valine, isoleucine, and leucine may reduce serum levels of phenylalanine.

This regimen was evaluated in 16 adolescents and young adults who were unable to obtain good dietary control of PKU but had behavioral or neuropsychological deficits that were relatively minor. Each was randomly assigned to receive the experimental mixture (valine, 150 mg/kg, isoleucine, 150 mg/kg; leucine, 200 mg/kg) or a control mixture of amino acids thought not to affect neutral amino acid transport. The 2 regimens were evaluated by neuropsychological tests and biochemical measures.

Attention and concentration are adversely affected in PKU. Attentional tests showed that patients who received the experimental mixture significantly improved over baseline and performed significantly better than those who received the control mixture. Baseline and control mixture results did not differ significantly. The Continuous Performance Test, which makes limited cognitive demands, was not significantly affected.

None of the functions tested deteriorated during treatment with valine, isoleucine, and leucine. The results obtained in this study confirm those of earlier experiments, which found some improvement in specific cognitive processes, suggesting that this treatment can help to maintain low serum levels of phenylalanine.

▶ Dr. Grant Morrow III, Professor and Chairman, Department of Pediatrics, Ohio State University, and Medical Director, The Children's Hospital, comments:

▶ Dr. Berry brings a new meaning to the phrase, "you are what you eat," by adding one's intellectual development to this concept. Despite the major impact of molecular biology on the field of inborn errors of metabolism, the practical, hands-on management of patients afflicted with PKU can still benefit from subtle improvements in dietary manipulation. Although early, appropriate dietary intervention has benefited most children, it is unfortunate that many patients with PKU still fail to reach their intellectual potential. The present study is yet another example of how scientists have extrapolated important observations in animals to successful therapy in humans and, hopefully, have helped to ensure more optimal development in children with PKU.—G. Morrow III, M.D.

Screening for Carriers of Tay-Sachs Disease Among Ashkenazi Jews: A Comparison of DNA-Based and Enzyme-Based Tests
Triggs-Raine BL, Feigenbaum ASJ, Natowicz M, Skomorowski M-A, Schuster SM, Clarke JTR, Mahuran DJ, Kolodny EH, Gravel RA (Hosp for Sick Children, Toronto; EK Shriver Ctr, Waltham, Mass; Harvard Med School; Univ of Florida)
N Engl J Med 323:6–12, 1990   3–3

The possibility that DNA-based screening can be used to identify carriers of Tay-Sachs disease in Ashkenazi Jews was prompted by the recent elucidation of the molecular basis of the 3 hexosaminidase A (HEXA) mutations in this population. Two mutations, a splice-junction mutation at the 5' end of intron 12 and another at the 4-bp insertion in exon 11, that cause infantile Tay-Sachs disease. A third mutation, a G-to-A nucleotide substitution in exon 7, accounts for the adult-onset form of the disease.

The DNA samples from 62 Ashkenazi obligate carriers were examined for these mutation sites by means of DNA amplification with the polymerase chain reaction followed by polyacrylamide-gel electrophoresis. In addition, the DNA-based test was used in 216 Ashkenazi carriers identified by the enzyme-based test widely used for screening for Tay-Sachs disease.

The 3 specific mutations accounted for all but 1 of the mutant alleles (98%) in the 62 Ashkenazi obligate carriers. Among the mutations that caused the infantile disease the insertion mutation accounted for 85% of the allelles, and the splice-junction mutation accounted for 15%.

One hundred seventy-seven of the 216 Ashkenazi carriers identified by the enzyme test (82%) had 1 of the specific mutations by DNA analysis: 79% had the insertion mutation, 18% had the splice-junction mutation, and 3% had the less severe exon 7 mutation. The DNA analysis did not identify a mutant allele in the remaining 39 subjects (18%). These were considered to be probably false positive, although there remains some possibility of unidentified mutations. In addition, DNA analysis identified the carrier status in 1 of 152 persons defined as noncarriers by the enzyme-based test.

The DNA test is a useful supplement to currently used diagnostic tests in screening for carriers of Tay-Sachs disease. The DNA test allows precise definition of the carrier state for the known mutations as and is simple enough to be performed in small centers.

▶ Dr. Michael M. Kaback, Professor and Chairman, Department of Pediatrics, University of California, San Diego, comments:

▶ Unquestionably, molecular technologies have already made major contributions to the diagnosis of genetic disease by identifying healthy individuals who are carriers (heterozygotes) of disease-related mutations, making these technologies enormously valuable in enhancing the specificity of genetic counseling. Genetics, however, is a science founded in the precepts of variability, spontaneous mutation, and expressivity. As we have learned with hemoglobin, and more recently from studies in cystic fibrosis and Duchenne type muscular dystrophy, multiple independent mutations (alleles) of any given gene are the rule rather than the exception. Although certain mutations in a given gene may be more common and account for the majority of mutant alleles in a defined population, they should not be expected to be the only ones. Accordingly, it is the specificity of mutation analysis, as described in this paper, that limits the application of this method as a screening test. It is the deficient or defective end product of the mutant gene that underlies the abnormal phenotype, the result of any 1 of possibly hundreds of different distinct mutations in the same gene. Therefore, the most effective way to conduct screening is to use method(s) directed first at the gene product or phenotype. If this is absent, altered, or deficient, then mutation analysis can be of great value in specifying which mutation is involved and, in turn, which clinical phenotype is to be expected.

More than 35 distinct mutations have been identified in the "Tay-Sachs disease gene," the locus on chromosome 15 that directs the production of the alpha-chain component of HEXA. Clearly, if only 3 mutations are evaluated and none are found, one cannot conclude that the individual tested is not a carrier for other mutations. Conversely, if reduced HEXA activity is observed, it is highly likely that the individual is a carrier of some mutation in this gene. Accordingly, the 39 subjects in the above study reported to be "probably false positive" are much more likely to be carriers of mutations other than the 3 that were analyzed. Clearly, molecular methods have an important role to play in carrier detection, but as an adjunct to screening tests rather than as a replacement for them.— M.M. Kaback, M.D.

Fumarylacetoacetase Measurement as a Mass-Screening Procedure for Hereditary Tyrosinemia Type I
Laberge C, Grenier A, Valet JP, Morissette J (Laval Univ Med Ctr, Ste-Foy, Quebec, Canada)
Am J Hum Genet 47:325–328, 1990   3–4

Fluorometric tyrosine determination on dried-blood spots is the primary neonatal screening test for tyrosinemia I (HT). Succinylacetone determination is then used when tyrosine MT: level is higher than a given threshold. However, blood tyrosine levels in newborns have decreased as a result of dietary changes and early discharge from the nursery, and tyrosine measurement has proved to be less discriminant. An enzyme-linked immunosorbent assay (ELISA) using a specific antihuman fumarylacetoacetase (FAH) antibody was developed to measure the deficient enzyme in HT in dried-blood spots. Immunoreactive FAH was measured retrospectively in 25 dried-blood samples from patients with proven HT and prospectively in 72,000 specimens received in a neonatal screening program.

None of the 25 dried-blood samples from patients with proven HT had detectable FAH. Of the 72,000 newborns screened prospectively, 34 had less than 12.5% of the reference adult FAH level. Using succinylacetone determination as a complementary test, 4 of these newborns were positive for this metabolite, and the other 30 had no detectable succinylacetone, for a false positive rate of 1:2,400.

These data demonstrate that immunoreactive FAH measurement can be used ;in mass neonatal screening for HT. However, because immunoreactive FAH is also measurable in red blood cells, blood transfusion before blood sampling for screening may yield false negative tests. Thus, being aware of a previous blood transfusion, an ELISA determination of FAH in blood spots could be used as a primary test in neonatal screening for HT.

▶ Chances are you were not thinking about fumarylacetoacetase this morning as you were having your coffee. This enzyme name is not one that normally rolls off the tip of one's tongue. In Quebec, however, it has received a lot of attention lately.

Canada has been ahead of the United States when it comes to neonatal screening, and screening for congenital hypothyroidism is a typical example of this. In Quebec, the incidence of HT is 1:17,000, and neonatal screening programs for HT have been in effect in Quebec for approximately 22 years. The rest of the world has not instituted HT screening because of problems with sensitivity and specificity related to measuring various metabolic intermediates on dried-blood spots. The people in Quebec, however, have found the solution to this problem. They have developed a specific assay for the primary enzyme defect in HT that has been attributed to fumarylacetoacetase. Assay for this enzyme can be done on dried-blood spots in the immediate newborn period.

Failure to diagnose HT with newborn screening will result in severe liver disease, renal tubular dysfunction, and progressive skeletal deformities suggestive of vitamin D-resistant rickets seen in the first few months of the infant's life. If you do make the diagnosis early, dietary restriction of phenylalanine and tyrosine allows temporary improvement in the HT, permits growth, and improves renal function. Late complications such as hepatocellular carcinoma may not be altered. Treatment is hardly perfect, and many infants do not survive with currently available medical treatment because of inadequate protein intake, severe infection, and hemorrhagic complications.

The ultimate answer to the treatment of HT may therefore come only by gene replacement therapy, years down the pike. In the meantime, however, liver transplantation is a totally appropriate option for those who fail medical management. Flye et al. (1) have shown remarkable success with liver transplantation for infants and children who would have otherwise died of HT.

I, for one, side with the Canadians and recommend adding HT to the disorders that should be screened for in the newborn period. Even if you could prevent a tiny number of liver transplants, screening would probably pay for itself. What's your vote?—J.A. Stockman, III, M.D.

Reference

1. Flye MW, et al: *Transplantation* 49:916, 1990.

The Clinical Features of Osteogenesis Imperfecta Resulting From a Non-Functional Carboxy Terminal Proα1(I) Propeptide of Type I Procollagen and a Severe Deficiency of Normal Type I Collagen in Tissues
Cole WG, Campbell PE, Rogers JG, Bateman JF (Univ of Melbourne; Royal Children's Hosp, Melbourne, Australia)
J Med Genet 27:545–551, 1990   3–5

Many patients with osteogenesis imperfecta (OI), particularly the lethal perinatal OI type II, have biochemical abnormalities of type I procollagen. The clinical, radiographic, and pathologic features of an infant with OI II were reviewed.

Infant was born at 35 weeks' gestation after an uneventful pregnancy and died after 20 minutes. His size for his gestational age was less than the 10th percentile. He had a relatively large calvarium, widely spaced eyes, and broad nasal bridge. The OI II resulted from a frameshift mutation that produced a truncated and functionless carboxy terminal propeptide of the proα1(I) chain of type I procollagen. There was a single uridine insertion after base pair 4088 of the preproα1(I) mRNA of type I procollagen. The extracellular matrix of bone and dermis showed incorporation of normal type I collagen only, resulting in a type I collagen content of about 20% of control tissues. The infant's radiographic features were most similar to those of OI IIB. The skeleton showed poor ossification with discontinuously beaded ribs and broad femora with multiple healed fractures of the diaphyses and metaphyses. There were hundreds of wormian bones within the calvarium. Endochondral and intramembranous ossification was grossly deficient. The bone was of a woven type without evidence of lamellar bone or Haversian systems and the osteoblasts did not mature into osteocytes. The femoral cortex contained Haversian canals that were surrounded by loose collagen, woven bone, and cartilaginous islands.

Osteogenesis imperfecta IIB can be subdivided into 2 types: one with helical mutations and normal and mutant type I collagen, and the other with carboxy terminal propeptide mutations and a severe type I collagen deficiency, but without mutant collagen in the tissue.

▶ Each year we select a small but significant number of articles that may not have widespread relevance to everyday practice but which represent new understandings or new descriptions of disorders previously unheard of. In this instance, we present a case of OI of the lethal perinatal type II. To say this differently, if you have ever seen a child with OI, it was not of this type, because these babies die very early. All we need to remember for now is that OI is a hereditary genetic disorder of connective tissues heralded by bone fragility, abnormal blueness of the sclerea, dentinogenesis imperfecta, and premature deafness. That is OI type II.

I trust that you don't mind being presented with these rarities of medicine periodically and are not disappointed by having them in the YEAR BOOK. One reader wrote in to say that rarity ought not to be commented on because the rarities of life are noninformative. I disagree, and to that letter writer I responded that he must recently have read Psalm 28:94—"Blessed is he who expects nothing, for he shall never be disappointed."—J.A. Stockman, III, M.D.

Geleophysic Dysplasia: A Storage Disorder Affecting the Skin, Bone, Liver, Heart, and Trachea
Shohat M, Gruber HE, Pagon RA, Witcoff LJ, Lachman R, Ferry D, Flaum E, Rimoin DL (Cedars-Sinai Med Ctr, Harbor/Univ of California at Los Angeles; Children's Hosp and Med Ctr, Univ of Washington, Seattle)
J Pediatr 117:227–232, 1990   3–6

Children with geleophysic dysplasia have typical facies, small hands and feet, short stature, hepatomegaly, and progressive cardiac disease. A small group of previously unreported cases was described to better delineate the clinical, radiographic, and morphologic characteristics of this condition.

Five children, 4 of whom were boys, were studied. Two of the patients were siblings. The facies were strikingly similar, characterized by a small nose, anteverted nostrils, broad nasal bridge, and long, thin upper lip with a flat, long philtrum. The patients had normal intelligence, development, and behavior. Growth delay occurred in infancy. The 2 patients who completed normal puberty had marked short stature with relatively lean body habitus. Hands and feet were small, with short, plump tubular bones and broad proximal phalanges. Those characteristics were associated with marked limitation in finger and wrist motion. After 3 years of age, the liver was enlarged. Two patients had mild mitral and tricuspid valve stenosis. Another had severe aortic stenosis. The child most severely affected died at 3½ years of age of airway obstruction caused by progressive tracheal narrowing. Lysosomal storage vacuoles were discovered in skin epithelial cells from 3 patients whose skin was studied, and in the tracheal mucosa, liver, cartilage, and macrophages of the patient who died.

The 5 patients exhibited the characteristic features of geleophysic dysplasia. The most significant determinant of prognosis appears to be progressive tracheal narrowing, a potentially lethal complication. The basic defect of geleophysic dysplasia, an autosomal recessive lysosomal storage disorder, is yet to be established.

▶ I bet you're wondering what geleophysic means. You will need an unabridged dictionary to track down the meaning of the term. What you'll find is that it translates into "happy-natured."

Geleophysic dysplasia is a term introduced by Springer et al. (1) in 1971 to designate an acrofacial dysplasia with a peculiar, pleasant facial appearance, short hands and feet (as a result of short, plump, tubular bones), short stature, and progressive cardiac valvular disease. It is the latter that is often quite problematic in these kids and ultimately discloses their true diagnosis. The pearl for this chapter of the YEAR BOOK is that if you ever see a child who you think has mitral, tricuspid, or aortic stenosis and also has a large liver (but not on the basis of heart failure), think happy-natured dysplasia. If you make a correct diagnosis, you will also have a smile on your face.—J.A. Stockman, III, M.D.

Reference

1. Springer JW, et al: *Lancet* 2:97, 1971.

Population-Based Study of the Developmental Outcome of Children Exposed to Chloride-Deficient Infant Formula
Willoughby A, Graubard BI, Hocker A, Storr C, Vietze P, Thackaberry JM, Gerry MA, McCarthy M, Gist NF, Magenheim M, Berendes H, Rhoads GG (Natl Inst of Child Health and Human Development, Bethesda, Md; Univ of South Florida, Tampa; Sarasota County Public Health Unit; Sarasota County Schools, Sarasota, Fla; Inst of Basic Research in Developmental Disabilities, Staten Island, NY)
Pediatrics 85:485–490, 1990   3–7

In 1978 and 1979, 20,000–50,000 infants in the United States were fed 2 soy-based infant formulas that were deficient in dietary chloride. Although acute signs and symptoms of exposure resolved with feeding of sufficient chloride diets, the long-term ill effects of this exposure were questioned. A population-based study was conducted to investigate the long-term cognitive effects of exposure to chloride-deficient infant formula.

Questionnaires were sent to houses of 3,639 first- and second-grade children attending public school in a southern county. The questionnaires ascertained feeding practices without reference to the subject of defective formula use. Of the 2,329 (64%) responses, 56 reported use of chloride-deficient formula. A total of 112 controls were selected from 310 users of other soy formulas and were matched for sex, feeding history, age, birth weight, and socioeconomic status. After exclusions and refusals, 42 exposed children and 66 controls were tested using the McCarthy Scales of Children's Abilities by examiners that were blinded to formula use.

The mean general cognitive index was 102.8 in children exposed to the chloride-deficient soy formula and 105.4 for the controls. The difference between groups was not significant, except for the low scores on the Quantitative Scale among exposed children. However, after adjusting for demographic differences, the mean scores on the general Cognitive Index were significantly lower among the exposed children than among controls, with the greatest difference in the Quantitative subscale. Suggestive differences were also observed in the Perceptual-Performance and Motor scales. These data demonstrate a small but statistically significant effect of chloride-deficient soy formula on the long-term developmental outcome of exposed children. Further studies are warranted to confirm these findings.

▶ Most of us have been following the chloride-deficient formula story for the better part of a decade. Recall that in 1978 and 1979, Syntex Laboratories, Inc., distributed 2 soy-based infant formulas that lacked adequate chloride. These formulas were NeoMullsoy and CHO-free. The chloride content of these formulas was found to be 1–2 mEq/L, substantially below the manufacturer's advertised concentration of 6 mEq/L. Although Syntex initiated a voluntary recall of the 2 products on August 2, 1979, it is estimated that the affected formulas were on the market in a chloride-deficient state from October 1978 to September 1979. Among the estimated 20,000–50,000 children exposed to these formulas during this time period, 141 cases of hypochloremic metabolic alkalosis were reported to the Centers for Disease Control. Some of these children suffered from lethargy, anorexia, irritability, poor weight gain, and gastrointestinal symptoms. In addition, some were documented to have unequivocal hypochloremia, hypokalemia, metabolic alkalosis, hematuria, hyperaldosteronism, and increased plasma renin levels. When chloride-sufficient diets were restored, these acute signs and symptoms resolved. The lingering issue, however, was the extent to which these children had or had not suffered any long-term problems ascribed to the use of these formulas.

These authors have been hot on the trail of the unresolved question of the last paragraph. As you can see from their data, they found a statistically significant, although small, effect of chloride-deficient formula on the long-term developmental outcome of exposed children.

Congress got into the act in 1980 when, as part of a congressional mandate set forth in the Infant Formula Act of 1980, it authorized a federally sponsored follow-up of these children. The following are highlights of the follow-up report: "In summary, we have found in children identified as having hypochloremia metabolic alkalosis, several incidences of significantly poorer performance than in control children. These differences suggest that compared with control children, these children may be at risk for deficits in language skills and expressive language abilities that require attention. However, the hypochloremic metabolic alkalosis group mean value of the scores in which the differences occurred were all within normal ranges. The greater likelihood of the affected children scoring outside the expected ranges . . . does suggest that these children may be at risk for deficits in language skills requiring expressive language ability attention. That the majority of children are performing at a normal level does not preclude the possibility that these children might have experienced developmental abnormalities at an earlier age."

You might very well suspect that the epilogue to the story regarding Neo-Mullsoy and CHO-free has not yet been written. Six or 7 years ago, I had an opportunity to cochair the abstract presentations in the general pediatrics section of the Society for Pediatric Research/American Pediatric Society. It was standing room only when the abstract on hypochloremic metabolic alkalosis resulting from use of these formulas was presented for the first time. It was standing room only because of all the lawyers. The parents of children who became ill wanted to know whether or not their children were damaged by these 2 formulas—and rightfully so.—J.A. Stockman, III, M.D.

Reference

1. Malloy MH, et al: *Pediatrics* 87:811, 1991.

Impact on Iron Status of Introducing Cow's Milk in the Second Six Months of Life

Penrod JC, Anderson K, Acosta PB (Florida State Univ, Tallahassee, Fla)
J Pediatr Gastroenterol Nutr 10:462–467, 1990   3–8

The adverse effects of iron deficiency have been well described. The impact on iron status of introducing cow's milk into the diet of infants during the second 6 months of life was investigated.

Nutrient intake was evaluated and iron status measured in 100 infants, aged 8 to 13 months. Forty-five infants were fed cow's milk as the primary beverage for at least 3 months before the study, and 55 were fed a milk-based infant formula. Nutrient intake for 40 infants in the first group and 45 infants in the second group was assessed. All of the infants were healthy. Most did not receive medications or supplements other than vitamins or fluoride for 3 weeks before the evaluation. Plasma albumin, iron, ferritin, transferrin saturation, and total iron-binding capacity were measured in blood taken from all infants.

Infants fed cow's milk had significantly lower mean iron and vitamin C intakes, plasma albumin, transferrin saturation, and ferritin than did infants fed formula. The frequency of low plasma iron, low transferrin saturation, and low plasma ferritin was significantly higher in the first group than in the second group. Fifty-eight percent of the infants fed cow's milk had 3 or more abnormal iron indices, compared with 23% of those fed formula.

Significant differences in iron status were found between the cow's milk-fed and formula-fed infants in this series. Feeding iron-fortified formula to infants to the age of 12 months apparently deters iron deficiency.

▶ Dr. Frank Oski, Given Professor of Pediatrics, the Johns Hopkins University School of Medicine, *the* expert on iron and cow's milk, comments:

▶ It is good to be back, particularly when it is an opportunity to comment on an article that confirms a previous observation (1) and supports the recommendation that whole cow's milk should not be consumed by infants during the first year of life. The 1991 YEAR BOOK included the abstract by Ziegler and associates (2) documenting the amount of occult gastrointestinal bleeding that occurred in infants during days 168 to 252 of life when they were fed the nasty white stuff. The risk of developing iron deficiency lurks in every bottle of pasteurized, homogenized whole cow's milk. Don't let your infant taste it, touch it, or even sniff it.—F. Oski, M.D.

References

1. Tunnessen WW Jr, Oski FA: *J Pediatr* 111:813, 1987.
2. 1991 YEAR BOOK OF PEDIATRICS, pp 83–85.

Relationship Between Infant Feeding and Infectious Illness: A Prospective Study of Infants During the First Year of Life
Rubin DH, Leventhal JM, Krasilnikoff PA, Kuo HS, Jekel JF, Weile B, Levee A, Kurzon M, Berget A (Albert Einstein College of Medicine; Montefiore Med Ctr, Bronx, NY; Yale Univ; Univ of Copenhagen; Gentofte Hosp, Hellerup, Denmark)
Pediatrics 85:464–471, 1990   3–9

The protective effects of breast-feeding against common infectious illnesses in early life have not been clearly demonstrated in developed countries. Correction was made for the methodological limitations that may account for the conflicting results, and 500 infants born consecutively in a university-affiliated community hospital in Copenhagen were studied prospectively for the first 12 months of life.

Information on feeding practices and illnesses were obtained from mothers of these infants through detailed monthly mailed questionnaires. The incidence of 4 categories of illnesses—gastroenteritis, upper respiratory illness, otitis media, and lower respiratory illness—was compared in breast-fed and formula-fed infants by using incidence density ratios that were controlled for major covariates.

The overall response rate was 73%. The percentage of infants who were completely or mostly breast fed decreased from 88% at age 1 month to 20% at age 12 months. The incidence densities of the 4 categories of illness did not differ significantly between feeding groups after adjusting for potential covariates such as birth weight, social class, day-care arrangements, number of siblings, family illness, and infant's age. Although there was a significant protective effect of breast-feeding on otitis media, this effect was no longer significant after adjusting for age.

These data suggest that breast-feeding does not provide substantial protection against common infectious illnesses during the first year of life in a largely middle-class urban population in a developed country.

▶ None of us is dumb enough to believe that this important article has broad applications to society as a whole. The carefully worded conclusion of the report must be read cautiously because the caveat stated is that breast-feeding does not provide substantial protection against *common* infectious illnesses in a *largely middle class* urban population in a *developed* country.

Among the health benefits of breast-feeding, 1 of the most important is a reduction in infant morbidity and mortality from infectious diseases. The magnitude of the benefit, however, appears to be conditional on economic factors, as the abstract indicates. This protective effect is far more striking in developing countries than in developed countries. The giant leap of faith needed to accept the results of this article is that the United States is a totally advantaged country, with no medical needs. Have you visited the South Bronx or South Chicago recently? Infants born into poverty should be considered to have been born into an undeveloped environment. It is only sensible to assume that such infants would benefit from being breast fed. Unfortunately, the mothers of these infants are among the least likely to initiate and continue breast-feeding (1).

Yes, there has been an increase in breast-feeding in less advantaged populations in this country, but the increases were smaller than those seen among the more affluent. Thus, the rich-vs.-poor differences actually rose over this period. Furthermore, if you believe that the trends now occurring in England will occur soon in the United States, there will be a precipitous fall in the prevelance of breast-feeding (2). If a similar decline is seen in the United States, particularly among the poor, it could have considerable adverse health consequences.

There are some unfortunate individuals who read the results of reports such as this one and embrace the results simply because they confirm the individual's bias that in a modern society, breast-feeding is no longer necessary. To these individuals, I would say, "All the Kookies are not in the jar."

To refresh your memory on all the positive benefits of breast-feeding, including protection from infectious problems, ask Allan S. Cunningham for a reprint of his excellent article entitled "Breast-feeding and health in the 1980's: A global epidemiologic review" (3). Allan's address is The Department of Pediatrics, Mary Imogene Bassett Hospital, Cooperstown, NY 13326. It's well worth the 29 cents it will cost you for the request.—J.A. Stockman, III, M.D.

References

1. Martinez GA, et al: *Pediatrics* 976:1004, 1985.
2. Emory JL, et al: *Arch Dis Child* 65:369, 1990.
3. Cunningham AS, et al: *J Pediatr* 118:659, 1991.

Prolonged Maternal Fluid Supplementation in Breast-Feeding
Dusdieker LB, Stumbo PJ, Booth BM, Wilmoth RN (Univ of Iowa Hosps and Clinics, Iowa City)
Pediatrics 86:737–740, 1990   3–10

Breast-feeding women commonly give inadequate milk supply as a reason for early weaning. The effect of increased maternal fluid intake on milk production after prolonged fluid supplementation was studied in 19 mothers.

The mothers were well nourished, and their infants were solely breast fed and thriving. The infants were between 90 and 120 days old. Fifteen of the women consumed at least a 25% increase in fluids above baseline for 7 days. The mean daily milk production was 767 mL at baseline and 744 mL for the increased fluid period. No significant change in milk production between baseline and increased fluid periods could be found. There was also no significant linear relationship between the percentage increase in fluid intake and percentage change in milk production.

Although a relationship could not be established between maternal fluid intake and increased milk production in this series, the women studied were different from the mothers of infants who do not thrive on breast-feeding. Mothers who are breast-feeding and whose infants are growing poorly may respond differently to increased fluid intake.

▶ Is nothing sacred in this world? Are we truly to believe that breast-feeding women should not be walking around sipping extra glasses of water? Habits do not die easily, nor do old wives tales, nor will the ritual of downing 3 or 4 extra glasses of water a day when you are breast-feeding.

The report by Dusdieker et al. is well done. I can find no flaw in the design or implementation of it. Thus, I must assume the conclusions are correct and that any woman who continues this practice has only herself to blame for the psychogenic diabetes insipidus caused by this ancient habit.

Not only do breast-feeding mothers not need extra water, their infants don't either. Not even in the tropics. When comparing 2 groups of infants (those who were solely breast fed vs. those who were breast fed plus being given supplemental water), investigators in India showed that infants who received supplemental water took less breast milk. Not only that, but the lesser quantity of breast milk was not made up for by the extra water they drank (1). Thus, if you have believed that infants in hot climates need extra water when they are being breast fed, you are wrong on that issue.

When the history of feeding practices during the 20th century is written, I am firmly convinced that only 1 rule of nutrition will stand the test of time: "Never eat prunes when you're hungry."—J.A. Stockman, III, M.D.

Reference

1. Sachdev HPS, et al: *Lancet* 337:929, 1991.

Transmission of Human Immunodeficiency Virus Infection by Breast-Feeding
Stiehm ER, Vink P (Univ of California, Los Angeles)
J Pediatr 118:410–412, 1991   3–11

Only 9 cases of transmission of HIV infection by breast-feeding have been described previously, 4 from Australia, 4 from Africa, and 1 from France. Now a case has been reported in the United States.

Female infant born in 1981 was the first child of a healthy woman aged 34 years and her healthy husband, both of whom lacked HIV risk factors and behavior. Elective section delivery was done at 36 weeks because of placenta previa. Breast-feeding continued exclusively for 3 months, and was supplemented for 5 months longer. Diarrhea developed at age 4 years during a trip to Haiti and shortly afterward the child became anemic and had hematuria, proteinuria, and splenomegaly. These abnormalities persisted, and oral candidiasis developed at age 5 years, when an HIV antibody test was strongly and repeatedly positive. Episodes of sinusitis and pneumonia ensued, with chronic diarrhea, chronic pancreatitis, and encephalopathy. Zidovudine treatment was given for 2 months with some response but was withdrawn because of neutropenia. The patient continued to deteriorate, and she died in 1988. Autopsy cultures showed *Mycobacterium avium-intracellulare* in the liver.

The patient's mother and brother (aged 2 years) were HIV-seropositive. A homosexual man who had engaged in high-risk activity and who was HIV-positive had been 1 of 12 donors of blood and plasma for the mother during postdelivery bleeding when her daughter was born.

The lack of parental HIV risk factors and the father's seronegativity suggest breast-feeding as the means of transmission in this case. Not all women who are infected or seroconvert post partum transmit HIV to their breast-fed infants. It seems reasonable, however, for HIV-positive women and those at risk to avoid breast-feeding their infants.

▶ Is it more likely that HIV can be transmitted to an infant through the milk of an infected mother or by exposure to an HIV-infected surgeon?

Obviously, the response to this question comes in 2 parts. The answer is commented on at length in the Infectious Disease chapter. At least in this country, all infants of HIV-positive mothers should be bottle fed. There is another side to this story, however, so read the commentaries in the Infectious Disease chapter.

On the other hand, should patients worry about contracting HIV from their doctors? I am sure that all of you kept tabs on the AMA convention in Chicago last June and the debate that surrounded this issue. At that time, only 1 individual in the country had been described who had contracted HIV from a health care provider (in that case a dentist). The chance of contracting AIDS from a physician must be terribly, terribly low. Of the 2,160 patients operated on by a surgeon who died of AIDS in 1989, none were found to have contracted this virus (1). The AMA's position as of July 1, 1990, has remained essentially the same, suggesting voluntary testing of individuals who feel that they may have a known risk factor. This is likely to change, however.

Whether or not the AMA's approach is correct could be subject to some debate, particularly as it applies to surgeons, who by virtue of operating on large numbers of people are automatically in a high-risk category no matter what "universal precautions" they take in the operating room.

No one is negating the right of a patient to know whether their physician is HIV-positive, but on the other side of the equation, it is much more likely that a physician will get AIDS from 1 of his or her patients than vice versa.—J.A. Stockman, III, M.D.

Reference

1. Mishu B, et al: *JAMA* 264:467, 1990.

Effect of Massive Dose Vitamin A on Morbidity and Mortality in Indian Children

Vijayaraghavan K, Radhaiah G, Surya Prakasam B, Rameshwar Sarma KV, Reddy V (Natl Inst of Nutrition, Hyderabad, India)
Lancet 336:1342–1345, 1990

3–12

Studies in Indonesia suggest that vitamin A supplementation reduces mortality rates by about 30%, even in mild vitamin A-deficiency states. To investigate further, the effect of vitamin A supplementation on morbidity and mortality in preschool children was evaluated in a prospective, double-blind, placebo-controlled study in Hyderabad, India. A total of 15,775 children, aged 1–5 years, received either 200,000 IU vitamin A or placebo every 6 months. Morbidity and mortality data were collected every 3 months.

Despite an association of mild xerophthalmia with increased respiratory infection but not diarrhea, vitamin A supplementation had no impact on morbidity. Likewise, there was no significant association between mild xerophthalmia and mortality. Mortality rates did not differ significantly between children who received vitamin A and those who received placebo. Mortality rates were highest in children who did not receive either vitamin A or placebo, possibly because the study subjects had more frequent contacts with the project staff. Vitamin A alone may not reduce child mortality.

Reduced Mortality Among Children in Southern India Receiving a Small Weekly Dose of Vitamin A

Rahmathullah L, Underwood BA, Thulasiraj RD, Milton RC, Ramaswamy K, Rahmathullah R, Babu G (Aravind Children's Hosp, Aravind Eye Hosp, Madurai, India; Natl Eye Inst, Bethesda, Md)
N Engl J Med 323:929–935, 1990

3–13

Some 20–40 million children worldwide have at least mild vitamin A deficiency. Several studies in Indonesia have reported that high-dose vitamin A supplementation significantly reduces mortality among infants and young children. However, these studies have been criticized on the basis of study design and lack of compliance data. To further define the role of vitamin A deficiency and its treatment in children, a 1-year, randomized, placebo-controlled trial was conducted in an economically and environmentally deprived area in southern India.

The study population consisted of 15,419 children between the ages of 6 months and 60 months who had been identified by trained enumerators in a house-by-house survey. Medical examination teams then performed ocular examinations, made anthropometric measurements, and recorded morbidity histories. All children with symptoms of xerophthalmia at the baseline examination were treated with a large-dose combination of vitamin A and vitamin E. The remaining children were randomly allocated to receive either a treatment solution containing 8.7 μmol of vitamin A and

46 μmol of vitamin E or a placebo solution containing 46 μmol of vitamin E alone. This dose of vitamin A would potentially be obtainable from foods. Community health volunteers visited each home weekly for 52 weeks to dispense the appropriate liquid supplement directly into the mouth of the study child and to record mortality and morbidity.

The baseline prevalence of xerophthalmia was 11%, and 7 children had active corneal involvement. Based on anthropometric measurements, 72% of the children were undernourished. Approximately one third of these children were stunted, 18% were stunted and wasted, and 23% were wasted.

During the 52-week surveillance period, 117 nonaccidental deaths occurred, 80 in the control group and 37 in the treatment group. Vitamin A administration reduced the age-adjusted total relative risk of mortality to .46 compared with nontreated children. Treatment with vitamin A reduced the relative risk of mortality in both sexes, but the reduction was somewhat greater among girls. The greatest reductions in risk occurred among children under 3 years of age and among chronically undernourished children. The symptom-specific risk of mortality was significantly associated with diarrhea, convulsions, and other infection-related symptoms. The mortality rate among children with xerophthalmia was approximately 50% higher than that among children without this condition. When adjusted for those who received a large dose of vitamin A, the treatment effect of the continued small dose persisted.

▶ There's been so much written about vitamin A this past year or 2 that it is difficult to tell where to begin a commentary on this subject.

Is vitamin A a magic bullet when it comes to decreasing morbidity and mortality in underdeveloped countries? If you read all the reports carefully, you will come to the conclusion that there is nothing particularly magical about vitamin A, and its relatively nonspecific effects cannot allow it to be "targeted" to any single disease. Nonetheless, the importance of vitamin A in maintaining immunity against infection in the face of malnutrition cannot be underestimated.

Since the discovery of vitamin A, when it was noted that deficient animals had an especially high prevalence of infection, reliable data have indicated an increased risk for certain infections among children in poor environments. Nonetheless, these observations have been largely overlooked. Several factors account for this. First, the eye signs of vitamin A deficiency are so striking that ophthalmologists have highlighted vitamin A deficiency as being only an ocular condition. Xerophthalmia, however, is simply a marker of an individual with a high risk of diarrhea or pneumonia. Another reason why vitamin A has been ignored is that assays other than plasma retinol have been conspicuously absent until recently.

Data documenting a decreased risk of infection, including diarrhea, come from various parts of the world. For example, in Indonesia, Sommer and colleagues (1) found a 34% decrease in mortality among children in villages where 200,000 IU of vitamin A were given to each child every 6 months. The risk of death or major complications during hospitalization for measles in South Africa was reduced by half among children receiving daily doses of vitamin A in the hospital (2).

If you think that all of these stories about vitamin A are made up or are otherwise preposterous, don't have a myth fit. Read all of the references, and make up your own mind. The annual cost to achieve these results has been estimated at only $1.64 to $2.20 per recipient, a small sum that still may be beyond the resources of some developing nations.—J.A. Stockman, III, M.D.

Reference

1. Sommer A, et al: *Lancet* i:1169, 1986.
2. Hussey GD, et al: *N Engl J Med* 323:160, 1990.

Sucrose and Delinquency: Behavioral Assessment
Bachorowski J-A, Newman JP, Nichols SL, Gans DA, Harper AE, Taylor SL (Univ of Wisconsin, Madison)
Pediatrics 86:244–253, 1990
3–14

Several studies have suggested that ingestion of sucrose may adversely affect the behavioral performance of juvenile delinquents, but these studies are hampered by serious methodological limitations. An interdisciplinary investigation was conducted to evaluate the biochemical and behavioral responses of juvenile delinquents to the ingestion of sucrose.

The subjects included 58 white and 57 black males aged 14 to 19 years. The controls included 39 white male subjects recruited from a public high school. In a double-blind challenge design the subjects were randomly assigned to a sucrose-loaded breakfast containing 78 g of sucrose or an aspartame-flavored breakfast containing less than 1 g of sucrose (no-sucrose). Behavioral assessment began 40 minutes after breakfast and continued for about 3 hours. Behavioral assessments included tasks that were relevant to delinquency and would be expected to occur after ingestion of sucrose.

Analysis of covariance indicated that performance after the sucrose-containing breakfast did not differ significantly from performance after the no-sucrose breakfast in both white and black delinquents. In fact ingestion of sucrose was associated with improved, rather than impaired, performance. Analysis of subgroups of juvenile delinquents indicated that those rated as hyperactive on the Achenbach Child Behavior Checklist showed better performance after a sucrose-containing breakfast, whereas those with less pronounced behavior problems performed better after the no-sucrose breakfast.

This study provides no evidence that ingestion of sucrose may compromise the behavioral performance of juvenile delinquents. Simple statements regarding the effects on behavior of ingesting sucrose are likely to be misleading, and individual difference variables should be considered when investigating the relationship between sucrose and behavior.

► I am certain that many parents were disappointed by the results of this study. The thought that behavioral disturbances in one's child might be organically determined by something as simple as the ingestion of sugar was an easy concept to use as a crutch in hard times. Well, folks, the crutch has been kicked out from under us. Shakespeare said it correctly in King Henry IV: "If sack and sugar be of fault, God help the wicked! If to be old and merry be a sin, then many an old host that I know is dammed." (1)

(For more on the topic of behavioral disturbances and CNS glucose metabolism, see the Neurology/Psychiatry chapter.)—J.A. Stockman, III, M.D.

Reference

1. Shakespeare W: *Henry IV Part II*. Act IV; scene 524; line 1598.

Blood Pressure, Fitness, and Fatness in 5- and 6-Year-Old Children
Gutin B, Basch C, Shea S, Contento I, DeLozier M, Rips J, Irigoyen M, Zybert P
(Columbia Univ, New York)
JAMA 264:1123–1127, 1990   3–15

Aerobic fitness, body fatness, and fat patterning are important predictors of cardiovascular disease in adults. Because there is evidence that cardiovascular disease originates during childhood, the influence of aerobic fitness, fatness, and fat patterning on blood pressure (BP) and lipids in children was evaluated in a cross-sectional manner. A total of 216 primarily Hispanic, inner-city 5- and 6-year-old children was studied. Aerobic fitness was measured with a submaximal treadmill test, and fatness was measured with 5 skin folds.

Diastolic BP was negatively correlated with fitness in both boys and girls and positively related to fatness for the boys. Systolic BP was positively related to fatness for the boys and girls, and negatively related to fitness among boys only when using heart rate at 5% grade as measure of fitness. Multiple regression models, including parental BPs, showed that fatness explained significant proportions of the variance in systolic BP for both the boys and girls and in diastolic BP for the boys. In addition, there was a tendency for central skin folds to explain significantly greater proportions of the variance in BP in boys, but not in girls. For both sexes, there was an inverse relationship between fitness and fatness.

At age 5 and 6 years, children exhibit some of the risk factors for cardiovascular disease seen in adults. Fitness and fatness appear to have an impact on current and future cardiovascular health, even as early as age 5 and 6 years.

► Dr. Hugh Allen, Professor of Pediatrics, Ohio State University; Chief, Division of Cardiology, Children's Hospital, comments:

► The message of this study is that at least for the inner-city, mainly Hispanic, population studied less physically fit 5- and 6-year-olds tended to be fatter and more hypertensive than fit children. A cause and effect relationship could not be shown, but the implication is certainly present. Fatness, inactivity, and hypertension are proven coronary risk factors in adults and may be early warning risk indicators in these children. Throw in hypercholesterolemia and smoking and you have a perfect early infarction milieu. Because this was a poor inner-city population, they are a target group for tobacco industry advertising, making the latter risk factor more likely than in a population subject to less advertising. Not being hypercholesterolemic is a function of picking the right grandparents and is therefore less controllable than the other risk factors. It will be interesting to see whether this particular cohort can be followed longitudinally to see what happens. Interventional attempts could also be studied. This important population base and research team forms an ideal pediatric Framingham-type study that should continue in Manhattan.—H.D. Allen, M.D.

Children's Frequency of Consumption of Foods High in Fat and Sodium
Simons-Morton BG, Baranowski T, Parcel GS, O'Hara NM, Matteson RC (Univ of Texas Health Science Ctr, Houston; Univ of Texas Med Branch, Galveston)
Am J Prev Med 6:218–227, 1990   3–16

As part of an investigation of childhood diet and physical activity, a survey was conducted among 943 third- to fifth-grade students in 4 Texas schools to assess the frequency of children's consumption of foods, particularly those high in fat and sodium. The children reported their food consumption for 3 days by using the food frequency questionnaire and 24-hour dietary recalls.

Twenty-five foods accounted for 64% of food choices across all meals. The most frequently consumed foods were breads, milk, hamburger or steak, soda pop, tomato sauce or tomatoes, and cheese. These 25 foods also accounted for 93.5% of breakfast choices, 76.4% of lunch choices, 70.5% of supper choices, and 76% of snack choices.

Fruits and juices accounted for 6% to 7% of total selections, and vegetables accounted for only 15.7% to 16.2% of selections. Fruits were more likely to be consumed for snacks, whereas vegetables were consumed at meals and for snacks. Seventeen of the top 25 foods for the total day and 13 to 16 foods for each meal or snack (table) exceeded the recommended levels for fat, saturated fat, or sodium by at least 50%.

A few items account for most of the food selections in children. Many of these foods are of limited nutritional value, and most are high in fat or sodium. These data provide a basis for planning interventions that target specific foods by meals or snacks.

▶ Our children now grow up in a society in which food is more cultural than nutritional. Cultural here means Taco Bell, Arby's, Wendy's, Burger King, and McDonald's. It's a fast-food, take-out world. When our daughter Jennifer indicates that she has a "yen" for something special, I fear she's going to call Tokyo to air express something payable only with "yen." Soon, I suppose, she'll be developing a "zen" for Tibetan food. In our household no one eats like a bird

Snacks: 25 Most Frequent Food Selections and Ratios of Observed to Recommended Total Fat, Saturated Fat, and Sodium for 3 Days

Food (N = 6,681)*	% of total selections	Cumulative % of total selections	Total fat† (observed % cal/30% cals)	Saturated fat† (observed % cal/10% cals)	Sodium† (observed mg/140 mg)
Soda pop	10.1	10.1	0.0	0.0	0.2
Hard candy/gum	6.6	16.7	0.0	0.0	<0.1
Candy bars	5.4	22.1	1.7	7.1	0.3
Fruit drink	5.0	27.1	0.0	0.0	0.1
Cookies/donuts	4.8	31.9	1.5	1.2	0.7
Ice cream	3.7	35.6	1.5	2.9	0.6
Potato/corn chips	3.5	39.1	1.9	1.7	1.1
Popsicles	3.0	42.1	0.0	0.0	0.1
Apples/applesauce	2.9	45.0	0.0	0.0	<0.1
Breads/buns/crust	2.8	47.8	0.5	0.4	1.5
Cake/cupcake/pie	2.7	50.5	1.1	1.4	1.5
Iced tea	2.3	52.8	0.0	0.0	0.0
Cheese	2.3	55.1	2.3	4.6	5.1
Grapes	2.2	57.3	0.2	0.1	<0.1
Ice cream bar	2.1	59.4	1.5	2.8	0.3
Orange/grapefruit	2.0	61.4	0.0	0.0	0.0
Banana	1.9	63.3	<0.1	<0.1	<0.1
Whole milk	1.9	65.2	1.3	2.5	0.9
Jello/pudding	1.8	67.0	0.4	0.7	1.5
Popcorn/pretzels	1.7	68.7	0.7	0.9	2.5
Olives/pickles	1.7	70.4	1.4	0.5	2.8
Low-fat milk	1.5	71.9	0.9	1.8	0.9
Crackers	1.5	73.4	1.6	2.4	1.4
Peanut butter	1.4	74.8	2.4	1.5	0.8
French fries	1.2	76.0	1.5	2.5	0.9

Note: For 943 children.
*Total number of choices.
†Ratios of 1.5 or greater considered excessive (50% above recommended values.)
(Courtesy of Simons-Morton BG, Baranowski T, Parcel GS, et al: Am J Prev Med 6:218–227, 1990.)

except the parakeet. On the other hand, our male teenager (James A. Stockman, IV) certainly eats like a horse but leaves behind the oats for the adults, indicating they need the fiber. Needless to say, mealtime is a sort of happening.

The above is probably not that atypical of many homes in America, so the report abstracted should come with no surprises: Kids have soda pop, pop tarts, burgers, pepperoni, and donuts for breakfast; french fries, tortillas, spaghetti, burgers, and soda pop for lunch; and burgers, spaghetti, fries, pickles and soda pop for supper. An average American diet.

There seems to be more need for nutritional education in our schools, however negatively our children view such guidance and however hopeless the effort. An example of the latter was the reception to the suggestion given to our middleschmerz kinder (Samantha) that the next time she grazed in the kitchen, perhaps she ought to fix herself a PB & J (my health favorite as a kid). Her response was rapid enough: "If God had wanted us to eat peanut butter, he would have lined the inside of our mouths with Teflon."

Maybe my grandfather was right. He lived into his 90s having bacon and eggs with toast for breakfast virtually every day of his life. He never exercised. I shall forever remember his most quotable quote: "Abstain from wine, women, food, and song . . . mostly song."—J.A. Stockman, III, M.D.

4 Allergy and Dermatology

Allergic Reactions to Milk-Contaminated "Nondairy" Products
Gern JE, Yang E, Evrard HM, Sampson HA (Johns Hopkins Univ, Baltimore; Mt Sinai Med Ctr, New York)
N Engl J Med 324:976–979, 1991   4–1

As many as 7.5% of children have adverse reactions to cow's milk. Such patients are advised to read product labels carefully to avoid inadvertent exposure to milk. Some reactions occur after ingestion of foods that are labeled "nondairy" or that contain milk products not listed on the label. Six patients were described who had adverse reactions after eating frozen desserts labeled "nondairy" or "pareve" or after eating processed meats with no milk products listed on their labels.

Six children who were allergic to milk had histories of adverse reactions minutes after they ate foods presumed to be milk-free. On every occasion, a parent had carefully read the product label. No other relevant allergies could be found to explain the children's reactions. Therefore, the

Milk-Protein Content of "Nondairy" Food Products

PRODUCT	CASEIN	WHEY	MILK PROTEIN
	micrograms/milliliter		
Tofulite (Lot a*)†	381	158	2202
Tofulite (Lot b)†	60	35	79
Tofulite (Lot c)†	219	90	468
Rice Dream bar (Lot a)†	343	148	1470
Rice Dream (Lot b)†	19	30	37
Rice Dream (Lot c)†	<1	<1	—
Giant Tofu	3	9	14
Ice Bean‡	5	12	171
A-Maize-Ing Delite‡	<1	<1	—
Oscar Mayer hot dog*§	136	5	70
Acme tuna	2060	2	2220

*The sample was from the same package as the food that caused a reaction in a patient.
†The product was made in a dairy-processing facility.
‡A soy-based dessert.
§The manufacturer confirmed that sodium caseinate had been added to the recipe but was not specifically listed on the label. The regulations of the Department of Agriculture at that time allowed sodium caseinate to be called a "natural flavoring."
(Courtesy of Gern JE, Yang E, Evrard HM, et al: *N Engl J Med* 324:976–979, 1991.)

foods that reportedly provoked the reactions in these children were tested for contamination with cow's milk. Sensitive enzyme-linked immunosorbent assays for milk proteins were used. Traces of milk protein were found in these "nondairy" foods in every case (table).

Persons who are allergic to milk, even those who read product labels carefully, may be inadvertently exposed to sufficient quantities of milk proteins to cause generalized reactions. Clinicians should consider this possibility in milk-sensitive patients who have adverse reactions of unclear origin. In addition, repeated exposure to hidden cow's-milk protein may exacerbate chronic conditions (e.g., eczema or rhinitis), or may delay the resolution of milk allergy through continued antigenic stimulation.

▶ My goodness, is there no way to protect ourselves from cows?

I bet you are wondering what specific foods the children in the abstract above ate. Two of them ate frozen tofu (Loft's Tofulite), 2 ate 1 bite of a beef hotdog (Oscar Meyer), 1 ate bologna (Oscar Meyer), and 1 ate a teaspoon of tuna fish (Acme). All had some degree of anaphylactic reaction. In the laboratory, each of these products was documented to have either casein, whey, or milk proteins by enzyme-linked immunosorbent assays.

How, pray tell, could milk have gotten into these "nondairy" food products? The manufacturers of the products were contacted. Although no specific errors in processing were identified with the tofu manufacturers, these products were manufacturered in plants that also did dairy processing. The manufacturer of the hot dog and bologna stated that the product recipes had recently been changed to include sodium caseinate, which was added to improve the texture of the processed meat. The levels of milk proteins measured in the sample of tofu represented the equivalent of approximately 2.5 mL of cow's milk per 120 mg serving of the dessert, and the sample of hot dog contained roughly the same amount of antigenic casein as .3 mL of milk. Even these small quantities were enough to induce anaphylaxis in these sensitized children.

Please don't blame Oscar Meyer for the error. Recall that they make the dog that kids like to bite. The Oscar Meyer hot dog and bologna labels, although they did not show the presence of sodium caseinate, were in compliance with current standards as defined by the Department of Agriculture, which is the organization responsible for regulating foods that contain more than 2% meat or poultry. Sodium caseinate, as noted, is frequently added as a binder. It was only on March 1, 1991, that sodium caseinate and other animal-derived or plant-derived food additives were required to be listed separately on the labels of foods regulated by the Department of Agriculture. A warning, however, is that foods that do not contain meat or poultry are regulated by the Food and Drug Administration, which operates under a different set of guidelines. Current regulations for this agency state that sodium caseinate and other "flavorings . . . may continue to be designated as such without specific ingredient declaration." Such is the common sense of federal bureaucracy!

The greatest problem with milk allergy, of course, tends to be with infants rather than with older children and adults. The latter 2 groups can read product labels and avoid milk-containing substances if they want to. Infants, however, are reliant on either breast milk or someone who puts the formula in their mouth. The treatment of choice for cow's-milk hypersensitivity in infants is total avoidance of cow-milk proteins. Soy formulas, meat-based formulas (no longer commercially available in the United States), and hydralized cow's-milk casein and whey formulas have been recommended for cow-milk hypersensitivity. We now know that soy hypersensitivity occurs in as many as 50% of children who are sensitive to cow's milk, so that it is not a logical formula to switch to. That leaves us with the hydrolysate formulas. The casein hydrolysates, Nutramigen and Pregestimil (Mead Johnson/Bristol Meyers), are generally regarded as safe and are approved as "hypoallergenic" for children with cow-milk hypersensitivity. Last year, the new hydrolysate formula, Good Start (H. A. Carnation Company) flunked out on this score and was not allowed to be labeled as hypoallergenic. Numerous reports of allergic reactions in cow-milk hypersensitive children were reported with Good Start. The most recent casein hydrolysate infant formula, Alimentum (Ross Laboratories) has been thoroughly tested (1) and appears to be in line with Nutramigen and Pregestimil as being "hypoallergenic."

"Hypoallergenic" does not mean "nonallergenic." Infrequently, children who are cow's-milk sensitive will react to these hypoallergenic formulas. A good example of this was recently reported by Saylor et al. (2). A young child who had developed a cow-milk hypersensitivity was described. After he had been off all dairy products for 3 years, it was thought worthwhile to attempt a challenge with a sip of one-quarter strength Nutramigen. The challenge was prompted by a decision to wean the patient's younger brother from the breast, and the child's mother needed to find a formula that would be safe to have in the house in case the 3-year-old accidently got into it. The challenge was undertaken in the pediatrician's office. Within seconds, the child has violent, blood stained emesis, conjunctival injection, generalized erythema, and wheezing that required immediate administration of epinephrine and diphenhydramine. To boot, during the next few weeks, ingestion of beef was associated with perioral hives. One month later, an episode of generalized erythema and persistent cough occurred while the child was visiting a grocery store. To make a long story short, this child wound up living on a diet consisting of water, rice, and chicken. Now it is difficult to blame all of this on cows, but none of this became a problem until the child was challenged with a cow-milk protein.

So how can we protect ourselves from the byproducts of cows? Not easy. My father used to have a saying "If cows could fly like birds, we'd all be carrying umbrellas." Unfortunately, the problem of cow-milk hypersensitivity doesn't have such a simple protective solution.—J.A. Stockman, III, M.D.

References

1. Sampson HA, et al: *J Pediatr* 118:520, 1991.
2. Saylor JD, et al: *J Pediatr* 118:71, 1991.

Exposure to House-Dust Mite Allergen *(Der p* I) and the Development of Asthma in Childhood: A Prospective Study
Sporik R, Holgate ST, Platts-Mills TAE, Cogswell JJ (Poole Gen Hosp, Dorset, England; Southampton Gen Hosp, Hants, England; Univ of Virginia)
N Engl J Med 323:502–507, 1990   4–2

The expression of atopy and allergic disease is dependent on exposure. In England, the majority of older children with asthma are sensitized to the house-dust mite. Because an infant's first exposure to aeroallergens may be an important determinant of later sensitization, a cohort of British children at risk for allergic disease because of family history were studied prospectively from 1978 to 1989. When the children were 1 year old, dust was collected from various sites in their homes and assayed for the house-dust mite allergen, Der p I. The procedure was repeated in 1989. The relationship between exposure to the house-dust mite allergen and the development of sensitization and asthma was analyzed.

Of the 67 children studied in 1989, 35 were atopic (by positive skin test), and 32 were nonatopic. Of 17 children with active asthma, 16 were atopic, and the same 16 were sensitized to the house-dust mite. The relative risk of active asthma was 14.6 in an atopic child and 19.7 in a child sensitized to the house-dust mite allergen. Skin reactivity to mites was positive by age 5 in 40% of the children with positive reactions at age 11.

The levels of mite allergen in the houses were generally high. The mean highest recorded levels of Der p I in the houses were 16.1 μg/g in 1979 and 16.8 μg/g in 1989. A trend toward increased sensitization with greater exposure at age 1 was observed at age 11. All but 1 of the children with asthma at age 11 had been exposed to more than 10 μg/g of Der p I in infancy. The relative risk of active asthma in any child was 4.8 with exposure to these levels. There was a weak inverse relationship between the level of exposure in infancy and the age at which the first episode of wheezing occurred, particularly among atopic children.

In addition to genetic factors, exposure in early childhood to the house-dust mite allergen appears to be an important factor in the subsequent development of asthma. Increased exposure to dust mites and other indoor allergens may be important factors in the recent increases in morbidity and mortality associated with this disease.

House Dust Mite Allergen Levels and an Anti-Mite Mattress Spray (Natamycin) in the Treatment of Childhood Asthma

Reiser J, Ingram D, Mitchell EB, Warner JO (Royal Brompton Hosp, London; Northwick Park Hosp, Harrow, England)
Clin Exp Allergy 20:561–567, 1990   4–3

Natamycin, a potent fungicide, decreases growth of the house-dust mite *Dermatophagoides pteronyssinus* (Dpt) in culture. The house-dust mite contributes to symptoms of allergy in children. A trial was undertaken to determine whether natamycin, sprayed onto mattresses, would benefit children with asthma who have mite sensitivity.

Forty-six children attending allergy clinics took part in the study. Their disease ranged from mild and episodic to chronic severe asthma requiring regular therapy. Mite sensitivity was confirmed by skin prick tests. Mattresses from the children's beds were sprayed once every 2 weeks for 3 months with either natamycin (500 mg per dose) or placebo. Because mites require humidity to thrive, absolute humidity, relative humidity, and humidity on the walls of the bedroom were monitored during the study period. Dust samples were obtained, and a blood specimen obtained from each child was analyzed for anti-Dpt IgE.

Levels of Dpt antigen *(Der p* I) in mattress dust were similar in the active and placebo groups at the end of the study. Changes in wall humidity were followed about a month later by changes in *Der p* I levels, but none of the other factors studied appeared to influence those levels. Furthermore, the children whose mattresses were treated did not have improved bronchial reactivity, lung function tests, or clinical symptoms.

The findings of this study do not justify the use of natamycin spray as part of an allergen avoidance regimen. Considerable reductions in *Der p* I must be achieved before reactivity is affected.

▶ *Dermatophagoides pteronyssinus* is the $10 term for the common house-dust mite. The report of Sporik et al. (Abstract 4–2) commented on later in this chapter by Dr. Hugh Sampson, suggests that the association of asthma with sensitization to house-dust mite allergen is a true cause and effect relationship in a large population of children with asthma. This implies that exposing children to a high level of foreign proteins in their homes could be regarded as an important health risk.

If you have not been following the house-dust mite saga, the allergen of this mite is a protein with a molecular weight of 24,000 and has been designated *Der p* I. The protein allergen has been cloned and identified as a simple enzyme cysteine proteinase. *Der p* I can be measured in house dust to give an index of the concentration of mite antigen and levels of exposure that presumably represent a risk for the development of asthma.

On the same theme, an airborne spore that is a particularly frequent trigger of asthma attacks during the summer and fall months has been described. This spore is *Alternaria alternata*. Osler once wrote that asthma was simply a "slight aliment that produces longevity." Unfortunately, in the last few years, we have noticed an increasing incidence of respiratory arrest or death among asthmatics in this country (see the commentary elsewhere in this chapter by Dr. Richard Evans). Part of this may be because of exposure to airborne spores and the common mold *A. alternata*. This is one of the most common atmospheric mold spores in the United States and reaches its highest abundance in grain-growing areas such as the Midwest. Inhalation of *A. alternata* spores may produce immediate asthmatic responses. There is strong circumstantial evidence that sensitivity to *A. alternata* is a risk factor in the marked increase in sudden severe episodes of asthma that has occurred in the Midwest. The season for *A. alternata* is between June and November. If you don't think this is a problem, read the report of O'Hollaran (1), which documents that if an individual has *A. alternata* skin-test reactivity, that individual has a 200-fold increase in the risk of respiratory arrest from asthmatic attacks.

So what do we do about *A. alternata* and the common house-dust mite? The only solution to *A. alternata* is for those in the plain states to move to the hills of the Northeast or Northwest (immunotherapy is not all that terribly effective). With respect to house-dust mites, there are things that you can do. First, you can find out whether there is a problem in your own house. Several testing kits have been developed that can aid in directing environmental control in the home. There is a recently marketed test, Acarex, that measures by-products of the mite. Which by-products you ask, pray tell? The by-product measured is feces. This test provides a semiquantitative estimate of mite concentration in household dust and is a nonprescription item that anyone can perform in the home. There are much more sophisticated assays, including an enzyme-linked immunosorbent assay for *Der p* I, available through reference laboratories. The value of such sophisticated DNA-based assays was verified in a report from the *Lancet* (2). If you are going to go to all the trouble of investigating your house for mites, you might as well also buy 1 of those cheap radon kits and really do it up right.

Once you know there is a problem in your home, the next step is to keep the house as "Mr. Clean" as possible. That includes meticulous vacuum cleaning. Proper vacuum cleaning, however, doesn't involve dragging out the old upright Hoover. It has been shown that these machines frequently increase airborne *Der p* I by simply blowing things around (3). The best thing available is a high-tech instrument for vacuuming that has a high-efficiency filter and goes by the trade name "Medivac." The latter is quite expensive. Recall that after Hoover was in office, all you could afford was a Hoover at the very most. Now that Bush is effectively demonstrating the long-term benefits of Reaganomics, we can't even afford a Hoover much less a Medivac. Then again, just think, with Bushnomics, we have a self-curing solution for the problem of carpets and the house-dust mite. One can no longer afford wall to wall carpeting, just maybe a throw rug here and there. Thank you, Mr. Bush, but then again, maybe next time I'll vote democratic so I can beat the bushes.

Well, this closes the commentary on *Dermatophagoides pteronyssinus*—the mite. If all this sounds like a "mite'ty tall story," let me tell you about cockroach allergens (4).—J.A. Stockman, III, M.D.

References

1. O'Hollaran MT: *N Engl J Med* 324:359, 1991.
2. Price JA, et al: *Lancet* 336:895, 1990.
3. Kaldra S: *Lancet* 49:336, 1990.
4. Lan JL, et al: *J Allerg Clin Immunol* 82:732, 1988.

Changing Patterns of Asthma Hospitalization Among Children: 1979 to 1987

Gergen PJ, Weiss KB (Ctrs for Disease Control, Hyattsville, Md; George Washington Univ)
JAMA 264:1688–1692, 1990   4–4

Asthma remains the leading chronic disease in childhood, and hospitalization rates for asthma have been increasing. To assess the reasons for this increase, the National Hospital Discharge Survey was used to evaluate the trends in asthma hospitalization among children younger than age 17 years under the *International Classification of Diseases, Ninth Revision, Clinical Modification (ICD-9-CM): 1979* to 1987.

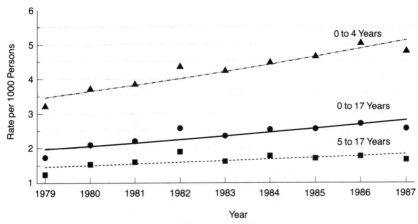

Fig 4–1.—Asthma hospitalization rates per 1,000 persons for United States infants, children, and youths aged 0 to 17 years. Symbols represent observed rates; lines represent trends based on log-linear regression. From National Center for Health Statistics, National Hospital Discharge Survey. (Courtesy of Gergen PJ, Weiss KB: *JAMA* 264:1688–1692, 1990.)

During this period asthma hospitalizations among children aged 0 to 17 years increased by 4.5% per year (95% confidence interval, 2% to 7.1%), from a rate of 1.73 per 1,000 in 1979 to 2.57 per 1,000 by 1987. The increase was largely the result of the increase in hospitalization among those aged 0 to 4 years, in whom the average percentage of change was 5% per year, compared with 2.9% per year among children aged 5 to 17 years (Fig 4–1). In the group aged 0 to 4 years black children had approximately 1.8 times the increase of white children. In this age group, hospitalizations for all diagnoses decreased by 4.6% per year, whereas admissions for lower respiratory tract disease remained relatively constant, with an insignificant decrease of 1.3% per year. Hospitalizations for acute and chronic-unspecified bronchitis decreased by 6.1%, but this decrease did not begin until 1983.

These findings suggest that a shift in coding from bronchitis to asthma does not appear to fully explain the increase. In addition to the overall increasing trend, the severity of asthma hospitalizations appears to be increasing, as reflected in the increasing percentage of admissions that require intubation or cardiopulmonary resuscitation.

Childhood hospitalization rates for asthma are increasing. The increase appears to be limited to children aged 0 to 4 years, particularly black children. This increase cannot be fully attributed to the implementation of ICD-9-CM in 1979.

Changing Patterns of Asthma Mortality: Identifying Target Populations at High Risk
Weiss KB, Wagener DK (George Washington Univ; Natl Inst of Allergy and Infectious Diseases, Natl Insts of Health, Bethesda, Md)
JAMA 264:1683–1687, 1990

4–5

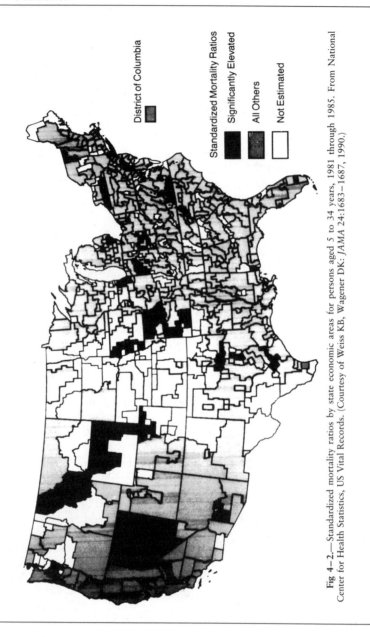

Fig 4–2.—Standardized mortality ratios by state economic areas for persons aged 5 to 34 years, 1981 through 1985. From National Center for Health Statistics, US Vital Records. (Courtesy of Weiss KB, Wagener DK: *JAMA* 24:1683–1687, 1990.)

Several reports have suggested an increasing trend in hospitalization for asthma and in asthma mortality since the early 1980s. Data from the US Vital Records on asthma mortality from 1968 to 1987 were used to describe the rates of change in asthma mortality among children and young adults aged 5 to 34 years with time and in small geographic areas. From 1968 through 1977 asthma mortality among persons aged 5 to

34 years steadily declined, for an estimated annual rate of 7.8%. From 1978 to 1987 asthma mortality increased at an annual rate of 6.2%. The rates increased significantly faster among children aged 5 to 14 years than among adolescents and young adults aged 15 to 34 years.

Small-area geographic analysis identified 4 areas with persistently higher asthma mortality than expected: New York City (New York), Cook County (Illinois), Maricopa County (Arizona), and Fresno County (California) (Fig 4–2). It appeared that 2 areas, New York City and Cook County, are driving, in part, the overall United States trend, with a combined annual increase in asthma deaths of 10.2% from 1979 to 1985. Neither changes in the International Classification of Disease coding nor more accurate diagnosis after autopsy accounted for the increasing mortality in the 1980s.

These data suggest there is an alarming reversal in asthma mortality since the late 1970s. Asthma mortality has increased in the 1980s at an annual rate of 6.2%, with the increase being particularly high among younger children.

▶ Richard Evans III, M.D., MPH, Professor of Clinical Pediatrics and Medicine, Northwestern University Medical School, and Head, Division of Allergy, Children's Memorial Hospital, comments:

▶ During recent years, there has been a trend toward increasing prevalence and severity of asthma, as evidenced by these studies. It is particularly disturbing to note that mortality has increased most among young children, blacks, and the poor. Although a greater willingness to diagnose asthma—and to hospitalize severe cases—may be reflected in the statistics, world literature suggests that there is a real escalation in the prevalence and morbidity of asthma apart from changes in classification, diagnosis, or more liberal hospitalization practices. Elevated air pollution certainly has to be considered as a likely factor, especially because urban dwellers seem to be disproportionately affected. It will be interesting to see how the current decline in cigarette smoking will affect future cases in infants and very young children in households where parents no longer smoke. Certainly there is enough evidence that smoking aggravates asthma in young children that pediatricians will want to warn new parents of the hazards of cigarette use. A possible area for future study will be the Middle East, where air pollution has reached tragic proportions as a result of long-burning oil-well fires.

Apart from air pollution, another disquieting factor emerges from these studies. It may be that the quality and/or availability of asthma care in the United States is declining, particularly in facilities serving the urban poor. At present, a major federally funded study is underway that may help set the direction for practical, cost-effective treatment programs for the disadvantaged population, but accessibility and quality of care will likely continue to be troubling issues as the government and health-care providers grapple with cost containment.

Clearly, childhood asthma remains an enigmatic disease in many ways. Lack of standardized diagnostic criteria still hampers effective epidemiologic study, as does the variance in study methodology. However, the foregoing reports and others here and elsewhere in the world have identified target populations at risk for increased morbidity and mortality from asthma. Now that we know, to some extent, who is at risk, we need to learn more about why and what can be done to reverse this distressing trend.— R. Evans III, M.D.

The Value of Immunotherapy With Venom in Children With Allergy to Insect Stings

Valentine MD, Schuberth KC, Kagey-Sobotka A, Graft DF, Kwiterovich KA, Szklo M, Lichtenstein LM (Johns Hopkins Univ)
N Engl J Med 323:1601–1603, 1990   4–6

Immunotherapy with insect venom is 97% effective in reducing the risk of sting-induced anaphylaxis, but the frequency of systemic reactions after challenge sting in untreated adults is approximately 60%. To determine which factors, in addition to a history of reaction and evidence of venom-specific IgE antibody, predispose patients to subsequent sting reactions, 242 children deemed at relatively low risk for severe reactions were studied. These children, aged 2 to 16 years, had systemic insect-sting reactions affecting only the skin. Each child had a positive skin-test reaction to 1 or more of 5 hymenopteran venoms, and 68 (28%) received immunotherapy with venom in a randomized fashion or based on the patient's (or parent's) choice.

During 4 years of observation, only 1 systemic reaction was observed in 84 stings that occurred in 36 patients treated with venom immunotherapy, for a rate of 1.2% of stings. In contrast, 196 stings in 86 untreated children resulted in 18 systemic reactions and a rate of 9.2%. The difference was significant. Of the latter, 16 reactions were considered milder than the reaction to the patient's originial sting, 2 were of similar severity, and none were considered severe.

The data confirm the efficacy of venom immunotherapy in preventing recurrence of systemic reactions after subsequent insect stings. Venom immunotherapy is probably unnecessary, however, for children whose reactions to insect stings are limited to the skin. It was not possible to determine characteristics predictive of repeat reactions because of the surprisingly low rate of reactions among untreated children.

▶ If you're not sure how deep the puddle is regarding the risk of insect stings, read on. Although fewer than 50 deaths from insect stings are recorded in the United States each year, the number of persons susceptible to allergic reactions from insect venom is estimated to be in the tens of millions. Hypersensitivity to insect venom is mediated by IgE antibodies, and although only 3% of the population has a history of a systemic reaction, such antibodies have been detected within 3 years after a sting in 20% of normal people. In the Northeast, bees and yellow jackets cause the majority of sting-induced allergic reactions, whereas imported fire ants are the primary offenders in the Southeast, as are wasps in the Southwest. The anaphylaxis produced by these insects is usually an all-or-none phenomenon—the victim either survives without sequelae or dies.

For almost 20 years, the investigators who authored the article abstracted above have been on the trail of what to do about insect-bite anaphylaxis. In 1974, they first reported in *The New England Journal of Medicine* that immunotherapy to treat patients who were allergic to insect stings was indeed appropriate (1). The Food and Drug Administration has given a green light to go ahead with immunotherapy, because it has been found that only about 12% of treated patients suffer any reactions to the desensitization injections, and only 9% of these (ergo less than 1% overall) are severe reactions. Treatment, however, is expensive, and the next task undertaken by these allergists from Johns Hopkins was to define carefully the indications for treatment. One reason for having to define better the indications was cost. It is not cost effective to treat the entire 3% of the population that has a history of systemic reactions. These authors decided to direct their attention initially to those who would benefit most with the least risk of adverse outcome: children with systemic insect-sting reactions whose previous reactions had been confined to the skin. The results: only 9.2% of stings in untreated children were found to lead to a subsequent systemic reaction, and because there was no progression to a more severe reaction, the Hopkins group has concluded that venom immunotherapy was quite unnecessary for most children who are allergic to insect stings. One giant step for allergists, 1 giant leap for kids.

Does this mean that no one should be desensitized? Absolutely not. Probably most adults should be desensitized. Venom immunotherapy is 97% effective in reducing anaphylaxis from stings in adults with previous systemic allergic reactions, and without therapy, up to 60% of such adults will have systemic reactions if stung again. The treatment is not a minor one. It must be given once or twice a week for several months and then monthly or at longer intervals for at least 3 to 5 years. If there is a significant risk for subsequent anaphylaxis from insect stings, patients should be advised to carry a syringe containing aqueous epinephrine. Three kinds are available: the EpiPen Junior and Senior, (.15 and .3 mg of epinephrine, respectively, Center Laboratories) and the Ana-Kit (.6 mg of epinephrine, which can be dispensed from the same syringe in .3-mg increments, Miles Laboratories).

It is fascinating to see how far immunotherapy has come. When I was a little shaver in the 1950s, I had to go in twice a week for "my shots" because I had bad hay fever. The quality of the stuff that was available in those days was extraordinarily questionable. I thought that the injections were more voodoo or black magic than science, and I think my allergist in Chadds Ford, Pennsylvania, did as well. He had a little plaque on the wall of his office that said "You can fool some of the people all the time and all the people some of the time. That's sufficient."

That was in the 1950s. We've come a long way since.—J.A. Stockman, III, M.D.

Reference

1. Lichtenstein LM, et al: *N Engl J Med* 290:1223, 1974.

It Is Chldren With Atopic Dermatitis Who Develop Asthma More Frequently if the Mother Smokes

Murray AB, Morrison BJ (Univ of British Columbia, Vancouver, Canada)
J Allergy Clin Immunol 86:732–739, 1990   4–7

A previous study has shown that a higher proportion of children of smoking mothers have eczema, compared with children of nonsmoking mothers. Because children with atopic dermatitis (AD) are at increased risk of asthma, it is hypothesized that children who have AD and are exposed to smoke from the mother are particularly at risk of asthma. Data on 620 nonsmoking children, aged 1–17 years, who were referred to an allergy clinic were evaluated. Parents were interviewed with regard to their smoking history and symptoms of AD and asthma in their children. Histamine bronchial-challenge tests were performed on 63 children aged 7 years or older who had a history of wheezing or asthma and who could perform the test reliably.

Children with a history of asthma were much more likely to have asthma if the mother was a smoker (79%) than if she was a nonsmoker (52%). Similarly, among those children in whom the diagnosis of AD had been confirmed, asthma was much more frequent in children of smoking mothers than in children of nonsmoking mothers. The prevalence of asthma was greater in both boys and girls with a history of AD if the mother was a smoker, but only in boys when the father was a smoker. In contrast, children with no history of AD were no more likely to have asthma whether the mother smoked or not. Multivariate logistic regression analysis showed that the risk of asthma was highest when the child had both AD and a mother who smoked. These data indicate that children with a history of AD are much more likely to have asthma if the mother is a smoker than if she is a nonsmoker.

▶ I still am firmly convinced that the reason God created tobacco was so that man could generate statistics.

I was not aware of the relationship between atopic dermatitis and maternal smoking and the subsequent risk of asthma. The authors of the article abstracted suggest that parents be advised not to smoke in the home. They should be told that there may be an increased risk of their child having asthma if they are smokers and their child has ever had atopic dermatitis.

Hopefully, but not with too much promise, we might think that parents will value the health of their children more than they do their own. As has been stated so many times in previous YEAR BOOKS, tobacco is a dirty weed. Warning labels on cigarette packages don't work, so maybe we should be calling on the weed-killing services of ChemLawn Corporation, International, to take care of the tobacco fields.—J.A. Stockman, III, M.D.

Xanthomas and the Inherited Hyperlipoproteinemias in Children and Adolescents

Maher-Wiese VL, Marmer EL, Grant-Kels JM (Brown Univ, Roger Williams Hosp, Providence, RI; Univ of Connecticut Health Ctr, Farmington)
Pediatr Dermatol 7:166–173, 1990   4–8

Hyperlipoproteinemias are associated with an increased risk of premature coronary artery disease. Xanthomas are known for their association with hyperlipoproteinemias, and their presence in children and adolescents are usually indicative of a more severe form of hyperlipoproteinemia. Hence, accurate and prompt diagnosis is essential.

Xanthomas in children may be the first clinical symptom of inherited hyperlipoproteinemias. There are 5 classifications of xanthomas associated with the different types of hyperlipoproteinemia. Eruptive xanthomas are common in types I and V hyperlipoproteinemias and occasionally in types III and IV (Fig 4–3A,B). The 2 xanthomas that are considered pathognomonic are intertriginous xanthomas in homozygous patients with type-II hyperlipoproteinemia and palmar crease xanthomas in patients with type-III disease (Fig 4–3C). Xanthelasmas are limited to patients with type-II disease. Tendinous and tuberous xanthomas are associated with type-II and type-III hyperlipoproteinemia. Xanthomas are uncommon in type-IV disease, but when present, they are usually of the eruptive, tuberous, or palmar type.

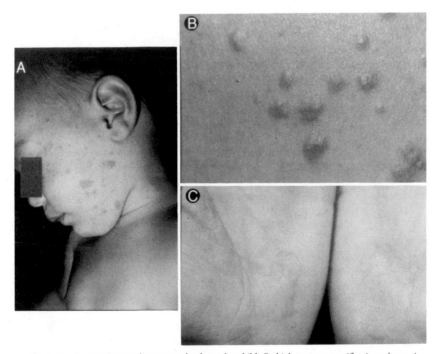

Fig 4–3.—**A,** eruptive xanthomas on the face of a child. **B,** high-power magnification of eruptive xanthomas on the back. **C,** palmar crease xanthomas. (Courtesy of Maher-Wiese VL, Marmer EL, Grant-Kels JM: *Pediatr Dermatol* 7:166–173, 1990.)

Differential Diagnosis of Childhood Bullous Pemphigoid

Disease	Clinical Features	Histologic Features	Immunopathologic Features
Acrodermatitis enteropathica	Autosomal recessive; periorificial and acral bullae after infant weaned; diarrhea; decreased serum zinc levels	Intraepidermal vesicles	Negative
Bullous urticaria pigmentosa	Darier's sign positive	Subepidermal bulla with mast cells and eosinophils	Negative
Epidermolytic hyperkeratosis	Autosomal dominant; bullae often present at birth	Intraepidermal bulla with granular degeneration and hyperkeratosis	Negative
Generalized herpes simplex	Grouped vesicles or bullae; multinucleated giant cells on Tzanck preparation	Intraepidermal vesicle with ballooning degeneration of keratinocytes	Negative
Bullous impetigo	Collarettes of scale around erosions; positive Gram's stain and bacterial culture	Intraepidermal bulla	Negative
Erythema multiforme	Target lesions	Subepidermal bulla; clumping of necrotic keratinocytes	Deposition of IgM and C3 in walls of superficial vasculature
Epidermolysis bullosa group	Inheritance pattern according to disease; milia formation in Dowling-Meara type	Site of bulla formation according to disease; electron-microscopic identification of cleavage plane	Negative
Incontinentia pigmenti	X-linked dominant; verrucous and pigmented lesions	Intraepidermal bulla with eosinophils; dyskeratotic keratinocytes	Negative
Congenital syphilis	Vesiculobullous lesions, especially on extremities; radiologic detection of skeletal involvement; serology	Intraepidermal bulla with superficial perivascular lymphoplasmocytic infiltrate	Negative

Disease	Clinical Features	Histology	Immunofluorescence
Toxic epidermal necrolysis	Flaccid bullae; Nikolsky's sign positive	Subepidermal bulla; necrosis of epidermis	Negative
Pemphigus vulgaris	Oral lesions often precede cutaneous flaccid bullae; Nikolsky's sign positive	Intraepidermal bulla with acantholytic cells	Epidermal intercellular deposition of IgG and C3
Childhood EBA	Bullae with acral distribution; milia and scarring	Subepidermal bulla with neutrophils	Linear deposition of IgG; occasional linear deposition of IgA, IgM, and C3; circulating IgG to EBA antigen
Bullous lupus erythematosus	Widespread tense bullae; positive ANA and signs of systemic lupus	Subepidermal bulla with neutrophilic papillary microabscesses	Granular or linear deposition of IgG, C3, and IgM; circulating IgG to EBA antigen best detected on salt-split skin
Herpes gestationes	Maternal history; vesicles, bullae, and urticarial plaques	Subepidermal bulla with eosinophils	Linear deposition of IgG and C3; serum herpes gestationis factor
Cicatricial pemphigoid	Bullae with scarring, predominantly affecting mucous membranes	Subepidermal bulla with eosinophils	Linear deposition of IgG and C3; circulating IgG
Childhood dermatitis herpetiformis	Symmetrically grouped vesicles and small bullae; gluten-sensitive enteropathy	Subepidermal bulla; papillary neutrophilic microabscesses	Granular deposition of IgA in dermal papillae
Chronic bullous disease of childhood	Vesicles and bullae in rosettes or clusters	Subepidermal bulla with eosinophils; occasional neutrophilic microabscesses	Linear deposition of IgA; no circulating autoantibodies

Abbreviations: EBA, epidermolysis bullosa acquisita; *ANA,* antinuclear antibody. (Courtesy of Nemeth AJ, Klein AD, Gould EW, et al: *Arch Dermatol* 127:378–386, 1991.)

Xanthomas are rare in children and adolescents. Hence, their presence warrants a more detailed history, physical examination, and laboratory analysis. Xanthomas may aid in the early detection of high-risk children with hyperlipoproteinemia.

Childhood Bullous Pemphigoid: Clinical and Immunologic Features, Treatment, and Prognosis

Nemeth AJ, Klein AD, Gould EW, Schachner LA (Univ of Miami)
Arch Dermatol 127:378–386, 1991   4–9

Bullous pemphigoid (BP) is an acquired immune bullous disorder that usually affects elderly persons; it is considered rare in childhood. In the youngest patient known to have BP, the condition was apparent before age 3 months.

Female infant, 2½ months, had multiple tense bullae on the palms and soles. She responded to steroid cream, but larger bullae appeared on the extremities, trunk, and neck 2 weeks later and progressed despite use of a nystatin-triamcinolone acetonide ointment (Fig 4–4). Results of cultures were negative. The mother had developed blisters on the thigh 3 times in the 2½ years before her child was born. A biopsy specimen showed a subepidermal bulla that exhibited type-IV collagen at its base (Fig 4–5), a typical finding in BP. Direct immunofluorescence (IF) study was strongly positive for C3 and IgG in perilesional skin. Results of indirect IF studies of maternal and infant sera and breast milk were negative. Treatment with prednisone, 1 mg/kg daily, led to rapid improvement. Cloxacillin also was administered. Prednisone was tapered over 4 months, and the patient has remained free of lesions for 3 years.

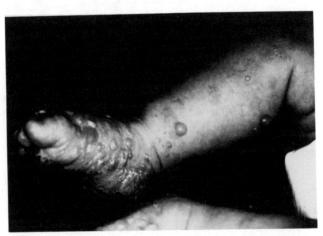

Fig 4–4.—Tense bullae distributed on the lower extremity with marked involvement of the foot (sole). (Courtesy of Nemeth AJ, Klein AD, Gould EW, et al: *Arch Dermatol* 127:378–386, 1991.)

Fig 4–5.—Photomicrograph of subepidermal bulla. Type IV collagen mapping of the basement membrane zone *(arrow)* shows type IV collagen at the bulla base. This is characteristic of bullous pemphigoid (oxidized diaminobenzidine-hematoxylin; original magnification ×50). (Courtesy of Nemeth AJ, Klein AD, Gould EW, et al: *Arch Dermatol* 127:378–386, 1991.)

Mucosal involvement is frequent in childhood BP (table, pg. 126). The cause of the disorder is not known, and suggested associations with various medications probably are coincidental. The best initial treatment is prednisone in a dose of 1 to 2 mg/kg daily. The course is usually, but not always, benign. Spontaneous remissions are not reported in childhood BP, in contrast to adult disease.

▶ Bullous pemphigoid is a rare but not unheard of problem in children. The skin lesions often begin as urticarial, irregularly bordered plaques reminiscent of erythema multiforme. Characteristically, tense, nongrouped, variably sized bullae arise on erythematous skin. Sites of predilection include the inner aspects of the thigh, the flexural surfaces of the forearms, the axillae, the lower part of the abdomen, the groin, and the palmar and plantar surfaces. Itching is a variable complaint. Until the early 1960s, bullous pemphigoid of childhood was lumped together with dermatitis herpetiformis.

As you might suspect, there could be much difficulty differentially diagnosing a child who has bullous pemphigoid from other bullous-type eruptions in infants and children. The only absolute way of making the diagnosis is by doing a skin biopsy. There is a very characteristic immunofluorescence with linear IgG deposition along the basement membrane zone in almost all patients. Complement (C₃) deposition is also found in virtually all bullous pemphigoid skin lesions in addition to the immunofluorescence positivity for IgG.

Other than bullous impetigo there aren't many "good" (easily treated) things that cause large blisters in kids. Once again, it may be advantageous to call the best dermatologist in your town and get some help on this one.—J.A. Stockman, III, M.D.

Ammoniated Mercury Ointment: Outdated But Still in Use

Aberer W, Gerstner G, Pehamberger H (Univ of Vienna; Municipal Hosp Stockerau, Stockerau, Austria)
Contact Dermatitis 23:168–171, 1990   4–10

Because of severe associated adverse effects (such as poisoning and high irritant and allergic potential) and its weak potency as an antiseptic or antipsoriatic agent, mercury is rarely used topically today, and a general prohibition of its use has been recommended. Data on 2 patients with severe allergic reaction to ammoniated mercury were reviewed to demonstrate that this agent is still in use and to promote awareness of its side effects.

Severe contact dermatitis developed in both patients after use of ammoniated mercury ointment for its postulated effect as an antiseptic. Patch testing confirmed the diagnosis. The lesions responded to oral and/or topical steroid treatment.

Topical mercurial agents are still widely used today, although more effective and less toxic drugs are available. The rate of complications from ammoniated mercury use remains relatively high. Allergy is frequent, considering that mercury is a weak allergen. Topical application can also cause systemic poisoning. Skin pigmentary changes can occur after prolonged topical use. Because of the availability of more effective and less toxic drugs, mercury ointment should be withdrawn from the market as a topical therapeutic agent.

Incidence of Acne Vulgaris in Patients With Infantile Acne

Chew EW, Bingham A, Burrows D (Royal Victoria Hosp, Belfast)
Clin Exp Dermatol 15:376–377, 1990   4–11

To determine whether infantile acne predisposes to teenaged acne, a retrospective study was conducted of patients treated for infantile acne between 1960 and 1970. Twenty-three (19 male) of the 74 patients seen at that time were successfully traced at 18 to 28 years later and completed a questionnaire. The control group consisted of 160 age-matched medical students. The severity of acne was classified according to the form of treatment received, topical therapy, systemic antibiotics, or isotretinoin.

The statistical power of the study was limited because of the small number of patients successfully traced. However, there was a trend toward a higher incidence and greater severity of acne vulgaris during the teenaged years among patients with a history of infantile acne, compared with the control group. Mean age at recurrence was 14.7 years, and 8.7% of study patients were treated with isotretinoin, compared with 1.3% in the control group.

This study supports the suggestion that infantile acne predisposes to adolescent acne, but further study in a larger population is necessary to settle the controversy.

Acne Fulminans

Goldstein B, Chalker DK, Lesher JL Jr (Med College of Georgia, Augusta)
South Med J 83:705–708, 1990   4–12

Acne fulminans is a rare and disfiguring disease that occurs almost exclusively in male adolescents. The clinical and laboratory features, pathogenesis, and therapy of this debilitating disease were reviewed.

The pathogenesis of acne fulminans remains obscure, but several studies suggest an immune-mediated phenomenon. The disease is characterized by an acute onset of noduloulcerative acne lesions, fever, and leukocytosis. It is associated with many problems, including stooped shoulders syndrome, weight loss, malaise, splinter hemorrhages, erythema nodosum, and polyarthritis. Various laboratory abnormalities have been reported in association with acne fulminans, including leukocytosis, anemia, thrombocytosis, and immunologic abnormalities. Radiographic abnormalities, such as lytic bone lesions and increased uptake with bone scans, have also been reported. Diagnosis may be particularly difficult in patients who have fever, weight loss, and arthralgia, and may even be delayed until acne lesions are recognized as significant findings. Current therapy for acne fulminans involves systemically administered corticosteroids, with doses of .5–1 mg/kg/day. Isotretinoin, .5–1 mg/kg/day, and/or systemically administered antibiotics can be used in combination with localized treatment. Early diagnosis and treatment is necessary to decrease the significant morbidity associated with acne fulminans.

▶ When the oldest of our 4 children, who are twins, turned teenagers, they both blossomed with acne. Fortunately, they are 20 this year and well on their way to time-induced recovery. Jenny, however, at one point along those years said to me that it would take a miracle to take care of her particular problem. She seemed relieved when I told her that I didn't believe in miracles, I relied on them. That's exactly what you have to do for some adolescents with acne.

One of the most extreme forms of acne carries the most extreme name, "acne fulminans." In 1959, Burns and Colville (1) described a 16-year-old boy who had mild acne for about a year preceding the onset of numerous exquisitely tender, deep, ulcerative acne lesions. These were associated with fever, arthralgias and myalgias. In 1977, Goldschmidt et al. (2) described 21 cases of what by then became known as "acne fulminans." Isolated cases of acne fulminans in patients with inflammatory bowel disease, alopecia totalis, inflammatory myositis, and associated with testosterone administration have been reported. Polyarthritis occurs in more than 75% of these patients. Treatment of these patients should be extremely aggressive, along the lines described in Abstact 4–12. The next time you see a child with rapidly progressing acne in association with fever, weight loss, and severe arthralgia, think acne fulminans, and act quickly. Referral to a dermatologist would be the better part of valor.

It is curious that human beings are the only creatures to suffer the consequences of acne. That is probably because, in common jargon, we are one of the few creatures on the earth that have our skin on the outside. Most creatures have fur. Herbert George Ponting said this differently:

"On the outside grows the fur side,
On the inside grows the skin side;
So the fur side is the outside,
And the skin side is the inside."

(Prepared by Mr. Ponting, the official photographer for the Scott Antarctic Exposition, for the *South Polar Times*, June 22, 1911).—J.A. Stockman, III, M.D.

References

1. Burns RE, Colville JM: *Arch Dermatol* 79:361, 1959.
2. Goldschmidt H, et al: *Arch Dermatol* 113:444, 1977.

Clinical Management of Port-Wine Stain in Infants and Young Children Using the Flashlamp-Pulsed Dye Laser

Nelson JS, Applebaum J (Beckman Laser Inst and Med Clinic, Irvine, Calif; Univ of California, Irvina)
Clin Pediatr 29:503–508, 1990

4–13

Port-wine stain (PWS), a congenital vasculopathy, occurs in about 3 infants per 1,000 live births, appearing most commonly on the face and neck (Fig 4–6*A*). The clinical management of PWS in infants and young children using the flashlamp-pulsed dye laser (FLPDL) was evaluated.

Irradiations are done with an SPTL-1 type FLPDL. High-intensity flashlamps excite the dye to produce visible photons at 585 nm. The laser can produce a 450-ms pulse at a maximum energy density of 10 J/cm². Energy densities used for treating lesions in infants and young children are typically 4.5–6.5 J/cm² and are calibrated with an energy meter. Laser energy is focused into a 1-mm core diameter quartz optical fiber that terminates in a microlens, focusing the laser radiation on a 5-mm circular spot of uniform light intensity (Fig 4–6*B*).

This new FLPDL produces excellent lightening of PWS in infants and young children without the adverse effects of hypertrophic scarring, permanent pigmentation abnormality, or textural changes that often occur with conventional laser systems. The treatment of this population, expected to benefit the most from early laser therapy, can now be done in a much safer manner (Fig 4–6*C*).

▶ Jerome M. Garden, M.D., Associate Professor, Departments of Dermatology and Pediatrics, Northwestern University Medical School, and Director, Laser Therapy, Divisions of Dermatology and Plastic Surgery, The Children's Memorial Hospital, comments:

▶ Attempts to treat patients with PWS effectively and safely have been ongoing for decades. This is in response to a desire to eradicate a lesion that is associated with potential bleeding and infection with aging and with psychosocial developmental problems. A long list of therapeutic methods has been promoted that in many instances fell dramatically short of expectations. Either ef-

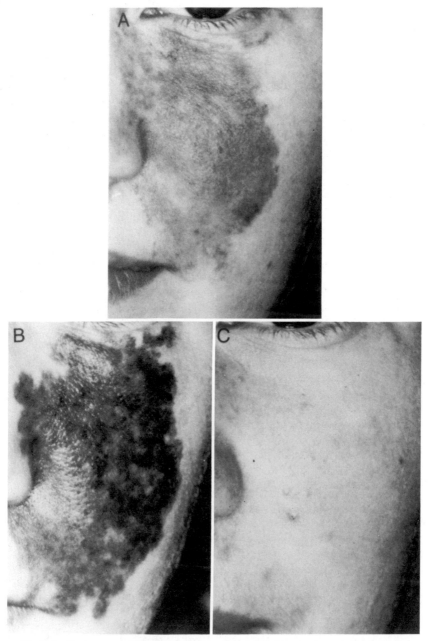

Fig 4–6.—Twelve-year-old female child with extensive left facial port-wine stain before treatment (**A**), immediately after irradiation of entire lesion (**B**), 6 months after completion of fourth treatment (**C**). (Courtesy of Nelson JS, Applebaum J: *Clin Pediatr* 29:503–508, 1990.)

fectivity had been limited, or adverse effects were unacceptable. This has been especially true in the pediatric population and has justifiably elicited a very cautious approach to the acceptance of any new therapeutic approaches and their purported claims of success.

The laser also has added its name to this group of expected saviors. The argon laser was heralded as a breakthrough, especially in 1970s. Being non-ionizing light, it was safe and indeed was more effective than most available modalities. However, adverse results of skin atrophy and depression and in the worse cases, scarring, would result. Again these adverse results were magnified in the pediatric patient.

It was not the concept of using laser light that was incorrect, but rather, that the technology was unavailable to optimize the potential. With the modification of the FLPDL in 1983 to selectively interact with cutaneous blood vessels, the Food and Drug Administration allowed investigation into the treatment of PWS in the adult and adolescent, and in 1986, in the pediatric patient as well. Several thousand laser treatments have been successfully delivered to pediatric patients with this newer laser. Its effectiveness has been remarkable but, more importantly, its safety is dramatic. There has not been any scarring. Unnatural pigmentary or skin texture changes are uncommon and only spotty. For the first time this laser has allowed the pediatric PWS patient an opportunity for therapy with an acceptable degree of safety.—J.M. Garden, M.D.

Suntan, Sunburn, and Pigmentation Factors and the Frequency of Acquired Melanocytic Nevi in Children: Similarities to Melanoma: The Vancouver Mole Study
Gallagher RP, McLean DI, Yang CP, Coldman AJ, Silver HKB, Spinelli JJ, Beagrie M (Univ of British Columbia, Vancouver)
Arch Dermatol 126:770–776, 1990   4–14

Although most studies of acquired benign nevi have involved adult populations, the frequency of moles increases rapidly in childhood and reaches the full adult burden by adolescence. Consequently, the role of various skin cancer risk factors in the occurrence of benign melanocytic nevi was examined in 913 white Vancouver school children aged 6 to 18 years.

Nevus counts were significantly higher in subjects with light skin, in those with a tendency to burn rather than tan when exposed to the sun, and in those who had numerous or severe sunburns in the past 5 years. Children with deeper tans tended to have fewer nevi than those who failed to tan. Also, nevus counts were higher in children who freckled than in those who did not.

These findings are similar to those obtained in studies of malignant melanoma in adults, and they suggest that strategies for lowering the risk of melanoma should begin with young children. A major effort is needed to educate parents about solar sensitivity in light-skinned children and to encourage them to see that their children use both protective clothing and effective sunscreens. Furthermore, public education should not be limited to traditional "sunspot" areas.

▶ When I was growing up, the worst thing you got from being out in the sun was a sunburn or a bad case of the freckles. Now we get an increased risk of melanoma and, as noted in this article, acquired melanocytic nevi. That wonderful glowing object out there in the center of our universe that gives and sustains life, unfortunately, produces ultraviolet (UV) light, which has few healthy effects.

What is confusing to many of us is the various wavelengths of UV light that cause problems and the very practical issue of which sunscreen should be used under what circumstances. Time for a little education on these matters.

Basically, there are 2 forms of UV that are important: UVA and UVB. Of UVB 280–320 nm and UVA 320–340 nm, UVB 280–320 nm is more energetic, but less UVB penetrates human epidermis, so dermal processes such as elastosis and wrinkling may be more closely related to UVA exposure. Sunscreens with high sun protection factors (SPF) are judged on the basis of their ability to protect skin against burning, and by implication against the development of skin cancer. Erythema is predominantly a UVB effect. Consequently, the SPF number on a tube of sun block tells us about burning and skin cancer but not about UVA protection. To say this a bit more simply, the main concern for human health involves 2 things: the carcinogenic impact of UVB and the cosmetic (wrinkling) effect of UVA. A higher SPF may protect you from burning, but it may not help you beat the odds against wrinkles. As an aside, in case you've forgotten, SPF numbers range from 2 to 50, and SPF is simply a measure of how long an individual can stay in the sun before burning. A person with fair skin who burns within 10 minutes without sunscreen could stay in the sun for 40 minutes before burning by using an SPF 4 product, according to the SPF theory.

Once again, if all this is confusing, the easiest way to remember this information is that UVA stands for aging and UVB stands for burning. Although both UVA and UVB can relate to skin cancer, UVB is the really bad actor. Thus far, the Food and Drug Administration has officially approved only 1 chemical, Parsol 1789, as a safe and effective screen for UVA. If you are worried about skin cancer and aging, buy the 2 products available in the United States with this agent: "Filteray" and "Photoplex", both of which contain Parsol.

To sum all this up, your standard off-the-shelf sunscreen with SPF 30 does a great job in terms of prevention of burning and reduction of skin cancer. It may not, however, prevent aging or do anything that will prevent those rare photo eruptions that are caused by UVA light. The latter include solar urticaria, and the light eruptions seen with erythropoietic protoporphyria, polymorphic light eruption, and systemic lupus erythematosus. The latter eruptions are caused by solar irritation of mast cells with release of histamines, etc., which can cause urticaria. If there is any 1 rule that will stead you well in life, it is: "Never scratch a mast cell."

Sorry for this somewhat rambling commentary, and many apologies for sun worshipers in the reading audience, because this commentary contains not a single ray of hope for you.—J.A. Stockman, III, M.D.

5 Miscellaneous Topics

Capillary Refilling (Skin Turgor) in the Assessment of Dehydration
Saavedra JM, Harris GD, Li S, Finberg L (State Univ of New York Health Science Ctr at Brooklyn)
Am J Dis Child 145:296–298, 1991   5–1

Pediatricians often use the decrease of skin elasticity and loss of skin turgor or increased capillary refilling time as signs in assessing dehydration, especially in children younger than age 2 years. However, no study to date has standardized the technique of timing skin turgor or assessing its accuracy as a predictor of the degree of dehydration in infants. The usefulness of skin turgor or capillary refilling in estimating the degree of dehydration in infants with diarrhea was investigated.

Two studies were done. The first involved 30 normal infants, aged 2–24 months. After the technique was standardized, capillary filling time was found to be more reproducible when the clinician applied just the amount of pressure to the fingernail bed needed to blanch it. The mean capillary refilling time in these children was .81 seconds. In the second study, 32 infants with diarrhea admitted to the hospital were examined. Capillary filling time was measured and correlated to the degree of dehydration as estimated from the difference in weight from the time of admission to weight after rehydration. A turgor time of 1.5 seconds or less indicated a less than 50-mL/kg deficit, or normalcy. A time of 1.5–3 seconds suggested a deficit of 50–100 mL/kg. Finally, more than 3 seconds indicated a deficit greater than 100 mL/kg.

With a little experience and without a stopwatch, a clinician can estimate an infant's hydration status. As with all clinical signs, however, even one as useful as this, variants will sometimes occur. Variants can usually be anticipated by a patient's overall condition and the circumstances in which he or she is found.

▶ I like this report, although I am not certain that it has as much clinical applicability as the authors suggest . . . "capillary refilling time measured in the fingernail bed is a valuable technique in estimating the degree of dehydration and should be part of the clinical assessment of an infant's hydration status." This implies that it can be used in almost all circumstances. One cannot ignore, however, the conclusion that a capillary refilling time of less than 1.5 seconds is normal or represents a deficit of less than 5% dehydration. A time of 1.5–3 seconds suggests a deficit of 5%–10%. A time longer than 3 seconds suggests a volume deficit of 10% or more. That was fairly clear from the report. The problem with the report is the difficulty that some will have reproducing the study's rigor. Indeed, it was a rigorously designed and well-executed study. An individual trying to reproduce these findings in practice or in an emergency room setting will have to be equally rigorous and learn all the caveat emptors associated with capillary refill times.

What are some of the things to be careful about with capillary refilling times? The time can be influenced by a number of factors, including the site at which the measure is made, the presence of edema, characteristics of the skin, and the cardiovascular status. Hypothermia, hyponatremia, and cardiac failure presumably will prolong the times. Fever may have the opposite effect. Hypernatremic states clearly do so. Hypernatremic dehydration appears to preserve skin elasticity and capillary refining times. The clinician must bear in mind each of these conditions when making a quantitative judgment. Severe malnutrition would not appear to affect capillary refilling times unless complicated by cardiac failure. On the other hand, the presence of edema resulting from kwashiorkor may result in capillary refilling times that are less reliable.

The major problem that I have with capillary refilling times is that I am probably going to miss a lot of the mild to moderately abnormal measurements. When a normal capillary refill time is .81 seconds, I know I'm in trouble, because my brain doesn't think that fast.

One final word of caution, if you decide to use capillary refilling times, don't use 2 watches. There's an old saying, "The man with 2 watches never knows what time it is."—J.A. Stockman, III, M.D.

Preparedness for Pediatric Emergencies Encountered in the Practitioner's Office

Altieri M, Bellet J, Scott H (Fairfax Hosp, Falls Church, Va; George Washington Univ; Georgetown Univ; Children's Hosp Natl Med Ctr, Washington, DC)
Pediatrics 85:710–714, 1990   5–2

The preparedness of the various emergency medical systems for the critically ill child with medical or surgical emergencies has been well examined. To ascertain the readiness of private pediatric offices to cope with life-threatening emergencies, questionnaires were sent to more than 400 pediatricians in the metropolitan Washington, DC, area. The survey elicited information on emergency equipment available, prearranged emergency plans, advanced life support training, and proximity of local emergency medical services.

Response rate was 40%. The most common office emergencies encountered were severe respiratory distress and seizures. Cardiac arrest and severe trauma occurred rarely. Only 50% of the physicians had prearranged emergency plans to deal with life-threatening emergencies, and 77% had some staff members certified in basic life support. Most offices were close to local emergency services. Half were within a 3-minute response time, and the other half were within a 10-minute response time. Oral airways, oxygen, and epinephrine 1:1,000 were the most readily available emergency equipment and drug, but most emergency cardiac drugs had expired shelf life.

The following recommendations to physicians who care for children are advocated to help them prepare in a cost-effective manner for life-

TABLE 1.—Recommended Emergency Equipment for Pediatric Offices

Equipment	Manufacturer/Model No.	Cost ($)
Oral airways		
Infant (no. 1, 55 mm)	Dynamed/A16437	7.80 per 6
Child (no. 2, 60 mm)	Dynamed/A16436	7.80 per 6
Small adult (no. 3, 80 mm)	Dynamed/A16435	7.80 per 6
Nasal airways		
Rusch (no. 12F)	Metro Medical/125200	5.00 each
Rusch (no. 14F)	Metro Medical/125200	5.00 each
Rusch (no. 16F)	Metro Medical/125200	5.00 each
Rusch (no. 20F)	Metro Medical/125200	5.00 each
Bag/valve/mask		
Hope III Child Resuscitator with relief valve	DynaMed/Y17202	118.00
Assorted pediatric masks		
Infant	Vital signs/5220	20.00 per 20
Toddler	Vital Signs/5230	20.00 per 20
Child/small adult	Vital Signs/5240	20.00 per 20
Oxygen		
Small oxygen tank (rental local vendors)		
Oxygen mask and nasal cannula		
Pediatric oxygen mask	Inspiron/001471	20.00 per 20
Nasal cannula	Satler Labs/1600-8	20.00 per 20
Portable suction equipment		
Ohmeda portable suction	Dynamed/Y17204	500.00
Endotracheal tubes		
3.0	Respiratory Support Products/N4022P	18.00 per 10
3.5	Respiratory Support Products/N4023P	18.00 per 10
4.0	Respiratory Support Products/N40424	18.00 per 10
5.5	Mallinckrodt/86268	18.00 per 10
6.0	Mallinckrodt/86448	18.00 per 10
8.0	Mallinckrodt/86113	18.00 per 10
Laryngoscope/blade		
Handle scope	Dynamed/Y43610	25.00 each
Blades		
Miller 00	Dynamed/Y43603	38.50 each
Miller 0	Dynamed/Y43604	38.50 each
Miller 1	Dynamed/Y43605	38.50 each
Miller 2	Dynamed/Y43606	38.50 each
Intravenous line drip setup		
Continue Flo Solution Administration Set	Travenol/2C071S	1.30 each
Arm boards (child)	Commander-Omni Co Inc/5124, 5126	33.40 per 50
Intraosseous bone marrow needle		
Jamshidi Disposable Illinois Sternal/Ilia Aspiration Needle, 15-gauge adjustable length	AHS/DIN1515	11.00 each
Syringes		
20-cc Becton Dickenson	Henry Schein Inc./987-2914	20.50 per 40
Nebulizer		
Medication Nebulizer Kit	Inspiron/37761	1.50

(Courtesy of Altieri M, Bellet J, Scott H: *Pediatrics* 85:710–714, 1990.)

threatening emergencies. All staff members should be trained in basic life support, and physicians should consider taking advanced cardiac life support courses. A formal emergency plan should be developed, and cost-effective emergency equipment and supplies should be available (Tables 1 and 2). Physicians should also know what services are available from their local emergency medical system.

▶ Dr. Sally Reynolds, Assistant Professor of Clinical Pediatrics, Northwestern University Medical School, comments:

▶ Over the last several years, an increased emphasis has been placed on pediatric emergency medicine. The development of fellowships in pediatric emer-

TABLE 2.—Recommended Emergency Drugs for Pediatric Offices

Drug	Cost ($ each)
Epinephrine	
1:1000 ampoules	0.75
1:10 000 prefilled syringes	7.00
Sodium bicarbonate: 50-mEq prefilled syringes	10.41
Atropine: 0.5-mg prefilled syringes	6.77
Valium: multidose vials	
5-mg/mL, 10-mL vials	14.43
10-mg/2-mL ampoules	3.25
Lidocaine: 100-mg prefilled syringes for intravenous administration	1.93
Calcium chloride	
10% ampoules	0.60
Prefilled syringes	6.12
Racemic epinephrine	
Albuterol for inhalation	11.00
Aminophylline: 250-mg vials (10 cm^3 25 mg/cm^3)	0.70
Glucose D5 ampoules prefilled syringes	6.30
Dilantin	
100-mg/2-mL prefilled syringes	5.00
250-mg/5-mL prefilled syringes for intravenous administration	5.40
Narcan	
Intravenous antibiotics: ampicillin	
Intravenous diphenhydramine (Benedryl): slow intravenous 50-mg ampoule	0.47
Intravenous steroids: Solumedrol	
Ipecac	

(Courtesy of Altieri M, Bellet J, Scott H: *Pediatrics* 85:710–714. 1990.)

gency medicine has led to a number of physicians with expertise in this area. In a previous study of Chicago-area physicians, only 42% of the physicians surveyed felt adequately equipped to handle a life-threatening event in the office (1). Pediatric emergency medicine physicians have attempted to aid their colleagues in office practice by being prepared for an emergency in a variety of ways. The authors have put together a list of equipment and drugs that will get a physician and his office staff through most situations. The majority of emergencies in this study were respiratory distress and seizures, yet only 51% of the offices had a bag-valve-mask available. Other recommendations include a staff that is certified in basic life support and a Pediatric Advance Life Support Course for the physician. Having all of the equipment available is not enough, the physician has to be able to use it effectively. This study may be the beginning of some guidelines for emergency care in the office setting.—S. Reynolds, M.D.

Reference

1. Fuchs S, et al: *Pediatrics* 83:931, 1978.

Professional Liability in a Pediatric Emergency Department
Reynolds SL, Jaffe D, Glynn W (Northwestern Univ; Children's Mem Hosp, Chicago)
Pediatrics 87:134–137, 1991   5–3

The risk of professional liability that results from care given in the pediatric emergency department is a growing concern. In a retrospective study, the patients, diagnoses, and outcome of all threatened and actual claims that originated in the emergency department of a pediatric teaching hospital from 1977 to 1988 were reviewed. From approximately 320,000 visits, 25 cases were identified by the hospital risk manager, and charts on 22 of these cases were available for analysis. The mean age was 3 years (range, 2 weeks to 13 years). The patients' payment status was private insurance in 10 cases and state public aid in 5; no third-party payment source was listed for 7.

Ten children were seen in the emergency department from midnight to 8 AM when no attending physician was present. Ten children were brought back to the emergency department with the same complaint within 2 weeks of the first visit. Eighteen children were discharged home. All had appropriate, adequately documented discharge instructions. Final diagnoses were minor trauma or abuse in 7 cases, neoplasms or chronic illnesses in 7, infectious diseases in 6, and appendicitis in 2 (table).

Diagnoses and Legal Outcome

Original DX	Final DX	Outcome
Seizures	Viral meningitis	Dropped
Otitis media	Dead on arrival 2 days later	Dropped
Gastroenteritis	Appendicitis	Dropped
Hepatitis A	Wilson's disease	Open
Carbon monoxide poisoning	Carbon monoxide poisoning	Dropped
Gastroenteritis	Tracheal stenosis	Unfounded
Hand laceration	Tendon injury	Settled
Viral illness	Meningococcemia	Dropped
Sexual abuse	Sexual abuse	Unfounded
Knee laceration	Missed foreign body	Settled
Candidal gastric tube infection	Ventricular peritoneal shunt malfunction	Settled
Cardiac arrest	Pacemaker failure	Dropped
Viral illness	Meningococcemia	Dropped
Viral illness	Child abuse	Dropped
Constipation	Medulloblastoma	Unfounded
Gastroenteritis	Brain tumor	Dropped
Diabetic ketoacidosis	Diabetic ketoacidosis	Open
Gastroenteritis	Appendicitis	Dropped
Viral illness	Toxic epidermal necrolysis	Dropped
Foreign body in esophagus	Foreign body in esophagus	Dropped
Viral illness	Peritonsillar abscess	Settled
Soft tissue trauma	Radial head dislocation	Settled

Quality-of-care issues were raised in 41% of cases during chart review before knowledge of the legal outcome. Legal claims were categorized as failure to diagnose in 16 cases and inappropriate treatment in 6. No claims went to trial. The families dropped their claim in 12 cases. Five patients received some payment, 3 claims were unfounded, and 2 remain open. Legal fees incurred in 16 cases during the 10-year period totaled $191,677, and $43,850 was paid to families.

Malpractice claims were uncommon in this pediatric emergency department. A disproportionate number of claims were filed by families of patients seen when an attending physician was not in the emergency room. No one specific diagnosis was overrepresented. The risk of professional liability was higher for those visiting the emergency department more than once for the same complaint. The cost of associated legal fees was more than 4 times the sum paid to families.

► As you might suspect, I know this particular hospital that did a review of its professional liability in the emergency room setting. I am proud that someone had the gumption to discuss this kind of sensitive issue in the literature so that we could all learn from it. What we see is that, although things are not perfect in teaching hospitals, generally a fine job is done. After analyzing over a third of a million visits to an emergency room, only 25 cases were identified by the hospital risk manager as ones that lead to some risk of professional liability. Of the 25 cases, 12 were dropped by the family, 5 patients received compensation, 3 claims were determined to be unfounded, and 2 were still on the docket. No claim had to go to trial; any claim with a settlement was settled out of court. It was interesting to see that the cost of managing the professional liability problem was 4 times greater than the actual amount of dollars paid to children and families ($191,677 vs. $43,850).

It is difficult to draw specific conclusions from this type of report. Malpractice claims do seem to be relatively uncommon in emergency departments. They seem to occur on a random basis with no single specific diagnosis showing up on a repetitive basis. Risk management techniques seem to do little, therefore, to alter the liability.

The easiest way to get out of a high malpractice environment is to take a step into Canada. Canadian physicians are only one fifth as likely to be sued for malpractice as their American counterparts (1). Presumably, this remarkable difference is attributed to a number of legal and institutional factors in Canada: the presence of universal health insurance, more generous programs of social welfare, limited use of contingent fees, the practice of having the losing party bear the cost of litigation, limited awards for pain and suffering, infrequent use of juries, and the effective defense work of the Canadian Medical Protective Association. Knowing the health care system in Canada and all of its problems (as well as fine points), I'm not sure the citizenry of the United States would opt for the Canadian system yet. The issue, however, is whether the malpractice situation has become so great in this country that we perhaps should resort to some of the better aspects of the Canadian system.—J.A. Stockman, III, M.D.

Reference

1. Coyte PC, et al: *N Engl J Med* 324:89, 1991.

Iatrogenic Illness in Pediatric Critical Care
Stambouly JJ, Pollack MM (Children's Hosp Natl Med Ctr, Washington, DC; George Washington Univ, Washington, DC)
Crit Care Med 18:1248–1251, 1990   5–4

Previous studies report an incidence of iatrogenic illnesses of up to 36% in hospital inpatients, but none has specifically addressed iatrogenic illness in the pediatric intensive care unit (PICU). In a prospective study, consecutive admissions to a PICU over 2 time periods totaling 6 months were studied to determine the incidence and outcome of iatrogenic illness, in pediatric patients.

Among the 541 patients admitted to the PICU, 25 (4.6%) were admitted because of an iatrogenic illness, defined as an adverse condition that occurred as a result of medical care independent of the child's underlying illness. Drug-induced conditions accounted for 8 (32%) of these admissions, including 6 respiratory failures occurring after anticonvulsant therapy. The remaining 17 admissions were the result of complications of medical-surgical acts, and 8 of these resulted in chronic complications. Diagnoses included chronic upper airway complications of neonatal intensive care in 6 patients, complications after tonsillectomy and adenoidectomy in 4, chronic postcardiac surgery complications in 2, cardiac catheterization complications in 2, and other miscellaneous conditions in 5. Only 1 (3.7%) patient died. The risk of dying among patients with iatrogenic illness was similar to that of other patients.

These data show that iatrogenic illness is a significant cause of PICU admission. Improved physician education about the potential risks of treatment and quality assurance programs may contribute to reducing the incidence of iatrogenic illness.

▶ Dr. James C. Fackler, Director, Multidisciplinary Intensive Care Unit and Director of Respiratory Therapy, the Children's Hospital Medical Center, Boston, comments:

▶ The work by Stambouly and Pollack, which examines PICU admissions for an iatrogenic cause, has important implications and reflects the multidisciplinary base of pediatric critical care. Although much is written about the complications that occur after critical care procedures and therapies (e.g., barotrauma from mechanical ventilation), this report identifies PICU admissions precipitated by "therapeutic misadventures" in many non-PICU patient-care areas. In a 6-month period in a PICU that receives all pediatric critical care patients except premature newborns and infants with major burns, approximately 5% (25 patients) of 581 PICU admissions were caused by iatrogenic complications. One third of the complications were drug side effects, and the remaining complications followed surgical or medical procedures. Nearly one half of the procedure-related complication group (8 of 17) were admitted to the PICU for an acute exacerbation of a chronic iatrogenic condition. Examples of chronic iatrogenic conditions were vocal cord paralysis and tracheal stenosis.

The authors ask (but do not answer): "Are these iatrogenic complications preventable?" Certainly, some complications are not preventable. Standard medical and surgical care is associated with finite risk. A similar study reports that 12.6% of admissions into an adult ICU had an iatrogenic cause. Yet, no pediatrician should be satisfied that the 5% iatrogenic PICU admission rate is half that reported in adult ICUs (1).

In the report of the adult ICU, about one half of the complications were "potentially avoidable." An example of such a group in the study by Stambouly and Pollack may be the 6 of 8 patients who suffered drug side effects caused by anticonvulsant drugs used for treatment of status epilepticus. Approximately 1 patient per month undergoes mechanical ventilation at Children's Hospital in Boston: to wit, identical circumstances. Although data are lacking, there is a strong bias that the fully expected respiratory depression represents overzealous therapy of status epilepticus, and may be avoided (2).

As codified pediatric critical care quality improvement efforts become increasingly multidisciplinary, screening admissions for iatrogenic complications becomes a simple and useful exercise. Only with such efforts, followed by open collaborative efforts with many generalists and specialists, will the minimum finite risk associated with excellent pediatric care be identified.—J.D. Fackler, M.D.

References

1. Trunet P, et al: *JAMA* 244:2617, 1980.
2. Freeman JM: *Pediatrics* 83:444, 1987.

Pediatric Trauma Triage: Review of 1,307 Cases
Jubelirer RA, Agarwal NN, Beyer FC III, Ferraro PJ, Jacobelli MC, Pfeifer WF III, Shah MA, Welch GW (Abington Mem Hosp, Abington, PA; York Hosp, York, Pa; Lancaster Gen Hosp, Lancaster, Pa; Community Med Ctr, Scranton, Pa; St Mary's Hosp, Langhorne, Pa; et al)
J Trauma 30:1544–1547, 1990   5–5

The guidelines for transfer of an injured child to a level I pediatric trauma center, as set forth in appendix J of the American College of Surgeons' *Hospital and Prehospital Resources for Optimal Care of the Injured Patient,* are based on the Pediatric Trauma Score (PTS) (Table 1) and a list of criteria (Table 2). The records of 8 level II trauma centers

TABLE 1.—Guidelines for Transfer to a Level I Center

Pediatric Trauma Score

	+2	+1	−1
Size	>20 Kg	10–20 Kg	<10 Kg
Airway	Normal	Maintained	Unmaintained
Systolic BP	>90 mm	50–90 mm	<50 mm
CNS	Awake	Obtunded	Coma
Open wound	None	Minor	Major
Skeletal	None	Closed	Open/multiple

Total points _____

Circle one variable (+2, +1, −1) from each line and add the scores for the total PTS. Any child whose PTS is 8 or less should be considered for transfer to a Level I pediatric trauma unit.

(From Jubelirer RA, Agarwal NN, Beyer FC III, et al: *J Trauma* 31:1544–1547, 1990. Courtesy of American College of Surgeons' Committee on Trauma: Hospital and Prehospital Resources for Optimal Care of the Injured Patient. Appendix J. Chicago, American College of Surgeons, 1987.)

were examined retrospectively to assess the relevance of appendix J to actual triage patterns.

The records of 1,307 patients were analyzed. Their average age was 8.27 years, and their average PTS was 9.71. Forty-three children were transferred to pediatric trauma centers and 24 died, 20 in the emergency room. Although 298 children met 1 or more of the criteria for transfer, 273 of these were not transferred. The 2 most common criteria for transfer were the need for pediatric intensive care unit admission and altered states of consciousness. No deaths occurred in patients not transferred who had met either of these 2 criteria.

Nineteen of 242 patients with a PTS ≤8, the recommended point for transfer, were transferred to a pediatric trauma center. There were 128 patients with both criteria for transfer and a PTS ≤8. There were 19 transfers and 19 deaths in this subgroup. Weight was an important component of PTS. There was a greater percentage of deaths and more transfers in children weighing <10 kg.

Trauma accounts for more deaths of children between the ages of 1 and 14 years than all other causes combined. Because most deaths occur during resuscitation, adult trauma centers must be able to handle pediatric trauma arrests. Children with a PTS >8 and who either require admission to the intensive care unit and/or have altered states of consciousness can be treated safely in the adult intensive care unit of a level II trauma center.

▶ If you want to read a delightfully enjoyable commentary, read that of Joseph Simon: "What is a Pediatric Emergency Physician?" (1). Dr. Simon was in a meeting at which a general pediatrician spoke up and asked rhetorically, "Isn't a pediatric emergency physician just a pediatrician who can sew lacerations and pass an ATLS course?" Dr. Simon sensed an "emergency," but re-

TABLE 2.—Referral Patterns for Hospitals Characterized
as 'Optimal' (Level I) and 'Limited' (Level II)

Level I	Level II
Patients having serious injury to more than one organ system.	Patients with single system injury who will not require ICU management and require a short length of stay.
Patients having one system injury who will require pediatric ICU care.	Patients with shock who require less than a one blood volume transfusion for stabilization.
Patients with signs of shock who require more than a one blood volume transfusion.	Patients with a single major long bone fracture.
Patients with fractures complicated by suspected neurovascular compartment injury.	Patients with stable, not serious head trauma who will not require ventilation or long-term rehabilitation.
Patients with potential for replantation of an extremity.	
Patients with suspected or actual spinal cord or column injuries.	
Patients with head injury having any one of the following:	
• orbital or facial bone fractures	
• cerebral fluid leaks	
• altered states of consciousness	
• changing neurologic signs	
• open head injuries	
• depressed skull fractures	
• required ICP monitoring.	
Patients suspected of requiring ventilatory or nutritional support.	

(From Jubelirer RA, Agarwal NN, Beyer FC III, et al: *J Trauma* 30:1544–1547, 1990. Courtesy of American College of Surgeons' Committee on Trauma: Hospital and Prehospital Resources for Optimal Care of the Injured Patient. Appendix J. Chicago, American College of Surgeons, 1987.)

sponded. Methodically he listed the many skills at the command of an emergency–medicine-trained pediatrician: the ability to use a slit lamp, to remove a nasal foreign body, to administer intravenous sedation, to direct cardiopulmonary resuscitation, to provide appropriate advice to emergency medical technicians working under field conditions, and to tap every orifice and every cavity of the body. Pediatric emergency medicine certainly has come of age within the last 2 decades.

Unfortunately, most injured children are not injured in an environment where they will be seen initially by a pediatric-trained emergency-medicine physician. The article abstracted is intended to show what the real world is like in community hospitals that do not have 24 – hour-a-day coverage by pediatric emergency – medicine-trained individuals. The conclusion of the report is very clear: adult trauma centers must be able to handle trauma arrests in children and must address the pediatric age group when planning trauma prevention activities. The tertiary care pediatric facility is just too far away if 80% of deaths occur during the initial resuscitation and stabilization.

Trauma remains the leading cause of death among children in North America over the age of 1, with blunt head injuries accounting for most of the deaths and injuries. Jaffe et al. (2) underscore that management of pediatric trauma requires an organized approach, combining diagnosis and treatment. The recommended sequence is as described by the Committee on Trauma of the American College of Surgeons. There are 4 distinct phases: the primary survey, the resuscitation, the secondary survey, and the definitive care. During the primary survey and resuscitation, the patient's condition is stabilized by identifying and correcting immediate threats to life — inadequate gas exchange (the airway and breathing) and inadequate perfusion of vital organs (the circulation). During the secondary survey, all important injuries are identified by a thorough head-to-toe examination. The plan for definitive treatment is then developed. These are the well known so called ABCs of resuscitation and/or stabilization.

This is a quiz question on pediatric trauma. Which month is the harbinger of all harbingers for trauma in children?

If you are thinking October (the last 2 weeks), you are absolutely correct. Three unrelated but simultaneous events occur that have been documented to increase the risk of certain kinds of trauma, making the end of October the worst time of the year as far as kids and trauma are concerned. These events are (1) change of seasons, (2) daylight saving time reverting to standard time, and (3) Halloween. The increase in after-school activities coupled with the sudden and much earlier occurrence of dusk results in children walking or riding a bike home at dusk or after dark. Recognize that on October 16, sunset is generally at 5:27 PM (daylight saving time). By October 31, it occurs at 4:07 PM (standard time), on average in the United States. One study from a Sacramento hospital (3) reported that 72% of all injuries occurred on the early evening shift.

These data may not apply to large city hospitals where everyone recognizes that shootings and falls out of windows are more likely in summertime when everyone is up and more active. But for the country as a whole, you'd better believe there was a reason why Hollywood made those Halloween series of movies. Jason lurks out there ready to traumatize. . .—J.A. Stockman, III, M.D.

References

1. Simon JE: *Pediatr Emerg Care* 6:219, 1990.
2. Jaffe D, et al: *N Engl J Med* 324:1477, 1991.
3. Spisso J, et al: *J Emerg Nursing* 16:339, 1990.

The Causes, Impact, and Preventability of Childhood Injuries in the United States: Childhood Suicide in the United States
Holinger PC (Rush Med College)
Am J Dis Child 144:670–676, 1990   5–6

Suicides by Age, Race, and Sex in the United States in 1985

Population Group

Age, y	Total	White Male	White Female	Nonwhite Male	Nonwhite Female
		No. of Suicides			
5-9	3	3	0	0	0
10-14	275	180	63	22	10
15-19	1849	1339	304	170	36
		Suicide Rate/100000 Population			
5-9	0.018	0.042	0	0	0
10-14	1.60	2.53	0.93	1.32	0.62
15-19	9.96	17.3	4.1	10.0	2.2

(Courtesy of Holinger PC: *Am J Dis Child* 144:670–676, 1990.)

Suicide is the second leading cause of death among 5- to 19-year-olds in the United States. The causes, impact, and preventability of childhood suicide in the United States were reviewed.

Childhood suicide rates increase with age (table). The rates for boys are higher than those for girls, and the rates for whites are higher than those for nonwhites. Childhood suicide rates tended to decrease in the 1940s and to increase from the mid-1950s to the late 1970s. For all groups other than white boys, the suicide rates have leveled off since then. Methods of suicide differ between older and younger children. Except for slightly higher rates of suicide by firearms, there have been no major changes in method since 1949. White boys, especially those aged 15 to 19 years, are at greatest risk.

Research suggests that most youths who kill themselves meet the criteria for diagnosable psychiatric disorders, such as affective disorder and personality disorders. A high percentage of suicide victims abuse alcohol or drugs. Comorbidity of affective disorders, personality disorders, or substance abuse seems particularly dangerous. One fourth to one half of youths who kill themselves have a family history of psychiatric disorder or suicide. An equal proportion made previous suicide attempts. The number and lethality of previous attempts correlate positively with an ultimate suicide. An increase in the proportion of teenagers in the population may create an increased risk of suicide in that cohort. Suicide cluster or contagion may also increase the risk of suicide among certain adolescent groups. Exposure to suicide through the media may be an additional risk factor, but this is controversial.

Primary prevention involves suicide prevention centers and agents, public education, training of professionals and paraprofessionals in suicidology, and understanding of population changes. Further research is needed on the identification of children at high risk, on factors that appear to enhance a suicidal outcome, and on the efficacy of various interventions.

▶ Katherine Kaufer Christoffel, M.D., MPH, Professor of Pediatrics, Northwestern University Medical School, comments:

▶ Injuries are the leading cause of death and disability during childhood after age 1 and in adolescence. Even under age 1 year, injury death rates are very high; however, they are not the leading cause of death in these children because deaths from perinatal causes and congenital anomalies are so common in infancy. This important fact is increasingly reflected in attention to and funding for pediatric injury prevention and treatment.

In 1989, the Centers for Disease Control's (CDC) Center for Environmental Health and Injury Control submitted a report to Congress on childhood injuries in the United States. That report was based in large measure on background papers prepared for CDC by expert consultants. Eight background reports addressed leading causes of pediatric injury (motor vehicle occupant injuries, drownings and near drownings, suicides, burns, brain injuries, pedestrian injuries, and violence), and 1 provided an overview of the price—in terms of mortality, morbidity, and costs—of this huge public health and medical problem. The June 1990 issue of the *American Journal of Diseases of Children* contains the CDC report to Congress and the 9 background papers, as well as several other papers on specific injury studies.

Each background paper reviews the epidemiology, costs, preventive approaches, and research needs relevant to the injury discussed. The importance of the information is indicated by several summary paragraphs from the CDC report:

"In 1986, more than 22,000 children aged 0 to 19 years died of injuries in the United States. These injuries included deaths from motor vehicle crashes, homicides, suicides, drownings, and fires and burns. Each year, an estimated 600,000 children are hospitalized for injuries, and almost 16 million children are seen in emergency departments for their injuries.

It is estimated that more than 30,000 children suffer permanent disabilities from injuries each year. The effects of such disabilities on children's development, daily living, and future productivity are great. The financial, emotional, and social effects of injuries on the family are enormous.

The costs of injuries to children are estimated to exceed $7.5 billion each year. Recent data suggest that these costs are considerably higher, with future productivity losses alone for fatalities in this age group amounting to more than $8 billion.

According to Fingerhut and Kleinman, "Childhood death rates in the United States are considerably higher than in other industrialized countries. Virtually all of the excess mortality among children in the United States is attributed to (unintentional) injury and violence." Differences in death rates among countries suggest that the United States' childhood death rates could be dramatically reduced by improving injury prevention and control. . . .

Priority injuries among children include those to motor vehicle occupants and those associated with homicide, assault and abuse, suicide and suicide attempts, drowning and near-drowning, pedestrian-vehicle collisions, and fire and burns. Among children, motor vehicles accounted for 47% of injury deaths in

1986. From 0 to 19 years of age, injuries to motor vehicle occupants are the major cause of death in the United States. Homicide is the second leading cause of injury death among children, accounting for 12.8%, while suicide ranks third with 9.6% of childhood injury deaths. Drowning, the fourth leading cause of injury death among children aged 0 to 19 years in the United States, accounts for 9.2% of injury deaths. Pedestrian injuries is the next ranking cause of injury death in children. . . . Fires and burns are the sixth major cause of injury death among persons aged 0 to 19 years, leading to 7.2% of deaths. Almost 30% of all childhood injury deaths result from a head injury. Injuries in the pediatric population disproportionately affect black and nonblack minority children. For some types of injury, black death rates are up to five times those for whites (1)."

For some of the injuries covered, the steps to prevention are clear; for example, increasing proper use of appropriate restraints for motor vehicle passengers through improved public education and laws (both content and enforcement). For others, no approach is proved, and all of the recommended options require further study. For these, progress toward prevention will require the implementation and evaluation of a variety of approaches (e.g., a combination of altered traffic controls and skill optimization may be needed to prevent pedestrian injuries).

Pediatricians have known for a long time that injuries are the greatest scourge facing their young patients. Increasingly, policy makers will be held accountable for failure to address this scourge. Inevitably, pediatricians will be called on to help with provision and coordination of care, research, prevention planning, and other matters. When these calls come, it will be helpful to have the June 1990 *American Journal of Diseases of Children* on the shelf for reference.—K.K. Christoffel, M.D.

Reference

1. Centers for Disease Control: *Am J Dis Child* 144:627, 1990.

Violent Death and Injury in US Children and Adolescents
Christoffel KK (Northwestern Univ, Chicago)
Am J Dis Child 144:697–706, 1990   5–7

Violence and suicide are leading causes of death among children. The literature on violent injury to American children and adolescents was reviewed. Homicide is among the leading causes of death in all age groups of childhood. Years of potential life lost increased by 44% in 1968– 1985, including a 93% increase in years of potential life lost because of firearm homicides. Youth homicide rates are peaking at progressively earlier ages, with successively lower peaks for successive cohorts. The 2 categories of childhood homicide are infantile and adolescent. Firearms are the leading means of death by homicide among children aged 12 years and younger. Nonfatal assaults by noncaregivers are about 100 times more frequent than homicides. Peer assaults include those by siblings and

Leading Categories of Causes of Death by Age: Children and Adolescents, 1985*

Cause of Death	<1 y Rank	<1 y Rate	1-4 y Rank	1-4 y Rate	5-9 y Rank	5-9 y Rate	10-14 y Rank	10-14 y Rate	15-19 y Rank	15-19 y Rate
Certain conditions originating in the perinatal period	1	508.6	9	1.0	9†	0.1	...	...	...	...
Accidents and adverse effects	6	23.7	1	20.0	1	11.9	1	13.2	1	44.2
Congenital anomalies	2	228.4	2	5.9	3	1.6	5	1.2	7	1.2
Malignant neoplasms†	+	+	3	3.8	2	3.6	2	3.4	4	4.6
Major cardiovascular disease	4	28.9	4	2.5	4	1.1	4	1.5	5	2.9
Homicide	10	5.3	5	2.4	5	1.0	4	1.5	3	8.6
Suicide	...	...	...	...	...	...	3	1.6	2	10.0
Symptoms, signs, and other ill-defined conditions	3	158.6	6	1.9	7	0.3	7	0.4	6	1.4
Meningitis	9	6.9	8	1.1	9†	0.1	10†	0.1	+	+
Pneumonia and influenza	5	18.8	7	1.5	6	0.5	8	0.3	8	0.5
Septicemia	7	8.1	10	0.6	9†	0.1	10†	0.1	+	+
Renal disease	8	7.4	+	+	9†	0.1	10†	0.1	+	+
Anemia	+	+	+	+	8	0.2	9	0.2	+	+
Chronic obstructive pulmonary disease and allied conditions	+	+	+	+	8	0.2	6	0.5	9	0.4
Asthma	+	+	+	+	8	0.2	7	0.4	10	0.3
All causes	...	1067.8	...	51.4	...	24.8	...	27.9	...	81.2

*The rates are per 100,000 population. Plus sign indicates a rate lower than the tenth leading category in age group.
†There are other categories with this same rate for this age group that are not in the top 10 causes for the other age groups.
(Courtesy of Christoffel KK: *Am J Dis Child* 144:697–706, 1990.)

nonsiblings. Rates of sibling violence are highest for younger children and for boys. The highly publicized phenomenon of "missing children" reflects mainly adolescent runaways and parent kidnappings. Risk-taking behaviors contribute to adolescent sexual assaults; 5%–7% of adolescent girls experience at least 1 sexual assault annually. Offenders are generally dates or boyfriends.

Analysis of data on childhood violence and homicide for 1985 revealed that 13% of all American murder victims in that year were aged 0–19 years, 60% of childhood homicide victims were aged 15–19 years, and 23% were aged younger than 5 years (table). Firearms were used in 55% of childhood homicides in 1985. Homicide rates for white boys are highest in infancy and the late teens; the pattern for white girls was similar. Homicide rates for blacks far exceed those for whites. For most categories of violent crime, the highest rates occur among adolescents aged 16–19 years, and the rate of simple assault is highest for those aged 12–15 years. Physical abuse exceeded sexual and emotional abuse at all ages. Surprisingly little is known about the origins of childhood violence or its prevention. The overriding unanswered question is: When will the control of such violence become a national priority?

▶ At the Society for Pediatric Research/American Pediatric Society/Ambulatory Pediatric Association meetings last spring, J. T. Maurer, M. J. Bartel, and R. R. Tanz had an abstract entitled, "Getting Away With Murder?: A Study of Unintentional Childhood Shootings." I think the data from that abstract identify 1 of the important issues regarding childhood injuries. The authors ask, "Is anyone held accountable when children are shot unintentionally (i.e., without intent for anyone to be injured), or are such shootings considered the cost of gun ownership in our society?" Using a database consisting of children less than 17 years of age who were treated at a single hospital between 1980 and 1990, these investigators identified 78 shooting victims, a quarter of whom were shot unintentionally. The vast majority of these shootings involved handguns. One fifth of the children died, and 40% suffered neurologic impairment. Most victims were male (68%) and nonwhite (53%). Of the victims, 58% were less than 10 years of age. The shooters were older: 79% were over 10 years of age, and 18 of the 19 were male. Although at least 11 local and state laws covering shootings were violated in the majority of cases, police were ambivalent about filing charges. Charges ultimately were filed against the shooter in only 21% of cases. Just half of these individuals were convicted. Gun owners were charged in 42% of the cases, but fewer than half were convicted. No one was ever imprisoned, and fines averaged only $150.

To look at the question from a different point of view, Y. D. Senturia, A. M. Teuscher, K. K. Christoffel, and the Pediatric Practice Research Group in Chicago presented an abstract at the same meeting that attempted to determine what proportion of households with children who go to pediatricians for routine care have firearms in the home. The Pediatric Practice Research Group includes private practitioners who care for a wide diversity of children with respect to socioeconomic backgrounds, from poor to extremely wealthy. Family ownership of a gun varied among practices, ranging from 6% of families to 53% of families (mean 29%) and by area of residence. Urban families had a 20% chance of having a gun in the house, suburban homes 31%, and rural homes 60%. The majority of firearms were stored in the bedroom. Although half of handguns were kept locked up, a high percentage (24%) were kept loaded all the time. Rifles tended not to be locked up, but fewer than 5% were kept loaded.

To say all this differently, the number of guns out there, loaded and ready to injure children, is enormous. The Brady Bill came none too soon.

There is an anonymous limerick that comes to mind when I think of the senselessness of the violence associated with handguns. It goes as follows:

"There was a little man, and he had a little gun,
And his bullets were made of lead, lead, lead;
He went to the brook, and saw a little duck,
And shot it through the head, head, head."

If anyone out there is aware of the name of the author of this limerick, let me know. I'd like to meet him or her.—J.A. Stockman, III, M.D.

Should You Cancel the Operation When a Child Has an Upper Respiratory Tract Infection?
Cohen MM, Cameron CB (Univ of Manitoba, Winnipeg)
Anesth Analg 72:282–288, 1991   5–8

Postponing an operation in a child with an upper respiratory tract infection (URI) is a common practice, but this practice may not always be feasible or practical. A large pediatric anesthesia database was used to compare the rates of intraoperative, recovery room, and postoperative adverse events in 1,283 children with a preoperative URI and 20,876 children without URI.

Children with a URI were 2 to 7 times more likely to have respiratory-related adverse events than children without URI (table). Other than significant disruptions in temperature regulations, children with URI were not at risk for any other adverse events. The increased risk for adverse respiratory events could not be attributed to the patients' age, physical status, site of operation, or emergency or elective status. However, the risk of respiratory complicatons was increased 11-fold if a child had a URI and had endotracheal anesthesia, compared with children without URI who had not undergone tracheal intubation.

The administration of anesthesia to a child with URI remains a controversial issue. General anesthesia in children with URI is associated with an increased risk of respiratory adverse events, and therefore these children require more observation and management during the perioperative period.

▶ Dr. Steven C. Hall, Associate Professor of Clinical Anesthesia, Northwestern University Medical School, comments:

▶ One of the most common and controversial clinical dilemmas facing pediatricians, anesthesiologists, and surgeons is the child with a possible URI. Should an elective surgical procedure be postponed if there is a URI present?

The average child experiences between 3 and 6 colds in a given year, with the prevalence greater from September to April. Because the acute phase usu-

Perioperative Events by Upper Respiratory Infection Status

	URI (n = 1,283)		No URI (n = 20,876)			
	n	%	n	%		Relative risk (95% CI)
Intraoperative events						
None	1,119	87.21	19,278	92.35	0.94	(0.89, 1.00)
Vomiting	12	0.94	131	0.63	1.49	(0.83, 2.67)
Arrhythmia	83	6.47	1,081	5.18	1.25	(1.00, 1.56)
Hypotension	3	0.23	26	0.12	1.88	(0.60, 5.83)
Temperature regulation	2	0.16	10	0.05	3.25	(0.80, 13.21)
Cardiac arrest	0		5	0.02	—	
Airway obstruction	44	3.43	158	0.76	4.53	(3.25, 6.31)*
Other respiratory	35	2.73	157	0.75	3.64	(2.52, 5.22)*
Drug complication	2	0.16	49	0.23	0.66	(0.18, 2.48)
Surgical	3	0.23	70	0.34	0.70	(0.23, 2.09)
Death	0		1		—	
Recovery room events						
None	1,075	83.79	18,290	87.61	0.96	(0.90, 1.02)
Laryngospasm	28	2.18	358	1.71	1.27	(0.87, 1.86)
Vomiting	60	4.68	1,308	6.27	0.75	(0.58, 0.97)*
Cardiovascular	0		38	0.18	—	
Temperature	12	0.94	131	0.63	1.49	(0.83, 2.67)
Airway obstruction	89	6.94	628	3.01	2.31	(1.85, 2.88)*
Other respiratory	26	2.03	111	0.53	3.83	(2.49, 5.82)*
Drug-related	1	0.08	34	0.16	0.50	(0.08, 2.77)
Surgical	14	1.09	265	1.27	0.86	(0.51, 1.46)
Postoperative events †						
Nausea and vomiting	193	19.67	4,175	26.00	0.76	(0.65, 0.87)*
Sore throat	11	1.12	195	1.21	0.93	(0.51, 1.68)
Headache	8	0.82	181	1.13	0.73	(0.36, 1.45)
Croup	37	3.77	107	0.67	5.66	(3.90, 8.21)*
Other respiratory	60	6.12	135	0.84	7.29	(5.37, 9.85)*
Temperature	33	3.36	251	1.56	2.15	(1.50, 3.09)*
Cardiovascular	3	0.31	29	0.18	1.69	(0.55, 5.23)
Surgical	22	2.24	284	1.77	1.26	(0.82, 1.95)
Other	14	1.43	259	1.61	0.89	(0.52, 1.50)
Death	0		1	0.01	—	

*$P \leq .05$ for URI compared with no-URI group.
†Rates per 100 charts reviewed. N = 981 for URI-only group; N = 16,055 for no-URI group.
(Courtesy of Cohen MM, Cameron CB: Anesth Analg 72:282–288, 1991.)

ally lasts 4–10 days, and the recovery period for normal respiratory function approaches 5 weeks (1), there may be little time for some children to have elective surgery performed when they are not in either an acute or recovery phase. Also, it is occasionally difficult to differentiate a URI from allergic rhinitis, chronic rhinorrhea related to teething or an underlying condition such as a cleft palate, or the prodrome of another infection, such as chicken pox or measles.

An increased incidence of laryngospasm, bronchospasm, desaturation, coughing, unexplained temperature elevation, atelectasis, croup, and pneumonia have been documented in children with a URI undergoing elective surgery (2–4). The concern about these complications has traditionally led practitioners to postpone surgery in children thought to have a cold. Although the likelihood of these complications had been widely accepted in the past, recent studies questioned the assumptions.

Tait and Knight, in a series of widely publicized papers, suggested that the presence of an uncomplicated URI does not increase complications for surgery

(5, 6). They did not find an increase in morbidity of children with URI symptoms having myringotomies under mask anesthesia, but they did suggest that the recovery period after the acute phase was associated with an increased incidence of complications. Interestingly, both children with a current URI and those with a recent URI exhibited significant desaturation during transport and recovery, demonstrating the need for supplemental oxygen in the recovery room.

The studies by Tait and Knight raised great controversy for 2 reasons. First, they struck at a "sacred cow" of anesthesia practice, the cancellation of surgery in the child with a URI. More importantly, the patients studied were not a population most people would cancel in the first place. The signs used to diagnose a URI in the studies were typical of nasopharyngitis or chronic nasal congestion, but not of a systemic illness. Children with productive cough, sneezing, hoarseness, fever, or rhonchi were excluded from the study. Recurrent signs of nasopharyngitis are quite typical in children with chronic serous otitis, recurrent tonsillitis, or an unrepaired cleft palate, and they are not usually grounds for postponement of elective anesthesia.

The study by Cohen approaches the problem from a demographic viewpoint, using quality assurance data (7). The study found marked increases in both intraoperative and postoperative complications, primarily respiratory, in children with a URI. The authors recommend postponement of surgery in children with signs of an acute URI, especially those under 5 years of age.

The various studies, including this one, suggest a 2-tiered approach. Children with an isolated nasopharyngitis, without signs of systemic or lower airway involvement, can probably undergo minor elective procedures without increased risk. However, surgery in the child with signs of fever, hoarseness, productive cough, "fussiness," purulent discharge, or rhonchi should be postponed until the child is asymptomatic. Also, because of the potential for residual atelectasis or reactive bronchospasm, any child with the history of a recent URI is a candidate for continuous measurement of oxygenation and supplemental oxygen in the recovery period.— S.C. Hall, M.D.

References

1. Betts EK: Pediatric outpatient anesthesia, in Rogers MD (ed): *Current Practice in Anesthesiology.* Toronto, BC Becker Inc, 1988, pp 137–139.
2. McGill WA, et al: *Anesth Analg* 58:33–333, 1979.
3. Olsson GL, Hallen B: *Acta Anaesthesiol Scand* 28:567–575, 1984.
4. DeSoto H, et al: *Anesthesiology* 68:276–279, 1988.
5. Tait AR, Knight PR: *Can J Anaesth* 34:300–333, 1987.
6. Tait AR, Knight PR: *Anesthesiology* 67:930–935, 1987.
7. Cohen MM, Cameron CB: *Anesth Analg* 72:282–288, 1991.

Burns From Hot Oil and Grease: A Public Health Hazard
Schubert W, Ahrenholz DH, Solem LD (Univ Hosp of Cleveland; St Paul-Ramsey Med Ctr, St Paul)
J Burn Care Rehabil 11:558–562, 1990   5–9

Fig 5–1.—A 2-year-old toddler reaching for a frying pan. The pan on the counter is just high enough for the contents to be out of sight and just low enough for him to be able to reach it. Even the smallest child would be able to reach the electrical cord. (Courtesy of Schubert W, Ahrenholz DH, Solem LD: *J Burn Care Rehabil* 11:558–562, 1990.)

There is little public awareness of the potential for burn injuries from hot oil and grease. The incidence, cause, and morbidity of burns caused by hot oil and grease were studied.

The charts of 1,818 patients hospitalized for burn injuries during a 10-year period were reviewed. Eighty-five (4.7%) burn injuries were caused by hot grease or oil. Mean age of the patients was 20 years (range, 6 months–64 years), but 34% of the patients were less than 8 years old. Seventy-eight of these burns occurred at home. The most common circumstance involved a child grabbing the handle or electric cord of a frying pan and pulling the hot oil down onto himself or herself (Fig 5–1). In adults, burns occurred while transporting hot oil or grease during a grease fire.

Mean total body surface area of second- and third-degree burns was

11.5% (range, .5–40%), and 58% of patients required split-thickness skin grafting. Three patients required intubation, and 1 required tracheostomy. Average length of hospital stay was 19.6 days.

Burns caused by hot oil or grease are common and may be on the increase. These burns are associated with considerable morbidity. The high boiling point, high viscosity, and potential combustibility of oil increase the potential soft-tissue damage, compared with scalds from hot water. Public education is needed to emphasize the hazards of burns from hot oil and grease. The dangers of children pulling on an appliance, the dangers of transporting hot oil, the importance of supervision while children are cooking, and the proper management of grease fires should be emphasized, particularly in homes with young children.

▶ It is curious that cooking foods like french fries in a pan with hot oil or in a deep frier is such a common American tradition. There seems to be little public awareness of the potential for burn injuries associated with this form of food preparation and the consequent impact on children. The picture of the 2-year-old from this article should be copied and used as part of anticipatory guidance by primary care providers. It might help to deter the "it could never happen to me" attitude of some parents.

At the same time that we are learning more about public health hazards related to burns, we are learning a lot more about how to treat them. Witness the recent success of burn grafts with cultured human skin, keratinocytes, and artificial skin, and most recently, the effects of recombinant human growth hormone in helping severely burned children. Herndon et al. (1) showed that if you administer recombinant human growth hormone (.2 mg/kg/day) to severely burned children, wound healing improves remarkably, and the previous hospital stay of 46 days decreases to just 32 days.

Well, parents, you have a choice. The choice seems fairly simple. Start learning about human recombinant growth hormone and in vitro cultivation of dermal cells, or better yet, learn to put things on the back burner.—J.A. Stockman, III, M.D.

Reference

1. Herndon DN, et al: *Ann Surg* 212:424, 1990.

Unintentional Injuries to Students at School
Langley JD, Chalmers D, Collins B (Univ of Otago, Dunedin, New Zealand; Dept of Education, Wellington, Dunedin)
J Paediatr Child Health 26:323–328, 1990   5–10

Unintentional injuries at school are a significant public health problem in New Zealand and elsewhere. The development of injury prevention policies has been hindered by a lack of national data on the circumstances of such injuries. The present study was designed to determine the incidence, nature, and circumstances of school injuries that resulted in death or hospitalization. The population at risk included full-time students aged 5 to 18 years.

National mortality data for 1977 through 1986 were analyzed. Coroners' files were reviewed to obtain details about the circumstances of the injuries. Cases that required hospitalization were identified from the national hospital discharge summary for 1986.

In the period reviewed 15 fatalities were identified. The circumstances of death were diverse, with the most frequent event being a fall (4 cases). There were 1,013 first admissions to the hospital, for an overall incidence rate of 152 admissions per 100,000 students per year. Injury rates decreased with increasing age. Boys had higher rates of injury than girls at all ages. More than three fourths of all injuries were fractures of the upper and lower extremities and intracranial injury. The 2 major causes of injury, falls and incidents involving striking against or being struck by a person or object, accounted for 89% of all incidents. The use of playground equipment and involvement in sports were 2 of the more common factors in many of the incidents.

School injury prevention policies should focus on children in their first 2 years of school. These policies should give special attention to falls from playground equipment, provision of equipment for sports, and sporting activities that minimize physical contacts. Policies should also emphasize the establishment of standardized injury referral procedures, first-aid training, and a standardized injury reporting system.

▶ From the day she started kindergarten, our youngest, Meredith Ashley, has said that schools weren't safe for your health. This was initially considered to be a subtle form of 5-year-old sports avoidance. Nonetheless, this past year, at age 13, during a mandatory gym class, as she walked unassisted (she should have been) on a balance beam, she fell off and fractured her radius. Maybe she has been right all along, and that is the point of the article abstracted above.

One of the most difficult tasks we have as parents is to transfer our supervision responsibility to the school. When doing this, we have to be certain that the school environment is a safe one. In a country as tiny as New Zealand, an average of 5 children are admitted to hospitals each day as a result of an injury suffered at school. Not all of these injuries occurred on the playground. In a large city such as Chicago, the injuries are much more likely to be student-to-student related, but that is still, in part, a school system's responsibility.

As parents, be proactive, but don't necessarily rely on your school board to solve the problem for you. My experience with the Chicago School Board has been fairly consistent. Given a sufficient number of people and an inadequate amount of time, they can create insurmountable opposition to the most inconsequential idea.

. . . Thank you New Zealand for telling a tale out of school.—J.A. Stockman, III, M.D.

Drownings in Minnesota, 1980–85: A Population-Based Study
Hedberg K, Gunderson PD, Vargas C, Osterholm MT, MacDonald KL (Minnesota Dept of Health, Minneapolis; Centers for Disease Control, Atlanta)
Am J Public Health 80:1071–1074, 1990   5–11

Drowning is the third most common cause of fatal, unintentional injury in the United States. Because a population-based incidence rate provides an accurate estimate of the risk of drowning, a population-based study of drowning, with emphasis on outdoor and recreational drownings, was conducted in Minnesota. Data were obtained from death certificates maintained by the Minnesota Center for Health Statistics and from fatal injury reports filed with the Minnesota Department of Natural Resources. Drowning rates were calculated using population data extrapolated from the 1980 census. The risk of drowning was estimated by the ratio of drownings to the number of water-related activities.

There were 541 drownings identified, for an annual incidence of 2.1 per 100,000 person-years. Mean annual incidence for males was 3.7 per 100,000 person-years, which was 5.3 times higher than that for females. Incidence rates were highest for persons 15 to 30 years old and for persons less than 5 years old.

Of the drownings, 62% occurred during the summer months, May through August, and involved boating (42%) and swimming (35%) events. Of the 135 drownings involving boating accidents, only 10% occurred while a personal flotation device was being used. Another 11% of drownings occurred during the winter months, December through February, and involved snowmobiles and motor vehicles breaking through ice on lakes and waterways (71%). The risk of drowning was highest during spring (March and April) and fall (October and November), when the ice on the lakes and waterway surfaces is starting to freeze or melt and is likely to be unsafe. These population-based data on drownings are vital to understand the causes of drowning and can be used to target prevention strategies, particularly in northern climates.

▶ This report from Minnesota is a bit skewed, although nonetheless quite interesting. You have to know a little bit about Minnesota to know why the data are so skewed. Minnesota is known as the "Land of 10,000 Lakes." Water covers 7,353 miles or 9.2% of the state's surface area. Lakes and waterways in Minnesota provide 4.2 million people with numerous recreational opportunities throughout the year, including swimming and boating in the summer and ice fishing in the winter. To say this somewhat differently, drownings in Minnesota are hardly typical of drownings in Sheboygan.

The national data on drownings show that drowning is the third leading cause of death for children aged 0–4 years and is second among unintentional injuries for older children. Throughout the country, swimming pool drownings are much more typical than lake drownings. The cost of caring for children with swimming pool-related accidents is currently estimated at between $460 and $650 million per year (1). The Minnesota contrast is the interesting seasonal variation in the causes of drowning, from falling through the ice in the middle of winter to boating injuries in the summer. Obviously, in Minnesota, to every season there is a turn.

What else have we learned this past year about drowning injuries? Actually, we have learned a great deal. We now know much more about the hazards of pool solar covers (2). Solar covers are the bubbly looking things that cost several hundred dollars (and look like they ought to be used as 5-cent packing material) and are used to cover pools to keep the heat in. Unfortunately, they can be quite dangerous. They are deceptive, giving the appearance of being able to be walked on by a 3-year-old or your family pet.

We also know that hot tub, spa, and whirlpool risks are unique to certain locations and populations. For example, if you are white and live in southern California, you have 2 chances per million of drowning in a hot tub, jacuzzi, or whirlpool. For much of the rest of the country, the risk is with our bathtub (3).

Personally, I think most in-house drownings occur in toilets, not bathtubs. This is simply a reflection of one of Murphy's Laws, which states that anything that falls onto the floor of a bathroom is as likely as not to bounce into the toilet.—J.A. Stockman, III, M.D.

References

1. Wintemute GJ: *Am J Dis Child* 144:663, 1990.
2. Norman J: *Pediatrics* 85:1114, 1990.
3. Shinaberger CS, et al: *Am J Public Health* 80:613, 1990.

Lisch Nodules in Neurofibromatosis Type 1
Lubs M-LE, Bauer MS, Formas ME, Djokic B (Univ of Miami; Miami Children's Hosp)
N Engl J Med 324:1264–1266, 1991   5–12

The most common clinical feature of neurofibromatosis type 1 in adults is the presence of Lisch nodules. In children, neurofibromatosis 1 can be difficult to diagnose. The prevalence of Lisch nodules in patients with neurofibromatosis 1 and their usefulness in its diagnosis were investigated in 167 patients, including 5 children with probable neurofibromatosis.

Lisch nodules were found in 73.7%. Only 5% of children younger than 3 years had Lisch nodules. Among those aged 3 to 4 years, the prevalence was 42%; among those aged 5 to 6 years, it was 55%. All 65 patients who were aged 21 years or more had Lisch nodules. The prevalence of Lisch nodules was higher than the prevalence of neurofibromas in all age groups except the youngest. Lisch nodules were never the only clinical sign of the disorder; café au lait spots were usually present as well (Figs 5–2 and 5–3).

In patients younger than 21 years, Lisch nodules are more likely to be present than neurofibromas, and they may therefore be helpful in making the diagnosis of neurofibromatosis 1 in younger patients. Because there

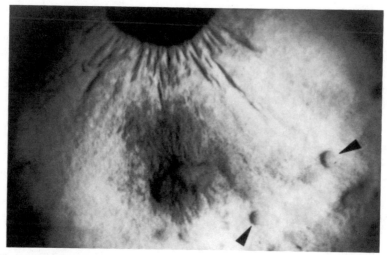

Fig 5–2.—Lisch nodules *(arrows)* on the iris of a 7-year-old patient with neurofibromatosis 1. The nodules are dome-shaped hamartomatous lesions that are clear to yellow or brown. (Courtesy of Lubs M-LE, Bauer MS, Formas ME, et al: *N Engl J Med* 324:1264–1266, 1991.)

appears to be no association between Lisch nodules and the overall clinical severity of neurofibromatosis 1, the presence or absence of the nodules cannot be used to predict its clinical course.

▶ Don't discount the importance of the Lisch nodule in the diagnosis and subclassification of neurofibromatosis. The tiny iris lesion known as the Lisch nodule is a critical part of how we look at the neurofibromatoses. They allow us to discriminate between types of neurofibromatosis and to distinguish between persons who bear a mutation at the neurofibromatosis 1 locus on the long arm of chromosome 17 and those who do not. The Lisch nodule has proved to be a valuable and reliable indicator of neurofibromatosis 1.

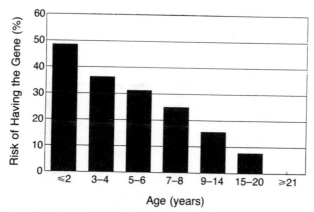

Fig 5–3.—Estimated risk of having the gene for neurofibromatosis 1 according to age in children with no Lisch nodules in whom the diagnosis was suspected but not proved. (Courtesy of Lubs M-LE, Bauer MS, Formas ME, et al: *N Engl J Med* 324:1264–1266, 1991.)

Just how reliable an indicator is the subject of the article by Lubs et al. abstracted above. Café au lait spots can be seen in many disorders, as can neurofibromas. If you have café au lait spots, neurofibromas, *and* Lisch nodules, however, you have what used to be called von Recklinghausen's disease, now more appropriately called neurofibromatosis 1. Thus, a simple, careful eye examination can be as useful as a DNA study for the diagnosis of this specific disorder.

A warning is in order. Dr. Vincent Riccardi, who probably has one of the largest experiences dealing with neurofibromatosis in children, cautions us in an editorial comment in *The New England Journal of Medicine* (1) that young children may not yet have had an opportunity to develop their Lisch nodules. It is his own experience over 13 years that some youngsters who are originally free of Lisch nodules eventually do acquire them later in life.

It has been 54 years since Professor Lisch described his now famous "bumps on the iris" in 1937. If you haven't started looking for them in patients with café au lait spots, the time to start is now.—J.A. Stockman, III, M.D.

Reference

1. Riccardi V: *N Engl J Med* 324:1285, 1991.

Hair Dryer Burns in Children
Prescott PR (Univ of Texas Southwestern Med Ctr, Dallas)
Pediatrics 86:692–697, 1990   5–13

Child abuse by burning is often reported in the literature. About 10% of all abusive injuries are inflicted burns. Three children burned with home hair dryers were studied.

The children were 3 girls, aged 16 months, 16 months, and 3½ years, respectively. The first child's burns were determined to have happened

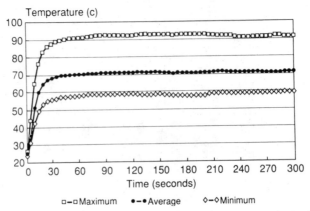

Fig 5–4.—High heat setting, 3-inch distance. (Courtesy of Prescott PR: *Pediatrics* 86:692–697, 1990.)

Time Required to Heat and Cool to 54° C (Seconds)

Dryer	Time to Reach 54°C			Time to Cool to 54°C After Heat Turned Off
	Low, 3-in	High, 3-in	High, on Grid	
1 (Case 1)	—*	9	4	304
2 (Case 2)	—†	16	3	172
3	—†	17	16	300
4	—†	9	7	210
5	255	9	6	255
6	290	18	9	130
7	—*	23	9	210
8	—†	22	9	274
9	50	8	6	186
10	—†	13	3	160

*No "low" setting.
†Never reached 54° C.
(Courtesy of Prescott PR: *Pediatrics* 86:692–697, 1990.)

accidentally while a babysitter was attempting to dry the infant's hair with a hair dryer. Because of a lack of previous experience with hair-dryer burns, other causes were suspected at first. In the second 2 cases, the burns were not accidental. The characteristics of each case, including other signs of abuse in the second and third child, aided in the final determination of accidental or nonaccidental injury.

Home hair dryers were tested to determine their heat output. The dryers quickly generated temperatures exceeding 110° C at the highest heat settings. After the dryers were turned off, the protective grills retained enough heat to cause full-thickness burns for as long as 2 minutes (Fig 5–4, table).

Accidental hair dryer burns caused by another person are possible. Such burns result only from the hot air. Children may also accidentally burn themselves by touching the protective grid while the dryer is on or just after it has been turned off. Deliberate burns are more likely to exhibit a full grid pattern and be deeper than accidental burns. Physicians must consider how consistent the burn is with the history, psychosocial factors, family makeup, past disciplinary practices, and previous Child Protective Services referrals in judging whether a hair dryer burn is accidental or deliberate.

▶ I have seen hair dryers used for everything from doing the final touches on a dog's bath, to melting frozen door locks, to drying fingernails (not my own). Given the attachment we have to them in our society, it's not likely that we will ever see a banning of them. What we need are more safety features built into them.

If you read this report carefully, you will learn that the heat of a hair dryer is sufficient to boil water (if you didn't electrocute yourself first). It's a wonder that the Underwriter's Laboratory has let these products get as far along as they have without paying attention to reports such as that of Prescott.

My prediction is that if appropriate safety features were engineered into every newly manufactured hair dryer, all the risks mentioned above would be eliminated within 6 months or less. That is based on the additional observation that the average life span of a hair dryer is 4.1 ± 1.9 months (for your average $15.95, 1,500-watt el cheapo, as currently passes the K Mart checkout counter).—J.A. Stockman, III, M.D.

Birth Interval Among Breast-Feeding Women Not Using Contraceptives
Rosner AE, Schulman SK (Schulman Med Associates, Maimonides Med Ctr, Brooklyn)
Pediatrics 86:747–752, 1990   5–14

The duration of postpartum amenorrhea and infertility appear to be affected by breast-feeding. The magnitude of this effect, however, is difficult to establish. Determining the effect would require a survey of a population with a large proportion of breast-feeding mothers who usually breast-feed for extended periods and who do not practice other methods of contraception. Such a population was found in the well-organized, ultra-Orthodox Jewish communities in New York City.

A questionnaire about birth interval in relation to formula-feeding and breast-feeding experiences was given to 112 Orthodox Jewish mothers. Thirty women used formula, and 236 breast-fed. None of the women used other methods of birth control. The mothers who breast-fed had longer birth intervals than those who used formula. Birth intervals preceded by breast-feeding were longer than those preceded by formula-feeding of the previous infant. Among breast-feeding mothers, there was a significant positive correlation between duration of breast-feeding and length of lactational amenorrhea and total birth interval. The age at which night feeding stopped was less strongly associated with lactational amenorrhea and total birth interval (table).

The duration of breast-feeding and of lactational amenorrhea influence the return of the mother's ability to conceive. The exact nature of this effect seems to be a combination of factors related to the quality of breast-feeding and the individual hormonal system of the mother.

Comparison of Matched Formula-Feeding and Breast-Feeding Experiences*

Characteristic	Formula-fed (n = 30)	Breast-fed (n = 30)	Statistically significant
Maternal height, in	63.9 (1.8)	63.9 (2.6)	No
Maternal weight, lb	144.7 (15.6)	136.8 (24.4)	No
Birth order of child	1.7 (0.9)	1.7 (0.9)	No
Age of mother at child's birth, y	21.5 (1.7)	22.1 (1.6)	No
Birth interval, mo	15.8 (4.9)	23.9 (10.0)	$P < .001$

*Values are mean (SD).
(Courtesy of Rosner AE, Schulman SK: *Pediatrics* 86:747–752, 1990.)

Anogenital Warts in Children: Clinical and Virologic Evaluation for Sexual Abuse
Cohen BA, Honig P, Androphy E (Univ of Pittsburgh; Univ of Pennsylvania; New England Med Ctr, Boston)
Arch Dermatol 126:1575–1580, 1990   5–15

The sharply rising incidence of anogenital warts in adults since 1980 is accompanied by an increase in reports of such lesions in young children, possibly as a result of sexual abuse. Seventy-three children seen in a 2-year period with anogenital warts were assessed for sexual abuse. One fourth of the group were aged 1 year and under. Females constituted 60% of the series.

Perianal and perigenital lesions typically were 2-mm to 3-mm papules

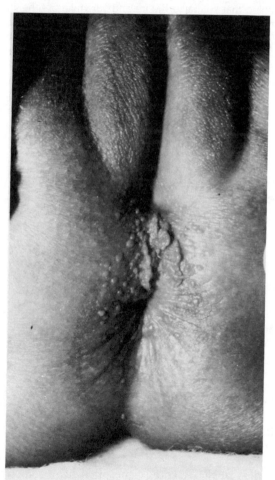

Fig 5–5.—Multiple condyloma and 2-mm to 3-mm flat papules in a 2.5-year-old girl. (Courtesy of Cohen BA, Honig P, Androphy E: *Arch Dermatol* 126:1575–1580, 1990.)

resembling flat warts (Fig 5–5). Warts on the scrotum and buttocks and in the inguinal region usually were larger discrete papules. Extragenital warts were present in 18% of patients. Sexual abuse was suspected or documented in 7 children. In half of the cases a close contact with warts was established and contacts most often had lesions on their extremities. Seven children reportedly had anal and/or genital lesions at birth.

Ascending infection may be a common source of involvement by human papillomavirus. Anogenital warts can be acquired at the time of delivery through an infected birth canal, from inadvertent contact with genital secretions, from direct contact with genital or extragenital warts, or through sexual abuse. Nonvenereal sources should be considered when lesions begin before age 3 years.

▶ There is nothing that will raise the ire and adrenalin of a health-care provider faster than finding warts in a child's anogenital area. As these authors point out, however, only in a minority of cases will these turn out to be the result of sexual abuse. Nonetheless, when you find them, you had better do some detective work.

The link between cervical dysplasia and cancer and the human papillomavirus is now an established and no longer controversial topic in adults. What we don't know, however, are the long-term implications for children who have this virus at an early age. Cohen and Honig would do well to keep track of these 70 prepubertal children to provide us with an answer to this long-term outcome question.

Read the excellent review of Charles F. Johnson (1) on the confusing ways in which sexual abuse presents itself clinically and anatomically. We need a lot more knowledge in this area, and Dr. Johnson appropriately quotes Goethe in this regard: "We see what we look for; we look for what we know."—J.A. Stockman, III, M.D.

Reference

1. Johnson CF: *Pediatrics* 87:722, 1991.

Aarskog Syndrome
Porteous MEM, Goudie DR (Duncan Guthrie Inst of Med Genetics, Glasgow, Scotland)
J Med Genet 28:44–47, 1991   5–16

The Aarskog syndrome, or facio-digital-genital syndrome, was first described in 1970 and is known to exist in 12 subjects living in western Scotland. However, the disorder is benign and consequently underdiagnosed. The syndrome has been assigned to the X chromosome, but this remains uncertain.

Female carriers of the Aarskog gene often have some features of the syndrome (table). They usually are short and many have hand or facial anomalies. Male patients with the syndrome share a very similar facial

Fig 5–6.—Three brothers with Aarskog syndrome. (Courtesy of Porteous MEM, Goudie DR: *J Med Genet* 28:44–47, 1991.)

appearance (Fig 5–6). Hypertelorism, a short nose with a wide philtrum, maxillary hypoplasia, and a broad nasal bridge are among the cardinal features of the syndrome.

Short stature in this syndrome is characterized by an increased upper-

Clinical Features in Aarskog Syndrome		
Clinical features	Glasgow series	Published cases
Hypertelorism	16/17	73/83
Ptosis	8/17	33/64
Downward slanting palpebral fissures	10/17	33/64
Short nose	12/17	30/45
Wide philtrum	12/17	76/87
Maxillary hypoplasia	12/17	72/87
Anteverted nares	14/17	28/36
Abnormal auricles	9/17	76/86
Broad nasal bridge	17/17	33/58
Crease below lower lip	8/17	72/82
Widow's peak	8/17	44/51
Short/broad hands	14/17	49/60
Brachydactyly	13/17	50/60
Syndactyly	9/17	36/56
Clinodactyly	15/17	42/65
Short 5th finger	15/17	22/28
Joint laxity	10/17	36/47
Single palmar crease	13/17	25/38
Broad, short, bulbous toes	12/17	21/28
Short stature (3rd centile)	15/17	71/81
Shawl scrotum	9/17	65/79
Cryptorchidism	6/17	54/77
Inguinal herniae	11/17	47/77
Prominent umbilicus	10/17	6/7
Pectus excavatum	3/17	31/57

(Courtesy of Porteous MEM, Goudie DR: *J Med Genet* 28:44–47, 1991.)

to-lower segment ratio. Scoliosis has been described, as well as splayed toes and metatarsus adductus. A shawl or overriding scrotum is characteristic, but it is not necessarily a constant feature; it is much less obvious with advancing age. Controlled observations reveal normal intelligence, and life expectancy is normal.

The differential diagnosis of Aarskog syndrome includes the Noonan and Robinow syndromes. Cardiac defects and major genital abnormalities are not present in the Aarskog syndrome.

▶ The rationale for including at least 1 syndrome in each YEAR BOOK is to make us aware of the unusual. I always have difficulty telling whether or not a certain set of features or characteristics in a given individual is indicative of a syndrome or merely the kind of variation that you see among your own relatives. I would suspect that the Aarskog syndrome was not described until 1970 for this very reason.

I hope that I have not alienated every member of my family such that I will never be invited again to a family reunion. Actually, that would be OK; family reunions are all relative anyway.—J.A. Stockman, III, M.D.

Effects of Medicaid Eligibility Expansion on Prenatal Care and Pregnancy Outcome in Tennessee
Piper JM, Ray WA, Griffin MR (Vanderbilt Univ)
JAMA 264:2219–2223, 1990   5–17

On the premise that removal of financial barriers to obtaining prenatal care by expanding Medicaid eligibility would reduce infant mortality in the United States, the federal government extended pregnancy coverage to include low-income, previously ineligible married women during their pregnancy. In July 1985 the Tennessee Medicaid program made this major regulatory change, and its effects on the use of early prenatal care and on the adverse pregnancy outcomes of low birth weight and neonatal death were studied.

Vital statistics on live singleton births in Tennessee for 12 months before the change (July 1, 1984 through June 30, 1985) and for 12 months after the change had been in effect for 1 year (July 7, 1986 through June 30, 1987) were linked with the Medicaid enrollment files to determine outcome rates. Data were not analyzed for the 12-month transition period immediately after the regulatory change.

The proportion of mothers enrolled in Medicaid increased from 22% in the year before the Medicaid expansion to 29% in the year after the transition. The increase was most pronounced among white married women younger than age 25 years with less than 12 years of education, among whom enrollment increased by 18%.

Compared with the year before the Medicaid change, there were no significant improvements in the use of prenatal care in the first trimester, the rates of very low and moderately low birth weight, and neonatal mortality, even among mothers for whom the coverage change was the greatest. An analysis of the timing of Medicaid enrollment relative to the delivery of the infant showed that two thirds of the mothers who enrolled did so after the first trimester.

These data fail to support the premise that expansion of Medicaid coverage per se will increase early use of prenatal care and decrease adverse outcomes of pregnancy. It appears that reduction in unfavorable perinatal outcomes in the United States may require addressing both the financial and nonfinancial barriers to prenatal care.

▶ Do you sense a mixed message when it comes to Medicaid coverage? Originally, Medicaid provided medical care for recipients of Aid to Families With Dependent Children, primarily unmarried mothers and their children. Pregnant women who were married were generally ineligible. A series of legislative changes enacted in the 1980s created a new category of eligible individuals: pregnant women whose eligibility was based solely on financial need compared with nationally set income criteria. More recent legislation on July 1, 1989, required that states cover pregnant women and infants with family incomes up to 75% of the poverty level, and on April 1, 1990, the requirement was 133% of the poverty level. This study from Tennessee suggests that, despite Medicaid expansion, the effects on use of prenatal care and pregnancy outcome are not nearly as positive as might have been expected. What are the reasons for this?

The reasons are probably multitudinous, including trying to get access to records and information. Nonetheless, the punch line is that findings do not support the premise that expansion of Medicaid coverage per se will increase early use of prenatal services and decrease adverse outcomes. Individuals eligible for Medicaid must overcome the apathy that has been generated about the program and its merits. One important nonfinancial barrier to prenatal care is the availability of providers who accept Medicaid patients. A 1985 National Survey of Fellows of the American College of Obstetrics and Gynecology suggested that only 63% of members provided services to Medicaid patients (1).

Despite the fact that eligibility for Medicaid has improved, the number of poor children has increased by 75% in the last 1 to 2 decades. Medicaid, which previously covered as many as 75% of poor children now covers about 50% of poor children (2). In fact, a recent survey by the Robert Wood Johnson Foundation sampled households across the United States in a random fashion and collected information about health coverage. Over 2,000 children were the subject of the analysis. Approximately 10% of the children in the survey had no medical insurance; 10% had no regular source of care; and 18% identified emergency rooms, community clinics, or hospital outpatient departments as their usual site of medical care (3). It was this latter group of individuals, the poor children in our society, who were less likely to have up-to-date immunizations. The only positive aspect of this is that these children will not, presumably, further challenge and bankrupt the Vaccine Compensation Fund.

Medicaid programs are basically designed by economists. It has been frequently said that if all the economists in the world were laid end to end, they still would not reach a conclusion. Economists, please ask for some help from those involved in health-care delivery. Maybe you could reach a conclusion.

All this proves 1 thing. Poverty, while not a disgrace, is certainly an inconvenience (in this country at least).—J.A. Stockman, III, M.D.

References

1. Committee on Health Care for Underserved Women, American College of Obstetricians and Gynecologists: *Obstetrics and Gynecological Services for Indigent Women: Issues Raised by an ACOG Survey.* 1988, p 8.
2. Roland D: *Ann Rev Public Health* 9:427, 1988.
3. Wood DL, et al: *Pediatrics* 86:666, 1990.

6 Neurology and Psychiatry

Cerebral Glucose Metabolism in Adults With Hyperactivity of Childhood Onset
Zametkin AJ, Nordahl TE, Gross M, King AC, Semple WE, Rumsey J, Hamburger S, Cohen RM (Natl Inst of Mental Health, Bethesda, Md)
N Engl J Med 323:1361–1366, 1990   6–1

Hyperactivity affects 2% to 4% of school-aged children, and its cause is unknown. It was hypothesized that cerebral glucose metabolism may differ between normal adults and those with a history of hyperactivity in childhood who continued to have symptoms.

To test this possibility, 50 normal, healthy control subjects and 25 patients, all adults, were studied. The patients were also the biologic parent of a hyperactive child. None of the study subjects had ever had stimulant treatment. Cerebral glucose metabolism was measured by administering 148 to 185 mega becquerel of $[^{18}F]$fluoro-2-deoxy-D-glucose intravenously to all subjects and patients while they performed an auditory attention task. A Scanditronix positron-emission tomograph with a resolution of 5 to 6 mm was used. Images were obtained for 30 minutes. Whole brain and regional rates of glucose metabolism were measured with computer assistance.

Adults with hyperactivity had a global cerebral glucose metabolism that was 8.1% lower than that of the control subjects. Glucose metabolism was significantly lower in the patients than in the controls in 30 of the 60 specific regions of the brain. The premotor cortex and superior prefrontal cortex were among the regions with the greatest reductions in glucose metabolism.

Both global and regional glucose metabolism is reduced in adults who have been hyperactive since childhood. The largest decreases were in the premotor cortex and superior prefrontal cortex, regions that have been shown to be involved in the control of attention and motor activity.

Attention Deficit Disorder in Children at Risk for Anxiety and Depression
McClennan JM, Rubert MP, Reichler RJ, Sylvester CE (Univ of Washington; Harborview Med Ctr, Seattle)
J Am Acad Child Adolesc Psychiatry 29:534–539, 1990   6–2

Many studies have reported on the increased frequency of attention and behavior problems, including attention deficit disorder (ADD), in depressed children. However, most of these studies have addressed comorbidity between AD and anxiety or depression, or both, by preselecting children with ADD.

In the present study the comorbidity between ADD and anxiety or depression, or both, was evaluated in children of parents with panic disorder, major depressive disorder, or with no diagnosis. A child received a diagnosis by a self-report, by a parent report, and by consensus, using a best estimate procedure. The study sample included 60 children from 33 panic proband families, 56 children from 31 depressed proband families, and 47 children from 25 control families.

Children of parents with depressive and panic disorder by the parents' reports and children of depressed parents by consensus had significantly higher prevalence rates of ADD, compared with children from control families. There was a significant association between ADD and anxiety or depression, or both, by parent report, child report, and consensus. When examined by age and gender groups, the rates of ADD were consistently higher in those with anxiety or depression, or both, particularly among male and younger children. The possibility of either a coexisting or a primary affective disorder should be considered in children referred for evaluation of ADD, particularly male and younger children.

▶ Let me see, I seem to have forgotten what this commentary is supposed to be about. Oh yes, it's on ADD.

The preceding 2 abstracts (Abstracts 6–1 and 6–2) look at the problem of attention deficit disorders/hyperactivity of childhood from radically different points of view. Certainly ADD, with or without hyperactivity, is a poorly understood, heterogenous disorder of unknown cause. It is a major clinical and public health problem estimated to affect 6%–9% of school-aged children, with symptoms persisting into adulthood. The validity of hyperactivity as a syndrome remains controversial, as does its treatment with stimulant medications. The study reported from *The New England Journal of Medicine* shows differences in cerebral glucose metabolism between hyperactive adults and normal adult controls, specifically in regions of the brain that have been postulated to be important in the control of preparation for motor activity, motor activity itself, and inhibition of inappropriate responses and attention. The overall symptoms of ADD are motor restlessness, attention difficulties, distractability, and impulsiveness.

Until the report abstracted in Abstract 6–1 was published, there were no hard-core data to unequivocally implicate neurochemical abnormalities as a cause for ADD. No consistent finding had previously emerged to implicate a specific neural transmitter, modulator, or neuroanatomical substrate. Only 1 other recent publication (1) has suggested a metabolic abnormality. The latter report, however, shows that children with ADD have significantly lower levels of plasma tyrosine, tryptophan, and phenylalanine. Because the report abstracted above appeared in the prestigious *New England Journal of Medicine,* I tend to favor the glucose story over the amino acid story, *if* there is a true metabolic basis for ADD. Certainly, one can not refute positron emission tomography scanning data with respect to glucose metabolism. These kids just don't burn as much sugar in their frontal lobes when they become adults. I suppose many parents are going to become depressed learning that too little sugar rather than too much may be a cause of ADD, but then again, many of these kids have a sweet tooth, perhaps hoping to overcome the diminished glucose use that is going on inside their calvaria. In any event, perhaps these data will put parent's minds to rest knowing that there may very well be an organic and/or metabolic cause of their child's problem.

It is this editor's impression that hyperactivity is reaching epidemic proportions in all age groups. We here in this country have become so tense and nervous that it's been years since I've seen anyone asleep in church—that's a bad sign. Chill out America!

Most of this tenseness may be related to our self-consciousness that maybe we are underachievers. In this regard, I believe in the "Fruit of the Loom" overview of our country: "Don't sell Americans shorts."—J.A. Stockman, III, M.D.

Reference

1. Bornstein RA, et al: *Psychiatr Res* 33:301, 1990.

Relative Efficacy of Long-Acting Stimulants on Children With Attention Deficit-Hyperactivity Disorder: A Comparison of Standard Methylphenidate, Sustained-Release Methylphenidate, Sustained-Release Dextroamphetamine, and Pemoline
Pelham WE Jr, Greenslade KE, Vodde-Hamilton M, Murphy DA, Greenstein JJ, Gnagy EM, Guthrie KJ, Hoover MD, Dahl RE (Western Psychiatric Inst and Clinic, Pittsburgh)
Pediatrics 86:226–237, 1990   6–3

Because of limited information on these drugs, the long-acting forms of stimulants are used in only a small percentage of children with attention deficit-hyperactivity disorder (ADHD). In a double-blind, placebo-controlled crossover trial, the relative efficacy of comparable doses of 3 long-acting stimulants were compared with a standard methylphenidate preparation.

Twenty-two boys aged 8 to 13 years with ADHD were treated with standard methylphenidate, 10 mg twice a day; with sustained-release methylphenidate (SR-20 Ritalin); pemoline, 56.25 mg; or a sustained-release form of dextroamphetamine (Dexedrine Spansule), 10 mg. The latter 3 long-acting preparations were given every morning with midday placebos. The children were participating in an 8-week summer treatment program involving recreational and classroom activities. The boys were evaluated on social behavior during group recreational activities, on classroom performance, and on performance of a continuous-performance task (CPT).

Generally, all 4 medications displayed equivalent and beneficial effects. All 4 drugs significantly reduced within-subject variability, with Dexedrine Spansule and pemoline producing the most consistent effects. The

CPT showed that all 4 drugs had detectable effects within 2 hours of ingestion and lasted for 9 hours. For the 15 children in whom continued treatment was recommended, 6 received Dexedrine Spansule, 4 received pemoline, and 4 received SR-20. Side effects such as loss of appetite and difficulty in falling asleep were more common in patients who received 1 of the 3 long-acting stimulants than in patients who received methylphenidate or placebo.

Although this study shows that the 3 long-acting stimulants provide beneficial effects equivalent to those of standard methylphenidate in children with ADHD, there are individual differences in drug responsivity. Additional studies that involve large samples and longer duration are warranted to define the effects of long-acting stimulants on ADHD.

▶ Dr. Sally Shaywitz, Professor of Pediatrics, Co-Director of the Center for the Study of Learning and Attention Disorders, Yale University School of Medicine, and the Director of the Learning Disorders Unit at the Child Study Center, comments:

▶ Beginning with the seminal report by Bradley over half a century ago of the positive effects of D-amphetamine, hundreds of studies have established that stimulants ameliorate many of the symptoms of ADD. Both clinical experience and controlled studies indicate that the time course for the peak effects of both amphetamine and methylphenidate range between 1 and 4 hours, a response time that frequently imposes significant limitations on the administration of these agents in children with ADD. Administration of a second dose of the stimulant 3–4 hours after the first dose can often circumvent the problem, but this may create logistic and social problems for the affected child. In this report, Pelham and his associates examine an alternate strategy—the use of stimulants with longer durations of action. Their findings indicate that a single morning dose of any of 3 agents (sustained-release methylphenidate, Dexedrine Spansules, or pemoline) are as effective as 2 doses of standard methylphenidate. Whether the longer-acting agents will continue to have an effect when given for months at a time remains to be determined, and this is noted by the authors.

This paper provides an important reminder of the complexity of the issues to be resolved if pharmacotherapy is to be incorporated as part of the treatment program for ADD. For example, although each of the medications, both the short-acting and the long-acting, were superior to placebo in improving aggressive behavior, the effects on classroom functioning, particularly on academic performance, were minimal. Not only were behavioral and cognitive symptoms differentially affected, but there were marked differences between observers—in this case, teachers and counselors—in their ratings of the same children. To further muddy the waters, behaviors often considered to be side effects of medications (e.g., irritability, tearfulness, and stomachaches) were as common or more common when the children were on placebo than when they were receiving many of the active medications. Whereas appetite suppression is a well-recognized side effect of stimulants, almost half of the children were rated to have loss of appetite while on placebo. Although use of the drugs had consistent positive effects on the indices assessed, at the conclusion of the study, no medication was recommended for one third of the children, primarily because of side effects.

The individual differences in responsivity found regarding which target symptoms were helped, which medication was most beneficial, and which side effects were observed, emphasizes the heterogeneity of the population of children currently labeled as having ADD. At this time, it is not possible to provide a single recommendation for treatment that could be generalized to all, or even most, children with ADD. We would agree with the authors that this study "highlights the need for controlled, individualized assessments of stimulant effects in every medicated child."—S. Shaywitz, M.D.

Reversal of Early Neurologic and Neuroradiologic Manifestations of X-Linked Adrenoleukodystrophy by Bone Marrow Transplantation

Aubourg P, Blanche S, Jambaqué I, Rocchiccioli F, Kalifa G, Naud-Saudreau C, Rolland M-O, Debré M, Chaussain J-L, Griscelli C, Fischer A, Bougnères P-F (Hôpital St Vincent de Paul, Paris; Hôpital des Enfants Malades, Paris; Centre Hospitalier, Lorient, France; Hôpital Debrousse, Lyon, France)
N Engl J Med 322:1860–1866, 1990   6–4

The inherited peroxisomal disease, X-linked adrenoleukodystrophy, is caused by a defective gene within the Xq28 region of the X chromosome. Initial attempts to treat the disease with bone marrow transplantation were unsuccessful, and some physicians thought that treatment might have accelerated neurologic deterioration. However, transplantation may have been performed too late. Bone transplatation must be performed after demonstration of CNS involvement, but early enough for some effects to be reversed.

Boy, 8 years, was a dizygotic twin who had normal motor and cognitive development throughout early childhood. Like his unaffected twin brother, he had scores below the middle range in school. At age 6½ years, he had a mild viral infection that triggered vomiting and coma. He was diagnosed with adrenal insufficiency after 2 additional episodes within the year. Six months later, the patient had dystonia and pyramidal signs and corresponding lesions of the internal capsules, pallidum, and caudate nuclei. He also had marked behavioral and cognitive changes. Symptoms rapidly worsened, and an MRI examination 1 month before transplantation showed that lesions of the pyramidal tracts now extended to the pons. The patient's mother was heterozygous for adrenoleukodystrophy. Two of her brothers had died in childhood from acute adrenal insufficiency, and her grandmother may have had an adult form of adrenoleukodystrophy. The patient underwent bone transplantation and dietary therapy. At 79 days after transplantation, the oxidation of very–long-chain fatty acids by peripheral-blood leukocytes derived from the donor was normal, and it remained so at 12 months after transplantation. Eighteen months after transplantation, plasma $C_{26:0}$ concentration and $C_{26:0}/C_{22:0}$ ratio were completely normal. Six months after transplantation, results of neurologic examination were similar to those before transplantation; however, verbal fluency was better, and the patient could participate normally in school. After 12 months, dystonia and pyramidal signs had disappeared, and the neurologic examination was normal. By 18 months, neurodiagnostic studies were normal.

In adrenoleukodystrophy, functional bone marrow cells from a donor may cross the blood-brain barrier and produce favorable effects on mechanisms leading to demyelination. Perivascular microglial cells—a subset of CNS cells—are derived from bone marrow. This finding may be particularly relevant in adrenoleukodystrophy. The results here support further evaluation of bone marrow transplantation for treatment of adrenoleukodystrophy.

▶ Why, pray tell, you might ask, would anyone want to entertain doing a bone marrow transplantation to treat a metabolic defect within the CNS? The answer to this question lies with a better understanding of exactly what goes on with children who have adrenoleukodystrophy. This is obviously a rare disorder and one that you may think is so infrequent that it does not deserve a place in the YEAR BOOK. Au contraire. The reason it is in the YEAR BOOK is to illustrate how we are manipulating genetic disorders these days.

In most cases, adrenoleukodystrophy is an X-linked inherited peroxisomal disorder caused by a defective gene at a very specific (Xq28) region on the X chromosome. Childhood adrenoleukodystrophy is characterized by multifocal demyelination of the CNS and adrenal insufficiency. The early symptoms include a variety of neuropsychological and neurologic manifestations. Lesions are readily detectable on MRI and are located in the subcortical white matter, the auditory and visual pathways, and the pyramidal tracts within the brain stem. Once the CNS manifestations occur, progression is rapid, leading to a vegetative state or death within an average of less than 3 years. The metabolic defect is characterized by impairment in the degradation of saturated very–long-chain fatty acids. These fatty acids accumulate in the cholesterol ester and ganglioside fractions of the patient's white matter and adrenal cortex as well as in plasma and red cells. The initial occurrence and death usually occur in childhood or early adolescence.

Until recently, the only treatment available was a diet containing glycerol trioleate and trierucate oils, with restricted intake of very–long-chain fatty acids. Dietary therapy was a temporizing measure at best. The rationale for bone marrow transplantation in cases of adrenoleukodystrophy relies on the hypothesis that functional bone marrow cells from the donor can cross the blood-brain barrier in the recipient and exert favorable effects on the mechanisms leading to demyelination. Studies in lower animals indicate that perivascular microglial cells, a subset of the CNS cells, are in fact derived from bone marrow.

Data from this report indicate that transplantation at a very early stage of brain involvement can reverse the demyelinating process of adrenoleukodystrophy. Unfortunately, the approach is unsuitable for most patients in whom neurologic deterioration is already extensive. Nothing works in the latter group of children. With the advent of assays for very–long-chain fatty acids in plasma, early diagnosis is now possible, and bone marrow transplantation will be much more widely used.

Bone marrow transplantation is now used to treat combined immunodeficiency syndromes, thalassemias, the Wiskott-Aldrich syndrome, lysosomal storage diseases, and osteopetrosis, all examples of genetic disorders. It is likely, however, that there will be a totally new therapy for X-linked adrenoleukodystrophy. Because this disorder represents a single-gene defect at a specific location, it is one of the genetic diseases that is an early candidate for human gene therapy.

Leon Rosenberg recently reviewed the treatment of genetic diseases (1). He said: "What kind of human diseases are candidates for human gene therapy? The answer is that somatic cell gene therapy can only be used for single-gene defects because it is only in this category of genetic disease that we have sufficient understanding to know which gene to isolate, clone, and intervene with. The most likely initial disease targets are beta thalassemia, or adenosine deaminase deficiency because bone marrow stem cells would be obvious and available cell targets. Thus, at best, gene therapy is currently applicable only to a small fraction of patients with genetic diseases. Lastly, when will human gene therapy be attempted in man? My guess is that the initial therapeutic trials will begin within the next five years."

Dr. Rosenberg's comments are now 2 years old. The clock is running, and if he's right, we should see some breakthrough in the next 3 years.—J.A. Stockman, III, M.D.

Reference

1. Rosenberg L: *Pediatr Res* 27:s10, 1990.

Mitochondrial Myopathy With a Defect of Mitochondrial-Protein Transport

Schapira AHV, Cooper JM, Morgan-Hughes JA, Landon DN, Clark JB (Royal Free Hosp School of Medicine, London; St Bartholomew's Hosp Med College, London)
N Engl J Med 323:37–42, 1990   6–5

Recent work focused on identifying the molecular basis of the mitochondrial myopathies has shown specific deficiencies of the iron-sulfur protein of complex III, or Rieske protein, and the 27.2-kilodalton subunit of succinate dehydrogenase.

Girl, 14 years, was evaluated because of weakness and exercise intolerance since early infancy. Her father was English, and her mother was Chinese. Her activities were restricted at school because of symptoms attributed to asthma. At 13 she had a progressive, generalized weakness requiring hospitalization. She was a normal-appearing girl with a waddling gait and difficulty rising from a squat. Mild myopathic changes in several muscles were revealed by electromyography. Lactate level was 1.05 mmol/L at rest, up to 4.91 mmol/L after exercise. Biopsy of the left vastus lateralis muscle showed that 9% of fibers had no cytochrome c oxidase. Succinate dehydrogenase was practically absent. Electron microscopy revealed small, superficial clusters of mitochondria with disordered labyrinthine cristae in many fibers. There were scattered intermyofibrillar mitochondria deep in the fibers that had similar features and substantial quantities of iron. Biochemical analysis showed decreased oxygen uptake with pyruvate, glutamate, and succinate, and low-normal rate with ascorbate. Cytochrome aa_3 levels were decreased, as were numerous cytochrome c activities.

Respiratory-chain polypeptide analysis showed a mild, generalized reduction of complex I, absence of the polypeptides that make up complex II, and a severe deficiency of the Rieske protein. Further study of the proteins reacting with the Rieske protein antibody showed that the human homogenate and mitochondrial proteins bound to identical cleavage sites with the test enzyme. Immunoblotting produced 26- and 22.5-kd bands; the lower-weight bands represented the mitochondrial fraction of Rieske protein in the homogenate. The patient was determined to have multiple respiratory-chain deficiencies, including specific polypeptide defects in succinate dehydrogenase and complex III.

The profound type of defect described produces death if widely distributed, although the patient under consideration had no clinical involvement outside of skeletal muscle. The only explanation for this type of transport defect is the existence of different precursor sequences or receptor types.

Molecular Basis of Different Forms of Metachromatic Leukodystrophy
Polten A, Fluharty AL, Fluharty CB, Kappler J, von Figura K, Gieselmann V (George-August-Universität Göttingen, Göttingen, Germany)
N Engl J Med 324:18–22, 1991   6–6

Metachromatic leukodystrophy is a lysosomal storage disorder caused by a deficiency of arylsulfatase A. Transmitted on an autosomal-recessive basis, it exists in 3 forms, depending on the patient's age at onset: late infantile (1–2 years), juvenile (3–16 years), and adult (>16 years). To understand the molecular defects in the different forms of the disease, mutations in the arylsulfatase A gene associated with metachromatic leukodystrophy were identified, and their frequencies were determined by allele-specific oligonucleotide hybridization in 68 patients with the disease.

Two alleles were identified. Allele I was associated with loss of the splice-donor site of exon 2, and allele A was characterized by substitution of leucine for proline at position 426. These 2 alleles accounted for about half of all arylsulfatase A alleles in the 68 patients with metachromatic leukodystrophy. Sufficient information was obtained for 66 patients to allow classification of their disease. All 6 patients who were homozygous for allele I had the late-infantile form of metachromatic leukodystrophy. Of the 8 patients who were homozygous for allele A, 6 had the adult form of the disease, and 3 had the juvenile form. Of the 7 patients with both alleles, all had juvenile-onset metachromatic leukodystrophy. Heterozygosity for allele I, with the other allele unknown, was usually associated with late-infantile disease. Heterozygosity for allele A was associated with a later onset of the disease. The clinical variability could be explained by the different levels of residual arylsulfatase A activity associated with these genotypes.

In metachromatic leukodystrophy, there is a clear correlation between the arylsulfatase A genotype and the clinical phenotype. Allele I is associated with the earlier and more severe late-infantile form of the disease. One copy of allele A produces the juvenile form, and two copies of allele A produce the mildest form, the adult-onset disease.

▶ Over the years, I have learned 4 principles of life: Never eat in a restaurant named Mom's, play poker with a guy named Doc, buy a car from a man named Frenchie, or accept anything at face value from a man named Bernie. I think I will add a fifth principle. To keep up on things like metachromatic leukodystrophy, arylsulfatase A deficiency, mitochrondrial myopathy, and topics like Rieske proteins, read *The New England Journal of Medicine.* These are the kinds of disorders and problems that we should have some remote familiarity with because they show up on certification and recertification examinations these days.

Frankly, I know relatively little about these disorders, and it would be foolish of me to attempt to educate you any further by quoting from some esoteric wisened source. To say it differently: "He who trains his tongue to quote from the learned sages will be known far and wide as being a smart ass."

Sorry I couldn't be more informative on these topics and for the profanity.—J.A. Stockman, III, M.D.

The Role of Plasmapheresis in Childhood Guillain-Barré Syndrome
Epstein MA, Sladky JT (The Children's Hosp of Philadelphia; Univ of Pennsylvania)
Ann Neurol 28:65–69, 1990   6–7

The effectiveness of plasmapheresis in the treatment of Guillain-Barré syndrome (GBS) in adults has been established. Plasmapheresis has been advocated in the treatment of childhood GBS under the assumption that results in adult studies can be extrapolated to children. To test this assumption, the records of 30 children admitted between 1984 and 1989 with the diagnosis of GBS were evaluated retrospectively. Seven patients were excluded because of mild disease.

Nine patients underwent plasmapharesis, and the other 14 served as historic control subjects. The 2 groups were similar in age, presenting symptoms, findings on initial physical examination, and antecedent illness. The maximal mean disability grading scales were virtually identical in both groups. Despite these similarities, the mean time to recover to grade 2 disease severity (independent ambulation) was significantly shorter in the plasmapheresis-treated patients, with a mean of 24 days

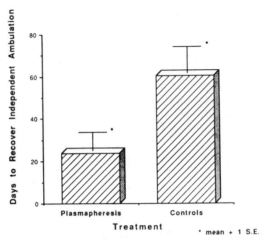

Fig 6–1.—Influence of plasmapheresis on recovery of ambulation in childhood GBS. Plasmapheresis-treated children reached grade 2 in a mean of 24 days, whereas children who received standard treatment did not reach this level until 60.2 days. *Bar* denotes standard error (SE). (Courtesy of Epstein MA, Sladky JT: *Ann Neurol* 28:65–69, 1990.)

compared with a mean of 60 days in control subjects (Fig 6–1). There were no significant complications from plasmapheresis.

Plasmapheresis diminishes morbidity in childhood GBS by shortening the interval until recovery of independent ambulation. However, until well-designed prospective trials are undertaken, plasmapheresis cannot be routinely advocated for all children with GBS.

▶ Whereas the effectiveness of plasmapheresis in the treatment of GBS has been established in adults, this report is the first to attempt to evaluate the role of plasmapheresis in the childhood form in a controlled fashion. Until now, data have not been available in children, in part because plasmapheresis is not without risk, and the natural history of the disease in children is generally more favorable. Note the inherent weaknesses of this 1 and only report regarding the beneficial role of plasmapheresis in children. It is a retrospective study, and many of the measures used to judge the effectiveness of plasmapheresis could not be determined accurately from the hospital records of the children evaluated. Nonetheless, plasmapheresis was well tolerated and, if nothing else, this report should serve as a prelude to well-designed prospective studies. Such prospective studies undoubtedly will require a comparison of plasmapheresis with the administration of intravenous gamma globulin. The latter treatment, judging from many anecdotal experiences, seems to be as effective as plasmapheresis.

The next time you run across a child with GBS, chances are that you will not just sit back and watch the illness go through its natural history. Despite the insufficient basis for therapeutic intervention, you probably will go on the offense and use intravenous gamma globulin or plasmapheresis. That is the Knute Rockne approach of winning: "The best offense is a strong offense."—J.A. Stockman, III, M.D.

Cesarean Section Before the Onset of Labor and Subsequent Motor Function in Infants With Meningomyelocele Diagnosed Antenatally

Luthy DA, Wardinsky T, Shurtleff DB, Hollenbach KA, Hickok DE, Nyberg DA, Benedetti TJ (Swedish Hosp Med Ctr, Seattle; Univ Hosp Med Ctr, Seattle)
N Engl J Med 324:662–666, 1991   6–8

The optimal management of meningomyelocele detected before birth is controversial. To assess the effect of labor and the type of delivery on the level of motor function, 200 infants with uncomplicated meningomyelocele seen during a 10-year period were followed-up. For fetuses with antenatal diagnosis of meningomyelocele without severe hydrocephalus, cesarean section was performed electively before the onset of labor.

The level of motor function, the score on the Bayley Mental Developmental Index, and the incidence of neonatal complications in 47 infants delivered by cesarean section before the onset of labor were compared with those of 35 infants delivered by cesarean section after a period of labor and another 78 infants delivered vaginally. There were no differences among groups in the size of the spinal lesions, but the mean anatomical level of the lesions was significantly lower in the vaginal-delivery group than the other 2 groups.

At 2 years of age, infants exposed to labor, whether delivered by cesarean section or vaginally, were 2.2 times more likely to have severe paralysis than infants in the pre-labor cesarean group (95% confidence interval, 1.7–2.8). The mean level of paralysis was 3.3 segments below the anatomical level of the spinal lesion in the pre-labor cesarean-section group compared with a mean 1.1 for infants delivered vaginally and .9 for infants delivered by cesarean section after a period of labor (table).

Characteristics of Pregnancy and Level of Paralysis, According to Exposure to Labor and Type of Delivery

VARIABLE	PRELABOR CESAREAN SECTION (N = 47)	LABOR PLUS CESAREAN SECTION (N = 35)	VAGINAL DELIVERY (N = 78)
	mean ±SD		
Gestational age at delivery (wk)	37.6±2.3	39.3±1.6*	38.9±4.1*
Length of labor (hr)	—	10.8±10.5	7.3±5.8†
Anatomical level of lesion (index)	21.1±3.2	21.0±3.4	22.5±1.9‡
Motor level of paralysis (index)§	24.4±2.9	21.9±4.6 ‖	23.7±2.8
Difference (motor − anatomical level)	3.3±3.0	0.9±4.1¶	1.1±2.3¶

*P < .05 for the comparison with the pre-labor cesarean-section group.
†P < .05 for the comparison with the labor plus cesarean-section group.
‡P < .001 for the comparisons with the pre-labor cesarean-section group and the labor plus cesarean-section group.
§At 2 years of age.
‖P < .001 for the comparisons with the pre-labor cesarean-section group and the vaginal-delivery group.
¶P < .001 for the comparison with the pre-labor cesarean-section group.
(Courtesy of Luthy DA, Wardinsky T, Shurtleff DB, et al: *N Engl J Med* 324:662–666, 1991.)

The 3 groups showed no differences in the frequency of neonatal complications or later intellectual performance. For the fetus with meningomyelocele without severe hydrocephalus, cesarean delivery before the onset
of labor may result in improved motor function over vaginal delivery or
cesarean delivery after a period of labor.

▶ It has been more than 6 years since we recognized that the outcome of a
baby born with meningomyelocele can be improved by planning a cesarean
section (1). Now we are also learning that delivery by cesarean section should
be timed to take place before even the earliest onset of labor. Babies born before the onset of labor have a lower risk of severe paralysis and, on average,
have motor neuron function that is 3.3 spinal segments better than would be
expected based on the anatomical level of their lesions. These results suggest
that "unsplinted" neural tissue and its blood supply may be traumatized by the
forces of labor, in which it has been demonstrated that the intrauterine pressure generated often exceeds 50 mmHg.

It would appear that the incidence of meningomyelocele, fortunately, is declining. It has dropped from 12 per 10,000 live births in 1970 to 6–8 per 10,000
live births in 1980. Declines since 1980 have been slight, however. There is a
lot of data now to suggest that prenatal vitamins may help to ensure closure of
the neural tube if given during embryonic development. Smithells et al. (2)
showed that the risk of neural tube defects diminished rapidly when women
who previously delivered a baby with a neural tube defect were given multivitamins, compared with similar women who were not (.7% vs. 4.6%). The mul-
tivitamin that seems to do the trick is folic acid. The claims made for the beneficial effect of folic acid are not universally accepted, however. Slattery et al. (3)
stated that there was a lack of evidence to support the recommendation that mul-
tivitamin supplements be used periconceptually to prevent neural tube defects.
Slattery et al. concluded that no decision could be made about the value or lack of
value of such supplements until more epidemiologic studies were reported.

Some of the above information is clearly history repeating itself. For example, midwife Catherine Schrader, who practiced in Holland between 1693 and
1741, carefully recorded the 3,100 deliveries in which she assisted (4). She
noted 6 cases of neural tube defect, or 1.9 per 1,000 deliveries, a much higher
rate than the .5 per 1,000 seen in the Netherlands today. The cases clustered
during 2 specific periods of time in which there was famine. Historians now
note that Ms. Schrader's data are an unusually accurate recording, suggesting
that there was a nutritional component, including folic acid deficiency, that
caused spikes in the incidence of neural tube defects in 18th century Holland.
What goes around seems to come around. Multivitamins are pretty cheap, and
if I were ever to become pregnant (a somewhat unlikely event), I certainly
would take them no matter what data did or did not support their use.—J.A.
Stockman, III, M.D.

References

1. Cherveak FA, et al: *Obstet Gynecol* 63:376, 1984.
2. Smithells RW, et al: *Lancet* 1:1027, 1983.

3. Slattery ML, et al: *Am J Epidemiol* 133:526, 1991.
4. Marland H: *Mother and Child Were Safe: The Memoirs of the Frisian Midwife, Catherine Schrader.* Amsterdam, Rodopi, 1987.

Seizures and Other Neurologic Sequelae of Bacterial Meningitis in Children
Pomeroy SL, Holmes SJ, Dodge PR, Feigin RD (Washington Univ School of Medicine, St Louis; Baylor College of Medicine, Houston)
N Engl J Med 323:1651–1657, 1990   6–9

Fewer children die of bacterial meningitis today, but some patients are left with neurologic deficits. To determine which features of acute illness predict chronic neurologic sequelae, 185 infants and children were followed prospectively for a mean time of 9 years after acute bacterial meningitis. Two thirds of infections were caused by *Haemophilus influenzae*, 16% were caused by *Streptococcus pneumoniae*, and 11% were caused by *Neisseria meningitidis*. Nearly one third of patients had seizures during the acute phase of meningitis.

When last evaluated, 14% of patients had a neurologic deficit. Sensorineural hearing loss was the most frequent deficit. Seven of the patients with deficits other than hearing loss had marked neuroradiological abnormalities, and 13 patients had afebrile seizures after the initial hospitalization. Those with serious deficits other than sensorineural hearing loss were at the highest risk of late seizures, and seizures during the acute phase strongly predicted late seizures. On multivariate analysis, however, persistent neurologic deficit was the only independent predictor of late seizures.

Children with persistent neurologic deficit after acute bacterial meningitis are at considerable risk of having epilepsy. Possibly inflammation leads to narrowing or spasm of cerebral vessels, with consequent cerebral flow impairment or thrombosis. Whether anti-inflammatory drug treatment early in the course of meningitis would alter this process is not clear.

▶ This report and the one of Taylor et al. (1), dealing with the sequelae of *H. influenzae* meningitis provide strong evidence for the need for vaccines to reduce the incidence of meningitis, but we already knew that. So what these reports do, then, is to refine our understanding of the sequelae, including seizures, of bacterial meningitis. Thank goodness for the introduction of HIB vaccine at 2 months of age.—J.A. Stockman, III, M.D.

The Risk of Convulsions: A Longitudinal Study of Normal Babies and Infants With Neonatal Damage in the First 6 Years of Life
Nalin A, Frigieri G, Cordioli A, Colò M, Tartoni PL(Univ of Modena, Italy)
Childs Nerv Syst 6:254–263, 1990   6–10

The cause of seizures in children is unknown in many cases. An extensive literature review and epidemiologic investigation were carried out to

Incidence (n = 1,000) of Convulsions in the Pathologic
and Control Groups

Year of life	Febrile convulsions		Epileptic convulsions	
	Control group	Patho-logical	Control group	Patho-logical
1st	12.6	23.9	2.5	21.5
2nd	12.6	16.27	2.5	2.3
3rd	4.2	4.7	–	–
4th	4.2	7.1	–	–
5th	–	–	2.5	2.3
6th	–	2.3	–	4.7
1st–6th	5.6	9.1	1.25	5.13

(Courtesy of Nalin A, Frigieri G, Cordioli A, et al: *Childs Nerv Syst* 6:254–263, 1990.)

determine the cause of seizures in the first 6 years of life and their corre-lation to perinatal events.

The risk of febrile or epileptic convulsions was investigated by the fol-low-up method. Two groups were studied. A group of 417 children who had any of a wide variety of neonatal disorders as term or preterm in-fants constituted the pathologic group. The control group was 400 healthy neonates born in the same period. Children had annual observa-tions until the age of 6. Verified seizures were placed into one of the fol-lowing categories: febrile convulsions, isolated afebrile convulsions, gen-eralized epilepsy, or partial epilepsy.

No significant difference in the incidence of febrile and epileptic con-vulsions was noted between the two groups. Epileptic encephalopathies and partial epilepsies were found only in the pathologic group, whereas isolated afebrile convulsions and generalized epilepsies were found in both groups. For the pathologic group, epileptic convulsions were more common in the first year of life. This group had a greater incidence of febrile and epileptic convulsions (table). Specific risk factors for convul-sions in childhood were established. For term infants, significant factors were birth-weight percentile higher than 90, asphyxia, neurologic syn-drome, and barbiturate treatment. Significant risk factors for premature infants were extreme prematurity, complicated delivery, asphyxia, apnea, and neurologic syndrome of the premature infant.

Risk of Seizure Recurrence Following a First Unprovoked Seizure in Child-hood: A Prospective Study
Shinnar S, Berg AT, Moshé SL, Petix M, Maytal J, Kang H, Goldensohn ES, Hauser WA (Montefiore Med Ctr, Bronx, NY; Yale Univ; Columbia College of Physicians and Surgeons, New York)
Pediatrics 85:1076–1085, 1990   6–11

To determine the magnitude of the risk of recurrence after a first un-provoked seizure, a prospective study of 283 children with unprovoked

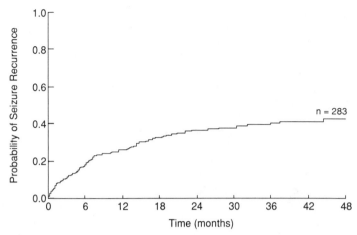

Fig 6–2.—Probability of seizure recurrence after first unprovoked seizure, Kaplan-Meier curve. (Courtesy of Shinnar S, Berg AT, Moshé SL, et al: *Pediatrics* 85:1076–1085, 1990.)

seizure were followed-up for a mean of 30 months (range, .2–65 months) from the time of first seizure. Their mean age at time of first seizure was 6.7 years.

Seizures recurred in 101 children (36%). The overall cumulative risk of seizure recurrence was 26% at 1 year, 36% at 2 years, 40% at 3 years, and 42% at 4 years (Fig 6–2). The mean time interval of recurrence was 9.2 months, and the greatest risk of recurrence was in the first few months after the first seizure. The risk of recurrence for the 47 children with a remote symptomatic first seizure was 53% at 2 years, which was significantly greater than the 33% risk for the 236 children with an idiopathic first seizure.

Among children with an idiopathic first seizure, the electroencephalogram (EEG) was the most important predictor of recurrence. The cumulative risk of recurrence at 2 years was 54% for the 81 children with abnormal EEG results, compared with 23% for the 138 children with normal EEG results. A family history of seizures was also an important predictor, but only when EEG results were abnormal. In children with remote symptomatic seizures, a history of previous febrile seizures or occurrence of partial seizures were significant risk factors for recurrence. Age at first seizure and duration of seizure did not affect recurrence risk in both groups. Most of the children (84%) were not treated with antiepileptic drugs or were treated for less than 2 weeks. Only 9% were treated for longer than 3 months. Treatment did not affect the risk of recurrence.

These data show that, even without treatment, most children with a first unprovoked seizure will not have a recurrence. These data also support the position of the American Academy of Pediatrics Committee on Drugs that most children with a first unprovoked seizure do not require therapy.

▶ Dr. John M. Freeman, Professor, Neurology and Pediatrics, The Johns Hopkins University School of Medicine, comments:

▶ Appropriate decision-making regarding the management of seizures requires understanding their natural history. We compare the chance of a recurrence and the consequences of such a recurrence with the risks and the consequences or side effects of the proposed treatment. If the risks of treatment exceed the benefits, treatment should be deferred. Shinnar and colleagues allow us to better understand the natural history of children after a first unprovoked afebrile seizure.

They find that, as with febrile seizures, approximately one third of children will have a recurrence. This risk was lower if the seizure was idiopathic, and the EEG result was normal; it was higher if the child had a prior neurologic insult or if the EEG was abnormal. Most recurrences were within the first year after the seizure. Should we use medication in an attempt to reduce that risk? That decision should depend on the consequences of the recurrence. Studies suggest that, as with febrile seizures, the consequences of a second afebrile seizure are low—death, neurologic, or intellectual problems do not occur, and even status epilepticus is exceedingly rare. If the consequences are low, does it matter if the chances of another afebrile seizure are 25%, 40%, or even 50%?

In modern decision-making, we multiply the risks and the consequences of a recurrence of an afebrile seizure and compare that outcome with the risks and consequences of some alternative, in this case treatment. Side effects of medication include allergic, idiosyncratic, and dose-related reactions such as liver or bone marrow problems and behavioral and, perhaps, intellectual side effects. The chance of a side effect varies with the medication, and the consequences of the side effects vary from minimal to severe.

We know from the study by Shinnar et al. that the recurrence risk after an afebrile seizure is low. We know from other studies that the consequences of a single recurrence are also low. Because the consequences of a recurrence are age-dependent and are less severe at a younger age, and because the effects of medication may be greatest on the developing brain, perhaps we should delay embarking on treatment with medication after the first afebrile seizure and thereby spare the child and the family the risks and consequences of medication side effects. We await studies of the recurrence risk after a second afebrile seizure.—J.M. Freeman, M.D.

Diphtheria-Tetanus-Pertussis Vaccine and Serious Neurologic Illness: An Updated Review of the Epidemiologic Evidence
Wentz KR, Marcuse EK (Univ of Washington; Children's Hosp and Med Ctr, Seattle)
Pediatrics 87:287–297, 1991
6–12

The safety of pertussis vaccine continues to be controversial. The most current epidemiologic evidence for serious neurologic illness associated with diphtheria-tetanus-pertussis (DTP) vaccine was studied.

Evidence published since the 1988 American Academy of Pediatrics Task Force Report on Pertussis and Pertussis Immunization was analyzed. The methodologic implications of some of the studies reviewed in that report were also examined. An association between DTP vaccine and serious acute neurologic illness was found. The magnitude of this relationship appears to range between 1 per 100,000 and 1 per 1 million immunizations. It is not known whether pertussis vaccine produces permanent brain damage. If it does, such damage is even more rare than serious acute neurologic illness.

The case-control study design offers the best chance of finding causal evidence on DTP vaccine and serious neurologic illness. The British National Childhood Encephalopathy Study is the only case-control study in the literature. Although bias and chance are not likely to account wholly for the rare association found between DTP vaccine and serious neurologic illness, this association has not yet been replicated by other case-control studies. In addition, the British National Childhood Encephalopathy Study does not show that DTP vaccine causes permanent brain damage.

Who Gets Treated? Factors Associated With Referral in Children With Psychiatric Disorders
Costello EJ, Janiszewski S (Duke Univ; Univ of Pittsburgh)
Acta Psychiatr Scand 81:523–529, 1990   6–13

A number of recent studies have suggested that most children with psychiatric disorders are not receiving psychiatric treatment. Yet it remains unclear why some disturbed children are brought to treatment and others are not. In the present community-based study children between the ages of 7 and 11 years were screened by using the Child Behavior Checklist (CBCL), and those scoring in the clinical range underwent further assessment to determine why fewer than half had been referred for treatment.

The 89 treated children were more likely than the 115 nontreated children to be black (44% vs. 24%), poor (41% vs. 20%), and male (76% vs. 53%). Treated children were twice as likely as nontreated children to be diagnosed as having a conduct disorder or a depressive disorder. However, the nontreated children had equal rates of attention deficit disorders, anxiety, oppositional disorders, and school failure. Teachers and, to a lesser extent, parents, reported more behavioral problems in the treated children.

The findings of this study are disturbing because factors other than severity of psychopathology, such as race, sex, poverty, and bad behavior in school, may determine which disturbed children receive mental health services. This means that many children in need of psychiatric intervention do not receive it. It often appears that children are more likely to receive treatment if their behavior upsets or annoys adults, particularly teachers.

▶ I can think of only 2 things to say about the preceding article. The availability of good patient care tends to vary inversely with the need for it in any given population. Second, everything in life is possible except skiing through a revolving door and getting to see a psychiatrist when you really need one.—J.A. Stockman, III, M.D.

7 Child Development

Pediatricians' Perceptions of Their Behavioral and Developmental Training
Breunlin DC, Mann BJ, Richtsmeier A, Lillian Z, Richman JS, Bernotas T (Inst for Juvenile Research, Chicago; Univ of North Carolina, Chapel Hill; Rush-Presbyterian-St Luke's Hosp, Chicago; Cook County Hosp, Chicago; Ramsey Clinic, St Paul, Minn)
J Dev Behav Pediatr 11:165–169, 1990   7–1

In 1978, the Task Force on Pediatric Education recommended that pediatric residents be trained in behavior-development pediatrics (BDP). The long-term impact of BDP training was evaluated by 80 graduates of a pediatric residency that required training in BDP. Questionnaires completed a mean 3.4 years after residency assessed their perceptions regarding the quality of BDP training, the value of behavior and development training for modern pediatric practice, their competence in applying behavior and development knowledge, and their desire to pursue additional training in behavior and development.

There was a significant overall effect of the quality of BDP training. Graduates consistently rated child development and anticipatory guidance/counseling as the best taught and most useful aspects of BDP training with which they felt most competent. These ratings were particularly high among graduates who received additional BDP training after residency. However, areas that were considered as integral components of training, such as psychosocial factors in physical illness and school issues, were rated lowest. Overall, there was very little commitment to receive additional training in BDP among respondents, but more than one third stated thay they would pursue additional training in behavior and discipline, child development, and school issues. Graduates who pursued additional BDP training rated their own competency and usefulness of BDP as greater than graduates who did not pursue such training.

These findings indicate that most graduates of residency programs that offer BDP training continue to value and use BDP knowledge and skills in their practice. The findings also suggest that graduates interpret the role of pediatrician to include identification and management of developmental and behavioral difficulties.

▶ Dr. Morris Green, Perry W. Lesh Professor of Pediatrics, Section of Behavioral/Developmental Pediatrics, Indiana University School of Medicine, comments:

▶ From 10% to 25% of patients seen in pediatric practice today are estimated to have developmental, behavioral, or learning problems. Although recent pediatric residency training related to these aspects of child health has been partly effective, as documented in this report, fuller realization of the pediatrician's potential contribution to the prevention, recognition, and management of these problems requires that these efforts be supplemented in practice by additional educational and organizational strategies.

Because personal experience with and direct responsibility for the care of thousands of patients are required to gain the maturity, judgment, observational skills, understanding, empathy, and data base required, the goal of full psychobiological competence of the pediatrician cannot be accomplished realistically in the 3 residency years.

In my view, the most effective and practical postresidency means to achieve such mastery is through participation in what I have termed Collaborative Office Rounds (COR groups). These groups consist of 7–8 pediatric practitioners, a pediatrician with special competence in behavior and development, a child psychiatrist, and a child psychologist who meet regularly every 2 weeks or so to discuss the diagnosis and management of patients being seen currently in the practice of 1 of the pediatricians. Several such COR groups have recently been funded by the Bureau of Maternal and Child Health.

Another seminal development now on the horizon is the collaborative effort of the American Psychiatric Association and the primary care specialties of pediatrics, internal medicine, family medicine, and obstetrics and gynecology to develop a classification system for mental disorders in primary care practices. The proposed Diagnostic and Statistical Manual for Primary Care (DSM-PC) will include an effective, user-friendly system to categorize the kinds of preventive, developmental, psychological, and psychobiological problems, including those concerned with chronic disease, seen daily in the pediatric office.

Such a nosology of mental disorders in children would permit practitioners to record both quickly and comprehensively the psychosocial, developmental, adaptational, and learning problems that they regularly identify in their practices. It is likely that such an official classification system would also lead to improved recording of psychosocial diagnoses by pediatricians, more relevant educational curricula, appropriate reimbursement, a clearer identity for behavioral pediatrics, greater diagnostic comfort for the clinician, and the data needed for further research in pediatric practice in relation to the kinds of psychosocial morbidity that is not commonly seen or discussed in teaching hospitals or psychiatric settings.

Another major stimulus to the provision of care that attends to the psychosocial and developmental aspects of child health would be the adoption of a resource-based relative value system for reimbursement of medical care. The current lack of adequate payment for level II and III ambulatory care that addresses the psychosocial and developmental aspects of child health is a major impediment to the inclusion of such cognitive services in pediatric practice today.

The institutionalization of these and the other changes now being explored will likely have a great impact on the content, organization, and structure of pediatric practice, education, and research in the 90s.—M. Green, M.D.

Psychological Functioning in Children With Cyanotic Heart Defects

DeMaso DR, Beardslee WR, Silbert AR, Fyler DC (The Children's Hosp, Boston)

J Dev Behav Pediatr 11:289–294, 1990   7–2

Survival in children with congenital heart disease (CHD) has increased markedly, but many children continue to experience a chronic illness, with repeated hospitalizations and operations. To determine the long-term impact of these chronic disorders on the child's psychological functioning, the relationship between CHD and psychological functioning was studied in 63 children with transposition of the great arteries and 77 with tetralogy of Fallot. Findings were compared with those in 36 children who originally had diagnoses of CHD but who recovered spontaneously without medical intervention. All children were less than 1 year of age at the time of diagnosis and underwent psychological testing between 5.5 and 6.3 years. A global assessment of psychological functioning was constructed from the parent clinical interview using a symptom check list and standard psychometric tests.

Children with transposition of the great arteries and tetralogy of Fallot had significantly poorer overall psychological functioning, greater CNS impairment, and lower IQs than the children who recovered spontaneously. Comparison between transposition of the great arteries and the tetralogy of Fallot groups was not significant. However, after controlling for the effects of IQ and CNS impairment, the differences between children with CHD and spontaneously recovered children were no longer significant.

The diagnosis of serious CHD does not appear to be associated with poorer emotional adjustment. In the absence of serious CNS and intelligence impairment, children with CHD are similar in psychological functioning to children who have never experienced serious CHD.

▶ Thank goodness for some cheerful news. A diagnosis of severe congenital heart defect does not appear to make a child more likely to have emotional disturbances in the absence of other confounding factors. Yes, there are certain diagnoses, such as transposition of the great vessels or tetrology of Fallot, that tend to fall at the end of a spectrum that is a bit less favorable, but on average, most kids with congenital heart disease seem to be doing quite well emotionally, without any need for intervention. I wish the same could be said for some of their parents, who rightfully and quite understandably may indeed need some help, especially around the time of surgical repair.

Because this is the first entry in the Child Development chapter, it may be worthwhile to give you a little bit of background on the *Journal of Developmental and Behavioral Pediatrics*. Not many readers of the YEAR BOOK OF PEDIATRICS subscribe to this particular journal. The Society for Behavioral Pediatrics, chartered in 1983, adopted as its' mission, "promoting developmental and behavioral research and teaching." (1). Toward this end, the Society assumed the sponsorship of an already successful journal, *The Journal of Developmental* and Behavioral Pediatrics. The journal and the annual meeting are currently the main educational activities of the society. There are approximately 1,450 paid subscribers to the Journal of Developmental and Behavioral Pediatrics. Of these, 528 are institutional subscriptions, and 330 receive the journal as members of the Society. Despite the fact that behavioral and developmental problems are fairly frequent in pediatrics, relatively few pediatric generalists subscribe. This is not a pitch for the journal, but simply a mention that this is a largely overlooked resource for those in primary care pediatrics. Those who do primary care may wish to thumb through the journal at your local hospital/medical center/medical school (or whatever is closest to you) library.—J.A. Stockman, III, M.D.

Reference

1. Friedman SB: *J Dev Behav Pediatr* 11:333, 1990.

The Life Expectancy of Profoundly Handicapped People With Mental Retardation
Eyman RK, Grossman HJ, Chaney RH, Call TL (Univ of California, Riverside; Univ of Michigan; Univ of California, Los Angeles; Loma Linda Univ)
N Engl J MEd 323:584–589, 1990   7–3

The life expectancy of individuals with mental retardation is shorter than that of the general population, but the life expectancy of profoundly handicapped people with mental retardation has not been established. Life-table estimates of life expectancy were generated for the 99,543 persons, aged <1 month–92 years, with developmental disabilities, including mental retardation, who received services from the California Department of Developmental Services between March 1984 and October 1987.

Three subgroups were identified based on 4 predictors of early death in mentally retarded persons. The predictors were deficits in cognitive function, limitations on mobility, incontinence, and the inability to eat without assistance. In additon to severe deficits in cognitive function and incontinence, 1,550 subjects in subgroup 1 were immobile and required tube feeding; 4,513 subjects in subgroup 2 were immobile but could eat with assistance; and 997 subjects in subgroup 3 were mobile but not ambulatory and could eat with assistance.

Immobile subjects had much shorter life expectancies than those who were mobile. In addition, immobile subjects who required tube feeding (subgroup 1) had a very short life expectancy, averaging an additional 4 to 5 years (Table 1). Those who could eat if fed by others (subgroup 2) had an average life expectancy of approximately 8 additional years (Table 2). In contrast, subjects who were mobile but not ambulatory (subgroup 3) had about 23 additional years of life expectancy.

Severe mental retardation is associated with a shortened life expectancy. Mobility is the best predictor of survival, and the need for tube

TABLE 1.—Life Table for 1,550 Profoundly Handicapped Persons
in Subgroup 1

Age Interval	Observed Death Rate	No. Living at Beginning of Interval (per 100,000)*	No. Dying during Interval (per 100,000)*	Average No. of Years of Life Remaining†
yr				
<1	0.45	100,000	41,354	3.3
1–4	0.27	58,646	37,623	4.1
5–9	0.21	21,022	13,755	4.8
10–14	0.20	7,268	4,734	4.8
15–19	0.22	2,534	1,737	4.5
20–24	0.25	797	583	4.4
25–29	0.22	214	144	5.4
30–34	0.18	70	41	7.0
35–39	0.07	29	8	8.9
40–44	0.19	20	13	6.4
45–49	0.14	8	4	8.1
50–54	0.00	4	0	9.2
55–59	0.20	4	3	4.2
≥60	0.39	1	1	2.6

*Of a hypothetical cohort of 100,000 children born alive. Values have been rounded.
†The average number of years of life remaining for a person who survives to the beginning of the age interval.
(Courtesy of Eyman RK, Grossman HJ, Chaney RH, et al: *N Engl J Med* 323:584–589, 1990.)

feeding is a strong predictor of mortality . Prognosis in profoundly handicapped, mentally retarded subjects is poor.

▶ There are many implications to this important study examining the life expectancy of profoundly handicapped people with mental retardation. One of the implications has to do with medical/legal aspects of the adverse neurologic outcome of complicated pregnancies, labors, and deliveries, and other devastating postpartum neurologic disorders. Medical/legal claims involving children are frequently based on an adverse neurologic outcome. The 2 most common specific issues relate to the diagnosis and treatment of meningitis and claims of injuries suffered in the perinatal period. Large settlements frequently are sought in these cases for a number of differing but interrelated reasons. For example, there is an implicit assumption that most children will have a long life span with expensive special needs that continue for many years. The report by Eyman et al. abstracted above provides evidence that this assumption is not correct. In a group of patients with severe or profound mental retardation who were immobile, incontinent, and who required tube feeding, only 59% were alive at 1 year of age, 21% at 5 years of age, 7.2% at 10 years of age, and 2.5% at 15 years of age.

With respect to additional factors that should be taken into consideration in

TABLE 2.—Life Table for 4,513 Profoundly Handicapped Persons in Subgroup 2

Age Interval	Observed Death Rate	No. Living at Beginning of Interval (per 100,000)*	No. Dying during Interval (per 100,000)*	Average No. of Years of Life Remaining†
yr				
<1	0.07	100,000	7,014	8.5
1–4	0.13	92,986	35,891	8.1
5–9	0.13	57,096	26,945	8.3
10–14	0.11	30,150	13,057	8.7
15–19	0.13	17,093	8,090	8.5
20–24	0.14	9,003	4,455	9.1
25–29	0.11	4,548	1,849	10.8
30–34	0.05	2,699	644	11.6
35–39	0.07	2,055	588	9.5
40–44	0.13	1,467	687	7.3
45–49	0.12	780	356	6.7
50–54	0.17	424	249	5.3
55–59	0.20	175	113	4.6
60–64	0.26	62	47	3.9
≥65	0.25	15	15	4.0

*Of a hypothetical cohort of 100,000 children born alive. Values have been rounded.
†The average number of years of life remaining for a person who survives to the beginning of the age interval.
(Courtesy of Eyman RK, Grossman HJ, Chaney RH, et al: *N Engl J Med* 323:584–589, 1990.)

malpractice claims is the frequently made statement that there is excess mortality in institutional settings, and that an individual's life would be prolonged with skilled nursing and attendant care at home or at a community-based facility. There are data to support this, but they are confounded by the fact that only those individuals with the most severe physical disabilities who require the most sophisticated care currently are being institutionalized.

If you wish to read more about this interesting, although highly complex, interrelationship between the medical and legal aspects of neurologic problems, including a full discussion of issues such as perinatal asphyxia, perinatal trauma, the difficulties that pediatricians face related to seizure medications, adverse reactions to immunizations, chloride-deficient formulas, bacterial meningitis, and other medical-legal complications, see the excellent review of Gerald Golden, Director of the Boling Center for Developmental Disabilities. The article appeared in *Current Problems in Pediatrics* (1). This is the best discussion of this timely and troublesome topic that I have ever read.—J.A. Stockman, III, M.D.

Reference

1. Golden GS: *Curr Prob Pediatr* 21:259, 1991.

Reported Practices of Pediatric Residents in the Management of Attention-Deficit Hyperactivity Disorder
Stancin T, Christopher N, Coury D (Case Western Reserve Univ, Ohio State Univ)
Am J Dis Child 144:1329–1333, 1990   7–4

Attention-deficit hyperactivity disorder (ADHD) is one of the most complex, controversial behavioral problems facing primary care pediatricians. The diagnostic, referral, and treatment practices for ADHD among pediatric residents from several training programs were examined.

In all, 124 residents completed the 94-question survey, which included items on the importance of 38 behavioral descriptors of childhood behavior disorders in the diagnosis of ADHD. The residents reported that they based their diagnoses on *Diagnostic and Statistical Manual of Mental Disorders, Revised Third Edition* behavioral criteria from multiple sources. They referred most children to other professionals for assessment, consultation, or treatment. Psychologists and behavioral pediatricians were the most common referral resource. A subset of residents referred to multiple consultants. In treating ADHD, residents reported that they most often relied on behavioral approaches. Many also prescribed stimulants, but most used treatment combinations. Few of the residents recommended dietary modifications in the treatment of ADHD.

In contrast, studies on practicing pediatricians have indicated that many use questionable diagnostic proceures or prescribe mostly stimulants alone to treat children with ADHD. Pediatric residents may be learning more acceptable practices in the diagnosis, referral, and treatment of this disorder.

▶ Dr. Barry S. Russman, Professor, Pediatrics and Neurology, University of Connecticut Medical School, and Chief, Pediatric Neurology, Newington Children's Hospital has long claimed that he has the problem discussed in the article abstracted. Nobody believes him, but he comments anyway:

▶ Today's practice of pediatrics demands that the physician become involved with the social, behavioral, and developmental aspects of children. Residency training directors must ensure that trainees are taught developmental pediatrics, including 1 of the most common disorders in children, namely, ADHD. Practicing pediatricians must be familiar with this disorder so that they can diagnose and manage patients with this disability as well as being able to diagnose and manage other disorders such as infectious diseases.

There are many explanations as to why some pediatricians are reluctant to care for the ADHD child, but 2 stand out. The diagnosis of ADHD is extremely difficult. According to the *Diagnostic and Statistical Manual of Mental Disorders, Revised Third Edition,* the child must exhibit 8 of 14 listed symptoms, which must be present for more than 6 months, and must have started before age 7. Further, "a criterion is met only if the behavior is considerably more frequent than that of most people of the same mental age." Experience with the behavior of children of different ages, in differnet situations, including the classroom, is necessary before a physician to make an ADHD diagnosis. Data about what constitutes excess activity has not been developed; therefore, a more objective method of diagnosing ADHD is needed. Future research should lead to the development of a method of differentiating primary ADHD from hyperactivity and a poor attention span that occurs only in specific situations such as language, for example. A child who is hyperactive in a language situation should not be labeled with the diagnosis of ADHD.

A second major concern with the management of such children is the time needed to satisfactorily help with their problem. The residents needed an average of about 45 minutes to complete the evaluation. The practicing pediatrician must take this factor into account when he or she becomes involved with this aspect of a child's health.

The good news is the encouraging information contained in the article by Stacin et al. that future pediatricians are being trained in this developmental disorder, observations in the office are not important when making the diagnosis, medication alone is not being recommended (rather, an understanding of the child's deficits and the relationship to the school setting, parents, siblings, and peers is emphasized), and dietary measures are not frequently used.—B.J. Russman, M.D.

Do Children With Autism Have March Birthdays?
Gillberg C (Univ of Göteborg, Göteborg, Sweden)
Arch Psychiatr Scand 82:152–156, 1990   7–5

Certain psychiatric disorders, especially schizophrenia, have been linked with birth at a certain period of the year. The month of March has been implicated in numerous studies. Research on seasonality and schizophrenia presumes that some environmental pathologic factor operates only during some months of the year. Foods linked with specific dates, vitamin deficiencies, or viral pandemics, especially influenza, may be factors. The birth dates of 100 people with "cryptogenic" autism born in counties in the western region of Sweden during a 22-year period were compiled. Birth dates of this group were compared with birth dates of 3 other groups: the general population of Sweden born in the same date range; 48 people with autistic-like disorders born in the same region and date range; and 20 people with Asperger syndrome born in the same region and date range.

An excess of March births was found in the group with autism. Common factors of sociodemographic characteristics such as low social class, urban dwelling in utero, and psychosocial disadvantage may also be significant in this group. The possible causes of autism, genetic determination or brain damage in utero, and their relation to seasonal variation in autism need further study.

▶ Would life be so simple as there being a relationship between being born in March and having autism? Frankly, I think these authors are barking up the wrong tree by trying to pin their hopes on such a thin theory. It could well be that a March baby is deprived for the first 3 months of life because its mother, having just delivered, may wish to enjoy spring without paying too much attention to her baby. Pretty far fetched, but so is the original premise.

What do we know about autism? A child usually begins to speak at about 12 months. During that first year, an internal map of the world is constructed from a mass of incoming sensory data. Once a certain degree of thought is achieved based on this experience, the child goes on to acquire a range of communication skills of which language is the most important. Cognitive development, therefore, depends on the evolution of thought processes that are themselves dependent on normal brain function. It follows that either damage to the neuronal substrait underlying the evolution of thought or environmental deficiencies that limit sensory experience will lead to cognitive deficits that occur clinically as disorders of communication, including autism. Such conditions are relatively uncommon, being seen in about 20–40 per 100,000 children.

The American Psychiatric Assocation, in its *Diagnostic and Statistical Manual of Mental Disorders, Revised Third Edition,* refers to conditions such as pervasive developmental disorders and identifies autistic disorders as the only recognized subset of disorders to have emerged. Autism is specifically identified as a syndrome characterized by a set of behavioral disorders that includes (1) qualitative impairment in reciprocal social interaction, (2) qualitative impairment of verbal and nonverbal communication and imaginative activity, and (3) a markedly restricted repertoire of activities and interest.

If you really want to bone up on autism, I suggest you read the excellent supplement to *Pediatrics* dated May 19, 1991 (1). This extensive review clearly indicates that autism does not have a single cause. Genetic and twin studies strongly suggest that, in some families, autism is inherited genetically, despite the fact that the rate of familial aggregation of classical autism is rather modest. Usually, CT, MRI, and routine EEG with or without evoked potentials add no critical information whatsoever to the evaluation/work-up of autistic children. Finally, it has been possible in recent years to make a quantitative histologic examination of the brains of several autistic individuals who coincidentally died. These autopsies have provided data on the anatomical basis of the disorder. Microscopic neuroanatomical abnormalities noted to date have been consistent in type and location. Subtle alterations in the size of neurons and the complexity of their processes and in the microarchitecture of the limbic and cerebellar circuits point to a defect in cellular development that began before birth. So far, none of the brains have had evidence of a gross destructive lesion or an infection (2).

In closing, the theory of a relationshp between being born in March and having autism is curious at best. This does not mean that March is not a miserable month, particularly in certain parts of the country. I spent 12 years in Syracuse, and I can tell you that 36 months of March were something else.—J.A. Stockman, III, M.D.

References

1. Denckla MB, Stanley J (eds): *Pediatrics* 87:suppl, 1991.
2. Bauman ML: *Pediatrics* 87:791, 1991.

Does SleepTight Work? A Behavioral Analysis of the Effectiveness of SleepTight for the Management of Infant Colic

Sosland JM, Christophersen ER (Univ of Kansas Med Ctr; Children's Mercy Hosp, Kansas City)
J Appl Behav Anal 24:161–166, 1991

7–6

Infant colic is common and distressing. Researchers have been studying specific interventions that may change the course of colic. The efficacy of SleepTight, an electromechanical device producing continuous vibration, was assessed in 6 infants.

SleepTight vibrates the baby's crib to simulate the action of a car traveling at 55 mph. Data on infant crying, parental use of SleepTight, and parental satisfaction were analyzed. The use of SleepTight was associated with a decrease in crying in 4 of the infants. The remaining 2 infants had slight increases in crying from baseline. Parental ratings of satisfaction ranged from very satisfied to very dissatisfied.

The findings are not completely consistent with the findings of previous research on the efficacy of SleepTight in infants with colic. A better understanding of this condition might be achieved if evaluation and treatment procedures matched the complexity and heterogeneity of infant colic. SleepTight may be most effective for a specific group of infants with relatively mild colic or for those who do not display physical symptoms such as excessive gas and abdominal pain.

▶ Dr. Mark Weissbluth, Associate Professor of Pediatrics, Northwestern University Medical School, comments:

▶ SleepTight is a vibro-acoustic device that supposedly imitates the auditory and kinesthetic effect of riding in a car at 55 mph. I'm not sure whether the designers had in mind my son's old Jeep or my new Saab. This pseudoscientific approach to soothing babies was heavily publicized after the original, and only, publication appeared as an abstract (1). However, Sosland and Christopherson did not find SleepTight to be effective treatment for colic. Also, Barr and associates in Montreal did not find that extra carrying, and presumably motion, cures colic (2). Similarly, in our study of colic (3), only 3% of infants usually responded to rhythmic rocking motions.

A parsimonious conclusion is that with increasing degrees of crying or fussing, there is decreasing effectiveness of vibratory motion (carrying or rocking) to reduce crying or fussing. Traditional approaches to calm babies, carrying them or using swings or cradles, soothe most babies most of the time, but these approaches are ineffective for those infants who cry or fuss the most. So, save your money if your infant has colic; the only sure cure is the passage of time.— M. Weissbluth, M.D.

References

1. Loadman WE, et al: *Pediatr Res* 182A, 1987.
2. Barr RG, et al: *Pediatrics* 87:623, 1991.

3. Weissbluth M, et al: *J Pediatr* 104:951, 1984.

Prevalence of Reading Disability in Boys and Girls: Results of the Connecticut Longitudinal Study
Shaywitz SE, Shaywitz BA, Fletcher JM, Escobar MD (Yale Univ; Univ of Texas at Austin)
JAMA 264:998–1002, 1990   7–7

Most target populations of reading-disabled children are selected on the basis of prior identification by their schools. A possible sample bias may therefore have resulted from the use of school-identified samples for studies of reading disability. It was hypothesized that the results of previous studies indicating an increased prevalence of reading disability in boys compared with girls reflected a bias in subject selection rather than a gender difference.

During this study of an epidemiologic sample of 215 girls and 199 boys, 2 groups of reading-disabled children were identified, 1 by research and 1 by school. There were no significant differences in the prevalence of reading disability in research-identified boys compared with research-identified girls in the second or third grade. Research identified 8.7% of second-grade boys and 6.9% of second-grade girls, and 9% of third-grade boys and 6% of third-grade girls as reading disabled. By contrast, school identification classified as reading disabled 13.6% of second-grade boys and 3.2% of second-grade girls, and 10% of third-grade boys, and 4.2% of third-grade girls.

School-identified samples are almost unavoidably subject to a referral bias. Reports of an increased prevalence of reading disability in boys may reflect this bias, rather than a real gender difference. Clinicians should not rely solely on schools for identifying reading-disabled children.

▶ Thank you Dr. Shaywitz et al. I always thought that teachers had it in for us boys. As Shaywitz et al. note, teachers rate boys as being significantly more active, less attentive, and less dexterous, and as having more problems in behavior, language, and academics than their female peers. This impression may lead to bias in referrals for reading disability. I can remember as a grade schooler that the boys in our class were always accused of being more klutzy and much less dexterous than our girl counterparts. In fact, I would have given my right arm to be able to be ambidexterous like Susie Pigtails who sat in front of me. What Shaywitz et al. are saying is that such a bias against boys may lead to inappropriate referral for reading disabilities—that the system can be inadvertently clogged by the poor judgment exercised by the source of the referrals.

While on the topic of handedness, do women of "advanced" maternal age tend to have left-handed offspring? While Cornan (1) concluded that there was a relationship in a study of 2,228 university freshman that indicated that higher maternal age was associated with a higher incidence of left-handedness, a more recent cohort study of all children born in the United Kingdom during 1 week in March, 1958 (a study known as the National Developmental Study), failed to show any relationship whatsoever between maternal age and whether you were likely to become right handed or left handed (2). As an aside, the Mc-Manus report didn't mention a word about autism and March.

For some time it has been supposed that older mothers have more stressful gestations and deliveries and that perinatal and prenatal stress relates to the appearance of left-handedness. Well, apparently, it just ain't so. Investigators who have hypothesized otherwise over the years apparently don't know their left hand from their right.—J.A. Stockman, III, M.D.

References

1. Cornan S: *N Engl J Med* 323:1673, 1990.
2. McManus IC: *N Engl J Med* 323:1426, 1990.

Nonhandicapped Very-Low-Birth-Weight Infants at One Year of Age: Developmental Profile

Williamson WD, Wilson GS, Lifschitz MH, Thurber SA (Baylor Univ, Houston; Texas Children's Hosp, Houston)
Pediatrics 85:405–410, 1990   7–8

The developmental profiles of 61 very low–birth-weight (VLBW) infants who had no major motor, sensory, or cognitive deficit were compared with developmental profiles of 28 term infants at age 1 year. Birth weights in the study group were less than 1,500 g. Development was assessed by using the Revised Gesell Developmental Schedules.

The VLBW infants were more likely than term infants to have significant discrepancies between fine motor or language ability and early problem-solving skills. In addition, they scored significantly below term infants with respect to adaptive, gross motor, fine motor, language, and personal-social function. Motor performance in the VLBW group correlated with bronchopulmonary dysplasia, intracranial hemorrhage, and time in hospital. Language performance correlated with intracranial bleeding and with birth weight.

Global cognitive scores are limited in depicting the developmental performance of VLBW infants. Comprehensive evaluation of all aspects of behavior is needed to properly assess these infants. Further studies will show whether early unevenness in development persists and affects performance in school.

▶ Dr. Marilee C. Allen, Associate Professor of Pediatrics, Johns Hopkins University School of Medicine, and Director of the NICU Developmental Clinic at the Kennedy Institute for Handicapped Children, comments:

▶ The relatively low incidence of major handicap (cerebral palsy, mental retardation) in VLBW preterm infants is well established in the literature. More recently, there has been increasing attention to more subtle CNS deficits in this population. A number of studies have suggested an increased incidence of visual perceptual deficits, language delays, clumsiness, fine motor problems, attention deficits, and school problems in preschool and school-aged children who were born prematurely. This study demonstrates that manifestations of subtle CNS dysfunction can be demonstrated in VLBW preterm infants as early as 1 year chronological age (10 months when age was corrected for degree of prematurity). Evaluation of each field or stream of development separately demonstrated differential performance for each stream: VLBW infants scored much lower than term infants in language and personal-social areas. Moreover, associations with perinatal risk factors were different for each stream (i.e., in addition to intracranial hemorrhage in both, language also correlated with birth weight and male gender and fine motor abilities correlated with bronchopulmonary dysplasia). These findings suggest differential causes for the subtle damage to the different streams of development in preterm infants.

This paper emphasizes the importance of evaluating and analyzing each stream of development separately. Most follow-up studies of preterm infants to date have relied on the Bayley Scale of Infant Intelligence, which averages an infant's abilities together into a mental and performance (motor) score. The Bayley Scale may be helpful in identifying major handicaps, but it is clearly inadequate when evaluating subtle CNS deficits. That these subtle CNS deficits may be very important functionally is suggested by the studies of preschool and school-aged children born prematurely.—M.C. Allen, M.D.

Preschool Age Children of Divorce: Transitional Phenomena and the Mourning Process
Stirtzinger R, Cholvat L (Univ of Toronto; Ontario)
Can J Psychiatry 35:506–513, 1990   7–9

There has been much learned about the role of attachment in continuous bonding and its particular sustaining role in times of crisis. Transitional objects and phenomena are important to persons, particularly in times of stress, change, or new situations. The role of the family home as an attachment object was studied in 57 preschool-aged children coping with the stress of a parental divorce.

The child's attachment to the famly home, based on strong desire for close proximity to it, was determined in 3 subgroups of children: the first group consisted of 19 children whose parents had divorced and who had not changed homes during the previous 2–12 months; a second group included 20 children whose parents had divorced and who changed homes; and a third group consisted of 18 children from intact families who moved away from the family home. There were no significant differences between groups regarding sex, school change, contact with noncustodial parent, siblings, birth order, and amount of time spent in the family home.

Children of divorce exhibited an increased level of attachment to the family home when compared with children of intact families who moved away from the family home. Furthermore, children of divorce who moved from the family home but showed a high attachment to it showed better behavior adjustment, both in externalizing expressions like aggression and delinquent behavior and in internalizing factors like depression and schizoid-like actions, compared with children of divorce who showed low attachment after moving from the family home and children who remained living in the family home after the divorce.

The family home takes an added significance on preschool children after divorce. This study presents a challenge to understanding the developmental intricacies of mourning for children of different ages and the role that object attachment plays for children in times of crisis.

▶ There has been so much written about the children of divorce that it seems inappropriate to say any more beyond what the abstract indicates about this study from the *Canadian Journal of Psychiatry*. Therefore, being totally bereft of any contributory thoughts on this topic, I will simply close this chapter on developmental pediatrics by repeating a question that was posed by Friman recently in the *American Journal of Diseases of Children* (1). The question is: "What would Linus do with his blanket if his thumb-sucking were ever treated?"

Well, now we have the answer. A study was undertaken in 39 thumb-sucking children who additionally had attachments to other objects such as teddy bears or blankets. The thumb-sucking habit was broken in these kids by use of a combination of adverse taste treatment and motivation. Adverse taste treatment basically means applying less than pleasant substances to the thumb twice a day or as required (2). The study results were very straightforward and have direct applicability or extrapolation to Linus. To say it differently, when Linus is older than 5 years, otherwise healthy, and is successfully treated for thumb-sucking, his interest in his blanket should diminish substantially (in fact to zero). He may not throw it away, but he will be much less likely to haul it around.—J.A. Stockman, III, M.D.

References

1. Friman PC: *Am J Dis Child* 144:1316, 1990.
2. Friman PC, et al: *Pediatrics* 78:174, 1986.

Impact of Pediatricians' Attire on Children and Parents
Marino RV, Rosenfeld W, Narula P, Karakureum M (Winthrop Univ Hosp; State Univ of New York at Stony Brook, Mineola, NY)
J Dev Behav Pediatr 12:98–101, 1991   7–10

Pediatricians try to develop trusting, comfortable relationships with both parents and children. The physician's attire has been shown to have a significant effect on patients' perceptions.

Fifty children and parents in an outpatient facility were shown 5 photographs of a female or male physician dressed differently (Figs 7–1 and 7–2). Dress ranged from formal to informal. A list of positive and nega-

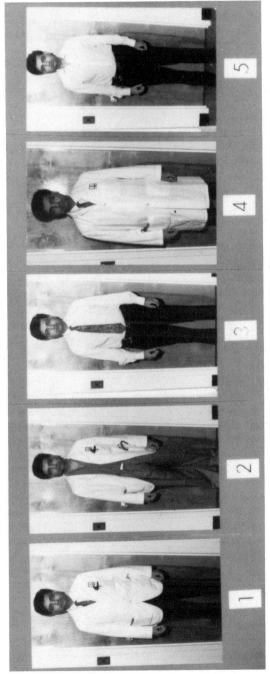

Fig. 7–1.— Male attire. (Courtesy of Marino RV, Rosenfeld W, Narula P, et al: *J Dev Behav Pediatr* 12:98–101, 1991.)

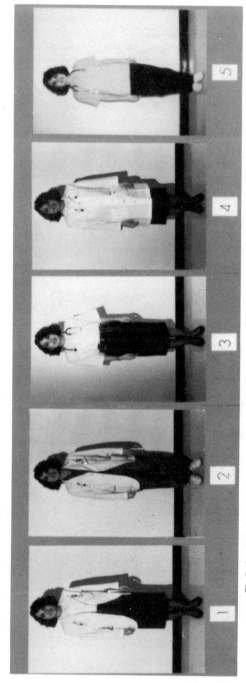

Fig 7–2.— Female attire. (Courtesy of Marino RV, Rosenfeld W, Narula P, et al: *J Dev Behav Pediatr* 12:98–101, 1991.)

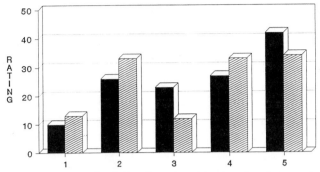

Fig 7–3.—Negative responses by children for male and female attire. (Courtesy of Marino RV, Rosenfeld W, Narula P, et al: *J Dev Behav Pediatr* 12:98–101, 1991.)

tive attributes was given to the parents and children, who were asked to match each picture to the attributes. Parents had a strong preference for the formally dressed woman and man. More than half the parents least liked the least formal attire. Children had no clear preferences for the male physician but preferred the female physician in the blouse and skirt. Although children also assigned negative attributes to the informal attire, it was not to the same degree as their parents (Fig 7–3).

Parents have stronger preferences than their children for physician attire. Although children apparently do not have strong positive preferences, they may respond negatively to informal attire.

▶ Dr. Sara Naureckas, Fellow in the Division of General Academic Pediatrics, and former Chief Resident, Children's Memorial Hospital, and Dr. Alan Friedman, Fellow in Pediatric Cardiology, Yale New Haven Medical Center, and former Chief Resident Physician, Children's Memorial Hospital, both comment:

▶ As we move toward the twenty-first century, it is clear that both medicine and fashion have made great strides. If ours were a perfect world, what a physician wears would not be as important as his or her ability to exercise sound medical judgment and to be compassionate. In our less than ideal world, however, it may be true that "You are what you wear."

It is well known that when kids reach school age, the opinions of their friends and classmates become increasingly important and may sometimes be in conflict with parental views and values. The authors of this article have shown that parents prefer more formally attired physicians. In this study of children aged 5 to 18 years, it is not surprising that parents could not predict which physician photo their children would prefer. One reason for this difference in physician preference may be the change in how the media presents doctors. We have gone from the formally dressed Drs. Kildare and Welby to the equally caring, competent, and kind, but much more casually and comfortably dressed, Drs. Joel Fleishman and Doogie Howser.

As pediatricians, we attempt to develop a trusting, comfortable, and effective relationship with both a parent and a chilld, 2 people who are widely discrepant in age and taste. Using the information in the article, we now have a good idea of what to wear to impress parents in the office brochure publicity photo. Based on recent trends, what kids might like best would be to have their pediatrician dressed like a green, pizza-eating reptile, better known as a Teenage Mutant Ninja Turtle.—S. Naureckas, M.D., and A. Friedman, M.D.

8 Adolescent Medicine

Marfan Syndrome in Adolescents and Young Adults: Psychosocial Functioning and Knowledge
Schneider MB, Davis JG, Boxer RA, Fisher M, Friedman SB (North Shore Univ Hosp, Cornell Univ Med College, Manhasset, NY)
J Dev Behav Pediatr 11:122–127, 1990   8–1

Little information on the psychosocial aspects of Marfan syndrome has been published. The adjustment of teenagers with this connective tissue disorder was investigated.

Twenty-two patients with Marfan syndrome, aged 11 to 24 years, were studied. The subjects were interviewed, then completed the Offer Self-Image Questionnaire and 2 additional questionnaires that elicited their concerns about the disorder, compliance with medical regimens, and knowledge of Marfan syndrome, as well as the impact of the syndrome on their level of psychosocial adaptation. The subjects' parents were also interviewed.

The adolescents showed normal psychosocial adaptation according to

Percent of Subjects Responding Correctly to General Knowledge Questions About Marfan Syndrome

Knowledge Area	% Correct Responses
Marfan syndrome is a genetic disorder	86
All organ systems are not necessarily equally involved	86
Beta-adrenergic blockers are commonly taken	82
A child can have Marfan syndrome even if their parents did not	73
Most serious risk of Marfan syndrome involves the cardiac system	73
Knows the function of beta-blockers	73
Defines Marfan syndrome in broad terms	59
Names 3 or more organ systems commonly involved in Marfan syndrome	59
Subject has a 50% chance of having offspring with Marfan syndrome	59
Pregnancy is a problem for females with Marfan syndrome	45
Severity of Marfan syndrome in an offspring is unpredictable	45

(Courtesy of Schneider MB, Davis JG, Boxer RA, et al: *J Dev Behav Pediatr* 11:122–127, 1990.)

the Offer Self-Image Questionnaire. However, they indicated that their lives would be significantly better without the syndrome, particularly with regard to their physical activity and self-image. The subjects most often expressed their concerns to their parents and less often to their physicians. Compliance with medical regimens was suboptimal. Their knowledge was weakest in areas pertaining to future childbearing (table).

Teenagers with Marfan syndrome appear to have normal psychosocial adaptation. However, physicians caring for such patients can enhance their ability to cope with Marfan syndrome by discussing self-image issues and disease-related concerns. Physicians should also encourage compliance with medical regimens and educate patients about the syndrome.

▶ You may think this entry is an odd one for the Adolescent Medicine chapter, but Marfan syndrome is becoming a "big deal" among teenagers. With a disorder that has an incidence of about 6 per 100,000 people and the increasing tendency toward large centralized school districts, you can be fairly sure that 1 or more children/adolescents in your own schools will have this disorder. Affected adolescents and young adults are often restricted from participation in contact sports, and they commonly are advised to take medications, particularly β-adrenergic blockers. Thus, teenagers with Marfan syndrome must limit their physical activities, sometimes chronically take medications, and are at increased risk for significant morbidity and early mortality. As adolescents, they additionally must begin to consider the implications of their disease on future childbearing, including the increased risk of mortality associated with pregnancy, because Marfan syndrome is an autosomal-dominant condition.

If you have not gained a great deal of familiarity with Marfan syndrome, chances are that you have not had much pressure put on you by your school district to help with identifying the young athlete who may have this disorder. In some areas, school physical examinations are intentionally designed to screen for Marfan syndrome to remove the high-risk child from competitive sports. Of the 22 cases reported in the study abstracted above, the correct diagnosis was suspected only twice by the child's primary pediatrician. Six of the 22 cases were detected after an abnormal eye examination, and a school physician or nurse identified 8 cases. In 2 of the cases, either a teacher or the child recognized what was going on because of a widely circulated recent issue of *Sports Illustrated* that very nicely and accurately covered the full range of risks associated with Marfan syndrome. Thus, pediatricians were the odd persons out when it came to initially making the diagnosis.

What can you say to a teenager who has recently been diagnosed with Marfan syndrome to help him or her cope with a disorder that can dislocate the lens and dilate or even rupture the aorta, in addition to other musculoskeletal, cardiovascular, pulmonary, and even CNS manifestations?

For one, you can tell the child that the cause of Marfan syndrome has finally been determined. This past year Kainulainen et al. (1) were able to locate the gene defect causing Marfan syndrome on chromosome 15. Although finding a cause does not equate to a cure, the discovery of the cause of Marfan syndrome will be of primary psychological benefit to patients. Many people, especially the parents of a child with a newly diagnosed sporadic case, respond to counseling and cope with the disorder much better if they realize that the cause is known and that there can never be a cure until the cause has been discovered. Parents also need to be reassured that the multidisciplinary program of prophylactic management developed over the last decade can lead to longer lives with less disability than the presence of a mutant allele would otherwise predict.

I think the greatest boost to a teenager with Marfan syndrome would come from confirmation that Lincoln indeed did have Marfan syndrome. He made it through life having accomplished a great deal, and knowing that he had the same disorder might be of some significant reassurance. As you may be aware, there is a variety of genetic material available to determine whether or not Lincoln had Marfan syndrome. Lockets of his hair and blood stains taken after his assassination would end or confirm the speculation that Abe's tall, gaunt frame and sunken eyes were manifestations of Marfan syndrome. Permission to pursue such scientific endeavors has been the topic of debate in Congress this past year. The diagnosis can easily be made on materials that are available without disintering the old boy. All one has to do is look for the chromosomal defect mentioned above.

If old Abe could be asked to give permission to have his genetic material examined, my bet is that, knowing it might help children, adolescents, and young adults understand their disease better, he would respond the same way he did in a letter to Secretary Stanton when he refused to dismiss Postmaster-General Montgomery Blair in July 1864. Mr. Lincoln said, "The truth is generally the best vindication against slander." I do not think Mr. Lincoln would have minded us knowing whether or not he had Marfan syndrome and, frankly, for society as a whole, knowing that it can't do him any harm now, it would be terrific if, in fact, he did have it for others who are now living.—J.A. Stockman, III, M.D.

Reference

1. Kainulainen K, et al: *N Engl J Med* 323:935, 1990.

Health Care Expenditure Patterns for Adolescents
Newacheck PW, McManus MA (Univ of California, San Francisco; McManus Health Policy, Inc, Washington DC)
J Adolesc Health Care 11:133–140, 1990   8–2

Data from the 1980 and first quarter 1981 National Medical Care Utilization and Expenditure Survey were used to determine total charges for inpatient hospital services, physician and nonphysician services, prescribed medications, and medical care equipment and supplies for 2,767 adolescents (aged 10 to 18 years). Family out-of-pocket expenses and other sources of payment were also assessed.

Average total per capita health care expenditures for this group were $525 in 1988 dollars (table). The average out-of-pocket expenses totaled $151. The burden of out-of-pocket expenses was not evenly distributed among the adolescents' families. The 10% of adolescents with the highest

	Average annual charges* ($)	Average paid out-of-pocket (%)
All adolescents	525	29
Age		
Early adolescence (10–14 yr)	349	28
Late adolescence (15–18 yr)	720	29
Gender		
Male	482	28
Female	569	30
Race		
White	573	29
Nonwhite	289	26
Poverty status		
Below poverty level	768	11
Above poverty level	491	33

Average Medical Care Charges and Out-of-Pocket Expenses for Adolescents

*Estimates are adjusted to 1988 dollars by using medical care component of Consumer Price Index.
(Courtesy of Newacheck PW, McManus MA: *J Adolesc Health Care* 11:133–140, 1990.)

out-of-pocket expenses accounted for 65% of all out-of-pocket expenses. White teens had medical expenses that were twice those of nonwhite teens, and teens whose families had incomes below the poverty level had substantially higher charges for medical services than teens from families with incomes above the poverty level. However, for impoverished adolescents family out-of-pocket expenses were lower on average.

Health insurance coverage was uneven in this sample. Although private health insurance was most common, a substantial minority of these teens were covered by public insurance or a combination of private and public insurance. Out-of-pocket expenses were related to the type of health insurance.

Financing strategies to improve access to care and decrease out-of-pocket medical expenditures for adolescents' families include creation of more private and public insurance products that are both affordable and accessible and provision of adequate catastrophic protection with reasonable annual out-of-pocket expense limits and adequate lifetime maximum benefit limits. Such strategies also include the development of basic and supplemental benefit plans and direct grant programs targeted at the special health care needs of teenagers.

▶ Dr. Iris F. Litt, Professor of Pediatrics, Stanford University Medical Center, and Director, Division of Adolescent Medicine, comments:

▶ The authors appropriately caution against accepting their finding of low per-capita expenditures as reflective of the actual status of the health of the nation's adolescents. Such data may underestimate true usage because of the survey's methodology. Information was provided by parents who may have been unaware of their adolescents' use of confidential health services or were unwilling to report use to preserve their own privacy. Such data most likely also reflect the difficulty adolescents have in identifying, accessing, and/or paying for health care, most often because of lack of insurance. One of 7 adolescents is without health insurance currently, including 1 in 3 who is poor yet not Medicaid-eligible. This group includes undocumented nationals of other countries, whose numbers have increased considerably in the decade since these data were collected.

The growing ethnic and cultural diversity of the country's adolescent population must also be considered in their health assessment and planning. The categorization of subjects as either "white" or "nonwhite," as was done in this study, fails to consider important genetic, cultural, regional, and socioeconomic factors that influence health status and delivery of care.

Among those adolescents who have health insurance, coverage is often lacking for the kinds of preventive or mental health problems needed for this age group. Legal requirements of parental consent may preclude use of family insurance for conditions that the adolescent may wish to keep confidential.

Inadequate training of health professionals to recognize and assess the age-appropriate health needs of adolescents further compromises the quality of the care they receive, even if adolescents can overcome barriers to access.

Expansion of Medicaid coverage, age-appropriate benefits in all insurance policies, and growth of school-linked health clinics are some of the strategies that may improve access for necessary health care and preventive services for adolescents.—I.F. Litt, M.D.

Association Between Parenthood and Problem Behavior in a National Sample of Adolescents
Elster AB, Ketterlinus R, Lamb ME (Univ of Utah, Salt Lake City; Natl Inst of Child Health and Human Development, Natl Insts of Health, Bethesda, Md)
Pediatrics 85:1044–1050, 1990   8–3

A previous study suggested an association between fatherhood and problem behaviors. Data from the National Longitudinal Survey of the Work Experience of Youth were used to evaluate the association between parental status and problem behavior among young women. Information regarding problem behaviors was obtained from a national sample of 1,263 urban and 388 rural young women who were aged 15 to 17 years when interviewed in 1980.

Based on the fertility data from 1985, each young woman was assigned to 1 of 3 parental status groups: school-aged mothers who were aged 18 years and younger at the birth of their first child, young adult mothers aged 19 to 21 years at the birth of their first child, and nonmothers who had not had a child by age 21 years.

Overall, urban youths had greater composite problem behavior scores than did rural youths, and white youths reported more problem behavior than did black youths. White youths were more likely to engage in truancy, running away, smoking marijuana, drinking alcohol, and using other drugs, whereas black youths were more likely to report school suspensions and fighting.

There was a clear association between problem behavior and the birth of a first chlid before age 19 years. The 3 parental groups appeared to be ordered in risk, with school-aged mothers most likely to have a history of problem behavior, followed by young adult mothers, and then by nonmothers. Compared with women who had never engaged in problem behavior, young urban women with 3 or more problem behaviors were twice as likely to have a child before age 21 years. Analysis of individual behaviors indicated that school-aged mothers were more likely than young adult mothers and nonmothers to report school suspension, truancy, running away, smoking marijuana, and fighting. These effects were more consistent for young urban women.

On average, adolescents who become pregnant and elect parenthood are likely to have engaged in problem behaviors before their pregnancy. These data can provide information for future studies that will address the risk of parental difficulties in these adolescents and the development of a risk appraisal instrument to identify adolescents at risk for becoming pregnant. Because the strength of the association between parenthood and problem behaviors appears to differ by type of community and racial group, prevention and intervention strategies will need to be sensitive to these types of ecological and cultural factors.

▶ Reading the adolescent medicine literature never fails to amaze me. There is such tremendous juxtaposition of differing kinds of problems. The topic of the article abstracted is a heavy one, and yet it immediately followed an article I was reading on "A Vocal Hygiene Program for High School Cheerleaders" (1). The latter article had nothing to do with foul language but rather with the management of the problem of hoarseness. I tell our medical students at Northwestern that everything in life is a bell-shaped curve. Well, when it comes to adolescent medicine problems, there are complications of being a cheerleader on 1 end of the bell-shaped curve, and at the other end I suppose would be substance abuse, HIV infection, and suicide.

Back to the article abstracted—the association between prior problem behavior and teen pregnancy. This is not a minor problem, and it certainly falls on the right-hand side of the bell-shaped curve in terms of seriousness, because along with substance abuse and delinquency, premature pregnancy ranks among the major health and social problems incurred by contemporary adolescents.

When I first approached reading this article, I thought that it was simply going to confirm preexisting prejudices common among health care providers that issues of poverty, race, and being in the inner city were dominant in terms of the bases of behaviors that lead to early pregnancy. I really shortchanged the study in that regard. These investigators have very thoughtfully examined the whole gamut of issues that explain the problem. One sees that black and white youth tend to be at risk for different problems. School suspension and fighting were more likely among black youth, whereas truancy, running away, smoking marijauna, and using other drugs were more likely among white youth. Hispanic youth, in general, had profiles more similar to white than to black youth. No report such as this is valuable unless it has some concrete implications. There are at least 3 that I could see. First, the degree of turmoil before pregnancy can be a predictor of how well adolescent mothers adjust to their new and varied roles after delivery. Second, prior problem behavior might be used as part of a risk appraisal to identify adolescents who are most likely to become pregnant. Third, because the strength of the association between parenthood and problem behaviors appears to differ by type of community and by racial group, prevention and intervention strategies will need to be sensitive to demographic and cultural factors.

Was life as complicated 50 years ago as it appears to be now for our teenagers? In the old days, it seemed as if boys were simply boisterous, and the only serious admonishment that we needed to make was that children should be seen and not obscene.—J.A. Stockman, III, M.D.

Reference

1. Aaron VL, et al: *Language, Speech, and Hearing Services in Schools* 22:287, 1991.

Assessment of Pubertal Maturity in Boys, Using Height and Grip Strength
Backous DD, Farrow JA, Friedl KE (Baylor Univ, Houston; Univ of Washington; Madigan Army Med Ctr, Tacoma, Wash)
J Adolesc Health Care 11:497–500, 1990   8–4

Several studies have suggested that pubertal maturity is predictive of sports injuries in adolescents. Although pubertal maturity is often taken as the measure of physical maturity, measures of strength and skeletal height may be more predictive of pubertal maturity. Several noninvasive measures of pubertal maturity, such as age, height, weight, body mass index, and maximum (right or left hand) and average grip strength with the hand-held dynamometer, were evaluated in 98 healthy boys (mean age, 14.8 years) and validated in a second sample of 99 healthy boys.

Stepwise discriminate functional analysis demonstrated that height and average grip strength were independent predictors of maturity. Boys were considered immature (Tanner stages 1 through 3) when average grip strength fell below 25 kg and height was less than 65 inches (165 cm), whereas boys who exceeded both of these measurements were considered mature (Tanner stage 4 or 5). When validated in the second sample of 99 boys, the method had a specificity of 100%, sensitivity of 93.5% for immature boys and 81% for mature boys, and overall efficiency of 85%. However, a subgroup of mature boys who met the height criterion but did not achieve the average grip strength for maturity was identified.

The use of height and grip strength is a practical, noninvasive method of classifying physical maturity in boys and screening for potential risk for sports injury. It appears that a subset of boys who are tall but weak may be at increased risk for certain types of sports injuries.

▶ What these authors are describing is a simple way of telling whether boys are pubertally mature, using 2 simple measurements: height and grip strength as determined by 1 of those little hand-held jobbies that tells you how many kilograms you can squeeze. These determinations were then compared with Tanner staging from the physical examination.

After reading this report in detail, I wondered why the authors just didn't rely on the Tanner staging itself. It doesn't take very long to do as part of a sports physical screening on a teenage male who is buck naked anyway. If you look carefully through the data, however, you will find an interesting finding, and that is that there is a significant gap of about 12 months between certain events. The data suggest that there is a small group of taller and generally pubertally mature (Tanner-wise) boys who do not yet possess the muscular strength of their peers of similar height. Presumably, it is this group who would otherwise waltz off onto the playing field with an increased risk of injury. Indeed, the latter has been documented in the soccer literature among a subset of this 'twixt and 'tween age group individuals (1).

So what is the point of all this? A simple determination of height and grip strength may go a long way to prevent sports-related injuries (that is still a testable hypothesis, however). For boys who are Tanner stage 3 to 4 whose grip strength is down, you can advise them to hang loose, it will only be another year or 2 before they can play with the best of them.

While on the topic of teenagers, your own teenaged daughter just got her driver's permit. Do you know what the greatest risk of her becoming involved with an accident is with respect to day of the week and time of day?

You would guess correctly if you guessed Friday, in the afternoon and evening. On nonschool days, however, accident rates start to increase about 7 AM and then rise steadily until late afternoon. Nighttime hours between 9 PM and 4 AM are especially high-risk times for adolescent drivers, particularly on nights that do not precede school days. Then again, don't worry about this, because *your* daughter isn't likely to be out that late at night anyway, is she? (2).—J.A. Stockman, III, M.D.

References

1. Backous DD, et al: *Am J Dis Child* 142:839, 1988.
2. Alexander EA, et al: *J Adolesc Health Care* 11:413, 1990.

**Trends in Teenage Smoking During Pregnancy
Washington State: 1984 Through 1988**
Davis RL, Tollestrup K, Milham S Jr (Washington State Dept of Health, Olympia)
Am J Dis Child 144:1297–1301, 1990   8–5

The *1990 Health Objectives for the Nation* called for a reduction of smoking prevalence in the general population to less than 25%, in youths aged 12 to 18 to less than 6%, and in pregnant women to less than half that of the nonpregnant population. To assess the progress made in Washington state toward achieving these goals in teenaged pregnant women, data on birth certificates from 1984 to 1988 were analyzed to determine smoking trends during pregnancy in teenagers aged 12 to 19 years who gave birth to a live infant.

There was a small but significant increase in the smoking prevalence among pregnant teenagers, from 32% in 1984 to 37% in 1988. Smoking prevalence varied with the mother's age, ethnicity, marital status, and amount of prenatal care. Smoking rates were highest among whites and native Americans. The prevalence among unmarried pregnant teenagers was higher than among those who were married. Smoking prevalence rates for pregnant teenagers in Washington state were greater than previously reported national rates for nonpregnant teenagers, and the differences did not appear to diminish over time.

There has been litle movement during the last 5 years toward meeting the *1990 Health Objectives for the Nation* with regard to smoking behavior of teenagers who become pregnant. In fact, smoking prevalence rates have increased.

Characteristics of Unmarried Adolescent Mothers: Determinants of Child Rearing Versus Adoption
Resnick MD, Blum RW, Bose J, Smith M, Toogood R (Univ of Minnesota; Children's Home Society of Minnesota; Minnesota Dept of Health, Minneapolis)
Am J Orthopsychiatry 60:577–584, 1990   8–6

The federal government has advocated adoption as an alternative to either abortion or child rearing for young adolescents. To determine the sociodemographic and personal attributes that characterize adolescents who place their children for adoption ("placer" group) and those who raise their children ("parent" group), 59 placers and a comparative group of 59 parents, aged 13–19 years, were interviewed. Most of the adolescents were white Catholic, or Protestant. There were no differences between groups in the number of pregnancies, abortions or miscarriages, or age of children, and level of education, but significantly more placers lived with both mother and father, whereas significantly more parents lived with the baby's father.

Adolescents who opted for adoption for their children were more likely to be of higher socioeconomic status and higher educational aspirations and to be from suburban residences. Placers were more likely to be frequent attendees of religious services. Placers were themselves more likely to be adopted, have adopted family members, and view adoption experience as positive, suggesting a learning process in considering and selecting pregnancy-resolution alternatives. Interestingly, one fifth of parents described their pregnancy as "planned," and 52% described themselves as "having reasons for getting pregnant." Most placers and parents described abortion as morally unacceptable or contrary to their religious beliefs. More than half of parents who had not chosen adoption explained that they were not emotionally capable of putting their child for adoption, whereas placers believed that adoption was in the best interest of their baby. More than one third of placers cited the importance of educational aspirations in their decision. Only 5% of placers, compared with 3 times that of parents, said that their decision was made because of preferences of the baby's father.

In addition to abortion or parenting, adoption is another pregnancy resolution alternative for the unmarried adolescent mother. This study provides data for discussions of interventions and appropriation of services for child-rearing or adoption for unmarried adolescent mothers. Physicians should encourage a more frank and open approach to the pregnancy resolution alternatives available to adolescents.

Sexual Activity and Problem Behaviors Among Black, Urban Adolescents
Ensminger ME (Johns Hopkins Univ)
Child Dev 61:2032–2046, 1990   8–7

It is not clear whether sexual activity should be considered in the same paradigm as adolescent substance use and assault. The relationships among these behaviors were examined in a series of 705 black inner-city adolescents who had been followed up since the first grade. Social behavior and parental supervision also were evaluated.

The most frequent patterns were a lack of problem behaviors; sexual activity only; and a combination of sexual activity, heavy substance use, and assault. Adolescents with multiple problems tended to differ from the others with respect to both behavior and parental supervision. Sexual intercourse correlated most closely with marijuana use and least closely with assault.

Male adolescents who were sexually active but had no problem behaviors resembled those without problem behaviors. In contrast, female adolescents who were sexually active but had no problem behaviors differed from their no-problem counterparts in family origin. They were more likely to have mothers who began bearing children while they were adolescents and mothers who did not finish high school.

A study of adolescent behaviors in combination appears useful for gaining an understanding of how deviant patterns develop. Because sexual activity often occurs along with other adolescent behaviors such as substance use, a comparison of those who are sexually active with those who are inactive, without regard to other behaviors, may yield findings that relate as much to substance use as to sexual activity itself.

▶ At first blush, selecting specific populations to examine problems such as adolescent sexuality may seem unusually narrow minded, if not frankly prejudicial. The complexity of individual issues, however, seems to dictate the necessity of this approach. Let me give you an example. Would you think that highly intelligent school-aged young women (including those in college) or delinquent Southern male adolescents are more likely to have altered their sexual practices to give better recognition to the problem of sexually transmitted diseases?

You would have answered wrong if you said college-aged women. MacDonald et al. (1) reported on a 1988 survey of 5,514 students in the first year of a community college or university. The results of their investigation were very clear. Highly intelligent young women must seem to enjoy taking risks, because their behavior has not been significantly modified overall. On the other hand, Elfenbein et al. (2) examined condom use by a population of delinquent Southern males. Of sexually active delinquent male adolescents admitted to a detention center in north central Florida over a 6-month period from 1987 to 1988, 70% reported routine use of condoms. A review of the medical records of a similar group of detainees from the same facility just 4 years earlier showed an almost twofold increase in the rate of condom use. When this group of adolescents was asked why they were using condoms, the predominant answer was to prevent sexually transmitted diseases (two thirds of the responders). Pregnancy was still fairly far down on the list, at only 33%. It used to be said that the best reason to go to college was so that you could get an education and avoid having to use your common sense. This doesn't seem to apply when it comes to thinking you are protected against sexually transmitted diseases simply because you are in the "correct" environment.

All of the above suggests that education, education, and more education, is needed. It is needed not only by the kids, but by the kids' parents. There is still too much ambiguity in the application of acceptable standards of behavior by parents. It is a strange country, isn't it when, if a 17-year-old girl develops gonorrhea, she is immediately socially stigmatized in a small community, but if a 17-year-old boy does that, it's simply a coming of age. In neither case is the sexually transmitted disease something to clap about.—J.A. Stockman, III, M.D.

References

1. MacDonald NE, et al: *JAMA* 20:3155, 1990.
2. Elfenbein DS, et al: *J Adolesc Health Care* 12:35, 1991.

Decreased Bone Density in Adolescent Girls With Anorexia Nervosa

Bachrach LK, Guido D, Katzman D, Litt IF, Marcus R (Stanford Univ; VA Med Ctr, Palo Alto, Calif)

Pediatrics 86:440–447, 1990 8–8

Osteoporosis is a recognized complication of chronic anorexia nervosa in adults. To determine whether bone mass is also reduced in younger patients with anorexia nervosa, bone mineral density of midradius, lumbar spine, and whole body, as measured by single- and dual-photon absorptiometry, were compared in 18 girls, aged 12–20 years who had anorexia nervosa and in 25 health control subjects of similar age. The role of body mass index, calcium intake, duration of illness and amenorrhea, and exercise in predicting the observed bone mass was evaluated.

Compared with healthy control subjects, patients with anorexia nervosa had significantly lower lumbar spine and whole bone mineral densities that correspond to deficits in bone mineral of 20% to 25%. Bone mineral density at the midradius was not significantly reduced. Of the 18 adolescents with anorexia nervosa, 12 showed marked osteopenia, with bone density greater than 2 standard deviations less than the normal mean for age. In half of these girls, the interval since diagnosis of anorexia nervosa was less than 1 year. Body mass index correlated significantly with bone mineral density in healthy control subjects and in patients with anorexia. Hence, the low bone density in patients with anorexia nervosa was commensurate with their low body mass index alone. Age at diagnosis and duration of anorexia nervosa correlated with bone mineral density, whereas calcium intake, exercise, and duration of amenorrhea did not.

Adolescent girls with anorexia nervosa frequently have marked deficits in bone mineral density. Because bone mineral in these patients corresponds to levels predicted from the normal regression of body mass and bone density, low body mass is a major predictor of bone deficit in adolescent girls with anorexia nervosa.

▶ Dr. Craig Langman, Associate Professor and Associate Chairman, Department of Pediatrics, and Director of the Section of Research Nephrology, Northwestern University Medical School and Children's Memorial Hospital, comments:

▶ Bachrach and colleagues studied adolescent women with anorexia nervosa and demonstrate that trabecular bone density was markedly diminished, and cortical bone density was preserved, when compared with control values. The best correlate of the change in vertebral mineral content was the markedly reduced body mass characteristic of the anorexic state. Why should pediatricians be interested in bone mineral density in women with anorexia nervosa?

The greatest percentage accumulation of bone mineral occurs during the childhood years, continuing through the mid to late 20s. Throughout the remainder of our life, we are losing bone and, unfortunately, if we drop our bone mineral density as measured in 1 of several lumbar vertebral or femoral regions to <1 g/cm^2, we may fracture even in the absence of trauma. The lay press has a feature on postmenopausal osteoporosis almost every week. However, there are some studies to suggest that the daughters of women with postmenopausal osteoporosis may have osteopenia despite normal menstruation and young age (late 20s to early 30s).

Thus, it may be that bone mineral density is an inherited condition, and may "track" quite similarly to the distribution of blood pressures in a population. The disorder called osteoporosis may represent not only enhanced dissolution of bone mineral during the initial period after menopause when estrogen is absent, but also, perhaps, occurs in a population in which "normal" bone mass accretion never occurred. If the latter possibility is allowed, it is not too difficult to see that pediatricians may be the best group to study and identify the mechanisms involved in the lack of bone mass accretion.

What are the components of bone mass accretion during childhood that may be abnormal and provide the background for enhanced losses of bone with menopause? Of course, these are unknown at present, but the list may include abnormalities of systemic hormones, local growth factors in bone, or preprogrammed changes in osteoblasts and/or osteoclasts themselves. Bachrach et al. have suggested that the disordered body composition of adolescent women with anorexia nervosa is most strongly correlated with osteopenia. However, the patients were amenorrheic and may have had multiple other hormonal abnormalities that had an impact on bone mass. Women with anorexia nervosa may serve to point out to us that in a most extreme circumstance, bone mineral accretion is reduced by 25%, and if it is not repaired quickly, this will surely lead to early-onset osteoporosis, as seen previously in studies of older women with the disease. Perhaps other chronic diseases of childhood may produce similar, though less dramatic, results as well.

Each of the potential areas of disturbance in the factors that govern bone mass accretion deserve careful study and attention in the correct populations to prove our thought that osteoporosis is actually a disease of childhood.—C. Langman, M.D.

Weight and Dieting Concerns in Adolescents, Fashion or Symptom?

Casper RC, Offer D (Michael Reese Hosp and Med Ctr, Chicago; Univ of Chicago)
Pediatrics 86:384–390, 1990

8–9

The relation of attitudes about weight and eating to psychological adjustment has not been evaluated in adolescents. To address this, 497 randomly selected adolescents, aged 16 to 18 who were in their senior year in 1 urban and 2 suburban midwestern high schools, were evaluated. Each student was interviewed and completed a brief 6-item screening scale to assess attitudes about body shape and dieting.

Nearly all adolescents reported feeling physically healthy and well. For boys, body satisfaction correlated strongly to a masculine physique, whereas for girls body satisfaction was associated most strongly with weight. Two thirds of female adolescents, compared with only a few boys (14%), were concerned with weight and dieting. Black females were less preoccupied with weight and dieting than were white females, but black males were more preoccupied with burning calories during exercise than were white males. For both males and females, increased weight and dieting concerns correlated highly with disturbances in body and self-image perceptions, mood, and overall psychopathology. Specifically, weight and dieting concerns were associated with depression for boys and with distress-depression irritation, vegetative depression, insomnia, and anxiety for girls. Furthermore, there was a trend for adolescents with weight and eating concerns to have used "uppers" or amphetamines.

Weight and dieting concerns are quite common among female adolescents but are surprisingly infrequent in male adolescents. Preoccupation with weight or dieting is likely to be associated with psychological problems for both male and female adolescents.

▶ The point to this report is in the authors' own words: "The fairly common fear of being overweight and thoughts about dieting experienced by contemporary female adolescents, in part, seem to reflect the greater aesthetic value that contemporary society places on thinness for women. Overall, the findings suggest that preoccupation with weight and/or dieting concerns in either male or female adolescents are likely to indicate psychological problems." Some surprise.

What should come as a surprise regarding teenagers are the results of a recent study reported in *The New England Journal of Medicine* describing the effects of variability of body weight and health outcomes from the Framingham population. Unless a teenager or adult is consistent about keeping off weight once dieting begins, fluctuation in body weight can have quite deleterious effects. Without question, the most frequent cause of fluctuation in body weight is dieting (1). It has been shown that employees of the Western Electric Company who put themselves through a single cycle of weight loss and then regained weight were at significantly increased risk for coronary artery disease (2). If dieting emerges as a major factor in body weight fluctuation and is a very adverse coronary risk factor, it will be important to evaluate further the public health implications of current weight-loss practices. At any time in this country, approximately 50% of American women and 25% of American men are dieting. These diets may be unsuccessful on the front end or the back end. We do not have good data on teenagers yet, but there are probably a fair percentage of teenagers who are also dieting, and implications for their health with respect to fluctuations in weight could be adverse as well.

So what is the conclusion of the preceding paragraph? If you are thin, stay thin. If you are fat, try to become thin. However, if you are fat and try to become thin, don't let yourself become fat again. If you are fat, become thin, and become fat again, you just added to your coronary risk factors, but that doesn't necessarily mean that you should not try to become thin again. Did you understand all that? If not, what follows we'll simply call "Stockman's Rule of Longevity":

Life Span In Years

THIN ▶ FAT → THIN ▶ FAT ? ▶ FAT → THIN → FAT ? ▶ FAT → THIN →
FAT → THIN ▶ ??

When all else fails, please accept the following advice, which is certainly applicable to most of us: "Moderation is for monks."—J.A. Stockman, III, M.D.

References

1. Lissner L, et al: *N Engl J Med* 324:1839, 1991.
2. Hamm BP, et al: *Am J Epidemiol* 129:312, 1989.

Triage Model for Suicidal Runaways
Rotheram-Borus MJ, Bradley J (Columbia Univ)
Am J Orthopsychiatry 61:122–127, 1991   8–10

Because adolescent runaways are at increased risk for suicidal behavior, a model program for triage of suicidal runaways was evaluated at 4 community-based agencies in a 30-month period. The program included 4 components: a 2-stage screening procedure to evaluate the risk for suicide and imminent danger, staff training, an agency protocol for triage of suicidal youths, and establishment of a multilevel mental health service network. A total of 741 runaways were screened during the study period.

The frequency of suicide attempts decreased significantly from 9 attempts in the 3-month period before implementation of the project to 2 attempts during the 18 months after its inception. Only 2% of the youths were referred for emergency psychiatric evaluation, and the psychiatrists' evaluations of suicidal tendencies concurred with the staff's decisions for triage. Furthermore, the project was continued or voluntarily implemented by community-based agencies. These results are encouraging and suggest that this triage model for suicidal runaways should be replicated to examine its generalizability to other community-based agencies.

Adolescent Suicide Attempters: Response to Suicide-Prevention Programs
Shaffer D, Vieland V, Garland A, Rojas M, Underwood M, Busner C (Columbia Univ; New York State Psychiatric Inst, New York)
JAMA 264:3151–3155, 1990   8–11

Suicide-prevention programs for high school students in the United States are growing rapidly. The impact of suicide-education programs on high-risk teenagers was investigated. Three suicide-prevention curricula delivered to 1,438 ninth- and tenth-grade students were identified. Sixty-three adolescents in these programs had made a suicide attempt and were considered at high risk. The attitudes of the high-risk teens were compared with those of 910 teenagers from the same population who had not attempted suicide.

Self-identified suicide attempters were less likely to endorse views consistent with the curricula at baseline. However, there was little evidence that the programs successfully influenced these views. Previous suicide attempters appeared to be more upset by the programs than nonattempters.

Purely educational programs such as the ones studied do not usually attempt to target high-risk adolescents. Their ability to change pathologic attitudes among high-risk students appears to be limited. Alternative methods that couple more efficient case identification with individualized assessment and intervention should be considered.

▶ According to statistics, more than 5,000 adolescents and young adults in this country (aged 15–24) will take their lives each year. This makes suicide the second leading cause of death among teenagers and young adults. During the last 25 years, the suicide rates, particularly for young men, quadrupled. If you add nonlethal suicidal behavior to these numbers, you will find that approximately 9% of high school students report that they have made a suicide attempt (1). If you want to translate this into your own community, between the ages of 15 and 19 years, 1 child in 10,000 in a school district or region will have a "successful" suicide, and many more children will have at least made a suicidal gesture.

Studies such as the preceding 2 (Abstracts 8–10 and 8–11) allow us to have a better understanding of the issues that face us as pediatricians when we are asked to consult with schools on issues that relate to teen suicide. There was an especially good review of our consultative role in this regard recently in *Pediatrics* (2), and the article is well worth taking the time to read. As we learn more and more about risk factors for attempted suicide, we learn how much more pervasive this problem is, and who among our children is especially at high risk. For example, 40% of 5,000 adolescent homosexuals who were recently surveyed indicated that they seriously considered attempting or had attempted suicide (3). These suicides are especially problematic, because the vast majority of psychiatrists believe that self-injurious acts on the part of homosexual adolescents are more serious and potentially more lethal than those of their heterosexual peers.

Ending a chapter on adolescent medicine with the topic of suicide is in a sense a "downer." The subject caused this editor to reflect on some current and not so current writings on the topic of suicide that may be appropriate to share. Fourteen years ago in his work, *The Good Word,* Willford Sheed took a rather pessimistic view of life when he said, "Suicide . . . is about life, being in fact the sincerest form of criticism life gets . . . the odds on any intelligent person having an unhappy childhood are better than fair, and the odds on a sad ending are off the board."

On the other hand, who can forget the words of Abraham Lincoln, in an address at the Young Men's Lyceum in Springfield, Illinois, on January 27, 1838: "If destruction be our lot, we must ourselves be its author and finisher. As a nation of freedom, we must live through all time, or die by suicide." We started this chapter with a commentary that included some thoughts about old Abe and we end the chapter with actual words of his. Thank you, sir.—J.A. Stockman, III, M.D.

References

1. Smith K, et al: *Suicide Life Threat Behav* 16:313, 1986.
2. Adler RS, et al: *Pediatrics* 86:982, 1990.
3. Remafedi G, et al: *Pediatrics* 87:869, 1991.

9 Therapeutics and Toxicology

Mercury Exposure From Interior Latex Paint
Agocs MM, Etzel RA, Parrish RG, Paschal DC, Campagna PR, Cohen DS, Kilbourne EM, Hesse JL (Ctrs for Disease Control, Atlanta; Enviromental Protection Agency, Edison, NJ; Univ of California, San Diego; Michigan Dept of Public Health, Lansing)
N Engl J Med 323:1096–1101, 1990   9–1

Because of their fungicidal and bactericidal properties, mercury compounds often are added to latex paint, including interior latex paint, to prolong shelf life. In August 1989, a boy, aged 4 years, had symptoms of acrodynia, a form of mercury poisoning, after exposure to paint fumes in a home recently painted with interior latex paint containing 4.7 mmol of mercury per liter. At that time, the Environmental Protection Agency's recommended limit was 1.5 mmol per liter. This case prompted a study to determine whether mercury exposure had occurred among other persons whose homes were recently painted with the same brand of interior latex paint. Indoor-air and urinary mercury concentrations were measured in 74 "exposed" persons living in 19 homes recently painted with the brand and in 28 "unexposed" persons living in 10 homes not recently painted with paint containing mercury.

Paint samples from the homes of exposed persons contained a median of 3.8 mmol of mercury per liter, and indoor air samples had a median mercury concentration of 10 nmol/m^3 (range, .5–49.9), exceeding the acceptable residential concentration of 2.5 nmol/m^3. In contrast, no mercury was detected in paint or air samples from the homes of unexposed persons. Furthermore, the median urinary mercury concentrations were significantly higher in exposed persons than in nonexposed persons. Among the exposed persons, children younger than age 10 years had the highest urinary mercury concentrations.

Significant exposure to mercury may occur in persons whose homes are painted with a brand of paint that contains mercury at concentrations approximately 2.5 times the Environmental Protection Agency's recommended limit. Children are at increased risk because vapors that contain mercury are heavier than indoor air and settle toward the floor.

▶ Any time there is a lead article in *The New England Journal of Medicine*, it commands a great deal of attention. The topic of this article and where it appeared is the stuff of which national news broadcasts are made. What the child described had, of course, is a case of acrodynia, or mercury poisoning. Acrodynia from paint is an unusual occurrence. It was reported in a 5-year-old boy almost 30 years ago after his house was painted with 1 of the first-generation latex paints that were then available (1).

Mercury is added to paint as phenylmercuric acetate and acts as preservative. Unfortunately, it becomes part of the volatile aroma that we are accustomed to after the painting of a room with latex paint. Phenylmercuric acid rapidly breaks down to form inorganic mercury, which can accumulate in the kidneys and enter the brain. It crosses the placenta, and affects the fetus. In children, inorganic mercury in high concentrations causes the symptom complex noted in this article. As you might suspect, most paint companies have voluntarily stopped using mercury as a stabilizer. Nonetheless, it was only a couple of years ago that the Environmental Protection Agency announced that compounds containing mercury could no longer be added to interior latex paint after August 20, 1990. They did not dictate, however, that interior latex paint containing mercury that was manufactured before that date should be removed from the market. Thus, there are probably large quantities of this material still around to endanger us and our children.

The risk of human mercury poisoning seems to continue. Workers in electrical industries and those in chloralkali plants are exposed to mercury vapors. Your mouth may also be a villain. Amalgam tooth fillings are another source of mercury and may currently be the chief source of exposure for a large segment of our current population. Vaporization of mercury may occur during chewing and for several minutes thereafter. Autopsy data indicate that brain mercury levels are approximately twice as high in people who have had fillings for many years as in those who have none. For more on this topic of mercury and our "chops" see the Dentistry and Otolaryngology chapter, where thoughtful recommendatons are given concerning what to do about this potential problem.

I bet you're wondering what the name of the paint company was that was the source of the intoxication noted above. It wouldn't take a rocket scientist to figure out who the manufacturer was if you could pick from a list of 5 potential names. The manufacturer was the Mercury Paint Company.

In concluding this commentary, you might be interested in the issue that the journal, *Nature* (2), raised as a new debate about mercury. It has to do with the mercury output of crematoriums. The hazard of fumes from industrial chimneys are well known. But is grandpa a health risk, even after he is dead? The point being made here is that, in the United Kingdom, 68% of the population are cremated sooner or later. Bearing in mind that those who are long in the tooth may have lost them and those who are young have frustrated their dentists, nonetheless, some 328 kg of mercury from dental amalgam may be released annually over the countryside of England and Wales. This is just over ½ gram per ex-person. Thus, the annual output of mercury from a low-level crematorium chimney in a well-populated area may exceed 2 kg. The author of the *Nature* article states that "opinions differ greatly as to the safe ambient exposure of mercury (1 vs. 50 $\mu g/m^3$), but as they say, there is no smoke without fire."

P.S. For the aficionados in the reading audience, the atomic number for quicksilver is 80, and mercury, the God of trade, is also the messenger for all other gods.—J.A. Stockman, III, M.D.

References

1. Hirschman SZ, et al: *N Engl J Med* 269:889, 1963.
2. Charney N: *Nature* 346:615, 1990.

Diphenoxylate-Atropine (Lomotil) Overdose in Children: An Update (Report of Eight Cases and Review of the Literature)
McCarron MM, Challoner KR, Thompson GA (Univ of Southern California, Los Angeles County/Univ of Southern California Med Ctr, Los Angeles)
Pediatrics 87:694–700, 1991   9–2

Diphenoxylate/atropine (DPX/ATR) is a commonly used antidiarrheal agent. Since 1965, 101 cases of DPX/ATR overdose in children have been reported. However, less than half of these cases have been described in detail. Eight cases of accidental DPX/ATR intoxication in young children were studied, and 28 cases found in the literature were reviewed.

Eight children, aged 18–30 months, were treated at 1 center. Only 1 child had a history suggesting atropine intoxication, with initial symptoms of cerebral excitement and flushed dry skin. Two children were seen with CNS and respiratory depression with miosis. The other 5 children did not have histories typical for atropine or opioid toxicity. Four had nonspecific findings of drowsiness and/or irritability, and 1, in addition to these, was ataxic and thirsty. One patient had acute onset of unexplained lethargy, head rolling, and generalized limpness. Three children were given syrup of ipecac 30 minutes to 4½ hours after the overdose. Four had gastric lavage 1½–15 hours after ingestion. Four were given oral activated charcoal, and 2 were given a cathartic. Only 2 received naloxone. There were no medical complications associated with the overdose. Twenty-eight additional cases reported since 1969 were also described (table).

Diphenoxylate/atropine overdose is primarily an opioid intoxication, which is sometimes associated with atropine toxicity. Atropine effects can occur before, during, or after opioid effects, contrary to popular belief. Treatment should include intravenously administered naloxone for depressed or inadequate respirations followed by continuous intravenous naloxone infusion, prompt gastric lavage, repeated activated charcoal administration, and close monitoring for 24 hours.

▶ I bet you didn't know that Lomotil is a weak, long-acting opioid derivative of meperidine (Demerol). I didn't know that until I read this report, but I should have, because Lomotil is a DEA Schedule II Controlled Substance.

In adults, a dose of 1 or 2 tablets of Lomotil contains only enough diphenoxylate to cause opioid effects in the GI tract, and it usually does not significantly alter the CNS. The same dosage in a child often results in overdose and may produce typical opioid effects such as CNS and respiratory depression. These manifestations of Lomotil overdose in children may be confusing to the physi-

Diphenoxylate/Atropine (DPX1ATR) Intoxication in Children: 28 Cases From the Literature

Year	First Author/ Reference	Cases (n = 28)	Amount Ingested DPX, mg	ATR, mg	Major Findings	Outcome
1969	Ament	2	100	1.0	Coma, apnea, miosis (1), tachycardia (1), flushed, fever, dry (1), hypotonic (1)	Recovered at
1973	Ginsberg	3	110*	1.1*	Lethargy, apnea (2), miosis, flushed, hypotonic	Recovered at
1971	Wheeldon	1	100	1.0	Lethargy, apnea	Recovered at
1969	Riley	1	75	0.8	Coma, respiratory depression†, miosis, fever, ataxic	Recovered at
1979	Curtis	1	68	0.7	Coma, apnea, Papilledema	Death
1969	Bargman	1	40	0.4	Coma, respiratory depression†, miosis, tachycardia, fever, hypotonic	Cortical blindness
1978	Curnock	1	38	0.4	Coma, apnea, miosis, flushed	Aspiration pneumonia
1969	Harries	1	30	0.3	Coma, respiratory depression†, apnea, cardiac arrest	Death
1973	Snyder	1	25	0.3	Coma, respiratory depression†, miosis, tachycardia, flushed, fever, dry, hypotonic	Recovered at
1965	Canby	1	20	0.2	Coma, apnea, tachycardia, fever	Recovered at
1969	Henderson	1	15	0.2	Coma, apnea, cardiac arrest, hypotonic, then rigid	Aspiration pneumonia
1980	Cutler	1	...	...	Coma, apnea, miosis, cardiac arrest, flushed, fever	Recovered at
1974	Rumack	13	15–100	0.2–1.0	Coma (12), respiratory depression (11), miosis (13), tachycardia (8), fever (2), rigid (1) Awake (1), Apnea (1)	Death (1) Aspiration pneumonia (2)

*One of 3 cases.
†Resp dep = respiratory depression or inadequate respirations.
(Courtesy of McCarron MM, Challoner KR, Thompson GA: *Pediatrics* 87:694–700, 1991.)

cian who sees the patient until the more recognizable atropine and/or typical diphenoxylate effects occur.

Naloxone is the treatment of choice for Lomotil overdose. Intravenous bolus doses of naloxone may be followed by a continuous intravenous naloxone infusion to prevent late recurrence of respiratory depression in severe intoxications. Inducing vomiting with syrup of ipecac is not recommended for asymptomatic patients, because CNS and respiratory depression may develop 1 or 2 hours after ingesting Lomotil tablets. Vomiting simultaneous with the onset of toxic symptoms should be avoided. Gastric lavage followed by activated charcoal is recommended. Because of the likelihood of reabsorption of diphenoxylate or its metabolate from the intestine, repeated administration of activated charcoal occasionally may also be needed. Naloxone by intravenous infusion may be an alternative to oral activated charcoal when the patient has intestinal ileus or gastric atony. Of course, whenever using repeated doses of activated charcoal, be sure that the patient is not losing so much fluid into the intestines that they are hemodynamically unstable.

Late opioid symptoms, probably caused by the metabolite diphenoxime, can occur 13 to 24 hours after ingestion. Therefore, at least 12 hours of monitoring and preferably 24 hours are required to detect both the initial and late symptoms.

On the subject of poisons, this last year was a big year for Robin Hood. Can you answer the following 2-part question: A certain tree supplied the wood for Robin Hood's bow and the fabeled English long bows in the battle of Agincourt. What is the tree, and what is the treatment of choice if a child eats its leaves, bark, or berries?

The answer to the first part of the question is the English yew tree. The leaves, bark, and berries of the yew can be lethal to humans. Yew ingestion is not a minor problem, because in many homes, this particular tree is brought into the house a week or 2 before December 25th of each year. The yew plant contains an alkaloid with powerful arrhythmogenic capabilities, similar to the cardiac glycosides in fox glove, oleander, lily of the valley, and monkshood.

How do you treat the problem? This was recently answered in a report of a 5-year-old autistic girl who nearly died after eating a piece of a yew plant. The physicians treating her used a rather novel therapy for her arrhythmias. Recognizing the cross similarities between compounds in the yew and cardiac glycosides, they empirically decided to treat the child with digoxin-specific FAB antibodies (Digibind). The child, on death's door, miraculously recovered. Before you jump for the Digibind, recognize that it is not specifically approved for this purpose, as it is for digoxin overdose.

What is the moral of all this? Next New Year's day, if your dog tries to eat half of your Christmas tree (assuming it is a yew), rush to your pharmacy and get all the Digibind you can find. If your cat does the same thing, turn on the Rose Bowl.—J.A. Stockman, III, M.D.

Efficacy of Sedation of Children With Chloral Hydrate
Rumm PD, Takao RT, Fox DJ, Atkinson SW (Brooke Army Med Ctr, San Antonio, Tex)
South Med J 83:1040–1043, 1990   9–3

Chloral hydrate is a safe and highly effective (almost 100% success rate) oral agent for sedation of children during diagnostic studies. However, at Brooke Army Medical Center, other drug combinations were used for sedation of these children because of a perceived high failure rate with chloral hydrate, particularly in younger or neurologically impaired children. Patient data and sedation scores were recorded in 50 children, aged 2 months to 14 years, who received chloral hydrate (mean dose, 58 mg/kg; range, 25–81 mg/kg) before a diagnostic study.

A single dose of chloral hydrate effectively sedated 43 children throughout the study, for an overall success rate of 86%. There were no side effects or complications. Of the 7 failures, 6 had known or suspected neurologic disorder. The failure rate was much greater in children with neurologic disorders (6 of 22, 27%) compared with normal children (1 of 28, 4%).

Chloral hydrate remains a safe and effective agent for children requiring sedation during diagnostic studies. Failure may be the result of a combination of errors, including delay of a planned study, inadequate dosing, or vomiting the drug. In addition, patients with neurologic disorders may not respond as easily to sedation with chloral hydrate.

Direct Hyperbilirubinemia Associated With Chloral Hydrate Administration in the Newborn
Lambert GH, Muraskas J, Anderson CL, Myers TF (Loyola Univ, Maywood, Ill)
Pediatrics 86:277–281, 1990   9–4

Chloral hydrate is widely used as a sedative-hypnotic in neonatal and pediatric patients. The only toxic effects attributed to chloral hydrate in the newborn include prolonged neurodepression and increased indirect serum bilirubin levels. Two retrospective analyses of the records of patients admitted to a neonatal intensive care unit during an 18-month period were made to test whether chloral hydrate can cause direct hyperbilirubinemia (DHB) in the newborn.

In the first analysis, 14 newborns who had nonhemolytic DHB were identified. Of these, 10 had received chloral hydrate, and the other 4 had definite causes of DHB.

In the second analysis, 44 newborns who had received more than 1 dose of chloral hydrate were identified. Of these, 10 had DHB, and the remaining 34 had normal direct bilirubin levels. Peak direct serum bilirubin levels were significantly higher and peaked much later in patients with DHB compared with patients without DHB. The mean total accumulative dose of chloral hydrate in patients with DHB was 1,035 mg/kg, significantly higher than the mean dose in patients without DHB (183 mg/kg). Furthermore, DHB occurred 6.8 days after chloral hydrate therapy was begun and resolved, at an average 5.4 days after therapy was discontinued.

Prolonged administration of chloral hydrate appears to be associated with DHB. In the newborn, this may be partially caused by the slow clearance of chloral hydrate's active and very toxic metabolite, trichloroethanol.

▶ This must have been the year of chloral hydrate. I have never seen so much written about a drug in so short a period of time. The article by Rumm et al. abstracted above (Abstract 9–3) and the Lambert et al. abstract that follows (Abstract 9–4) show us that chloral hydrate is still efficacious, but it can produce side effects. The side effects are beginning to attract more and more attention. In a Letter to the Editor in *Science,* M. T. Smith (1) raises questions about the use of chloral hydrate as a sedative for children undergoing dental and/or medical procedures. He suggests that chloral hydrate is a toxic metabolite of the rodent carcinogen trichloroethylene and is a mutagen and chromosome-damaging agent. If you do a little mathematics, the average 15 kg child may require 900 mg of chloral hydrate for sedation, a dose equivalent to drinking 1 liter of water a day contaminated with 5 parts per billion of trichloroethylene. The EPA says this is equal to the maximum amount of trichloroethylene that an individual is allowed in 1,000 years of life. This is all based, of course, on Dr. Smith's assumption of the relationship between trichloroethylene and chloral hydrate.

Some editorial asides about chloral hydrate. First, having personally prescribed the drug many times in specific situations where I thought it was needed for sedation-pain relief, I found it didn't work. You may have a similar impression about the value of this drug.

There is a misimpression that many of us have that the drug is appropriate for sedation and analgesia. The drug is appropriate for sedation, but of course, it is not an analgesic. So, the next time you attempt to do a lumbar puncture using chloral hydrate, the sedated patient is likely to wake up and scream at you. If you think about using chloral hydrate as a sedative and an analgesic, not only are you kidding yourself, you are also hurting the child. You'd be better off taking the chloral hydrate yourself.

The answer to appropriate sedation, in some instances, may be the use of intravenous ketamine. In 1 study that examined this drug, it proved to be a wonderful alternative to conventional sedation in a pediatric intensive care unit (2). An initial bolus of .5–1.0 mg/kg administered over 2 to 3 minutes, followed by continuous infusion of 10 μg/kg/min is very effective. As with any intravenous anesthetic, cardiorespiratory effects should be monitored. The wonderful plus of ketamine is that it produces amnesia and analgesia in addition to sedation. The magic bullet we are looking for?—J.A. Stockman, III, M.D.

References

1. Smith MT: *Science* 250:359, 1990.
2. Tobias JD: *Crit Care Med* 33:819, 1990.

Fetal Alcohol Syndrome in Adolescents and Adults
Streissguth AP, Aase JM, Clarren SK, Randels SP, LaDue RA, Smith DF (Univ of Washington; Univ of Vancouver; Albuquerque, NM)
JAMA 265:1961–1967, 1991   9–5

Fetal alcohol syndrome (FAS) is the leading known cause of mental retardation in the United States. The physical and mental manifestations of this syndrome in adolescence and adulthood have not been well documented. The first systematic follow-up study to examine adolescent and adult manifestions of FAS included 61 adolescents and adults with alcohol teratogenesis.

The facies of patients with FAS or fetal alcohol effects were not as distinctive after puberty. However, the patients tended to remain short and microcephalic. Their weight was somewhat closer to the mean. The range of intelligence quotient (IQ) socres was wide, the mean being 68. Average academic functioning was at the second- to fourth-grade levels, and arithmetic deficits were most characteristic. Maladaptive behaviors were common and included poor judgment, distractibility, and difficulty perceiving social cues. The patients' family environments were remarkably unstable. On average, they had lived in 5 different principal homes in their lifetimes. Sixty-nine percent of the biologic mothers were known to be dead.

The natural history of FAS can now be followed through adolescence and into adulthood. Major psychosocial and lifelong adjustment problems characterize most of these patients.

▶ This is an important report. It is the first report that I am aware of to follow the individual affected by fetal alcohol syndrome well into adulthood. It causes one to wonder how many retarded adults may actually suffer from the fetal alcohol syndrome because, as this report has documented, after puberty the facies of patients with the fetal alcohol syndrome no longer are distinctive or characteristic.

It is sad to say, but the characteristic facies may not even be recognizable to the average care provider in the nursery. Little et al. (1) examined the medical records of 40 infants born to 38 alcohol-abusing mothers to determine the frequency of the fetal alcohol syndrome. Six infants fully conformed to the diagnostic criteria, but fetal alcohol syndrome was not noted in a single medical record.

You may have heard about an article from Australia that contends that mild to moderate alcohol use during pregnancy does not hurt babies. Walpole et al. (2) found 665 women who had ingested no more than 1 ounce of absolute alcohol per day (equivalent to 2 drinks of liquor, 2 glasses of wine, or 2 cans of average-strength beer). Not a single fetus of these women appeared to show any evidence of the fetal alcohol syndrome. If you have not read this report, don't, and feel fortunate that you have not seen it. It is mentioned here only for completeness sake, because it is so widely referenced. It is a poor study with no long-term follow-up. I personally will write the editor of the *Journal of Epidemiology and Community Health* to ask the head size of the manuscript reviewer who gave it an acceptance.

Before going off the topic of alcohol, recognize that Swedish drivers with a sweet tooth may find themselves in trouble with the law. Beginning on July 1, 1989, Sweden lowered the blood alcohol limit for drivers to remarkably low levels, based on the observation that virtually any level of blood alcohol can impair coordination. The problem with sweet tooths is based on the observation of

Hunnisett et al. (3), who found ethyl alcohol in the blood of 311 of 510 volunteers 1 hour after the ingestion of 5 gm of sugar. This phenomenon is well described and is called the "auto-brewery syndrome." It probably depends on the fermentation of sugar by blood gut flora. Blood alcohol levels that are in the illegal range under the new Swedish laws have been reported. If blood alcohol is positively related to the quantity of carbohydrate consumed, then cookie consumers and chocoholics should beware: cookies contain 66 g of carbohydrate per 100 g, and plain chocolate contains 65 g of carbohydrate per 100 g.

If plain old chocolate causes so much trouble, one might as well go whole hog and indulge in chocolate liqueurs. I don't indulge in alcohol or chocolate. Instead, because this is the Toxicology chapter . . . waiter, please would you bring me a Perrier. Extra benzene please.—J.A. Stockman, III, M.D.

References

1. Little BB, et al: *Am J Dis Child* 144:1142, 1990.
2. Walpole I, et al: *Epidemiol Community Health* 44:297, 1990.
3. Hunnisett A, et al: *J Nutr Med* 1:33, 1990.

Apnea and Seizures Caused by Nicotine Ingestion
Singer J, Janz T (Wright State Univ, Dayton, Ohio)
Pediatr Emerg Care 6:135–137, 1990   9–6

Nicotine poisoning has been known to result from overindulgence in tobacco products and from ingestion of smoking or chewing tobacco. A new product, nicotine gum (Nicorettes), which is used for therapy of smoking addiction, can also cause toxicity. Two young children had seizures after apparently ingesting the gum product and cigarette butts.

Boy, 20 months, was brought to the hospital after suffering a generalized, tonic-clonic seizure. During transit the paramedics noted shallow ventilation and emesis. On arrival at the emergency department, the child was apneic, in a persistently tonic state, with eyes deviated left. Treatment included tracheal intubation, artificial ventilation, and an infusion of phenytoin. The child was able to be extu-

TABLE 1.—Nicotine Content of Smoke
and Smokeless Tobacco Products

Product	Range (mg)
1 whole cigarette	13–19
1 cigarette butt	5–7
1 cigar	15–40
1 g wet snuff	5–30
1 g dry snuff	12–16
1 g chewing tobacco	2–8
1 piece Nicorette	2

(Courtesy of Singer J, Janz T: *Pediatr Emerg Care* 6:135–137, 1990.)

232 / Pediatrics

TABLE 2.—Signs and Symptoms After Nicotine Exposure

Gastrointestinal	Cardiorespiratory	Autonomic	Neurologic
Nausea	Hyperpnea	Headache	Confusion, disorientation
Vomiting	Hypertension	Palpitations	Lethargy, coma
Abdominal pain	Dysrhythmia	Agitation	Miosis, blurred vision
Diarrhea	Respiratory depression	Hyperactivity	Hypotonia, weakness
Dry mouth	Apnea	Insomnia	Hyporeflexia, areflexia
Salivation	Hypotension	Tremor	Major motor seizure

(Courtesy of Singer J, Janz T: *Pediatr Emerg Care* 6:135–137, 1990.)

bated after 4 to 6 hours, when his respiratory efforts improved. A urine drug screen revealed nicotine, and the child's father reported that Nicorettes were present in the home.

Oral doses of nicotine as small as 1 to 4 mg can produce toxic effects in nonhabituated adults. Children may show signs and symptoms of toxicity after consuming 3 cigarette butts or a single Nicorette (Table 1). Gastrointestinal symptoms occur first, within 15 to 90 minutes of ingestion. The other effects of nicotine toxicity are quite variable (Table 2). Cardiovascular instability, CNS dysfunction, and neuromuscular blockade may cause death if supportive care is not provided.

Although nicotine poisoning produces a variety of stimulant and depressive effects, pharmacologic therapy is rarely necessary. Animal studies have shown that even severe toxicity can be treated with attention to airway, ventilation, and circulation. A urine toxicology screen using chromatography can verify nicotine ingestion. Parents should be made aware of the potential danger of tobacco products.

▶ Table 1 and Table 2 pretty much say it all. Anyone who thinks that cigarettes are healthy for you (or anything else that contains or produces nicotine) need only review this report. Oral doses as small as 1–4 mg of nicotine may be associated with toxic effects in nonhabituated adults. Toddlers who consume either a single whole cigarette, 3 cigarette butts, 1 cigar butt, or a single Nicorette may exhibit signs and symptoms of nicotine toxicity.

Although it is hard to imagine why kids chew cigarette butts, they sometimes do. Any adult who smokes and leaves their butts around ought to have theirs kicked.—J.A. Stockman, III, M.D.

Poisonings in Laboratory Personnel and Health Care Professionals
Binder L, Fredrickson L (Texas Tech Univ RAHC-El Paso)
Am J Emerg Med 9:11–15, 1991   9–7

Intentional poisoning in laboratory personnel and health care workers differs qualitatively from poisonings encountered in the general population. In contast to poisoning by cleaning substances, analgesics, and cosmetics among lay persons, a different distribution of poisonings is seen in

TABLE 1.—Substances Producing Methemoglobin

Acetanilid	Nitrogen oxide
Acetophenetidin	Nitroglycerol
(phenacetin)	Pamaquine
Amyl nitrite	Para-bromoaniline
Aniline derivatives	Para-chloroaniline
Anilinoethanol	Para-nitroaniline
Antipyrine	Pentaerythritol tetranitrate
Benzocaine	Phenetidin
Bismuth subnitrate	Phenylazopyridine
Chlorates	Phenylenediamine
Chlorobenzene (oral)	Phenylhydroxylamine
Chloronitrobenzene (oral)	Piperazaine (also EKG changes)
Diaminodiphenylsulfone	Plasmoquine
Dimethylaniline	Prilocaine
Dinitrobenzene	Primaquine
Dinitrophenol	Pyridium
Ethyl p-aminobenzoate	Quinones
(idiosyncracy)	Resorcinol
Hydroquinone (oral)	Sulfonamides
Metachloroaniline	Sulfones
Methylene blue (IV)	Tetranitromethane
Nitrates (if reduced)	Tetronal
Nitrites	Trional
Nitrobenzene	Toluidine
(Dinitrobenzene)	Trinitrotoluene
Nitrochlorobenzene	Vegetables (spinach)

(Courtesy of Binder L, Fredrickson L: *Am J Emerg Med* 9:11–15, 1991.)

educated laboratory and health care personnel. Barbiturates, carbon monoxide, cyanide and its derivatives, azides, and methemoglobin-inducing chemicals are the 5 most common poisons encountered in these personnel.

When there is no history of exposure, barbiturate poisoning should be highly considered in knowledgeable personnel who have profound metabolic depression, when pill fragments are found on gastric lavage, and after other potential causes are excluded through metabolic work-up and cerebral CT scanning. Diagnosis of carbon monoxide poisoning should be suspected from history of potential exposure, new onset of arrhythmias or myocardial ischemia, new onset of lactic acidosis, altered mental status, seizure, fundoscopic findings of equal cherry-red coloration of retinal arteries and veins, and an oxygen saturation gap of 5% or more.

Cyanides, azides, and methemoglobin-inducing chemicals are used commercially and at home; therefore, eliciting a history of availability in the workplace or home may be useful. Subtle clues to cyanide poisoning include patient's occupation and cyanide availability, aroma of bitter almonds to the gastric aspirate, unexplained and severe lactic acidosis, unexplained cherry-red coloration of retinal arteries and veins on fundos-

TABLE 2.—Diagnosis of Unknown Poisoning
in Knowledgeable Personnel

Poison	Diagnostic Clues
Barbiturates	Characteristic clinical presentation in knowledgeable personnel. Pill fragments on gastric lavage (refutes other metabolics/CNS diagnoses). Exclusion of other potential diagnoses through metabolic workup and CT scanning. Barbiturate level or tox screen. Hypothermia. Pinpoint pupils, nystagmus.
Carbon monoxide	History of potential exposure (found unconscious in car, garage, at fire). New onset of arrhythmias/myocardial ischemia. New onset lactic acidosis, altered mental status, seizure. Equal "cherry-red" coloration of retinal arteries and veins. Oxygen saturation gap > 5%.
Cyanide	Availability to victim in workplace or home. Aroma of "bitter almonds" to gastric aspirate. Unexplained "cherry-red" coloration of retinal arteries and veins. Oxygen saturation gap > 5%. Anion gap metabolic acidosis (unexplained). Fire victims. New onset seizures. Pulmonary edema.
Azides	Availability to victim in workplace or home. Pungent aroma to gastric aspirate. Unexplained and severe lactic acidosis. Alternating CNS restlessness and atony. Positive ferric chloride testing of gastric aspirate (red precipitate). Headache and nausea in resuscitation team members.
Methemoglobin-inducing chemicals	Availability to victim in workplace or home. Bitter "petrochemical" smell of certain chemicals. Cyanosis refractory to oxygen. "Chocolate brown" appearance of blood.

(Courtesy of Binder L, Fredrickson L: *Am J Emerg Med* 9:11–15, 1991.)

copy, a positive Lee-Jones assay of gastric aspirate, and an oxygen saturation gap of 5% or greater.

The patient's occupation is also a clue to diagnosis of azide poisoning, along with a pungent aroma to the gastric aspirate, unexplained lactic acidosis, alternating restlessness and atony with evidence of progressive cellular anoxia, and positive ferric chloride testing of gastric aspirate. Headache and nausea may occur among members of the resuscitation team as a result of inhalation of azoimide gas from the victim's exhaled air and gastric aspirate. Poisoning with methemoglobin-inducing chemicals (Table 1) should be suspected in the presence of a bitter petrochemical smell of certain chemicals, cyanosis refractory to oxygen, and chocolate-brown appearance of blood.

The emergency physician faces a dilemma when presented with an unresponsive patient or unknown poisoning in knowledgeable personnel. In these cases, the emergency physician should undertake meticulous physical and laboratory examinations and should consider the clinical presentation of these poisons (Table 2).

▶ The subject of poisoning is always intriguing because it has an air of mystery. Let's see how good you are with the following "who done its?"

First, in the play and film *Amadeus,* it was suggested that Salieri, out of jealousy, managed to drive Mozart into his grave. Writers have speculated that this was done by poisoning. Is this true?

Not so says Dr. John Davies who, after reviewing all available information, concluded that Mozart died from the following: streptococcal infection, resulting in Henoch-Schönlein syndrome, resulting in renal failure, resulting in iatrogenic excessive venosections, followed by cerebral hemorrhage and terminal bronchopneumonia (1). I enjoyed reading this book a great deal and gained even greater respect for Mozart and all he accomplished. I also realized how old I was getting. When Mozart was my age, he had been dead 11 years.

Second who done it: Four members of a family come to a hospital with headache, nausea, and abdominal pains. They give a history of drinking unrefrigerated milk the previous evening. A tentative diagnosis is made of infective gastroenteritis, until a few hours later when 4 more members of the family come to the hospital complaining of the same symptoms, but they didn't drink the milk. What additional questions might you ask?

You might ask how the family prepared their meals. In this instance, a visit to the family house revealed a barbeque grill sitting in the middle of the living room. All the members of the family were poisoned with carbon monoxide (2).

If you think that this is farfetched, note the problem in Korea. Korea has one of the highest hospital admission rates for carbon monoxide poisoning. There, heating is commonly achieved with the "Ondol" system, by which charcoal briquettes are burned directly under the floor on which people sleep. The system is economical but there is always a danger that gases will seep up through inapparent cracks in the floor. Each year in Korea there are thousands of admissions for carbon monoxide poisoning and hundreds of deaths (3).

Last, you are on the southwest coast of Taiwan and you suddenly realize that a peculiar form of peripheral artery disease seems to be endemic in the population. What is going on?

You are seeing what is known as "black foot disease." This is caused by chronic arsenic poisoning, highly endemic to Taiwan. The disease was first described in 1954, when researchers noted that residents in the area had been using artesian well water containing arsenic for more than 35 years. This produces a clinical illness comparable to atherosclerosis obliterans, resulting in gangrene of the extremities (3).—J.A. Stockman, III, M.D.

References

1. Landon HCR, et al: *Mozart, 1791, The Last Year.* New York, Schimer Books, 1989.
2. Gasman GD: *West J Med* 153:656, 1990.
3. Chen CJ: *Lancet* 2:442, 1990.

The Total Iron-Binding Capacity in Iron Poisoning: Is It Useful?
Tenenbein M, Yatscoff RW (Univ of Manitoba, Winnipeg; Manitoba Poison Control Ctr, Winnipeg)
Am J Dis Child 145:437–439, 1991   9–8

A serum iron concentration higher than the total iron-binding capacity (TIBC) is frequently used as a criterion for starting deferoxamine treatment in patients with iron poisoning. However, some patients with iron poisoning with TIBC determinations above the reference range have a normalization of those values with a drop in serum iron concentration. This phenomenon may be a laboratory aberration.

This hypothesis was tested in vitro. The addition of iron to test serum samples produced a related increase in the TIBC. Changing the assay by providing additional adsorbent prevented this occurrence. The reproducibility of the TIBC as done by 500 laboratories on 10 different reference samples was then determined. The mean coefficient of variation, 16%, was considered to be unsatisfactory.

Total iron-binding capacity is a labor-intensive procedure that prolongs turnaround time. It can be unreliable during acute hyperferremia, and its interlaboratory reproducibility under normoferremic conditions is not acceptable. In addition, the relationship between exceeding the TIBC by the serum iron concentration and clinical iron toxicity has never been established. Total iron-binding capacity should therefore not be used as an indication for initiating deferoxamine treatment in patients with acute iron poisoning.

▶ This report adequately demonstrates that TIBC is not useful. If you even remotely think about ordering it while the patient is being treated with deferoxamine, you are really going to make some bad misjudgments. Deferoxamine, by providing binding sites for iron, causes falsely elevated measurements of

TIBC. This may lead to the premature withdrawal of deferoxamine in patients with acute iron intoxication. Deferoxamine does not interfere with the determination of iron itself (1); therefore, keep the serum iron, look for the pink tinge in the color of the urine as a indicator that deferoxamine is working, and toss out the TIBC. It is worthless.

One more toxicologic pearl. There is a difference in the peak serum iron concentration following the ingestion of medicinal iron as opposed to the iron that is present in chewable vitamins. Whereas medicinal iron salts produce a maximum mean serum iron concentration very soon after ingestion, the iron in chewable vitamins will not reach its peak level in the serum until 4–5 hours after the vitamins are taken (2).—J.A. Stockman, III, M.D.

References

1. Bentur Y, et al: *J Pediatr* 118:139, 1991.
2. Ling LJ, et al: *Am J Emerg Med* 9:24, 1991.

Valproic Acid-Induced Cytopenias: Evidence for a Dose-Related Suppression of Hematopoiesis
Watts RG, Emanuel PD, Zuckerman KS, Howard TH (Univ of Alabama at Birmingham)
J Pediatr 117:495–499, 1990   9–9

Valproic acid (VPA) is used in high doses as a single anticonvulsant agent. The primary side effect, thrombocytopenia, is usually believed to be of idiosyncratic or immunologic origin. The additional side effects of neutropenia and erythrocyte aplasia are of unknown cause. A dose-dependent suppression of bone marrow erythroid progenitors by VPA was observed.

Boy, 16 years, had been treated with a combination of clonazepam, VPA, and acetazolamide for a mixed seizure disorder. When the patient showed increased lethargy and worsening cognitive function, the clonazepam and acetazolamide were discontinued and the dosage of VPA was increased to 2,500 mg/day. At this time, the patient had normal hematologic values. After 6 months of VPA monotherapy, the patient was admitted for evaluation of severe anemia. Therapy with VPA was discontinued, and the patient received a single transfusion of packed erythrocytes. Two weeks after discontinuation of VPA therapy, there was a spontaneous recovery from the red cell aplasia. Mean corpuscular volume returned to baseline levels by 1 month, but the resolution of neutropenia took several months.

In bone marrow cultures from healthy adults, VPA caused a dose-related suppression of neutrophilic and erythroid marrow colony growth in vitro. Close hematologic monitoring of patients receiving VPA therapy, especially in high doses, is crucial. Though hepatic damage is the most feared complication of VPA therapy, the hematologic side effects of anemia, thrombocytopenia, and neutropenia may also have serious consequences.

▶ There seems to be no end to the complications that VPA can cause. Now we see that it can produce anemia and neutropenia. Not only does it produce anemia, but it also produces the kind of anemia that scares the dickens out of hematologists—anemia caused by red cell aplasia in association with an increased mean corpuscular volume. The hematologist who sees a child with red cell aplasia and a high mean corpuscular volume is usually concerned about serious stem cell damage to the bone marrow, such as is seen in the Diamond-Blackfan syndrome, leukemia, and preleukemia. Valproic acid apparently produces an effect on DNA that is similar to the effect of stem cell insults on DNA (that may be stretching it a bit, but never let it be said that YEAR BOOK doesn't stretch a point when a point needs to be made). Valproic acid is a great drug when it is needed. It is even a better drug when it isn't used.

On the subject of "V" drugs, are you aware of the association between valium and amnesia and what the latest is in this regard?

We should be aware of the potential for amnesia after the use of intravenous valium. Lurie et al. (1) described a 30-year-old man who was being evaluated for upper gastric pain. He underwent an uneventful upper endoscopy. Sedation was maintained by a slow intravenous infusion of valium (10 mg). Shortly after the procedure, while still on the endoscopy table, the patient wanted to know when he was going to have his endoscopy. He was told he already had it, whereupon he said he was being lied to, became abusive, broke into a tantrum, assaulted his physician, and had to be restrained by several members of the staff. The only thing that would calm him down was a second endoscopy.—J.A. Stockman, III, M.D.

Reference

1. Lurie Y, et al: *Lancet* 2:576, 1990.

Hepatic Fibrosis With the Use of Methotrexate for Juvenile Rheumatoid Arthritis
Keim D, Ragsdale C, Heidelberger K, Sullivan D (Univ of Michigan Hosp)
J Rheumatol 17:846–848, 1990   9–10

Methotrexate (MTX) is currently under study in the treatment of juvenile rheumatoid arthritis (JRA). Hepatic fibrosis is a serious complication of MTX therapy, and there is very little known about the subsequent risk of this complication in JRA. A patient with JRA was seen in whom hepatic fibrosis developed after 3 years of MTX therapy.

Girl, 17 years, was treated with MTX for JRA for 3 years after aspirin, penicillamine, and choline salicylate failed to control the disease. A liver biopsy specimen at 1½ years of MTX therapy and about 6 years after onset of disease showed normal findings (grade I). A second elective liver biopsy specimen obtained 2 years later showed evidence of hepatic fibrosis, interpreted as grade III-A. Liver function tests were normal. The cumulative dose of MTX was about 1.3 g.

This case provides evidence of structural hepatotoxicity with the use of MTX for JRA. This patient is the first of 8 patients reported in whom hepatotoxic changes developed during the course of MTX therapy for JRA. Except for the use of aspirin in this patient, which had been discontinued at the time of the first biopsy, and the largest cumulative dose of MTX relative to the other patients, this patient has no other known risk factors for MTX toxicity. Periodic liver biopsy is recommended to monitor hepatotoxic changes resulting from MTX. In this patient, liver function tests did not correlate with the development of hepatic fibrosis.

Iatrogenic Hypocalcemic Tetany
Edmondson S, Almquist TD (Naval Hosp, San Diego)
Ann Emerg Med 19:938–940, 1990   9–11

Sodium phosphate enemas are commonly used in both adults and children, but they can produce serious electrolyte imbalance. Hypocalcemic tetany developed in a child after the use of adult sodium phosphate enemas.

Boy, 4 years, was given 3 adult-sized sodium phosphate enemas for constipation during a 2-day period. He complained of muscular stiffness and inability to move his extremities. Except for tetanic contractions of the muscles of the legs and arms, other neurologic findings were unremarkable. Initial calcium level was 5.2 mg/dL, and phosphate level was 17.5 mg/dL. Intravenous calcium was administered, and there was rapid resolution of symptoms. The electrolyte imbalance normalized with oral calcium supplementation.

This case highlights the potential harmful effects of sodium phosphate enemas. In this case, hypocalcemia results when serum calcium is bonded with an extrinsic substance. Treatment consists of correcting the underlying disease and calcium replacement when serum calcium level is less than 5 mg/dL or if hypocalcemic symptoms are present.

▶ For more on the topic of calcium metabolic abnormalities, see the Nutrition and Metabolism chapter.

Because Abstract 9–11 says it all when it comes to sodium phosphate enemas causing iatrogenic hypocalcemic tetany, this commentary will deal with a slightly different phenomenon that also involves an agent that alters metabolic processes. See if you can figure out what is going on here.

Two individuals engaged in a sporting activity note a change in the taste of carbonated beverages to an unpalatably acidic taste. What sporting activity were these individuals engaged in, and what medication were they taking?

Well, you get a star for your forehead if you answered mountain climbing and acetazolamide. Acetazolamide (Diamox) is commonly recommended for prophylaxis of acute mountain sickness. This carbonic anhydrase inhibitor is also widely used in the management of glaucoma. During an expedition to Peru and Bolivia, a little-reported effect of acetazolamide was noted (1). On drinking carbonated sodas, the subjects reported the above taste abnormalities. Presumably, the mechanism for the alteration in taste was the inhibition of carbonic anhydrase by acetazolamide. Such inhibition would cause carbonic acid, present in all carbonated sodas, to be taste perceptible. In individuals not taking a carbonic anhydrase inhibitor, carbonic acid is broken down almost instantaneously by this enzyme at the mucosal level.

Two thoughts about the above: Remember the next time you prescribe acetazolamide, the consequences could be in bad taste. Also, as many in the reading audience are quite familiar with this editor's aversion to exercise, I cannot fail but to warn those who engage in sporting activities such as those previously mentioned in this commentary. "If at first you do not succeed, so much for mountain climbing and skydiving."—J.A. Stockman, III, M.D.

Reference

1. McMurdo MET, et al: *Lancet* 337:1190, 1990.

Spina Bifida in Infants of Women Treated With Carbamazepine During Pregnancy
Rosa FW (Food and Drug Administration, Rockville, Md)
N Engl J Med 324:674–677, 1991   9–12

Previous studies have reported on the association between exposure in utero to carbamazepine and spina bifida. To investigate this association further, a cohort of women receiving Medicaid benefits who took antiepileptic agents during pregnancy and who delivered from 1980 to 1988 was studied. Only infants with spina bifida identified at the time of delivery were considered.

Four infants with spina bifida were born to 1,490 women who were taking antiepileptic drugs during pregnancy, and 32 of those were born to 107 women taking carbamazepine alone (table). The lack of independent association of phenytoin, barbiturates, or primidone with spina bifida indicates that, unlike valproic acid (VPA), those drugs do not confound concurrent maternal exposure to carbamazepine.

In a review of available cohort studies of carbamazepine exposure of fetuses, 9 cases of spina bifida were reported among the 984 exposures in utero to carbamazepine, for a relative risk of about 13.7 (95% confidence limits, 5.6 and 33.7) times the expected rate. The relative risk of spina bifida associated with exposure in utero to carbamazepine as compared with unconfounded exposure to other antiepileptic drugs was 6.8 (95% confidence limits, 2.4 and 19.1). The relative risk associated with carbamazepine as compared with VPA was .6 (95% confidence limits, .2

Infants With Spina Bifida Born to Women Taking
Antiepileptic Agents During Pregnancy,
1980 Through 1988

DRUG	CASES OF SPINA BIFIDA/NO. OF PREGNANT WOMEN TAKING DRUG	
	TOTAL *	UNCONFOUNDED TOTAL †
Barbiturates	3/1058	1/1018
Phenytoin	1/469	0/444
Carbamazepine	3/107	2/99
Primidone	1/62	0/50
Valproic acid	1/47	0/39
Total	4/1490	—

Note: The women were all Michigan residents and Medicaid recipients.
*Total refers to the total number of infants born to women taking the drugs alone or in combination. Thus, there was a total of 4 infants with spina bifida born to women who had taken the following drugs: carbamazepine and phenobarbital (child born in 1981); carbamazepine, valproic acid, and primidone (child born in 1982); carbamazepine, phenytoin, and mephobarbital (child born in 1985); and phenobarbital (child born in 1985).
†*Unconfounded total* refers to the totals derived after the removal of the following confounding factors: concurrent use of valproic acid or carbamazepine by women taking barbiturates, phenytoin, or primidone; concurrent use of valproic acid by women taking carbamazepine; and concurrent use of carbamazepine by women taking valproic acid.
(Courtesy of Rosa FW: *N Engl J Med* 324:674–677, 1991.)

and 1.7). This analysis of all available data indicates that exposure to carbamazepine without concurrent exposure to VPA carries a 1% risk of spina bifida.

▶ For an extensive discussion and an update on the neonatal management of spina bifida, see the Newborn and Neurology/Psychiatry chapters of this YEAR BOOK.—J.A. Stockman, III, M.D.

Effectiveness of an Antihistamine-Decongestant Combination for Young Children With the Common Cold: A Randomized, Controlled Clinical Trial
Hutton N, Wilson MH, Mellits ED, Baumgardner R, Wissow LS, Bonucelli C, Holtzman NA, DeAngelis C (Johns Hopkins Univ)
J Pediatr 118:125–130, 1991   9–13

Physicians frequently prescribe antihistamine-decongestant combinations to treat upper respiratory tract infection (URI) in young children. However, no randomized, controlled clinical trials have confirmed the efficacy of such drugs. A study was done to test the hypothesis that antihistamine-decongestant combinations offer no clinically significant relief of the symptoms of URI in young children.

Ninety-six children were randomly assigned to 1 of 3 treatment groups: antihistamine-decongestant, placebo, or no treatment. Follow-up telephone interviews with parents were conducted approximately 48 hours after the children were taken to the clinic. The parents were asked about the child's overall status and the duration of symptoms. At the outset of the study, approximately two thirds of the parents believed that their children needed medicine for cold symptoms. At follow-up, 64% of the children were thought by their parents to be considerably better—67% of the treatment group, 71% of the placebo group, and 57% of the no-medicine group. Parents who believed their child needed medicine reported greater improvement of symptoms at the follow-up, regardless of which treatment group their child was assigned to.

The results do not support the use of antihistamine-decongestant preparations in young children with the common cold. When prescribing such drugs, the physician should weigh the risk of adverse reaction or accidental ingestion by young family members against the perceived benefit.

▶ Dr. Jack L. Paradise, Professor of Pediatrics University of Pittsburgh Medical School, and Medical Director of the Ambulatory Care Center, Children's Hospital of Pittsburgh, comments:

▶ Praise is due the authors of this report for tackling in earnest a mundane but tough problem: Assessing the effectiveness of treatments for the common cold is no simple task. The requirements for such a study are formidable and extend well beyond a randomized, double-blind trial design. One must identify a group of subjects who are reasonably certain to have no more than a cold, and in particular, not paranasal sinusitis. One must characterize the subjects demographically and clinically. One must specify pertinent outcome measures. These measures must be assessed by unbiased observers of assured reliability. One must decide in advance on a "clinically important" degree of improvement that, if found, would justify recommending the treatment's use. If the treatment's risks and cost are low, as is the case here, one should logically settle for a relatively small degree of improvement. However, to demonstrate either the presence or the absence of a small degree of improvement with a high degree of confidence requires a large sample size. One must monitor the extent of compliance with the assigned treatment regimens. Of course, one must analyze the data (as in this case, reasonably complex) properly, and consider possible sources of bias. And finally, one must limit conclusions narrowly to those supported by the analysis, and generalize those conclusions only to the extent warranted by the compositon of the study population.

All of this is a tall order, and the intrepid investigators who set out to fill it faced many built-in constraints, some clearly insurmountable. Probably the most important of these stemmed from the special nature of their available study population: inner-city children of low socioeconomic status whose parents deemed them ill enough to be brought for care to a hospital outpatient department. Given the study's limitations on this and other of the grounds referred to above, the statement that "the results . . . do not support (the use of) an antihistamine-decongestant preparation for young children with the common cold" is fair and appropriately conservative. Unfortunately, however, for those of us pooh-poohers hungry for a bit of certainty, neither do the results conclusively discredit use of an antihistamine-decongestant for that purpose. Accordingly, until a study with all of the requisite, stringent elements appears, we will have to continue to rely on plain old clinical experience, or prejudice, or both, to justify our naysaying to parents. Meanwhile, we can thank the authors for reminding us that the utterly commonplace remains an intellectually challenging area for clinical research.—J.L. Paradise, M.D.

10 The Genitourinary Tract

Treatment of Posterior Hypospadias by the Autologous Graft of Cultured Urethral Epithelium
Romagnoli G, De Luca M, Faranda F, Bandelloni R, Franzi AT, Cataliotti F, Can-
cedda R (Ospedali Galliera, Genoa, Italy; Universitá di Palermo, Italy; Universitá
de Genova, Genoa, Italy; Istituto Nazionale per la Ricerca sul Cancro, Genoa)
N Engl J Med 323:527–530, 1990   10–1

Keratinocytes derived from normal human skin can be cultivated in vitro to form a patch of epidermis suitable for grafting. The keratinocytes possess an intrinsic capacity for site-specific differentiation that becomes fully expressed when grafts of cultured epidermis are transplanted to different parts of the body. In an application of this principle to human urethral mucosa, epithelial cells were cultured in vitro and transplanted to form the anterior urethra in 2 patients with congenital hypospadias.

A 1–2-mm biopsy specimen of urethral mucosa was obtained from the urethral meatus of each patient. The urethral cells were cultured, and confluent sheets of epithelium were available for grafting 16 and 18 days after the biopsies. At surgery, a cultured epithelial graft was placed on the connective tissue of the prepared wound on the ventral aspect of the penis, sutured, and covered by an occlusive dressing (Fig 10–1). Ten days later, the underlying connective tissue covered with the urethral epithelium was dissected, and a new urethra was surgically constructed. The new urethra was connected to the original urethral meatus immediately in 1 patient and 6 months later in the other patient. Except for small, easily repaired fistulas, no complications were noted. At 6 and 18 months after surgery, urination and erectile functions were normal, and no strictures or fistulas were present. Endoscopic examination of 1 patient a year after surgery showed morphologically normal urethral mucosa.

Autologous grafts of cultured urethral epithelium were successfully used to form the anterior urethra in patients with congenital hypospadias. This technique offers considerable functional improvement over traditional skin grafting.

▶ One could really let one's mind run wild with the possibilities that are generated by the concepts underlying the procedures described in the article abstracted above. Read on.

In about 20% of cases of hypospadias, the urethral opening is all the way back at the base of the penis, and there is no anterior urethra at all. Historically,

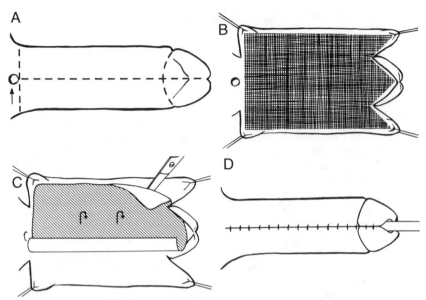

Fig 10–1.—The surgical procedure. **A,** the form of posterior hypospadias treated. The *arrow* indicates the urethral meatus; *broken line* indicates the incision performed on the ventral aspect of the penis to prepare the receiving bed for the cultured epithelium. **B,** the cultured epithelium mounted on petroleum gauze and placed on the connective tissue of the prepared wound. **C,** the construction of the new urethra by dissecting the connective tissue *(arrows)* covered by urethral epithelium. The *hatching* indicates the epithelium. **D,** the new urethra was sutured over a stent, and the operation was completed by suturing the 2 skin flaps together. (Courtesy of Romagnoli G, De Luca M, Faranda F, et al: *N Engl J Med* 323:527–530, 1990.)

treatment in these cases has required extensive reconstruction of the anterior urethra, usually with autographs of flaps of contiguous skin which is transferred with a vascular pedicle, the same way that certain types of extensive skin grafts would be transferred. When you do the latter, however, there may be present with the engrafted cells pilosebaceous skin units. Because this skin now makes up one's urethra, that can obviously lead to problems such as a hairy, sweaty urethra. Not much fun having one of those things around.

To obviate the above problems, a few years ago a surgical procedure was described in which autographs of bladder mucosa were used to form the penile urethra in boys with hypospadias. This can produce a good functional result, but the approach requires extensive surgery to the bladder. Now comes an entirely new approach to producing massive numbers of urethral mucosal cells.

Keratinocytes derived from normal human skin can be cultivated in vitro (1). These cells can be used to form a stratified patch of epidermis suitable for grafting on the sites of burns and skin defects caused by the removal of giant nevi or chronic leg ulcers. Very recently, autologous skin keratinocytes have been used successfully to line the mastoid cavities of patients with postoperative otorrhea. Not only do these cells engraft, but they also tend to engraft with a site-specific differentiation. This means that they grow as cells from the site from which they were originally obtained. For example, epithelial cells derived from the palate that are cultivated in vitro and then reimplanted will reconstitute cellular structure identical to palatal epithelium.

What was done in this report was pretty straightforward. Cells were obtained from this child's urethral meatus, which was at the base of his penis. The cells were taken to the laboratory and cultivated there. In the laboratory, a biopsy specimen's cellular size can be remarkably amplified. One cell can become 10,000 cells. You can grow whole sheets of penile urethral mucosal cells. Having these sheets available, you then go back to the patient and perform the surgery noted in the figure. You simply splay open the length of the penis, make a suitable bed for the tissue to be put into, roll everything back up around a catheter, wait for everything to heal, whip out the catheter (carefully), and you have a normally functioning penis.

Not only is there a normally functioning penis, it functions in every normal way. It sustains normal urination without an increased risk of infection. Furthermore, it has elastic properties that will allow a boy to have a normal erection. To put it simply, cultured urethral keratinocytes will become the "spandex" of the penis of the 90s for boys with complex hypospadias.—J.A. Stockman, III, M.D.

Reference

1. Rheinwald JC, et al: *Cell* 6:331, 1975.

Laparoscopy for the Nonpalpable Testis: How to Interpret the Endoscopic Findings
Castilho LN (Hospital Samaritano de Campinas, São Paulo, Brazil)
J Urol 144:1215–1218, 1990   10–2

The ideal diagnostic method for evaluating patients with nonpalpable testes remains to be defined. Classically, exploration has been the method of choice. In the present study 38 patients aged 2 to 33 years with 45 nonpalpable testes were evaluated by laparoscopy under general or epidural anesthesia.

Laparoscopy was technically successful in 36 of 38 patients (94.7%). The other 2 had intestinal adhesions. Of the 24 testes identified in the abdominal cavity, 15 were atrophic, 2 had no epididymal connection, and 7 were normal in appearance. All were found between the external iliac vessels and internal inguinal ring.

The same type of anesthesia was used in 32 patients (84.2%) who underwent exploration. There was complete correlation between laparoscopic and operative findings with regard to the presence or absence of the testis. Sixty percent of the testes sought were present, with all but 1 in the abdomen; 40% were absent. Except for 3 cases of emphysema, only 1 complication occurred.

Diagnostic laparoscopy is equally as effective as exploration in the evaluation of patients with nonpalpable testes, and the risk of complications is low. A scheme to interpret endoscopic findings has been proposed. A confirmatory operation is not necessary when the hypoplastic spermatic vessels end blindly in the pelvis or enter the internal inguinal ring followed or not by a vas deferens, and for a vas deferens alone ending blindly in the pelvis or entering the internal inguinal ring (the vanishing testis).

A confirmatory operation also is not necessary if no vascular, ductal or testicular structure is found under laparoscopic examination (testicular absence). Low and limited inguinotomy must be performed for spermatic vessels of normal appearance, followed or not by a vas deferens entering the internal inguinal ring, which suggests that the testis is probably in the inguinal canal.

▶ There are basically 2 reasons to find a nonpalpable testis. One is to locate it so that you can surgically perform an orchidopexy. The other is to completely exclude its absence because an unoperated, undescended testis cannot be allowed to be left in place because of the increased risk of malignant transformation. The ideal method to investigate the nonpalpable testis has not been found to date, but many methods have been described, including hormonal therapy to attempt to descend the testis, pneumoperitoneography, herniography, ultrasonography, venography, arteriography, CT scanning, MRI scanning, exploration, and finally laparoscopy, the topic of the article abstracted.

You might think that abdominal laparoscopy has been around only since Dr. Fiber Optic invented his instrument. Not so. Laparoscopy originated in Europe at the turn of this century. You can imagine how much you could see without the current elaborate telescopic lens systems and fiber optics that have been available only in the last 2 decades. To look for a nonpalpable testis, the abdomen is inflated with a gas (usually under general anesthesia), and the structures around the internal inguinal ring are looked at carefully. In this report, all 24 testes found endoscopically were between the internal ring and the external iliac vessels.

Based on the experience from this report, which is consistent with the information found in other reports, it seems fairly clear what kind of scheme should be used to interpret endoscopic findings. A confirmatory operation after endoscopy is unnecessary for hypoplastic spermatic vessels ending blindly in the pelvis or entering the internal ring, followed or not by a vas deferens, or for a vas deferens alone ending blindly in the pelvis or entering the internal inguinal ring (the vanishing testis). A confirmatory operation is unnecessary if no vascular, ductal, or testicular structure is found under laparoscopic examination (testicular absence). Low and limited inguinal surgery must be performed for spermatic vessels of normal appearance, followed or not by a vas deferens entering the internal ring (the testis probably is present in the inguinal canal). When laparoscopic examination is technically unsatisfactory, for whatever reason, surgical exploration is indispensable.

Laparoscopy for the above purposes is always reminiscent of a fishing expedition. In this case, if you can catch just 1 fish, take a good look at it and put it back in where it's supposed to be, it will have been well worth the effort. That is laparoscopy as opposed to surgical exploration. Surgical exploration is like draining the pond to find the 1 and only fish that may or may not even be there.—J.A. Stockman, III, M.D.

Abnormalities of Lipoprotein Metabolism in Patients With the Nephrotic Syndrome

Joven J, Villabona C, Vilella E, Masana L, Albertí R, Vallés M (Hospital de Sant Joan, Reus, Spain; Unitat de Recerca de Lipids, Reus; Hospital Germans Trias y Pujol, Badalona, Spain; Hospital Valle de Hebrón, Barcelona, Spain)
N Engl J Med 323:579–584, 1990   10–3

Hyperlipidemia is a striking feature in nephrotic syndrome, but its cause and nature remain uncertain. Serum lipids and apoproteins were measured in 57 patients, aged 15 to 81 years, with untreated nephrotic syndrome who had normal renal function and no confounding metabolic disorders. In addition, the kinetic indices of low-density lipoprotein (LDL) were studied in 6 patients and again in 3 of these 6 patients after recovery.

Compared with 57 normal control patients matched for age, sex, and weight, those with nephrotic syndrome had significantly increased serum concentrations of cholesterol, triglycerides, phospholipids, and LDL and very low density lipoprotein (VLDL) fractions. However, the relative proportions of these lipids and lipoprotein fractions were similar to those in normal subjects. The largest percent increase was in the serum apoprotein B, which correlated well with the increased LDL values. The relative proportions of lipids were positively correlated with increased serum concentrations of apoproteins B, C-II, C-III, and E, suggesting quantitative rather than qualitative differences in the lipoproteins. Lipiduria was present in all patients with nephrotic syndrome, probably reflecting the excretion of high-density lipoproteins, although no intact immunoreactive apoprotein A-I was found in the urine. Serum albumin concentrations correlated inversely with serum lipid concentrations. Kinetic studies of LDL metabolism showed an increased production of LDL apoprotein B, which returned to normal after recovery. Fractional catabolic rates were similar to those in normal persons.

Patients with the nephrotic syndrome and hyperlipidemia appear to have a selective increase in LDL apoprotein B synthesis. The increases in serum concentrations of LDL cholesterol, other lipids, and apoprotein B apparently result from reversible increases in lipoprotein production.

▶ This year has been a good news-bad news story with respect to our understanding of the nephrotic syndrome in children. Part of the good news is the subject of the abstract above. We now have a much better understanding of the lipid metabolic abnormality in patients with the nephrotic syndrome. We all know that such patients have elevated cholesterol levels. Because some children with nephrotic syndrome go on to have a long-term course, there has been concern that the hyperlipidemia may do them some harm. This is speculative, but there has been enough concern about this problem that some have suggested that such children be treated with various lipid-lowering therapies.

Patients with the nephrotic syndrome have increased concentrations of cholesterol, triglycerides, and phospholipids in serum and in the VLDL and LDL fractions of serum (no new news here), but the proportions of the individual components of the serum lipoprotein fractions are in fact similar to those of normal subjects. To say it differently, the whole system is simply revved up. The suspicion here is that there is a stimulus that triggers a pan-increased production of these lipid fractions, which are, of course, related to various protein carriers. The culprit presumably is the patient's hypoalbuminemia and low plasma oncotic pressure. The normal reaction of the body under these circumstances would be to compensate by producing other particles that are oncotically active. One of the most oncotically active particles is apoprotein B. If you produce a lot of this substance, you are going to produce an increase in the various fractions of lipids that are so commonly elevated in the nephrotic syndrome.

The conclusion of all this is pretty straightforward. These findings suggest that the hyperlipidemia is not the result of decreased receptor uptake but rather is the result of increased production and treatment directed toward inhibiting LDL synthesis—for example, with the hydroxymethylglutaryl-CoA-reductase inhibitors. That's good news.

Also good news is the recent understanding that steroid-sensitive nephrotic syndrome in children may be genetic. For a long time there has been some suspicion that the predisposition for this disease is inherited. A European survey that excluded cases of congenital nephrotic syndrome found that 63 of 1,877 nephrotic children had affected family members (1). Monozygotic twin studies also confirm this. Unequivocally confirming it is a recent report from Lagueruela et al. (2), who showed that HLA "extended haplotypes" run in families of children with the nephrotic syndrome. An "extended haplotype" is a linkage among several different HLA antigens that is more than a random chance. This study suggests that the presence of one of these haplotypes contributes enormously to susceptibility to this steroid-sensitive disease.

So what about the bad news? The bad news lies in 2 areas. One has to do with the ever-increasing numbers of patients described with the nephrotic syndrome who have it as a result of the use of nonsteroidal anti-inflammatory drugs (3). Be careful when using such drugs. They are being suggested to patients as alternatives for aspirin and acetaminophen.

Last, on the bad news side, is the knowledge that HIV infection can produce a nephrotic-like syndrome on the basis of a focal and segmental glomerulosclerosis. If you ever run across a patient with HIV infection with a positive dip stick in the urine for protein, think HIV or an associated sexually transmitted disease such as syphilis as a potential cause (4).—J.A. Stockman, III, M.D.

References

1. White RHR: *Int Arch Eur Surg Clin Nephrol* 1:215, 1983.
2. Lagueruela CC, et al: *Kidney Int* 38:145, 1990.
3. Robinson J, et al: *Pediatrics* 85:844, 1990.
4. Kusner DJ, et al: *N Engl J Med* 324:341, 1991.

Continuous Arteriovenous Hemofiltration/Dialysis Improves Pulmonary Gas Exchange in Children With Multiple Organ System Failure

DiCarlo JV, Dudley TE, Sherbotie JR, Kaplan BS, Costarino AT (Children's Hosp of Philadelphia; Univ of Pennsylvania, Philadelphia)
Crit Care Med 18:822–826, 1990   10–4

In children with multiple organ system failure, excess lung water that results from the combined effects of fluid resuscitation, capillary leak phenomena, and renal failure can exacerbate pulmonary gas exchange. The role of continuous arteriovenous hemofiltration with or without countercurrent dialysis (CAVH/D) in the treatment of children with multiple organ system failure was evaluated in 8 children, aged 6–19 years, with coexistent renal and respiratory failure. In all of these patients, pulmonary edema was the major feature causing abnormal pulmonary function; 6 patients had acute respiratory distress syndrome.

Before CAVH/D, patient weight increased to 65.2 kg because of fluid accumulation. After 48 hours of CAVH/D, the mean weight decreased significantly to 60.3 kg. Similarly, pulmonary gas exchange improved significantly as evidenced by increase in arterial oxygen pressure-fraction of inspired oxygen from 137 to 208; positive end-expiratory pressure remained unchanged or decreased. In patients with net negative fluid balance, improved oxygenation was associated with a decrease in pulmonary capillary wedge pressure and greater reduction in weight. Colloid oncotic pressure also increased significantly. Volume of parenteral nutrition increased markedly, whereas blood urea nitrogen and serum creatinine levels remained unchanged. Except for transient hypotension that promptly responded to albumin infusion, no other hemodynamic instability attributable to CAVH/D therapy was noted.

These data show that CAVH/D improves pulmonary gas exchange in children with multiple organ system failure, possibly by removal of body and lung water or by enhancing clearance of mediators associated with pulmonary dysfunction. In addition, CAVH/D enhances nutritional intake in these patients. The procedure is associated with minimal hemodynamic changes and infrequent complications.

Continuous Hemodiafiltration in Children

Bishof NA, Welch TR, Strife CF, Ryckman FC (Univ of Cincinnati; Children's Hosp Research Found, Cincinnati)
Pediatrics 85:819–823, 1990   10–5

Continuous arteriovenous hemofiltration is an effective treatment of acute renal failure in patients with multisystem dysfunction. However, the procedure may not be sufficient for control of azotemia. Either hemodialysis or peritoneal dialysis is an alternative method, but may be undesirable in these unstable patients. Continuous arteriovenous hemodiafiltration (CAVHD) may alleviate this problem. In addition to removal of excess plasma water, CAVHD facilitates solute removal (Fig 10–2). This technique has been increasingly used in severely ill adults. The use of CAVHD in 4 children was studied.

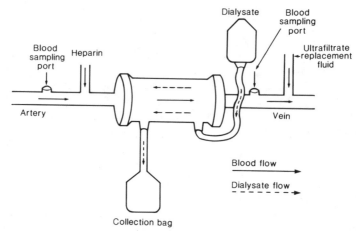

Fig 10−2.—Schematic illustration of continuous arteriovenous hemodiafiltration system. (Courtesy of Bishof NA, Welch TR, Strife CF, et al: *Pediatrics* 85:819−823, 1990.)

One child had perinatal asphyxia and oliguria while on extracorporeal membrane oxygenation, 2 patients had Burkitt's lymphoma and tumor lysis syndrome, and 1 patient had septic shock several months after a bone marrow transplant. All had acute renal failure and contraindications to hemodialysis or peritoneal dialysis. Continuous arteriovenous hemodiafiltration was performed from 11 hours up to 7 days. In 1 patient, urea clearance with CAVHD was 2−4 times that expected from ultrafiltration removal alone. None of the patients had worsening of cardiovascular status or required increased pressor support during CAVHD. The 2 patients with tumor lysis syndrome survived, and both eventually recovered normal renal function.

Continuous arteriovenous hemodiafiltration is a safe and effective renal replacement therapy in critically ill children with multiorgan failure. The technique may be particularly useful in children with massive tumor lysis.

▶ Dr. Richard Cohn, Associate Professor of Clinical Pediatrics, Northwestern University Medical School, and Director, Section of Clinical Nephrology, Children's Memorial Hospital, comments:

▶ If the pediatric hematologists are taking over the world (1), then the pediatric nephrologists are taking over the intensive care units. The dialytic options available to nephrologists, intensivists, and neonatologists are numerous and often confusing (2).

What is not confusing is that control of extracellular volume and solute removal is now possible in infants and small children, provided vascular (or peritoneal) access is supplied. Until the mid1980s, dialysis for extremely ill children was available mainly as hemodialysis, an efficient, but intermittent treatment that rapidly removed volume as well as solutes. The decrease in both circulating volume and plasma osmolality often caused major hemodynamic instability.

Continuous hemofiltration was a less efficient but more gentle form of intravascular volume reduction, which also allowed for the replacement of removed fluid with enteral or parenteral alimentation. However, this form of therapy often did not remove adequate solute in patients with severe azotemia.

In the above article, Bishof et al. describe the process of continuous hemodiafiltration in children. The slow removal of volume by hemofiltration, which is predominantly convection mediated, is *combined* with the slow removal of solute by dialysis, which is predominantly diffusion mediated. Because this procedure is carried out continuously (24 hours a day), the treatment provides gentle, efficient removal of solute combined with removal of large volumes of fluid, allowing for hyperalimentation and transfusions of necessary blood products. This procedure is especially useful for patients on chemotherapy for "bulky tumors" and for catabolic patients with significant azotemia. It is also used approximately half the time for patients on extracorporeal membrane oxygenation. For pediatric patients, a blood pump is used in almost all cases, because cardiac output may not suffice to drive the system and so that tight regulation of the blood flow rate into the filter is maintained.

Despite these advances, it must be remembered that patients for whom these modalities are used are often critically ill. Frequently, these patients have multiorgan failure and require vasopressor support. Heparin must be used as an anticoagulant, with its inherent risk of systemic bleeding. Nevertheless, as the article indicates, recovery occurs in many patients, and the majority will recover normal renal function. There are certain to be additional advances in this field in the 1990s; it is likely that the nephrologist will maintain a constant role in the critical care setting, especially in these times of bone marrow, liver, and other organ transplants.— R. Cohn, M.D.

References

1. 1991 Year Book of Pediatrics, p 276.
2. Morganstern B: *Pediatr Nephrol* 4:645, 1990.

Renal Transplantation in Infants
Najarian JS, Frey DJ, Matas AJ, Gillingham KJ, So SKS, Cook M, Chavers B, Mauer SM, Nevins TE (Univ of Minnesota, Minneapolis)
Ann Surg 212:353–367, 1990
10–6

To determine the role of renal transplantation in the treatment of renal failure in the young child or infant, the long-term results of 79 kidney transplants performed in 75 infants aged younger than 2 years in 1965–1989 were reviewed (Fig 10–3). Of the children, 23 were 12 months old or younger. Renal failure was caused by hypoplasia and obstructive uropathy in 52% of patients and by oxalosis in 11%. Infants were considered for transplantation when they were undergoing or about to begin dialysis. There were 75 primary transplants and 4 retransplants; 63 donors were living related (LRD), 1 was living unrelated, and 15 were cadaver donors (CAD). All had intra-abdominal transplants with arterial

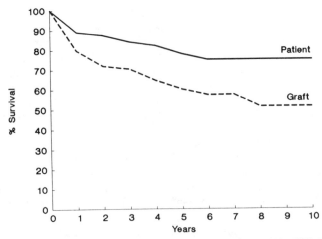

Fig 10–3.—Patient and graft survival for primary transplants in infants (1965–1989). (Courtesy of Najarian JS, Frey DJ, Matas AJ, et al: *Ann Surg* 212:353–367, 1990.)

anastomosis to the distal aorta. Before 1983, routine splenectomy was performed, and immunosuppressive protocol included azathioprine, Minnesota antilymphoblast globulin, and methylprednisolone. In 1984, splenectomy was abandoned, and in addition to immunosuppressive therapy, patients received donor-specific transfusions preoperatively. Other non–donor-specific transfusion patients and cadaver transplant recipients received sequential therapy with cyclosporine postoperatively.

During an average follow-up of 60 months, 48 (64%) infants were alive with functioning grafts. Since 1983, patient survival at 1 year has been 95%; at 5 years survival has been 91%. Graft survival was 96% at 1 year and 82% at 5 years. Patient and graft survival were significantly improved with cyclosporine therapy, and patient survival was significantly better for LRD recipients compared with CAD recipients. Oxalosis was associated with decreased patient and graft survival. Outcome did not differ between infants aged 12 months or younger and those aged 12–24 months, or between infants and older children.

There were 16 deaths (21%), including 5 early deaths from coagulopathy and infection and 11 late deaths from postsplenectomy sepsis, recurrent oxalosis, infection, and other causes. There have been no deaths since 1983. Thirty grafts were lost. The major cause of graft loss was rejection in 15 patients; other causes were death with functioning grafts in 7, recurrent oxalosis in 3, and technical complications in 3. Overall, 52% of patients did not experience rejection episodes. The mean creatinine level in patients with functioning grafts was .8 mg/dL. Early postoperative complications included fever, atelectasis, ileus, and reactions to Minnesota antilymphoblast globulin. Late complications included infections, small-bowel obstruction, ureteral complications, and metabolic abnormalities. Although the infants were small for their age at the time of transplantation, successful transplants resulted in increased growth, head circumference, and development. Renal transplantation can be performed in infants aged younger than 2 years with the same patient and graft survival rates achieved in older children and adults. Furthermore, patients with successful transplants have improved growth and development with excellent rehabilitation. Early transplantation should be the preferred method of treatment for end-stage renal disease in infants.

The Use of Cadaver Kidneys for Transplantation in Young Children
So SKS, Gillingham K, Cook M, Mauer SM, Matas A, Nevins TE, Chavers BM, Najarian JS (Washington Univ; Univ of Minnesota, Minneapolis)
Transplantation 50:979–983, 1990   10–7

The role of cadaver kidney transplantation in infants and young children with end-stage renal disease has been questioned, particularly before the use of cyclosporine. Before 1984, cadaver kidney transplantation in young children was frequently associated with poor patient and graft outcome. To assess the current risk of cadaver kidney transplantation in children, outcomes in the era of low-dose cyclosporine as part of a quadruple immunosuppressive regimen were compared with outcomes in the era of triple-drug immunosuppression before 1979.

Between 1963 and 1989, 44 cadaver kidney transplantations were performed in 42 children younger than age 6 years. Of these, 19 were performed between 1984 and 1989 using a quadruple-drug regimen consisting of Minnesota antilymphocyte globulin, azathioprine, prednisone, and cyclosporine. The other 25 were performed before 1984, without the use of cyclosporine. Twenty-five transplants were performed in children younger than 3 years of age. Follow-up periods ranged from 1 to 18 years.

Overall, patient survival rates were 77% at 1 year and 69% at 4 years; graft survival was 54%. After adoption of the quadruple-drug immunosuppressive regimen, the 1-year patient survival increased significantly, from 53% before 1979 to 90% since 1984. Similarly, 1-year graft survival improved significantly from 40% to 78% in recipients younger than 6 years of age and from 22% to 82% in recipients younger than 3 years of age. With the quadruple-drug regimen, 1-year and 4-year graft function rates for children less than 6 years of age were 83% for first cadaver transplants and 72% for second cadaver transplants. These results were essentially the same as in older children and adults. However, even with quadruple-drug immunosuppression, 1-year graft function was significantly poorer in kidneys from donors less than 4 years old (50%) than in kidneys from donors more than 4 years old (87%). Serial height measurement in 15 children after transplantation showed that 8 (53%) had accelerated growth, 5 (33%) had normal-velocity growth, and only 2 (14%) had poor growth.

With quadruple-drug immunosuppression, cadaver renal transplantation from adults or pediatric donors older than age 4 is a viable alternative in the management of end-stage renal disease in young children.

There is, however, little evidence that cadaver kidney transplantation in children less than 1 year old is safe or effective.

▶ We have written a lot about renal transplantation in prior YEAR BOOKS, so this commentary will digress a bit to deal with some other aspects of chronic renal disease. Let's touch on a variety of topics.

This year has seen the double-edged sword of using or not using aluminum hydroxide as a phosphate-binding agent for control of hyperphosphatemia in patients with chronic renal disease. Although aluminum hydroxide is an excellent phosphate-binding agent, it can and regularly does produce aluminum intoxication in patients with chronic renal disease. This is not a trivial problem, because aluminum in bone markedly accelerates the effects of renal osteodystrophy. A study has shown, however, that calcium carbonate is actually more effective than aluminum hydroxide in binding phosphate, with essentially none of the toxicity seen with aluminum (1).

There has been a lot of other new information about aluminum with which you should be familiar. Elevated plasma aluminum levels are being reported in normal infants who receive antacids containing aluminum (2). In these infants, aluminum-containing antacids were given to help manage gastroesophageal reflux. The levels of plasma aluminum were high enough that it could not be safely assumed that they would not result in some damage to these infants, although none was noted during the short time covered by this report. Even a single exposure to large quantities of orally ingested aluminum can produce a problem. Take, for example, the situation on July 6, 1988, in Cornwall, England. On that day, at the Lowermoor Water Treatment Works, 20 tons of 8% aluminum phosphate solution were inadvertently deposited directly into a water tank (contact tank) rather than into the central storage processing tank. The contact tank was downstream of pH monitors at the water works, so the contaminated water was directly distributed into households and industrial buildings. Aluminum phosphate is added to water largely to balance pH. That same day, some of the 20,000 consumers noted that the water had an unpleasant metallic taste, and a few had some initial symptoms. Two individuals who drank the water felt ill for more than 8 months, and on more careful examination (including bone biopsies) they showed evidence of severe aluminum toxicity, including aluminum deposition into bones (3). If that can happen in 1 day with a high dose in adults, imagine what can happen to babies.

We now have a better understanding about who does and who does not get polycystic kidney disease. Suppose, for example, that while taking a medical history and performing a physical examination, you discover that a family member of the patient has polycystic kidney disease, and you want to find out whether the child you are examining may carry the genetic defect (an autosomal-dominant problem). You may think this is an unfair question, because this is a rare disorder. In fact, it is not rare. About 1 in 1,000 persons carries a mutant gene for the condition. Polycystic kidney disease is responsible for up to 9% of cases of end-stage renal disease in the United States. The condition could be diagnosed before symptoms occur by the use of ultrasound, which may detect renal cysts. In children, however, these cysts are usually so small that they are undetectable, becoming larger and more numerous as the child gets older.

If you really want to find out whether a child has polycystic kidney disease of the autosomal variety, you may need to examine the short arm of chromosome 16. This has been determined to be the locus for the autosomal-dominant polycystic kidney disease gene, designated TKD1. Only 4% of families with this disorder have the disorder because of a mutation elsewhere on the genome (4).

The last new bit of information relative to chronic renal disease has to do with a better understanding of the relative risk of this problem for blacks, whites, and American Indians.

Blacks are 4 times more likely to develop end-stage renal disease than whites. Other racial and ethnic groups may also be at greater risk for renal failure. For native American Indians living in the United States, the overall risk of end-stage renal disease is approximately threefold higher than for whites. Little is known about the incidence of end-stage renal disease in Hispanic Americans. Blacks have a disproportionately lower number of kidney transplants than whites, particularly with respect to kidneys from a living donor. In contrast, the number of native Americans who have primary transplantation of cadaver kidneys or kidneys from living related donors, is proportionate to the number of native Americans with new onset end-stage renal disease and is quite comparable to the corresponding rates among whites.

To understand the reason for this racial disparity, you will need to read the excellent special article by Kasiske, et al. (5), who speculated that differences in the frequencies of ABO blood groups and the major histocompatibility-complex antigens, inadequate financial coverage, knowledge that the outcome after transplantation is worse in blacks than in whites, cultural barriers, and other socioeconomic factors all affect the rate of transplantation in these differing ethnic groups.

No one ever said that life was fair, but the injustices relative to organ transplantation that are racially based are just not right. The latter situation simply underscores the fact that if you think the world is against you, it doesn't necessarily mean it isn't.—J.A. Stockman, III, M.D.

References

1. Salusky IB, et al: *N Engl J Med* 324:527, 1991.
2. Tsou VN, et al: *Pediatrics* 87:148, 1991.
3. Eastwood JV, et al: *Lancet* 336:462, 1990.
4. Parfrey PS, et al: *N Engl J Med* 323:1085, 1990.
5. Kasiske BL, et al: *N Engl J Med* 324:302, 1991.

Chronic Renal Disease and Pregnancy Outcome
Cunningham FG, Cox SM, Harstad TW, Mason RA, Pritchard JA (Univ of Texas Southwestern Med Ctr, Dallas)
Am J Obstet Gynecol 163:453–459, 1990   10–8

From 1971 through 1988, 37 women with pregnancies complicated by chronic renal insufficiency were followed prospectively. Of these, 26 had moderate renal insufficiency, and 11 had severe renal insufficiency. The maternal, fetal, and perinatal outcomes in these groups were compared.

Common maternal complications included anemia, chronic hypertension, and preeclampsia. Renal function deteriorated in 5 patients with moderate renal insufficiency and in 1 patient with severe renal insufficiency. These 6 patients were followed up for a mean 5 years after delivery. Five were chronically hypertensive, and 4 required dialysis an average 30 months after delivery. Of 7 patients with stable renal function during pregnancy, 6 showed deterioration at a mean 39 months after delivery. Blood volume expansion in women with moderate renal disease was normal, whereas women with severe disease had significantly attenuated expansion. Serial creatinine clearances increased during pregnancy in half of the women with moderate insufficiency and in none of the women with severe renal disease.

There were 30 live-born infants, and 6 pregnancies either aborted spontaneously or were electively terminated before 26 weeks' gestation. The only perinatal mortality was 1 third-trimester fetal death. Preterm delivery complicated 13 (40%) of 32 pregnancies. Compared with women who had severe renal insufficiency, those with moderate renal insufficiency were more likely to be delivered of live births (88% vs. 64%) and had a lower incidence of fetal growth retardation (35% vs. 43%) and preterm delivery (30% vs. 86%). Mean birth weights in the moderate and severe renal disease groups were 2,500 and 1,520 g, respectively, and birth weights correlated inversely with maternal serum creatinine concentration (Fig 10–4).

Pregnancy in women with moderate to severe renal insufficiency commonly is complicated by chronic hypertension, preeclampsia, and anemia. Perinatal complications include midpregnancy losses and low birth weight (from preterm delivery, fetal growth retardation, or both). Despite the high incidence of maternal morbidity, adverse perinatal outcome is not prohibitive, with 80% of pregnancies resulting in live-born infants.

▶ Dr. Michael Socol, Professor of Obstetrics and Gynecology, Northwestern University Medical School, comments:

▶ Preconceptual counseling for the woman with chronic renal disease must address 2 major issues. Will long-term renal function be compromised by the pregnancy? Is perinatal outcome adversely affected, and if so, what complications can be anticipated?

Fortunately, pregnancy does not impair renal status in those women with chronic renal disease and normal or only mildly decreased renal function. Prognosis is more uncertain for patients with moderate (preconception serum creatinine of 1.4–2.5 mg/dL) or severe (serum creatinine >2.5 mg/dL) insufficiency. Uncontrolled hypertension is now recognized as the principal factor predisposing patients to renal deterioration, but women with lupus nephropathy, membranoproliferative glomerulonephritis, and perhaps immunoglobulin A and reflux nephropathies may also be at increased risk.

Perinatal complications include superimposed preeclampsia, fetal growth re-

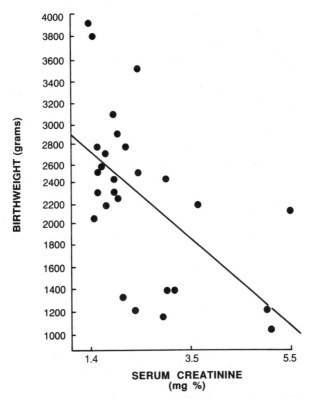

Fig 10–4.—Comparison of birth weights of 29 live-born infants with maternal serum creatinine concentrations (Spearman's correlation coefficient = −.6252, P = .001). (Courtesy of Cunningham FG, Cox SM, Harstad TW, et al: *Am J Obstet Gynecol* 163:453–459, 1990.)

tardation, preterm delivery, and stillbirth. Pregnancy outcome is directly related to the severity of renal insufficiency and chronic hypertension. Consequently, some authors have discouraged conception if the serum creatinine level exceeds 1.5 mg/dL and diastolic blood pressure is above 90 mm Hg. It should be kept in mind, however, that these criteria are somewhat arbitrary and possibly are too conservative. Even though "normal" pregnancy is unusual when the preconception creatinine level is higher than 3.0 mg/dL, successes have been documented and include patients requiring dialysis.

The current report is encouraging for women with moderate or severe renal insufficiency. Worsening renal function, defined as a ≥50% increase in creatinine concentration during pregnancy, occurred in only 5 of 26 patients with moderate insufficiency and only 1 of 11 patients with severe insufficiency. Whereas preterm birth, fetal growth retardation, and preeclampsia were common, particularly in those patients with chronic hypertension, 80% of pregnancies resulted in live-born infants. If the 6 pregnancies terminated before 26 weeks of gestation are excluded, perinatal mortality was limited to a single third-trimester fetal death.

Patients with chronic renal disease definitely should be managed in a tertiary center and, ideally, should receive preconceptual counseling about maternal and fetal risks. Sustaining a successful pregnancy will be related to the degree of functional renal impairment and chronic hypertension. Renal disease with hypertension and azotemia impairs fertility, but with the availability of hemodialysis and transplantation even these patients may consider pregnancy. If a patient decides to attempt pregnancy after appropriate appraisal of potential complications, chronic renal disease should not be viewed as an absolute contraindication to this endeavor.—M. Socol, M.D.

Renal Venous Thrombosis in Infants and Children
Ricci MA, Lloyd DA (Univ of Pittsburgh; Children's Hosp of Pittsburgh)
Arch Surg 125:1195–1199, 1990   10–9

Before 1964, an aggressive surgical approach to renal venous thrombosis in infants and children was recommended. Since then, success with supportive treatment alone has been reported.

A review of 46 cases, spanning 32 years, showed that the last surgical procedure (nephrectomy) for renal venous thrombosis was performed at the study hospital in 1978. Since then, 9 of 10 neonatal patients treated nonoperatively have survived. In recent years, sonography has confirmed the diagnosis with 92% accuracy. In earlier years, diagnosis was frequently supported by intravenous pyelography, with an accuracy of 79%. Of 21 patients diagnosed during life, 4 were treated surgically, and 3 of these survived. Of the 17 patients treated nonoperatively, 14 (82%) survived, including 5 patients with bilateral disease.

Early diagnosis by sonography and supportive nonoperative therapy provides the best success in patients with renal venous thrombosis. There is no clear benefit of surgical intervention in the acute phase. In selected patients, thrombolytic therapy may be of value.

▶ This review demonstrates how far we have come in terms of our understanding of what to do with renal vein thrombi. It wasn't until the 1960s that people stopped operating on every child and adult with a renal vein thrombosis. As a house officer in training, a renal vein thrombosis was suspected any time a patient (neonate or otherwise) had hematuria, proteinuria, and a unilateral abdominal mass. The diagnosis was confirmed with intravenous pyelography. Every now and then, you had to argue with an old-timer surgeon who wanted to remove the thrombosed kidney. Arguing with an old-timer surgeon usually meant throwing yourself bodily over the patient to spare that patient the knife. More than 1 pediatric house officer came close to having his or her own kidney ripped out by an angered attending physician.

Nonetheless, the approach characterized by "tincture of time" has proved to be correct. In the vast majority of patients with renal vein thrombosis, the problem is adequately resolved. Careful attention to the cause of the difficulty and meticulous medical management of the specific problem are needed. As was noted in this series, the survival rate approached 90% for children of all ages with renal vein thrombosis and, in the vast majority of these survivals, renal function returned.

In the 1990s, dealing with a renal vein thrombosis requires only a high index of suspicion, an ultrasound machine, and a little patience. Every now and then, a drop or 2 of heparin helps as well.—J.A. Stockman, III, M.D.

Idiopathic Hypercalciuria: Association With Isolated Hematuria and Risk for Urolithiasis in Children
Stapleton FB, the Southwest Pediatric Nephrology Study Group (Baylor Univ Med Ctr, Dallas)
Kidney Int 37:807–811, 1990
        10–10

When hematuria in children is not associated with proteinuria, red blood cell casts, or a family history of glomerular disease, its significance remains unclear. Several limited studies have suggested a link between isolated hematuria and increased urinary calcium excretion in children. A prospective multicenter study was undertaken to determine the frequency and prognostic importance of hypercalciuria in children with hematuria.

Seventy-six of the 215 children enrolled in the study had urinary calcium excretion greater than 4 mg/kg/day while ingesting their routine diets. Compared with children who had normal urinary calcium excretion, those with hematuria and hypercalciuria were likely to be male, to be white, to have a family history of urolithiasis, and to have gross hematuria and calcium oxalate crystalluria.

Renal biopsies performed in 10 patients with urinary calcium excretion of .4–2.5 mg/kg/day revealed 3 cases of IgA glomerulonephritis, 3 cases of glomerular basement membrane thinning, and 1 case of proliferative glomerulonephritis. Oral calcium loading tests showed renal hypercalciuria in 26 children and absorptive hypercalciuria in 15. The tests were not diagnostic in 35 children.

Follow-up information for 1–4 years was available for 184 patients. Urolithiasis or renal colic developed in 8 of 60 hypercalciuric patients but in only 2 of 124 patients with normal urinary calcium excretion. Hypercalciuria in a child with otherwise unexplained hematuria suggests a risk for developing urolithiasis, but other causes of hematuria should also be considered.

▶ Dr. Craig Langman, Associate Professor of Pediatrics, Northwestern University Medical School, and Director, Section of Research Nephrology, Children's Memorial Hospital, comments:

▶ The article by Stapleton et al., representing the Southwest Pediatric Nephrology Study Group's (SWPNSG) description of children with hematuria and hypercalciuria, demonstrates several important findings. Most importantly, they have laid to rest the idea that hematuria-associated hypercalciuria is an isolated finding in Chicago and Memphis by studying patients in diverse geographic areas including Texas, Oklahoma, Arkansas, Colorado, and Utah. Perhaps just as importantly, the SWPNSG represents one of the few ongoing "study" groups in pediatric nephrology since the dissolution of the International Study of Kidney Diseases in Children. You remember that the latter study group made important inroads in our understanding of the natural history and treatment recommendations for children worldwide with minimal change nephrosis and some of its variants. The majority of the clinically relevant questions in pediatric nephrology cannot be answered by the experience of 1 center, and the combined efforts of the SWPNSG serve to remind us that, except for the cancer study groups, there are few national study groups in all of pediatrics. We might take a valuable lesson from the SWPNSG in organizing across institutional boundaries.

What importance is the demonstration of a "disease" called idiopathic hypercalciuria in children? Even the short-term data provided by Stapleton et al. demonstrate that 8 of 60 children with hypercalciuria formed a renal stone, and most had many. This is compared with only 2 of 124 children with normal urinary calcium excretion who formed stones. Just as important are new data in adults with idiopathic hypercalciuria, demonstrating that fracturing osteopenia is not an infrequent occurrence (1). Anecdotally, we have seen 2 patients in the past 12 months who fractured bones without trauma and who carried the diagnosis of idiopathic hypercalciuria, suggesting that the disturbance in bone metabolism may extend into the childhood forms as well. Thus, the marker of the hypercalciuric state, hematuria, may give us an early glimpse of what must now be viewed as a systemic bone and mineral disturbance: enhanced absorption of calcium through the intestinal tract, excessive renal excretion in the absence of differences of serum parathyroid hormone levels, and the added problem of dissolution of bone mineral stores, with resultant fractures.

The data from the study by Stapleton and his colleagues at the SWPNSG serve to remind us that idiopathic hypercalciuria is a frequently occurring genetic disease, and many children who have it may suffer a morbid event related to it. Based on other data, some children may develop a long-term defect in normal bone mass accretion. This article serves the additional purpose of reminding pediatricians of the need to coalesce our important questions into collaborative working groups to effectively help our patients.—C. Langman, M.D.

Reference

1. Bataille P, et al: *Kidney Int* 39:1193, 1991.

Soft Tissue Calcification in Pediatric Patients With End-Stage Renal Disease
Milliner DS, Zinsmeister AR, Lieberman E, Landing B (Mayo Clinic and Found, Rochester, Minn; Children's Hosp of Los Angeles, Calif)
Kidney Int 38:931–936, 1990   10–11

In adults, soft-tissue calcification is a well-recognized complication of uremia, resulting in ischemic necrosis, cardiac arrhythmias, and respiratory failure. Soft-tissue calcifications in children, however, are considered rare. Prompted by a report of sudden death from pulmonary calcinosis in

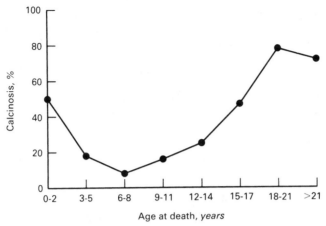

Fig 10–5.—Prevalence of calcinosis by age in pediatric patients with end-stage renal disease who underwent postmortem examination at Children's Hospital of Los Angeles. (Courtesy of Milliner DS, Zinsmeister AR, Lieberman E, et al: *Kidney Int* 38:930–936, 1990.)

an adolescent after renal transplantation, the clinical, biochemical, and autopsy data on 120 pediatric patients with uremia who were undergoing dialysis or who had undergone renal transplantation were retrospectively reviewed.

There were soft-tissue calcifications in 72 (60%) patients. Of these, 43 (36%) had systemic calcinosis involving the blood vessels, lung, kidney, myocardium, coronary artery, CNS, and gastric mucosa. Vascular calcification was always accompanied by deposits in other organs. The prevalence of calcinosis was 50% from birth to age 2 years, was low during early childhood, and increased steadily throughout childhood and adolescence (Fig 10–5). There were focal calcifications in 29 patients; 48 had no soft-tissue calcifications. Multiple logistic regression analysis showed that the use of vitamin D or its analogues, type of vitamin D prescribed, peak calcium × phosphorus product, age at onset of renal failure, and male sex were jointly associated with calcinosis. Oral vitamin D therapy had the strongest association with calcinosis, particularly with the use of the more potent analogue calcitriol.

After adjusting for other variables, the duration of renal failure, peak serum calcium levels, serum calcium and serum phosphorus levels at death, and primary renal diagnosis were not significantly associated with calcinosis. Cardiopulmonary calcinosis was a contributory factor in the death of 11 patients. Soft-tissue calcification is a significant problem in young patients with advanced renal disease, suggesting a role for vitamin D analogues in the pathogenesis of soft-tissue calcification.

▶ Data from this series confirm that soft-tissue calcification is a significant problem in young patients with advanced renal disease. Lung, myocardium, and coronary arteries are frequent sites of calcium deposition, with clinically significant and, in some cases, fatal consequences. In fact, a sudden death from pulmonary calcinosis in an adolescent following renal transplantation prompted the review from Los Angeles Children's Hospital abstracted above.

The message here is fairly clear. Go lightly with the vitamin D, otherwise you may turn your patient to stone.

By the way, a turning to stone is the current theory of the terminal illness suffered by Lot's wife in the Old Testament. Recall that according to the Old Testament, "The Lord caused to rain upon Sodom and Gomorrah brimstone and fire and hereover the cities and all the plain and all the inhabitants of the cities." Recall also that God forewarned Lot to flee the city but not to look back as the inferno began. Unfortunately, during the escape, Mrs. Lot looked back at the devastating conflagration and she "became a pillar of salt."

Current theory has it, however, that she became a pillar of something else (1). The theory is that by turning back, Mrs. Lot was hit full in the face by a hot blast of air of high CO_2 content causing her P_{CO_2} to skyrocket upward along with her body temperature. Two powerful forces would have forced the free calcium in Mrs. Lot's blood upward. The lowering of her pH and tissue release of calcium would do this. At a partial pressure of only 10^{-1} atmospheres of CO_2, a free calcium concentration of 10^{-4} M would have occurred, and only 3% of the total available in blood would have been necessary to initiate calcite formation. At the same time that all of this was going on, the increased free calcium, more likely than not, triggered muscle contraction, with instant spread of rigor. Simultaneous rigor, with the instantaneous formation of calcite, caused her to "turn to stone," which must have given the vague resemblance of being turned into a pillar of "salt." Mrs. Lot died instantly of a disease known as "rigor carbonatus."

Whether or not this is true, it is fascinating, isn't it, how modern science serves to corroborate and even elucidate medical events described in the Bible.—J.A. Stockman, III, M.D.

Reference

1. Klotz IM: *J Royal Soc Med* 81:397, 1988.

Predicting Treatment Outcome in Nocturnal Enuresis
Devlin JB, O'Cathain C (Eastern Health Board, Dublin)
Arch Dis Child 65:1158–1161, 1990   10–12

Childhood nocturnal enuresis has been treated, with varying degrees of success, by drugs and behavioral conditioning. Reported cure rates for the enuresis alarm range from 30% to 100%. A program of treatment using the alarm was evaluated, and an attempt was made to identify variables related to a successful outcome.

The study group included 127 children consecutively referred to an enuresis clinic. Most (83%) had primary enuresis, because they had never acquired nocturnal continence. The remaining (22%) children, classified as having secondary enuresis, had started wetting again after being reliably dry at night for at least 6 months.

The children were encouraged to assume full responsibility for the program. During a baseline period of 8 weeks, they kept a chart recording wetting frequency and the time and size of the wet spot. The alarm was then given to the children to be used until a period of 21 consecutive dry nights was achieved. A further course of the alarm was tried in the event of relapse.

As a result of the baseline behavioral recording period, 22 children became dry. Eight children were lost after the initial visit, and 1 other was referred for surgical management. Of the remaining 96 children who had a trial of the enuresis alarm, 84% achieved an initial successful outcome of 42 consecutive dry nights. Nine of 11 children who relapsed and required further treatment became dry again. At 6-month follow-up, the variables significantly affecting outcome were stress in the family and the child's distress about the wetting. At 12 months, psychiatric disorder in the child, an absence of the child's concern about wetting, and developmental delay in the child adversely affected outcome.

When these variables were removed, the rate of success for the enuresis alarm exceeded 90%. This study confirms the role of conditioning treatment and the importance of encouraging the child and the family. Problems such as family stress and medical or psychological factors should be considered when undertaking this form of treatment.

Routine Admission Urinalysis Examination in Pediatric Patients: A Poor Value
Mitchell N, Stapleton FB (Univ of Tennessee; LeBonheur Children's Med Ctr, Memphis)
Pediatrics 86:345–349, 1990

10–13

Some hospital bylaws require routine urinalysis at the time of admission. Because of a recent trend toward performing only those routine procedures that are cost-effective, the value of routine urinalysis has been questioned. A study was undertaken to determine how rigorously the hospital bylaws for routine urinalysis were adhered to, the impact of screening urinalysis on patient care, and whether the cost-effectiveness of this screening test justifies its implementation.

During the months of June and November 1987, there were 2,695 hospital admissions to a day-care unit or inpatient medical or surgical services. Of these, urinalyses were considered essential for diagnosis or therapy in 543 patients; these patients were excluded from the analysis. Of the remaining 2,152 patients eligible for screening, only 30% (145 of 476) of a day-care unit and 35% (587 of 1,676) of inpatient admissions had an admission urinalysis.

Of the 732 screening urinalyses performed, results were abnormal in 20%. The frequency of abnormal results did not differ between the medical and surgical admissions or between the months of June and November. The most common abnormalities on initial urinalyses were pyuria and hematuria. Only 38% of the abnormal admission urinalysis results were followed by another urinalysis or urine culture. Subsequent urinalyses showed persistent abnormalities in 58%, but most subsequent abnormal results were not evaluated further. In addition, only 37% had chart documentation that the urinalyses were evaluated. Urinary tract infection was diagnosed in 6 patients, and no other diagnoses or changes in management were made. The total cost of initial urinalyses and follow-up tests for these 732 patients during the 2 months was $23,465, which translated to a cost of $3,911 for each of the 6 urinary tract infections diagnosed.

When hospital bylaws mandate admission urinalysis, this requirement is often ignored, and abnormal results are often unappreciated or not pursued. In addition, this study demonstrates the great cost of this screening test with little apparent benefit in detecting renal disease.

▶ Dr. Thomas Welch, Director, Division of Nephrology, Childrens Hospital Medical Center, Cincinnati, comments:

▶ Fifteen years ago, Dodge and associates examined the usefulness of the urinalysis as a screening procedure in healthy school-aged children (1). This widely quoted study suggested that the yield of important renal disease from screening urinalyses in such a population did not justify the costs that were generated. In response to this and a number of other supporting studies, many have suggested that urinalysis is not a necessary component of routine health maintenance visits.

Such studies, of course, have not addressed the usefulness of the urinalysis in hospitalized children. It could certainly be argued that patients entering the hospital are not "healthy" and that important information could be obtained from screening tests. In a child about to undergo elective surgery, for example, there could be a significant benefit to the detection of unrecognized urinary tract infection (pyuria), diabetes mellitus (glycosuria), or chronic nephritis (hematuria or proteinuria).

Although such a screening procedure may seem reasonable, careful studies have not supported it. Another 1990 publication, for example, reviewed 486 children admitted for elective surgery (2). Of these, 15% had abnormal urinalyses; in only 2 cases, however, was the abnormality considered important enough to cancel surgery. Neither of these children was subsequently found to have significant urinary tract disease. Interestingly, 1 of these patients later required emergency surgery to handle a complication that resulted from cancellation of the elective procedure.

Mitchell and Stapleton have provided us with additional observations on the "routine" urinalysis. Urinalyses were costly, and the yield of important findings was small. Two other findings were surprising considering our current litigious atmosphere. The hospital's bylaw-mandated urinalysis requirement was often ignored, and most of the abnormalities detected were not pursued. Pediatricians should examine their own hospital requirements on this matter and work to eliminate this costly, unnecessary ritual. The study of Mitchell and Stapleton will provide ammunition for such policy reviews.—T. Welch, M.D.

References

1. Dodge WF, et al: *J Pediatr* 88:327, 1976.
2. O'Connor ME, Drasner K: *Anesth Analg* 70:176, 1990.

Clinical Evaluation of a Rapid Screening Test for Urinary Tract Infections in Children
Shaw KN, Hexter D, McGowan KL, Schwartz JS (Children's Hosp of Philadelphia; Univ of Pennsylvania, Philadelphia)
J Pediatr 118:733–736, 1991   10–14

A rapid test for measuring leukocyte esterase (LE) activity recently became available on a dipstick combined with a nitrite test. Some hospitals now use this test in lieu of microscopic assessment or cultures to save money. However, these rapid screening tests have not been studied thoroughly in clinical settings. The diagnostic performance of the LE-nitrite urine dipstick was compared with microscopy and quantitative urine culture in a pediatric emergency department.

All 491 children seen in a pediatric emergency department in an 8-month period who had a urine specimen collected when a laboratory technician was available were enrolled in the study. Using a positive quantitative urine culture as the standard, the sensitivity, specificity, and positive and negative predictive values for LE, nitrite, and combined LE-nitrite dipstick results were determined. The combined dipstick test detected urinary tract infection as well as the urinalysis and had fewer false positive results. The predictive value of a negative dipstick test result was 98% overall. In children younger than age 2 years, however, neither the dipstick nor the urinalysis could detect all urinary tract infections.

Combined LE and nitrite dipstick testing is as successful as microscopic assessment of spun urine in detecting urinary tract infections in children seen in a pediatric emergency room. The combined dipstick test, particularly when done by the physician during the physical examination, is much faster and less expensive than urinalysis. The combined LE and nitrite dipstick test should be used instead of urinalysis for rapid urinary tract infection screening, except when clinical findings indicate examination of the sediment for casts.

▶ These investigators have served us very well. They have shown us that a routine urinalysis is no longer necessary as a screening tool to detect a urinary tract infection. A simple dipstick using a leukocyte esterase and nitrite test will, indeed, suffice.

The years 1990 and 1991 were the years of the "urinalysis bashing." We saw a lot written about the value or lack of value of examination of urine during that time. For example, Mitchell et al. (Abstract 10–13) examined just how useful routine admission urinalysis was for hospitalized children. This study was performed at the University of Tennessee, and 2,695 patients admitted to a day-care or inpatient unit over 2 months were evaluated. Some 500 children were excluded from the analysis because they were expected to have an abnormal urinalysis. Of the remaining examinations, 20% were abnormal, with equal proportions in both medical and surgical patients. Pyuria was the most prevalent abnormality, and hematuria was second. Only 38% of these abnormalities were followed with a repeat urinalysis, and 58% showed persistent abnormalities. However, only 6 patients had a change in management or a specific diagnosis because of the initial urinalysis. In these 6 patients (6 of 2,695), a diagnosis of a urinary tract infection was made. As you might suspect based on the article by Shaw et al. (Abstract 10–14), pyuria is an extremely poor way to screen for a urinary tract infection. Thus, Mitchell et al. concluded that the routine screening urinalysis had little if any value for patients being admitted to the hospital. The total cost of urinalysis in the 2-month study period alone was $23,465, which computes to approximately $4,000 per diagnosis of urinary tract infection. You don't have to go to a cost-effective analysis expert to figure out that routine urinalyses are not a bargain.

The next issue then is whether or not there is any value to routine dipstick testing of the urine. A dipstick, although a labor-saving device, still is not without some expense. The average dipstick costs about $3. Would you believe that in the United States about $150,000,000 are spent each year on routine dipsticking of urines. A report on this topic in *JAMA* suggested that indiscriminate routine dipsticking without an indication may be a waste of precious health care dollars (1).

As an alternative, you might want to simply "eyeball" a urine specimen. You might find that your eyes are as good, or almost as good, as a urine culture in telling whether or not a urine is infected. Investigators have shown that if a freshly voided urine appears "crystal clear" or can be made to become crystal clear by the addition of 2 drops of acetic acid, which dissolves phosphate crystals, it is extraordinarily unlikely that the urine will be culture positive. Rawal et al. documented this information (2). Before you take a lot of time to criticize or find potential flaws with this observation, please read the article. Cloudy urine may or may not be culture positive, but "crystal clear urine" is overwhelmingly not likely to be. Now there's a reasonable pearl.

This commentary will close with one last curio. It is an observation by Labbe (3), who noted that of 31 boys aged 5 to 15 years seen in his office with a first urinary tract infection, none required investigation of the anatomy of the urinary tract. Why? All 10 boys had caused, unknowingly, their own urinary tract infection by injecting water into their urethra while taking a bath or a shower. The instruments used were a syringe in 4 cases, a rubber bulb in 3 cases, a plastic bottle in 2 cases, and a hand-held shower massager. So what is the principle here? The principle is pretty straightforward. If you diagnose a urinary tract infection in a boy, do a very careful history to see whether the cause is that described by Labbe. If it is, you can skip the VCUG and renal ultrasound. Write a prescription that has 3 parts: (1) change the shower head, (2) remove all extraneous objects from the bath and shower, (3) if necessary, substitute for #2 a rubber duckie. I can't imagine that the latter would do any harm.—J.A. Stockman, III, M.D.

References

1. Woolhandler S, et al: *JAMA* 262:1215, 1989.
2. Rawal K, et al: *Lancet* 1:1228, 1990.
3. Labbe J: *Pediatrics* 86:703, 1990.

11 The Respiratory Tract

Digital Clubbing and Pulmonary Function Abnormalities in Children With Lung Disease
Paton JY, Bautista DB, Stabile MW, Waldman AE, Nassar AG, Platzker ACG, Keens TG (Childrens Hosp, Los Angeles)
Pediatr Pulmonol 10:25–29, 1991   11–1

Digital clubbing has long been associated with certain diseases of the chest and abdomen. The correlation between digital clubbing and pulmonary function was investigated in 147 children, adolescents, and young adults with a wide range of respiratory conditions. The mean age was 14 years.

The patients were divided into 7 diagnostic groups: 44 had cystic fibrosis, 20 had asthma, 28 had scoliosis, 10 had malignancy, 10 had interstitial pulmonary disease, 8 had collagen vascular disease, and 27 had miscellaneous chest wall anomalies, congenital syndromes, and so on. The mean arterial oxygen pressure (PaO_2) was 81 mm Hg, and the mean forced expiratory volume in 1 second (FEV_1) was 60% of predicted. Digital clubbing was diagnosed in 43 patients. Patients with digital clubbing had a PaO_2 of 69.4 mm Hg, whereas those without clubbing had a PaO_2 of 88.3 mm Hg. There was digital clubbing in 46% of hypoxic patients, compared with only 5% of normoxic patients. The ratio of distal phalangeal depth to interphalangeal depth (DPD/IPD) was negatively correlated with PaO_2 in patients with cystic fibrosis and interstitial fibrosis. All other patients, except for asthmatics, had weak negative correlations. The overall DPD/IPD ratio was correlated significantly with PaO_2; DPD/IPD was correlated with other lung function abnormalities only for patients with cystic fibrosis.

The presence of digital clubbing is associated with abnormalities of pulmonary function, particularly abnormally low PaO_2. The association can be seen most clearly in patients with cystic fibrosis and interstitial lung disease. This may reflect the prolonged duration of exposure to hypoxemia in these diseases.

▶ It is amazing how far back descriptions of problems that still escape our understanding go. For example, since the time of Hippocrates, the association between digital clubbing and certain diseases of the chest and abdomen has been recognized (1). The earliest descriptions of asbestos hazards are from the ancient Roman times. Small quantities of chrysotile (meaning white) asbestos appeared to have been extracted several thousand years ago in Northern Italy. Mining in that era was carried out by slaves and criminals. Plautus noted that there was no place so much like hell as the stone quarry (2). The elder Pliny is given credit for referring to the use of respiratory protection against asbestos:

"Faciem laxis fesicis inligint ne in respirando pernicilem pulveram trahunt" (they tied bladders over their faces to prevent the inhalation of pernicious dust as they breathed) (3). If you find any of this classical background of interest, see the story relating asbestos to the Romans in the *Lancet* (4).

We in the United States tend to be a bit myopic about the worldwide causes of digital clubbing. Do you know what the most common cause of digital clubbing is worldwide? The cause is indoor air pollution in developing countries. Where there are no air conditioning systems, the condition of air inside houses, shops, and offices is largely determined by the quality of the inside air and by any exchange that occurs with the external air. Thus, indoor levels of carbon monoxide in houses bordering roads that carry heavy traffic are important health hazards. Heating and cooking fumes are even more troublesome, especially at night or during cold seasons, because of inadequate ventilation and because of the use of fuels in the middle or at the lower end of the "energy ladder."

If you are not familiar with the term "energy ladder," it is used by environmentalists to describe the bell-shaped curve of what constitutes cooking and heating fuels. Globally, the lowest rung of this ladder is occupied by the burning of dried animal dung, twigs, or grass. Next come crop residues. These are followed by wood and then charcoal. On the higher rungs there are the nonbiomass fuels such as coal, coke, and kerosene. Then come piped and bottled gases. Electricity, at the top of the ladder, is the cleanest but also the most expensive form of energy.

"Developed" countries have begun to address these problems. Take, for example, the United Kingdom. Until the 1950s, the most common cause of chronic bronchitis and emphysema in London was environmental pollution. Only in 1952, after the death of several prized cattle being exhibited at the Smithfield Show in London and the subsequent deaths of almost 25,000 human inhabitants of the city during a period of dense smog, was there finally introduction of stiff anti-pollution measures (5). Within a decade, air pollution was reasonably well controlled within that city. By contrast, last year, it was noted that about a third of women over the age of 50 in the rural Ladakh region of Kashmir—very few of whom smoked—have chronic obstructive airway disease (6). In Nepal, where both chronic bronchitis and cor pulmonale are common, the main cause of these diseases in women is exposure to smoking fumes rather than to tobacco smoke (7). One of the most interesting statistics I read last year was that the most frequent cause of fluorosis in China (this problem is epidemic in certain parts of China) is not from fluoridation of drinking water—practically unheard of in that country—but rather use of coal with high fluoride content!

It is interesting to see how man, on the death of a few cows, occasionally stumbles over the truth. Unfortunately, most of time man simply picks himself up and stumbles on. It is time to do something about the environment. It's sickening.—J.A. Stockman, III, M.D.

References

1. Hansen-Flaschen J: *Clin Chest Med* 8:287, 1987.
2. Plautus: *Captivi*, v. 999.

3. Pliny: *Natural History*, 23, 60:122.
4. Brown K, et al: *Lancet* 336:445, 1990.
5. Editorial: *Lancet* 2:1549, 1990.
6. Chen S: *World Health Stat Q* 43:127, 1990.
7. Pandey MR: *Br J Dis Chest* 70:251, 1976.

Risk Factors for Adolescent Cigarette Smoking: The Muscatine Study
Reimers TM, Pomrehn PR, Becker SL, Lauer RM (Univ of Iowa, Iowa City)
Am J Dis Child 144:1265–1272, 1990   11–2

Most studies on adolescent cigarette smoking involve a cross-sectional survey. As smoking among adolescents is a developmental phenomenon with different risk factors exerting their influence at different times, a longitudinal study was conducted of 443 students who were followed up from early to late adolescence. Students in grades 8–11 completed a multi-item questionnaire to examine the longitudinal influences of several behavioral and social variables on smoking behavior and to assess whether the influence of these factors changes over time.

An increase in the percentage of regular smokers was observed throughout adolescence, from 2.7% in grade 8 to 14.7% in grade 11, particularly among boys (table). Experimenting with smoking was more frequent as adolescents matured. Several factors tended to distinguish ad-

Percentage and Number of Cases Categorized as Nonsmokers, Experimenters, and Regular Smokers by Grade and Sex*

Grade, Sex	Nonsmoker	Experimenter	Regular Smoker
	% (No.)		
8th			
Total	86.9 **(385)**	7.2 **(32)**	2.7 **(12)**
M	86.9 (185)	7.0 (15)	3.3 (7)
F	87.0 (200)	7.4 (17)	2.2 (5)
9th			
Total	83.1 **(368)**	9.5 **(42)**	4.3 **(19)**
M	81.2 (173)	10.8 (23)	4.7 (10)
F	84.8 (195)	8.3 (19)	3.9 (9)
10th			
Total	80.8 **(358)**	7.0 **(31)**	9.3 **(41)**
M	80.8 (172)	5.6 (12)	10.8 (23)
F	80.9 (186)	8.3 (19)	7.8 (18)
11th			
Total	68.4 **(303)**	12.4 **(55)**	14.7 **(65)**
M	63.8 (136)	13.6 (29)	16.9 (36)
F	72.6 (167)	11.3 (26)	12.6 (29)

*Percentages do not add to 100% because of a small percentage of persons who did not "fit" the definition of non-smoker, experimenter, or regular smoker across grades.
(Courtesy of Reimers TM, Pomrehn PR, Becker SL, et al: *Am J Dis Child* 144:1265–1272, 1990.)

olescents who smoked regularly from their nonsmoking peers, including previous smoking status, close association with friends who smoke, less attachment to parents, poor school performance, less involvement in extracurricular school activities, and fewer negative and more positive perceptions of cigarette use. Many of these factors were present as early as grade 8. Among these factors, previous smoking status and association with friends who smoke were consistently associated with an adolescent's future smoking status.

Efforts to prevent cigarette smoking should begin early, at age 12–13 years. Children who are at risk for cigarette smoking may be identified by their attitudes, by peer and parental relationships, and by involvement in school activities. Hence, strategies that promote nonsmoking behavior should be directed not only toward the child but also toward influences within the child's home and school environment.

Who Profits From Tobacco Sales to Children?
DiFranza JR, Tye JB (Univ of Massachusetts, Fitchburg; Baystate Med Ctr, Springfield, Mass)
JAMA 263:2784–2787, 1990   11–3

The addiction that fosters tobacco use can be thought of as a childhood disease. The quantity of tobacco purchased by American youth, the monetary value of these sales, and the profits realized by the tobacco industry were investigated.

Two estimates, 1 conservative and 1 comprehensive, were made of cigarette consumption by children aged younger than 18 years (table). When the average of the 2 was used in further computations, the results indicated that more than 3 million American children consume 947 million packs of cigarettes and 26 million containers of smokeless tobacco each year. These tobacco products equal annual sales of $1.26 billion. About 3% of tobacco industry profits come directly from the sale of cigarettes to children, which is illegal in 43 states. About half of the tobacco indus-

Estimated Annual Consumption of All Smokers Aged 8–17 Years, Comprehensive Method

Age, y	Smoking Category	No. of Smokers	No. of Cigarettes per Day Self-Reported Rate	Adjusted Rate	No. of Packs per Year
8-11	<Daily	393 800	0.20	0.278	1 999 000
8-11	Daily	117 600	4.00	5.560	11 940 000
12-17	<Daily	1 822 000	2.00	2.780	92 500 000
12-17	Daily	3 109 000	13.73	19.080	1 083 000 000
Total	. . .	5 442 400*	. . .	. . .	1 190 000 000*

*Columns do not add because of rounding.
(Courtesy of DiFranza JR, Tye JB: *JAMA* 263:2784–2787, 1990.)

try's profits of $3.35 billion a year comes from sales to people who became addicted to nicotine in childhood. Tax revenues to the federal and state governments from cigarette sales to children are about $152 million and $173 million, respectively. These figures dwarf governmental expenditures on smoking and health.

Amost all current state laws on the distribution of tobacco to children are ineffective because they cannot be practically enforced. Communities adopting more restrictive ordinances or regulations that have been more successful share several features. Decriminalizing the offense by making it a civil, rather than a criminal, offense allows ticketing as a means of enforcement. Sting operations allow for effective enforcement with minimal expenditure of community resources. Local licenses are required for tobacco vendors, and meaningful penalties, such as substantial monetary fines and license revocation, should be enforced when laws are violated. Finally, these communities have bans or restrictions on vending machines and the distribution of free samples.

▶ The question poised in the title of the article abstracted above is, of course, rhetorical. The whole issue of tobacco smoking seems to center around a balance scale, with money and advertising at one end of the scale, and the antitobacco campaign at the other.

The earliest antitobacco campaign on record was in 1604 when King James I (no relation) imposed a tax on tobacco imported from the new world in an attempt to limit the "Custome lothesome to the Eye, hateful to the Noise, and harmefull to the Braine, and dangerous to the Lungs" (1). That campaign has accumulated some speed since then, at least in the United States. In this country, the consumption of cigarettes has declined by almost one third, with about 38 million adults having quit smoking. Unfortunately, cigarette consumption over 20 years has increased 400% in less developed countries such as India.

While all of this has been going on, the United States has become the number 1 exporter of cigarettes, with total exports of 118.5 billion cigarettes in 1988, an astounding 18% increase in that year alone. This does not mean that other countries do not manufacture their own cigarettes, or at least tobacco. It has been estimated that the growing of tobacco in underdeveloped countries usurps the place of food crops that could feed an estimated 10 to 20 million people. There are also potential environmental effects of tobacco that go even beyond the tobacco smoke itself in other parts of the world. In most underdeveloped countries of the world that grow tobacco, the tobacco is flue-cured by wood smoke. This requires the felling of massive quantities of trees. For example, in Tanzania, 12% of all trees are felled for the sole purpose of curing tobacco.

As far as warning labels and recognition of health hazards are concerned, unfortunately, only 6 countries throughout the world require health warning labels on cigarette packaging. The brand name of the most popular cigarette in Kenya, for example, is "Life."

What we need here is more emphasis on warning individuals and less tobacco advertising. It has been noted previously in the YEAR BOOK that the cigarette industry has a very circuitous way of getting around even the ban on cigarette advertising on television. Take, for example, how much exposure you had to cigarette advertising if you watched a recent Marlboro Grand Prix Motor Race. In an effort to verify the extent of television viewer exposure of cigarette brands, in spite of the ban on such promotions, a video tape recording was made of a nationally telecast automobile race, the Marlboro Grand Prix, which was shown on July 16, 1989 (2). An observer, a medical student with a moderate interest in automobile racing, viewed the 1½ hour program 6 times. During the first viewing, the observer made a list of categories to enable him to tabulate the various kinds of visual exposure that took place regarding the Marlboro brand name. On the second viewing, he measured the length of time the word Marlboro or its red Chevron logotype was visible on the screen. On the third viewing, he counted the smaller billboards and the banners that were posted along the raceway retaining wall. On the fourth time through, the observer counted the number of spoken mentions of Marlboro, as well as the number of exposures of the Marlboro car, which remained in almost constant view, regardless of its standing in the race. During the fifth and sixth viewings, the observer recorded all other visual exposures of the Marlboro name.

So what were the results? As required by law, the television announcers at no time referred to the race as the Marlboro Grand Prix, but rather the "New Jersey Meadowlands Grand Prix presented by Nissan." However, there were 5,993 times at which the Marlboro name could be seen during the telecast. Of these, 4,998 were shots of raceway signs. During the 93 minutes of the broadcast, the Marlboro name could be seen for 46 minutes.

All of this indirect "free" advertising caught the eye of the advertising journal, *Sponsors Report*. They calculated the monetary value of Marlboro's television exposure during the above telecast. This calculation showed that Marlboro received $1,280,505 of free television advertising time during that one race alone. Recall that the Public Health Cigarette Smoking Act of 1969 prohibits the promotion of cigarette brands on television and calls for enforcement of the law by the Attorney General of the United States. The law requires a $10,000 fine for each violation. Were that law to be applied to the telecast of the 1989 Marlboro Grand Prix, a fine on the order of $59,330,000 would have been appropriate. Needless to say, there was no such fine.

One last question closes this long commentary. Is it ethically possible for the United States to continue to permit unrestricted marketing and sale of a substance more addictive and more hazardous to human health than any other known substance?

The answer is obviously as rhetorical as the title of the article abstracted. Tobacco fields are indeed "killing fields."—J.A. Stockman, III, M.D.

References

1. Stebbins KR: *Soc Sci* 30:227, 1990.
2. *Current Probl Pediatr* (in press)

Exposure of Children With Cystic Fibrosis to Environmental Tobacco Smoke

Rubin BK (Univ of Alberta, Canada)
N Engl J Med 323:782–788, 1990   11–4

Children with cystic fibrosis may be at increased risk of harm from exposure to tobacco smoke. A group of children with cystic fibrosis was studied to determine the effects of smoke on their clinical status, growth and nutrition, and pulmonary function.

The children were studied before and after they attended a 2-week, smoke-free summer camp for children with cystic fibrosis. The study group comprised 43 children, 18 girls and 25 boys, mean age 108.9 months. Of these, 24 (56%) came from households with smokers. A dose-dependent relationship was noted between cigarettes smoked per day in the home and overall severity of disease. Severity of disease was assessed by age-adjusted hospital admissions, peak expiratory flow rate, weight and height percentile, midarm circumference, and triceps skin-fold thickness. These effects were most significant in girls.

When the 24 children from households with smokers were considered separately, the dose-dependent relationship held only for number of hospital admissions and for height. Of the 21 children who had good lung function and the 27 children who had normal weight for their height at the start of camp, those who came from households with a smoker gained significantly more weight during camp than those who came from smoke-free homes.

Passive exposure to tobacco smoke seems to adversely affect the growth and health of children with cystic fibrosis. However, other variables cannot be ruled out in this study, including social and economic factors that may determine whether there was a smoker in the home and the nutritional status of the children. Further studies of smoking and cystic fibrosis are needed.

▶ Children with cystic fibrosis are no more immune to the effects of secondary smoke than anyone else. Obviously, they are at even higher risk than the average individual who is passively smoking.

Passive smoking starts in our intrauterine environment and continues until the day we die. With respect to intrauterine environment, there is recent information that extends our knowledge of what happens to the babies of women who smoke while they are pregnant. Were you aware that there is a very significant association between smoking in women and the occurrence of a single umbilical artery in their infants (1)? Also, children born to women who smoke 10 or more cigarettes per day during their pregnancy have lower McCarthy Scales of Children's Abilities at age 3 (2). Last, it is now estimated that 17% of lung cancers among nonsmokers can be directly attributed to high levels of exposure to second-hand cigarette smoke during childhood and adolescence (3).

There is an interesting new initiative going on to find a way to decrease the risk of cigarette smoking. This is based on the landmark recognition by the U.S.

Surgeon General in 1988 that smoking is an addiction to nicotine and resembles the kind of addiction seen with drugs such as heroin, cocaine, and alcohol (4). Thus, it is clear that there is a central paradox with cigarette smoking: Although people smoke for nicotine, they die mainly from the tar and other unwanted components in the smoke. Why can't manufacturers figure out a way to deliver the pure addictive product, nicotine, without the concomitant pollutants? That way we would have only 1 problem on our hands (nicotine) rather than 2 (nicotine plus cancer).

The pressure for the above obviously led to the development of nicotine chewing gum, largely used for individuals who want to withdraw from smoking. If you want to, you can mimic the effect of cigarette smoking by using a nicotine vapor inhaler (5). At least 5 pharmaceutical companies have skin patches at varying stages of testing, and the clinical use of such patches is licensed in some countries. Other products undergoing clinical trials include nasal nicotine spray, nicotine lozenges, and a nicotine vapor puffer (6). Although these nicotine replacement products are marketed as aids to stop smoking, might they eventually replace tobacco on the open market?

The core of this issue lies with the addictiveness of nicotine itself. It is the nicotine that people cannot easily do without, not the tobacco. As a drug delivery system, the modern cigarette is a highly efficient device for getting nicotine into the brain, but it is also a very "dirty" one.

The first effort in the United States along the lines suggested above came in 1988 when a major U.S. tobacco company released details of a highly innovative type of cigarette that heats rather than burns tobacco (7). It is a nearly perfect low tar cigarette. Unfortunately, far from welcoming it into the market place, the AMA, the Heart and Lung Association, the American Cancer Society, and others combined to petition and speak against it at a special hearing before a subcommittee of the House of Representatives (8). The government eventually labeled the product as a nicotine delivery system, and attempts to market it as a tobacco product ultimately were abandoned by R.J. Reynolds.

Can't some smart person in the reading audience of the YEAR BOOK figure out a way to deliver nicotine in what looks like a cigarette but isn't? Obviously, you are asking yourself the question, isn't there a risk to nicotine itself? The answer is that there is no known role of nicotine in tobacco-related cancers, neither is it implicated in obstructive lung disease. Nicotine can interact with gases such as carbon monoxide to exacerbate cardiovascular disease, however.

The lyricist, Otto Harbach, authored the words: "When a lovely flame dies, smoke gets in your eyes." Do you think Harbach was foreshadowing the demise of cigarette smoking when he penned those lyrics in 1933?—J.A. Stockman, III, M.D.

References

1. Lilja GMC: *BMJ* 302:569, 1991.
2. Sexton N, et al: *Int J Epidemiol* 19:72, 1990.
3. Janerich DT, et al: *N Engl J Med* 323:632, 1990.
4. *Report of the Surgeon General.* Washington, DC, Dept. of Health and Human Services, 1988.

5. Feyerabent C, et al: *J Pharm Pharmacol* 42:450, 1990.
6. Russell MAH, et al: *JAMA* 257:3262, 1987.
7. *Chemical and Biological Studies on New Cigarette Prototypes That Heat Instead of Burn Tobacco.* Winston-Salem, N.C., R.J. Reynolds Tobacco Co., 1988.
8. *U.S. House of Representatives Subcommittee on Health and Environment Hearing.* Washington, D.C., U.S. Government Printing Office, 1988, Serial no. 100—68.

Aerosolα_1-Antitrypsin Treatment for Cystic Fibrosis

McElvaney NG, Hubbard RC, Birrer P, Chernick MS, Caplan DB, Frank MM, Crystal RG (Natl Heart, Lung, and Blood Inst; Natl Inst of Diabetes and Digestive and Kidney Diseases; Natl Inst of Allergy and Infectious Diseases; Natl Inst of Health, Bethesda, Md; Emory Univ)

Lancet 337:392–394, 1991

11–5

In cystic fibrosis, neutrophil-dominated inflammation of the respiratory epithelium results in a chronic epithelial burden of the destructive enzyme, neutrophil elastase. In a new approach to the treatment of cystic fibrosis, suppression of this burden was attempted using α_1-antitrypsin (α_1AT), the main inhibitor of neutrophil elastase in 12 patients with cystic fibrosis.

The patients received α_1AT by aerosol, 1.5–2 mg/kg every 12 hours, for 1 week. Bronchoalveolar lavage showed pronounced neutrophil-dominated inflammation. The amounts of α_1AT, active neutrophil elastase, and antineutrophil elastase capacity in the respiratory epithelial lining fluid (ELF) obtained by bronchoalveolar lavage were measured.

Aerosol α_1-antitrypsin treatment increased α_1AT levels in the ELF to 2–3 times greater than baseline, suppressed the active neutrophil elastase, increased the antineutrophil elastase capacity and the amount of α_1AT/neutrophil elastase complexes, and reversed the ability of respiratory ELF to interfere with neutrophil killing of *Pseudomonas* species. No adverse effects were noted.

Aerosol α_1AT treatment may effectively prevent damage to the respiratory epithelium by neutrophil elastase and augment host defense on the respiratory epithelial surface in patients with cystic fibrosis. These preliminary findings are sufficiently convincing to support further clinical trials.

▶ Dr. Hans Wessel, Professor of Pediatrics, Northwestern University Medical School, and Chief of the Division of Pulmonology, Children's Memorial Hospital, comments:

▶ The recent spectacular advances in the understanding of the genetics of cystic fibrosis, the underlying basic defect and the molecular basis of the inflammatory responses to persistent bacterial infection with *Pseudomonas aeruginosa* have led to the investigation of a number of new therapies for cystic fibrosis. The above study by McElvaney et al. represents one of these new approaches, demonstrating in 17 patients the efficacy of an α-1-antitrypsin aerosol to suppress neutrophil elastase, a destructive proteolytic enzyme that contributes significantly to direct injury to airway epithelium, interferes with normal host defenses by cleavage of immunoglobulins and complement, and inhibits phagocytosis and killing of *Pseudomonas sp.* by neutrophils.

The following are other new approaches to therapy:

1 The use of recombinant DNAse aerosol to promote cleavage of high-molecular DNA derived in abundance from inflammatory cells, a process that contributes significantly to the highly viscous properties of cystic fibrosis sputum.

2 The use of amiloride, a sodium transport blocker, to improve mucociliary clearance and cough clearance of cystic fibrosis sputum.

3 A number of laboratories are pursuing approaches to gene therapy of cystic fibrosis that are based on incorporation of the normal gene into appropriate vectors (retrovirus, cytomegalovirus, vaccinia, plasmids), with a high affinity for respiratory epithelium. Preliminary studies have demonstrated expression of the normal gene in cystic fibrosis epithelial cells.

None of these exiting new approaches will result in a permanent cure for cystic fibrosis. However, if they prove to be clinically feasible and safe they may profoundly alter the natural history of treated cystic fibrosis by achieving a further large increase in life expectancy for these patients and by eliminating much of the lengthy and frequent inpatient care that they require.—H. Wessel, M.D.

Pseudomonas cepacia: **A New Pathogen in Patients With Cystic Fibrosis Referred to a Large Centre in the United Kingdom**
Simmonds EJ, Conway SP, Ghoneim ATM, Ross H, Littlewood JM (St James's Univ Hosp; Seacroft Hosp, Leeds, England)
Arch Dis Child 65:874–877, 1990   11–6

New species of pseudomonads, particularly *Pseudomonas cepacia*, have been recognized recently as important pathogens. Infection with *P. cepacia* has become increasingly frequent in patients with cystic fibrosis in North America. To investigate further, the records of 160 patients with cystic fibrosis seen in a large cystic fibrosis center in the United Kingdom during the past 6 years were studied retrospectively.

Between 1984 and 1989, *P. cepacia* infection was identified in 11 patients, with a maximum prevalence of 7% in 1988. Of the 90 (56%) patients chronically infected with pseudomonads in 1989, 8 (9%) had *P. cepacia* infection. The patients were aged 4.7–21.7 years at the time of their first sputum isolate of *P. cepacia*, and infection persisted for .3–4.7 years. Mortality rate was 27% compared with 7% among patients with chronic *Pseudomonas aeruginosa* infection during the same period. Of the 3 patients who died, 2 deteriorated rapidly shortly after infection despite appropriate antibiotic therapy. Of the 8 survivors, 3 had deteriorated quickly and 5 remained clinically stable. *Pseudomonas cepacia* was the only isolate in 1 patient, whereas the other 10 patients had mixed infection with *P. cepacia* and *P. aeruginosa*. *Pseudomonas cepacia* isolates were resistant to colomycin, aminoglycosides, and ciprofloxacin. The risk of infection was not associated with patient to patient transmission or use of nebulized antibiotics.

Pseudomonas cepacia is an important new pathogen in patients with cystic fibrosis. Survival is reduced among patients with *P. cepacia* infection, and current treatment regimens apparently cannot reverse the rapid deterioration that occurs in some patients.

▶ *Pseudomonas cepacia* has become an important, if not a critical, pathogen among cystic fibrosis patients. Pulmonary infection with this organism results in rapid clinical deterioration and death in some patients with cystic fibrosis. In others, prolonged colonization is associated with increased morbidity and shortened survival. Pulmonary colonization by *P. cepacia* is generally refractory to antibiotic treatment. The introduction of *P. cepacia* into the cystic fibrosis population has been one of the most devastating factors affecting long-term prognosis.

Because there is no magic bullet in terms of stamping out this organism, prevention would seem to be foremost on everyone's mind. Until recently, however, it wasn't even known how somebody got this particular strain of bacteria. The epidemiology of *P. cepacia* has been controversial. The clustering at certain cystic fibrosis centers and the high risk of colonization associated with recent hospital admissions suggest nosocomial acquisition and person-to-person transmission. Nonetheless, *P. cepacia* has rarely been recovered from hospital environmental surfaces or respiratory treatment equipment. Transmission between cystic fibrosis patients in the hospital has not been documented. The principal obstacle to documentation of such transmission has been lack of methods to identify distinct *P. cepacia* strains. Now we have the ability to do that. LiPuma et al. (1) showed the transmission of *P. cepacia* from one cystic fibrosis patient to another, and they suggested that any unnecessary contact between colonized and noncolonized cystic fibrosis patients should be avoided.

Before closing this commentary, let's update what we now know about the genetic abnormality of cystic fibrosis. There has been an explosion in information in this regard since Riordan et al. (2) reported cloning of the defective gene in cystic fibrosis 3 years ago. The most common gene abnormality affecting the cystic fibrosis transmembrane conductance regulator gene is known as delta F508. This is a deletion of 3 base pairs in the first nucleotide-binding fold of the gene. Unfortunately, there are more than 50 other mutations that have been found within the CFTR gene. This large number of mutations makes any mass screening for carriers of cystic fibrosis relatively unfeasible at this time (see last year's YEAR BOOK). In the United Kingdom, however, population screening for heterozygotes has been thought to be desirable nonetheless, and pilot screening programs are being initiated (3).

Even if the new information about these various mutations that cause cystic fibrosis has not led to screening, it has shed a great deal of insight into the clinical variation that is seen in patients with cystic fibrosis. Most patients with cystic fibrosis either are homozygous for the delta F508 abnormality (about 80% of cystic fibrosis patients) or are heterozygous for the delta F508 and some other mutation (about 19%). We now have learned from 2 different reports what are the clinical differences between those who are homozygous or heterozygous for the delta F508 gene. Those who are homozygous have been observed to have earlier onset of symptoms, to require more pancreatic enzyme substitution, and to have a calculated yearly incidence of chronic *Pseudomonas aeruginosa* infection as well as yearly mortality rates that are greater than in heterozygous patients (4). Another study has shown that patients who are heterozygous for delta F508 have lower sweat chloride values at diagnosis and almost normal nutritional status (5).

Thus, the variable clinical course of patients with cystic fibrosis can be attributed in part to specific cystic fibrosis genotypes. It seems hard to imagine, but the preceding sentence could not have been written a year and a half ago. Such is the speed with which we are accumulating knowledge about the inner-link between the molecular biology of cystic fibrosis and its clinical manifestations.—J.A. Stockman, III, M.D.

References

1. LiPuma JJ, et al: *Lancet* 2:1094, 1990.
2. Riordan JR, et al: *Science* 245:1066, 1989.
3. Brock DJH: *Am J Hum Genet* 47:164, 1990.
4. Johansen HK, et al: *Lancet* 337:631, 1991.
5. Kerem E, et al: *N Engl J Med* 323:1517, 1990.

Microbiology of Empyema in Children and Adolescents
Brook I (Uniformed Services Univ of the Health Sciences, Bethesda, Md)
Pediatrics 85:722–726, 1990   11–7

The role of anaerobic bacteria in empyema in children and adolescents has rarely been demonstrated. A retrospective study of the microbiology of empyema in 72 children and adolescents, aged 3 months to 17 years and 8 months, seen during a 13-year period, was evaluated. Only specimens processed for aerobic and anaerobic bacteria are included.

A total of 93 organisms were isolated, including 60 aerobic and 33 anaerobic bacteria (table). Aerobic bacteria only were isolated in 67% of the patients, anaerobic bacteria only were isolated in 24%, and mixed aerobic and anaerobic bacteria were isolated in 10%. Overall, anaerobic bacteria were recovered in 33% of patients, mostly in patients older than age 6 years. The predominant anaerobic bacteria were *Bacteroides* sp., anaerobic cocci, and *Fusobacterium* sp. The predominant aerobic or facultative bacteria were *Haemophilus influenzae, Streptococcus pneumoniae,* and *Staphylococcus aureus.* There was β-lactamase activity in at least 1 isolate in 37% of patients, including all 8 tested *S. aureus* and 7 *Bacteroides fragilis* group, 3 of 10 *H. influenzae* group, 2 of 4 *Bacteroides melaninogenicus* group, and 1 of 2 *Klebsiella pneumoniae.* Empyema in most patients with pneumonia was caused by *S. pneumoniae* and *H. influenzae,* whereas anaerobes were mostly isolated in empyema that developed after aspiration penumonia, lung abscess, spreading infection of oral or dental origin, and subdiaphragmatic abscess. The importance of

Bacterial Isolates in 72 Cases of Empyema in Children and Adolescents

Aerobic and Facultative Bacteria	No. of Isolates	Anaerobic Bacteria	No. of Isolates
Streptococcus pneumoniae	13	*Peptostreptococcus* sp	4
Streptococcus pyogenes	3	*Peptostreptococcus magnus*	2
α hemolyticus streptococci	5	*Peptostreptococcus micros*	1
γ hemolyticus streptococci	4	*Peptostreptococcus anaerobius*	1
Streptococcus faecalis	2	*Veillonella parvula*	1
Staphylococcus aureus	10		
Haemophilus influenzae	15	*Propionibacterium acnes*	2
		Clostridium perfringens	1
Escherichia coli	2		
Klebsiella pneumoniae	3	*Fusobacterium nucleatum*	5
Pseudomonas aeruginosa	2	*Fusobacterium necrophorum*	1
Proteus mirabilis	1		
		Bacteroides sp	2
		Bacteroides fragilis	3
		Bacteroides distasonis	1
		Bacteroides thetaiotaomicron	3
		Bacteroides melaninogenicus	2
		Bacteroides intermedius	3
		Bacteroides oris-buccae	1

(Courtesy of Brook I: *Pediatrics* 85:722–726, 1990.)

anaerobic bacteria in empyema in children and adolescents is demonstrated.

▶ Empyema generally occurs as an extension of pneumonia or lung abscess or is spread as a result of abscesses of the retropharynx, mediastinum, perivertebral area, or skin. Empyema can also occur after external introduction of organisms from trauma or surgery.

The microbiology of empyema obviously is dependent on the cause of the primary infection, not the secondary one (the empyema). Most cases of *Streptococcus pneumoniae* and *haemophilus influenzae* are associated with pneumonia. The recovery of anaerobic bacteria is mostly associated with aspiration pneumonia, lung abscess, subdiaphragmatic abscess, and abscesses of dental or oral pharyngeal origin.

Before moving off subjects involving the lung, pleural, and mediastinum, recognize 2 recently described conditions: "the belch" pneumomediastinum and the "sax orgy" pneumomediastinum. These are somewhat different variations on the same theme. In the former, a previously healthy, nonsmoking, 18-year-old man was admitted to the hospital with chest pain radiating to his neck. The pain had started a few minutes after he belched. On chest x-ray film, he had a pneumomediastinum and subcutaneous emphysema. Presumably, the pneumomediastinum was a complication of increased alveolar pressure associated with the belching (1).

The second case was that of a 24-year-old man who was admitted to a Pennsylvania emergency room with symptoms of substernal pain, breathlessness, and difficulty swallowing. Physical examination demonstrated subcutaneous emphysema, and a chest x-ray showed mediastinal emphysema. The patient had been well until the evening before admission, when he first noticed these symptoms after 3 hours of vigorous continuous saxophone playing (2).

The solution to the above problems is in the prevention. Rolaids would have prevented 1 problem. Obviously, the second patient should have learned how to practice "safe sax."—J.A. Stockman, III, M.D.

References

1. Aguado J, et al: *Lancet* 2:1390, 1990.
2. Snyder RW, et al: *N Engl J Med* 323:758, 1990.

Home Care for Ventilator-Dependent Children: Psychosocial Impact on the Family
Quint RD, Chesterman E, Crain LS, Winkleby M, Boyce WT (Univ of California Med Ctr, San Francisco)
Am J Dis Child 144:1238–1241, 1990   11–8

There are an increasing number of children discharged from hospitals undergoing assisted ventilatory therapy. Although their care at home has resulted in lower costs and improvement in medical condition and developmental outcomes, little has been said about the impact of home ventilatory care on the families. A survey was conducted of 18 northern California families caring for ventilator-dependent infants and children, aged 9 months to 18 years, to understand the family impact of caring for these children in the home. Information on the family demographics; financial, social, and personal impact on the family; and parental coping mastery of the care of a ventilator-dependent child at home were elicited using a confidential structured interview and the Impact on Family Scale.

Most of the ventilator-dependent children were younger than age 6 years (55%). Most had CNS conditions (67%) and 1 or more concomitant medical conditions (83%). All but 1 of the families were intact, with 50% relying on Medicaid funds and 44% relying on private insurance to cover costs of home care (table). Out-of-pocket expenses in relation to child's home care were more than $1,000 in 83% of families; 72% of the families had in-home nursing care.

The perceived family impact, as measured on the Impact on Family Scale, was similar for both the primary caretaker and the spouse. However, primary caretakers showed significantly reduced Coping subscale scores when the duration of in-home ventilation was longer than 2 years. Specifically, primary caretakers exhibited poorer scores on items that measure family closeness and self-esteem with longer duration of home ventilatory care.

Primary caretakers of ventilator-dependent children show reduced cop-

Financial and Nursing Supports of Children
Receiving Home Ventilatory Care

	No. (%)
Financial	
Insurance coverage	
Private	4 (22)
HMO	4 (22)
Medicaid (Medi-Cal)	9 (50)
CCS	1 (5.6)
% of medical costs	
covered by insurance	
60-80	7 (39)
80-100	11 (61)
Nonreimbursed	
expenses (12 mo	
before interview)	
$0-$999	3 (17)
$1000-$1999	9 (50)
≥$2000	6 (33)
Nursing	
Average h/d of home	
nursing	
0	3 (17)
1-8	2 (11)
9-16	9 (50)
17-24	4 (22)
Lack of privacy	
(n = 17 families)	
With spouse	
Yes	12 (71)
No	5 (29)
With children	
Yes	7 (41)
No	10 (59)
With friends	
Yes	4 (24)
No	13 (76)

Abbreviations: HMO, health maintenance organization;
CCS, California Children's Services Program.
(Courtesy of Quint RD, Chesterman E, Crain LS, et al:
Am J Dis Child 144:1238–1241, 1990.)

ing with increased duration of child's assisted ventilation. This finding may be of practical relevance for physicians who care for ventilator-dependent children. This finding also may be important for those involved in the formulation of health policies. If this finding is confirmed in future studies, there would be a need to re-evaluate the use of ventilator technology in the home.

▶ Dr. James M. Perrin, Associate Professor of Pediatrics, the Harvard Medical School, comments:

▶ Dr. Quint and his colleagues have helpfully documented some of the issues that face families who care for ventilator-assisted children at home. The demands on these families include much time devoted to caretaking, loss of privacy when sharing home space with nurses, and the financial burdens of equipment and supplies, home modifications, or just paying high electric bills. The study documents families' extensive out-of-pocket expenses and confirms that most families, despite the extensive demands on their time and resources, want to keep their child at home.

The process of family adjustment to a ventilator-assisted child at home is complex. This study suggests that the family impact does not decrease with time, but that family coping skills may diminish. Yet, it is risky to draw longitudinal conclusions from a cross-sectional study of only 18 families. There may be several patterns of family adjustment. The complicated stresses of the transition from hospital to home resolve after 3 to 6 months for most families, who then have a more predictable routine and feel more comfortable with their own caretaking skills. Problems often arise later when home nursing staff must be replaced or when the child undergoes a major transition, such as entering school or adolescence. The first cadre of home care personnel is mainly recruited and trained through a tertiary care center. Families have the task of recruiting and training replacements themselves. The choice in this study of 2 years as the line between "short-term or long-term" home management may miss the impact on families at times of transition.

Although the finding of less effective coping skills in "long-term" care families may reflect burnout and exhaustion or uncertainty, the children and families too may be different. Some children's need for ventilator assistance decreases with time, often within 2 years of going home. These children likely tax families' coping abilities in ways different from children with more long-term ventilator needs. Other family variables (e.g., social support, access to respite care, social class) may also affect coping skills.

Quint et al. describe well the multiple demands on families caring for ventilator-assisted children. If these needs receive greater attention, perhaps we can develop appropriately coordinated, comprehensive services for these children and families, including a continuum of services from hospital to home, with available respite services and the types of community-based extended care centers mentioned in the paper.—J.M. Perrin, M.D.

Extracorporeal Membrane Oxygenation for Hydrocarbon Aspiration
Scalzo AJ, Weber TR, Jaeger RW, Connors RH, Thompson MW (St. Louis Univ; Cardinal Glennon Children's Hosp, St. Louis)
Am J Dis Child 144:867–871, 1990   11–9

Extracorporeal membrane oxygenation (ECMO) has been used for more than a decade in neonates with predictably fatal pulmonary failure and in adults with reversible acute pulmonary and cardiac insufficiency. However, the heart-lung bypass procedure has had limited use in older children with other pulmonary disorders. Two infants aged 15 and 16 months were treated successfully with ECMO after hydrocarbon aspiration.

Infant, 15 months, was hospitalized after aspirating an undetermined amount of baby mineral oil. His condition deteriorated, requiring intubation. Both left and right pneumothoraces occurred, and his pulmonary status progressively worsened. After transfer to a children's hospital with a pediatric intensive care unit, the infant was given a trial of high-frequency ventilation. When his hypoxemia did not improve, he was prepared for ECMO. Vascular access was achieved through a right common carotid arterial cannula and a right internal jugular venous cannula. Blood transfusions and total parenteral nutrition were required. The infant continued to receive ECMO for 12 days, a period complicated by recurrent pneumothoraces, hemorrhage, and infection. Because of the risks of continued ECMO, the infant was weaned from the bypass procedure at this time. His blood gas values gradually improved, and he made a complete respiratory recovery, but he had right cerebral hemispheric abnormalities.

Ingestion of hydrocarbons remains a significant cause of childhood morbidity. Conventional management results in a high percentage of deaths. These 2 cases represent the first reports of ECMO for the treatment of hydrocarbon aspiration. Because of the neurologic complications in the first child, the second was cannulated through a sternotomy and was free of neurologic sequelae. Thus ECMO is a potentially life-saving option in cases of hydrocarbon aspiration.

▶ The applicability of ECMO for respiratory failure seems limited only by certain diagnoses and the patience of the people who are involved with operating the ECMO equipment. It would seem logical to use ECMO for patients with respiratory failure resulting from hydrocarbon aspiration. It certainly turned the tide in the patient described above.

One wonders why someone doesn't start using artificial surfactant in some of these patients as well because hydrocarbons strip surfactant from the alveolar lining. I would be willing to bet that we will see some articles soon addressing the role of surfactant in illnesses other than respiratory distress syndrome.

For more on the topic of ECMO, see the discussions in the Newborn chapter of this year's YEAR BOOK.—J.A. Stockman, III, M.D.

Childhood Deaths From Toy Balloons
Ryan CA, Yacoub W, Paton T, Avard D (Univ of Alberta Hosp; The Edmonton Board of Health, Edmonton; Canadian Inst of Child Health, Ottawa, Ont, Canada)
Am J Dis Child 144:1221–1224, 1990   11–10

Accidental deaths by choking in childhood can occur from toy rubber balloons. Data on 4 children who died of suffocation by rubber balloons in Canada and the epidemiology of rubber balloon-related deaths in children in the United States were reviewed. Uninflated toy balloons were involved in 3 deaths, and 1 death involved an inflated balloon that the child bit. Initially, 2 children were partially obstructed and conscious, but they progressed to complete airway obstruction after blind sweeps of the pharynx. Spontaneous efforts and first-aid efforts, including the Heimlich maneuver, were ineffective in dislodging the balloon.

In 1973–1988, the United States Consumer Product Safety Commission reported at least 121 rubber balloon-related deaths in children. The highest mortality occurred in infants, but 25% of deaths occurred in children aged 6 years and older. Of the 15 choking deaths related to children's products, 43% were caused by toy balloons. Of all children's products, toy balloons are the leading cause of childhood choking deaths in the United States. Parents, caretakers, physicians, and policymakers should be alerted to the dangers of rubber toy balloons, and preventive efforts should be directed toward a ban on this type of balloon and the development of safer alternatives.

▶ Tragedies involving rubber balloons generally involve uninflated balloons or balloon pieces. The management of the child who has an obstructed airway from a rubber balloon is no different from the management of anyone who has foreign body airway obstruction. That is fairly clear-cut. What is not so clear-cut is how to prevent such occurrences.

A complete ban on rubber balloons would eliminate the impact of choking deaths from children's products. This is not likely to be the solution. In lieu of that solution, the authors of the article abstracted above offer the following guidelines to help reduce the risk of death from balloon aspiration:

• Adults should always blow up balloons for children and supervise children while they are playing with balloons.
• Older children should be warned of the dangers of chewing or sucking on balloons.
• Rubber balloons should be banned from hospitals, day care centers, and schools.
• Toy manufacturers and importers should put safety warning messages on balloon packages.
• Redesign the product. This is not easy when it comes to rubber balloons, but with the introduction in the last 10 years of helium-filled aluminum balloons, there is an alternative to the rubber balloon and the shattering consequences that can occur when pieces of it are inhaled.

As a last note on balloons and the hazards they pose, the hazard isn't only to our children but also potentially to our environment. Birds, fish, and even a 590-kg leather-backed turtle were recently found washed ashore in New Jersey, starved to death when balloons that were released in the atmosphere during celebrations were eaten and then unfortunately lodged in the stomachs of the animals. An encouraging and positive step to protect both children and the environment was the recent action by the Governor's Highway Safety Program in North Carolina to stop using balloons as promotional exercises by state and local agencies (1).

Manufacturers of rubber balloons, if you don't care about our children, at least think of the birds, fishes, and turtles.—J.A. Stockman, III, M.D.

Reference

1. Jones PJ: *Tar Heel Centerline* 1:1, 1989.

12 The Heart and Blood Vessels

The Erythrocyte Sedimentation Rate in Congestive Heart Failure
Haber HL, Leavy JA, Kessler PD, Kukin ML, Gottlieb SS, Packer M (Mount Sinai School of Medicine, New York)
N Engl J Med 324:353–358, 1991

12–1

The belief that the erythrocyte sedimentation rate is low in patients with congestive heart failure stems primarily from observations published in a single report in 1936. These observations previously were unchallenged. This notion was reexamined.

The sedimentation rate in 242 patients referred for treatment of chronic heart failure was measured. Sedimentation rates were low (<5 mm/hr) in only 10% of these patients, and rates were increased (>25 mm/hr) in 50%. Patients with low or normal sedimentation rates had more severe hemodynamic abnormalities than those with high rates. These patients had lower cardiac indices and higher mean right atrial pressures. Sixty-six percent of the patients with a low or normal sedimentation rate had New York Heart Association functional class IV symptoms compared with 42% of patients with increased rates. After 1–3 months of treatment, patients with rates that decreased showed little hemodynamic or clinical response. However, both cardiac performance and functional status improved in patients whose rates increased. Sedimentation rate and plasma fibrinogen level were correlated. Changes in the sedimentation rate during treatment had an inverse relationship with changes in mean right atrial pressure. The 1-year survival among patients with low or normal sedimentation rates was 41% compared with 66% among patients with elevated rates.

The erythrocyte sedimentation rate is not characteristically low in patients with congestive heart failure. The depression of the sedimentation rate, however, appears to reflect a state of severe cardiac decompensation.

▶ Why pray tell, in the 1990s, would the erythrocyte sedimentation rate continue to arouse any interest? It still seems to, though.

For more than 50 years, it has been taught that patients with congestive heart failure have low erythrocyte sedimentation rates. Medical students even attempt to memorize mnemonics for the 11 common causes of a very low sed rate (these include anorexia nervosa, hypofibrinogenemia, a beta lipoproteinemia, sickle cell anemia, pyruvate kinase deficiency, hereditary spherocytosis, congestive heart failure, nephrotic syndrome, steroid therapy, aspirin administration, and serum sickness). In any event, you can scratch congestive heart failure from the list. The notion that the erythrocyte sedimentation rate is low in patients with congestive heart failure was based on a single report of Paul Wood in 1936 (1). He noted a striking retardation of the sedimentation rate in patients who had acute pulmonary congestion and peripheral edema resulting from heart failure. What Haber, et al. have shown in the present report is that the sed rate is less than 5 mm per hour in only 10% of patients with congestive heart failure, whereas half of their study subjects had an erythrocyte sedimentation rate of more than 25 mm per hour. Only in the most severe cases of congestive heart failure was there a lowering of the ESR, presumably on the basis of alterations and impairment of hepatic fibrinogen formation.

The difference between 1936 and 1991 is pretty straightforward. Few patients have such persistent cardiac decompensation as was noted 50 years ago.

The low erythrocyte sedimentation rate of congestive heart failure bids its fond farewell to us medical folks and joins the ranks of medical folklore. I shall shed a tear over this loss as I try to figure out a new mnemonic for a slightly shorter list of causes of a low erythrocyte sedimentation rate. Please do not write to find out what the old mnemonic was. As with most of what we learned in medical school, it could best be described as being somewhere between "colorful" and "obscene."—J.A. Stockman, III, M.D.

Reference

1. Wood P: *Q J Med* 5:1, 1936.

Diagnosis and Management of Infantile Marfan Syndrome
Morse RP, Rockenmacher S, Pyeritz RE, Sanders SP, Bieber FR, Lin A, MacLeod P, Hall B, Graham JM Jr (Mary Hitchcock Mem Hosp, Hanover, NH; Johns Hopkins Univ, Baltimore; Children's Hosp, Boston; Brigham and Women's Hosp, Boston; West Penn Hosp, Pittsburgh; et al)
Pediatrics 86:888–895, 1990   12–2

The diagnosis of Marfan syndrome is uncommon early in infancy. Marfan syndrome was diagnosed in a group of infants in the first 3 months of life. Experience with these infants was evaluated, and the literature on additional cases was studied.

Marfan syndrome was diagnosed in 22 severely affected infants before the age of 3 months, and an additional 32 cases were located in the literature. Serious cardiac disease was found in 82% of the new group and in 94% of those reported in the literature. Congenital contractures occurred in 64% of the new group and 47% of those reported in the literature. Other useful clinical findings were arachnodactyly, dolichocephaly, a characteristic facies, a high-arched palate, micrognathia, hyperextensible joints, pes planus, anterior chest deformity, iridodenesis, megalocornea, and dislocated lenses. Echocardiography was a helpful noninvasive tool for defining the extent of cardiovascular involvement and following its

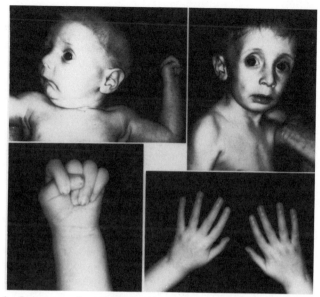

Fig 12−1.—Patient at age 2 months. Left, with contractural arachnodactyly, dolichocephaly, megalocornea, micrognathia, and deep-set eyes. By age 1 year (right), facial features persisted with ectopia lentis seen at age 4 months and rsolution of contractural arachnodactyly by age 5 months. Aortic root dilation with mitral and tricuspid valve prolapse were evident at birth. Studies of type 1 and type 3 collagen appeared normal. The patient is alive with significant cardiac morbidity at age 4 years. (Courtesy of Morse RP, Rockenmacher S, Pyeritz RE, et al: *Pediatrics* 86:888−895, 1990.)

course. Mitral valve prolapse, valvular regurgitation, and aortic root dilation were characteristic cardiac findings in early life. Cardiac function ranged from normal to poor and tended to worsen. Of the 22 new patients, 3 infants died in the first year of life (Figs 12−1 and 12−2).

When Marfan syndrome is diagnosed early in life, morbidity and mortality may be high. The prompt recognition of this phenotype can facilitate management and counseling. Most severe cases appear to result from a sporadic mutation in a single germ cell of 1 parent. Many familial cases may have milder manifestations, may be harder to diagnose in infancy, and may have a better prognosis.

▶ This must be the year of Marfan syndrome. Perhaps appropriately so, because so much has been learned about it in recent times.

Marfan syndrome, an inherited multisystem disorder with a variable phenotype, is serious, largely because of its cardiovascular complications, which cause 95% of the deaths in patients with the condition and reduce the mean life expectancy by up to 40%. With the new information from the study abstracted above, we may need to reduce that longevity downward because most of the historic data on this topic has not included a diagnosis of Marfan made in early infancy. A diagnosis made at that time portends an extremely poor prognosis with very early death. You might want to read the commentary in the Adolescent Medicine chapter on adolescents with Marfan syndrome.

Diagnostic manifestations

Skeletal

    Anterior chest deformity, especially asymmetric pectus

    Excavatum/carinatum

    Dolichostenomelia not due to scoliosis

    Arachnodactyly

    Vertebral column deformity

        Scoliosis

        Thoracic lordosis or reduced thoracic kyphosis

    Tall stature, especially compared with unaffected first-degree relatives

    High, narrowly arched palate and dental crowding

    Protrusio acetabulae

    Abnormal appendicular joint mobility

        Congenital flexion contractures

        Hypermobility

Ocular

    Ectopia lentis*

    Flat cornea

    Elongated globe

    Retinal detachment

    Myopia

Cardiovascular

    Dilation of the ascending aorta*

    Aortic dissection*

    Aortic regurgitation

    Mitral regurgitation due to mitral valve prolapse

    Calcification of mitral annulus

    Mitral valve prolapse

    Abdominal aortic aneurysm

    Dysrhythmia

    Endocarditis

Pulmonary

    Spontaneous pneumothorax

    Apical bleb

Skin and integument

    Striae atrophicae

    Inguinal hernia

    Other hernia (umbilical, diaphragmatic, incisional)

Central nervous system

    Dural ectasia*

        Lumbosacral meningocele

    Dilated cisterna magna

    Learning disability (verbal-performance discrepancy)

    Hyperactivity with or without attention deficit disorder

Fig 12–2.—Diagnostic criteria for Marfan's syndrome. Listed in approximate order of decreasing specificity. Major manifestations are indicated by asterisk. (From Morse RP, Rockenmacher S, Pyeritz RE, et al: *Pediatrics* 86:888–895, 1990. Courtesy of Beighton P, dePaepe A, Danks D, et al: *Am J Med Genet* 29:581–593, 1988.) *(cont'd on p. 295)*

Requirements for diagnosis
In the absence of an unequivocally affected first-degree relative:
Involvement of the skeleton and at least two other systems; at least one major manifestation
In the presence of at least one unequivocally affected first-degree relative:
Involvement of at least two systems: at least one major manifestation preferred, but this will depend on the family's phenotype
Urine amino acid analysis in the absence of pyridoxine supplementation confirms absence of homocystinuria
Conditions most often considered in differential diagnosis
Homocystinuria
Familial or isolated mitral valve prolapse syndrome
Familial or isolated annuloaortic ectasia (Erdheim disease)
Congenital contractural arachnodactyly
Stickler syndrome

Fig 12–2 (cont.).

There are a number of psychological overtones to this diagnosis, in addition to the anatomical ones.

Not only can you make a diagnosis of Marfan syndrome in infancy, if you want to, you can make it in utero because the chromosomal defect is now understood. It was nearly a century ago when the first Professor of Pediatrics in Paris, Antoine Marfan, described a young girl with long, spider-like fingers and other curious skeletal anomalies. It wasn't until 1943, a year after Marfan's death, that involvement of the aorta was identified. By the time McKusik, in 1955, showed that disease of the aorta accounted for most deaths, it was well recognized that Marfan syndrome was an autosomal-dominant disorder. Not until 1988 was there common agreement regarding the conditions necessary for the diagnosis. The current diagnostic criteria were established at the 7th International Congress on Human Genetics in 1986 and refined at the 1st International Symposium on Marfan Syndrome in 1988.

These refinements in diagnosis were 1 small step. The giant step, however, has been the identification of the specific genetic disorder that is located on chromosome 15 (1). It is now suspected that the specific defect in Marfan syndrome relates to the microfibrillar system and not to elastin itself. Fibrillin is a component of the elastin-associated fibrils, which are critically important for maintaining blood vessel integrity (including the aorta) and provide a framework for other tissues in the body, including the skin, lung, and the skeleton. If you wish to read more of the interesting developments regarding Marfan syndrome, see the excellent review of this topic by Pyertiz (2).

Marfan syndrome has now made the list of high hitters for missed diagnoses by pediatricians, especially as related to school physicals and permission for participation in sporting activities. Read as much about this syndrome as you can, unless you want to be the odd man or woman out.—J.A. Stockman, III, M.D.

References

1. Kainulainen K, et al: *N Engl J Med* 323:935, 1990.
2. Pyertiz RE, et al: *N Engl J Med* 323:987, 1990.

Cardiovascular Effects of Caffeine Therapy In Preterm Infants
Walther FJ, Erickson R, Sims ME (Univ of Southern California; Los Angeles County-Univ of Southern California Med Ctr, Los Angeles)
Am J Dis Child 144:1164–1166, 1990   12–3

Theophylline and caffeine are frequently used in the neonatal intensive care unit. A previous study indicated that theophylline therapy increased left ventricular output in preterm infants by a combination of positive inotropic and chronotropic effects, but it lacks a pressor effect. The effects of caffeine on cardiovascular function and blood pressure were studied in 20 clinically stable premature infants. In 10 infants caffeine citrate was given intravenously at a loading dose of 20 mg/kg and a maintenance dose of 5 mg/kg every 24 hours. The other 10 infants acted as a control group.

Compared with the control group, left ventricular output and stroke volume, as measured by a combination of 2-dimensional and pulsed Doppler echocardiography, increased significantly on days 1 to 7 of caffeine therapy. This was accompanied by an increase in mean arterial blood pressure on days 1 to 3, but the heart rate did not change significantly.

These data indicate that caffeine has positive inotropic and pressor effects in clinically stable premature infants. These changes should be taken into consideration when making decisions on what type of methylxanthine to use in preterm infants.

▶ Methylxanthines, specifically theophylline and caffeine, are used frequently in the neonatal intensive care setting. Theophylline and caffeine are used similarly to treat apnea of prematurity and to assist weaning of preterm infants from mechanical ventilation. Whereas there are extensive data on theophylline therapy showing that it increases left ventricular output by a combination of increasing contraction and cardiac rate, theophylline does not increase blood pressure. On the other hand, what we see from this report is that caffeine can cause changes in blood pressure, and although these changes are small, they may potentially contribute to periventricular-intraventricular hemorrhage in susceptible preterm infants.

All of the above is not to say that the administration of caffeine may not have an indication for newborn infants, it's just that it may not be good for them. In fact, it may be just as bad for them as it is for us adults.

To say the above paragraph differently, caffeine isn't a terrific substance. Many a person has gone to their sarcophagus by what they have put into their esophagus.—J.A. Stockman, III, M.D.

Aortic Thrombosis After Umbilical Artery Catheterization in Neonates: Prevalence of Complications on Long-Term Follow-Up

Seibert JJ, Northington FJ, Miers JF, Taylor BJ (Univ of Arkansas; Arkansas Children's Hosp, Little Rock)
AJR 156:567–569, 1991   12–4

In a previous study of neonates assessed for aortic thrombosis with abdominal sonography, 21 of the 81 infants had sonographically detectable aortic clots. The long-term complications of leg growth, renal abnormalities, and blood pressure abnormalities were documented in this group of 21 children.

Five of the infants died in the neonatal period, 4 were lost to follow-up, and 2 were excluded because of unrelated renal abnormalities. Ten children from the original group were available for reassessment at 36 to 42 months of age. Those children were compared with an age-matched control group of 7 children who did not have aortic thrombi. In the study group, 3 infants had blood pressures greater than the 95th percentile; 6 had blood pressures between the 50th and 95th percentile. The height of 4 infants with aortic thrombosis was less than the fifth percentile for age. One child had a 1-cm discrepancy in leg-length measurements, and 7 had a .5- to 2-cm discrepancy between legs in either thigh or calf circumference. No evidence of residual clot in the aorta or renal vessels was found on Doppler sonography. All children had a normal flow in both renal arteries and veins.

Infants with known aortic thrombosis should have long-term follow-up to detect potential problems. Even when neonatal aortic thrombosis resolves, complications in these infants can result in renovascular hypertension and leg-growth abnormalities.

▶ Dr. Maureen Andrew, Professor of Pediatrics and Pathology, McMaster University Medical Centre and the Hospital for Sick Children, Toronto, comments:

▶ Seibert and colleagues report on the frequency and nature of long-term morbidity associated with thrombotic complications of umbilical artery catheters (UAC). Other authors have previously reported on the presence or absence of long-term morbidity from UAC-associated thrombi; however, the results have not been uniform. The discrepancies reflect several parameters including study design (selected patients vs. cohort studies), inclusion or exclusion of control populations, objective testing to demonstrate the presence of asymptomatic as well as clinically symptomatic UAC thrombi, the decade from which the population was identified, and finally, the outcome parameters measured. The study by Seibert was a cohort study of asymptomatic and symptomatic UAC thrombi documented by ultrasound in 81 consecutive infants with UAC. Twenty-one of the 81 infants were identified to have a UAC thrombus, and of these, 10 were available for follow-up. Although there was no residual thrombus detected by ultrasound, all of the infants had at least 1 clinical abnormality documented in the form of hypertension, abnormal renal function, and/or discrepancies in leg measurements. The conclusions of this study and of other reports in the literature clearly indicate that there is long-term morbidity associated with UAC thrombi, and all underscore the need for further, more comprehensive follow-up studies to fully delineate the magnitude of the problem. In particular, follow-up studies are needed of asymptomatic UAC thrombi, because most of the data available, including the study by Seibert et al., focus on symptomatic UAC thrombi. Based on the results of 6 prospective angiographic studies, there is a high rate (10%–95%) of asymptomatic UAC thrombi.

The presence or absence of significant long-term morbidity from UAC thrombi will dictate the approach to initial management. Both prophylactic and therapeutic approaches can be considered. Although there is strong evidence from 4 controlled studies that the use of low-dose heparin prolongs the patency of UAC, there is no convincing evidence that prophylactic heparin as currently used decreases the number or size of UAC thrombi. However, it is probable that prophylactic anticoagulant therapy can be effectively and safely manipulated to prevent UAC thrombi. In addition to prevention strategies, more aggressive screening for the presence of asymptomatic UAC thrombi and clinical trials of treatment would be warranted if the long-term morbidity is significant.—M. Andrew, M.D.

Percutaneous Femoral Venous Catheterization in Preterm Neonates
Abdulla F, Dietrich KA, Pramanik AK (Louisiana State Univ, Shreveport)
J Pediatr 117:788–791, 1990   12–5

The use of percutaneous femoral venous catheterization has not been reported in preterm neonates, probably because of the potential for increased catheter-associated sepsis related to groin hygiene and the rare occurrence of complications such as septic arthritis of the hip. The feasibility and safety of percutaneous femoral venous catheterization in critically ill preterm neonates was studied prospectively and compared with the use of similar catheters in nonfemoral peripheral venous sites.

A total of 120 percutaneous silicone rubber central venous catheters was inserted in 95 critically ill preterm neonates in a neonatal intensive care unit. Sixty-three were placed through the femoral vein (Fig 12–3), and 57 were placed through nonfemoral veins.

The percutaneous femoral venous technique was successful in 90% of attempts, compared with 84% success in the nonfemoral group. Percutaneous femoral venous catheterization was completed in 20 to 75 minutes. The only complication was accidental femoral artery puncture in 18%, which was easily controlled without adverse sequelae. Complications in the nonfemoral group included frequent hematoma formation.

There was no significant difference in the mean duration of catheter stay or rate of sepsis between the 2 groups. There were no gram-negative or other enteric infections in the femoral group, and no site infections were noted even though the catheters stayed in place for up to 60 days. Clot formation was frequent in both groups, possibly because of prolonged interruption of the lines to change fluids or administer antibiotics.

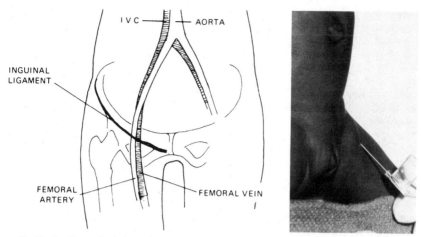

Fig 12–3.—Femoral vein lies inferior to inguinal ligament and medial to femoral artery. Needle is directed into femoral vein approximately 1 cm below inguinal ligament and .5 cm medial to maximal pulse of femoral artery. Introducer needle is advanced at 30 degrees toward umbilicus. *Abbreviation: IVC,* inferior vena cava. (Courtesy of Abdulla F, Dietrich KA, Pramanik AK: *J Pediatr* 117:788–791, 1990.)

Percutaneous femoral venous catheterization appears to be as safe and effective as nonfemoral catheterization in critically ill preterm neonates. Further studies are warranted to define the use of this technique in the premature neonate.

▶ The preceding 2 articles (Abstracts 12–4 and 12–5) deal with vascular access and complications thereof. My hat is off to anyone who can catheterize the femoral vein of a tiny preterm infant percutaneously. One might logically think that the risks of destroying this vessel, of injuring the hip capsule, or of other local complications would be extremely high. Apparently this is not so in experienced hands. It is probably best for each of us to leave these technical procedures to those who are expert at doing them. When I need an arterial cutdown, I call a close friend who is a cardiovascular surgeon. He can get those catheters in in a fraction of the time that other people take—he's a real "Phantom of the Artery."

One of the long-term complications of umbilical artery catheterization is occlusion of 1 or the other of the renal arteries, with resultant kidney loss and/or hypertension. Because this YEAR BOOK has no articles on hypertension, I will ask a couple of questions on this topic and related matters.

Is hypertension associated with preeclampsia and preterm labor more common among women resident physicians?

The answer is yes. Preeclampsia with hypertension and preterm labor (but not preterm delivery) are more common among women physicians than among their male resident classmates' wives (8.8% vs. 3.5%, and 11.3% vs. 6%, respectively) (1). This was not a particularly easy study to design, because so many residents are married to other residents. It seems perfectly obvious why so many house officers marry one another—one good 'tern deserves another.

300 / Pediatrics

The second question having to do with hypertension is a little far afield and has to do with the drug minoxidil, which is used less as an antihypertensive than it is as a drug to grow hair. With respect to the latter attribute, in addition to minoxidil, what may be the best way to get hair to grow on your head?

Fracture your skull. Ravin, an endocrinologist, has observed that individuals with fractures of their lower extremities develop a growth of lush, terminal hair on the skin over the fracture (2). There are probably some among us who would be willing to risk the experiment of sustaining multiple fractures to see what the effect might be up top.—J.A. Stockman, III, M.D.

References

1. Hatch MC, et al: *N Engl J Med* 324:629, 1991.
2. Ravin N: *N Engl J Med* 323:350, 1990.

Determinants of Hemoglobin Concentration in Cyanotic Heart Disease
Gidding SS, Bessel M, Liao Y (Children's Mem Hosp, Chicago; Northwestern Univ, Chicago)
Pediatr Cardiol 11:121–125, 1990   12–6

There is currently no consensus regarding expected values of hemoglobin for a given degree of hypoxemia. Variables that might destabilize systemic oxygen transport, thereby determining a clinically useful relationship between hemoglobin concentration and aortic oxygen saturation were identified.

Two hundred seventy-two children with cyanotic congenital heart disease who had undergone cardiac catheterization were evaluated to determine the effects of chronic hypoxemia, iron stores, and age on hemoglobin concentration. All had aortic oxygen saturation of less than 93%. Common diagnoses included tetralogy of Fallot (60), complex transposition (34), and tricuspid atresia (31). The children's mean age at the time of the study was 4.4 years.

For the group as a whole, mean oxygen saturation was 82%, and mean hemoglobin concentration was 16.3 g/dL. Red cell mean corpuscular volume above the 90th percentile was found in 72% of children, and hemoglobin concentration was higher in this group than in children with a mean corpuscular volume in the tenth to 90th percentile or below the tenth percentile. Multiple regression analysis showed that age and oxygen saturation were associated with hemoglobin in children presumed to be iron sufficient and with oxygen saturation of greater than 75%. In children older than age 11 years, significant correlations between hemoglobin concentration and oxygen saturation were not present.

Aortic oxygen saturation is not the only important determinant of hemoglobin concentration in patients with cyanotic congenital heart disease. Hemoglobin concentration increases with increasing age, and diminished iron stores lower hemoglobin concentration. These results may be applied to children younger than age 11 years to calculate the adequacy of the erythrocytic response.

▶ This is an important report. It is important not only for the cardiologist or hematologist, but it is also critically important for the primary care pediatrician. All must be cognizant of what the expected normal values are for hemoglobin and mean corpuscular volume (MCV) and what the risks are for the development of iron deficiency with or without anemia. Several studies have documented an increased risk of cerebral vascular accidents associated with the development of iron deficiency in children less than 6 years of age who have concomitant cyanotic congenital heart disease (1). To say this differently, one must know the normative ranges for hemoglobin and MCV in patients with cyanotic congenital heart disease to detect the early signs of iron deficiency anemia. The data of Gidding et al. tell us what the normative numbers are. You will need to read this article in detail to figure out what an expected hemoglobin level is, because it depends on both the age and the degree of desaturation seen in any particular patient with cyanotic congenital heart disease. As a rule of thumb, however, the mean hemoglobin concentration is between 16 and 17 g/dL in the average patient whose arterial oxygen saturation is 82%.

Patients with cyanotic congenital heart disease also tend to be somewhat macrocytic. Fifty-one percent of these patients had MCVs greater than the 97th percentile for age and sex and an additional 21% had MCVs between the 90th and 97th percentile. If you are not sure what the "normal" percentage ranges for MCV are based on age, the figures are in the *Harriet Lane Handbook*. They are also in an excellent review on iron deficiency by Dallman et al. (2).

So, what are Gidding et al. telling us? They are telling us that if you don't want to run the risk of stroke, check the hemoglobin level. If the hemoglobin level is more than 1.0 g/dL below what you expect it to be, be concerned about iron deficiency. Be more concerned if the MCV for that patient is below the 90th percentile for normal MCVs for that patient's age. The occurrence of these 2 findings means that the patient could develop a stroke and needs to be treated with iron.

The reason why patients with iron deficiency and cyanotic congenital heart disease develop strokes is pretty straightforward. They have polycythemia. Iron deficiency makes the red cell membrane very nondeformable. The combination of polycythemia and a nondeformable red cell membrane markedly increases the whole blood viscosity.

We tend to examine the nail beds to decide whether somebody with heart disease is significantly cyanotic. Be wary of doing that in school-aged girls, young women, and older adult females. Why? Chances are some will have in common the "nail polish sign." Mehan (3) observed that females of all ages with cyanotic congenital heart disease tend to use nail polish to conceal the cyanotic tinge of their nails. This is a particular problem in parts of the world such as India, where many children with cyanotic congenital heart disease are not operated on. The practice of painting nails may lead to diagnostic errors. Mehan suggests that, with awareness of the possible significance of painted nails, a bottle of acetone would go a long way to overcome this curious but important problem. Remember the "nail polish sign."—J.A. Stockman, III, M.D.

References

1. West DW, et al: *J Pediatr* 117:266, 1990.
2. Dallman PR, et al: *Am J Clin Nutr* 33:86, 1980.
3. Mehan VK: *Lancet* 2:62, 1990.

Cardiomyopathy and the Use of Implanted Cardio-Defibrillators in Children

Kaminer SJ, Pickoff AS, Dunnigan A, Sterba R, Wolff GS (Univ of Miami; Tulane Univ; Univ of Minnesota, Minneapolis; Cleveland Clinic Found)
PACE 13:593–597, 1990   12–7

Despite aggressive medical therapy, prognosis is uniformly poor in children and adults with cardiomyopathy and ventricular dysrhythmias. The use of automatic implantable cardiodefibrillators significantly improves survival in adult patients, but the device has been used rarely in children. The value and feasibility of automatic implantable cardiodefibrillators were demonstrated in 4 young patients.

Four patients with cardiomyopathy and refractory ventricular dysrhythmias were managed with automatic implantable cardiodefibrillators. Two of these patients were the youngest and the smallest known patients to have these devices, and one of them received the first programmable model. After implantation, the patients experienced several episodes of ventricular tachycardia or fibrillation that were cardioverted by the device. The patients adjusted well to the presence of the defibrillator. One patient is awaiting cardiac transplantation.

The use of automatic implantable cardiodefibrillators may improve life expectancy in young patients with cardiomyopathy and malignant ventricular dysrhythmias. This may allow time for definitive therapy in the form of transplantation.

▶ D. Woodrow (better known as Woody) Benson, Jr., M.D., Ph.D., Professor of Pediatrics, and Chief of the Division of Pediatric Cardiology, Northwestern University Medical School/Children's Memorial Hospital, is a world's expert in electrophysiology. He comments:

▶ The clinical histories of the 4 patients reported on emphasize an unappreciated dimension of the cardiomyopathy problem. That is, cardiomyopathy usually connotes dysfunction of the pumping action of the myocardium. This was relatively subtle in the reported cases. What is illustrated by these cases is the periodic, life-threatening electrical instability (dysfunction) of the heartbeat in some patients with cardiomyopathy. The essential, unanswered question is how to identify such patients before cardiac arrest occurs. Which patient with extrasystoles is a potential cardiac arrest victim? Which ostensibly normal child with syncope is a potential cardiac arrest victim?

This paper demonstrates the feasibility of using a relatively new "high-tech" device in relatively young children with medically refractory, life-threatening ventricular rhythm disturbances. However, as we all know from our experience with major and minor home appliances, no man-made device is perfect. Interested readers are referred to a paper by Kron et al., which reviews experience with 40 patients less than 20 years old who received the automatic implantable cardioverter-defibrillator (AICD) between 1980 and 1989 (1). In a median follow-up of 28 months, 5% of patients died suddenly in spite of AICD, and 27% received an inappropriate shock. We still have a long way to go to understand the essential problem in "electrocardiomyopathy" patients. Until better answers are available, the AICD appears to be a useful adjunct to managing selected patients.—D.W. Benson, Jr., M.D., Ph.D.

Reference

1. Kron IL, et al: *J Am Coll Cardiol* 16:896, 1990.

Immunosuppressive Therapy in the Management of Acute Myocarditis in Children: A Clinical Trial
Chan KY, Iwahara M, Benson LN, Wilson GJ, Freedom RM (The Hosp for Sick Children, Toronto)
J Am Coll Cardiol 17:458–460, 1991   12–8

There is evidence that acute myocarditis leads to dilated cardiomyopathy, making effective treatment even more important. The value of steroid therapy was examined in 13 consecutive infants and children seen from 1984–1989 with biopsy-proved acute myocarditis.

The mean patient age was 5.7 years. Twelve of the 13 patients had congestive heart failure, and all but 1 of the patients had a structurally normal heart. Prednisone was begun in a dose of 2 mg/kg daily and was tapered to 0.3 mg/kg over 2 months. One patient received azathioprine as well.

Repeat endomyocardial biopsy showed histologic improvement in all 8 patients evaluated and elimination of inflammatory infiltrate in 6. Two patients continued to receive prednisone. One patient died of persistent low cardiac output and multisystem dysfunction. In surviving patients, heart failure stabilized and resolved within a week of the start of treatment. Ten patients regained a normal ECG a mean of 4.5 months after treatment.

Immunosuppression effectively reduced myocardial inflammation in these patients and improved cardiac function. Two of the present patients relapsed when treatment was withdrawn but again improved when treatment was reinstituted.

▶ Acute myocarditis can be a fulminating, relentless illness that results in significant morbidity and mortality. Additionally, there is evidence to suggest that it is a cause of dilated cardiomyopathy. Beyond the infancy period in childhood, cardiomyopathy is probably the single most common indication for cardiac transplantation. Thus, any effective therapy for acute myocarditis will have substantial impact not only on the acute process, but also on the incidence of end-stage dilated cardiomyopathy and its transplantation implications. The use of immunosuppressive agents in the treatment of acute inflammatory myocarditis, referred to in the abstract, has been controversial, and there have been no published, controlled series. There is emerging, however, an absolutely fascinating background that clearly justifies the role of immunosuppressive drugs.

Take, for example, our understanding of what causes dilated cardiomyopathy. Until lately, evidence for enteroviral (usually Coxsackie B virus) involvement in chronic cardiac disease in man was largely circumstantial, based on reports of high titer Coxsackie B virus-specific neutralizing antibody present in patients with myocarditis and dilated myocardiopathy. Now, with the advent of molecular biologic probes, enteroviral RNA has been detected in endomyocardial biopsy specimens from patients with myocarditis and dilated myocardiopathy (1). Approximately half of all patients show viral RNA in myocardial biopsies.

What does all this mean? Evidence suggests that patients who have myocarditis caused by enteroviruses have a poorer outcome (2). There are 2 explanations of why viruses do in the heart. The first is that cardiac damage results from persistent but defective viral replication, which in and of itself damages the heart. The more likely possibility is virus-induced alteration of major histocompatibility complex antigen expression and consequent exposure of cardiac neoantigens to the immune system.

How prednisone works is still unknown. The mechanism of action, however, may be related to a very interesting protein that you probably have not heard of before known as "perforin." Activated cytotoxic T lymphocytes can kill virus-infected target cells by contact-dependent release of granule proteins. One of these proteins, perforin, creates characteristic pores in the membrane of a wide variety of target cells. The presence of pores alters the osmotic equilibrium across the cell membrane, leading to an influx of water and eventually to cell death. The name "perforin" obviously was coined by somebody who linked it to its ability to "perforate," or put holes in, cell membranes.

Young et al. (3) showed conclusively that perforin is produced by lymphocytes and natural killer cells in acute human myocarditis lesions presumed to be viral in origin. Electron microscopy performed by these investigators has shown ultrastructural membrane lesions in myocardial cells consisting of 15–20 nm pores that are the characteristic hallmark of perforin action.

So we have come full circle. Chan et al. showed us that prednisone can work. Young et al. show us why it should work. It presumably works by inhibiting T lymphocytes that otherwise would release perforin, which would drill holes in myocardial cells, killing them and doing somebody in during the course of myocarditis.

If this story is correct, we should be able to target immunosuppressive therapy in a much more specific way rather than simply using a drug such as prednisone. For example, why hasn't anyone used OKT3 (the monoclonal antibody against cytotoxic T cells)? I venture to guess that some time in the next 5 years, somebody will produce a monoclonal antibody against perforin. It is a protein, and it shouldn't be hard to make a monoclonal antibody against it. This editor of the YEAR BOOK likes to make predictions such as those above. I'll stand behind the prediction that somebody will make a monoclonal antibody against perforin, the agent that punches holes in cell membranes. Anyone want to punch holes in this prediction?—J.A. Stockman, III, M.D.

References

1. Byers PH, et al: *Proc Natl Acad Sci USA* 78:775, 1981.
2. Editorial: *Lancet* 336:971, 1990.
3. Young LHV, et al: *Lancet* 336:1019, 1990.

Cardiac Localization of Eosinophil-Granule Major Basic Protein in Acute Necrotizing Myocarditis

deMello DE, Liapis H, Jureidini S, Nouri S, Kephart GM, Gleich GJ (St Louis Univ; Cardinal Glennon Children's Hosp, St Louis; Mayo Clinic and Found, Rochester, Minn)

N Engl J Med 323:1542–1545, 1990   12–9

Löffler's endocarditis, characterized by eosinophilic pancarditis, muscle necrosis, and arteritis, is usually associated with systemic diseases. Fulminant acute necrotizing eosinophilic myocarditis occurred in the absence of extracardiac disease in 2 patients. Two previously healthy children, aged 14 years and 22 months, respectively, had initial viruslike illness followed by sudden and progressive cardiac decompensation. One patient showed a pattern of infarction on ECG and 1 showed peripheral eosinophilia. Death occurred within hours of onset of dyspnea.

In both children, autopsy showed acute, extensive necrotizing eosinophilic myocarditis. Indirect-immunofluorescence stain for major basic protein of eosinophil granules showed intense staining of eosinophils (cellular staining) and extracellular staining within necrotic myocardium. There was no evidence of arteritis. Neither patient had evidence of drug-induced hypersensitivity or parasitic infestation. Extracardiac disease at autopsy was largely related to cardiac failure. Although rare, fulminant acute necrotizing eosinophilic myocarditis can occur in the absence of extracardiac disease.

▶ The report of the death of these 2 children is truly scary. Both children died within hours of the onset of the first symptom of congestive heart failure. They both died of a fulminant necrotizing myocarditis, with a myocardium that was infiltrated with eosinophils.

The association between eosinophilia and endomyocarditis has been documented previously. A form of Löeffler's endocarditis, characterized by eosinophilic pancarditis, muscle necrosis, and arteritis, is usually a feature of certain systemic diseases, including the hypereosinophilic syndrome, eosinophilic leukemia, polyarteritis nodosa, drug-induced hypersensitivity, bronchial asthma, biliary tract carcinoma, or parasitic disease. These 2 children had sudden cardiac deterioration after a short illness, presumably viral, and died within a few hours of fulminant acute necrotizing eosinophilic myocarditis. The clinical features of these 2 patients differ from the usual picture of Löffler's endocarditis. Both patients were previously healthy and had an initial virallike illness followed by sudden fulminant cardiac decompensation and death within hours of the onset of dyspnea. In both, the chief finding at autopsy was acute, extensive necrotizing eosinophilic myocarditis. These patients had no evidence of parasitic infection, no evidence of hematologic malignancy, and no evidence elsewhere of a systemic vasculitis. Both patients had received a drug (1 had taken ampicillin, and the other had taken Dilatin). These drugs can cause hypersensitivity myocarditis, but the clinical picture of previous patients who developed this as a result of drug sensitivity was not at all like the fulminant course seen in these 2 patients.

I personally have seen only 1 case of eosinophilic pancarditis, and that was in a child with acute lymphocytic leukemia, whose leukemic cells produced a T cell mediator that stimulated the production of eosinophils. That child had fulminant congestive heart failure as the predominant symptom, not leukemia. The next time you see any child with myocarditis and he or she is going downhill rapidly, make sure that the cardiologist gets an endomyocardial biopsy ASAP. If it turns out to be one of these rare cases of eosinophilic myocarditis, in the absence of any other systemic disease, chances are that therapy is not going to be successful.—J.A. Stockman, III, M.D.

Late Cardiac Effects of Doxorubicin Therapy for Acute Lymphoblastic Leukemia in Childhood

Lipshultz SE, Colan SD, Gelber RD, Perez-Atayde AR, Sallan SE, Sanders SP (Children's Hosp, Boston; Dana-Farber Cancer Inst, Boston; Harvard Med School)
N Engl J Med 324:808–815, 1991   12–10

Cardiotoxicity has been associated with doxorubicin treatment. The long-term effects of this agent, however, have not been established. The cardiac status of a group of children treated for acute lymphoblastic leukemia with doxorubicin 1–15 years earlier was assessed.

One hundred fifteen children, all in continuous remission, were studied. Eighteen had received 1 dose of doxorubicin, and 97 had received multiple doses. The single doses totaled 45 mg/m^2 of body-surface area; multiple doses totaled 228–550 mg/m^2, with a median of 360. A median of 6.4 years had elapsed since the end of treatment.

Fifty-seven percent of the children had abnormalities of left ventricular afterload or contractility. The most significant predictor of abnormal cardiac function was the cumulative dose of doxorubicin. Seventeen percent of those given 1 dose had slightly increased age-adjusted afterload, and none had reduced contractility. However, 65% of those given at least 228 mg had increased afterload and/or reduced contractility. Increased afterload resulted from decreased ventricular wall thickness, not from hypertension or ventricular dilatation. According to a multivariate analysis of patients given at least 228 mg, the only significant predictors were a higher cumulative dose, which predicted reduced contractility, and an age of younger than 4 years at the time of treatment, which predicted increased afterload. In 71% of 34 patients assessed serially, afterload increased progressively. Reported symptoms did not correlate well with indices of exercise tolerance or ventricular function. Eleven children had congestive heart failure within 1 year of doxorubicin treatment. Five of these children had recurrent heart failure 3–10 years after completing doxorubicin therapy. Two needed heart transplantation. None of the children had late heart failure as a new event.

The treatment for 1 potentially fatal childhood disease may cause another serious, potentially fatal disease. There was an unexpectedly high incidence of late cardiovascular abnormalities in this series. The contribution of doxorubicin to the cure of children with cancer must be balanced against the later effects of treatment and the influence on the child's quality of life.

▶ It is not likely that most of the reading audience of the YEAR BOOK is giving doxorubicin. On the other hand, with the marked improvement in survivorship of children with both hematologic and solid tumor malignancies, you may very well be involved with the long-term follow-up of such children. If you are, take heed of this report. It shows that over half of children who receive anthracyclines have abnormalities of the left side of their heart 1 to 15 years later. Each of the children in this report was treated in what was considered to be an appropriate way with these drugs.

When anthracyclines are given to treat malignancy, the pediatric oncologist is very careful to monitor therapy. Basically, this means doing an echocardiogram not too long after the first administration of the drug and before each subsequent administration of the drug (these drugs are given cyclically). The drug is stopped if there is any abnormality seen. Furthermore, the total quantity of the drug is always kept below a "ceiling" level that is known to produce cardiac toxicity. For example, the incidence of congestive heart failure in patients receiving more than 550 mg/m^2 doxorubicin is about 30% (1). What the article above shows us is that no matter how careful we are, we are still going to run into long-term problems. What we need is a more sensitive test. One such test may be noninvasive exercise echocardiography. Using the latter technique, Yeung et al. (2) showed that children who have normal myocardial function at rest can have impaired myocardial responses, as measured by a change in the shortening fraction of the left side of the heart on echocardiography, a response to the physiologic stress of exercise.

What does all this mean? It means that, although we are reaping all the benefits of being able to cure various childhood malignancies, at the same time we are sowing the seeds of several long-term complications of therapy, one of which is cardiac damage. The benefit-risk ratio, at least as far as we understand it right now, favors what we are doing to these kids, but the scale is beginning to tilt slightly. Let's keep our fingers crossed.—J.A. Stockman, III, M.D.

References

1. Blum RH, et al: *Ann Intern Med* 80:249, 1974.
2. Yeung ST, et al: *Lancet* 337:816, 1991.

Follow-Up Results of Balloon Angioplasty of Native Coarctation in Neonates and Infants

Rao PS, Thapar MK, Galal O, Wilson AD (Univ of Wisconsin, Madison; King Faisal Specialist Hosp and Research Ctr, Riyadh, Saudi Arabia)
Am Heart J 120:1310–1314, 1990   12–11

Although initial experience with balloon angioplasty of native coarctation in neonates and infants has been poor, subsequent experiences are encouraging. The intermediate long-term results of balloon angioplasty for native aortic coarctation in neonates and infants younger than age 1 year are evaluated.

Nineteen infants, aged 3 days to 12 months, underwent balloon angioplasty of native aortic coarctation in a 60-month period. Thirteen infants had severe associated cardiac defects. Indications for balloon angioplasty included congestive heart failure and/or hypertension not controlled by medical management. Immediate results showed a significant reduction in peak-to-peak systolic pressure gradient from 39 to 11 mm Hg and an increase in coarctation segment size from 2.2 to 4.7 mm. One death (5%) occurred 2 days after angioplasty because of associated cardiac defect; none of the infants required immediate surgical intervention.

Sixteen infants had follow-up cardiac catheterization at a mean 12 months after balloon angioplasty and clinical follow-up at a mean 36 months. The other 2 infants were either lost to follow-up or not enough time had elapsed for restudy. The residual peak-to-peak systolic pressure gradient across the coarctation (mean, 22 mm Hg) and coarcted segment size (mean, 4.4 mm) remained improved significantly compared with pre-angioplasty values. Five (31%) infants had recoarctation: 2 underwent surgical resection, and 3 underwent repeat balloon angioplasty, all with success. None of the patients had aneurysm.

Considering the previously reported higher mortality and morbidity rates associated with coarctation surgery in neonates and infants younger than age 1 year, despite similar recoarctation rates and the findings of this study, balloon angioplasty is recommended as the procedure of choice for relief of symptomatic native aortic coarctation in neonates and infants younger than age 1 year.

▶ Dr. Alexander Muster, Professor of Pediatrics, and a member of the Division of Cardiology, Northwestern University Medical School and Children's Memorial Hospital, comments:

▶ The effectiveness of a new medical intervention is judged by its long-term results and by how it compares with already existing alternatives. The intermediate-term balloon angioplasty follow-up (longest: 5 years) for native coarctation of the aorta in infants described by Rao et al. should resolve some of the controversy surrounding this procedure.

Some of the concepts of Dr. Rao et al. regarding the usefulness of balloon dilatation procedures were developed while these authors were working in a third world country, where appropriate surgical alternatives are not easy to come by. Nevertheless, presumably based on more recent experience in the United States, the authors advocate balloon angioplasty as the treatment of choice for native coarctation of the aorta in neonates and infants.

Comparing the surgical experience with coarctation repair, which dates back to 1953, with the more recent angioplasty results could be interpreted as an attempt by the authors to sway the reader toward their viewpoint. In the more recent surgical series, patients with significant associated lesions usually undergo corrective or palliative surgery along with coarctation repair. Whether this accounts for the higher mortality in the surgical series is not discussed in this article. The rate of recoarctation seems comparable for the two methods.

The ideal outcome of any medical procedure is complete cure. Neither surgery nor balloon angioplasty for native coarctation has achieved this ideal so far. However, surgery is constantly seeking and developing new and better techniques to improve the immediate and long-term results. Expectations for total elimination of residual pressure gradients by surgery seem realistic. No substantial improvement in angioplasty techniques can be anticipated in the foreseeable future. If so, balloon angioplasty for native coarctation in infants and children will have to be considered, at least at the present state of the art, a palliative procedure.—A. Muster, M.D.

Preoperative Transcatheter Closure of Congenital Muscular Ventricular Septal Defects
Bridges ND, Perry SB, Keane JF, Goldstein SAN, Mandell V, Mayer JE Jr, Jonas RA, Casteneda AR, Lock JE (Children's Hosp, Boston; Harvard Med School)
N Engl J Med 324:1312–1317, 1991   12–12

Surgical repair of muscular ventricular septal defects is more risky than the repair of membranous defects. This is especially true for muscular ventricular septal defects associated with complex heart lesions. Approaching the defect through an incision in the systemic ventricle can produce late ventricular dysfunction. The preoperative transcatheter closure of muscular ventricular septal defects remote from the atrioventricular and semilunar valves, followed by the surgical repair of associated defects, was studied.

Twelve patients, aged 10 months to 20 years, were selected jointly for this treatment by a cardiologist and cardiac surgeon. Preoperative transcatheter umbrella closure of 21 defects was attempted. Half of the patients had associated complex heart lesions, and the remainder of the patients had undergone pulmonary-artery banding to decrease the amount of left-to-right shunting. Severe ventricular septal deficiency was present

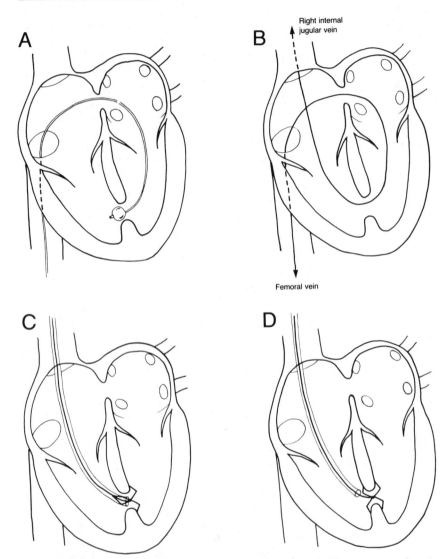

Fig 12–4.—Technique of transcatheter closure of a ventricular septal defect. A venous catheter is advanced across the atrial septum (through either a naturally occurring atrial septal defect or an atrial septal puncture) and into the left ventricle; the ventricular septal defect is then crossed from left to right (panel A). The end-hole catheter is then used to place a long guidewire (panel B). In some patients, 1 end of the wire passes out the right internal jugular vein, as shown; in others, both ends pass out the femoral veins. This wire is used to guide the placement of a long sheath that is used to deliver the Clamshell device (panel C). The device consists of 2 umbrellas, connected back to back, each with 4 arms; for simplicity, only 4 of the 8 arms are shown (panel D). (Courtesy of Bridges ND, Perry SB, Keane JF, et al: *N Engl J Med* 324:1312–1317, 1991.)

in half the cases. All defects were closed successfully. There were no major complications. Subsequent cardiac procedures for associated conditions in 11 cases resulted in a mean pulmonary-to-systemic flow ratio of 1.1, indicating a minimal residual left-to-right shunting. The last patient was still awaiting surgery. After a follow-up of 7–20 months, none of the patients had died, needed reoperation, or had late complications (Fig 12–4).

The usefulness of a prospective, collaborative approach between pediatric interventional cardiologists and pediatric cardiac surgeons in the treatment of complex congenital heart disease is confirmed. Such an approach using transcatheter closure followed by surgical repair may reduce the rates of operative mortality, reoperation, and left ventricular dysfunction in children with muscular ventricular septal defects.

▶ You may think that transcatheter (nonsurgical) closure of ventricular septal defects (VSDs) is a bit too risky in comparison with surgical correction. This is not necessarily so, and you have to read this article in some detail to figure out why. Specifically, the patients chosen for this procedure were those who would be at unusually high risk of surgical complications. These were not straightforward, simple VSDs. Indeed, at the Boston Children's Hospital where the transcatheter procedures in this report were done, a surgical mortality of 14% is what drove these surgeons and cardiologists to look to some other vehicle for closing these unusual VSDs. The mortality was almost always related to ventricular dysfunction which, presumably, is an effect of the incision into the heart muscle.

Contrast the relatively serious problems of surgery with the lack of any serious complications in all but 1 patient in the abstract above. The 1 patient who had a problem was a high-risk patient with other difficulties.

Contrast this also with the status of closure of atrial septal defects (ASDs). Transcatheter techniques for closure of atrial defects have been available for more than 2 decades, yet the approach has not achieved widespread usage. The reason for this is that, with current techniques of cardiopulmonary bypass (the first bypass procedure was used in 1953 to correct an ASD), the surgical mortality is, or should be, essentially zero. Nonetheless, this last year there have been 2 major reports of transcatheter closure of an ASD with a new type of instrument known as a "double umbrella with a clam shell configuration." This instrument uses spring tension to attach the umbrella, which closes the atrial septal defect. Rome and coworkers (1) achieved successful transcatheter occlusion of defects in 32 of 34 strictly selected patients. Only 1 episode of major morbidity occurred in a single patient who was at a high risk. After 1 to 2 years, no significant complications were noted. A study by Hellenbrand et al. (2) combined transesophageal echocardiography with fluoroscopy to guide transcatheter closure of defects. With this dual imaging technique, successful closure was accomplished in 10 of 11 patients aged 1 to 46 years. Minor residual leaks were seen in only a few patients. These latter successes will have to be watched very carefully, again in light of the surgical results, which are virtually free of any complications except hospitalization and pain associated with the "knife."

A concluding comment regarding ASD is pretty straightforward. Lessons learned from the past provide our directions for the future, as was so ably proven in the report by Murphy et al. (3). The lesson from the past is that if you are going to repair an ASD, do it early. The experience at the Mayo Clinic over a 30-year interval of follow-up showed that patients who underwent repair before

24 years of age lived as long as someone who never had an ASD. If you waited until you were over 41, you lived only about half as long. Don't wait for pulmonary hypertension to set in.

These catheter closures of ASDs and VSDs are absolutely fascinating feats of biomedical engineering. Who cares if the things leak a little bit. That happens with age anyway, or as my grandmother once told me, "You know you're getting old when everything dries up or starts to leak."—J.A. Stockman, III, M.D.

References

1. Rome JJ, et al: *Circulation* 82:751, 1990.
2. Hellenbrand WE, et al: *Am J Cardiol* 66:207, 1990.
3. Murphy JG, et al: *N Engl J Med* 323:1645, 1990.

Long-Term Outcome After Surgical Repair of Isolated Atrial Septal Defect: Follow-Up at 27–32 Years
Murphy JG, Gersh BJ, McGoon MD, Mair DD, Porter CJ, Ilstrup DM, McGoon DC, Puga FJ, Kirklin JW, Danielson GK (Mayo Clinic and Found, Rochester, Minn; Univ of Alabama, Birmingham)
N Engl J Med 323:1645–1650, 1990   12–13

Long-term survival is poorly documented in patients treated for atrial septal defect in the early era of cardiac surgery. A 3-decade follow-up of 123 patients who had repair of an isolated septal defect in 1956–1960 was studied. The mean age at surgery was 26 years. Three fourths of the patients were symptomatic at the time of operation.

The 30-year actuarial survival rate for those who were operated on was 74% compared with 85% for age- and sex-matched controls. Perioperative mortality was 3.3% in this series. Long-term survival was compromised only for patients who were aged 25 years and older at the time of surgery. Late cardiac events occurred in 57% of patients at least aged 25 years at operation but in only 15% of patients aged 24 years or younger at operation (table). Apart from age, pulmonary artery systolic pressure was a significant independent predictor of long-term survival. Late heart failure, stroke, and atrial fibrillation all occurred more often in older patients. Atrial fibrillation/flutter persisted in 13 of 19 patients after operation. Of 104 patients in sinus rhythm preoperatively, 77% remained in sinus rhythm during long-term follow-up.

Patients operated on for atrial septal defect before age 25 years have an excellent outlook. Ivalon sponge no longer is considered suitable for patch closure of atrial septal defects. All patients should be monitored for late atrial arrhythmia.

▶ Dr. Dan G. McNamara, Professor of Pediatrics, and Emeritus Chief, Pediatric Cardiology Section, Baylor College of Medicine, comments:

▶ This long-term follow-up of patients after surgical closure of isolated atrial septal defect confirms the need to correct this anomaly during childhood or ad-

Summary of Late Cardiac Events According to Age
at Operation

EVENT	≤24 YR (N = 62)	>24 YR (N = 61)
Stroke	0	8
Transient ischemic attacks	0	2
Heart failure	2	15
Complete heart block	0	2
Implantation of permanent pacemaker	2	3
Valvular heart surgery	1	1
Reoperation for atrial septal defect	1	0
Myocardial infarction	0	4
Infective endocarditis	2	0
Pericarditis	1	0
Total	9	35
	(15%)	(57%)

(Courtesy of Murphy JG, Gersh BJ, McGoon MD, et al: *N Engl J Med* 323:1645–1650, 1990.)

olescence. Pediatric heart centers have recognized and promoted nationwide adherence to this principle.

The authors compared early (30 days) and late (27–32 years) mortality and morbidity with 2 variables: age at operation (for 123 patients) and presence or absence of preoperative elevation of pulmonary artery pressure ($\geq$40 mm Hg peak systolic pressure in 101 patients).

There were no perioperative deaths among patients 2–11 years and 12–24 years, and at 27 years follow-up, there were no differences in longevity compared with age- and sex-matched controls in the general population. In patients 25–40 years and 40–62 years, however, there were 4 perioperative deaths, and 27-year survival rates were only 80% for the 25–40 year age group compared with 91% for controls and 40% in the 41–62 year age group compared with 59% in controls.

When repair was performed in older patients, both fatal and nonfatal cardiac events occurred in 57% compared with 15% in younger patients.

The size of the left to right shunt was the same in all age groups and was unrelated to pulmonary artery pressure. Thus, early and late survival and morbidity are not solely explained by pulmonary hypertension. Rather, age alone is the more important independent predictor of outcome. Although pediatricians have no role in managing the adult patient with atrial septal defect, pediatricians do have a responsibility to try to identify this anomaly in their patients, and when the defect is suspected should encourage the parents to obtain definitive evaluation followed by surgical repair well before the child becomes an adult.

The 2 tasks that this reviewer proposes are not always very easy to accomplish, however. The diagnosis of atrial septal defect is often first made in the adult. The murmur is usually rather faint in the child, but close attention to the second heart sound reveals noticeable wide splitting. In most patients growth is normal, and subjective exercise tolerance is usually unaffected until adulthood.

Parents and some physicians are often understandably reluctant to agree to open-heart surgery in a healthy-appearing asymptomatic child, but an awareness of the invariably progressive and irreversible deterioration in cardiac function beginning in early adult life should clarify the need for a preventive medicine approach to correct management of this common defect.—D.G. McNamara, M.D.

Congenital Brain Anomalies Associated With the Hypoplastic Left Heart Syndrome

Glauser TA, Rorke LB, Weinberg PM, Clancy RR (The Children's Hosp of Philadelphia; Univ of Pennsylvania, Philadelphia)
Pediatrics 85:984–990, 1990   12–14

Palliative cardiovascular surgery has offered hope for long-term survival for infants with the hypoplastic left heart syndrome (HLHS), a congenital disease that was previously considered a uniformly fatal condition. To define the nature and incidence of coincident developmental and acquired neuropathology with this disorder, the medical records and postmortem reports of 41 infants with HLHS seen during a 52-month period were reviewed to define the type, frequency, and clinical presentation of the developmental brain anomalies in these infants. The mean patient age at death was 31 days.

Overall, 29% of infants had either a major or minor CNS abnormality. There were overt CNS malformations in 4 (10%) infants, including holoprosencephaly in 1 and agenesis of the corpus callosum in 3. Micrencephaly, defined as brain weight at autopsy more than 2 SDs below the mean for age, occurred in 9 (27%) infants, and 8 (21%) had cortical mantle malformations. There were clinically apparent dysmorphic features in 17 (41%) infants, and 7 had recognizable patterns of malforma-

Patterns of Malformation Recognized
in Infants With Hypoplastic Left
Heart Syndrome

Malformation Pattern	No. of Cases
Holt-Oram	1
Smith-Lemli-Optiz	1
VATER association	1
Monosomy X	2
Trisomy 18	2

Abbreviation: VATER, vertebral defects-anal atresia-tracheoesophageal fistula with esophageal atresia-radial and renal dysplasia.
(Courtesy of Glauser TA, Rorke LB, Weinberg PM, et al: *Pediatrics* 85:984–990, 1990.)

tion (table). The absence of dysmorphic features did not preclude overt or subtle CNS malformations, but the presence of dysmorphic features also did not indicate an underlying brain anomaly reliably. The incidence of micrencephaly was significantly greater in infants with HLHS as 1 of multiple malformations compared with those in whom HLHS was an isolated abnormality. Among infants with HLHS with no recognizable malformation, the occurrence of developmental neuropathology was more likely among those who were small for gestational age, microcephalic, or had ocular abnormalities. Major or minor CNS anomalies are relatively common in infants with HLHS. These infants deserve careful genetic, opthalmologic, and neurologic evaluations, imaging studies of the intracranial anatomy, and long-term neurologic follow-up.

▶ Dr. Jackie Noonan, Professor and Chairman, Department of Pediatrics, University of Kentucky, and Chief of Pediatric Cardiology, Chandler Medical Center, comments:

▶ The high incidence of developmental brain anomalies associated with HLHS reported by these authors is in sharp contrast to a previous clinical study reporting a low incidence of extracardiac anomalies (12%) in such infants (1). This study, however, is retrospective and limited to those infants who underwent a complete postmortem examination. The ascertainment bias introduced is quite striking. Prospective studies have always shown a definite male predominance in HLHS (2/3 male and 1/3 female). In this study, 22 of the 41 infants were female, and 80% of those with developmental neuropathology were female. In a previous postmortem study from the same institution (2), 23 (28%) of 83 patients with HLHS had a chromosomal abnormality, mendelian dominant disorder, or a major extracardiac abnormality. Of these 23 infants, 15 were female. Of interest is the relatively high incidence of Turner syndrome among females with HLHS. Future studies should look more critically at the specific anatomical defects present in relation to extracardiac anomalies. Aortic valve atresia, the most common form of HLHS, has a strong male preponderance, whereas mitral atresia with a patent aortic valve is of equal sex distribution. The underlying pathogenesis and cause involved in HLHS may differ among the various anatomical types of HLHS.

This study would suggest that infants with a recognizable pattern of malformations are more likely to undergo a complete postmortem examination than the typical male infant whose cardiac lesion has been well defined by cardiac ultrasound, and who has no other obvious extracardiac malformation. This study also clearly suggests that a female with HLHS requires a careful evaluation for associated defects, including a karyotype. Careful physical examination, including measurement of head circumference, should be done in all infants, and any infant with congenital heart disease should be suspect for associated extracardiac anomalies.—J. Noonan, M.D.

References

1. Greenwood RD, et al: *Pediatrics* 55:485, 1975.
2. Natowicz M, et al: *Pediatrics* 82:698, 1988.

Use of Cholesterol Measurements in Childhood for the Prediction of Adult Hypercholesterolemia: The Muscatine Study

Lauer RM, Clarke WR (Univ of Iowa)
JAMA 264:3034–3038, 1990   12–15

Whether screening for cholesterol in school-aged children predicts those who, as adults, will require continued surveillance or intervention was investigated in a cohort of 2,367 children aged 8–18 years. The group was evaluated on several occasions and followed to ages 20–30 years. The criterion serum cholesterol level, suggested by the National Cholesterol Education Program as the lowest prompting surveillance and intervention in adults, was 200 mg/dL.

Among those children whose cholesterol levels were above the 75th percentile on at least 2 occasions, 75% of the girls and 56% of the boys failed to qualify for intervention as adults. Of those having levels exceeding the 90th percentile, 57% of girls and 30% of boys still failed to qualify.

Screening based on multiple estimates of total serum cholesterol in children yields an inaccurate classification of significant numbers of children with respect to adult cholesterol levels. General screening of all children should be approached cautiously, because data on the costs, risks, and benefits of intervention strategies to be used in children remain unavailable. Many individuals who have high cholesterol levels as children have normal levels as young adults, even without intervention.

▶ Dr. Louis A. Barness, Professor of Pediatrics, University of Wisconsin, Madison, the master of things that go into infant's and children's stomachs, comments:

▶ The studies of Lauer and Clarke are important data for the basis of the recommendations of the National Cholesterol Education Program for Children and Adolescents. One recommendation that has raised controversy is that cholesterol screening be limited to those children and adolescents with a family history of atherosclerotic events or high serum cholesterol levels.

Even so eminent a statistician as Frank Oski objects to this recommendation, because only about 50% of those children and adolescents with elevated serum cholesterol will be identified. Unappreciated, however, are a number of overriding factors supporting the committee recommendation.

As indicated by Lauer and Clarke, tracking of serum cholesterol levels is relatively poor—not nearly as good as tracking of blood pressure levels. Other factors include the rarity of atherosclerotic events in the first 2 or 3 decades of life, the expected lowering of cholesterol levels for the population when the recommended diet limiting fat to 30% of the calories is followed, the potential harm from improperly labeling children "at risk," and the greater importance of detecting those with a genetic predisposition for atherosclerosis. Also considered were the expense of universal screening, technical errors in determinations, and the limited experience in the use of cholesterol-lowering drugs in children.—L.A. Barness, M.D.

Sudden Death in Young Competitive Athletes: Clinicopathologic Correlations in 22 Cases

Corrado D, Thiene G, Nava A, Rossi L, Pennelli N (Univ of Padua, Italy)
Am J Med 89:588–596, 1990   12–16

Clinicopathologic studies of the pathologic substrates of sudden death in youth are rare. Underlying disease is usually a clinically silent cardiovascular disorder that might not have been diagnosed or even suspected.

Twenty-two sudden deaths in northern Italy that occurred between 1979 and 1989 were studied by postmortem assessment. The 19 male and 3 female athletes were aged 11–35 years. Sudden death occurred during or just after a competitive activity in 18 cases. In 10, sudden death was the first indication of an underlying problem. Death was the result of arrhythmic cardiac arrest in 17 athletes, with right ventricular cardiomyopathy (also called "right ventricular dysplasia") being found most often, followed by atherosclerotic coronary artery disease, conduction system pathology, anomalous origin of right coronary artery from the wrong aortic sinus, and mitral valve prolapse.

Sudden death was attributable to "mechanical" causes in 2 patients; 1 had a pulmonary embolism and 1 had an aortic rupture. In 3 athletes the cause of death was cerebral. All of those with right ventricular cardiomyopathy died during competitive activity. Most had a history of palpitations or syncope, or both. Available ECG tracings revealed inverted T waves in precordial leads or left bundle-branch block ventricular arrhythmias, or both.

In this area in northern Italy right ventricular cardiomyopathy is not so rare among the cardiovascular diseases associated with the risk of arrhythmic cardiac arrest. It appears to account for most cases of sudden death in young athletes. Prodromal symptoms and ECG signs can alert physicians to the possibility of this disorder.

▶ This report is of 18 cases of sudden death occurring during or immediately following a sporting activity. The most common abnormality found at autopsy was cardiomyopathy followed closely by atherosclerotic coronary artery disease. A patient here or there had a conduction system disease, an anomalous right coronary artery, or mitral valve prolapse. There were deaths from pulmonary embolism, rupture of the aorta, and cerebrovascular accident.

Because cardiomyopathy was discussed earlier in this chapter, what follows is a brief overview of what is going on in the world of fat, the second most common cause of sudden death in the athlete (atherosclerosis). See how well you can answer the next series of questions about dietary fat.

First, is it necessary to remove the skin from a chicken before it is cooked to reduce the content of fat in the final preparation? To rephrase the question, although a chicken is not a migratory bird, does the fat in a chicken's skin migrate into the meat when you cook it?

The answer to this question is actually fairly straightforward. It is certainly not a paltry (poultry) question. Most individuals, even those who need to be on a low fat diet, would indicate their preference to see their chicken with the skin on when it is served. Is it okay to serve this way and simply remove the skin at the table, then eat the chicken? There is no significant difference in the fat content of chicken cooked with or without the skin on (1). Thus, even though you can't have your skin and eat it too, you can certainly cook your chicken fully clothed and visually enjoy it, however temporarily, before it is skinned and ingested.

Second question: What is Methuselah gene?

No one knows for sure, but Helen Boley may have it. She made the front page of the *Wall Street Journal* on Friday, April 5, 1991. The *Wall Street Journal* doesn't always only report financial news. It reports news of importance in other arenas as well. In any event, Helen Boley, a petite 61-year-old, is thought to be the only person on record who was born with 2 copies of what now is known as the "Methuselah gene." Scientists have been in search of the Methuselah gene ever since the first description of the biblical patriarch who was said to have lived more than 900 years. As far as can be determined, Mrs. Boley inherited the gene for long life from her mother and a second copy of the same gene from her father. Evidence of Mrs. Boley's Methuselah genes lies in her cholesterol level, which she had done for routine cholesterol screening. Her high density lipoprotein fraction of cholesterol (the protective variety) was 200 mg/dL. Half that level would have most of us cashing in our life insurance policies as being unnecessary. The dangerous form of cholesterol (LDL) in Mrs. Boley was a mere 100 mg/dL. Mrs. Boley's family all lived to ripe old ages except her father, who died of colon cancer at 64.

Third question: Which of the following 2 methods will extract cholesterol from meat: cooking it and draining off excess fat or subjecting the meat to meticulous trimming?

The answer is neither. Almost all the cholesterol is in the muscle-cell membranes within the meat and very little is in the "fat" itself. On the other hand, triglyceride in meat is principally in fat cells interspersed between muscle cells of meat. For this reason, it is extremely difficult to extract the cholesterol from meat simply by cooking it and draining off the excess fat. Meticulous trimming will get rid of some triglyceride but does little to lessen cholesterol. Don't give up hope, however, if you're a meat lover. Chemistry has entered the kitchen. If you take raw ground beef, pork, lamb, or poultry and cook it in vegetable oil heated to 195° F, the vegetable oil will penetrate into the meat and replace saturated fat with the unsaturated fat of the vegetable oil. This reduces the cholesterol content of cell membranes by over 50%. If you heat the mixture to a slightly higher temperature for a few additional minutes (230° F, 5 minutes) to brown the meat, you can pour off the oil. Then simply rinse the meat in boiling water and voila, you have low cholesterol ground meat with a good flavor, which can be used in spaghetti, sauces, chili, meat loaf, or soups. Don't expect it to look or taste like a T-bone steak, however (2). Jeff Smith, if you're reading this commentary, you are free to abstract the above for your next *Frugal Gourmet* cookbook.

The last question is: Name the actor and the movie in which the star jumps to the top of the prison camp pecking order by winning a bet to eat 50 eggs in 1 hour.

That was Paul Newman in the 1967 film, *Cool Hand Luke*. As noble a feat as that was, this past year, an 88-year-old man was described who for more than 15 years had eaten 25 eggs a day with no known side effects. He was fit and healthy physically. The way he got away with this was studied extensively (3). This man somehow had a body that absorbed only 18% of dietary cholesterol, a body that produced half of the endogenous cholesterol that we synthesize, and produced bile acids that sopped up manyfold the cholesterol of the rest of you and me. Where he got the money to buy 25 eggs a day at age 88 is beyond me given the price of dairy products these days. This gentlemen certainly had a lot to crow about.—J.A. Stockman, III, M.D.

References

1. Dieleman L, et al: *N Engl J Med* 323:759, 1990.
2. Small DB, et al: *N Engl J Med* 324:73, 1991.
3. Kern F: *N Engl J Med* 324:896, 1991.

The Upper Limit of Physiologic Cardiac Hypertrophy in Highly Trained Elite Athletes

Pelliccia A, Maron BJ, Spataro A, Proschan MA, Spirito P (Comitato Olimpico Nazionale Italiano, Rome; Natl Heart, Lung, and Blood Inst, Bethesda, Md)

N Engl J Med 324:295–301, 1991   12–17

In "athlete's heart," the increase in the thickness of the left ventricular wall is usually mild. However, it may be more marked in some athletes, creating a diagnostic problem for clinicians trying to distinguish the physiologic hypertrophy of the athlete's heart from pathologic forms of hypertrophy (e.g., hypertrophic cardiomyopathy). This distinction is important because most cases of sudden death in athletes are probably attributable to hypertrophic cardiomyopathy. Left ventricular dimensions were measured echocardiographically in a large group of highly trained athletes.

The 947 elite athletes studied participated in a wide variety of sports. The thickest left ventricular wall measured was 16 mm. Wall thicknesses in the range suggestive of hypertrophic cardiomyopathy—13 mm or greater—were found in only 16 athletes, or 1.7%. Fifteen of these athletes were rowers or canoeists, and 1 was a cyclist. Therefore, the incidence of wall thicknesses of 13 mm or greater was 7% among rowers, canoeists, and cyclists. None of the 728 participants in 22 other sports had thicknesses in this range.

Left ventricular wall thicknesses of 13 mm or greater are very uncommon in highly trained athletes and appear to be virtually confined to athletes training in rowing sports. These thicknesses are also associated with an enlarged left ventricular cavity. The upper limit to which the wall thickness may be increased by athletic training appears to be 16 mm. Athletes with greater thicknesses and a nondilated left ventricular cavity are likely to have primary forms of pathologic hypertrophy.

▶ This is an interesting study. An athlete who exercises vigorously and regularly will have an increase in the thickness of the ventricular wall. Although this thickness is usually mild, it may be more substantial in some athletes and may actually create the diagnostic problem of distinguishing the physiologic hypertrophy of the athlete's heart from the pathologic form of hypertrophy seen with hypertrophic cardiomyopathy. The latter disease in an athlete can lead to sudden death, so this is important in differential diagnosis.

To examine this question, the study abstracted above looked at a population of 1,000 elite athletes who had trained over long periods, the majority of whom had attained international recognition for their athletic prowess. Among these 1,000 athletes, the thickest left ventricular wall measured was 16 mm. Wall thickness within a range compatible with the diagnosis of hypertrophic cardiomyopathy (≥13 mm) was seen in only 16 subjects (1.7%). Of these, 15 were rowers or canoeists, and 1 was a cyclist. The wall was equal to or greater than 13 mm thick in 7% of 219 rowers, canoeists, and cyclists but in none of 728 participants in 22 other sports. On the basis of these data, it was concluded that a left ventricular wall thickness equal to or greater than 13 mm is very uncommon in highly trained athletes and is virtually always confined to athletes training in rowing sports. In the latter group of individuals, the upper limit of normal must now be raised to 16 mm. Therefore, athletes with a ventricular wall thickness of more than 16 mm are likely to have primary forms of pathologic hypertrophy, such as hypertrophic cardiomyopathy.

In these days of fine sailboats and motorboats, it strikes this editor that rowers and canoeists must be nuts. Then again, I never worry about these fine athletes reproducing their exercise gene. For the jocks among you, recognize that tightly fitting athletic supporters can reduce the number of ejaculated sperm by almost 90%. I consider this the 1,299th reason not to exercise.—J.A. Stockman, III, M.D.

13 Blood

Effects of Intravascular, Intrauterine Transfusion on Prenatal and Postnatal Hemolysis and Erythropoiesis in Severe Fetal Isoimmunization
Millard DD, Gidding SS, Socol ML, MacGregor SN, Dooley SL, Ney JA, Stockman JA III (Northwestern Univ)
J Pediatr 117:447–454, 1990
13–1

The hematologic course of isoimmunized fetuses was studied to evaluate the effects of intravascular, intrauterine transfusion (IUT) on prenatal hemolysis and erythropoiesis and postnatal anemia in this condition. Serial determinations of hemoglobin, Kleihauer-Betke stains to detect fetal hemoglobin-containing erythrocytes, and plasma erythropoietin (EPO) measurements were made prenatally, at birth, and postnatally in 12 isoimmunized fetuses treated with IUT. Sensitizing antibody titer and reticulocyte count were also measured in 5 fetuses. The mean gestational age at first IUT was 26 weeks.

Before the first IUT, before the final IUT, and at birth, mean values for hemoglobin were 6.1, 9.1, and 11.3 g/dL, respectively. Reticulocyte counts were 22.7%, .5%, and .9%; fetal hemoglobin-containing erythrocyte levels were 100%, 1.6%, and 1.5%; and EPO levels were 12, 56, and 756 mU/mL, respectively. All but 1 fetus, who died in utero, were born by cesarean section at a mean gestational age of 35 weeks. Only 1 infant required exchange transfusion. Postnatally, all 10 surviving infants became profoundly anemic, and all but 1 required simple blood transfusions. Before the first postnatal blood transfusion, mean hemoglobin concentration was 6.2 g/dL, mean reticulocyte count was .8%, mean EPO level was 23 mU/mL, and sensitizing antibody titer remained markedly elevated. The EPO levels increased in the fetus or neonate only when hemoglobin levels fell below 5 g/dL.

Intravascular transfusions in isoimmunized fetuses partially correct fetal anemia, suppress fetal erythropoiesis, and thereby decrease fetal hemolysis. Postnatally, these infants have progressive, often prolonged anemia. The absence of reticulocytosis, relatively low EPO level, and elevated titers of sensitizing antibody typically persist for months. The intrauterine and postnatal anemia in isoimmunized fetuses treated with IUT may be attributable to both hemolysis of newly formed erythrocytes by circulating antibody and suppressed erythropoiesis.

▶ The first 3 articles selected for inclusion in this chapter in one way or another have to do with erythropoietin. This abstract delineates what happens before delivery and in the first 2 to 3 months of life in infants who are affected with erythroblastosis fetalis.

Multiple blood samples were obtained from these infants before birth as part of the routine management of Rh incompatability. What was seen was that, quantitatively, these fetuses did not produce the markedly elevated levels of erythropoietin that would be seen in children and adults with the same low levels of hemoglobin. Thus, in utero, the fetuses were not compensating for the hemolytic anemia they were experiencing. Almost all of these infants received intrauterine transfusions. Because of this, when they were born there were no sensitized cells to cause hyperbilirubinemia, and the infants, of course, did not require exchange transfusion. Infants such as these may require multiple booster transfusions over the first 4 to 8 weeks of life and sometimes longer. It has been assumed that the reason they require such booster transfusions is that the high level of anti-D antibody in these infants (remember that they have not had it removed by exchange transfusion) eliminates any new red blood cells they make that contain the D antigen. What this study shows is that during the first few months of life, these infants do not respond with appropriate levels of erythropoietin when they become anemic. This suggests that these infants might be candidates for the administration of recombinant erythropoietin, and this is currently under investigation.

The ability to sample blood from the umbilical cord of infants has revolutionized the diagnosis and management of scores of disorders. Pericutaneous umbilical blood sampling requires a very seasoned obstetrician, one who is willing to have a large number of patients referred to him or her and who has enough patience to sit at the opening of a spinal needle as it is guided ultrasonically to the umbilical cord in utero. Specially trained obstetricians seem to make this fairly routine these days. The wife of a friend of mine, an obstetrician who does this kind of work, told me that she asked her husband over dinner what his day was like. He simply commented that he had a busy day at the orifice (of the needle, that is).

The article that follows deals with the status of recombinant erythropoietin as part of the management of the anemia of prematurity.—J.A. Stockman, III, M.D.

Effects of Recombinant Human Erythropoietin in Infants With the Anemia of Prematurity: A Pilot Study
Halpérin DS, Wacker P, Lacourt G, Félix M, Babel J-F, Aapro M, Wyss M (Hôpital Cantonal Universitaire, Geneva, Switzerland)
J Pediatr 116:779–786, 1990   13–2

Anemia of prematurity is characterized by reduced bone marrow erythropoietic activity and low serum erythropoietin (Epo) levels. Because bone marrow and circulating erythroid progenitors in premature infants display normal proliferation and differentiation in vitro in the presence of recombinant human erythropoietin (rHuEpo), a clinical trial was undertaken to stimulate endogenous Epo production in infants with anemia of prematurity and thereby provide a new therapeutic alternative to the otherwise potentially hazardous Epo transfusions. Starting at 21–33 days of life, 7 infants with anemia of prematurity received rHuEpo in doses of 75 to 300 U/kg/wk for 4 weeks. All patients received elemental iron and vitamin E oral supplements.

Baseline serum Epo level was low in all patients (mean, 9.9 mU/mL). After rHuEpo therapy, the number of reticulocytes increased significantly from a mean baseline count of 75×10^9/L to 165×10^9/L on day 14 of treatment. Six patients had correction or stabilization of anemia, with an estimated increase in total erythrocyte volume of 49% during therapy vs. a predicted increment of 18% in the absence of rHuEpo. One patient showed a decline in hematocrit level during treatment. Three of the responders showed a secondary fall in hematocrit level during or after therapy was discontinued. Serum iron and ferritin levels decreased rapidly during therapy. A transient early thrombocytosis and a slight decline in absolute neutrophil count was seen in most patients. Treatment was well tolerated.

Recombinant human erythropoietin treatment may correct or stabilize anemia of prematurity, but its effects may be limited by a variety of factors that include iron availability. Controlled clinical trials are warranted to confirm this limited but encouraging experience.

Recombinant Human Erythropoietin for a Jehovah's Witness With Anemia of Thermal Injury

Boshkov LK, Tredget EE, Janowska-Wieczorek A (Univ of Alberta Hosp; the Canadian Red Cross Blood Transfusion Service, Edmonton, Alberta)
Am J Hematol 37:53–54, 1991   13–3

Recovery from extensive burns is often accompanied by moderate to severe anemia. Burn victims frequently need many red cell transfusions. Recombinant human erythropoietin was used in a burn victim who refused blood transfusion.

Man, 52, was hospitalized with a burn injury on his hands and face and inhalation injury. His hemoglobin was 15.4 g/dL and his hematocrit was .45 on admission. He had split-thickness skin grafting of both hands on the second day. Eight days after the injury, his hemoglobin was 8 and his hematocrit was .24. An additional 4-unit blood loss was anticipated from facial grafting. The patient, however, was a Jehovah's Witness and refused blood transfusion. He had an inappropriately low reticulocyte count at .007%. His serum iron, total iron-binding capacity, and saturation were also decreased. Human recombinant erythropoietin was given intravenously on day 10 at 300 U/kg daily for 7 days, then at 150 U/kg 3 times a week for 3 weeks. This therapy produced a tenfold rise in reticulocyte response and a rise in hemoglobin from 7.4 to 10.4 g/dL over 12 days. The patient also had a marked improvement in clinical status, with a resolution of confusion and improved wound healing. Bone marrow studies on day 10 of treatment showed the presence of iron and erythroid hyperplasia. Split-thickness skin grafting of the face was done 14 days after treatment was initiated. Although the patient's hemoglobin dropped from 10.4 to 7.4 g/dL after the procedure, it rose to 10.1 over the next 14 days of recombinant human erythropoietin therapy. At this time, the patient was discharged.

The use of recombinant human erythropoietin markedly improved this patient's clinical condition, permitting earlier grafting, improved wound healing, and earlier discharge from the hospital. Despite elevated endogenous erythropoietin levels, the patient was reticulocytopenic.

▶ This is the last in the triology of reports on recombinant erythropoietin. The use of recombinant erythropoietin for a Jehovah's Witness who has a sluggish ability to make his own blood would seem almost heaven sent. Patients with thermal injuries frequently become anemic to the point of requiring blood, and they often have an inability to manufacture red cells. This problem can be over-driven by the administration of recombinant erythropoietin.

There are many applications for the use of recombinant erythropoietin. It can be used to correct the anemia of patients with AIDS who are on drugs such as azidovudine (1) and it is ideal for the anemia of malignancy (2). One of its most important usages relates to helping an individual increase the amount of blood he or she can electively donate for their own surgery. Autologous blood transfusion has increased more than tenfold in the last 3 years (3). This practice is now widely endorsed for 2 reasons: the patient's blood is the safest blood, and blood procured in anticipation of elective surgery will add to the national blood inventory. I bet you weren't familiar with the fact that 1 unit of self-donated blood can be procured from a patient every 72 hours until 72 hours before surgery, as long as the patient's hematocrit remains equal to or greater than 33% (American Association of Blood Banks Standard). Iron supplements must be given, even if the patient is not iron deficient. Thus, many units of self-donated blood can be procured over an interval of up to 42 days, which is currently the maximum storage interval for liquid blood. If you want to go beyond that point, the blood can be frozen and stored for years.

So how does recombinant erythropoietin relate to self-donations of blood? If recombinant erythropoietin is administered to you while you are donating your own blood, you can donate 41% more red blood cells, even though you may donate exactly the same number of units of blood. In other words, erythropoietin helps to keep your hemoglobin up when you are attempting to donate a number of units quickly (4).

The applications for use of recombinant erythropoietin continue to expand. It's still not too late to buy some stock in its manufacturer.—J.A. Stockman, III, M.D.

References

1. Fischl M, et al: *N Engl J Med* 322:1488, 1990.
2. Ludwig H, et al: *N Engl J Med* 322:1693, 1990.
3. Goodnough LT, et al: *Vox Sang* 601:1, 1990.
4. Goodnough LT: *Trans Med Rev* 4:228, 1990.

Vitamin C Deficiency in Patients With Sickle Cell Anemia
Chiu D, Vichinsky E, Ho S-L, Liu T, Lubin BH (Children's Hosp Oakland Research Inst, Oakland, Calif; San Francisco State Univ)
Am J Pediatr Hematol Oncol 12:262–267, 1990   13–4

Deficiency of fat- and water-soluble antioxidants could be a determinant in the pathogenesis of sickle cell disease, and peroxidative damage to red cell membranes may contribute to the pathophysiology of the disease. The authors previously reported a deficiency of vitamin E in patients with sickle cell disease. Because vitamin C, a water-soluble antioxidant, may have a major role in regeneration of vitamin E, vitamin C deficiency in sickle cell disease was examined. The antioxidant systems in sickle cell patients and possible causes of vitamin E deficiency were also analyzed.

Leukocyte vitamin C, which reflects total body reserve, was measured by a modified 2,4-dinitrophenylhydrazine method. Hemoglobin levels and white blood cell (WBC) counts were also taken. Decreased leukocyte vitamin C in the cellular antioxidant systems was found in 50% of 18 patients with sickle cell anemia. None of the 12 control patients showed vitamin C deficiency. Patient age was not a factor. A statistically significant correlation was found between leukocyte vitamin C levels ($r = -.62$) and serum ferritin concentration ($.01 < p \le .025$). No correlation was found between leukocyte vitamin C levels and either hemoglobin concentration or WBC count.

Increased use may be a factor in vitamin C deficiency in patients with sickle cell disease. Vitamin E deficiency and peroxidative stress, both reported in patients with sickle cell disease, may be related to vitamin C deficiency. The patient's hypermetabolic state may also be a factor. Low tissue vitamin C levels (less than .08 mM) greatly enhance microsomal lipid peroxidation. The enhanced peroxidative stress may in turn cause a decrease in vitamin C levels, creating a vicious circle. The mechanisms of vitamin C deficiency and the pathophysiologic consequences remain to be established.

▶ Dr. Alan Cohen, Associate Professor of Pediatrics, University of Pennsylvania School of Medicine, and Attending Hematologist, the Children's Hospital of Philadelphia, comments:

▶ The 500-year-old story of vitamin C has not lacked drama. In 1498, shortly after his fleet of 4 ships rounded the southern tip of Africa, Vasco daGama wrote that "many of our men fell ill here, their feet and hands swelling, and their gums growing over their teeth so that they could not eat." Fortunately, daGama's crew shortly encountered 2 Moorish trading boats, and after buying oranges, "it pleased God in his mercy that . . . all our sick recovered their health. . . ."

In 1747, James Lind, a surgeon on the H.M.S. Salisbury, conducted what has been described as the first controlled trial in clinical nutrition. In the face of an outbreak of scurvy during a cruise in the English Channel, he divided 12 affected sailors into 6 treatment groups. Maintaining a similar basic diet for all subjects, Lind gave 2 sailors oranges and lemons for 6 days. The remaining sailors received such tasty concoctions as half a pint of sea water a day (group 3) or a medicinal paste made from nutmeg, garlic, mustard seed, a Peruvian tree resin, radish root, and gum myrrh (group 6). With no formal statistical analysis (after all, the numbers were small) Lind concluded that "oranges and lemons were the most effectual remedies for this distemper at sea."

In 1976, the Nobel laureate Linus Pauling concluded from his studies that, "there is a continually increasing body of evidence that the optimum intake of vitamin C decreases both the morbidity and mortality with heart disease, cerebrovascular disease, and cancer, as well as infectious diseases in general." He predicted that increased intake of vitamin C would extend life expectancy by 12 to 18 years. In contrast to the few oranges and lemons eaten by Lind's subjects, Pauling himself took 12 grams of vitamin C a day when well and 40 grams a day at the first sign of a cold.

These are tough acts to follow. The vitamin C saga continues to unfold, however, frequently at a finer level of investigation. The study by Chiu et al. illustrates the role of vitamin C as a multifaceted biological co-factor. The low level of vitamin C found by these investigators in some patients with sickle cell disease is strongly correlated with increased iron stores and probably results in part from the catalytic effect of the excessive iron. Low vitamin C levels may, in turn, reduce the antioxidant capabilities of the red cell, augmenting the oxidative damage to the erythrocyte membrane and perhaps contributing to the pathophysiology of sickle cell disease. This study may lack the religiousness of daGama, the drama of Lind, and the assuredness of Pauling, but it is another important step in understanding the biological role of vitamin C and its possible relationship to a wide variety of human diseases.—A. Cohen, M.D.

Outpatient Management of Febrile Illness in Infants and Young Children With Sickle Cell Anemia

Rogers ZR, Morrison RA, Vedro DA, Buchanan GR (Univ of Texas, Dallas; Children's Med Ctr, Dallas)
J Pediatr 117:736–739, 1990   13–5

Because of the potential for a fulminant course, febrile illness in young children with sickle cell anemia is treated promptly with parenteral antibiotics and usually requires hospitalization. A 36-month study evaluated the effectiveness, safety, and cost-effectiveness of outpatient management of febrile children with sickle cell anemia. The children were managed according to a standardized protocol.

The protocol calls for a prompt evaluation by a physician, complete blood cell count and blood culture, and intravenous dose of ceftriaxone or cefuroxime before any test results are available. The decision to continue outpatient treatment or to hospitalize the patient is individualized based on the child's age and apparent toxic appearance, height of the fever, changes from steady-state hematologic values, recent compliance with prophylactic penicillin therapy, and parental ability to return if the child's condition should deteriorate. All discharged patients were given oral antibiotics.

A total of 211 visits were made by 74 febrile children younger than age 5 years with homozygous sickle cell disease or sickle cell β^+-thalassemia disease. In 76 visits (36%) patients were admitted to the hospital and in 135 visits (64%) patients were managed on an outpatient basis. Parenteral ceftriaxone was given to 168 children, and cefuroxime was given in

Temperature (° C)	Patients	Episodes by age category* 0-12 Mo	13-24 Mo	25-60 Mo	Patients admitted (%)
38.0-38.9	81	12/34	4/23	5/24	26
39.0-39.9	59	11/18	6/20	9/21	44
40.0-40.9	27	4/6	10/16	1/5	56
>41.0	1	1/1	—	—	100

Initial Temperature, Age, and Disposition

*Number of patients admitted/total number of study patients in each age group.
(Courtesy of Rogers ZR, Morrison RA, Vedro DA, et al: *J Pediatr* 117:736–739, 1990.)

30. Only 6 of 210 initial blood samples (2.9%) grew pathogenic organisms, including *Streptococcus pneumoniae* in 4 cases. *Haemophieus influenzae* in 1, and *Salmonella* group D in 1. These children with bacteremia were aged 14 to 23 months. All had markedly elevated temperatures and were admitted because of a clinical impression of sepsis. No growth was evident on blood drawn 12 to 24 hours after the initial dose of ceftriaxone.

More than half of the children with an initial temperature of greater than 39° C were safely managed as outpatients (table). There was only 1 death during the study. Cost analysis showed that outpatient management resulted in a minimal saving of $1,200 per febrile event.

Outpatient management of selected infants and young children with sicke cell anemia and fever is believed to be a safe, effective, and economical alternative to routine hospitalization. Multi-institutional prospective studies following a similar protocol will be needed to define the limits of this approach.

Usefulness of Red Cell Distribution Width in Association With Biological Parameters in an Epidemiological Survey of Iron Deficiency in Children

Mahu JL, Leclercq C, Suquet JP (Hôp Bichat, Paris)
Int J Epidemiol 19:646–654, 1990   13–6

The red blood cell distribution width (RDW) is a quantitative measure of red blood cell anisocytosis that can be readily obtained on automated hematology counters. Although some studies have shown its diagnostic usefulness in detection of iron deficiency, the RDW is not usually used in epidemiologic investigations. Using a Technicon model H-6000 counter, the diagnostic usefulness of RDW in iron deficiency, in association with usual biochemical and hematologic parameters of iron status, was studied in a representative sample population of 384 children, aged 6 months to 6 years. The Pearson correlation coefficients and specificity and sensitivity of RDW were tested comparatively with the more traditional parameters of iron status, including serum ferritin (Fri), total iron-binding capacity (TIBC), serum iron (SI), transferrin saturation (TSat), free erythrocyte protoporphyrin (FEP), mean corpuscular hemoglobin concentra-

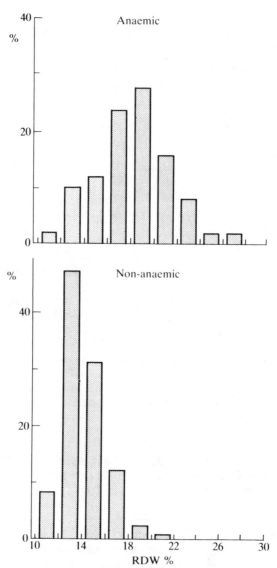

Fig 13–1.—Histogram of RDW values in anemic (Hb < 11 g/dL; n = 52) and nonanemic (n = 329) children. (Courtesy of Mahu JL, Leclercq C, Suquet JP: *Int J Epidemiol* 19:646–654, 1990.)

tion (MCHC), mean corpuscular hemoglobin (MCH), mean corpuscular volume (MCV), and hemoglobin concentration (Hb).

The prevalence of anemia (Hb<11 g/dL) was 13.6%. The Pearson correlation coefficient for iron storage parameters (Fri) and circulating iron parameters (SI, TSat, TIBC) were greater with RDW, MCV, and MCH than with Hb. The distribution of RDW was significantly different between anemic children and nonanemic children, and the mean RDW was significantly higher in anemic children (20.2% vs. 16.1%) (Fig 13–1). In addition to RDW of 18%, other hematologic parameters used as iron deficiency criteria were MCV < 70 fl, MCH < 22 pg, MCHC < 32%, FEP > 35 μg/dL whole blood, TIBC > 85 μmol/L, TSat < 10%, and Fri < 12 μg/L. The combination of sensitivity and specificity was best for RDW and worst for MCHC. These data suggest that the use of RDW in association with traditional parameters of iron status in epidemiologic studies would be worthwhile.

▶ These authors went to great lengths to show that the RDW works as a tool in the detection of iron deficiency. To quote from their article: "Statistical analysis was carried out using Pearson correlation coefficients, variance analysis, Duncan's multiple-range test, chi-square test, and Fisher's chi-square exact test."

I know about chi and Fisher, but I thought Pearson was a syndrome, and Duncan made donuts. This kind of statistical analysis seems to be overkill when attempting to prove a point. Red cells, when they become iron deficient, develop anisocytosis and poikilocytosis. They vary in size and shape and that increases the red cell distribution width when using electronic counting equipment. It's as simple as that. In my book, the RDW (although complimentary to things like hemoglobin concentration and MCV) alone is one of the very best screening tests for iron-deficiency anemia. No questions asked.—J.A. Stockman, III, M.D.

Lead Poisoning and Thalassemia Trait or Iron Deficiency: The Value of the Red Blood Cell Distribution Width
Bhambhani K, Aronow R (Children's Hosp of Michigan, Detroit; Wayne State Univ)
Am J Dis Child 144:1231–1233, 1990   13–7

The red blood cell (RBC) distribution width (RDW) is a quantitative measure of RBC size variation or anisocytosis that is readily measurable with automated electronic particle counters. Reports have suggested that microcytosis and anemia occur less often in childhood lead poisoning uncomplicated by iron deficiency or thalassemia trait. The cause of microcytosis and anemia was investigated using RDW in 21 consecutive patients with lead poisoning, who were aged 15 months to 8.5 years, and in 7 nonrandomly selected patients with iron-deficiency anemia and lead poisoning.

Based on mean corpuscular volume (MCV), 10 children had normal MCV levels (>72 fL), and all had RDWs in the normal range (<15). The other 11 patients had microcytosis (MCV, <72 fL). The thalassemia trait (α or β) was found in 9 children; 1 had both a thalassemia trait and iron deficiency, and 1 had iron deficiency. The RDW was less than 17 (range, 13.6–16.6) in patients with the thalassemia trait and more than 17 (range, 19–25.1) in patients with iron deficiency. Hence, including the 7 additional patients with iron deficiency and lead poisoning, the mean

RDW in all 9 patients with iron deficiency was 19.3 (range, 17.7–25.1). These data confirm previous reports that microcytosis in children with lead poisoning is not caused by lead, but rather by a coexistent iron deficiency or thalassemia trait. The RDW is a valuable and rapid procedure to assess the cause of microcytosis in childhood lead poisoning. Iron deficiency is most likely to occur in patients with an RDW greater than 17.

▶ The data from this study confirm the information provided by the preceding abstract. Patients who are found to have lead poisoning (most are picked up by elevations in free erythrocyte porphyrin screening tests) who also have an elevated RDW, are quite likely to be iron deficient. It has been known for a long time that the most common cause of microcytic anemia in association with lead poisoning is not lead poisoning but rather iron deficiency.

On the topic of lead, can you answer the following question: Your Aunt Matilda dies, leaving you her Steuben glass collection. Is it safe to store your prized brandy in the lovely crystal decanter that you have just inherited?

The answer to this question is certainly yes, assuming you don't drink the brandy. Such crystal is made with high concentrations of lead. Lead compounds, when added to molten quartz, yield a glass with high density and durability and a special brilliance. Most lead crystal vessels now contain as much as 24%–32% lead oxide. In a recent report from New York City, Dr. Joseph Graziano was curious about whether or not leaded decanters and glasses would be a source of lead exposure for individuals drinking from them (1). He found that alcoholic beverages stored in crystal decanters steadily increase in lead concentration over time, and spirits kept in decanters for a long time may achieve lead concentrations comparable to those in the notorious sweetened wines of Roman times. In case you have forgotten, the Romans added lead salts to wine to make it sweeter. Brandy stored in a leaded crystal decanter for 5 years has 21,530 μg/L of lead that has been leeched from the glass. The U.S. Environmental Protection Agency maximum allowable lead level in drinking water is 50 μg/L, which is currently being decreased to a more stringent 20 μg/L or less.

The above data produce an interesting paradox. Infrequent drinking from such a decanter would result in a rare but large dose of lead. Frequent drinking would result in repeated smaller doses because presumably one would empty the decanter and refill it fairly quickly. If all of this weren't bad enough, if you pour wine into a crystal wine goblet, lead begins to leech from the crystal within minutes.

As intriguing as all these data are, those who enjoy fine brandy and the crystal containers that hold the brandy are likely to hazard the risk of lead poisoning. Much of the rest of the world merely has to worry about the lead solder in their old stock of Budweiser cans.—J.A. Stockman, III, M.D.

Reference

1. Graziano J: *Lancet* 337:141, 1991.

Hereditary Spherocytosis Associated With Deletion of Human Erythrocyte Ankyrin Gene on Chromosome 8

Lux SE, Tse WT, Menninger JC, John KM, Harris P, Shalev O, Chilcote RR, Marchesi SL, Watkins PC, Bennett V, McIntosh S, Collins FS, Francke U, Ward DC, Forget BG (Harvard Med School; Yale Univ; Univ of California, Irvine; Integrated Genetics, Inc, Framingham, Mass; Duke Univ)

Nature 345:736–739, 1990   13–8

In studies of families with hereditary spherocytosis (HS) and balanced translocations involving chromosomes 8 and 12, the *SPH2* locus has been mapped to chromosome 8p. Other studies suggest that *SPH2* represents ankyrin. Genomic DNA from 2 unrelated HS patients with chromosome 8 deletions were hybridized to probes for erythrocyte ankyrin and the anion exchanger AE1 to test this possibility.

The ratio of ankyrin signal to AE1 signal was approximately .5 in both children. It was thought that the children had 1 deleted ankyrin gene, because AE1 was likely to be a single-copy gene. This also strongly suggested that ankyrin was encoded at the *SPH2* locus. The ankyrin gene's position, in terms of the chromosome's fractional length relative to the terminus of the short arm (FLpter), corresponded to band 8p11.2. Examination of lymphoblastoid cells showed only one hybridization signal per cell, in both metaphase spreads and interphase nuclei. Thus, only one copy of the ankyrin gene was present. Two hybridization signals were seen in control cells. On cohybridization with probes for both ankyrin and c-*myc*, c-*myc* was found on both chromosomes 8, but ankyrin was found on only one. The red cells of the affected children were deficient in ankyrin, with lesser deficiencies of spectrin and protein 4.2.

The human erythrocyte ankyrin gene appears to be located at chromosome 8p11.2, most likely at *SPH2*. In HS patients with involvement of *SPH2*, ankyrin, spectrin, and protein 4.2, deficiencies probably cause the spherocytosis and hemolysis. More typical HS patients have lesser deficiencies of spectrin and ankyrin.

▶ I bet that you want an English translation of what you have just read in this abstract. Well, here it comes.

Hereditary spherocytosis is a relatively common hemolytic anemia. It is thought to be caused by a deficiency or dysfunction of spectrin, ankyrin, and/or possibly other membrane proteins. By word of a little more clarification, the inner side of the human red blood cell membrane is laminated (literally held together) by a protein network. Spectrin is 1 of the very necessary proteins that "glues the red cell membrane together." Spectrin itself has to be held in place by another protein. Things that hold things in place frequently are called anchors. The protein that anchors spectrin is called "ankyrin." It is almost as simple as that.

Spectrin deficiency has been found to be the most common abnormality in hereditary spherocytosis (1). In some patients, the spectrin deficiency may be the result of a deficiency or dysfunction of ankyrin, which is not able to hold spectrin appropriately in place. Have you ever heard of the disorder known as hereditary pyropoikilocytosis? That is a hereditary hemolytic anemia in which the red blood cells are very misshapen, and they become markedly more abnormal when the blood is heated in a laboratory (hence its name, "pyro–"). That disorder is characterized by a partial deficiency of spectrin, and in this disorder the spectrin itself is abnormally structured. In the common type of hereditary elliptocystosis, the molecular defect involves a spectrin dysfunction, similar to hereditary pyropoikilocystosis. In hereditary elliptocystosis, however, the cells contain near or near-normal amounts of spectrin.

So there you have it. As Lux et al. noted in the above article, we even know the chromosome on which the gene exists for the production of ankyrin. Some individuals with hereditary spherocytosis have it on the basis of a deletion in the gene that encodes for ankyrin on chromosome 8.

If all of this seems fairly sophisticated, it is. However, anything that is caused by a chromosomal deletion may ultimately have a molecular biologic cure in the not too distant future. If you care for or are participating in the care of someone with hereditary spherocytosis, stay tuned to the story as it evolves.—J.A. Stockman, III, M.D.

Reference

1. Liu S–C, et al. *Blood* 76:198, 1990.

Variable Clinical Severity of Hereditary Spherocytosis: Relation to Erythrocytic Spectrin Concentration, Osmotic Fragility, and Autohemolysis
Eber SW, Armbrust R, Schröter W (Univ Hosp of Göttingen, Germany)
J Pediatr 117:409–416, 1990   13–9

Hereditary spherocytosis is the most common erythrocyte membrane defect. Clinical symptoms are variable, making differential diagnosis difficult. Quantitative laboratory criteria were developed on the basis of clinical history, hematologic data, autohemolysis, and osmotic fragility.

The clinical characteristics of 80 patients (63 children and 27 healthy relatives) were evaluated. Routine hematologic determinations were made, and osmotic fragility, autohemolysis, erythrocyte spectrin content, and erythrocyte membrane lipid phosphorus were measured and correlated with disease severity. Four categories emerged (table). The first category is spherocytosis as a trait in symptom-free relatives of patients with recessively inherited disease. Mild (category 2) and moderate (category 3) spherocytosis are observed largely in patients with dominantly inherited disease. Severe spherocytosis (category 4), characterized by recessive inheritance and transfusion dependence, was found in 2 patients. The erythrocyte spectrin concentration was normal in carriers and in patients with mild spherocytosis but was significantly reduced in the moderate to severe states of the disease.

Splenectomy may be performed to avoid decreased vitality, formation of gallstones, and severe hemolytic and aplastic crises that require transfusions. Patients with mild spherocytosis do not require splenectomy dur-

Classification of Spherocytosis and Indications for Splenectomy

Classification	Trait	Mild spherocytosis	Moderate spherocytosis	Severe spherocytosis*
Hemoglobin (gm/L)	Normal with relation to age	110-150	80-120	60-80
Reticulocyte counts (%)	≤3	3.1-6	≥6	≥10
Bilirubin (μmol/L)	≤17	17-34	≥34	≥51
Reticulocyte production index	<1.8	1.8-3	>3	
Spectrin per erythrocyte† (% of normal)	100	80-100	50-80	40-60
Osmotic fragility				
Fresh blood	Normal	Normal to slightly increased	Distinctly increased	Distinctly increased
Incubated blood	Slightly increased	Distinctly increased	Distinctly increased	Distinctly increased
Autohemolysis				
Without glucose (%)	<10	≥10	≥10	≥10
Correctability (%)	>60	>60	0-80	50
Splenectomy	Not necessary	Usually not necessary during childhood and adolescence	Necessary during school age before puberty	Necessary, possibly not before yr 3 of life

*Value before transfusion.
†Normal (mean ± SD): $226 \pm 54 \times 10^3$ molecules per cell.
(Courtesy of Eber SW, Armbrust R, Schröter W: *J Pediatr* 117:409–416, 1990.)

ing childhood and adolescence. Splenectomy should be done for patients with moderate to severe spherocytosis. Most patients with less than 80% of normal spectrin content require splenectomy.

Prolonged Survival in Patients With Beta-Thalassemia Major Treated With Deferoxamine

Ehlers KH, Giardina PJ, Lesser ML, Engle MA, Hilgartner MW (New York Hosp—Cornell Med Ctr, New York; North Shore Univ Hosp, Manhassett, NY)
J Pediatr 118:540–545, 1991   13–10

Despite advances in the understanding and treatment of β-thalassemia major, most persons with this disease remain transfusion dependent. Since the 1960s, these patients have been treated with a chelation program to reduce the iron burden. Whether this painful, cumbersome, and costly process prolongs life has not been established definitively. The effect of hypertransfusion and chelation with deferoxamine on length of survival was investigated using the Kaplan-Meier product limit method to analyze longevity.

Seventy-one patients treated between 1960 and 1976 received a low-transfusion regimen and no chelation. Those patients had an estimated median age of survival of 17.4 years. Eighty patients beginning hypertransfusion between 1976 and 1978 and chelation with deferoxamine survived to a median age of 31 years. Data on 70 patients treated with hypertransfusion and deferoxamine were available to calculate the ratio of total milligrams of transfusional iron to cumulative grams of deferoxamine. The 24 patients who died had a total iron burden greater than 1.05 g/kg, and a ratio exceeding 31. Those patients had poor compliance with chelation or a late start of treatment, with an inability to receive enough deferoxamine before they died. Arrhythmia requiring treatment preceded death in all but 1 patient, as did cardiac failure. Of 41 similarly iron-loaded survivors, 33 had a ratio of less than 31. Only 3 of those patients had an arrhythmia, and 5 had cardiac failure (Fig 13–2).

Hypertransfusion and chelation with deferoxamine appear to prolong survival in patients with thalassemia major. In this series, compliance with deferoxamine chelation was a significant factor in delaying cardiac complications and death. Patients who adhere to a vigorous program of chelation may enjoy a longer, symptom-free life.

▶ Last year we commented on the potential role of bone marrow transplantation as part of the treatment of transfusion-dependent homozygous β-thalassemia. We also mentioned the increasing understanding we have of oral iron chelators. In the last year, however, not many children have undergone bone marrow transplantation for this condition, presumably because of the relative risks of the procedure vs. the potential of many years of well being that these children now have. There is very little to note in terms of progress with respect to oral iron chelators either.

This is not to say that there is not some good news. Ehlers et al. have clearly

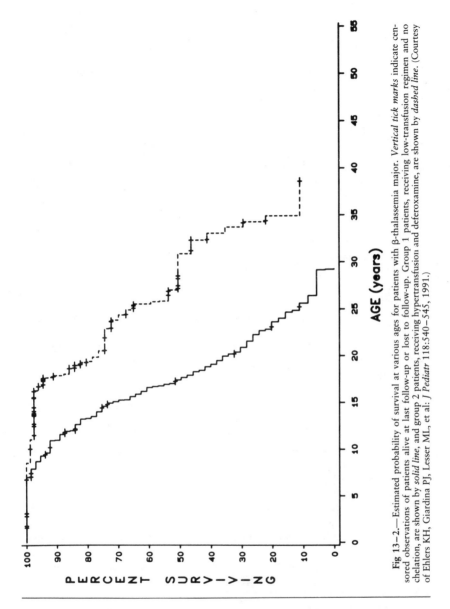

Fig 13–2.—Estimated probability of survival at various ages for patients with β-thalassemia major. *Vertical tick marks* indicate censored observations of patients alive at last follow-up or lost to follow-up. Group 1 patients, receiving low-transfusion regimen and no chelation, are shown by *solid line,* and group 2 patients, receiving hypertransfusion and deferoxamine, are shown by *dashed line.* (Courtesy of Ehlers KH, Giardina PJ, Lesser ML, et al: *J Pediatr* 118:540–545, 1991.)

documented that the life span of a patient with homozygous β-thalassemia has approximately doubled in the last 30 years. In the days before deferoxamine, the longest that someone with thalassemia major was likely to survive was the mid to late teens. Now, survivorship to an average age in the fourth decade of life is to be expected if the patient is compliant with the rigorous therapy needed. Furthermore, if iron chelation therapy is begun early in life (10 years or younger), there is a 90% chance that a patient with β-thalassemia major will develop normal gonadal function and sexual development (1). In the 1960s it was unheard of for a transfusion-dependent individual with thalassemia to progress through puberty with normal sexual maturation.

The longer life span and greater overall "normality" of patients with thalassemia major occurs at a price. That price is the daily subcutaneous administration of deferoxamine. This drug can affect vision and hearing and can cause certain other problems as well. Sometime in the next century, I am quite certain that people in medicine will be looking at what we are doing right now and chuckling a little bit about how primitively and indirectly we dealt with disorders such as transfusion-dependent thalassemia. Well, we're doing the best we can.—J.A. Stockman, III, M.D.

Reference

1. Bronspiegel-Weintrob N, et al: *N Engl J Med* 323:713, 1990.

The Epidemiology and Clinical Aspects of the Hemolytic Uremic Syndrome in Minnesota

Martin DL, MacDonald KL, White KE, Soler JT, Osterholm MT (Minnesota Dept of Health, Minneapolis)
N Engl J Med 323:1161–1167, 1990
                                        13–11

The frequency of hemolytic uremic syndrome appears to be increasing; however, few population-based studies have documented this trend. A retrospective population-based study of hemolytic uremic syndrome was conducted on residents of Minnesota under the age of 18 from 1979 through 1988. The study evaluated the frequency of disease occurrence, clinical illness, and predictors of disease severity and outcome. Investigators also examined risk factors in a case-control study. With identifying information from 170 hospitals, investigators reviewed medical records of all patients less than 18 years old with a diagnosis of hemolytic uremic syndrome. Death records were also reviewed.

Investigators identified 117 patients with hemolytic uremic syndrome. There was a mean annual increase in incidence from .5/100,000 child-years in 1979 to 2.0/100,000 child-years in 1988. *Escherichia coli* 0157:H7 was identified in 13 of 28 stool specimens. In patients with typical hemolytic uremic syndrome, elevated polymorphonuclear leukocyte counts at hospital admission, a shorter prodromal period, and bloody diarrhea were predictive of severe disease (table). The case-control study found that children who attended large day care centers were more likely to have the syndrome that those who did not. Though day-care attendance might be a risk factor, the population-attributable risk suggests that day care could account for no more than 16% of cases. Four children died, yielding a fatality rate of 3.4%.

Hemolytic uremic syndrome and *E. coli* 0157:H7 infection are becoming important clinical and public health problems. This syndrome is associated with considerable morbidity, and its incidence is increasing, particularly in young children. Some cases may be prevented by early recognition of *E. coli* 0157:H7 infection and by public warnings against serving

Symptoms of 117 Patients With Hemolytic Uremic
Syndrome in Minnesota, 1979 Through 1988

SYMPTOM	NO. OF PATIENTS (%)
Diarrhea	101 (86)
Vomiting	88 (75)
Bloody diarrhea	69 (59)
Abdominal cramps	60 (51)
Fever	57 (49)
Respiratory symptoms	22 (19)
Lethargy	21 (18)
Seizures	20 (17)
Pallor	17 (14)

(Courtesy of Martin DL, MacDonald KL, White KE, et al: *N Engl J Med* 323:1161–1167, 1990.)

raw milk or undercooked hamburger to young children. At present, only 2 states require reporting of hemolytic uremic syndrome. Other states should consider requiring this as an index of *E. coli* 0157:H7 infection to monitor trends in occurrence of disease and to identify outbreaks quickly.

Treatment of Aplastic Anemia With Antilymphocyte Globulin and Methylprednisolone With or Without Cyclosporine

Frickhofen N, Kaltwasser JP, Schrezenmeier H, Raghavachar A, Vogt HG, Herrmann F, Freund M, Meusers P, Salama A, Heimpel H, German Aplastic Anemia Study Group (Univ of Ulm, Ulm, Germany)
N Engl J Med 324:1297–1304, 1991   13–12

After bone marrow transplantation, immunosuppression is the best treatment for aplastic anemia. Antilymphocyte globulin or cyclosporine are most effective. Although patients have been successfully treated with combinations of these agents, no controlled study of such combination therapy has been published. The results of treatment with antilymphocyte globulin and methylprednisolone with or without cyclosporine were evaluated.

Eighty-four patients not eligible for bone marrow transplantation were enrolled in the randomized, multicenter trial. Forty-one patients received antilymphocyte globulin and methylprednisolone, and 43 patients received these agents plus cyclosporine. Significantly more patients in the cyclosporine group had a complete or partial remission at 3 months (65%) than patients who did not receive cyclosporine (39%). At 6 months, 70% and 46%, respectively, had a complete or partial remission. Patients with severe or very severe aplastic anemia benefited most from the regimen that included cyclosporine. At 6 months, 65% of these patients had a response to treatment compared with 31% of such patients who did not receive cyclosporine. Granulocyte and hemoglobin levels normalized in most responders, but platelet counts remained subnormal in 61% of the patients. Ten of 52 responders—3 in the cyclosporine group and 7 in the other group—had a relapse 4–37 months after therapy. The actuarial survival of all patients receiving cyclosporine and all patients not receiving cyclosporine was 64% and 58%, respectively. Among those with severe or very severe disease, survival was 80% and 44%, respectively. The side effects of cyclosporine were substantial but reversible.

Patients with aplastic anemia seem to respond better to a combination of cyclosporine, antilymphocyte globulin, and methylprednisolone than to antilymphocyte globulin and methylprednisolone alone. The difference in response is most apparent among patients with severe disease who responded at a rate nearly twice that of patients not given cyclosporine.

▶ Dr. Bruce M. Camitta, Professor of Pediatrics, Medical College of Wisconsin, comments:

▶ Acquired aplastic anemia results from damage to pluripotent hematopoietic stem cells. The defect (deficit) can be cured by allogeneic marrow transplantation in 70%–80% of children and young adults. However, only 25%–30% of affected individuals have a matched, related donor.

Autoimmune marrow suppressive phenomena are present at diagnosis in half of patients with aplastic anemia. This does not prove causality, however, nor does response to immunosuppressive drugs, because these agents may have other nonspecific effects (mitogenicity, release of colony-stimulating factors, or stem cell toxicity).

Antilymphocyte globulin alone improves the hematologic status of 50%–70% of patients with aplastic anemia. Responses to cyclosporine of corticosteroids alone are less frequent (approximately 25%). The study of Frickhofen et al. suggests that adding cyclosporine increases the response rate to antilymphocyte globulin plus corticosteroid therapy. However, several caveats are in order (1). Responses to immunosuppressive therapy are usually incomplete. Most patients have residual hematologic deficits and decreased marrow reserve (2). Late relapses of aplasia may occur in 10%–30% of patients. Several patients in the current study remain dependent on cyclosporine (3). Follow-up is still somewhat short. Significant survival differences after 3–5 years would be more reassuring (4). Finally, other authors report that 10%–40% of patients with aplastic anemia may eventually develop paroxysmal nocturnal hemoglobinuria, myelodysplastic syndromes, or acute nonlymphocytic leukemia. This may reflect further damage to defective stem cells.

Immunosuppressive therapy currently has an important role in the treatment of patients with aplastic anemia. However, we should not be lulled into complacency by favorable initial responses. In the words of Lawrence Peter Berra, "It ain't over til it's over."—B.M. Camitta, M.D.

A Controlled Trial of Interferon Gamma to Prevent Infection in Chronic Granulomatous Disease

Gallin JI, Malech HL, Weening RS, Curnutte JT, Quie PG, Jaffe HS, Ezekowitz RAB, (Internatl Chronic Granulomatous Disease Cooperative Study Group)
N Engl J Med 324:509–516, 1991   13–13

In chronic granulomatous disease, an uncommon inherited disorder of phagocytes, defective production of the reactive intermediates of oxygen predisposes patients to recurrent, severe pyogenic infections. In vitro and in vivo studies have shown that interferon-γ may partly correct the metabolic defect in phagocytes. The effectiveness of interferon-γ in reducing the frequency of serious infections associated with chronic granulomatous disease was studied in 128 patients enrolled in a randomized, double-blind, placebo-controlled trial. The median age was 15 years.

Interferon-γ, 50 μg/m², or placebo was given subcutaneously 3 times a week for as long as 1 year. Fourteen of the 63 patients given interferon had at least 1 serious infection, compared with 30 of the 65 given placebo. Twenty serious infections occurred in the interferon group, compared with 56 in the placebo group. Interferon proved beneficial regardless of patient age, use or nonuse of prophylactic antibiotics, and mode of inheritance of disease. However, measures of superoxide production by phagocytes did not change significantly. Patients tolerated interferon well, with no signs of serious toxicity.

Interferon-γ is effective and safe for patients with chronic granulomatous disease. The drug substantially reduces the frequency of serious infections. Interferon-γ should be given to patients with chronic granulomatous disease as prophylaxis against infections, either alone or, preferably, with prophylactic antibiotics.

Hematologic Manifestations in Pediatric HIV Infection: Severe Anemia as a Prognostic Factor

Ellaurie M, Burns ER, Rubinstein A (Albert Einstein College of Medicine, Bronx, NY)
Am J Pediatr Hematol Oncol 12:449–453, 1990   13–14

Adult HIV infection results in a broad spectrum of pathologic conditions, including widespread damage to the hematopoietic system. A longitudinal study was undertaken to assess the hematologic manifestations of HIV infection in a large cohort of children.

The hematologic profiles of 100 children with HIV infection were compared with those of uninfected infants who had transplacentally acquired maternal anti-HIV antibodies and with those of HIV-negative infants born to intravenous drug-abusing, HIV-uninfected mothers (table). Anemia was present in 94% of the HIV-infected infants and was a major predictor of disease progression. In 91% of those with a hematocrit less than 25%, the course of the disease was rapidly fatal. Leukopenia occurred in 47% and thrombocytopenia occurred in 33% of HIV-infected children. Children with opportunistic infections had the most severe neutropenia.

Main Hematologic Abnormalities in Childhood HIV Disease

	Group A * (N = 100) %	Group B † (N = 22) %	Group C ‡ (N = 25) %
Anemia	94	31	32
Leukopenia	47	22	12
ANC <1500/mm³	41	23	12
ANC <1000/mm³	20	9	0
Lymphopenia	36	0	0
Thrombocytopenia	33	0	8
Pancytopenia	10	0	0

Abbreviations: ANC, absolute neutrophil count.
*HIV-infected children.
†HIV-uninfected infants born to an HIV-infected mother.
‡HIV-infected infants born to HIV-uninfected intravenous drug-abusing mothers.
(Courtesy of Ellaurie M, Burns ER, Rubinstein A: *Am J Pediatr Hematol Oncol* 12:449–453, 1990.)

No evidence of suppression of any component of hematopoiesis by passively acquired antibodies to HIV could be found.

Hematopoietic aberrations in HIV-infected children appear to be more frequent and severe than those in adults. Hematologic manifestations in pediatric HIV disease may be caused by viral interference with fetal hematopoiesis.

▶ Acquired immune deficiency disease, which is transmitted by blood, is caused by a virus that produces a very complex secondary set of hematologic problems in and of itself. Specifically, it causes anemia, neutropenia, and thrombocytopenia.

Far and away, anemia is the most frequent hematologic manifestation of HIV infection in children. Ninety-four percent of all HIV-infected children are anemic. Although a third of these patients have red cell antibodies, the pathophysiology of the anemia is most consistent with the anemia of chronic infection.

The neutropenia of HIV is seen in just under half of infected children. Fortunately, the counts do not fall to so dramatically low levels as to be a significant risk for bacterial infection. The mechanism of the neutropenia in HIV-infected children is not known.

Thrombocytopenia can be a major source of difficulty in babies and children with HIV. It is often the first sign of the infection. For this reason, if you are doing viral titers as part of the workup of someone that you think has an autoimmune thrombocytopenia, add HIV to the list of viral causes (along with EBV, CMV, etc.). During the course of HIV infection, elevated levels of platelet-associated IgG and/or circulating immune complexes are seen, which shorten platelet survival to the point at which the patient can no longer maintain normal platelet counts.

The management of the anemia of HIV is expectant. In those few patients in whom transfusions might be thought necessary, recombinant erythropoietin will usually suffice (see the earlier commentary on this topic in this chapter). The neutropenia of HIV generally requires no therapy. The thrombocytopenia, however, can be quite problematic and is managed in the same way that the thrombocytopenia of any autoimmune variety is treated.

Most of us think that hematology consists of 4 things: red cells, white cells, platelets, and clotting. Very little is known about the clotting aspect of HIV, at least until recently. Patients with HIV infection have normal routine clotting screening tests. They do, however, have physical problems that would suggest a hypercoagulable state. For example, AIDS patients frequently develop a retinopathy very similar to the proliferative retinopathy seen in diabetics. On April 29 of this past year, at the annual meeting of the Association for Research in Vision and Ophthalmology in Sarasota, investigators from Northwestern University and Rush-Presbyterian-St. Luke's Medical Center in Chicago, using a test (thromboelastography), which measures the actual coagulation of whole blood, found that clotting activity was much faster and stronger in AIDS patients, perhaps partially accounting for some of the vascular disease that these patients develop.—J.A. Stockman, III, M.D.

Intravenous Anti-D Treatment of Immune Thrombocytopenic Purpura: Analysis of Efficacy, Toxicity, and Mechanism of Effect
Bussel JB, Graziano JN, Kimberly RP, Pahwa S, Aledort LM (New York Hosp; North Shore Hosp, Manhasset Long Island; Mount Sinai Med Center, New York)
Blood 77:1884–1893, 1991

13–15

Intravenous Anti-D has been used in the treatment of immune thrombocytopenic purpura (ITP). Exploration of the mechanism of Anti-D, however, has been limited. The clinical efficacy of intravenous Anti-D therapy and its mechanism of effect were studied in 43 Rh^+ patients with ITP who had not had splenectomy and 3 who had splenectomy.

Patients who did not undergo splenectomy had a mean platelet increase of 95,000/μL. Acute platelet responses were greater in children than in adults. Response was unaffected by HIV status and thrombocytopenia duration. Maintenance treatment was given as needed. The mean interval between infusions was 24 days. The patients who had undergone splenectomy had no platelet response at all. Infusions were completed in less than 5 minutes, and toxicity was minimal (Fig 13–3).

The effect of intravenous Anti-D treatment is apparently not limited to Fc receptor blockade, the generally accepted mechanism of Anti-D effect. There was no correlation of parameters of hemolysis with platelet increase. Also, there was a 48- to 72-hour delay before platelet increase. The change in monocyte Fc receptor I expression tended to correlate with platelet increase. The in vitro production of antibodies to sheep red blood cells was increased after intravenous Anti-D infusion.

In this series, children responded to treatment better than adults. Five of 14 children with chronic ITP could discontinue treatment at a mean 13 months. Patients with HIV infection responded as well as those with

IV ANTI-D FOR ITP

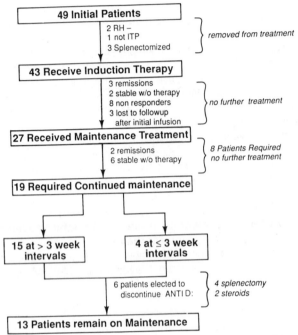

Fig 13–3.—Flow diagram showing outcome of the 49 patients who received intravenous Anti-D treatment. Six patients were removed from analysis (top of the figure), including 3 who had undergone splenectomy before treatment; 3 additional patients were lost to follow-up. In addition, patients did not receive maintenance for either of 2 reasons: sustained response to initial treatment or failure to respond to initial treatment. (Courtesy of Bussel JB, Graziano JN, Kimberly RP, et al: *Blood* 77:1884–1893, 1991.)

classic ITP. Toxicity was minimal. Evidence suggests that the FcR interactions of Anti-D-coated red blood cells may have immunomodulatory effects.

▶ One of the things that brings the most displeasure to a pediatric hematologist is the patient who fails to respond promptly or easily to treatment for ITP. In the past, the standard treatment of ITP included steroids followed by splenectomy if the patient did not get better within 6 months to a year. Now we can string these patients out for very long periods of time with intermittent high dose pulse steroids or the use of intravenous gamma globulin (IgG). The latter, which seems to be the treatment of choice these days for such patients, is quite expensive. What Bussel et al. hit on is a perfectly acceptable alternative for some of these patients. This is the use of Anti-D (that is the "D" as in Rhesus blood group, commercially available for prevention of Rh sensitization under the brand name of RhoGam). If you inject Rh positive patients who have ITP with Anti-D, there will be an increase in the platelet count in the majority of such patients. Part of the mechanism of action here could be that antibody-coated red blood cells are producing a reticuloendothelial (Fc) blockade. To say this differently, it's like putting maple syrup in the oil of your car engine—it gums everything up. This allows antibody-coated platelets to remain in the circulation. The beauty of using Anti-D is its cost effectiveness. Fifty bucks of Anti-D is roughly the equivalent of about $500–$1,000 worth of intravenous IgG.

Please don't rush out to your local supermarket (pharmacy) to order Anti-D for your patients with ITP. The only preparation of Anti-D in North America that can be administered intravenously is a Canadian product (WinRho), which is prepared by the Winnipeg Rh Institute of the University of Manitoba, Winnipeg, Canada. It is not licensed in the United States for use in anyone: not a pregnant woman, not a postpartum woman, and not a patient with ITP. It is only available on experimental protocol, at least at this writing. What we do have in the United States (RhoGam) is an intramuscular preparation, and it doesn't do anything for the patient with ITP except hurt when you administer it.—J.A. Stockman, III, M.D.

Estimation of the Risk of Thrombocytopenia in the Offspring of Pregnant Women With Presumed Immune Thrombocytopenic Purpura
Samuels P, Bussel JB, Braitman LE, Tomaski A, Druzin ML, Mennuti MT, Cines DB (Univ of Pennsylvania; Cornell Univ)
N Engl J Med 323:229–235, 1990   13–16

Clinicians still debate the optimal management of immune thrombocytopenic purpura (ITP) during pregnancy. The risk of severe neonatal thrombocytopenia remains uncertain. The risk of neonatal thrombocytopenia and hemorrhage in infants born to mothers with ITP or presumed ITP was estimated and whether or not platelet-antibody testing plus maternal history of the condition is useful in identifying neonates at risk for thrombocytopenia was determined by studying the index pregnancy outcome in 162 women.

Two maternal features predicted a low risk of severe neonatal thrombocytopenia: the absence of a history of ITP before pregnancy and the absence of circulating platelet antibodies in women with a history of the condition. Eighteen (20%) of the 88 neonates born to women with a history of ITP had severe thrombocytopenia, compared with 0 of the 74 infants born to women who first had thrombocytopenia during pregnancy. Eighteen (26%) of the 70 neonates born to women with a history of ITP with circulating platelet antibodies had severe thrombocytopenia. None of the infants born to women with a positive history but without circulating antibodies had this condition (Fig 13–4).

In this series, the risk of severe neonatal thrombocytopenia in infants born to women with no history of ITP before pregnancy and in infants whose mothers had a history of the condition but did not have circulating platelet antibodies was 0%. Thus, the absence of a history of this condition or the presence of negative results on circulating-antibody tests

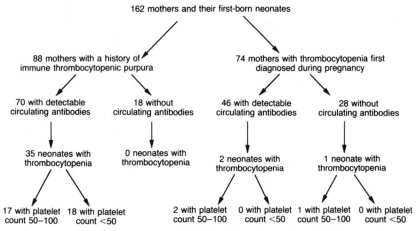

Figure 13–4.—Identification of high-risk and low-risk neonates in the study. The relation between the neonatal platelet counts after the index pregnancy, the maternal history, and the results of indirect antiglobulin tests in all 162 patients are shown. Platelet counts indicated are ×10⁻⁹/L. (Courtesy of Samuels P, Bussel JB, Braitman LE, et al: N Engl J Med 323:229–235, 1990.)

in pregnant women means that the risk of severe neonatal thrombocytopenia in their infants is minimal.

▶ The optimal care of pregnant women with ITP remains uncertain because there is a poor correlation between maternal and neonatal platelet counts. Additionally, there has been no noninvasive method to predict severe neonatal thrombocytopenia, which has led obstetricians to use fetal scalp sampling, percutaneous umbilical blood sampling, and delivery by cesarean section in women with ITP. If you believe these authors, if a women did not have ITP before she became pregnant, and if circulating platelet antibodies were not detectable, that woman's chances of having a significantly thrombocytopenic baby are zero. Are these data so convincing that all such pregnancies require no intrauterine blood sampling and no cesarean section? That leap of faith must be further explored, but it is certainly the $64 question. I hope that no baby's life will be lost if the authors' speculations are incorrect.—J.A. Stockman, III, M.D.

The Molecular Genetic Analysis of Hemophilia A: A Directed Search Strategy for the Detection of Point Mutations in the Human Factor VIII Gene
Pattinson JK, Millar DS, McVey JH, Grundy CB, Wieland K, Mibashan RS, Martinowitz U, Tan-Un K, Vidaud M, Goossens M, Sampietro M, Mannucci PM, Krawczak M, Reiss J, Zoll B, Whitmore D, Bowcock S, Wensley R, Ajani A, Mitchell V, Rizza C, Maia R, Winter P, Mayne EE, Schwartz M, Green PJ, Kakkar VV, Tuddenham EGD, Cooper DN (MRC Clinical Research Centre, Harrow, England; Thrombosis Research Inst, London)
Blood 76:2242–2248, 1990   13–17

It is important to characterize the point mutations occurring in the factor VIII gene of patients with hemophilia A not only to understand the basis of CpG hypermutability but also to relate the structure of the factor VIII protein to its function. A systematic screening technique was used to describe CpG sites in the factor VIII gene in DNA samples from patients with hemophilia A.

The DNA from blood samples from 793 unrelated patients with hemophilia A was isolated for investigation. A directed search strategy was used to screen for point mutations in 8 potentially hypermutable CpG dinucleotides at sites that were thought to be functionally important: codons-5; 336; 372; 427; 583; 795; 1,689; and 1,696. The DNA samples were amplified by polymerase chain reaction and screened by oligonucleotide hybridization.

Sixteen patients had point mutations that were consistent with a model of 5-methylcytosine (5mC) deamination. New recurrent mutations were shown at codon 336, CGA → TGA; 372, CGC → TGC; 372, CGC → CAC; and 1,689, CGC → TGC. The sites were thought to be important as cleavage sites for activated protein C or thrombin. The remaining arginine codons screened showed further novel C → T transitions, which resulted in the creation of TGA termination codons. Within and among different ethnic groups and CpG sites, differing mutation frequencies were demonstrated. The differences probably resulted from differing levels of cytosine methylation, though there is no direct evidence of this conclusion.

New examples of recurrent mutation of CpG dinucleotides have been found in the factor VIII gene that causes hemophilia A. These mutations are consistent with a model of 5mC deamination. If CpG mutability is shown to correlate with methylation status, then the methylation status of specific CpG sites in a given gene should be established before labor-intensive screening is done.

▶ The molecular genetics of hemophilia A are pretty complex, aren't they? If you made it through the first sentence of the abstract, you know 99.9% more information regarding hemophilia than most of the rest of the medical world. This abstract, as with the one on hereditary spherocytosis, requires some degree of explanation. Let's start with the basics and move up.

We know that hemophilia A is an X-linked bleeding disorder affecting about 1 in 5,000 males. It is caused by a deficiency of factor VIII, a cofactor in the activation of factor X by factor IXa. Hemophilia A has been maintained in the population by an equilibrium between a loss of defective factor VIII genes, because of the low reproductive fitness of some affected individuals, and the gain of new mutations. Thus, patients not known to be related usually carry different mutations. The search for the Holy Grail when it comes to hemophilia is finding out what all the point mutations are within the gene complex that encodes for the factor VIII molecule. The article abstracted is an exploration in search of a strategy to detect all of these point mutations. This is not an easy task for several reasons. The factor VIII molecule itself is one of the longer proteins of its sort (2,332 amino acids). The gene that makes the protein is large and complex. Because different families with hemophilia have different gene abnormalities within that complex that cause the hemophilia, the story becomes even more complex when attempting to translate molecular biologic information into medical care. For example, the enormous potential variety of mutations causing hemophilia, even though within a single gene, complicates DNA-based carrier and prenatal diagnosis, because no single useful DNA probe can be prepared to detect gene defects in all carriers and affected fetuses. For this reason, carrier and first trimester prenatal diagnosis has to be based on the tracking of defective genes within specific families by means of DNA markers situated either within or at some distance from the gene itself. This procedure provides very limited help to families of isolated cases (probably 50% of the total).

To overcome these difficulties, rapid procedures must be developed to detect mutations in all the essential regions of the factor VIII gene. So far, such developments have been hindered by the size and complexity of the gene. That is pretty much the message of the abstract above.

With all this complexity, it must seem a minor miracle that so large a gene has already been cloned and that a recombinant factor VIII product is currently being tested. The introduction in the mid-1960s of factor VIII concentrates was thought to represent a milestone in the management and treatment of hemophilia. With the transmission of hepatitis B, delta hepatitis, hepatitis C, and HIV, it turned out to be more of a death sentence for some patients than a milestone. The human recombinant anti-hemophiliac factor VIII, being a purely synthetic product, has none of these risks. In the first 107 patients studied, Schwartz et al. (1) found that this recombinant factor VIII worked as well as plasma-derived factor VIII. Furthermore, it did not cause the formation of factor VIII inhibitors to any greater extent than natural factor VIII. Obviously, this material will replace all preexisting products, no matter what its final cost.

In summary, there is a lot to be learned about the many, many genetic point mutations that can cause hemophilia. Soon, there will be an important new treatment product available. If you have to be born with hemophilia, now is a much better time than even 20 years ago.—J.A. Stockman, III, M.D.

Reference

1. Schwartz RS, et al: *N Engl J Med* 323:800, 1990.

Prevalence of Hepatitis C Virus Antibody in a Cohort of Hemophilia Patients
Brettler DB, Alter HJ, Dienstag JL, Forsberg AD, Levine PH (Med Ctr of Central Massachusetts-Mem, Worcester; Natl Insts of Health, Bethesda, Md; Massachusetts Gen Hosp, Boston; Harvard Med School)
Blood 76:254–256, 1990   13–18

Infections with transfusion-transmitted viruses were common among hemophilia patients before the introduction of viral-inactivated factor concentrates. Recently an assay for detection of antibody to hepatitis C virus (HCV) was developed.

To determine the prevalence of antibody to HCV, a group of 131 hemophiliacs with a median age of 25.8 years was studied. All but 2 of the patients had used factor concentrate that had not undergone viral inactivation. Serum samples were obtained from the patients and tested for the presence of an antibody to HCV (anti-HCV).

The overall prevalence of HCV antibody was 76.3%. The antibody was detected in 74% of 118 patients with hemophilia A and in 67% of 12 patients with hemophilia B. There was no significant difference between the anti-HCV negative and anti-HCV positive groups in age, amount of non–heat-treated factor concentrate used, or level of aminotransferase. There was, however, a positive association between HCV antibody and the presence of antibody to hepatitis B core antigen and antibody to HIV.

A subgroup of 31 patients was tested twice for HCV antibody at intervals of 35 to 71 months. Twenty-five of these patients were repeatedly seropositive, 4 were repeatedly seronegative, and 2 went from seropositive to seronegative.

The findings of this study confirm the high prevalence of HCV infection in patients with hemophilia and support the causative role of the virus in the development of chronic liver disease in these patients. To prevent new cases of HCV, plasma donors should be tested for anti-HCV. In addition, improved methods of viral inactivation must be developed.

▶ Soon after the introduction of pooled clotting factor concentrates in the late 1960s and early 1970s, a rise in the incidence of acute hepatitis in hemophiliacs was reported in the United States. This was initially called acute non-A, non-B hepatitis. Early on it was thought that the hepatic dysfunction caused by non-A, non-B hepatitis was mild and self-limiting. Later it became clear that in a substantial number of patients, the liver disease was severe and progressive, advancing to cirrhosis in many. Unfortunately, the whole picture became obscured by the advent of HIV into the equation in the early 1980s. Relatively recently it was shown that hepatitis C virus (HCV) was the major causative agent of parenterally transmitted non-A, non-B hepatitis. What this report does is to show how common hepatitis C infection is among heavily transfused hemophiliacs. The majority of these patients have had this virus transmitted to them, and many of them have chronic active hepatitis as a consequence.

The real trick in this whole story is how to prevent new cases of HCV infection for "virgin" hemophiliacs. The authors of this report suggest that improved methods of viral inactivation must be developed along with improved testing of plasma donors. The former is already being done, and so is the latter. These, together, are not in and of themselves likely to be the answer to the whole problem. No viral inactivation technique is foolproof. Furthermore, we now know that screening blood donors for HCV antibody, although helpful, misses a fair number of infectious donors. For example, Esteban (1), in a large study of 280 transfusion recipients, showed that screening of blood donors for anti-HCV antibody prevented only about half of the cases of transfusion-associated hepatitis. Presumably, there are HCV-infected individuals out there who remain seronegative for extended periods. They will be missed by such antibody screening. The next time you get a transfused unit of blood, if it's not your own, you stand a small risk of getting non-A, non-B hepatitis of the HCV variety, even though that unit of blood will have been HCV-antibody screened.

To summarize all of the above differently, keep in good health. Drive safely. If you can talk a blood bank into storing your own blood away frozen so that when you need it, it will be there, try. Just hope that when you do need that blood, you can stay alive long enough for it to thaw out. The bottom line here is pretty straightforward: Don't let anybody slip you a unit of blood unless it is absolutely, unequivocally indicated, and then only if you've been given the right of first refusal to donate to yourself.—J.A. Stockman, III, M.D.

Reference

1. Esteban JI: *N Engl J Med* 323:1107, 1990.

Assessment by Gene Amplification and Serological Markers of Transmission of HIV-1 From Hemophiliacs to Their Sexual Partners and Secondarily to Their Children
Hewlett IK, Laurian Y, Epstein J, Hawthorne CA, Ruta M, Allain J-P (Ctr for Biologics Evaluation and Research, Bethesda; Hôp Bicetre, Kremlin-Bicetre, France; Abbott Labs, North Chicago, Ill)
J AIDS 3:714–720, 1990
13–19

An increased risk of transmitting viruses, especially HIV-1 is a drawback to the use of plasma pools in preparing blood products for hemophiliacs. Serologic studies have suggested significant viral transmission from infected hemophiliacs to their sex partners. Serologic markers were used to examine the transmission of HIV-1 infection from men with hemophilia A to their female sex partners and secondarily to their children. The HIV genome was detected by the polymerase chain reaction (PCR).

Twenty-eight men with hemophilia participated in the study. Sixteen had used condoms irregularly or not at all. Five of 27 female sex partners were seropositive for HIV-1. Eleven others were seronegative but PCR positive. The findings were confirmed by examining serial serum samples and paired samples of DNA from serum and peripheral blood mononuclear cells. Infection, as detected by the PCR, was transmitted to 60% of exposed children, including 1 child of a seronegative but PCR-positive mother.

It appears that the HIV-1 genome can be transmitted without inducing active, persistent infection. Transmission can be prevented by safe sex practices, including the regular use of condoms. The mechanism of transmission and the potential pathogenicity of the transmitted viral genome remain uncertain.

▶ A distinct minority of sexually active hemophiliacs are HIV negative. This report clearly shows how easily these men infect their spouses and how the spouses can bear infected children. In this regard, the risk of transmission from a patient with hemophilia is no different than from an individual who is an HIV-infected drug addict. It's a shame to have to make this latter statement, but it is true. To date, there have been virtually no studies showing what the true impact is of being a husband and knowing that you have hemophilia and are HIV infected. Care providers will tell you to practice safe sex, which simply implies the use of condoms. If you were an infected hemophiliac, would you take that advice and remain sexually active? Would you recognize that, as a contraceptive, condoms are not 100% effective, so how could they be 100% effective in the prevention of HIV transmission? One can think of no more difficult decision that a hemophiliac has to make.

Two last comments about HIV infection. One has to do with the risks that medical house staff experience, and the other has to do with a recently described new mode of transmission of HIV.

The number of house staff who are potentially exposed to serious HIV contamination appears to be growing. Between January and March 1989, at 3 teaching hospitals: Moffitt, Long Hospital-San Francisco General Hospital, and the San Francisco Veteran's Hospital, a survey of internal medicine residents revealed that 36% recalled being exposed to blood from patients at high risk for having HIV infection. An additional 19% recalled an accidental exposure to documented HIV-infected blood. Approximately 80% of these exposures were needle-stick injuries, and the remainder were mucosal splashes (1). What is even more disturbing than the above statistics is the fact that 70% of needle-stick injuries recalled by subjects went unreported. The principle reasons for not reporting were time constraints, perception that the needle-stick injury did not represent a significant exposure, lack of knowledge about reporting mechanisms, and concern about confidentiality and professional discrimination. The latter sentence encompasses a multitude of professional failures on all of our parts when it comes to our genetic heritage, our residents.

Regarding a recent description of a new mode of transmission of HIV infection was the report of a truck driver from New Jersey who got his HIV by "gay bashing." This was an individual who denied homosexual exposure or intravenous drug abuse. He and his work colleagues, however, on weekends would go out "gay bashing." They sought out places frequented by gay men and systematically beat them. This particular man frequently recalled sustaining small lacerations on his hands while administering these beatings. During blood screening related to a routine application for life insurance, HIV seropositivity was found (2). The author of Exodus (Exodus 21:24) must have had this individual in mind when it was written, "Eye for an eye, tooth for a tooth, hand for a hand, foot for a foot."—J.A. Stockman, III, M.D.

References

1. Mangione CM, et al: *Am J Med* 90:85, 1991.
2. Carson P, et al: *Lancet* 337:731, 1991.

14 Oncology

Trends in Survival for Childhood Cancer in Britain Diagnosed 1971-85
Stiller CA, Bunch KJ (Univ of Oxford, Oxford, England)
Br J Cancer 62:806–815, 1990
14–1

To date, the only detailed analysis of childhood cancer survival rates using population-based data from England, Scotland, and Wales covered children registered during 1962–1970, with a brief addendum for 1971–1974. The survival rates were reviewed for children from these countries whose diagnoses were made between 1971 and 1985.

The series analyzed included more than 15,000 childhood cancers. Highly significant improvements in survival were noted for many major diagnostic groups. Between 1971–1973 and 1983–1985, the actuarial 5-year survival rate rose from 37% to 70% for children with acute lymphoblastic leukemia, from 4% to 26% for those with acute nonlymphoblastic leukemia, from 76% to 88% for those with Hodgkin's disease, from 22% to 70% for those with non-Hodgkin's lymphoma, from 61% to 72% for those with astrocytoma, and from 24% to 42% for medulloblastoma. Additionally, the actuarial 5-year survival rates increased from 15% to 43% for neuroblastoma, 58% to 79% for Wilms' tumor, 17% to 54% for osteosarcoma, 26% to 61% for rhabdomyosarcoma, 59% to 94% for malignant testicular germ-cell tumors, and 43% to 77% for malignant ovarian germ-cell tumors. The 2 main diagnostic groups for which there was no evidence of any trend were retinoblastoma and Ewing's sarcoma. Retinoblastoma already had an excellent prognosis, with a 5-year survival rate of more than 85%. For Ewing's sarcoma, the survival rate remained below 45%. For all groups except Hodgkin's disease, survival rates in Britain remained below those in the United States (table).

The increases observed in population-based survival rates for many major diagnostic groups reflect the substantial advances in the treatment of a wide range of childhood cancers since 1970. These improvements occurred at a time when increasing numbers of children were treated at specialist centers participating in national and international clinical trials and studies. This centralization of care may provide the opportunity for further improvements in the prognosis of many childhood cancers.

▶ As you can see from the table, the stellar improvements that are being seen in Great Britain roughly parallel those occurring here in the United States. If a television reporter were to ask us what is now the 5-year survival for a child with "cancer," the response would have to be 70%–75% overall. This, of course, is a meaningless statistic, but then again the question wasn't all that great either. What is of importance are the trends in individual malignancy survivorship. Here we have seen improvements in virtually every childhood malig-

351

Five-Year Survival Rates (%) for Childhood Cancer in England, Scotland, and Wales and the United States, 1973–81

	England, Scotland, and Wales (present study)	United States (Young et al., 1986)
Leukaemia	43	51
ALL	51	59
ANLL	12	20
Hodgkin's diseases	86	84
NHL	36	51
Ependymoma	30	32
Astrocytoma	60	66
Medulloblastoma	33	41
Neuroblastoma*	24	50
Retinoblastoma	87	88
Renal tumors	70	76
Osteosarcoma	27	43
Ewing's sarcoma	36	48
Rhabdomyosarcoma†	42	54

*US data may include up to 2 cases of paraganglioma.
†US data exclude embryonal sarcoma.
(Courtesy of Stiller CA, Bunch KJ: Br J Cancer 62:806–815, 1990.)

nancy except retinoblastoma, which has a cure rate that is hard to beat anyway. In Great Britain, improvement in survival rates for patients with Ewing's sarcoma has not occurred. There have been slight improvements in the United States, although the overall response rate is not that terribly different than it was 10 to 15 years ago.

It is difficult to tell where the next major breakthrough will be in the treatment of various types of childhood malignancy. If a manager of a financial portfolio were investing time instead of dollars, they would invest time in those areas that would have the greatest yield. Science doesn't work quite that way. As much effort is going into retinoblastoma and childhood leukemia (the results of survivorship here are also already good) as into glioblastoma of the brain (where the survivorship is not nearly as good). That is simply the nature of science.—J.A. Stockman, III, M.D.

Cancer Risk Among Children of Atomic Bomb Survivors: A Review of RERF Epidemiologic Studies

Yoshimoto Y (Radiation Effects Research Found, Hiroshima)
JAMA 264:596–600, 1990

14–2

At present, microcephaly among in utero-exposed children of atomic bomb (A-bomb) survivors is the only teratogenic effect of ionizing radiation exposure observed in human beings. An increased prevalence of mental retardation has recently been related to A-bomb radiation exposure during weeks 8 through 15 of gestation. Because somatic and germinal mutations are considered to promote cancer through many mechanisms, possible radiation-induced, somatic mutations in A-bomb survivors could increase their cancer risk compared with that of the general population. The Radiation Effects Research Foundation (RERF) has carried out studies for many years to investigate the possible genetic effects of biochemical mutations and cytogenetic abnormalities. Untoward pregnancy outcomes have been studied, as well as the survival of children born to A-bomb survivors. These studies have failed to reveal any significant genetic effects.

Epidemiologic studies of cancer risk in children of atomic bomb survivors were carried out at the RERF. There were 2 groups of children: (1) in utero-exposed children, born to mothers who were pregnant at the time of the bombings of Hiroshima and Nagasaki, and (2) the F_1 population, conceived after the atomic bombings and born to parents of whom 1 or both were atomic bomb survivors.

From 1950 to 1984 only 18 cancer cases were confirmed among the in utero sample; however, cancer risk did appear to increase significantly as maternal uterine dose increased. The first patient was a girl who died of liver cancer at age 6 and was reported to have been mentally retarded. The second was a girl who had Wilms' tumor at age 14 and who died of stomach cancer at age 35. These 2 cases were the only childhood cancers that developed before age 15. All other individuals from the in utero population had cancer in adulthood, the earliest being at age 18.

Forty-three cancer cases were noted in the F_1 population between May 1946 and December 1982. All of these patients were less than 20 years old. For this group, cancer risk did not seem to increase significantly as parental gonadal dose increased. Follow-up of this population will determine changes in the patterns of adult-onset cancer.

The RERF information is inconclusive concerning a relationship between leukemia risk and paternal radiation exposure in the 6 months before conception. This is because of the few leukemia cases and the limited number of children born between May 1945 and December 1946 (about 2% of the total sample).

▶ Are we to take comfort from the results of this report? It shows no unusual increased risk of malignancy in individuals who were exposed in utero to the atomic bombings of Hiroshima and Nagasaki. Neither does it show any increased risk of malignancy to children conceived after the atomic bombing who were born to parents, 1 or both of whom were blast survivors. If these results hold up, that is better news than what otherwise might have been seen, but these data do not tell the whole story. You must read an article by Yamazaki et al. (1).

Yamazaki, et al. go beyond the oncologic complications of the atomic bomb blast and examine the overall outcome of those who were still in utero in August 1945. They report a marked increase in perinatal loss and significant vulnerability of the developing fetal brain to radiation injury. The most critical period appeared to be 8–15 weeks postfertilization, corresponding to that time in development when neuronal production increases and there is migration of immature neurons to their cortical site of function.

Perhaps the most vivid picture of what went on over 45 years ago comes from interviews with the mothers of the Kinoko-Kai, the "mushroom cloud auxillary." Mothers of the Kinoko-Kai each have in common a retarded child or a child with microcephaly who was prenatally exposed at the time of the bombings in Hiroshima and Nagasaki. The mothers themselves recall the effects of the powerful blast on their well-being. Most report a lengthy period of lassitude during which they experienced high fevers and bloody diarrhea. Alopecia was almost universal. This radiation-induced illness continued to affect them during the remainder of their pregnancies. Most of these women gave birth to their babies in February 1946. Virtually every infant was described as being listless in the first few months of life. One mother recounted an infant who had no hair growth until 2 years after birth. All the babies were able to be adequately fed because the radiation effect on the mother did not compromise lactation. Evidence of the neurologic damage became apparent when most children enrolled in school and developmental mental delay was readily detected. A fair percentage of these now adults are institutionalized and are called "pika," the Japanese term for flash.

I had a troublesome time finishing the *JAMA* paper of Yamazaki. I personally believe that every politician in a "nuclear" country should be forced to read what happens to the innocent bystanders when there is an inability to resolve war except in such a horrific way.—J.A. Stockman, III, M.D.

Reference

1. Yamazaki JM, et al: *JAMA* 264:605, 1990.

A Prospective Study of Hyperparathyroidism in Individuals Exposed to Radiation in Childhood
Cohen J, Gierlowski TC, Schneider AB (Michael Reese Hosp and Med Ctr, Chicago; Univ of Illinois, Chicago)
JAMA 264:581–584, 1990   14–3

Radiation treatment in the head and neck have been associated with increasing incidence of various tumors, including tumors of the thyroid, salivary glands, nerves, and breast. Since 1974 patients who received radiation treatment during childhood for benign conditions in the head and neck area had been followed-up prospectively. Data from these patients were studied to determine the effects of childhood irradiation on the parathyroid glands.

Of the 4,297 patients who received radiation to the tonsils before age 16 years, 2,923 (68%) were located and evaluated. Thirty-two of these patients had hyperparathyroidism. The average latency period was 34.7 years (range, 19.8 to 45.7 years). The incidence of hyperparathyroidism was 18.7 per 100,000 person-years among patients younger than age 40 years and 171 per 100,000 person-years for patients between the age of 40 and 60 years, a 2.9- and 2.5-fold increase, respectively, over that expected in the general population.

Thyroid cancer occurred in 31% of patients with hyperparathyroidism, compared with 11.2% of patients who had thyroid cancer but no parathyroid tumors, for a relative risk of 2.8. Age at treatment, total dose, and sex did not reliably predict the occurrence of parathyroid tumor.

Patients with a history of head and neck irradiation have a twofold to threefold risk of developing hyperparathyroidism. These findings emphasize the importance of calcium measurements in the evaluation of patients with a history of childhood radiation for benign conditions in the head and neck.

▶ If you are between the ages of 22 and 60, this article could have pertinence to you. We all know that radiation was commonly used as a treatment for benign conditions of the head and neck, predominantly for enlarged tonsils, but sometimes also for an enlarged thymus. This modality of therapy was especially prevalent from the early 1930s through the mid-1950s. Thus, people who are at risk range in age roughly from 20 to 60, depending on exactly when they were treated. A long overlooked risk of tumor formation has been that within the parathyroid glands. We have tended to focus all too intensely on the thyroid without thinking of those little nubbins of tissue that lie embedded in the back of the thyroid gland. Anyone having had such therapeutic radiation stands 2½ to 3 times greater than normal risk of hyperparathyroidism developing during the remainder of their life. Actually, this is probably an underestimate because all at-risk people have yet to develop their disease.

The authors of this study suggest that if one's history is positive for such a risk exposure, that individual's health should be monitored with periodic testing of calcium levels. It is difficult to say whether this is a correct way to approach the problem, because there has been little information about the sensitivity and specificity of serum calcium assays relative to the detection of subclinical and clinically apparent hyperparathyroidism. A physical examination might help. It probably will not pick up the parathyroid nodule. What it will pick up is the possibility of a thyroid tumor. If you read this report carefully, you will find that 84% of patients with hyperparathyroidism also develop thyroid tumors, including thyroid cancer (31%). More often than not, the parathyroid abnormality was found when the physical examination led to the suspicion of a thyroid tumor.

Thank goodness our ankles, toenails, and the rest of our feet are relatively inert objects. Many thousands more of us had our feet irradiated when we tried on shoes in the late 1940s and early 1950s in those funny little view boxes in the local shoestore than there are patients who ever had their tonsils irradiated. Has anyone ever looked for long-term sequelae of devotees of Buster Brown shoe stores? Is it possible that my 7½ E could have been or should have been a 10? We'll never know.—J.A. Stockman, III, M.D.

Second Primary Tumors Following Radiotherapy for Childhood Cancer
Hawkins MM (Radcliffe Infirmary, Oxford, England)
Int J Radiat Oncol Biol Phys 19:1297–1301, 1990   14–4

Survivors of childhood cancer appear to be at increased risk for second primary tumors (SPTs). The incidence of SPTs was determined in a cohort of 9,279 survivors of childhood neoplasms other than retinoblastoma treated in Great Britain before 1980.

An analysis of this cohort found almost 5 times the number of malignant tumors that would be expected in control populations. The cumulative risk of SPT by 25 years from 3-year survival was 3.7%. Even in the absence of radiotherapy and chemotherapy, the excess of SPTs was about 4 times the number expected. Radiotherapy appeared to be involved in the development of many of these.

Survivors of CNS tumors had 5 times the number of expected malignant neoplasms observed. The excess of thyroid and connective tissue tumors in these patients was statistically significant. In those who had not undergone radiotherapy and chemotherapy, the number of SPTs observed was similar to that expected. Survivors of Wilms' tumor had almost 8 times the number of expected tumors. The risk of SPT was increased by 12-fold in patients with Wilms' tumor who had received radiotherapy but no chemotherapy. Secondary leukemia appeared to occur more often among children with more recently diagnosed cancer.

A previous study found the risk of SPT after heritable retinoblastoma to be 13 times that expected. In patients with other cancers who did not receive radiation or chemotherapy, the development of SPT may also result from an inherent genetic predisposition. Although the number of patients in whom SPTs develop accounts for only a small proportion of those who are cured, it is important to monitor survivors of childhood cancer, especially those who have undergone radiotherapy or received multiple cytotoxic drug regimens.

▶ This is a very extensive report, giving follow-up on almost 10,000 survivors of childhood malignancy. The risk of a secondary malignancy was somewhere between 6 and 9 times higher than in the population at large, depending on the precise form of therapy that was given to treat the original disease. These data are not necessarily new, but they confirm the suspicions that we have seen in the literature previously that all such children need to be followed well into adulthood to be certain that they do not survive 1 malignancy only to die of another later on.

How do adult survivors of modern treatment for childhood cancer achieve their life goals? Do they move through their later lives smoothly, or is it a bumpy ride? Green et al. (1) tracked down 227 former pediatric cancer patients who were now close to 30 years of age to see how they were doing. Here is what they found. Approximately 11% of the survivors reported some form of employment-related discrimination. If they worked for a corporation, they did get health insurance (better than 90% were insured in this circumstance). When it came to life insurance, the story was somewhat different. Life insurance could be purchased only by 60% of the full-time employed men and 55% of the women. These percentages are significantly lower than those reported for the United States population at large. Twenty-four percent of those with life insurance indicated that they had some significant difficulty getting it. Only some 50% of subjects were married or lived as married, a percentage significantly lower than the rest of the United States. Women aged 20 to 24 years were the most unlikely to marry, and women aged 35 to 44 years had a signif-icantly higher rate of divorce than similarly aged women throughout the rest of the country. Although there was no statistical significance related to the follow-ing observation, many former patients indicated that their diagnosis and treat-ment for childhood cancer influenced their decision to have or not have chil-dren.

One of the problems that we have as pediatricians is that we often don't get to see the entire natural course of a disease and/or the complications of its treatment. The children who survive cancer treatment pass on to the internist or adult oncologist for follow-up. We may feel proud of the job that we have done (and rightfully so), but we really don't have "the big picture." Read the Green article. It does provide the bigger picture.—J.A. Stockman, III, M.D.

Reference

1. Green DM, et al: *Cancer* 67:206, 1991.

Late Deaths After Treatment for Childhood Cancer
Hawkins MM, Kingston JE, Wilson LMK (Univ of Oxford, England)
Arch Dis Child 65:1356–1363, 1990
14–5

Knowledge of the pattern of mortality among patients who survive for at least 5 years after childhood cancer may provide further understanding of late relapse and late effects of treatment. To address this, 749 deaths occurring among 4,082 patients surviving for at least 5 years after the diagnosis of childhood cancer in Britain before 1971 were evaluated.

The causes of death among the 738 cases in which there was sufficient information were recurrent tumor in 74%, a second primary tumor in 8%, a medical condition related to treatment of the tumor in 7%, a trau-matic death unrelated to the tumor or its treatment in 5%, and any other cause unrelated to the tumor or its cause in 6%. The good long-term prospects for 5-year survivors of childhood non-Hodgkin's lymphoma, neuroblastoma, retinoblastoma, Wilms' tumor, or soft tissue sarcoma were confirmed, with less than 10% of patients dying of recurrent tumors during the next 15 years. In contrast, more than 25% of 5-year survivors of Hodgkin's disease, ependymoma, medulloblastoma, and Ewing's tu-mor, and more than 50% of 5-year survivors of acute lymphoblastic leu-kemia, died of recurrent disease during the same period. Deaths resulting from acute lymphoblastic leukemia were largely attributable to CNS re-lapse at a time when CNS prophylaxis was not given routinely.

When compared with mortality rates in the general population, there was a threefold increase in the expected number of deaths from non-neo-plastic causes and a fivefold increase in the expected number of deaths from cardiovascular causes, mainly as a result of myocardial infarction and cerebrovascular accidents. There was no evidence of an excess num-ber of deaths from suicide, but there was a threefold increase in the ex-pected number of deaths from accidents after tumors of the CNS. Of the deaths from causes related to treatment, 2 groups of potentially avoidable deaths were identified. The first group included deaths from endocrine failure in patients with craniopharyngioma and panhypopituitarism who experienced addisonian crises in periods of stress related to infection. The second group involved children with problems related to postradiation fibrosis.

The investigation relates to patients treated for childhood cancer before 1971. The pattern of mortality after the more recent treatment regimens, in which chemotherapy is being used more extensively, will probably be different.

▶ Childhood cancer: Cure at what cost? At first this question may seem rhetorical given the downside to no treatment. As the article abstracted indicates, there are late deaths after treatment for childhood cancer. Some of these deaths are specifically related to the treatment, others are only indirectly related. Deaths, of course, are the tip of the iceberg. There is a greater degree of morbidity in terms of endocrine sequelae to a variety of therapies. Renal dysfunction happens on occasion as a consequence of radiation (such as for Wilms' tumor); the use of cisplatinum causes significant glomerular damage; the alkyalating agent, ifosfamide, produces tubular dysfunction; and the frequent use of amnioglycoside antibiotics is associated with renal toxicity. Cardiovascular effects of treatment were noted in the chapter on the Heart and Blood Vessels. Late cardiomyopathy is being increasingly reported. We are all familiar with neuropsychological sequelae of treatment. Fertility may be affected, although this is a relatively infrequent problem. One good piece of news is that there is no increased incidence of congenital anomalies in children of patients who receive chemotherapy for cancer in childhood and adolescence (1).

Earlier in this chapter we mentioned the risk of secondary primary tumors. On average, this risk is on the magnitude of about 3% of survivors, 15 years from the time of diagnosis. Social problems have also been noted elsewhere in the chapter. Part of the problem of the social adaptation difficulties that some children run into later in life is the misunderstanding of what they went through early in childhood. For example, a recent study from this country showed that 14% of survivors of childhood malignancy were unaware of their initial diagnosis (2).

These are the effects of the treatments that we have given, and they are the effects that have to be lived with. With the overall cure rate for childhood malignancy somewhere in the 70%–80% range, and recognizing that 1 child in 600 develops cancer before their 15 birthday, very soon there will be at least 1 survivor of childhood cancer for every 1,000 young adults in our population. Some of these young adult survivors are not particularly happy with the outcome of their malignancy. Recently, there has been a rash of law suits by these patients against their original attending physician because of the late effects of treatment (3).

To go back to the opening question in this commentary—childhood cancer: cure at what cost? I think Thoreau put it much more eloquently than could this editor: "The cost of a thing is the amount of what I call life which is required to be exchanged for it immediately or in the long run."—J.A. Stockman, III, M.D.

References

1. Green DM, et al: *N Engl J Med* 325:141, 1991.
2. Byrne J, et al: *Ann Intern Med* 110:400, 1989.
3. Miller DR: *Am J Dis Child* 142:114, 1988.
4. Thoreau HD: *Walden*, 1856.

A Comparison of Induction and Maintenance Therapy for Acute Nonlymphocytic Leukemia in Childhood: Results of a Pediatric Oncology Group Study

Steuber CP, Civin C, Krischer J, Culbert S, Ragab A, Ruymann FB, Ravindranath Y, Leventhal B, Wilkinson R, Vietti TJ (Baylor College of Medicine, Houston; Johns Hopkins Univ; Pediatric Oncology Group Statistical Office, Gainesville, Fla; Univ of Texas MD Anderson Cancer Ctr, Houston; Emory Univ; et al)
J Clin Oncol 9:247–258, 1991   14–6

There have been improvements in induction response and disease-free survival in the treatment of childhood acute nonlymphocytic leukemia (ANLL) in the past 15 years. Postremission therapy seems to be needed, but its intensity and duration have not been defined. The results of a Pediatric Oncology Group (POG) phase III randomized trial of induction and continuation chemotherapies were assessed in 256 children with previously untreated ANLL.

Induction therapy consisted of vincristine, cytarabine, and dexamethasone (VADx) or daunorubicin, cytarabine, and thioguanine (DAT). Treatment with DAT produced a superior complete remission (CR) rate (82% vs. 61%). Postremission therapy involved either standard 2-cycle therapy or a more intensive 4-cycle regimen administered for 2 years. Patients in the 2 continuation regimens had comparable outcomes. The overall complete continuous remission rate for the best combination of induction and continuation therapies at 2 years was .50; at 3 years, .35; and at 4 years, .34. Selected clinical and laboratory parameters showed differences in induction responses that favored DAT induction but did not influence subsequent disease-free survival. The 2 subgroups that responded better to 4-cycle continuation treatment were patients with French-American-British classification M1/M2 disease and patients older than 10 years at time of diagnosis.

Although no statistically significant differences were found between the 2 continuation therapy regimens, there was a trend favoring the more intense 4-cycle arm, in which there were demonstrable differences in certain subgroups. The overall 2-year complete continuous remission rate for patients given DAT induction and 4-cycle continuation therapy was 50%, equivalent to that seen in contemporary pediatric ANLL trials.

▶ Dr. William M. Crist, Chairman, Department of Hematology-Oncology, St Jude Children's Research Hospital, comments:

▶ Progress in treatment and supportive care over the last 20 years has improved the cure rate of children with acute myeloid leukemia (AML) from virtually nil to between 20% and 40%. However, recent progress has been slow, and variations in chemotherapy, including the highly intensified regimens used over the last decade, have had minimal impact on treatment outcome in this biologically heterogenous group of malignancies. In this report and others, the relatively poor prognosis of children with AML stands in striking contrast to the generally favorable outlook for children with most other common pediatric malignancies. Further, prognostic factor analysis has not defined subgroups of patients with distinctly different prognoses, precluding the development of risk-directed therapies designed to improve the therapeutic index. Currently, autologous and allogeneic bone marrow transplantations performed during remission are associated with approximately 30% and 50%–70% chances of cure, respectively. As increasing numbers of patients are undergoing transplants, novel approaches to the problems of donor availability and graft vs. host disease are being developed. The eradication of residual leukemia that occurs during remission by using immune modulators such as interleukin 2 to stimulate antileukemic effector cells is being actively evaluated. Finally, recent success in laboratory-based research has provided important insights into the pathogenesis of some subtypes of AML, including acute promyelocytic leukemia with the (15;17) and AML with the t(8;21). The expectation is that improved understanding of the complex process of malignant transformation will lead to new and more effective approaches to treatment.—W.M. Crist, M.D.

Improved Outcome in Childhood Acute Lymphoblastic Leukaemia With Reinforced Early Treatment and Rotational Combination Chemotherapy
Rivera GK, Raimondi SC, Hancock ML, Behm FG, Pui C-H, Abromowitch M, Mirro J Jr, Ochs JS, Look AT, Williams DL, Murphy SB, Dahl GV, Kalwinsky DK, Evans WE, Kun LE, Simone JV, Crist WM (St Jude Children's Research Hosp, Memphis; Univ of Tennessee, Memphis)
Lancet 337:61–66, 1991   14–7

Results from several clinical trials suggest that intensification of early treatment may help to prevent drug resistance in childhood acute lymphoblastic leukemia (ALL). Whereas most of these strategies have been used for patients with poor prognoses, the present study also included patients with more favorable prognoses.

The study group included 358 consecutive untreated patients (median age, 5 years). A 4-agent remission induction therapy was reinforced with teniposide plus cytarabine and high-dose methotrexate with leucovorin rescue, followed by rotational combination chemotherapy. Patients achieving complete remission were randomized according to prognosis to conventional continuation treatment or to 4 pairs of drugs rotated weekly or every 6 weeks. In addition to intrathecal therapy given to all patients, those with higher risk received 1,800 cGy cranial irradiation and those with CNS leukemia received 2,400 cGy cranial irradiation after 1 year of remission.

Complete remission was achieved in 99% of the lower-risk group and in 95% of the higher-risk group. At a median follow-up of 40 months, 4-year event-free survival estimates were 73% for the group as a whole, 81% for lower-risk patients, and 69% for higher-risk patients. In the 6-year study period, 62 relapses occurred, most in the bone marrow. Secondary acute myeloid leukemia developed in 8 of the children with poorer prognoses. Multivariate analysis showed that a leukocyte count above $50 \times 10^9/l$, CALLA-negative blasts, and a pseudodiploid or hypodiploid karyotype independently predicted an unfavorable outcome.

Treatment was generally well tolerated, and the children received most courses as outpatients. The regimen described here may cure 69% to 77% of ALL patients under 18 years. In lower-risk patients, the high 4-year event-free survival rate suggests that intensive early therapy and conventional postremission treatment may often be adequate to secure durable remissions.

Systemic Exposure to Mercaptopurine as a Prognostic Factor in Acute Lymphocytic Leukemia in Children

Koren G, Ferrazini G, Sulh H, Langevin AM, Kapelushnik J, Klein J, Giesbrecht E, Soldin S, Greenberg M (Hosp for Sick Children, Toronto; Univ of Toronto)
N Engl J Med 323:17–21, 1990   14–8

Although remission is successfully induced in more than 90% of children with acute lymphocytic leukemia (ALL), 30% to 40% of these children have a relapse. Oral mercaptopurine and methotrexate are typically part of the maintenance therapy given during remission. Recent research has shown that the bioavailability of oral mercaptopurine can vary widely, raising concerns about the effects of this on the risk of relapse.

Whether lower systemic exposure to mercaptopurine increases the risk of relapse was investigated in 23 children receiving maintenance therapy for ALL. Eleven children were considered to be at low risk of relapse and 12 were considered to be standard risk on the basis of disease features. Ten children relapsed. Those who did and did not relapse were comparable in mean age, hemoglobin level, mean daily dose of mercaptopurine, weekly dose of methotrexate, and total number of days during which mercaptopurine and methotrexate were interrupted. The 2 groups did differ significantly however in the mean area under the mercaptopurine concentration-time curve attained by a dose of 1 mg mercaptopurine per square meter of body surface area. That value was 1,636 nmol/L times minutes in those who relapsed and 2,424 nmol/L times minutes in those who did not. This resulted in a significantly lower total daily systemic exposure to mercaptopurine in children who had relapses. The tendency also appeared when those at low risk and those at standard risk were analyzed separately.

The prognosis of childhood ALL is adversely affected by low systemic exposure to oral mercaptopurine during maintenance therapy. Children beginning maintenance treatment should be studied to establish the pharmacokinetics of mercaptopurine, and doses should be tailored to achieve an appropriate systemic exposure.

▶ Anyone who has ever been involved with actually managing a child with acute lymphocytic leukemia knows what a juggling act one goes through to adjust the maintenance medication of these patients. Maintenance medication usually means the daily, biweekly, or weekly administration of the combination of 6 mercaptopurine and methotrexate. One starts off with a certain dose based on an average expected response per meter squared of body surface area or per kilogram of body weight and then finagles that dose up or down depending on how the patient tolerates the medication in terms of blood counts or any other systemic toxicities. At the end of treatment, virtually no 2 children have been treated quite the same way because of the many variables that are involved.

This study shows us that 1 variable has not been taken into account previously—the pharmacokinetics of the drug that is given every day, 6 mercaptopurine. Indeed, in any 1 patient, variations as high as 50% can be seen in the area under the curve of the pharmacokinetics of this particular drug. The authors of this study recommend that it is important to have a rough understanding of precisely how to dose a patient by doing a pharmacokinetic study and then repeating the study every few months. For practical reasons, no one is going to that much trouble now, and frankly, it would make an already complex management even more complex.

In addition to the pharmacokinetics of drugs such as 6 mercaptopurine, there are a few other things that should be taken into account with respect to maintenance chemotherapy in children with acute lymphocytic leukemia. For example, there is a drug interaction between trimethoprin-sulfamethoxazole and methotrexate. Trimethoprin-sulfamethoxazole causes methotrexate to accumulate to much higher levels than might ordinarily be expected. Also, when giving these drugs, it may be worthwhile to look to see how fat a child is. If a child is at or above the 75 percentile weight for height (an index of the fat body mass) you achieve lesser and lesser serum concentrations of 6 mercaptopurine when the drug is given on a meter-squared basis.

Life was quite a bit simpler before the pharmacologist invented pharmacokinetics. They are here to stay, and if we want to achieve better results from treatment of cancer, we will probably have to do more than simply write prescriptions based on body weight or surface area.—J.A. Stockman, III, M.D.

Hodgkin's Disease in Children: Correlation of Clinical Characteristics, Staging Procedures, and Treatment at the University of Minnesota

McClain KL, Heise R, Day DL, Lee CKK, Woods WG, Aeppli D (Univ of Minnesota, Minneapolis)
Am J Pediatr Hematol Oncol 12:147–154, 1990   14–9

To determine the optimal therapy for children with Hodgkin's disease, data on 63 children who were evaluated for clinical and laboratory findings at their initial appearance and at the end of therapy in 1965–1983 were retrospectively reviewed.

The initial erythrocyte sedimentation rate (ESR) was greater than 50 mm/hour in 50 patients, including 13 of 14 with relapses. Only 1 of 3 patients with an ESR less than 50 mm/hour had a relapse compared with 16 of 29 with an ESR greater than 50 mm/hour. The size of the mediastinal mass at diagnosis did not correlate with the survival rate. Lymphangiography yielded 2 of 4 false positive and 8 of 28 false negative results. Abdominal CT scans of 14 patients were neither false positive nor false negative.

The overall survival rate was 89%, with a 71% disease-free survival rate after median follow-up of 10.5 years. In 7 of 22 patients with positive staging laparotomy, relapses occurred, despite radiotherapy for 3 patients with stage IA and IIA disease, chemotherapy alone for 2 with stage IIB disease, and chemotherapy plus radiotherapy for 1 with stage IIIB and 1 with stage IVB disease. Of patients without evidence of Hodgkin's disease at laparotomy, 6 of 34 relapsed, including 1 patient with stage IA and 5 with stage IIA disease who received radiotherapy alone. Chemotherapy with a variety of regimens, with or without radiation therapy, gave poor results for the treatment of stage III and stage IV disease, with 6 of 7 patients relapsing. After 3.5 years of follow-up, the disease-free survival rates were 92% for patients with stage I disease, 81% for those with stage II disease, 78% for those with stage III disease, and 40% for those with stage IV disease.

Pediatric patients with Hodgkin's disease had an increased chance of relapse if they had an ESR greater than 50 mm/hour, although size of mediastinal mass did not predict outcome. Combined modality treatment is recommended for patients with stage II and IV disease; combination therapy may be the best treatment for all children with Hodgkin's disease.

Intracranial Ependymomas in Children
Goldwein JW, Leahy JM, Packer RJ, Sutton LN, Curran WJ, Rorke LB, Schut L, Littman PS, D'Angio GJ (Univ of Pennsylvania, Fox Chase Cancer Ctr, Grandview Hosp, Southern Wisconsin Radiotherapy Ctr, Children's Hosp of Philadelphia)
Int J Radiat Oncol Biol Phys 19:1497–1502, 1990   14–10

Less than 10% of pediatric brain tumors are ependymomas. The treatment of these tumors is very controversial. Treatment of intracranial ependymomas in children was studied to determine the role of prophylactic craniospinal irradiation and to define prognostic factors that would identify patients needing more aggressive treatment.

Forty-nine children and 2 young adults were treated at 1 center between 1970 and 1988. Thirty-three tumors were infratentorial, and 18 were supratentorial. Fifteen patients had total or near-total tumor resection, and 36 had partial resection or biopsy. Eighteen patients received postoperative irradiation alone, 4 received chemotherapy, and 26 were given a combination. Median follow-up was 7.75 years. The 5-year actuarial survival rate was 46%. The 5-year actuarial progression-free rate was 30%. Twenty-nine of the 30 patients with progression had a local progression; 1 died before the site of failure could be discovered. Six patients also had disease outside the primary site at relapse, 3 of whom had craniospinal irradiation. Patients whose tumor dose exceeded 4,500 cGy and white persons had significantly better local control. Survival was not significantly affected by extent of resection, histology, location, use of cranial or craniospinal irradiation, or the use of chemotherapy.

The single most important factor in treatment failure in children with intracranial ependymoma is the inability to control local disease. In this series, it was not possible to identify the role of chemotherapy, extensive surgery, or prophylactic cranial or craniospinal irradiation in improving local control or survival. The most favorable prognostic factors appear to be older age, higher local radiation dose, and white race.

▶ Dr. Henry S. Friedman, Professor of Pediatrics, Duke University Medical Center, comments:

▶ Ependymomas represent approximately 10% of all pediatric brain tumors, with the majority occurring in children less than 5 years of age. Although these tumors can be seen in both the infratentorial and supratentorial compartments, ependymomas occur most frequently in the region of the fourth ventricle. Conventional therapy for this tumor has consisted of surgical intervention followed by radiotherapy, with an overall survival of approximately 40%–70% in large, modern pediatric series (1). Children less than 3–4 years of age at diagnosis have been reported to have a substantially worse prognosis, consistent with the observations reported by Goldwein et al. in the article abstracted above. The search for more effective intervention for this tumor has generated several controversies regarding the biology and therapy of ependymoma including the following: (1) What is the significance of anaplastic features? (2) What is the significance of extent of surgical resection? (3) What are the appropriate radiotherapy ports for treatment of ependymoma? and (4) What is the role of chemotherapy in the treatment of this tumor?

Although there clearly are prognostic implications associated with the degree of malignancy of astrocytomas, this does not appear to be true in ependymoma, with several reports demonstrating findings similar to those of the present report. However, unlike the observations of Goldwein et al., several other studies have clearly shown an increase in survival for patients undergoing gross total resection as opposed to those who undergo subtotal resections (2, 3). The results of the Pediatric Oncology Group studies strongly suggest a marked increase in survival following gross total resection (4). It is clear that initial surgical intervention for ependymoma should consist of maximal tumor resection, a goal most frequently accomplished by the experienced pediatric neurosurgeon.

The controversy concerning the appropriate volume of radiation therapy, specifically the choice of local treatment or craniospinal irradiation, has been eloquently discussed in the literature. Although there are differing opinions, the most recent studies suggest that local radiotherapy is adequate for all children with infratentorial ependymoma unless there is evidence of leptomeningeal tumor dissemination (1). The ultimate cure of ependymoma appears to be limited by failure at the primary site. This has generated enthusiasm for approaches designed to increase local control, such as the use of hyperfractionated radiotherapy planned by the Pediatric Oncology Group.

The role of chemotherapy in the treatment of ependymoma remains poorly defined. However, it is clear that this tumor is sensitive to several chemotherapeutic agents, including cisplatin (5) and a combination of vincristine/cyclosphamide (4). Although previously published studies have failed to demonstrate a survival advantage associated with adjuvant chemotherapy for patients with ependymoma, the most active agents have not been tested in this setting. Future studies evaluating the efficacy of cisplatin, vincristine, and cyclophosphamide will more precisely evaluate whether the addition of this modality will have an impact on survival.

Children with ependymomas, indeed, children with all brain tumors, should be treated at academic institutions providing care by pediatric neurosurgeons, pediatric radiotherapists, and pediatric oncologists. Those children who survive brain tumors are frequently damaged by the tumor or the therapies chosen to provide curative intervention. The role of pediatric endocrinologists, pediatric neuropsychologists, and pediatric neurologists is critical if these children are to maximize their quality of life. As with children with other neoplasms, children with brain tumors must be referred to academic centers that are able to provide comprehensive multidisciplinary care.—H.S. Friedman, M.D.

References

1. Kun LE, et al: *Ped Neurosci* 14:57, 1988.
2. Nazar GB, et al: *J Neurosurg* 72:408, 1990.
3. Healy EA, et al: *Neurosurgery* 28:666, 1991.
4. Duffner P: personal communication.
5. Friedman HS, Oakes WJ: *J Neuro-oncol* 5:217, 1987.

Prognostic Value of Immunocytologic Detection of Bone Marrow Metastases in Neuroblastoma
Moss TJ, Reynolds CP, Sather HN, Romansky SG, Hammond GD, Seeger RC
(Children's Cancer Study Group, Pasadena, Calif)
N Engl J Med 324:219–226, 1991   14–11

Conventional bone marrow examination has been a routine means of clinically staging neuroblastoma. Specific immunostaining of malignant cells by using monoclonal antibodies should be a more sensitive procedure and may increase the detection of metastases. Bone marrow aspirates from 197 patients with newly diagnosed neuroblastoma were examined for tumor cells by using immunoperoxidase staining with monoclonal antibodies (immunocytologic analysis) and examination of smears and specimens obtained by trephine biopsy (conventional analysis).

Forty-six percent of the patients had tumor cells on routine smears and trephine biopsy specimens, and 67% had tumor cells on immunocytologic analysis. The latter study detected metastasis in 34% of patients who were thought to have localized or regional disease. In cases of widespread disease, the immunocytologic study detected tumor cells that were not apparent on conventional study.

When stage II or III disease was diagnosed in patients older than age 1 year, those with occult marrow metastasis did poorly, whereas those who were free of metastases did well. In patients who had stage IV disease before age 1 year, those with few or absent marrow metastases did relatively well.

Immunocytologic study is both a sensitive means of detecting marrow metastases of neuroblastoma and a good prognostic guide. The present findings illustrate the biological heterogeneity of neuroblastoma.

▶ Dr. Garrett Brodeur, Associate Professor of Pediatrics and Genetics, Washington University School of Medicine, comments:

▶ This paper by Moss and colleagues raises at least 3 interesting points concerning the current management of patients with neuroblastoma. First, immunocytologic evaluation of bone marrow aspirates provides additional sensitivity in detecting metastatic disease and may obviate the need for trephine biopsies in the routine staging of patients. Indeed, a standard "cocktail" of monoclonal antibodies could aid in the assessment of neuroblastoma involvement of other metastatic sites, such as lymph nodes, liver, and skin. It would be ideal if a specific panel of monoclonal antibodies could be used for such purposes by all major pediatric oncology divisions or centers. Second, the approach used by the authors represents a means of quantitative assessment of bone marrow involvement by neuroblastoma cells. Indeed, it may be useful for the International Neuroblastoma Staging System (1) to adopt this approach (or some modification of it) for the assessment of marrow disease. The techniques of mononuclear cell separation from bone marrow aspirates and immunocytology are available in most major medical centers, and this approach may obviate the need for the addition of 2 marrow biopsies, as currently recommended. Furthermore, it would permit a more quantitative assessment of tumor involvement, as well as tumor response to various therapeutic modalities. Third, the detection of occult marrow involvement in patients with localized or regional disease clinically had prognostic significance in their study, at least in subsets of patients. Although it was not the focus of this paper, it is unfortunate that some comparison was not made to other prognostic markers for neuroblastoma. These include: (1) genetic features of the tumor cells, such as N-myc amplification (2, 3), tumor cell DNA content (4, 5), and deletion of the short arm of chromosome 1 (6, 7); (2) histopathology (8); and (3) serum markers, such as ferritin (9, 10), neuron-specific enolase (11), or lactate dehydrogenase (12). It is likely that clinical features such as patient age and stage, including the assessment of marrow involvement, will be combined with biologic markers of prognosis, such as those mentioned above, to define risk groups that are very accurate in predicting the clinical aggressiveness of the tumor (13). This, in turn, will permit the selection of the therapeutic agents and intensity that are most appropriate for each individual patient's tumor.—G. Brodeur, M.D.

References

1. Brodeur GM, et al: *J Clin Oncol* 6:1874, 1988.
2. Brodeur GM, et al: *Science* 224:1121, 1984.
3. Seeger RC, et al: *N Engl J Med* 313:1111, 1986.
4. Look AT, et al: *N Engl J Med* 311:231, 1984.
5. Look AT, et al: *J Clin Oncol* 9:581, 1991.
6. Christiansen H, et al: *Br J Cancer* 57:121, 1988.
7. Hayashi Y, et al: *Cancer* 63:126, 1989.
8. Shimada H, et al: *J Natl Cancer Inst* 73:405, 1984.
9. Hann HWL, et al: *N Engl J Med* 305:425, 1981.
10. Hann HWL, et al: *Cancer Res* 45:2843, 1985.
11. Zeltzer PM, et al: *Cancer* 57:1230, 1986.
12. McWilliams NB, et al: *Pediatr Res* 23:344, 1988.
13. Brodeur GM: *Brain Pathol* 1:47, 1990.

Screening for Neuroblastoma at 3 Weeks of Age: Methods and Preliminary Results From the Quebec Neuroblastoma Screening Project

Tuchman M, Lemieux B, Auray-Blais C, Robison LL, Giguere R, McCann MT, Woods WG (Univ of Minnesota, Minneapolis; Univ Hosp Ctr of Sherbrooke, Sherbrooke, Quebec)
Pediatrics 86:765–773, 1990   14–12

Neuroblastoma, an embryonal neural crest tumor, is the most common solid cancer in young children. A large study was undertaken in Quebec to determine the impact of screening infants for the preclinical detection of neuroblastoma on the population-based mortality from this tumor.

All infants born in Quebec in a specified 5-year period are to be screened at 3 weeks and again at 6 months. Urinary homovanillic acid and vanillylmandelic acid determinations are made from dried filter paper samples. Thin-layer chromatography is used for initial qualitative screening with confirmatory quantitative screening done by gas chromatography-mass spectrometry (GC-MS).

In the first 6 months of the screening of 3-week-old infants, 41,673 neonates were tested. Eleven percent were also tested by GC-MS and were referred for assessment to exclude neuroblastoma. Four infants had neuroblastoma, 1 had a calcified adrenal gland, and 4 had no tumor. An additional 3 infants had a clinical diagnosis of neuroblastoma before the screening age of 3 weeks. A neuroblastoma that did not secrete homovanillic acid or vanillylmandelic acid was diagnosed clinically in another infant who had had negative screening results (Fig 14–1).

This screening program uses a 2-stage approach. The first stage is

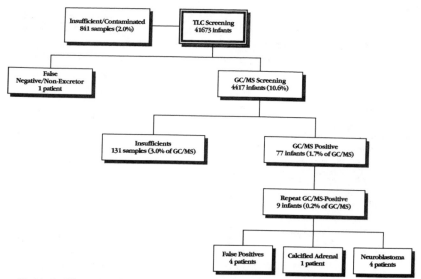

Fig 14–1.—Illustration of statistics for the first 6 months of screening of 3-week-old neonates in the Quebec Neuroblastoma Screening Study. *Abbreviations: TLC,* thin-layer chromatography; *GC/MS,* gas chromatography-mass spectrometry. (Courtesy of Tuchman M, Lemieux B, Auray-Blais C, et al: *Pediatrics* 86:765–773, 1990.)

rapid, qualitative, reproducible, inexpensive, and can eliminate at least 90% of the samples. The more laborious and expensive quantitative stage involves the GC-MS assay, which is very sensitive and specific. Combining the qualitative and quantitative tests into a screening program minimizes their respective disadvantages.

▶ Dr. Susan Cohn, Assistant Professor of Pediatrics, Northwestern University Medical Center, and Division of Hematology/Oncology, Children's Memorial Hospital, comments:

▶ Although children with neuroblastoma account for only 8% of the total cases of childhood cancer diagnosed each year, 15% of cancer deaths in children are caused by this tumor. The prognosis is particularly poor for patients who are over the age of 1 year and have advanced disease (< 20% 5-year survival rate) (1). Children who are less than 1 year of age have a better outlook than older children, and patients with localized disease fare better than those with advanced disease. Thus, the use of mass screening to detect neuroblastoma preclinically before the patient is 1 year of age and before the disease is widespread is an exciting concept.

Tuchman and colleagues are currently studying the impact of screening infants for neuroblastoma in a controlled population-based study in Quebec. Preliminary results suggest that neuroblastoma can indeed be detected in asymptomatic infants as young as 3 weeks of age by analyzing urine for the presence of abnormal quantities of homovanillic acid (HVA) and vanillylmandelic acid

(VMA) using thin-layer chromatography and gas chromatography-mass spectrometry. Neuroblastoma has also been detected in asymptomatic infants in Japan, where nationwide screening for neuroblastoma has been done since 1985 by measuring catecholamine metabolites in urine collected from 6-month-old infants using high performance liquid chromatography (HPLC) (2). However, although detecting neuroblastoma by screening has proved to be feasible, it has not been shown that preclinical detection of neuroblastoma leads to reduced mortality and morbidity from the tumor.

The impact of mass screening has been difficult to determine from the Japanese data because population-based incidence and mortality data have not been reported. Only survival rates have been provided. In addition, it has become clear that neuroblastoma is a heterogenous disease. The neuroblastomas that are seen clinically as localized disease, for example, are biologically distinct from those tumors that are widely disseminated. Furthermore, the genetic make-up of an individual neuroblastoma appears to be determined early and remains constant. Thus, "good prognosis" neuroblastoma does not evolve into "poor prognosis" disease.

To date, virtually all of the neuroblastomas that have been detected by the mass screening programs in Japan and Quebec have had favorable clinical and biological features (i.e., "good prognosis" disease) (3). Conversely, neuroblastoma patients missed by the mass screening program in Japan have been reported to have tumors with unfavorable clinical and biological features and have had poor outcomes (4). Most of these patients were seen clinically after the age of 12 months with advanced disease, and 50% of the tumors have been *N-myc* amplified (a biologically unfavorable characteristic). Thus, further data from population-based mortality studies like the 1 currently ongoing in Quebec, comparing screened and unscreened populations, are needed before the impact (if any) of presymptomatic detection of neuroblastoma on mortality can be assessed.—S. Cohn, M.D.

References

1. Silverberg E, et al: *Cancer* 40:9, 1990.
2. Sawada T, et al: *Prog Clin Biol Res* 271:525, 1988.
3. Murphy SB, et al: *Lancet* 337:344, 1991.
4. Nishi M, et al: *Pediatr Res* 26:603, 1989.

Current Diagnosis and Treatment of Pheochromocytoma in Children: Experience With 22 Consecutive Tumors in 14 Patients
Caty MG, Coran AG, Geagen M, Thompson NW (Univ of Michigan; CS Mott Children's Hosp, Ann Arbor, Mich)
Arch Surg 125:978–981, 1990   14–13

Pheochromocytoma is rare in childhood. From 1970 through 1988, 22 pheochromocytomas were treated in 14 children aged 6 to 18 years. Mean follow-up was 69 months.

Ten children had sustained hypertension. Other symptoms included diaphoresis, fatigue, headache, and flushing. Seven had familial pheochromocytoma, including 3 with the multiple endocrine neoplasia syndrome.

Among the 22 tumors were 8 adrenal, 4 bilateral, and 6 extra-adrenal. Most tumors were localized with CT and ^{131}I-metaiodobenzylguanidine (MIBG) scanning. In all but 1 patient, the findings on CT and MIBG scans agreed. Computed tomography failed to show bilateral adrenal tumors in 1 patient.

Four children had bilateral adrenalectomy. Eight adrenal and 6 extra-adrenal tumors were resected. All patients underwent preoperative α-blockade with phenoxybenzamine and β-blockade with propranolol for the control of perioperative hypertension, and none of the patients experienced complications related to inadequate control of hypertension. At follow-up 9 evaluable patients remained normotensive without medications. Preoperative localization of pheochromocytoma with MIBG scanning provides accurate diagnosis of adrenal and extra-adrenal tumors, allowing resection of this rare tumor with complete cure.

▶ We don't tend to think very much about the likelihood of a child having a pheochromocytoma, because this is a rare tumor in children. The problem with rare tumors is that we tend to not include them on our differential diagnosis list. This is particularly true of pheochromocytoma because the symptoms can be so unusual (hypertension, sweating, flushing, etc.).

Read this report carefully. The introduction of MIBG scanning technology now provides an accurate way to diagnose pheochromocytoma located either in the adrenal gland or at any other site in the body. To say this differently, if the differential diagnosis of pheochromocytoma even remotely enters your mind, order an MIBG scan.—J.A. Stockman, III, M.D.

Retinoblastoma in Older Children
Shields CL, Shields JA, Shah P (Thomas Jefferson Univ, Philadelphia)
Ophthalmology 98:395–399, 1991   14–14

The incidence of retinoblastoma in the United States ranged from 1 in 15,000–20,000 live births. The annual incidence of retinoblastoma in children, aged 0–4 years, is 10.9 per million; in those 5 years and older, it is .6 per million. A study was made of children who were older than 5 years of age when retinoblastoma was diagnosed.

Of 400 consecutive patients with retinoblastoma, 34 (8.5%) were older than age 5 years at initial diagnosis. The tumor was active in 26 children (76%). These 26 children were found to have several unique characteristics. Their median age was 6 years; the oldest was age 18 years. Twenty patients (77%) volunteered symptoms that prompted an eye examination. Nine had leukocoria; 9 had reduced vision; 4 had strabismus; 1 had pain; 1 had floaters; and 2 had no symptoms. All 26 children had unilateral sporadic retinoblastoma. Misdiagnosis before referral was common in this group of children. Five had vitrectomy for presumed

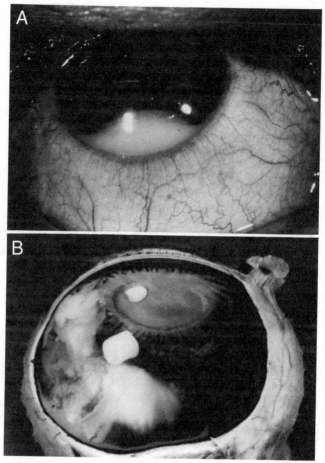

Fig 14–2.—A, girl, aged 16 years, with a hypopyon that was later determined to be an endophytic retinoblastoma after vitrectomy. **B**, gross specimen of the enucleated eye in the same patient shows the fluffy, endophytic retinoblastoma. (Courtesy of Shields CL, Shields JA, Shah P: *Ophthalmology* 98:395–399, 1991.)

vitreous hemorrhage or endophthalmitis when the retinoblastoma was unsuspected. One patient had cryotherapy for presumed Coats' disease, and 1 was observed for 7 months for presumed vitreous hemorrhage (Fig 14–2).

Active retinoblastoma can occur in children older than 5 years of age, and it may produce atypical clinical features in this age group. Clinicians should seriously consider retinoblastoma in children who have signs of unexplained vitreous hemorrhage or endophthalmitis, even if they are older than age 5 years.

▶ The average age at diagnosis of retinoblastoma (when there is no family history) is 24 months in unilateral cases and 13 months in bilateral cases. Retinoblastoma is diagnosed in nearly 90% of all patients before 5 years of age. Thus, it is a bit startling to see that almost 10% of patients were beyond the traditional age group in the series abstracted above. We don't tend to think of this tumor as a cause of eye problems in the older child, adolescent, or adult. We should, however, based on this new information.

Retinoblastoma has been the focus of much research, because in about one third of cases the predisposition of cancer is dominantly inherited from affected parents. Early detection of retinoblastoma ensures a better prognosis, both for vision and for life. Until recently, the only available method of detection for an at-risk child was regular full-eye examination under anesthesia. In practical terms, this meant that all children at risk for neuroblastoma on clinical grounds were screened in this manner on a routine regular basis. This was problematic because the retinoblastoma mutation is not fully penetrant (not all subjects carrying the dominant mutant gene showed the tumor), and the disease is able to "skip" a generation or 2. Thus, there is often a considerable investment in screening a small number of patients who are not at risk themselves.

The story regarding the specific diagnosis of neuroblastoma and the prenatal diagnosis has changed remarkably. We now know that retinoblastoma susceptibility is related to a family of recessive genes (tumor-suppressive genes) which, if inactivated, can express retinoblastoma and other soft tissue tumors (1). These genes are located on chromosome 13q14. With restriction fragment length polymorphism studies, retinoblastoma can be diagnosed in the majority of fetuses and newborns at risk for the inheritable form of the disease long before the tumor develops. This technology would allow clinical testing procedures to focus on those patients at high risk of developing retinoblastoma, and it would make prenatal testing an option (2).

The last thing in the world one wants to do is to miss a diagnosis of retinoblastoma. The cure rate currently in the United States approaches 90% if you make the diagnosis early.—J.A. Stockman, III, M.D.

References

1. Chance WG, et al: *N Engl J Med* 323:1457, 1990.
2. Onadim ZO, et al: *Arch Dis Child* 65:651, 1990.

Cancer in the Families of Children With Soft Tissue Sarcoma
Birch JM, Hartley AL, Blair V, Kelsey AM, Harris M, Teare MD, Jones PHM (Christie Hosp and Holt Radium Inst; Royal Manchester Children's Hosp, Manchester, England)
Cancer 66:2239–2248, 1990   14–15

The cancer family syndrome involves soft-tissue sarcoma in children and young adults and early-onset breast cancer in their mothers and close relatives. In a previous study, an excess of breast cancer was found in the mothers of 143 children with soft-tissue sarcoma. These observations were extended to include specific cancers among 754 first-degree relatives (mothers, fathers, and siblings) of a population-based series of 177 children with soft-tissue sarcoma.

There were 40 cancers among the first-degree relatives, compared with 24.82 expected (relative risk, 1.61; 95% confidence interval, 1.15–2.19). There was no excess of cancers in fathers, but there was an excess of borderline significance in the mothers and a significant excess in the siblings. There were significant excesses of carcinoma of the breast in mothers and siblings and gliomas in siblings. A step forward multivariate Cox analysis showed 3 variables in the index child that were independently associated with high cancer risk in relatives. These factors were age younger than 24 months at diagnosis; histologic type, embryonal rhabdomyosarcoma or other and unspecified soft-tissue sarcoma; and male sex.

This study shows a significant excess of cancers in first-degree relatives of population-based series of children with soft-tissue sarcoma. The pattern of cancers is consistent with the Li-Fraumeni syndrome. It is possible to identify a subgroup of children whose relatives are at high risk of early cancer onset.

▶ The cancer family syndrome was first described in 1969 by Li and Fraumeni (1). As noted in the abstract, this usually involves a child who has a soft-tissue sarcoma. A young adult parent also has a malignancy either preceding or following that of the child. The most common adult malignancy is breast cancer in the mother. Adrenocortical tumors and brain tumors also have been found to occur in excess numbers in these families, along with osteosarcoma, leukemia, melanoma, lung cancer, laryngeal cancer, and a few other carcinomas as well.

Although not a great deal is known about the cancer family syndrome, this report adds a better understanding of the type of child who is likely to have a parent or parents at risk for this problem. When should you worry? You should worry if you have a boy who is less than 24 months of age and is diagnosed with an embryonal rhabdomyosarcoma or an unspecified soft-tissue sarcoma. In that situation, the likelihood of the cancer family syndrome occurring is over tenfold greater than with other forms of childhood malignancy. That is an astounding conclusion, but one that is substantiated by the data.

This is the last commentary in the Oncology chapter so we will close with a question that has an oncologic basis. What is the relationship of meat, fat, and fiber intake to the risk of colon cancer?

This is not a silly question. There is indeed such a relationship. Nutritional factors are strongly suspected as being important in causing colon cancer. The hypothesis that diets high in fat cause colon cancer is based on increased rates of this cancer in various countries where the per-capita consumption of red meat and animal fat is high and the consumption of fiber is low. Until recently, this was only a hypothesis. However, a recent prospective study of young women (2) showed that the relative risk of colon cancer in women who ate beef, pork, or lamb as a main dish everyday was increased 2.5-fold, compared with those reporting consumption less than once a month. The ingestion of fish and chicken without skin was related to a significantly decreased risk.

The report by Willett et al. is a landmark article from which the following lessons can be concluded: Don't ask "Where's the beef?" Don't go "whole hog." Definitely avoid "going on the lamb." Better still, be known for the personality trait of having "gone fishin" and best yet, don't write off this report as "for the birds." . . . Eat a few instead.—J.A. Stockman, III, M.D.

References

1. Li EP, Fraumeni JF Jr: *Ann Intern Med* 71:747, 1969.
2. Willett WC, et al: *N Engl J Med* 323:1669, 1990.

15 Ophthalmology

The Fixed and Dilated Pupils of Premature Neonates
Isenberg SJ, Molarte A, Vazquez M (Harbor/Univ of California at Los Angeles
Med Ctr, Torrance; Univ of California, Los Angeles)
Am J Ophthalmol 110:168–171, 1990

15–1

A previous study of the pupils of premature infants found that most did not respond to light, although a few did. To better characterize the pupils of preterm neonates, 30 premature newborns were examined on a weekly basis. Pupil diameters in relative darkness and light responses were measured for comparison as the infants matured.

None of the infants had ocular or potentially confounding systemic abnormalities. At the time of study entry, all were less than 31 weeks' postconceptional age. The initial measurement of pupil diameter, at a mean of 7.8 days after birth, was made in the darkest environment that would permit observation. Examinations were repeated weekly until the pupils showed a response to light of at least .5 mm.

At the initial examination, in relative darkness, the mean pupil diameter was 3.9 mm, and the cornea had a mean diameter of 7.5 mm. No pupil demonstrated a response to light at this time. The mean postconceptional age at which a light response of at least .5 mm was evident was 30.6 weeks (Fig 15–1). Pupil measurements became progressively smaller with age.

The cause of the dilated pupil in preterm neonates is not known, but it may be related to the immature development of ocular muscles. The mydriatic effect of the dilator pupillae may precede the miotic effect of the sphincter, producing a net mydriasis in the premature infant. Anatomical

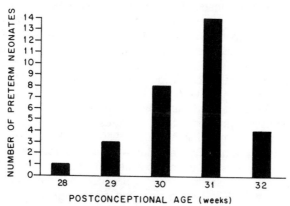

Fig 15–1.—Postconceptional age at which the pupils first responded to light (600 ft-c). (Courtesy of Isenberg SJ, Molarte A, Vazquez M: *Am J Ophthalmol* 110:168–171, 1990.)

changes in the iris may prevent the pupil from responding to light. Because of the changes occurring as the infants mature, conclusions based on mydriasis and unresponsiveness to light should be delayed until about 32 weeks' postconceptional age.

▶ I don't know why there is so much interest in knowing the pupil size of preterm and term infants. Not that the information that has been generated in recent years is not significant. It is simply that its significance does not even seem to be applied in the nursery setting, at least not in those that I am acquainted with. It takes time to measure these pupils, and any measurement must be done under controlled circumstances. Nonetheless, the data to date can be summarized in a few short sentences. At 26 weeks of postconceptional age, the pupils of a preterm infant have a mean diameter of 4.7 mm in relative darkness. The cornea at this age is only 7.0 mm. Thus, the pupil is wide—very wide. One can only assume that the reason for this (since no one has been able to determine the cause of this pupillary dilation) is that infants are begging you to look in their eyes to be sure they don't develop retinopathy of prematurity. After 26 weeks, the pupillary diameter gradually decreases progressively to reach a mean of 3.4 mm at 29 weeks. The earliest time you can expect a response to flashing a light in the eye is at 30.6 ± 1.0 weeks of postconceptional age. There is a modestly wide range for the latter (28 to 32 weeks). Even though the pupil doesn't respond until 28–32 weeks, the average newborn infant will blink in response to a bright light, showing that at least some portion of the optic pathways are, in fact, working.

If you read all the work done by the Isenberg group (the authors of the above article) you can come to several understandings. You should be able to define what constitutes an abnormally dilated or constricted pupil in a term or near term neonate. If you use the standardly held criteria that normal lights are within 2 standard deviations of the mean, the pupils of term or near term infants should be considered abnormally dilated if their diameter exceeds 5.4 mm or abnormally constricted if their diameter is less than 1.8 mm. Without question, if a pupil doesn't respond to light after 32 weeks, there is something wrong with the baby. As simple as these statements are, it took a lot of work to generate the data behind these statements. Many kudos to Isenberg et al. for their efforts. The best recognition of their efforts would be to use the data on a regular basis as part of the evaluation of at-risk preterm and term infants.

On a slightly different topic, did you know that this is the golden anniversary of "retinopathy of prematurity?" Yes, it was in 1942 that Terry first reported the extreme prematurity and "fibroplastic overgrowth of persistent vascular sheath behind each crystal lens" (1). It is interesting to see what has happened with retinopathy of permaturity. In the late 1950s and 1960s, everyone thought that retinopathy of prematurity was licked—we recognized that oxygen played "some role" in its cause and the management of infants was therefore altered. Unfortunately, the complacency that the disorder no longer existed was misplaced. By the late 1970s, with greater and greater survivorship of infants of extremely low birth-weight, at least 8% of babies born weighing under 1 kg at birth were blind (2). Currently, most data suggest that the frequency of blindness in the first year of life in survivors of this weight range remains constant at 4%–5%.

With respect to the retinopathy of prematurity, there has been a lot of fadism regarding management. Vitamin E is one typical example of a transient fad (i.e., in one era and out the other). We now know that it just doesn't work. It seems perfectly obvious that, when it comes to the eyes, the only sight that is 20/20 is hindsight.

We'll end a few of the commentaries in this chapter with some questions. This is a pearl for those who love the PERLA part of a physical examination. The question is, when infants are asleep, are the pupils dilated, unchanged, or constricted in the average term infant? Don't ask how this information was generated, because it is difficult to conceive of how one can determine pupil size with the lid closed, but the answer is that, when asleep, the pupil of an infant's eyes constrict rather than dilate (as does your's and, hopefully, mine). This is a consequence of decreasing inhibitory innervation to the oculomotor nucleus, which occurs at this age (3). Is that or is that not an interesting perla?—J.A. Stockman, III, M.D.

References

1. Terry TL: *Am J Ophthalmol* 25:203,
2. Saigal S, et al: *J Pediatr* 105:969, 1984.
3. Loewenfeld IE:, in Thompson HS, et al. (eds): *Topics in Neonatal Neuro-ophthalmic Development*, Baltimore, Williams & Wilkins, 1979, p. 124.

Retinopathy of Prematurity-Induced Blindness: Birth Weight-Specific Survival and the New Epidemic
Gibson DL, Sheps SB, Uh SH, Schechter MT, McCormick AQ (Univ of British Columbia; British Columbia Ministry of Health, Vancouver)
Pediatrics 86:405–412, 1990

15–2

In a recent population-based study in British Columbia, a significant increase since the mid-1960s in the incidence of retinopathy of prematurity (ROP)-induced blindness in infants with birth weights 750–999 g was found. The increased incidence of ROP-induced blindness in live-born infants may be attributed to increasing birth weight-specific survival.

All cases of ROP-induced blindness in infants born in the province from 1952 to 1986 were identified using the British Columbia Health Surveillance Registry (table). In addition, the birth records for the 1,299,740 infants born in British Columbia in the same period, and the death records of 22,940 British Columbia-born infants who died in the province before the end of the first year of life were linked using a combination of probabilistic and manual record linkage techniques. The birth weight-specific incidence rates of ROP-induced blindness in live-born infants and first-year-of-life survivors were calculated using these linked

Retinopathy of Prematurity-Induced Blindness in British Columbia, 1952–1986: Birth Weight-Specific Rates Per 10,000 First-Year Survivors

Birth Year	Birth Weight Category					Total Survivors*
	500–749 g	750–999 g	1000–1499 g	1500+ g	Not Known	
1952–54		2381.0	887.6	2.1	14.4	4.5
1955–59			142.5	0.1	10.4	0.4
1960–64			133.9	0.1	31.2	0.4
1965–69	833.3	444.4	96.2			0.5
1970–74	769.2	350.9	54.8	0.1	476.2	0.5
1975–79	1666.7	526.3	46.9	0.1		0.8
1980–84	545.5	486.7	35.3		416.7	0.9
1985–86	689.7	500.0				0.8
1952–86	675.7	480.3	103.0	0.2	21.0	0.9

*Includes birth weight not known.
(Courtesy of Gibson DL, Sheps SB, Uh SH, et al: *Pediatrics* 86:405–412, 1990.)

records and those from the British Columbia Health Surveillance Registry.

Weight-specific incidence rates of ROP-induced blindness were highest during the original epidemic from 1952 to 1954, in both live-born infants and first-year survivors. In infants who weighed 500–749 g at birth, the incidence of ROP-induced blindness increased steadily in both live-born infants and first-year survivors from 1965 to 1975. After 1975, the incidence continued to increase in live-born infants but decreased in survivors. In infants who weighed 750–999 g at birth, the incidence of ROP-induced blindness in live-born infants from 1965 to 1986 increased continually, whereas the incidence in survivors remained stable. In infants who weighed 1,000–1,499 g at birth, the slight trend toward decreasing

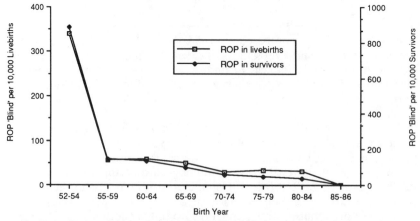

Fig 15–2.—Retinopathy of prematurity (ROP)-induced blindness per 10,000 liveborn infants and per 10,000 survivors: infants who weighed 1,000–1,499 g. (Courtesy of Gibson DL, Sheps SB, Uh SH, et al: *Pediatrics* 86:405–412, 1990.)

rates observed in live-born infants since the end of the original epidemic was more pronounced (Fig 15–2).

A new epidemic of ROP-induced blindness in infants who weighed less than 1,000 g at birth is confirmed. However, this increasing incidence of ROP-induced blindness in live-born infants is primarily a function of increasing birth weight-specific survival.

▶ Dr. Dale Phelps, Professor of Pediatrics and Ophthalmology, and Director of the Program in Neonatology, University of Rochester Medical Center, comments:

▶ Although we faithfully keep seeking a new iatrogenic cause to magically eliminate this frustrating disease, there are no answers yet. The relatively small number of children who were blind because of ROP (n = 114 over 34 years) in this study represents a valiant effort on the part of the authors to analyze all cases in a defined population base (British Columbia), and it is remarkable that with so few cases in any 1 time/birth-weight cell that the data are so consistent with prior individual hospital reports. About 5% of survivors who weighed under 1 kg at birth and about .4% of those who weighed 1–1.5 kg at birth are blind from ROP. The observed increase in the percent blinded in the 1 particular time period (1975–1979) in just 1 birth-weight group (500–749 g) is more likely to be a function of small cell size than a true change. The percent of survivors affected is not climbing, just the number of survivors. Therefore, the perceived increase is unlikely to be some new iatrogenesis that neonatologists are offering, but remains the same unknown that we have faced since 1954, when the excessive oxygen portion of the equation was removed. Whereas we can be pleased that our increased numbers of very low–birth-weight survivors are not suffering an increased rate of ROP blindness, we still have not learned how to prevent ROP blindness in all cases.

These data and continued similar monitoring should facilitate appropriate planning by agencies that provide services to the visually impaired.—D. Phelps, M.D.

Intestinal Giardiasis Associated With Ophthalmologic Changes
Mantovani MP, Giardino I, Magli A, di Martino L, Guandalini S (Univ of Naples, Italy)
J Pediatr Gastroenterol Nutr 11:196–200, 1990   15–3

Symptomatic giardiasis usually involves the gastrointestinal (GI) system, although cases of the parasitic infection have also been associated with skin, respiratory, and nervous system manifestations. Several studies have noted a connection between giardiasis and ocular alterations. This connection was examined in a group of children with giardiasis and GI symptoms.

The patient group included 49 boys and 41 girls with a mean age of 6.9 years. Each child was being treated for a first episode of diagnosed giardiasis. An ophthalmologic study was performed at this time, at 15 and 30 days after treatment, and subsequently every 3 months for 1 year. The children and their family members were each treated with a single dose of tinidazole. Two control groups were also examined, 1 composed of healthy children seen for routine check-ups and another of children with GI symptoms but no history of parasitosis or infectious disease.

Ocular alterations were found in 10 of the 90 children with giardiasis. No such abnormalities had been noted in their previous ophthalmologic check-ups. Eight had an extensive "salt and pepper" degeneration of the pigmented epithelium. In 1 case the pigmented epithelium showed atrophic areas; another had a small, hard exudate in the left eye. One of the 2 remaining children had slight discoloration of the temporal half of the optic disk; the other was affected by chorioretinitis.

A single dose of tinidazole resulted in negative parasitologic check-ups in 86 children; only 4 required a second dose. Opthalmologic follow-up for 1 year failed to reveal alteration of the salt and pepper-type degeneration or of the optic disk discoloration. No significant ocular alterations were observed in either of the control groups. Thus, children with symptomatic giardiasis should be monitored for ophthalmologic changes.

▶ The fact that *Giardia lamblia* can cause such significant eye disease is news to me. This interesting report shows us that ophthalmic complications should always be suspected and looked for in children with GI symptoms diagnosed as giardiasis. Take a very careful examination of the eye grounds and look for the salt and pepper-type necrosis described in this paper. This is the same type of clinical finding that may be seen with congenital syphilis and with certain types of bacterial and parasitic infections (toxoplasmosis and onchocerciasis). As this article indicates, the retinal findings do not appear to go away over time.

If you want to read more about the commonality of problems shared between the GI tract and the eye, see the interesting commentary of Gary Diamond (1). Diamond reviews the multiplicity of things that link the eye and gut: inflammatory bowel disease, amoebiasis, toxoplasmosis, echinococcosis, cystoicercosis, trichinosis, toxocariasis, Zellweger syndrome, Alagille syndrome, and giardiasis, as noted above.

So what is the question for this commentary? It goes as follows: a 1-month-old boy comes to the emergency room of your hospital with a horrified mother who states "a worm has crawled out of my son's eye." The child lives in the city of Atlanta. On examination you find what appears to be a larva, approximately 2 mm long, which emerges from the lacrimal punctum. After this has been removed, a second larva emerges. What is going on and what is the treatment of choice?

What is going on is fairly straightforward: the larvae belong to the family Calliphoridae. To be more scientific, the child had a fly egg in his eye (2). The disorder, of course, is known as external ophthalmomyiasis, which follows the deposition of eggs or larvae by the pregnant female fly on or near the conjunctiva. The fly doesn't have to land on the eye to deposit the larvae, they can be dropped by the female without her landing (a form of non-kamikazi dive-bombing).

You may recall from a previous commentary in the YEAR BOOK in 1985 that occasionally fly larvae can penetrate the globe, causing internal ophthalmomyiasis. These larvae leave characteristic hypopigmented tracks in the subretinal tissue as they move about, sort of like footprints in the sand.

If you don't like this question so far, you won't like the part of the answer that has to do with management. The management of external ophthalmomyiasis consists of mechanically removing each and every one of the larvae. This can usually be accomplished by instilling a local anesthetic into the eye and removing the larvae with forceps or a cotton tip swab. If the little creatures start squiggling around on you, a 5% solution of cocaine or 2% solution of lidocaine can paralyze the larvae, facilitating their removal. Don't forget to turn the eyelids inside out otherwise you're going to have an unhappy camper the next day because you may have missed 1 or more additional larvae. The management of internal ophthalmomyiasis includes the use of steroids to suppress inflammation, photocoagulation of the larvae, and surgical removal of the larvae. The visual outcome of this condition is usually poor, however.

Finally, of all the infectious things noted in the above commentary, the one that is most easily preventable is that caused by cat-associated toxoplasmosis. Get rid of the cats. If you are not sure what a cat is, just look it up in the dictionary, and you will find the definition: Cat (n) the crab grass in the lawn of civilization.—J.A. Stockman, III, M.D.

References

1. Diamond G: *J Pediatr Gastroenterol Nutr* 11:147, 1990.
2. Rao S, et al: *Pediatr Infect Dis J* 9:675, 1990.

Brittle Cornea Syndrome: An Heritable Connective Tissue Disorder Distinct From Ehlers-Danlos Syndrome Type VI and Fragilitas Oculi, With Spontaneous Perforations of the Eye, Blue Sclerae, Red Hair, and Normal Collagen Lysyl Hydroxylation
Royce PM, Steinmann B, Vogel A, Steinhorst U, Kohlschuetter A (Univ of Zürich, Switzerland; Univ of Hamburg, Germany)
Eur J Pediatr 149:465–469, 1990   15–4

Brittle cornea syndrome is a rare, autosomal recessively inherited disorder bearing a certain resemblance to fragilitas oculi and the type VI (ocular) form of the Ehlers-Danlos syndrome (EDS VI). Data were reviewed on a patient with typical signs of brittle cornea syndrome who had additional features that clearly differentiate this syndrome from the classic form of EDS VI.

Girl, 4 years, had the characteristic features of brittle cornea syndrome of brittle corneas, blue sclerae, and red hair. She had healthy, consanguineous Syrian parents, and had a male cousin who apparently had the same condition. The red hair in the girl and her cousin was otherwise unknown in the family. Between ages 2–3 years, the child had 3 ruptures of the cornea, once in the left eye and twice in the right eye. Her skin was soft and velvety to the touch, her joints were hyperextensible, and her auricles were dysplastic with unusually soft cartilage.

The clinical phenotype in this patient bore some resemblance to both EDS VI and fragilitas oculi, which is not clearly distinguished as a distinct entity from EDS VI. The patient did not have the abnormality of collagen lysyl hydroxylation characteristic of EDS VI. The most striking finding was fiber and cell-free spaces in the dermis, although the significance of this finding in a patient with brittle cornea syndrome is not clear.

► The term "brittle cornea syndrome" was first used about a dozen years ago in the description of an autosomal recessively inherited disorder in 2 siblings of a consanguinous Tunisian Jewish family. The syndrome is characterized by red hair, blue sclerae, and brittle corneas (1). In the affected individuals, the corneas were so brittle that they ruptured or perforated spontaneously. At first this seemed like an uncommon disorder, but it quickly became obvious that if you were in Tunis, and were Jewish, and had red hair, you had a reasonable likelihood of having the "brittle cornea syndrome."

What the report above does is to suggest that the "brittle cornea syndrome" is part of a generalized connective tissue disturbance most closely analogous to Ehlers-Danlos syndrome. The abnormality in Ehlers-Danlos syndrome has now been tracked down to a defective hydroxylation within collagen.

The next time you see an individual with red hair and blue sclerae, be a little bit concerned. There are many causes of blue sclerae, and we as pediatricians should be familiar with all of these. One of the causes, however, is this so-called "brittle cornea syndrome." As an aside, the other causes of blue sclerae in children include iron-deficiency anemia, osteogenesis imperfecta, inherited disorders of connective tissue (including Ehlers Danlos syndrome), collagen disorders, prolonged steroid therapy, and myasthenia gravis. The average red-haired young lady with blue sclerae is more likely to have iron deficiency, not "brittle cornea syndrome." In 1908, Osler first described blue sclerae in iron-deficient, undernourished teenaged girls. It is amazing how he continues to have lessons for us all. A recent article in Lancet (2) notes that blue sclerae have a specificity of 94% in the diagnosis of iron-deficiency anemia, with a sensitivity of 87%. Think about that a little bit, and the next time you need to make a diagnosis of iron deficiency, look someone straight in the eye.—J.A. Stockman, III, M.D.

References

1. Ticho U, et al: *Br J Ophthalmol* 64:175, 1980.
2. Kalra L, et al: *Lancet* 2:1267, 1986.

The Iris in Williams Syndrome
Holmström G, Almond G, Temple K, Taylor D, Baraitser M (Hosp for Sick Children, London)
Arch Dis Child 65:987–989, 1990   15–5

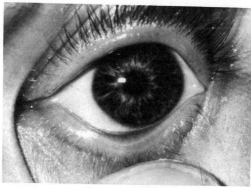

Fig 15–3.—Stellate pattern of iris in a patient with Williams syndrome. (Courtesy of Holmström G, Almond G, Temple K, et al: *Arch Dis Child* 65:987–989, 1990.)

Williams syndrome was characterized in 1961 as including mental deficiency, elfin facies, and supravalvular aortic stenosis. Reports in 1963 noted the association with infantile hypercalcemia, and the phenotype has gradually been expanded. The most common features of Williams syndrome are early feeding difficulties, mild growth retardation and mental deficiency, friendly and outgoing personality, hoarse voice, small wide-spread teeth, and variable cardiovascular anomalies. A stellate pattern of the iris (Fig 15–3) and a high incidence of blue irides have also been reported.

Slides of 80 eyes of children with Williams syndrome were compared with 240 control slides. The 320 slides were shown in random order to 7 observers. The observers were ophthalmologists or geneticists. A stellate pattern was noted more often in the irides of patients with Williams syndrome (51%) than in those of controls (12%). The stellate pattern was difficult to detect in heavily pigmented irides. Fifty percent of the patients with Williams syndrome and 51% of the controls had blue irides.

The stellate pattern of the iris was found in at least half of the patients with Williams syndrome and was therefore considered diagnostically important. Differences in the color of the iris were not significant between patients and controls. Clinical experience in discriminating the stellar pattern of the iris was found to be helpful in diagnosis of patients with Williams syndrome.

▶ When Williams first described his syndrome in 1961 (1) it was simply a triad of "mental deficiency, a characteristic elfin facies, and supravalvular aortic stenosis." Soon we learned that it was frequently associated with early onset hypercalcemia. The characteristic features of Williams syndrome include the above plus early feeding difficulties, a friendly outgoing personality, hoarse voice, small wide-spaced teeth, and variable cardiovascular anomalies, only 1 of which is supravalvular aortic stenosis. The face of these patients is characterized by malar flattening, full cheeks and lips with an open mouth, long philtrum, depressed nasal bridge, short palpebral fissures, periorbital fullness, and epicanthal folds.

We now see that patients with Williams syndrome are more than 50% likely to have the stellate iris pattern seen in Figure 15–3. This is thought to be caused by hypoplasia of the stroma of the iris. This finding is so characteristic that if you think a child may have Williams syndrome and you see the stellate pattern in the iris, you are home scot-free with the correct diagnosis.

If you have never had an opportunity to meet a child with Williams syndrome, I encourage you to go out and do so and learn about this disorder. As they get older, these children are absolutely delightful with respect to their personality. They won't mind in the least if you want to look in their eyes. They will be very obliging and, if nothing else, you will change your definition of iris to be "that part of the eye that smiles," as in "when iris eyes are smiling."— J.A. Stockman, III, M.D.

Reference

1. Williams JCP, et al: *Circulation* 24:1311, 1961.

Mutations Within the Rhodopsin Gene in Patients With Autosomal Dominant Retinitis Pigmentosa
Dryja TP, McGee TL, Hahn LB, Cowley GS, Olsson JE, Reichel E, Sandberg MA, Berson EL (Harvard Med School, Massachusetts Eye and Ear Infirmary, Boston)
N Engl J Med 323:1302–1307, 1990   15–6

Night blindness is an early indication of retinitis pigmentosa. The rod photoreceptors, which are responsible for night vision, use rhodopsin as the photosensitive pigment. Mutations in the rhodopsin gene in patients with autosomal dominant retinitis pigmentosa were studied.

Three mutations were found in the human rhodopsin gene. Each mutation occurred exclusively in the affected members of some families with autosomal dominant retinitis pigmentosa. Two mutations were C-to-T transitions, which involved separate nucleotides of codon 347. The third mutation was a C-to-G transversion in codon 58. Each mutation corresponded to a change in 1 amino acid residue in the rhodopsin molecule.

None of 106 unrelated normal control subjects had these mutations. The incidence of these 3 mutations was then added to that of a previously reported mutation involving codon 23, and 27 of 150 unrelated patients with autosomal dominant retinitis pigmentosa were found to carry 1 of these 4 defects in the rhodopsin gene. All 27 had abnormal rod function on their electroretinograms.

In some patients autosomal dominant retinitis pigmentosa is caused by 1 of a variety of mutations of the rhodopsin gene. Patients with the mutation involving codon 23 are probably descended from a single ancestor.

▶ If you think that retinitis pigmentosa is an extraordinarily rare disorder, chances are that you have missed 1 or more children who ultimately become blind as teenagers or adults. As a genetic problem, the incidence at birth for this disorder is about 1 in 3,500. To express this number a little bit differently, for every child who develops leukemia, there will be someone out there with retinitis pigmentosa. Most of us know 1 or more children, either under our care or in our community, with leukemia. There could be about the same number of children out there with undiagnosed retinitis pigmentosa.

Patients with retinitis pigmentosa characteristically report the occurrence of night blindness during early to late adolescence and lose vision in their midperipheral visual field and then far peripheral field in adulthood. Most are legally blind by age 40, with a central field of less than 20 degrees in diameter. Virtually all patients lose central field vision as well by age 50–80. No minor disease!

Retinitis pigmentosa is genetically quite heterogenous. It is transmitted as an autosomal dominant trait in some families, an autosomal recessive trait in other families, and an X-linked trait in still others. The importance of the article abstracted above is that it provides a clear linkage between a chromosomal abnormality and the product of that chromosome, rhodopsin, as the cause of retinitis pigmentosa. The chromosome in question is chromosome 3. These investigators have found that the gene encoding rhodopsin is on the 3q portion of the chromosome. Night blindness, as noted, is the early symptom of retinitis pigmentosa. The rod photo receptors in the retina are responsible for night vision and use rhodopsin as the photosensitive pigment. The primary defect in retinitis pigmentosa would then appear to be a problem with rhodopsin. This is consistent with the finding of abnormal rod function on electroretinography in all patients tested with this disorder so far.

Although there is no magic bullet to cure retinitis pigmentosa, now that the highly probable cause of it has been described, it is more than worthwhile for you to recognize that there may be a patient in your practice who has the problem and is just waiting to be diagnosed by you.—J.A. Stockman, III, M.D.

Ocular Manifestations of Patients With Circulating Antineutrophil Cytoplasmic Antibodies

Pulido JS, Goeken JA, Nerad JA, Sobol WM, Folberg R (Univ of Iowa Hosps and Clinics, Iowa City)
Arch Ophthalmol 108:845–850, 1990   15–7

Antineutrophil cytoplasmic antibodies (ANCAs) are associated with certain systemic vasculitides, particularly Wegener's granulomatosis (WG) and microscopic polyarteritis. In patients with ocular findings and little evidence of systemic disease, ANCA titers may prove useful when deciding whether invasive biopsy specimens may be necessary to establish the diagnosis of vasculitis. The ocular findings in 6 patients with systemic vasculitis and positive ANCA titers were examined.

Four patients had WG, 1 had microscopic polyarteritis, and a histopathologic diagnosis could not be made in 1. For all 6 patients, a diagnosis could not be made from the original histopathologic findings. Two patients with WG were initially referred for ocular manifestations, and the ANCA titers, along with biopsy findings, helped confirm the diagnosis.

Ocular findings included ptosis, bilateral lacrimal gland masses, proptosis, choroidal folds, episcleritis, phlebitis, retinal and vitreous hemorrhage, keratitis sicca, and bilateral central scotomas. The ANCA testing, in conjunction with clinical and biopsy findings, helped to establish the diagnosis of systemic vasculitis.

The use of ANCA assay should be considered in patients with eye symptoms of possible vasculitis, especially in the presence of scleritis. A prospective study should be undertaken to define the clinical significance of ANCA testing in patients with ocular findings suggestive of systemic vasculitis.

▶ There is a hematologic cause for every problem that effects man. You simply have to find it.—J.A. Stockman, III, M.D.

An Investigation of the Clinical Use of Botulinum Toxin A as a Postoperative Adjustment Procedure in the Therapy of Strabismus
McNeer KW (Med College of Virginia, Richmond)
J Pediatr Ophthalmol Strabismus 27:3–9, 1990   15–8

The success of surgery for strabismus depends on adjusting extraocular muscle (EOM) length and force dynamics to optimal balance. Even with optimum postoperative binocular alignment, the result may become unstable, necessitating more surgery. In 1973, the injection of botulinum toxin A into human EOM was suggested as an alternative way to treat strabismus. Data on 47 patients who had 71 postoperative EOM injections as an adjustment procedure reviewed retrospectively.

In 15 consecutive patients with esophoria who were treated with medial rectus injections, there were no significant refractive errors. In 4 older patients with esophoria, the mean deviation was reduced from 10 to 3 prism diopters at 135 weeks. In 12 patients with exophoria, the distance deviation was decreased from 18 to 6 prism diopters at 115 weeks. Ptosis and transient, unintended vertical deviations were the only side effects. It was difficult to determine whether botulinum toxin A changed the time span of the clinical course in these patients; however, when it was effective, it was very convenient.

▶ This, of course, is hardly the first report of the use of botulinum toxin for the treatment of strabismus. In fact, the Food and Drug Administration has recently approved botulinum toxin (Oculinum) as a therapeutic agent in patients with various muscle disorders. The toxin exerts its paralytic action by rapidly and strongly binding to presynaptic cholinergic nerve terminals. The treatment of muscle with botulinum toxin results in an accelerated loss of junctional acetylcholine receptors. Paralysis and nearly complete decline of motor and plate potentials occur within a few hours after the injection of botulinum toxin.

If you think that I knew all of this off the top of my head, you are mistaken. I found out about the details of exactly how botulinum toxin works in an excellent review by Jankovic et al. (1). Their article is well worth your reading. You will discover in that review that the commercially available botulinum toxin is simply a culture of clostridial botulinum toxin that is established in a fermentor, grown and harvested by acidification and centrifugation, and further purified for commercial use. There is 1 other product available elsewhere in the world (Dysport), which is manufactured in the United Kingdom. The British toxin is almost 20 times more potent.

The use of botulinum toxin as part of the management of strabismus was the very first initial application of this toxin therapeutically. It was used to weaken extraocular muscles. There are now many uses that are both approved and are being considered for approval. Botulinum toxin is the treatment of choice for blepharospasm, and it is now routinely used for many forms of dystonia. For us in pediatrics, the most common dystonia that we deal with is spasmodic torticollis. For individuals such as myself, it is the treatment of choice also for writer's cramp (believe it or not). It is regularly being used as part of the management of a variety of tremors (such as those associated with Parkinson's disease, tics, segmental myoclonis, and other hyperkinetic movement disorders). Many individuals with multiple sclerosis are disabled by spasticity, and botulinum toxin injected into adductor leg muscles has resulted in dramatic improvement in muscle tone in affected individuals. The effects of botulinum toxin on spasticity in children with cerebral palsy are currently under evaluation.

You can let your mind run wild with potential applications for things that are "spazzed" out and theoretically might respond to botulinum toxin. If you can think of anything, chances are it has already been tried. For example, botulinum toxin has been used to improve bladder function in patients with spasmodic bladders caused by spinal cord injury. It has been used to treat spasm of the rectal sphincter (the medical term for this is animus). It works wonders in the latter disorder, especially for those who have intractable constipation, because once used, the trap door (or back door) is then open. I have seen no reports of the use of botulinum toxin to help youngsters with highly retractile testis. I suppose we will be seeing reports of its use for such uptight situations soon.

Curiously, there are no absolute contraindications to injections of botulinum toxin except a history of hypersensitivity to the toxin (none yet reported) and infection at the site of injection. No teratogenicity has been observed. A word to the wise, however, would suggest that if you are going to have this stuff injected into you, be sure that the person with the syringe knows a good deal about human anatomy.

One final thought, and this is for the veterinarians in the reading audience of the YEAR BOOK, if there are any. Why don't you think about using botulinum toxin to produce a pharmacologic "debarking" of pet dogs whose masters demand that you make them silent. Botulinum toxin will work (it is used in humans for laryngeal dystonia), is much more humane, and after a few months, its effects will wear off, by which time the dog will probably have forgotten how to bark anyway. I bet it would work. Please quote me on this one.—J.A. Stockman, III, M.D.

Reference

1. Jankovic J, et al: *N Engl J Med* 324:1186, 1991.

The Eye in the CHARGE Association

Russell-Eggitt IM, Blake KD, Taylor DSI, Wyse RKH (Hosp for Sick Children, London; Inst of Child Health, London)
Br J Ophthalmol 74:421–426, 1990
15–9

The CHARGE association includes patients with at least 4 features prefixed by the letters of the mnemonic: Coloboma, Heart defects, Atresia of the choanae, Retarded growth and development, Genital hypoplasia, Ear anomalies and/or hearing loss. Facial palsy is also common. The incidence and range of ocular features in the CHARGE association were studied in 50 patients seen at a center concerned with the management of this entity.

Ocular abnormalities occurred in 44 of 50 patients (88%) with the CHARGE association. Of these, 41 (82%) had typical coloboma, and 2 had atypical colobomas with normal fundi. Colobomas affected the posterior segment in 38 patients, with involvement of the optic disk in all but 7 eyes. In some cases, the coloboma was subtle and occurred as a defect of the retinal pigment epithelium inferonasal to the optic disk. Other ocular abnormalities seen were microphthalmos in 21 patients, squint in 17, nystagmus in 12, and optic nerve hypoplasia in 4 (table). Facial palsy occurred in 22 patients, including 4 with an associated disorder of vertical eye movement. Refractive errors occurred in 36 patients.

Pediatricians should be aware of these features because some of them (e.g., choroidoretinal coloboma) may be occult until retinal detachment occurs. Facial palsy should also be considered a major feature of the CHARGE association.

Reported Ocular Features in Syndromes With Systemic Features in Common
With the CHARGE Association

	CHARGE	CATEYE	GOLDENHAR	VACTERL	DIGEORGE	EDWARDS
Coloboma	*	*	*		*	*
PHPV	*					
Epibulbar dermoids			*			
Lid coloboma	*		*			
Ocular motility disorder	*		*			
Optic nerve hypoplasia	*		*			

(Courtesy of Russell-Eggitt IM, Blake KD, Taylor DSI, et al: *Br J Ophthalmol* 74:421–426, 1990.)

▶ By now, just about everybody in pediatrics is or should be familiar with the CHARGE association. The tip-off invariably is the finding of coloboma. Although the presence of coloboma is hardly specific to the CHARGE syndrome, in the presence of the other findings, you can quickly make a clinical diagnosis. Remember that coloboma are also seen in cat eye, Goldenhar, the DiGeorge, and the Edwards syndromes.

We will close the Ophthalmology chapter of the YEAR BOOK with a description of a new disorder of the 1990s, "air-bag keratitis." Even though airbags have been around for more than a decade, it has only been in the last couple of years that Lee Iacocco has made them a household (garage) appliance. Recently, a 2-year-old boy was described who was an unrestrained passenger in a 2-car motor vehicle accident. The boy was thrown from the rear seat to the front, landing face up under the dashboard. The driver's airbag had inflated and burst. Following the accident, there appeared to be a problem with the child's eyes. When seen in the emergency room, he had erythema of the facial skin and eyelids and moderate conjunctiva injection. Both corneas showed focal clouding, and his tears were very alkaline (pH 8.5–9.0 in both eyes). The eyes were irrigated with Ringer's solution until the pH returned to normal. One month after the accident, the child had 20/40 vision in the right eye and 20/30 in the left, with residual small corneal scars (1).

To understand what is going on here, it must be recognized that, when an airbag inflates, it does so subsequent to a spark ignition of sodium azide that yields nitrogen gas, ash, and a small amount of sodium hydroxide. These products most likely were responsible for the ocular injuries and facial burns sustained by this patient. If you are ever first on the scene of an accident and an airbag has been involved which has ruptured, prompt irrigation of the eyes is the emergency treatment of choice and should be done as soon as possible, even in the field. The problem just described seems to be well known to everyone except physicians. For example, the National Highway Traffic Safety Administration has published a document "Emergency Rescue Guidelines for Air-Bag Equipped Cars" (2) that describes the potential for such a complication.

Please do not interpret the above comments regarding air bags as a suggestion on this editor's part that it is better to live in the past than it is to live with current technologies. The only beneficial thing about living in the past is that it's cheaper.—J.A. Stockman, III, M.D.

References

1. Ingraham HJ, et al: *N Engl J Med* 324:1599, 1991.
2. National Highway Traffic Safety Administration. *Emergency Rescue Guidelines for Air-Bag Equipped Cars.* Washington, D.C., Government Printing Office, 1990.

16 Dentistry and Otolaryngology

Dental Enamel Defects in First-Degree Relatives of Coeliac Disease Patients

Mäki M, Aine L, Lipsanen V, Koskimies S (Univ of Tampere; Univ Hosp of Tampere; Finnish Red Cross Blood Transfusion Service, Helsinki, Finland)
Lancet 337:763–764, 1991   16–1

Ingestion of gluten results in permanent-tooth enamel defects distributed chronologically in all 4 sections of dentition. Such defects are strongly associated with celiac disease in children. A study was done to determine whether dental changes can be used to screen for this disease among apparently healthy relatives of patients with the disorder.

Fifty-six healthy, first-degree relatives of patients with celiac disease underwent dental examination and small bowel biopsy. Twenty-five subjects had celiac-type general permanent-tooth enamel lesions. Seven subjects had histologic evidence of the disease, and all of these had enamel lesions. The celiac-type enamel changes were highly associated with HLA-DR3. Most of the DR3 alleles belonged to the extended haplotype A1; B8; DR3 group.

Dentists who are aware of celiac disease in a family should be able to identify family members who would benefit from gastroenterologic assessment. However, the celiac-type dental enamel defects may also occur without active celiac disease.

▶ For more on the topic of celiac disease, see this year's YEAR BOOK chapter on Gastroenterology. There is a lot happening with this "old timer" these days, only 1 aspect of which is the fact that you can screen for celiac disease by looking at someone's teeth. It is sort of like looking a gift horse in the mouth when it comes to rapid diagnosis.

Enough said on the topic of celiac disease. There are several other dental-related items that are worthy of mention.

Fluoride continues to receive a lot of attention. About 2 years ago, a study suggested that rats fed high diets of fluoride had an increased risk of a rare kind of bone cancer. The Food and Drug Administration (FDA), however, states that there is no evidence that fluoride causes cancer in humans, and the Public Health Service has issued a declaration that "Optimal fluoridation of drinking water does not pose a detectable cancer risk to humans." These 2 agencies, however, stress that we must use the right amount of fluoride and not too much. About 95% of toothpaste sold in the United States contains fluoride, and the FDA review panel has "encouraged parents to instruct their children to use only a small amount of toothpaste and to rinse carefully after brushing their teeth." If you want to read more about fluoride and cancer, see the *New York Times,* February 20, 1991.

A corollary of this news report appeared in the *St. Petersburg Times* on April 25, 1991 (page 18A). A science writer reported that Dr. William J. Blot, a National Cancer Institute researcher, had recently completed a study showing a strong link between the use of alcohol-containing mouthwashes and oral and pharyngeal cancer. Individuals who use alcohol-containing mouthwashes may have up to a 90% increased risk of such cancers. The disclaimer with the latter report, of course, is that many users of mouthwash do so to mask "smoker's breath," a more established cause of oral and pharyngeal carcinoma.

The other hot topic with respect to fluoride this past year has been the potential risk of consumption of bottled water. The sale of bottled water has increased 70% in the last 5 years. It is a "chic" alternative to tap water, given the high profile of environmentalists, who are suggesting that our tap water is contaminated with pesticides, herbicides, and heavy metals such arsenic and other toxins. Consequently, sales have skyrocketed. So what is the issue with fluoride and bottled water? Bottled water testing is carried out by the FDA's Safe Drinking Water Act legislation. Bottled water is not required to be fluoridated. Some brands contain no fluoride, and others may contain more than 4.0 ppm of fluoride. It has been estimated that 10% of all children in the United States are now using bottled water as their primary source of drinking water. Those who drink bottled water as their primary source of drinking water seem to have about a 75% chance of receiving greater than an optimal amount of fluoride. The highest fluoride content is in mineral water processed in France (1–3).

Finally, to make a long story longer, let's not forget toothpaste. Is it better to spit out the toothpaste or swallow it after brushing? The answer to this question comes in several parts. First, you don't need more fluoride, so for that reason, it is better to spit out. Second, there may be a link between toothpaste and Crohn's disease. This theory goes all the way back to 1939 when Burrill B. Crohn was told by Emanuel Libman (the brillant clinician and discoverer of Libman-Sachs disease) that it was his theory that toothpaste might be involved in the pathogenesis of regional enteritis. Sullivan et al. (4) point out that toothpaste contains a variety of inorganic metals and salts, many of which have been shown in experimental models to produce granulomatous lesions in the intestine. Even more recently, Florence et al. (5) documented that insoluble particles as small as 50 nm are taken up by the gut mucosa, mainly through the Peyer's patches. Thus, biodegradable material is taken up by lymph nodes draining the GI tract.

Finally, there was a report of a 21-year-old nonsmoking woman with a history of asthma every time she brushed with Crest tartar control toothpaste (Proctor and Gamble, Cincinnati, Ohio). She didn't have this problem when she used a gel-based toothpaste. The difference between the 2 types of toothpaste is an artificial flavoring that is used in the tartar control toothpaste (6).

One last note regarding teeth. I recently learned that the first rule of dentistry taught in dental school is do not talk to your patient until the drill is in his or her mouth. Knowing that explains a lot.—J.A. Stockman, III, M.D.

References

1. McGuire S: *N Engl J Med* 321:836, 1989.
2. Flaitz CM, et al: *Quintessence Int* 20:847, 1989.
3. Tate WH, et al: *J Pediatr* 117:419, 1990.
4. Sullivan SN, et al: *Lancet* 2:1096, 1990.
5. Florence AT, et al: *Lancet* 1:1580, 1991.
6. Spurlock BW, et al: *N Engl J Med* 323:1845, 1990.

The Effects of Nutritional Quality and Frequency of Consumption of Sugary Foods on Dental Caries Increment
Lachapelle D, Couture C, Brodeur J-M, Sévigny J (Université Laval, Québec)
Can J Public Health 81:370–375, 1990   16–2

Reports on the role of sugary foods in the development of dental caries are conflicting. A longitudinal study was conducted to determine the association of dietary quality with dental caries increment in 232 children aged 11 years. With the help of their parents, the children completed a 3-day dietary record, which included 1 weekend day. The nutritional quality of the child's diet was evaluated by using a quality index based on the eating frequency of foods recommended in food guides. Two oral examinations 20 months apart were performed, and the dental caries increment was evaluated with the DMFS index.

The subjects were divided into 3 groups based on their nutritional quality index. For the total sample and for boys and girls considered separately, the mean dental caries increment decreased as the nutritional quality of the diet increased. However, the analysis of variance did not show any significant differences between the mean caries increment for the 3 groups. Furthermore, there was no significant association between frequency of consumption of sugary foods and caries increment. There was also no association between nutritional quality and oral hygiene or between the mother's education and the children's frequency of consumption of sugary foods.

This study shows no strong association between dietary factors and dental caries. It appears that children with the highest dental caries increment may not necessarily have poor nutrition or consume sugary foods more frequently.

▶ It is refreshing to see an article on sugar causing problems related to tooth decay. With all the "hype" going on about the risks of mercury in dental amalgam, we seem to have lost sight of the fact that a risk far greater than mercury is having no teeth at all because of sugar-induced caries. This is not meant to say that there may not be any problem with mercury exposure from "silver" fillings. What is the current information in this regard?

There seems to be no issue that autopsy data indicate that brain mercury levels are approximately twice as high in people who have had fillings for many years as those with no fillings. Those with fillings have elevated blood and urine mercury levels as well. Vaporization of mercury from amalgam fillings occurs during chewing and for several minutes thereafter. Both the Canadian Dental Association and the American Dental Association claim that this is not a major health risk. Not so, says Lorschider et al. (1). These investigators note that the estimated dietary intake of mercury from air, water, and food averages 3.09 μg. A "silver" amalgam tooth filling weighs 1.5–2.0 g, and 50% of the filling is elemental mercury. Estimates of amalgam mercury doses absorbed daily range from 1.2 to 27 μg, with a consensus average of 10 μg. In individuals with many fillings, the dose can be as high as 100 μg.

The American Dental Association has stated that amalgam mercury exposure is insignificant compared with eating fish or seafood (2) and that tuna fish salad is a far greater mercury source than fillings (3). However, the average fish-eating person in the United States consumes 18.7 g of fish per day, containing an average mercury concentration of only .27 μg/g, yielding a daily mercury intake of 5.0 μg, with a lesser amount than that being absorbed (4).

In all fairness to our dentists, you should listen to what they have to say. What they say may be found in the *Clinical Research Associates Newsletter,* volume 15, issue 2, February, 1991. What follows is a lengthy extraction from that Newsletter entitled, "Silver amalgam and its alternatives—1991." I apologize for the somewhat long-winded comments that follow, but I think they are important for you to read because this is what your dentists are reading and telling their patients.

"Recently, controversy about silver amalgam use has been revived due to media exposure. Clinical Research Associates' survey with 10,000 responses showed that currently 94% of dentists use amalgam as major Class 2 restorative material, and 6% do not use amalgam at all. Research and/or empirical evidence supports both sides of the question. Practicing dentists and patients must make the decision together on whether or not to use amalgam in this confusing time. What follows are questions asked most commonly by patients.

- Does the American Dental Association support silver amalgam use? Yes, as do the National Associations of almost all countries of the world.
- Has the FDA granted approval to market silver amalgam? Yes. In 1976, under a grandfather clause after enactment of Medical Device Amendments, Food, Drug, and Cosmetics Act and again in 1987 when it was classified as a product not requiring further study and efficacy data.
- Are any states considering eliminating silver amalgam use? Yes, there are anti-amalgam lobbys active in several U.S. states.
- Should a dentist remove silver amalgam restoration on a patient's request? Maybe. There appears to be no problem in doing this if: a) the patient is advised that currently there is not sufficient evidence to justify amalgam removal for 'health reasons'; b) advantages, disadvantages, and risks of such removal are explained to the patient; and c) signed consent is obtained.
- Should a dentist advocate removal of silver amalgam for health reasons? No. Some dentists may not realize this violates the principles of ethics and codes of professional conduct of the American Dental Association and some other national organizations as well.
- Are there any known problems associated with removal of silver amalgam

restorations? Yes, but they are minimal: a) trauma to teeth and pulp tissue; b) increased release of mercury vapor during removal; c) cutting away tooth structure; and, d) placement of silver amalgam with restorations that have less research and could later be found to be more toxic than amalgam.
- Do persons with silver amalgam restorations have more mercury in their blood than those without amalgam? Yes, but this small amount of mercury is several times less than amounts shown in research to have been caused by eating one or more fish per week.
- Do recent studies on sheep by Canadian researcher, Mary Vimi, indicate that mercury in dental restorations is a potential problem for humans? To be decided. There has been significant debate on the relation of these sheep studies to humans. However, on November 20, 1990, the Canadian Dental Association sent a communication to its members critiquing the Vimi study reaffirming the Association's acceptance of amalgam, and asking for continuing research on the subject of toxicity of dental amalgam.
- Have signs and symptoms of multiple sclerosis been related to silver amalgam? No. Leaders of the Multiple Sclerosis Society recently stated in writing that multiple sclerosis has no relation to silver amalgam dental restorations and they were very critical of the *60 Minutes* television program that recently aired for inferring this relationship.
- Should patients be advised before silver amalgam placement that there is mercury in this material? Yes, in view of increased litigation, it appears prudent to advise patients of any therapy that is being contemplated, along with alternatives, advantages, disadvantages, known risks and costs.
- Is there adequate research on potential toxicity of materials suggested as replacements for silver amalgam restorations? No. Material most likely to be used is composite resin. There has been very little research documenting the effect of composite resin components that are released from restorations over time. Small particles of glass fillers, metals of numerous types, and resin matrix debris can enter the digestive system. Also, questions remain unanswered concerning breakdown products of dental cements used with cast gold, ceramic, and other materials out of which inlays, onlays, and crowns are constructed. In addition, various metals in gold alloys have had little biologic research.
- Are there alternatives for silver amalgam at this time? Yes, but none has the universal usefulness of silver amalgam. There are many important characteristics to consider in the selection of alternative materials."

To close this unusually lengthy commentary on a controversial topic, let me simply add that we must continue the search for verifiable data.— Let's fight truth decay.—J.A. Stockman, III, M.D.

References

1. Lorschider FL, et al: *Lancet* 337:1103, 1991.
2. American Dental Association: *ADA News* December 1, 1989, p 6.
3. American Dental Association: *J Am Dent Assoc* 120:395, 1990.
4. Clarkson TW, et al: *EPA Bulletin*, No 600/8/84/019 F, 1984, pp 314–319.

Use of a Palatal Stabilizing Device in the Prevention of Palatal Grooves in Premature Infants
Fadavi S, Adeni S, Dziedzic K, Punwani I, Vidyasagar D (Univ of Illinois, Chicago)
Crit Care Med 18:1279–1281, 1990   16–3

Acquired palatal grooves have been reported in intubated neonates, particularly after prolonged orotracheal intubation. Because the persistence of these palatal grooves may affect the child's phonation and future dental and orofacial development, a study was undertaken to determine whether a palatal stabilizing device (PSD) may prevent palatal grooving in premature intubated neonates.

In a prospective, randomized fashion, 26 premature infants requiring endotracheal intubation were assigned either to an experimental group (n = 12) that received an intraoral acrylic PSD within 24 hours of intubation (Fig 16–1) or a control group (n = 14). Birth weights ranged from 540 to 1,740 g, and gestational age ranged from 24 to 36 weeks. Mean duration of intubation was 38 days for the control group and 33 days for the experimental group.

Postextubation palatal impressions showed normal palatal structures in all 12 infants in the experimental group. In contrast, all 14 infants in the control group showed palatal grooving ranging from 2 to 7 mm in depth (Fig 16–2). The most severe grooving patterns occurred in infants intubated for more than 30 days with a correlation coefficient between the intubation period and groove depth of r = .92. The PSD is an effective device in preventing palatal grooving in intubated premature infants and requires little change in routine care.

▶ In 1984, Erenberg and Nowak (1) warned us that as many as 48% of infants who require orotracheal intubation demonstrate a palatal groove after the tube is removed. By definition, a palatal groove is an architectural deformity of the

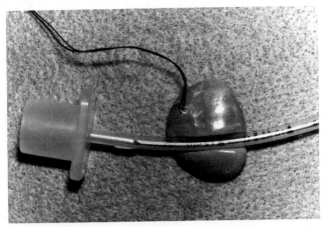

Fig 16–1.—Palatal stabilizing device with endotracheal tube in place. (Courtesy of Fadavi S, Adeni S, Dziedzic K, et al: *Crit Care Med* 18:1279–1281, 1990.)

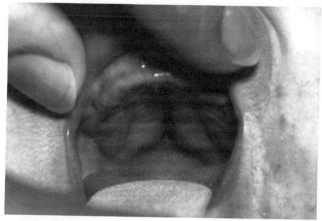

Fig 16–2.—Infant with palatal groove ≥ 5 mm in depth. (Courtesy of Fadavi S, Adeni S, Dziedzic K, et al: *Crit Care med* 18:1279–1281, 1990.)

palate caused by external pressure from the orotracheal tube. What Fadavi et al. are telling us in the article abstracted above is that we can mold an appliance to fit around the tube so that the tube will rub against the mold and not the palate. This prevents the development of a palatal groove.

If you want to read another article on this topic, read that of Fadavi et al., in the *Clinics of Preventive Dentistry* in 1990 (2). Then again, don't bother, it is exactly the same material presented in 2 different journals. You be the judge as to whether this is an important enough topic to clone itself with only a minor change in lineage of the authors.—J.A. Stockman, III, M.D.

References

1. Erenberg A, Nowak AJ: *Am J Dis Child* 138:974, 1984.
2. Fadavi S, et al: *Clin Prev Dent* 12:9, 1990.

Bacteremia in Children Following Dental Extraction
Coulter WA, Coffey A, Saunders IDF, Emmerson AM (The Queen's Univ of Belfast; Royal Belfast Hosp for Sick Children)
J Dent Res 69:1691–1695, 1990
16–4

To determine the incidence of postextraction bacteremia in children after dental manipulation, blood was collected for culture 1–2 minutes after tooth extraction in 58 patients aged 2–13 years. The effects of the number and type of teeth extracted, oral hygiene, gingival health, presence of abscess, and antibiotic prophylaxis on the incidence and intensity of bacteremia were assessed.

Postextraction blood cultures were positive in 20 of the 32 (63%) patients who did not receive antibiotics, compared with 9 of 26 (35%) children who received antibiotic prophylaxis with penicillin, amoxycillin, or erythromycin because of the increased risk of infective endocarditis.

Identification and Incidence of Microorganisms in Postextraction
Bacteremia in Children

Micro-organism	Total Number of Isolates	Number of Patients from which Isolated
Streptococcus sanguis	13	8
Streptococcus mitior	11	8
Streptococcus milleri	3	2
Streptococcus sp.	4	2
Actinomyces sp.	12	5
Bacteroides sp.	9	5
Lactobacillus sp.	4	3
Veillonella sp.	10	7
Corynebacterium sp.	5	3
Other identified sp. *	12	8
Non-characterized	5	3
Total	88	

Note: Strict anaerobes represent 26.5% and streptococci, 37.3% of characterized isolates.
*Identified species include *Fusobacterium, Haemophilus, Capnocytophaga,* and *Bacterionema.*
(Courtesy of Coulter WA, Coffey A, Saunders IDF, et al: *J Dent Res* 69:1691–1695, 1990.)

Hence, antibiotics significantly reduced the incidence of bacteremia. The intensity of bacteremia was small; 80% of cultures had 2 colonies per milliliter of blood. The agar-pour plate method, which facilitated the growth of anaerobes, was significantly better in detecting bacteremia than the broth culture method. A high proportion of isolates were recovered under anaerobic culture. Of the 88 bacterial strains isolated, 22 were strict anaerobes and 16 were microaerophilic (table). The remainder were mainly streptococci, particularly *Streptococcus sanguis* and *Streptococcus mitior,* which were generally sensitive to the antibiotics used. There was no correlation between the incidence of bacteremia and the plaque and gingival indices, the number and type of teeth extracted, and presence of abscess.

All children at risk of infective endocarditis require antibiotic prophylaxis before tooth extraction, because it is impossible to predict clinically the likelihood or magnitude of transient bacteremia. Penicillin, amoxycillin, and erythromycin are recommended for prophylaxis.

▶ The 63% incidence of bacteremia in this group of children is of the same order as that reported by Peterson and Peacock some 15 years ago (1). This provides compelling evidence for the absolute need for antibiotic prophylaxis when indicated.

Notice the word when in the above paragraph. We are still learning more about when we should and should not use antibiotic prophylaxis to prevent bacterial endocarditis. For example, should you use prophylaxis for simple adjustment of orthodontic appliances in children with structural heart disease? The current guidelines of the American Heart Association do not suggest so, but this may not be true. Biancaniello et al. (2) recently described 2 young teenagers who got into serious trouble because they did not conform to any guideline published by the American Heart Association. One was a 13-year-old boy who was admitted to the hospital with a spiking temperature of over 40° associated with rigors and a 10-pound weight loss during the preceding 6 weeks. Ten days before the onset of fever, according to the patient's mother, his orthodontist had adjusted the wires on his braces. An echocardiogram confirmed the presence of vegetations on the right aortic cusp and severe destruction of the aortic valve, which ultimately required replacement. It was impossible to tell whether the aortic valve was normal before all the damage occurred.

The second case was that of a 14-year-old girl admitted with a 3-week history of fever up to 39° C. She also had weight loss, fatigue, and headache. She was known to have had a small ventricular septal defect. An echocardiogram showed a small vegetation on the septal leaflet of the tricuspid valve. Blood cultures in her, as in the other teenager, were positive.

The American Heart Association will have to pay careful attention to these reports. They have a fairly profound significance because, at least in our area, most orthodontists leave appliances on for a little over 2 years and adjust them as frequently as every 5 weeks. This would markedly explode the requirements for antibiotic prophylaxis use, but if it prevents things such as replacement of aortic valves, it is well worth the effort required.—J.A. Stockman, III, M.D.

References

1. Peterson LJ, et al: *Circulation* 53:676, 1976.
2. Biancaniello TM, et al: *J Pediatr* 118:248, 1991.

Bacteremia With Otitis Media
Schutzman SA, Petrycki S, Fleisher GR (Boston)
Pediatrics 87:48–53, 1991   16–5

Otitis media is a common illness in young children. Reports of the incidence of bacteremia in otitis media have ranged from 1.5% to 5.8%. A study of febrile children with otitis media was undertaken to determine the occurrence of associated bacteremia, factors related to an increased risk of bacteremia, and the outcome of patients with bacteremia.

From charts studied at a children's hospital, 2,982 patients were identified who were aged 3–36 months, had temperatures ≥39° C, and had otitis media without other evident bacterial infectious foci. Blood cultures, obtained at the discretion of the treating physician, were drawn for 1,666 children. All patients were treated with orally administered antibiotics and were then discharged.

Fifty of the cultures (3%) were considered bacteremic; most (39) grew *Streptococcus pneumoniae*. The incidence of bacteremia increased at higher temperatures, and younger children were more likely to be bacteremic. When the 50 patients with bacteremia were reevaluated, 9 were found to have continued fever, 3 had persistent bacteremia, 1 had pneu-

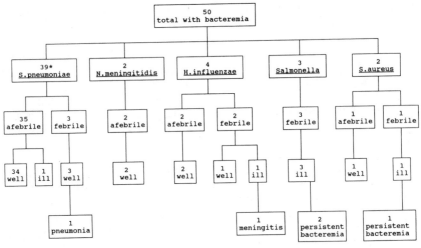

* 1 lost to follow-up

Fig 16–3.—Clinical outcome of children with bacteremia according to organism. *S. pneumonia = Streptococcus pneumoniae; N. meningitidis = Neisseria meningitidis; H. influenzae = Haemophilus influenzae; S. aureus = Staphylococcus aureus.* (Courtesy of Schutzman SA, Petrycki S, Fleisher GR: *Pediatrics* 87:48–53, 1991.)

monia, and 1 had meningitis (Fig 16–3). All of these children recovered after antibiotic therapy without major complications.

Although only about half of the children had blood cultures drawn, these were patients with younger age and higher mean temperatures—factors associated with an increased risk of bacteremia. Thus the rate of bacteremia in the entire group of children should not exceed 3%. The potential benefit of performing a blood culture must be weighed against the cost, inconvenience, and discomfort of the procedure.

▶ As a house officer, every time I saw a highly febrile youngster, I was "tickled pink" when I found a red eardrum and nothing else in an otherwise nonseptic-looking patient. It put my mind at ease knowing I had little to be worried about from that point on. This report, however, reminds us that up to 5% of infants and children with otitis media who have temperatures of greater than 40° will be bacteremic. Even at lesser temperatures, there is still some risk of bacteremia. Approximately one fifth of the bacteremic patients came home to haunt the care provider. Within this latter category of patients, persistence of fever, persistence of bacteremia, the development of pneumonia and meningitis were noted. To say all this differently, of all patients with bilateral otitis media, .6% will go on to have a more complicated course. Only 1 in 1,500 will have a problem such as pneumonia or meningitis subsequently. Nonetheless, we should not be changing our approach to the management of a febrile child with otitis media. Oral antibiotics (assuming the child otherwise looks satisfactory) are good enough.

Before closing out this commentary, we will ask the question, "Does the infrared tympanic membrane thermometer work?"

The answer to this is maybe yes, maybe no, maybe we don't know as yet. Current tympanic membrane thermometers consist of a probe tip covered by a disposable polyethylene speculum, an infrared-sensing handle, and a base module that translates the accumulated infrared energy into a temperature reading. Kenney et al. (1) seem to think that the instrument is quite effective, especially in view of the labor cost savings in terms of time associated with use of the instrument. Ross (2) reviewed the instrument known as "First Temp" and concluded as well that tympanic membrane thermometers offer several significant advantages over glass-mercury and electronic devices presently being used. However, because of conflicting data regarding the accuracy of the tympanic membrane thermometer, he suggests that additional studies are needed before everyone rushs out and buys one of these thermometers. The conflicting data in part were reported at the Ambulatory Pediatric Association meetings in spring 1991. Oral and/or rectal temperatures were compared with tympanic membrane temperatures in 1,159 children from the Children's Memorial Hospital in Chicago (3). The authors concluded that the First Temp tympanic membrane thermometer is not a reliable indicator of fever in children because of its imprecision and significant variability. The manufacturer has indicated that it is working on a new generation of First Temp, which will be called "Genius," to solve this problem.

Conclusion: The first generation of tympanic membrane thermometers may fall into the same classification as hair restorers. They both appear to be balderdash.—J.A. Stockman, III, M.D.

References

1. Kenney RD, et al: *Pediatrics* 85:855, 1990.
2. Ross SP: *Pediatr Emerg Care* 6:299, 1990.
3. Nypaver M, et al: *Proc Ambulatory Pediatric Association*, Spring meeting, New Orleans, 1991.

Otitis Media in Infancy and Intellectual Ability, School Achievement, Speech, and Language at Age 7 Years
Teele DW, Klein JO, Chase C, Menyuk P, Rosner BA, and the Greater Boston Otitis Media Study Group (Boston City Hosp; Boston Univ; Harvard Med School)
J Infect Dis 162:685–694, 1990   16–6

Children with frequent episodes of acute otitis media and effusions of the middle ear (MEE) experience some degree of conductive hearing loss during their illness. In young children such hearing loss occurs at a time when language and other skills are acquired. Results of previous studies that have related MEE to later delay or impairment of speech, language, or cognitive abilities have been inconclusive.

A series of 194 children with a history of MEE were evaluated at age 7 years. The children were stratified by estimated time spent with MEE during the first 3 years of life: fewer than 30 days, 30–129 days, or 130

Cognitive Ability at Age 7 Years by Estimated Days With Middle
Ear Effusion (MEE) During First 3 Years of Life

Estimated days with MEE

IQ test	<30	30–129	⩾130
Full scale	113.1*†	107.5*	105.4†
Verbal	111.5‡§	106.5‡	105.8§
Performance	112.2†‖	108.3‖	104.1†

Note: Cognitive ability is expressed as mean IQ by WISC-R after adjusting for socioeconomic status and gender. Time spent with MEE is natural log of time with effusion (days + 1). Intervals with MEE were selected to produce 3 groups of about equal size.
*P = .007.
†P = .001.
‡P = .026.
‖Not Significant.
§P = .008.
(Courtesy of Teele DW, Klein JO, Chase C, et al: *J Infect Dis* 162:685–694, 1990.)

days or more. The third group included a disproportionate number of boys, children with siblings, and those who had ventilation tubes. After controlling for confounding variables, a significant association was noted between estimated time spent with MEE during the first 3 years of life and lower scores on tests of cognitive ability (table), speech and language, and school performance at age 7 years. Children with MEE during the first 3 years of life had significantly lower scores in mathematics and reading on the Metropolitan Achievement Test. Articulation and the use of morphological markers were similarly affected. Scores on the full-scale Wechsler Intelligence Scale for Children, revised, were lowest for those children who had the longest experience of MEE (105.4) and highest for those who had the least (113.1).

The hearing loss experienced by children with MEE appears to have an effect on later intellectual ability, success in school, and speech and language capabilities. Time with MEE after the age of 3 years did not significantly affect these measures. Thus effective intervention to prevent MEE in infancy may help children to reach their intellectual and linguistic potential.

▶ Dr. Herbert L. Needleman, Professor of Pediatrics, University of Pittsburgh Medical School, comments:

▶ What the developmental sequelae of otitis media are is a high-stakes question. The disease is among the commonest in pediatric practice, and were it to be followed by impaired CNS function, it could be among the most important causes of language and school problems.

The study by Teele et al. is one of the more rigorous investigations of the problem, and their report of IQ deficits, lower achievement in math and reading, and speech problems must be taken seriously. An earlier forward study of otitis media and IQ by Silva et al. (1) reported similar findings, further strengthening the inference drawn here.

Teele et al. studied subjects prospectively, and their sample has adequate statistical power. Subjects were chosen in an unbiased fashion, the examiners were all trained in the diagnosis, and the psychological raters were blind to the health status of the subjects. Weaknesses of the study are lack of early measures of performance and hearing and the use of a clinical diagnosis of the disease to classify subjects. None of these invalidate the author's findings. Indeed, because there is no reason to believe that they are systematically assigned to 1 group, they are type II biases, and they increase the risk of missing a true finding. Reducing these errors could be expected to increase the size of the otitis media effect. Some critics of this and other studies have failed to take into account the fact that biases often are not symmetrical. Listing biases is not enough, the direction of the bias' impact should be determined—whether toward or away from the null.

Any study that attempts to isolate the effects of any single threat to the CNS from the multiple agents that affect development is guaranteed to elicit controversy. The influences on child development factors are manifold, the measurement of CNS performance imprecise, and the classification of exposure to the noxious agent subject to error. Many studies of otitis media and child development have shown deficits in cognitive or language function, and some have failed to find an effect. When this happens, reviewers tend to tally the votes, and then conclude that no conclusion can be drawn. This approach seriously degrades the data. If there were no effect of otitis media on development, only 1 study in 20 would be expected to show an effect on the basis of chance. A 50/50 tally is therefore strong evidence of an effect. Narrative reviews of issues like this may be expected to dwindle in the future as quantitative syntheses of data (known as meta-analysis) grow in number and sophistication.—H.L. Needleman, M.D.

Reference

1. Silva PA, et al: *J Learn Disabil* 19:165, 1986.

Amoxicillin or Myringotomy or Both for Acute Otitis Media: Results of a Randomized Clinical Trial
Kaleida PH, Casselbrant ML, Rockette HE, Paradise JL, Bluestone CD, Blatter MM, Reisinger KS, Wald ER, Supance JS (Children's Hosp of Pittsburgh; Univ of Pittsburgh)
Pediatrics 87:466–474, 1991   16–7

Antimicrobial drugs have been the customary treatment for acute otitis media in children for nearly 40 years. Controversy continues, however, on the optimal duration of treatment, the advantage of adding myringotomy, and the desirability of routinely treating the disease at all. A prospective, randomized trial was done to determine the efficacy of amoxicillin in the treatment of nonsevere acute otitis media and the comparative efficacy of amoxicillin alone, myringotomy alone, and amoxicillin and myringotomy combined.

Five hundred thirty-six infants and children with acute otitis media were assigned to 1 of 6 consistent year-long regimens. Nonsevere episodes were treated with either amoxicillin or placebo, and severe episodes were treated with amoxicillin, amoxicillin plus myringotomy, or, in children aged 2 years or more, placebo and myringotomy. Nonsevere episodes had better outcomes in patients treated with amoxicillin than with placebo. In children with nonsevere episodes at study entry, those assigned to amoxicillin had less average time with effusion during the succeeding year than those given placebo. Recurrence rates in these 2 groups, however, were comparable. In children aged 2 years and older, severe episodes resulted in more initial treatment failures when treated with myringotomy alone compared with amoxicillin with or without myringotomy. Overall, patients with severe episodes treated with amoxicillin alone and those treated with amoxicillin and myringotomy had comparable outcomes.

Children with acute otitis media should be routinely treated with amoxicillin or an equivalent antimicrobial drug. The routine use of myringotomy, alone or with amoxicillin, is not warranted.

▶ You can be sure of 1 thing in life: in each year's YEAR BOOK you will read something about therapy for otitis media. When will it ever end?

The issue raised by the article abstracted above is whether or not myringotomy adds anything to the initial management of acute otitis media. Several points are quite clear from this extraordinarily well designed study. Regarding nonsevere otitis media, outcomes are consistently more favorable in those treated with antibiotics (in this case, amoxicillin) than in those who receive no treatment at all. This is no great surprise, despite trends in England away from treatment of mild otitis media. Further, in the management of severe otitis media, the data suggest that treatment with myringotomy alone may be inadequate. Furthermore, the routine addition of myringotomy to amoxicillin is probably not advantageous either. This is not to say that children with severe pain in their ears, those whose symptoms do not resolve with simple antibiotic management, or those in whom suppurative complications develop should not undergo a myringotomy.

This year is the silver anniversary of an article by Lecks, Kravis, and Wood that addressed the value of steroids as part of the management of serous otitis media (1). Believe it or not, these very same investigators recently have concluded, after a quarter of a century's experience with intranasal steroids, that they may work (2). At the same time that the report by Lecks et al. was appearing, Podoshin et al. (3) reported that oral prednisone at a dose of 1 mg/kg/day, when combined with amoxicillin, was significantly more effective than amoxicillin alone in the treatment of persistent otitis media with effusion. Berman et al. (4) concluded the same thing in a report from the University of Colorado. They combined steroids with trimethoprim sulfamethoxazole and found the combination to be better than antibiotic alone.

Before you rush to the pharmacy for topical or oral steroids, read the very thoughtful commentary on this whole subject by Macknin (5) who reviewed the world's literature from 1967 to the present time. He concludes that "it appears that antibiotics plus steroids might offer at least a temporary beneficial effect in clearing middle ear effusion. However, in 1991, large prospective blinded placebo controlled studies with long-term follow-up are still needed to define what, if any, role steroids should play in the management of middle ear disease." Enough said on the topic of steroids and middle ear effusions.

A question: You see all the advertisements on television about purchasing the toothbrush recommended most by dentists. What are the prescribing preferences of pediatricians when it comes to front-line antibiotic treatment for otitis media?

The answer to this should come as no surprise. In a survey done at the National Pediatric Infectious Disease Seminar in New Orleans in 1990, 88% of the respondents chose amoxicillin as their first-line therapeutic agent for otitis media. As a back-up for failure of amoxicillin therapy in otitis media, the following drugs were used: Bactrim/Septra, 34.8%; Ceclor, 27.8%; Pediazole, 19.5%; Augmentin, 16.9%; Suprax, 1%; and Ceftin, 0% (6).

Middle ear disease is an incredibly intricate affair, and more than one researcher has fallen into the pitfalls associated with studies of problems in this arena. All of the answers are not in as yet, and to the investigators in Pittsburgh who have worked so hard in this area, we say keep your chin up. The essence of research is to recognize that, although Mother Nature makes things complex, she is not wicked. The answers will ultimately come.—J.A. Stockman, III, M.D.

References

1. Lecks HI, et al: *Clin Pediatr* 6:519, 1967.
2. Lecks HI, et al: *Clin Pediatr* 30:174, 1991.
3. Podoshin L, et al: *Otolaryngol Head Neck Surg* 116:1404, 1990.
4. Berman S, et al: *Pediatr Infect Dis J* 9:533, 1990.
5. Macknin L: *Clin Pediatr* 30:178, 1990.
6. Nelson JD, et al: *Pediatr Infect Dis J* Newsletter 16:11, 1990.

A Comparison of Postoperative Bleeding Incidence Between General and Local Anesthesia Tonsillectomies

Kennedy KS, Strom CG (Naval Hosp, Portsmouth, Va; Naval Hosp, Oakland, Calif)
Otolaryngol Head Neck Surg 102:654–657, 1990   16–8

Bleeding is the most frequent complication after tonsillectomy. To ascertain the role of anesthesia in postoperative tonsillectomy bleeding, 192 patients, aged 2–56 years (mean age, 18 years) who underwent tonsillectomy were interviewed 30 days after operation. Patients having local anesthesia were injected with 1% lidocaine containing 1:100,000 epinephrine.

Postoperative bleeding occurred in 3 (3%) of 105 patients who had general anesthesia and 13 (15%) of 87 patients who had local anesthesia. When the results were re-evaluated considering that no patients age younger than 9 years old had the procedure under local anesthesia, the incidence of postoperative bleeding remained significantly higher in patients who received local anesthetic (15%) than in those who received general anesthesia (4%) and those who received locally infiltrated epinephrine during general anesthesia (6%). Bleeding was more common after the first 24 hours postoperatively (secondary bleeding). Sex and history of peritonsillar abscess had no effect on the incidence of postoperative bleeding.

Interestingly, 4 patients who bled were treated by physicians other than the operating surgeon. None of the patients required blood transfusion, and no deaths occurred. These data suggest that postoperative tonsillectomy bleeding is more common after local anesthesia than after general anesthesia. The incidence of postoperative tonsillectomy bleeding may be underestimated because patients may be treated by other physicians and may not inform the operating surgeon.

▶ The easiest way to have no problems related to a tonsillectomy is not to do the tonsillectomy in the first place. There are still far too many tonsillectomies being performed without adequate indication. The fact that there will be less bleeding under general anesthesia than with local anesthesia for a tonsillectomy should give no consolation either to parents who permit their children to have this procedure or to the surgeons doing it. Frankly, the only person who should be permitted to perform an unwarranted tonsillectomy is someone who previously has had a tonsillectomy himself or herself and was not afforded the benefits of either general or local anesthesia.—J.A. Stockman, III, M.D.

Changes in Tonsillar Bacteriology of Recurrent Acute Tonsillitis: 1980 vs 1989

Timon CI, McAllister VA, Walsh M, Cafferkey MT (St James' Hosp; Trinity College, Dublin)
Respir Med 84:395–400, 1990   16–9

To assess the changes in tonsillar microbiology that have occurred over the past 10 years, 2 groups of patients with recurrent acute tonsillitis who underwent tonsillectomy 9 years apart were studied. Tonsillectomies were performed in 33 patients, aged 2.5–17 years, in 1980, and in 58 patients, aged 3–33.5 years, in 1989. A tonsillar swab was obtained before operation from each patient.

In the 1980 study, normal flora was isolated from 60% of the tonsil surface specimens and 24% of the deep-tissue specimens. In the 1989 group, 45% of the patients had normal flora on superficial tonsil swabs, and none of the patients had normal deep-tissue cultures. *Hemophilus* species predominated in the deep-tonsil cultures performed in 1980 and remained the most frequent pathogen isolated from tonsillar tissue in 1989. The incidence of *Haemophilus influenzae* in tonsillar tissue increased from 39% in 1980 to 62% in 1989. Furthermore, only 2% of the *H. influenzae* isolates of 1980 were β-lactamase producers compared with 44% of the 1989 isolates. *Staphylococcus aureus* has also become more prominent over time, increasing from a 6% incidence in 1980 to a 40% incidence in 1989. Few anaerobic organisms were cultured.

In both study groups, the throat swabs grew mostly organisms commensal to the upper respiratory tract, but the deep tonsillar tissue excised at tonsillectomy carried significant growths of pathogens, thus supporting the diagnostic inadequacy of superficial throat swabs. In view of the high incidence of β-lactamase-producing organisms found in the 1989 study, it is recommended that penicillin or ampicillin should no longer be used as the agents of choice in blind therapy for recurrent acute tonsillitis, but that penicillinase-resistant antibiotics should be prescribed.

▶ Dr. Itzhak Brook, Professor of Pediatrics, Uniform Military Services Medical School, comments:

▶ Recurrent pharyngotonsillitis caused by group A β-hemolytic streptococci (GABHS) continues to be a serious clinical problem. Failure to eradicate the streptococci from patients treated with penicillin occasionally can lead to rheumatic fever and, rarely, to glomerulonephritis. As a last resort, many physicians refer their patients for elective tonsillectomy. One explanation for this penicillin failure is that repeated penicillin administration results in a shift in the oral bacterial microflora, with selection of β-lactamase-producing bacteria (BLPB) (e.g., strains of *Haemophilus* sp., *Staphylococcus aureus, Moraxella catarrhalis,* and *Bacteroides* sp.) which, by degrading penicillin in the area of the infection, can protect not only themselves but also penicillin-susceptible pathogens.

The study by Timon et al. explored for the first time the dynamics of tonsillar infection in 1 location (Dublin, Ireland) over a period of 9 years. They compared the microbiology of deep and superficial tissues of the tonsils in the non-inflamed status and determined the incidence of BLPB. Although anaerobes were not vigorously sought in this study, Timon et al. showed that a significant increase occurred between 1980 to 1981 in the recovery rate of the 2 BLPB: *S. aureus* and *H. influenzae.* They also confirmed that more pathogens including GABHS can be found in the core of the tonsils rather than on the surface. This suggests that GABHS may be "shielded" from penicillin therapy in the core of the tonsils by the BLPB.

Because clinicians only obtain surface cultures of tonsils, they may miss GABHS in the non-inflamed tonsils. Whether these discrepancies also explain the difficulties in recovery of GABHS in acute tonsillar infection is yet to be determined.

It is evident from this report, as well as from several others, that the microbiology of tonsillitis may vary in different geographic locations. Although what is common to all sites where studies were performed is the growing number of tonsils that harbor BLPB, these bacteria may vary at different locations. Whether these differences mean that different antimicrobials should be used to eradicate GABHS recurrent tonsillitis is yet to be ascertained. The antimicrobials that showed superior efficacy to penicillin in eradicating GABHS as well as both the aerobic and anaerobic BLPB are clindamycin or the combination of amoxicillin and clavulanic acid. Although second and third generation cephalosporins have superior efficacy against *S. aureus* and *H. influenzae* compared with penicillin, they are less effective than clindamycin or amoxacillin and clavulanic acid against anaerobic BLPB.—I. Brook, M.D.

Dentofacial Development in Long-Term Survivors of Acute Lymphoblastic Leukemia: A Comparison of Three Treatment Modalities
Sonis AL, Tarbell N, Valachovic RW, Gelber R, Schwenn M, Sallan S (Children's Hosp; Dana Farber Cancer Inst; New England Med Ctr Floating Hosp, Boston)
Cancer 66:2645–2652, 1990   16–10

   Although the prognosis for children with acute lymphoblastic leukemia has improved, a high incidence of acute oral complications has been seen after completion of therapy. Both chemotherapeutic agents and radiation therapy (RT) may cause dental problems.
   The effects of 3 treatment approaches on dental and facial development were compared retrospectively in 97 children who had undergone chemotherapy alone, chemotherapy plus 1,800-cGy cranial irradiation or chemotherapy plus 2,400-cGy irradiation. All were younger than age 10 years when therapy began, were in continuous remission when studied, and were evaluated at least 5 years after the diagnosis of acute lympho-

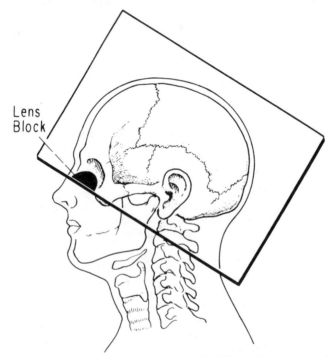

Fig 16–4.—Typical cranial field for CNS prophylaxis. The field includes the entire cranial meninges. The inferior border of the fields are positioned along a line that extends from the inferior orbital ridge to approximately 1 cm below the mastoid tip to the middle of the second cervical vertebra. (Courtesy of Sonis AL, Tarbell N, Valachovic RW, et al: *Cancer* 66:2645–2652, 1990.)

blastic leukemia. The field of irradiation for CNS treatment included the entire cranial meninges (Fig 16−4).

Panoramic radiographs, obtained on all patients, were examined for dental abnormalities and classified according to a dental disturbance severity scale. For purposes of analysis, patients were divided into 6 groups according to age (younger or older than age 5 years) and type of treatment. The lowest mean disturbance severity rating (.64) was in children who were age 5 years or older at diagnosis and who received no radiation therapy. The highest such rating (16.25) occurred in the younger children who had received the higher radiation dosage; craniofacial effects of therapy were observed only in this subgroup. Abnormalities included tooth agenesis, arrested root development, microdontia, and enamel dysplasias.

The overall incidence of abnormal dental development was high and occurred in 94% of all children and 100% of those younger than age 5 years at diagnosis. The relatively high position of the maxillary permanent posterior teeth in the younger children placed those teeth in the direct field of irradiation. Therapy-altered pituitary function may also play a role in abnormal craniofacial development.

▶ This abstract pretty much says it all. One related thing that is not mentioned in this article is the potential that there may be alterations in the architecture of the airway that can result in other sequela such as recurrent otitis media, which either directly or indirectly can result in hearing problems. Please add long-term survivors of acute lymphocytic leukemia to the list of children at high risk for both the problems noted in the abstract and for potential hearing difficulties.

On the topic of hearing, we are frequently asked who should and should not have audiology screening. What follows is a 1990 position statement by the Joint Committee on Infant Hearing, which was comprised of representatives from The American Speech & Hearing Association, The American Academy of Otolaryngology, the American Academy of Pediatrics, and the Council on the Education of the Deaf. The criteria established for audiology screening in infants is as follows:

- Birth weight of 1,500 grams or less.
- Need for prolonged neonatal resuscitation associated with acidosis, shock, neurologic sequelae, or respiratory disease (e.g., may include Apgar score of 0–3 at 5 minutes, failure to initiate spontaneous respiration by 10 minutes, or those with hypotonia persisting to 2 hours of age).
- Congenital infection known or suspected to be associated with sensorineural hearing impairment such as toxoplasmosis, syphilis, rubella, cytomegalovirus, and herpes.
- Bacterial meningitis.
- Craniofacial anomalies including morphologic abnormalities of the pinnae and ear canal, absent philtrum, low hairline, and cleft palate.
- Hyperbilirubinemia at a level exceeding indication for exchange transfusion.
- Family history of congenital or delayed onset childhood sensorineural impairment.

- Ototoxic medications including but not limited to the aminoglycosides used for more than 5 days (e.g., gentamicin) and "loop" diuretics used in combination with aminoglycosides.
- Prolonged mechanical ventilation for a duration equal to or greater than 5 days (e.g., persistent pulmonary hypertension, meconium aspiration syndrome).
- Stigmata or other findings associated with a syndrome known to include sensorineural hearing (e.g., Waardenburg syndrome, Usher's syndrome, or Trisomy 21).
- Other reasonable suspicion.

I hope that you find the above list helpful in your practice.—J.A. Stockman, III, M.D.

Massive Adenopathy in Oropharyngeal Tularemia; C.T. Demonstration
Umlas S-L, Jaramillo D (Children's Hosp, Boston)
Pediatr Radiol 20:483–484, 1990   16–11

The radiologic manifestations of oropharyngeal tularemia, an uncommon cause of exudative pharyngitis and cervical lymphadenopathy, have not been described. The CT findings were helpful in diagnosing tularemia in a small boy with massive nodal enlargements.

Boy, 3½ years, had a 5-day history of sore throat, enlarged cervical nodes, and fever. Lateral cervical radiography showed thickening of the retropharyngeal tissues in the upper cervical region. Contrast-enhanced CT of the neck revealed marked adenotonsillar enlargement (Fig 16–5) with areas suggestive of early abscess formation in the adenoids. Retropharyngeal swelling and moderate bilateral cervical and submandibular adenopathy were also evident. Although 14 days of

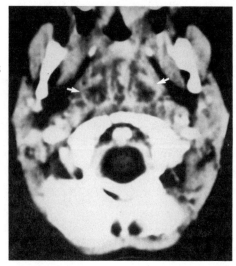

Fig 16–5.—Contrast-enhanced CT scan during first admission to hospital shows enlarged adenoids with inhomogeneous enhancement surrounding areas of low attenuation *(arrows)*. (Courtesy of Umlas S-L, Jaramillo D: *Pediatr Radiol* 20:483–484, 1990.)

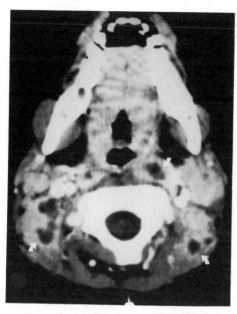

Fig 16–6.—Contrast-enhanced CT 3 weeks after scan in Figure 16–5 shows multiple areas of low attenuation with rim enhancement within nodal masses and in retropharyngeal space *(arrows)*. (Courtesy of Umlas S-L, Jaramillo D: *Pediatr Radiol* 20:483–484, 1990.)

penicillin and cefuroxime therapy produced a rapid resolution of symptoms, residual oropharyngeal swelling persisted at discharge. Five days after discharge the fever recurred along with new enlargement of the cervical nodes. Contrast-enhanced CT of the neck showed multiple areas of low attenuation with rim enhancement in the retropharyngeal tissues. Additional multiloculated masses with low attenuation centers and enhancing septa, which were consistent with abscess formation, were noted in the posterior cervical nodal chains (Fig 16–6). Smaller nodes along the internal jugular chains were enlarged but not necrotic. Gentamicin and oxacillin were given intravenously after serum tularemia titers were analyzed. All but the largest node responded to this treatment. Surgical drainage was needed for that node. The patient was discharged after 17 days of antibiotic therapy and remains well.

The oropharyngeal form of tularemia is usually seen in children and results from ingestion of the anaerobic gram-negative bacillus *Francisella tularensis*. Clinicians should consider tularemia in the differential diagnosis of massive adenotonsillar enlargement and extensive necrotic cervical adenopathy, particularly is endemic areas.

▶ The next time you see massive oropharyngeal lymphadenopathy on physical examination or on CT/MRI scanning that is suggestive of tularemia, ask the parents whether there are any pets at home named Flopsy, Mopsy, Cottontail, or Peter.

This editor shall not make snide remarks about rabbits as has been customary with cats. People who besmirch such kindly creatures as rabbits are mud slingers, and mud slingers do nothing but lose ground.—J.A. Stockman, III, M.D.

17 Endocrinology

Effect of Deslorelin Dose in the Treatment of Central Precocious Puberty
Pescovitz OH, Barnes KM, Cutler GB Jr (Indiana Univ Med Ctr, Indianapolis;
Natl Inst of Child Health and Human Development, Bethesda, Md)
J Clin Endocrinol Metab 72:60–64, 1991   17–1

Long-acting luteinizing hormone-releasing hormone (LHRH) analogues (LHRHas) are effective in the treatment of central precocious puberty, but no studies have determined the lowest effective dose of any of the presently available LHRHas. A double-blind study was conducted to determine the efficacy of deslorelin at dosages lower than the 4 μg/kg·day, which was previously known to suppress gonadotropins, linear growth, and skeletal maturation.

In 29 children with central precocious puberty, deslorelin was administered subcutaneously at 4 μg/kg·day for the initial 3 months. Thereafter, the patients were randomly assigned to 1 of 3 daily doses of deslorelin: 4 μg/kg (9 patients), 2 μg/kg (11 patients), or 1 μg/kg (9 patients). After 15 months, they resumed therapy at 4 μg/kg·day for 1 year.

The groups did not differ in terms of chronological age, bone age, pretreatment growth rate, or Tanner stage at the onset of therapy. Clinical and hormonal responses were also similar during the first 3 months of LHRHa therapy. Also, there were no significant differences during the 15-month treatment with 1, 2, or 4 μg/kg·day of deslorelin in terms of pubertal stage, linear growth velocity, rate of skeletal maturation, sex steroid levels, mean luteinizing hormone (LH) or follicle-stimulating hormone (FSH) levels, or peak FSH response to LHRH stimulation or to a dose of deslorelin. Peak LH responses to LHRH stimulation or to a dose of deslorelin were highest in children treated with the lowest dose.

Deslorelin given at 1 μg/kg·day may not effectively suppress the gonadotropin response to a dose of LHRH or deslorelin. A dosage of 2 μg/kg·day may have an efficacy similar to that of a dosage of 4 μg/kg·day. Until the efficacy of the 2-μg/kg dosage is confirmed in a larger study, considering that no toxicity has been reported with the larger dosage, it is recommended that deslorelin be given at 4 μg/kg·day in the treatment of children with central precocious puberty.

▶ Deslorelin is the first long-acting LHRH analogue to be used in the treatment of central precocious puberty. Following its introduction, an additional 5 other agonist/analogues have been developed as well. They have changed our understandings regarding the classification of pure premature sexual development.

It was once thought that premature sexual maturation of gonadal origin (in other words, excluding adrenal disorders) consisted of only 2 conditions, central precocious puberty and isolated premature thelarche. Central precocious puberty is often called idiopathic precocious puberty and is gonadotropin-dependent. It is brought about by the premature onset of pulsatile gonadotropin-releasing hormone secretion. In this situation, the sequence of pubertal development is normal, but the advance in epiphyseal maturation ultimately compromises adult stature. By contrast, isolated premature thelarche usually starts in girls under the age of 2, and the changes are confined to breast development. The growth rate is normal, and the condition resolves spontaneously. With the advent of gonadotropin-releasing hormone analogues, we have learned that if there is no response to treatment, puberty is independent of gonadotropin-releasing hormone secretion. For example, "familial testotoxicosis" is a form of gonadotropin-independent precocious puberty in which the serum may contain a testis stimulating factor. Gonadotropin-independent precocious puberty in girls is rare, seen almost exclusively in association with the McCune-Albright syndrome. Central precocious puberty in boys is almost always a serious condition associated with CNS space-occupying lesions.

The Food and Drug Administration has approved these gonadotropin-releasing hormone agonists/analogues. There appear to be minimal side effects of therapy with them. In girls with the central precocious puberty, the complete cessation of menstruation, cessation or regression of secondary sexual development, restoration of age-appropriate behavior, decrease in the velocity of growth to that appropriate for skeletal age, and slowing or cessation of skeletal maturation allowing normal adult stature is to be expected with treatment. Therapy needs to be monitored relatively frequently at 1 to 3 month intervals. The goal is complete cessation of treatment with gonadotropin-releasing hormones.

Don't think that agents such as deslorelin are just for kids. In fact, their widest use is not in children. Agonists produce a biochemical castration in adult males with prostatic cancer that results in relief of bone pain, decreases in serum and alkaline phosphatase levels, and dramatic remissions of metastatic bone disease. Women who have difficulty with uterine fibroids can have this problem taken care of with the agonist analogues. The same is true for women with endometriosis. These agonists can also be used for the management of polycystic ovary disease. They have done a fantastic job in assisting women to become pregnant through the in vitro fertilization technology. Pretreatment of 10 to 14 days with a gonadotropin-releasing hormone analogue now permits the induction of ovaluation by exogenous gonadotropins at an exact predictable point in time.

Finally, and somewhat unexpectedly, it has been found that a wide variety of tumors appear to have gonadotropin-releasing hormone receptors. Treatment with gonadotropin-releasing hormone agonists has proven helpful in the management of breast, pancreatic, ovarian, and pituitary tumors.

It was just 30 years ago that we knew virtually nothing about the secrets underlying normal pubertal development. Now the secrets have been revealed. At the rate at which we are developing these agonists/analogues and finding out what they can do, there won't even be secrets left in a few years.—J.A. Stockman, III M.D.

Preserving Adult Height Potential in Girls With Idopathic True Precocious Puberty
Kreiter M, Burstein S, Rosenfield RL, Moll GW Jr, Cara JF, Yousefzadeh DK, Cuttler L, Levitsky LL (Univ of Chicago)
J Pediatr 117:364–370, 1990
17–2

Idiopathic true precocious puberty is defined as the onset of isosexual pubertal changes before age 8. The only permanent physical sequela is reduced adult height. A prospective study compared presenting features of 21 girls with precocious puberty with and without evidence of reduced adult height potential.

Fourteen girls with impaired adult height prognosis (group 1) were re-examined after treatment with intranasal nafarelin, a gonadotropin-releasing hormone (GnRH) agonist. The criterion for treatment was a deterioration in predicted height as indicated by a loss of ≥5 cm on sequential bone age determinations at least 5 months apart or a predicted adult height of less than 152.5 cm. The 7 girls with a prognosis of unimpaired height (group 2) were followed without therapy. Initial estradiol levels were greater in group 1. Nafarelin therapy in group 1 suppressed the pituitary-gonadal axis. After transient reduction in height potential in girls with the youngest bone ages, the 2 years of treatment slightly improved predicted heights from 150.7 ± 2.1 to 152.7 ± 2.0 cm ($P < .05$). Height predictions increased from 165.4 ± 3.0 to 168.7 ± 4.1 cm ($P < .05$) in group 2.

Therapy with GnRH agonist apparently preserves height potential in girls with an initially impaired height prognosis. It seems necessary to achieve rapid (within 6 weeks) and complete suppression of the pituitary-gonadal axis when GnRH therapy is instituted. Optimal treatment might include a higher GnRH dose during the first 6 months or a combination therapy with antigonadal or antisteroidal agents. Height potential was preserved without therapy in patients with a good initial height prognosis. It is believed that GnRH analogues should be used conservatively until long-term safety and benefits are confirmed.

► Dr. Dennis Styne, Professor and Chairman, Department of Pediatrics, University of California, Davis Medical Center, comments:

► Hypothalamic gonadotropin-releasing hormone is secreted in episodic bursts every 90 to 120 minutes, with increased amplitude occurring during puberty. Such increased GnRH secretion causes greater episodic release of gonadotropins, which subsequently causes increased concentration of plasma sex steroids, leading to secondary sexual development. If this process occurs early, the condition is central or true precocious puberty. Exogenous GnRH may be administered in similarly timed boluses to cause such pulsatile release of gonadotropins. However, if GnRH is administered in a constant infusion, the pituitary gonadotrope, after a brief period of increased secretion, decreases gonadotropin secretion. Alterations of the 6th amino acid of the GnRH decapeptide and of its n-terminal can increase its potency and duration of action. Thus, a

single dose of such a superactive analogue is experienced by the pituitary gonadotrope as a constant infusion of GnRH and a daily single dose or a monthly
time-release dose will suppress gonadotropin secretion. These superactive
GnRH analogues appear to be the ideal medical treatment for central precocious puberty.

In this article, nafarelin, 1 of the superactive GnRH analogues, is again shown
to be effective in suppressing gonadotropin secretion, causing decreased sex
steroid secretion and cessation of the progression of secondary sexual characteristics. Most authorities feel that GnRH analogues are an excellent and safe
treatment for central precocious puberty. The authors have demonstrated that
those patients most likely to achieve impaired adult heights because of severe
manifestations of central precocious puberty and advancement of their bone
ages benefit the most from GnRH analogues. Conversely, those most mildly
affected with central precocious puberty and with the least progression under
observation are suggested to avoid a reduction in height potential and may not
need to be treated. Their evidence is consistent, but their patients, and indeed
the majority of patients treated with GnRH analogue, have not yet reached
their final adult height. Although height predictions certainly are useful to determine whether an undue advancement of bone age is occurring in a given patient with precocious puberty, the proof or refutation of the hypothesis presented will occur when a large number of patients reach final adult height and
fusion of their epiphyses.—D. Styne, M.D.

The Little Women of Loja: Growth Hormone-Receptor Deficiency in an In-bred Population of Southern Ecuador

Rosenbloom AL, Aguirre JG, Rosenfeld RG, Fielder PJ (Univ of Florida; Inst of
Endocrinology, Metabolism, and Reproduction, Quito, Ecuador; Stanford Univ)
N Engl J Med 323:1367–1374, 1990
17–3

Laron-type dwarfism is characterized by the clinical appearance of isolated growth hormone deficiency with increased serum levels of growth
hormone and reduced serum levels of insulin-like growth factor I (IGF-I).
It has been described in only about 50 patients. The condition is caused
by a deficiency of the cellular receptor for growth hormone and is transmitted as an autosomal recessive trait. Growth hormone-receptor deficiency was studied in an inbred population of southern Ecuador.

Nineteen female patients and 1 male patient aged 2 to 49 years were
investigated. All were members of an inbred Spanish population (Fig 17–
1). Seventeen were from 2 large pedigrees. Among the 13 affected sib-
ships were 19 affected and 24 unaffected sisters and 1 affected and 21
unaffected brothers. The patients' heights ranged from 10 to 6.7 standard
deviations below the normal mean height for that age in the United
States. Fifteen patients had limited elbow extensibility. All had blue
scleras. Affected adults had relatively short extremities. All 4 affected
women older than age 30 years had hip degeneration. All affected children had increased basal serum levels of growth hormone. These levels

Fig 17–1.—Family of patients 8, 9, and 10. *From left to right:* sister aged 25 years (height 158.8 cm); brother aged 18 years (164.7 cm): patient 9; father aged 52 years (165 cm); patient 8; brother aged 12 years (135.9 cm); sister aged 8½ years (115.4 cm); mother aged 46 years (156.7 cm), holding patient 10. (Courtesy of Rosenbloom AL, Aguirre JG, Rosenfeld RG, et al: *N Engl J Med* 323:1367–1374, 1990.)

were normal to moderately elevated in the adult patients. The serum level of growth hormone-binding protein ranged from 1% to 30% of normal. The concentrations of IGF-I were low, as were serum levels of IGF-II and growth hormone-dependent IGF-binding protein-3.

In this inbred population the high incidence of growth hormone-receptor deficiency has resulted in a clinical picture that resembles Laron-type dwarfism and differs from it mainly in the marked predominance of affected female patients. This population may be genetically related to other populations reported to have Laron-type dwarfism, but with the genetic defect linked to a trait resulting in the early death of most affected male fetuses.

▶ I know you've been waiting all your life to learn about the Little Women of Loja. The Little Women of Loja form a group of individuals with short stature resulting from a form of dwarfism known as "Laron" dwarfism. This is a very specific form of short stature caused not by growth hormone deficiency but rather by growth hormone-receptor deficiency. Aside from the Little Women of Loja, there have been only approximately 50 cases described of the Laron-type dwarfism, which is characterized by the clinical appearance of isolated growth hormone deficiency with elevated serum levels of growth hormone and decreased serum levels of insulin-like growth factor I (IGF-I, previously known as somatomedin C). Laron dwarfism is caused by a deficiency of the cellular receptor for growth hormone and is traditionally transmitted as an autosomal trait. The difference between the Little Women of Loja and the typical Laron-type dwarfism is that the Little Women of Loja are all females, and no males have been described, not very typical of an autosomal recessive disorder. It is thought that the genetic defect linked to their trait results in the early death of most affected males.

The conclusion that the above disorders are caused by abnormal or deficient cellular growth hormone receptors is supported by the finding of abnormal binding of growth hormone to liver membranes in 2 patients (1) and by the absence of the structurally related serum growth hormone-binding protein in affected persons.

What you do for these people is not to give them growth hormone, because it doesn't work. However, Walker et al. (2) found that you can bypass the need for growth hormone by directly giving replacement with IGF-I. The latter is a peptide hormone presumed to mediate most of the growth-promoting actions of growth hormone. The latter investigators have given an 11-day infusion of recombinant IGF-I to an 8-year-old boy with growth retardation unresponsive to growth hormone. It produced all of the expected biochemical changes that growth hormone might have.

If all of this sounds a bit complicated, I'm with you. The time has long since passed when anyone other than an endocrinologist should be caring for a child who requires treatment for short stature. What I did learn from reading articles related to this topic is that we have come a long way in our basic understanding of the entire process of growth. For example, the receptor for growth hormone on all of our cells (including red blood cell precursors) is related to a specific gene located on chromosome 5. It is an abnormality in that gene that is understood to be the cause of Laron-type dwarfism.

In closing this commentary, let's pose a query. When does a pygmy become a pygmy?

In response to this question, it has been strongly suggested that the short adult stature of African pygmies is the result primarily, if not solely, of the absence of accelerated growth at puberty. Not so says Bailey (3). Bailey has observed the birth of 51 female pygmies and has followed their height every 6 months. At less than 1 year of age, these pygmies were already below the third percentile for height in comparison to U.S. female growth charts. This short stature continued to fall progressively off the chart over the first 5 years of life, indicating that pygmies are pygmies from birth. Thus ends the riddle of pygmy short stature.—J.A. Stockman, III M.D.

References

1. Eshet R, et al: *Isr J Med Sci* 20:8, 1984.
2. Walker JL, et al: *N Engl J Med* 324:1483, 1991.
3. Bailey RC: *N Engl J Med* 323:1146, 1990.

Reproducibility of Growth Hormone Testing Procedures: A Comparison Between 24-Hour Integrated Concentration and Pharmacological Stimulation

Zadik Z, Chalew SA, Gilula Z, Kowarski AA (Kaplan Hosp, Rehovot, Israel; Univ of Maryland, Baltimore; Hebrew Univ, Jerusalem)
J Clin Endocrinol Metab 71:1127–1130, 1990   17–4

The growth hormone (GH) provocative tests are the most common diagnostic procedures used for the evaluation of GH deficiency. Because the clinical usefulness of a diagnostic procedure is greatly influenced by its reproducibility, the variability of the integrated concentration of GH (IC-GH), a measure of the physiologic secretion of GH, was compared with that of provocative stimulation tests.

Provocative stimulation tests with arginine, insulin, or clonidine were performed twice within 6 weeks in 113 prepubertal children referred for evaluation of growth retardation. In 40 of these children, the IC-GH test was performed twice within 4 weeks.

There was a highly significant correlation between the 2 measurements of IC-GH, whereas a moderate correlation was noted between the first and second pharmacologic GH stimulation tests. For the latter, clonidine had the highest reproducibility. The reproducibility of the IC-GH test was significantly better than that of the provocative tests.

The IC-GH test yields consistently more reproducible results than the provocative tests and should be a highly suitable method for clinical diagnosis and research on GH deficiency.

▶ It is no sin to be short in the United States, but it doesn't appear to be a virtue either. Were you aware that business school graduates more than 6 feet tall receive a starting salary 12.4% higher than shorter graduates (1). In last year's YEAR BOOK, we commented that the taller candidate for president has won 80% of the elections in this century. Of all the presidents, only 2 have been shorter than average for an American man at the time of election.

The increased availability of recombinant growth hormone has produced a virtual unlimited supply of it. Recently, Allen and Fost (2) examined the whole issue of who should and who should not receive recombinant growth hormone. They concluded that access to potentially efficacious growth hormone could not be ethically denied to non–growth hormone-deficient children who in fact might be made taller with exogenous growth hormone. However, because of the enormous expense, and because of concerns that universal access would not ameliorate the disadvantages of short stature, they suggest that it is appropriate to restrict access, even within the group of children responsive to growth-hormone. As a starting point, they propose that treatment be limited to those for whom height is not merely a relative disadvantage but a serious handicap, arbitrarily defined as below the first percentile. They insist that the central point is that handicap and growth hormone responsiveness should be the criteria for treatment, not the cause of handicap or the ability to pay. Most importantly, they emphasize that height is not a reliable predictor of happiness and self-esteem. With a cost of $35 per milligram of recombinant growth hormone, (which can translate easily into $5,000 to $30,000 per year per child treated) you can spend the same amount of money on other things in life that can increase your self-esteem.

With all the above having been said, it is still necessary to be sure that somebody is or is not growth hormone-deficient before you blunder into using growth hormone not knowing exactly what you are treating. The article abstracted above shows that pharmacologic stimulation of growth hormone is no longer a necessary test in all patients. There are less invasive, simpler ways of determining whether somebody is growth hormone-deficient. This has been substantiated by Donaldson et al. (3). You can even measure a 24-hour urine growth hormone excretion as a non-invasive, accurate, and useful screening test for growth hormone deficiency (4).

In closing this commentary, it is amazing how we as adults take pride in the way we think we should appear and the demands we make on physicians to make us be that way. Proof positive of this is the lying we do about ourselves. It has been documented that the majority of driver application forms list women as weighing 115 pounds and every living man as being 6' tall with a full head of brown hair. How surprising is it then that parents of short kids walk into a doctor's office and, having read about recombinant growth hormone, insist on its administration. They must think that they are going into an ice cream parlor where the rule of thumb is, "if a customer wants vanilla, give them vanilla." Doctoring is just not that simple, and these families need to know that.—J.A. Stockman, III M.D.

References

1. Deck L: *Psychology Today* 5:102, 1971.
2. Allen DB, Fost NC: *J Pediatr* 117:16, 1990.
3. Donaldson DL, et al: *J Clin Endocrinol Metab* 72:647, 1991.
4. Kohno H, et al: *J Clin Endocrinol Metab* 71:1496, 1990.

Adult Height in Boys and Girls With Untreated Short Stature and Constitutional Delay of Growth and Puberty: Accuracy of Five Different Methods of Height Prediction
Brämswig JH, Fasse M, Holthoff M-L, von Lengerke HJ, von Petrykowski W, Schellong G (Univ Children's Hosp, Münster and Freiberg, Germany)
J Pediatr 117:886–891, 1990   17–5

The accuracies of 5 commonly used methods of height prediction in estimating adult height were evaluated in children with untreated short stature and constitutional delay of growth and puberty (CDGP). Height predictions calculated by the Bayley-Pinneau, Roche-Wainer-Thissen (RWT), target height, and Tanner-Whitehouse Mark I (TW-MI) and Mark II (TW-MII) methods were compared with final adult height in 37 boys and 32 girls. All had initial heights at or less than the third percentile for chronologic age and a bone age retardation of 2 years or more. Height predictions were calculated for the group as a whole and for pa-

tients with parents of normal and short stature. Initially, mean chronologic ages were 14.8 years for boys and 12.87 years for girls. Mean ages
at follow-up were 23.14 years for boys and 21.05 years for girls.
Mean adult heights were 170.4 cm for boys and 157.8 cm for girls,
both within the lower range of normal. For boys, the RWT method offered the best estimate, underestimating adult height by .53 cm for the
total group. The target height and Bayley-Pinneau methods overestimated
adult height by 1.73 and 3.10 cm, respectively, whereas the TW-MI and
TW-MII methods underestimated adult height by 7.31 and 4.17 cm, respectively. For girls, no method was superior in estimating adult height.
Adult height was overestimated by the target height method by .65 cm
and by the RWT method by 2.64 cm. The Bayley-Pinneau method underestimated by .84 cm, the TW-MI method by 2.05 cm, and the TW-MII
method by 1.75 cm. The differences between predicted and adult height
in girls were generally smaller than those in boys.

Children with short stature and CDGP usually reach an adult height in
the lower range of normal. Although the accuracies of the commonly
used methods of height prediction are generally better for girls than for
boys, each method differs in accuracy and tendency to overestimate or
underestimate adult height.

Constitutional Delay of Growth: Expected Versus Final Adult Height
LaFranchi S, Hanna CE, Mandel SH (Oregon Health Sciences Univ, Portland)
Pediatrics 87:82–87, 1991   17–6

The condition known as constitutional delay of growth and puberty
(CDGP) is thought to be a variation of normal growth with a clear familial tendency. There is a male preponderance in CDGP, the most common
cause of short stature among children referred to pediatric endocrinologists. Children with CDGP are expected to grow for a longer duration
than average and eventually achieve a height normal for their genetic potential. Whether these children do, in fact, reach their expected height
was investigated.

The records of children with CDGP seen at 1 clinic between 1975 and
1983 were examined. Of 357 subjects who met the study criteria, 71
were of an age when they would have been expected to reach adult
height. Forty-two of these subjects, 29 men and 13 women, were located.
When their adult heights were measured, the average age of the men was
24 years and the average age of the women was 20.5 years. There was a
positive family history of CDGP in 88% of the men and 29% of the
women, both primarily in their fathers.

Final adult heights were significantly less than target heights (table).
Men had a final adult height of 1.2 SD, and women had a final adult
height of 1.3 SD below the 50th percentile for adults. Although there was
some genetic contribution to shortness in these subjects, the fathers were
still 5.2 cm taller than their sons and the mothers were 5.1 cm taller than
their daughters.

Final Adult Height of the Subjects, Parental Heights, Predicted Heights, and Target Heights (Mean ± SD)

	Males (n = 29)	Females (n = 13)
Mean age at contact, y	23.9 ± 2.2	20.5 ± 3.6
Final adult height, cm	169.5 ± 4.5	156.4 ± 3.8
Predicted height,* cm		
BP	171.4 ± 4.5	155.6 ± 4.3
RWT	169.6 ± 4.8	160.1 ± 4.2‡
Parental height,† cm	174.7 ± 4.5‡	161.5 ± 5.1‡
Target height, cm	174.6 ± 4.5‡	161.7 ± 5.5‡

*BP, Bayley-Pinneau method; RWT, Roche-Wainer-Thissen method.
†Under males are fathers' heights; under females are mothers' heights.
‡P < .002 vs. final adult height.
(Courtesy of LaFranchi S, Hanna CE, Mandel SH: *Pediatrics* 87:82–87, 1991.)

There may be an overlap of CDGP and a disturbance of human growth hormone secretion and function. But these individuals may not have met their target height because of a selection bias in the group—they were the shortest children referred to a subspecialty clinic. It is not possible, however, to exclude a pathologic process.

▶ The preceding 2 abstracts are disturbing. The first of the 2 (Abstract 17–5) deals with the final height of children with constitutional delay of growth and suggests that the standards that we use for height prediction are off, thus accounting for why so many children fail to achieve the height that we anticipate they will. The second abstract (Abstract 17–6), on the other hand, suggests that there is nothing wrong with the prediction curves, it's just that kids with constitutional short stature ultimately turn out to be shorter than the definition of this disorder is intended to imply. Constitutional short stature simply implies a delay in maturational processes, which eventually straightens itself out and allows an individual to achieve a "normal" height. Apparently, there are some children with constitutional delay of growth in whom human growth hormone secretion or function in childhood, while apparently normal, is not normal and does not allow these children to reach what for them should be their normal adult height. To say this differently, these children might indeed be candidates for growth hormone administration. These 2 abstracts challenge our traditional definition of constitutional delay of growth.

We are now learning more about all of these growth disturbances, and the introduction of recombinant growth hormone has come none too soon. The product, however, is both a good news and not quite so good news affair. The good news is that it certainly works in most instances. Schwartz et al. (1) found that 87% of children with short stature less than the first percentile who have no underlying organic disease to account for the short stature will respond adequately to exogenous growth hormone. Although not doing a perfect job, growth hormone is doing very nicely by girls with Turner syndrome (2). For the elderly, we are seeing an increasing number of reports about potential benefits of growth hormone administration (3). As in growth hormone-treated children, therapy in the elderly results in an increase in lean body mass and a decrease in adipose tissue mass. Muscle strength improves. Cholesterol levels even drop. Obviously, the use of growth hormone for the elderly is extraordinarily controversial, but its effects are similar to the effects of the swimming pool water on Don Ameche, Wilfred Brimley, and Jack Gilford in the films, *Cocoon 1 and 2.*

Please don't think that growth hormone treatment doesn't carry any theoretical hazards. It does. The possibility that growth hormone treatment may increase the risk of cancer certainly needs long-term investigation. There are concerns about an increased risk of leukemia in growth hormone-treated children (4). In vitro, human growth hormone enhances the proliferation of leukemic blast cells (5). Walker et al. (6) warn us that recombinant growth hormone produces profound metabolic effects, which should cause us to limit its use in otherwise healthy children until the mechanism of its action is more clearly elucidated. Finally, growth hormone has been given to children with chronic renal failure who are not growing well, and it does assist growth (7). However, Ree et al. (8) have reported deterioration of renal function in 2 children with renal disease treated with recombinant growth hormone, and a third case has been added by Watson (9). It is speculated that growth hormone causes hyperfiltration by increasing glomerular filtration rates.

In the previous commentary we said "If a customer wants vanilla, give them vanilla" when referring to the demands being made for recombinant growth hormone. The mixed blessings associated with recombinant growth hormone should caution us to warn those who want "vanilla" that the buyer must beware.—J.A. Stockman, III M.D.

References

1. Schwartz ID, et al: *Am J Dis Child* 144:1092, 1990.
2. Rongen-Westerlaken C, et al: *Acta Paediatr Scand* 79:658, 1990.
3. Editorial Comment: *Lancet* 337:1131, 1991.
4. Stahnke N, et al: *Eur J Pediatr* 148:591, 1989.
5. Estrov Z: *J Clin Oncol* 9:394, 1991.
6. Walker JM, et al: *Lancet* 336:1331, 1990.
7. Johannson G, et al: *Acta Paediatr Scand Suppl* 370:36, 1990.
8. Ree DL, et al: *Arch Dis Child* 65:856, 1990.
9. Watson J: *Lancet* 337:108, 1991.

Preservation of Physiological Growth Hormone (GH) Secretion in Idiopathic Short Stature After Recombinant GH Therapy

Wu RHK, St Louis Y, DiMartino-Nardi J, Wesoly S, Sobel EH, Sherman B, Saenger P (Montefiore Med Ctr/Albert Einstein College of Med, New York; Genentech, Inc, South San Francisco)
J Clin Endocrinol Metab 70:1612–1615, 1990 17–7

Recombinant growth hormone (GH) is being used successfully for children with idiopathic short stature (ISS), but the effect of recombinant GH on spontaneous GH secretion is unknown. To assess the recovery of spontaneous GH secretion 48 hours after the cessation of recombinant GH therapy, 11 prepubertal children with ISS whose GH responses after provocation were 10 ng/mL or greater were studied. The treatment group included 7 children who received recombinant GH, .1 mg/kg 3 times a week, and a control group included 4 children. Because of low body weight, 1 child in each group had 12-hour overnight studies; GH samples were obtained from the others every 20 minutes for 24 hours. Samples were obtained before the start of GH therapy and 48 hours after the end of 12 months of therapy. Additionally, 3 children in the treatment group underwent a 24-hour study after 6 months of treatment.

The GH secretion profiles showed similar numbers of peaks, mean concentrations, peak amplitudes, and secretory rates before and after treatment. Mean GH and peak GH amplitude were greater at 6 months than the means of the treatment group at the beginning and end of treatment; this difference was not significant. Somatomedin-C levels increased from .42 to 1.25 U/mL in the treatment group, and from .56 to 1.16 U/mL in the control group. In the latter group this increase was attributable to 1 patient who entered puberty during the study period, whose somatomedin-C level increased from .72 to 2.5 U/mL.

Recombinant GH therapy in children with ISS does not appear to interfere with endogenous pulsatile secretion of GH. In growing children, the GH secretory system appears to be quite resilient. Further studies are needed to confirm these findings after long-term treatment.

Final Height in Boys With Untreated Constitutional Delay in Growth and Puberty
Crowne EC, Shalet SM, Wallace WHB, Eminson DM, Price DA (Royal Manchester Children's Hosp; Christie Hosp, Manchester, England)
Arch Dis Child 65:1109–1112, 1990.   17–8

Although short stature caused by constitutional delay in growth and puberty (CDGP) is an extreme of normal development rather than a clinical disorder, it can cause considerable clinical problems. Many patients remain unhappy despite promises of normal growth to come. Psychological distress may affect behavior and school performance and may even persist into adult life. The natural history and psychological impact of the growth pattern in boys with CDGP were investigated.

Forty-three boys with short stature as a result of CDGP were followed until they reached final height. At initial diagnosis, their mean chronological age was 14 years; bone age delay, 2.7 years; standing height SD score, −3.4; and predicted adult height SD score, −1.3. The final adult SD score, measured at 21.2 years of age, was −1.6. The difference between final height and predicted adult height was not significant, but the difference between final height and measured midparental height was significant.

According to results of psychological questionnaires, the CDGP group

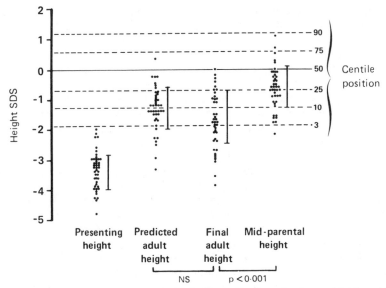

Fig 17–2.—Presenting height, predicted adult height, final height, and midparental height standard deviation score for 43 boys with constitutional delay in growth and puberty. (Courtesy of Crowne EC, Shalet SM, Wallace WHB, et al: *Arch Dis Child* 65:1109–1112, 1990.)

did not differ significantly from a control group in self-esteem, marital status, or employment state. Self-esteem was not correlated with final height, but 25 patients indicated that their growth delay had affected their success at school, work, or socially. Twenty stated that they would rather have had treatment to advance their growth spurt (Fig 17–2).

The more frequent use of active medical treatment to advance growth in boys with CDGP is supported. Although boys with CDGP reach their predicted heights, they are still short for their families.

▶ Dr. Felix Conte, Professor of Pediatrics, University of California, San Francisco Medical Center, comments:

▶ The report of Wu et al. (Abstract 17–7) demonstrates that alternate-day growth hormone administration at a dose of .1 mg/kg/day for 1 year has little or no effect on physiologic growth hormone. The discrepancy between the conclusions of this study and those previously published, which demonstrated feedback inhibition by exogenous growth hormone, can be resolved by analogy with pituitary-adrenal suppression. Dose, frequency, and duration of therapy are all critical factors when assessing feedback inhibition. In general, alternate-day therapy is less apt to cause suppression than daily therapy. Realistically, growth hormone feedback inhibition does not have the same clinical significance as adrenal suppression, with its possibility of manifest cortisol deficiency. More important questions to the clinician are the efficacy, as well as side effects, of pharmacologic dose growth hormone therapy in short non–growth hormone-deficient children.

Sixty to eighty percent of short, non-growth hormone-deficient children with constitutional delay in growth and development and/or genetic short stature respond to growth hormone administration with a significant acceleration in growth velocity (>2 cm/yr) (1–3). However, growth velocity diminishes with time (1–3), bone age may advance in parallel with growth acceleration (2), and the onset and tempo of puberty may be accelerated (1, 4, 5). Data on final heights in a small cohort of patients treated with a regimen similar to that reported by Wu et al. revealed that only 15% of patients were significantly (>4.0 cm) taller than predicted height after 1–8 years of therapy (6). What happened? Analysis of the data suggests that any height gained before the onset of puberty was lost in the majority of children as a consequence of the effects of growth hormone on the tempo of puberty and the rate of bone maturation (6). Thus, current data suggest that growth hormone will allow only a small percentage of non–growth hormone-deficient children to grow taller. Which ones? How do you select them? These are as yet unanswered questions. Perhaps our goal should not be to make short, non–growth hormone-deficient children taller as adults, but simply to accelerate their growth rate to ameliorate their extreme short stature and its concurrent psychological problems during childhood. What about larger doses of growth hormone (7) and GnRH analogue to delay pubertal maturation? Experimental trials to evaluate these questions are presently in progress. In any event, each day I am reminded of the fact that I have not yet ascended to the level of "godfather." Hence, I cannot grant short, non-growth hormone-deficient children (or their parents) their wish to be tall. I can make them an offer they can refuse—daily growth hormone shots at a cost of $10,000 to $40,000 per year with no guarantee about final height and with the possibility of side effects.

Crowne et al. (Abstract 17–8) and La Franchi and co-workers (8) have demonstrated that the final heights of untreated individuals with constitutional delay in growth and puberty are not significantly different from predicted heights but are in the lower range of target height. Thus these children do not appear to grow to their genetic potential. La Franchi et al. postulated that this discrepancy betweeen final height and genetic potential can be explained by selection bias, because only the shortest children with constitutional delay in growth and puberty (>2 SD below the mean) were studied by both groups (8). This conclusion is supported by a study from Sweden that reported final heights on 183 randomly selected children from birth to maturity (9). The late maturing males were 6.5 cm taller than the early maturing males and 4.2 cm taller than the normal maturing males. No significant difference in final height related to age of onset of puberty was noted in females. However, this data is of little consolation to the short adolescent male (>14 years) who is disturbed by his stature as well as his lack of puberty. As Crowne et al. noted, these young men usually want therapy to bring about the development of secondary sexual characteristics as well as to initiate a growth spurt. Numerous studies over the past 30 years have shown that a short course of "low dose" testosterone or oxandrolone will initiate a growth spurt, engender the development of secondary sexual characteristics, and have little or no effect on final height (10–14). In this respect, there is no evidence that growth hormone is as effective as testosterone or oxandrolone in patients with constitutional delay in growth and puberty

(15), and its effect on final height in these patients is still to be determined.—F. Conte, M.D.

References

1. Kaplan SL, et al: in Isaksson O, et al (eds): *Growth Hormone: Basic and Clinical Aspects.* Amsterdam, Excerpta Medica, 1987.
2. Wit JM, et al: *J Pediatr* 115:720, 1989.
3. Hintz RL, et al: *Pediatr Res* 457:79A, 1991.
4. Van der Werff ten Bosch JJ, et al: *Neth J Med* 32:217, 1988.
5. Darendeliler F, et al: *Acta Endocrinol (Copenh)* 122:414, 1990.
6. Kaplan SL: personal communication, 1991.
7. Walker J, et al: *J Clin Endocrinol Metab* 69:253, 1989.
8. La Franchi S, et al: *Pediatrics* 87:83, 1991.
9. Hagg U, et al. *Ann Hum Biol* 18:47, 1991.
10. Kaplan JG, et al: *J Pediatr* 82:38, 1973.
11. Richman R, et al: *N Engl J Med* 319:1563, 1988.
12. Kaplowitz PB: *Am J Dis Child* 143:116, 1991.
13. Rosenfeld RL: *J Clin Endocrinol Metab* 70:559, 1990.
14. Tse W-Y, et al: *J Pediatr* 117:588, 1990.
15. Buyukgebiz A, et al: *Arch Dis Child* 65:448, 1990.

Creutzfeldt-Jakob Disease in Pituitary Growth Hormone Recipients in the United States

Fradkin JE, Schonberger LB, Mills JL, Gunn WJ, Piper JM, Wysowski DK, Thomson R, Durako S, Brown P (National Inst of Diabetes and Digestive and Kidney Diseases, Bethesda, Md; Centers for Disease Control, Atlanta; Natl Inst of Child Health and Human Development, Bethesda, Md; Food and Drug Admin, Rockville, Md; Westat Inc, Rockville, Md; et al)
JAMA 265:880–884, 1991

The occurrence of 3 deaths from Creutzfeldt-Jakob disease (CJD) in young hypopituitary patients in 1985 led to withdrawal of pooled cadaver pituitaries for growth hormone treatment. All 3 patients had been treated with pituitary-derived human growth hormone years earlier. A study was undertaken to determine the prevalence of CJD in those given human growth hormone acquired through the National Hormone and Pituitary Program.

The 6,284 confirmed recipients were 9.6 years of age on average when treatment began, and received growth hormone for an average of 3.9 years, most often for idiopathic hormone deficiency. Seven neuropathologically confirmed cases of CJD have occurred in this population. Six patients had ataxia and imbalance—not altered mentation as is seen in sporadic cases. One patient died in the preclinical phase of the disease.

All 7 cases were among nearly 700 patients treated before 1970. A large majority of those exposed have not yet passed the incubation phase of CJD. Affected patients received growth hormone for a median of 100 months, compared with 41 months for all patients starting treatment before 1970. No case clustering was noted in a particular treatment center, and no single lot of hormone was implicated. No primate yet has developed CJD after the intracerebral administration of growth hormone. Testing has included lots from one of the batches of glands common to all 7 cases.

The duration of treatment appears to be a major risk factor for CJD. Contamination of pituitary growth hormone probably involves a low titer of infectivity distributed among multiple preparations.

▶ If you have been following the story of the relationship between the administration of human growth hormone and Creutzfeldt-Jakob disease in past YEAR BOOKS, the story is becoming more clear. In 1985, 3 deaths resulting from Creutzfeldt-Jakob disease, a fatal degenerative neurologic disorder affecting mentation and/or movement, occurred in young hypopituitary patients who in years past had been treated with pituitary-derived growth hormone. When these cases were recognized, the National Institutes of Health (NIH) terminated distribution of human pituitary derived growth hormone. Fortunately, shortly thereafter, the recombinant product became available. The NIH has initiated a study in conjunction with the Centers for Disease Control and a private research group to determine how many cases of Creutzfeldt-Jakob disease have resulted from pituitary-derived growth hormone. Among the 6,284 patients who received human growth hormone through the NIH program, 7 cases of neuropathologically confirmed Creutzfeldt-Jakob disease have been identified to date. All 7 cases received growth hormone therapy before 1970. Because the average interval from treatment to onset of disease appears to be about 15 years, there are still a majority of potentially exposed patients who have not attained the prerequisite incubation period for expression of Creutzfeldt-Jakob disease (1).

What is extraordinarily intriguing is the fact that we now may understand why some people do and some people do not get Creutzfeldt-Jakob disease when exposed to the agent that causes it. The clue to this has come from a group of Libyan Jews. Worldwide, the incidence of Creutzfeldt-Jakob disease is 1 to 2 cases per million population with a few exceptions. Among Libyan Jews, it occurs more than 100 times more frequently. Until quite recently, the cultural or culinary practices of Libyan Jews have been invoked to explain the high incidence of this disorder. The favored culprit has been lightly cooked sheep brain. The consumption of sheep eyeballs has also been a proposed mode of transmission. Transmission through consumption of sheep brain was an attractive hypothesis because ritualistic cannibalism of human brain is thought to be responsible for the spread of kuru among the Fore people of New Guinea. Oral transmission of the scrapie agent is now suspected as the cause of bovine spongiform encephalopathy or "mad cow disease." Scrapie is a transmissible neurodegenerative disease of sheep similar to Creutzfeldt-Jakob disease in humans; however, there is no evidence that flocks whose meat had been eaten by Libyan Jews have a higher than usual incidence of scrapie.

So what is the link between Libyan Jews and those who have come down with Creutzfeldt-Jakob disease after administration of human growth hormone? The answer to this question comes from the recent description by Hsiaio et al. (2), who have found a single nucleotide (G switching to A) change at the first position of codon 200 on the chromosomes of Libyan Jews who develop

Creutzfeldt-Jakob disease. Creutzfeldt-Jakob disease is caused by organisms known as prions, and this gene site is now called the prion-protein gene. In the June 15 issue (1991) of the *Lancet,* Collinge et al. (3) closed the circle, showing that of the 6 patients who developed Creutzfeldt-Jakob disease after the administration of human growth hormone, 4 had the exact same prion-protein gene abnormality that was recently described in Libyan Jews. This would then seem to prove that there is a genetic susceptibility to Creutzfeldt-Jakob disease that allows genetically susceptible individuals to become infected when exposed to prion-type organisms such as those that were contaminating human growth hormone before the 1980s. These are very important findings, because it would suggest that the many thousands of individuals who received human growth hormone are likely to do quite well because the incidence of this genetic abnormality is quite low.

A quiz question to end this commentary: How long does the scrapie virus survive internment?

This may seem like a stupid question, but it really isn't. Earlier in this commentary, it was suggested that infected sheep carrying scrapie could be a cause of a neurodegenerative disorder. In any event, if you take scrapie-infected hamster brain homogenates and mix them with soil and bury all this, after 3 years, this virus still survives in the ground (4). In Iceland, where scrapie is particularly common among sheep, the sheep are often plowed under when they bite the dust. The investigators from the *Lancet,* in making recommendations to protect human beings as well as animals, suggest "that the practice of plowing under the carcasses of animals dying of scrapie bovine spongiform encephalopathy be abandoned and that such animals should be excluded as a source of bone meal and fertilizers unless it is first autoclaved."

Even a sheep isn't allowed to turn over in its grave any more.—J.A. Stockman, III M.D.

References

1. Fradkin JE, et al: *JAMA* 265:880, 1991.
2. Hsiaio K, et al: *N Engl J Med* 324:1091, 1991.
3. Collinge J, et al: *Lancet* 337:1441, 1991.
4. Brown P, et al: *Lancet* 337:269, 1991.

Plasma Prorenin Activity and Complications in Children With Insulin-Dependent Diabetes Mellitus

Wilson DM, Leutscher JA (Stanford Univ, Stanford, Calif)
N Engl J Med 323:1101–1106, 1990   17–10

Patients with insulin-dependent (type I) diabetes often have proliferative retinopathy or nephropathy. Not only are the pathogeneses of these complications unclear, but there is no method to predict which patients are at higher risk of these complications, except possibly by association with a family history of hypertension. Increased plasma proreinin activity has been found in patients with type I diabetes who have microvascular complications. To determine whether increasing levels of plasma prorenin activity can predict the development of complications in children and adolescents with diabetes, 135 patients with type I diabetes with a mean age of 10.3 years were studied during 468 outpatient visits. At the first visit, all patients were normotensive on a diet that did not restrict sodium, and none were taking any medications that alter plasma renin activity. Plasma prorenin activity was measured in all patients and in 54 control children and adolescents.

The mean plasma prorenin activity among the 32 patients aged older than 10 years who had uncomplicated diabetes was 8.43 ng of angiotensin I per liter·second, significantly greater than the 7.06 mean from 37 controls of the same age. The mean plasma prorenin activity among the 9 patients aged older than 10 years who had retinopathy or overt albuminuria was 13.09 ng of angiotensin I per liter·second. When sequential plasma prorenin activity measurements were obtained for 34 patients aged 10 years or older with uncomplicated diabetes, 14 patients had at least 1 increased value. Evidence of retinopathy or overt albuminuria appeared in 8 of these patients; these complications developed in only 1 of 20 patients with consistently normal plasma prorenin values. The increased plasma prorenin activity values in the 8 patients in whom complications developed preceded the complication by at least 18 months. Increases in plasma prorenin activity precede the development of retinopathy or nephropathy in adolescents with diabetes by as much as 36 months. Increased values for plasma prorenin activity in children with type I diabetes indicates a high risk of complications.

▶ Dr. Robert J. Winter, Professor of Pediatrics, and Associate Chairman for Medical Education, Northwestern University Medical School, comments:

▶ The diabetes story is reading more and more like a Sherlock Holmes tale all the time, with a new chapter every few months. For years we struggled with how best to treat diabetes (and we still do struggle with that), but every now and again some sleuth unravels a more basic understanding of what causes diabetes or how to predict it or its complications. The association of histocompatibility loci (HLA antigens) with diabetes and with an autoimmune predilection, the detection of antibodies to components of the insulin-producing beta cells, and aberrations of first phase insulin response to the intravenous glucose tolerance test as predictors of type I diabetes (1) all help to create a "whodunit" sense to predicting diabetes. With the autoimmune cause for insulin-dependent diabetes virtually assured, the potential development of less toxic immunosuppressives than cyclosporine holds promise for the prevention of diabetes in those detected by these means to be in the early stages of progression toward the disease.

If diabetes cannot yet be easily or permanently prevented or cured, what can we do to predict the deterioration of long-term microvascular complications all too common in those who have the disease for 20 years or more? Certainly the retinopathy story reads as another fascinating tale, having evolved a decade ago into the now widely accepted fact that retinopathy detected at its earliest stages can be treated wtih aggressive use of the argon laser, thus preventing further deterioration and blindness. Early detection is of paramount importance, thus behooving primary care physicians caring for patients with type I diabetics to examine the fundi carefully and recommend annual ophthalmologic consultation. Such practice has saved countless diabetics from blindness over the past decade.

Another scourge of long-term diabetes is nephropathy, and diabetes is now the leading cause of end-stage renal disease in this country. Until recently, little could be done to predict or prevent diabetic nephropathy, and once detected little could be done to prevent the inexorable decline to end-stage disease. Although renal transplantation in the diabetic is showing promise, it remains a "too little, too late" approach to prevent this complication. About a decade ago the presence of microalbuminuria (minute quantities of albumin detected by a highly sensitive assay) was described and later proved to herald overt albuminuria and uremia (2). This ability to predict subsequent nephropathy became more important with the recognition that a low protein, low phosphorus diet (.6 gm/kg/day of protein in adults) would retard the progression of renal disease (3). Although this has recently been challenged (4), a low protein diet remains one of the few approaches to this critical problem.

In this report by Wilson and Luetscher we are now potentially taken even 1 step earlier in this detection effort. It would appear that elevated plasma prorenin activity is antecedent to the presence of microalbuminuria, and if corroborated by others may serve to detect the very earliest tendency for diabetic renal disease. A combination of controlled dietary protein and use of angiotensin enzyme inhibition before the onset of hypertension (5) may prove to be extraordinarily useful in protecting the diabetic kidney from its disastrous progression toward renal failure.

While we are awaiting preventions or cures for diabetes, and while we struggle with controlling the metabolic aberration well enough to prevent complications, a good number of Sherlock Holmes' are giving us greatly needed approaches to early detection and treatment of complications before substantial morbidity or mortality ensue. Elementary, my dear Watson!—R.J. Winter, M.D.

References

1. Chase HP, et al: *J Pediatr* 118:838, 1991.
2. Viberti GC, et al: *Lancet* 1:1430, 1982.
3. Zeller K, et al: *N Engl J Med* 324:78, 1991.
4. Locatelli F, et al: *Lancet* 337:1289, 1991.
5. Cook J, et al: *J Pediatr* 117:39, 1990.

A Novel Testis-Stimulating Factor in Familial Male Precocious Puberty

Manasco PK, Girton ME, Diggs RL, Doppman JL, Feuillan PP, Barnes KM, Cutler GB Jr, Loriaux DL, Albertson BD (Natl Inst of Health, Bethesda, Md; George-town Univ Hosp)

N Engl J Med 324:227–231, 1991   17–11

Familial male precocious puberty is a gonadotropin-independent form of precocious puberty with unknown causes. To determine whether the plasma of boys with familial male precocious puberty contains a novel stimulator of testicular testosterone production, a bioassay using adult male cynomolgus monkeys was developed.

Plasma was obtained from 12 boys with the condition, 7 normal prepubertal boys of similar ages and with similar plasma gonadotropin levels, and 1 boy with hypogonadotropic hypogonadism. The plasma was infused into the testicular artery of adult male cynomolgus monkeys pretreated with gonadotropin-releasing hormone antagonist to inhibit the endogenous secretion of gonadotropins. Testicular venous effluent was collected every 15 minutes for 3 or 5 hours, and testosterone levels were measured.

Compared with baseline, the mean peak testosterone response was significantly increased in the monkeys infused with plasma from the boys with familial male precocious puberty than in those infused with plasma from normal boys and from the boy with hypogonadotropic hypogonadism in the 3-hour studies. Plasma from 92% of the boys with familial male precocious puberty and 12.5% of the normal prepubertal boys stimulated a response greater than 195% of baseline values. In the 5-hour studies, the mean peak testosterone response compared with baseline was significantly higher in monkeys infused with plasma from 3 boys with familial male precocious puberty than in those infused with plasma from 3 normal prepubertal boys. The mean area under the testosterone response curve was significantly greater in the animals infused with plasma from the boys with familial male precocious puberty in the 5-hour studies but not in the 3-hour studies. There may be a circulating testis stimulating factor in the plasma of boys with familial male precocious puberty. The production of such a factor would explain the biological nature of this condition.

▶ Dr. Edward O. Reiter, Professor of Pediatrics, Tufts University Medical School, and Chairman of Pediatrics, Baystate Medical Center, comments:

▶ Isosexual precocious puberty has been classified as being either gonadotropin-dependent or gonadotropin-independent. True or central precocious puberty, the most common variety of sexual precocity, results from premature activation of the hypothalamic pituitary gonadal axis. In this condition, factors within the CNS normally preventing initiation of pulsatile gonadotropin-releasing hormone release by the hypothalamic arcuate nucleus are prematurely eliminated, and sexual precocity ensues. In contradistinction, gonadotropin-independent precocious puberty is characterized by those forms of sexual precocity that are not mediated by pituitary gonadotropins. These include such entities as human chorionic gonadotropin-producing tumors, neoplasms of the adrenal, ovary or testes, the McCune-Albright syndrome, and the syndrome described in this paper by Manasco et al., namely, male-limited autosomal dominant, familial precocious puberty (MLFPP) or, as more robustly characterized, "testotoxicosis" (1).

The clinical syndrome of gonadotropin-independent sexual precocity (or "testotoxicosis" or MLFPP) is characterized by wide variability not only in the clinical course, but also in the final height outcome in large patient kindreds. Strikingly progressive pubertal maturation at a young age is often a central feature. All of the signs and symptoms of androgen excess are usually present. The increased testicular volume relative to the amount of systemic virilization, however, is not nearly as prominent in true gonadotropin-mediated precocious puberty. Although accelerated sexual development dominates the early clinical picture, the complete syndrome also may include progression to what appears to be normal gonadotropin secretory dynamics in adolescence and young adulthood and, finally, to premature gonadal failure with gonadotropin hypersecretion by middle age (2).

The concept that the sexual precocity of "testotoxicosis" is "gonadotropin-independent" stems from the finding that levels of both immunoreactive and bioactive gonadotropins have been either undetectable or meager both during basal secretion and also in response to exogenous stimulation of gonadotropin-releasing hormone. In contrast to the somewhat analogous syndrome of thyrotoxicosis, however, there have been no "Leydig cell-stimulating immunoglobulins" as yet identified. In a study generally supporting the report of Manasco et al. Holland presented evidence for a serum gonadotropin-like activity both in a mouse Leydig cell bioassay system, and in a rat ovarian membrane radioreceptor assay system (3). As in this study by Manasco and co-workers, in which plasma was infused in vivo into the testicular artery of adult cynomolgus monkeys, the results of Holland's in vitro assays showed substantial variability. Although such studies suggest their existence, the nature of these putative gonadotropin-like factors has not been further characterized.

In contrast, an extensive literature has arisen describing intratesticular regulation of androgen production (4). Such studies at least lend credence to the notion that a primary dysregulation of gonadal androgen production by local peptide modulators, rather than the postulated circulating gonadotropin-like factor, could underlie the syndrome of testotoxicosis.—E.O. Reiter, M.D.

References

1. Rosenthal SM, et al: *J Clin Endocrinol Metab* 57:571, 1983.
2. Reiter EO, et al: *N Engl J Med* 311:515, 1984.
3. Holland FJ: *Endocrinol Metab Clin North Am* 20:191, 1991.
4. Skinner MK: *Endocr Rev* 12:45, 77, 1991.

An Aromatase-Producing Sex-Cord Tumor Resulting in Prepubertal Gynecomastia

Coen P, Kulin H, Ballantine T, Zaino R, Frauenhoffer E, Boal D, Inkster S, Brodie A, Santen R (Pennsylvania State Univ, Hershey; Univ of Maryland)
N Engl J Med 324:317–322, 1991   17–12

Gynecomastia in prepubertal children is usually attributable to increased production of endogenous estrogen. Excessive production of estrogen may result from increased levels of endogenous substrate or aromatase activity, or both. Elevated aromatase activity in gonadal tissue without an increase in androgenic substrate has not been reported until now.

Boy, 4 years, had a 1-year history of painless, bilateral breast enlargement. His father had Peutz-Jeghers syndrome, but no one else in the family had gynecomastia, endocrine tumors, or reproductive problems. The boy had rectal polyposis consistent with this syndrome at his age. He had high levels of estradiol in testicular venous serum, high peripheral serum estradiol-to-testosterone ratios after stimulation with human chorionic gonadotropin, and increased aromatase activity in the testicular homogenates. All of these findings supported the supposition that the boy's gynecomastia resulted from increased testicular aromatase activity. He had accelerated skeletal maturation, with a bone age of 10 years. His testicular tumors were composed of sex cords that formed annular tubules, with hyalinization of the tubular basement membranes.

This and previously reported cases show that male as well as female patients with Peutz-Jeghers syndrome may have sex-cord tumors. The incidence in boys is probably higher than once believed.

▶ This abstract may have left you a little cold, wondering what really was going on with this child and why what he had was so important. Let me go beyond the abstract and explain.

As noted, gynecomastia in prepuberal children usually results from an increase in the production of endogenous estrogen. This was not true in this child. Thus, the search was on for some other cause. Over expression of functional proteins, including enzymes, commonly occurs in reponse to neoplastic transformation. Steroid-producing tumors may secrete multiple hormones in excess, presumably as a reflection of enhanced activity of several steroidogenic enzymes. In this patient, the excess production of a tumor-related enzyme was specifically pinpointed to a single enzyme, aromatase. So what does aromatase do? Estrogen biosynthesis involves the transformation of steroid precursors to androgens and then the conversion of androgens to estrogens by the enzyme aromatase. Thus, in this boy, the normal amounts of steroids that were being produced by him were converted by aromatase to estrogen in excess of what normally would have happened, and this caused his gynecomastia. The elevations in estrogens were only modest and could not be detected. The elevated aromatase enzyme pinpoints the testis as the source of the problem. Because there was a family history of Peutz-Jegher syndrome, it was a correct assumption that there had to be a testicular tumor.

I was not previously aware of the association betwen Peutz-Jegher syndrome and gonadal tumors, but there is one. It can also cause estrogen-secreting ovarian tumors and precocious puberty in girls. As you know, Peutz-Jegher syndrome is an autosomal dominant disorder. So finally, all the above makes some sense. Individuals with the Peutz-Jegher syndrome should be watched for the development of gynecomastia.

It isn't often that a single case report makes it into *The New England Journal of Medicine* as a feature article. Be impressed by this report: It added a tremendous amount of new insight into the causes of gynecomastia in children, the relationship between Peutz-Jegher's syndrome and gynecomastia, and new information on an enzyme that I had never heard of when I was in medical school.—J.A. Stockman, III M.D.

Assessment of Gonadal Maturation by Evaluation of Spermaturia
Schaefer F, Marr J, Seidel C, Tilgen W, Schärer K (Univ Children's Hosp, Heidelberg, Germany; Univ Hosp, Heidelberg)
Arch Dis Child 65:1205–1207, 1990   17–13

The detection of spermatozoa in the urine is a quick, non-invasive method of assessing the achievement of exocrine testes function during male puberty. Because spermaturia is a discontinuous phenomenon, the value of this method as a screening instrument is limited. The sensitivity and specificity of repetitive morning urine sampling was evaluated in 129 healthy peripubertal boys aged 10.1 to 17.8 years. Sediments from 1,120 first morning urine samples obtained for 10 consecutive days were analyzed for the presence of spermatozoa and correlated with the state of sexual maturation.

The proportion of subjects with sperm-positive urine increased from pubic hair stage (PH) 1 to PH 5 from 6% to 92%, respectively, with a steep rise between PH 2 and 3. Estimated median age at first positive spermaturia (spermarche) was 14.1 years, with a 95% confidence interval of 13.5 to 14.9 years (Fig 17–3). At PH 1 to 4 all positive urine samples were found within the first 5 days of collection, whereas at PH 5 the cumulative frequency of spermaturia increased up to day 8.

Repetitive morning urine sampling is a simple, non-invasive procedure

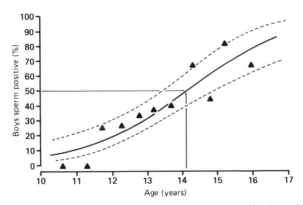

Fig 17–3.—Probit analysis of median age at spemarche. Age was grouped in 6-month intervals. Triangles represent unsmoothed percentages of sperm-positive individuals per age group. Solid curved line indicates smoothed sigmoid probability curve, dotted lines indicate 95% confidence intervals. (Courtesy of Schaefer F, Marr J, Seidel C, et al: *Arch Dis Child* 65:1205–1207, 1990.)

for assessing spermatogenic activity in pubertal boys and may be used as a qualitative screening test for testicular damage in this population.

▶ Girls have menarche. Now we can state that boys have spermarche. Spermarche occurs at an average age of 14.1 ± .6 years (2 SD).

To document this, these authors have collected the first morning urinary void for 2 consecutive weeks from each boy included in this study. Thus, for the 100+ boys evaluated, a total of 1,120 urine specimens were examined for the presence of spermatozoa.

Examining large numbers of urine specimens for sperm is a very socially acceptable way of telling whether or not a boy has come of age in a noncontroversial scientific way. As you might suspect, there could have been a much more straightforward way of obtaining specimens than that chosen. Chances are, however, that parents' permission for their boys to do this would have not been easily obtained. On the other hand, it's fair to say that the boys would probably have been up for it.—J.A. Stockman, III M.D.

18 The Musculoskeletal System

Osteoarthrosis and Congenital Dysplasia of the Hip in Family Members of Children Who Have Congenital Dysplasia of the Hip
Hoaglund FT, Healey JH (Univ of California, San Francisco; Hosp for Special Surgery, New York)
J Bone Joint Surg 72-A:1510–1518, 1990   18–1

A previous study suggested that congenital dysplasia of the hip may be associated with a higher prevalence of osteoarthrosis among family members of an affected child than in the general population. To investigate further, 408 siblings, parents, and grandparents of 78 children with congenital dysplasia of the hip were studied. Measurements of the acetabulum on pelvic radiographs were evaluated for signs and sequelae of congenital dysplasia.

In 4 mothers and 6 siblings, congenital dysplasia of the hip had been diagnosed during childhood. In the siblings the diagnosis was made on the basis of clinical examination and was confirmed on radiographs. None of the remaining 91 siblings had evidence of congenital dislocation of the hip or of acetabular dysplasia. Of the 312 parents and grandparents examined, 15 (5%) had osteoarthrosis of the hip, but only 4 had superolateral osteoarthrosis, which may be a residuum of congenital dysplasia. Furthermore, acetablular coverage in adults, as measured by the center-edge angle of Siberg, did not differ significantly from that of controls.

The greater prevalence of congenital disease of the hip in mothers and siblings of children with congenital dysplasia of the hip is consistent with a multifactorial inheritance. Acetabular dysplasia in family members is likely to be the result of subluxation or dislocation rather than being inherited.

Neonatal Screening and Staggered Early Treatment for Congenital Dislocation or Dysplasia of the Hip
Burger BJ, Burger JD, Bos CFA, Obermann WR, Rozing PM, Vandenbroucke JP (Univ Hosp, Leiden, The Netherlands; Elizabeth Gasthuis, Haarlem, The Netherlands)
Lancet 336:1549–1553, 1990   18–2

Doubt remains about the reliability of screening for congenital dislocation of the hip (CDH) in neonates and the value of early treatment. In a

9-year period, 14,264 consecutive newborn infants were screened for CDH. At the first visit, the infant's hips were examined by Barlow's method, and the family history of CDH was recorded.

Of the screened infants, 140 had positive Barlow tests, and abduction was started immediately; 133 had doubtful Barlow tests. These infants underwent radiography at 5 months of age and were treated if CDH was present. Of the infants who had negative Barlow tests, 685 had a positive family history and also underwent radiography at 5 months of age and were treated if CDH was present; 13,306 had no family history of CDH. Of the infants who had negative Barlow tests and no family history of CDH, 596 were seen again at 5 months of age, and 4,365 underwent review at 2 years of age. In all, 5 groups were analyzed (Fig 18–1).

Dislocation was missed at primary screening in 3 children (.02%), confirming the reliability of the screening test. Nineteen children (14%) who were Barlow doubtful proved to have dysplasia at 5 months. Dysplasia was also seen at 5 months in 15% of the children who had negative Barlow test but a positive family history and in 2 to 3% of children in the reference group. The high percentage of children with positive family histories who had dysplasia at 5 months underlines the role of hereditary factors in dysplasia. Of the 140 infants in whom treatment was started immediately, 17% had relapse dysplasia after therapy withdrawal, 3%

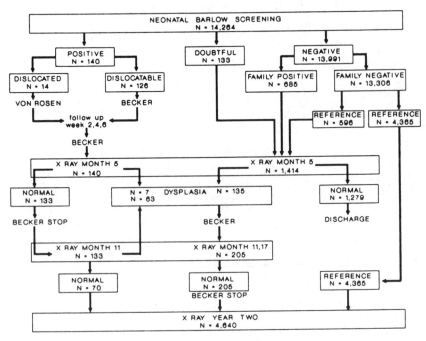

Study protocol.

Fig 18–1.—Study protocol. (Courtesy of Burger BJ, Burger JD, Bos CFA, et al: *Lancet* 336;1549–1553, 1990.)

had avascular necrosis, and 78% were normal at age 2 years. When treatment was started at 5 months, dysplasia relapse did not occur, only 1% had avascular necrosis, and 53% to 63% were normal at age 2 years. Although the initial 78% response to early treatment in the neonatal period seems good compared with the 53% to 63% success rate after late treatment, avascular necrosis was considerably more frequent among children treated during the neonatal period. For children with dislocatable hips, a wait-and-see treatment strategy with ultrasonography or radiography at 5 months of age is recommended.

▶ This article created quite a ruckus when it appeared. It not only implied, but recommended, that it is safer overall, and just as efficacious, to delay treating CDH for up to 5 months. The responses to this theory came quickly. Dr. Gellis, in *Pediatric Notes,* said, "I have difficulty just watching that long."

A somewhat more conservative view of delay in treatment was that reported by Gardiner and Dunn (1), who reported on 79 infants with CDH that was diagnosed by ultrasound. These infants were put into 1 of 2 randomized groups: those who underwent immediate splinting and those who underwent sonographic surveillance for 2 weeks. Infants in the latter group had splints put on at 2 weeks of age if instability persisted. It persisted in only 11 of the 38 subjects. Thus, in this latter group, the majority of infants were spared any treatment and its consequent risks. The problem with what Gardiner et al. describe, however, is the medical costs involved with repeated ultrasound. That aside, and assuming there is the ability to provide follow-up, it would seem that the approach of Gardiner et al. makes the most sense.

Why does screening for CDH remain such a controversial topic? This was recently addressed in an editorial to The *Lancet* in which it was commented: "To answer this question one has to remember the ingredients of a successful screening program. Not only should the disorder be clearly identifiable and its natural history understood, but the program itself should be simple, reproducible, reliable, and preferably inexpensive. Moreover, the natural outcome of the condition should be amendable to modification with treatment that is both safe and dependable. Congenital hip dysplasia does not fulfill all of these criteria. The terminology exemplifies the dilemma: congenital dislocation, instability, dysplasia, and displacement have all been used interchangeably" (2).

Ever since Ortolani (3) introduced his now commonly used screening test for neonatal hip instability, we have been looking for a better way to screen for this disorder. There was even a point at which routine radiographs in the newborn period became popular in certain parts of the world. Now, ultrasound has come of age. In Austria and Germany, all children are now screened by ultrasound at birth. In the United States a selective approach is used. This basically implies screening anyone who is detected by physical examination or anyone with a higher-than-average risk of hip instability (for example, those born by breech delivery, those with Down syndrome, those with congenital joint laxity such as that seen in association with the Ehlers-Danlos syndrome). The great advantage of these kinds of combination screenings is that ultrasound is safe and may be repeated to monitor progress, albeit at some monetary cost.

Missing a CDH or not treating it when treatment is indicated is a problem. It is estimated that about 30% of adults who ultimately have their hips replaced have this done as a consequence of acetabular dysplasia resulting from problems very early in life. On the other hand, you cannot ignore the complications of over-vigorous treatment. Suzuki et al. (4) reported some degree of avascular necrosis in 36 of 220 difficult-to-reduce hips. The latter group included some complex cases but shows an end of the spectrum in terms of the risks associated with overtreatment. As has been said elsewhere in this book, all of life is a bell-shaped curve. You can do harm by failing to treat, and you can do a lot of harm by overtreating when it isn't needed. Try to work somewhere in the middle of the bell-shaped curve and you will get the best results. You only get one chance at dealing with a newborn's hip to get the best outcome. If something goes wrong, it's all downhill from there. . . .—J.A. Stockman, III, M.D.

References

1. Gardiner HM, et al: *Lancet* 336:1553, 1990.
2. Editorial Comment: *Lancet* 337:947, 1991.
3. Ortolani M: *Paediatria* 45:129, 1987.
4. Suzuki S, et al: *J Bone Joint Surg* 72a:1048, 1990.

Economic Evaluation of Neonatal Screening for Congenital Dislocation of the Hip
Tredwell SJ (British Columbia Children's Hosp, Vancouver)
J Pediatr Orthop 10:327–330, 1990   18–3

Congenital dislocation of the hip (CDH), when detected soon after birth, can be treated successfully and less invasively than with later operative correction. Neonatal screening has shown dislocatable and subluxable hips to be present in 5 to 9 newborns per 1,000.

To determine the cost benefit of a neonatal hip screening program at 2 hospitals in British Columbia, the costs of neonatal screening and treatment of CDH were compared with the costs of treating established cases of CDH. When such costs were examined, it was estimated that neonatal screening and treatment of 1,000 infants could save $15,717 (Canadian) over the costs of surgical care for 1,000 unscreened infants.

This model assumes a 100% detection rate with a zero false-negative rate. With a false-negative rate of .03/1,000, based on previous studies of more than 100,000 infants, the economic benefit of screening would be $15,143/1,000 live births. Although the actual cost benefit would vary at other institutions, neonatal screening for CDH clearly has economic value.

▶ Dr. H. Theodore Harcke, Director of Medical Imaging, the Alfred I. duPont Institute, comments:

▶ Routine screening of all newborn infants is a controversial issue. Clark et al. (1) showed that screening of all infants who had risk factors or an abnormality on physical examination did not reduce the prevalence of late cases in their practice. Based on a comparison of clinical screening and screening with ultra-sonography, Tonnis et al. (2), concluded that all newborns should be screened because more disorders are detected by ultrasound than by clinical examination. The present study addresses the economics of screening and properly identifies key factors. Newborn screening in Europe has led to as many as 19.3% of all screened infants being placed in some kind of treatment protocol (2). The timing of screening is a point for consideration. Screening infants who are 6 weeks old identifies persistent abnormalities early enough for treatment but allows for resolution of minor abnormalities seen in the newborn period that dictate a follow-up examination. The disadvantage of late screening is the difficulty in ensuring that the entire population is examined (3).—H.T. Harcke, M.D.

References

1. Clarke NMP, et al: *J Bone Joint Surg* 71-B:9, 1989.
2. Tonnis D, et al: *J Pediatr Orthop* 10:145, 1990.
3. Harcke HT, Kumar SJ: *J Bone Joint Surg* 73-A:622, 1991.

Late-Onset Tibia Vara (Blount's Disease): Current Concepts
Thompson GH, Carter JR (Case Western Reserve Univ)
Clin Orthop 255:24–35, 1990   18–4

There are 3 types of idiopathic tibia vara, or Blount's disease: infantile, which has its onset between the ages of 1 and 3 years and is most common; juvenile, onset between 4 and 10 years; and adolescent, onset at 11 years or older. The latter 2 groups are considered late-onset forms of tibia vara.

In a 19-year period, 47 children underwent surgery for tibia vara. In 15 patients (32%) the onset of the disease was classified as late-onset. The reported experience comprised 22 knees in the 15 children; there were 13 knees in 8 juvenile-onset patients and 9 knees in 7 adolescent-onset patients. Fourteen of the patients were black. There were no significant clinical, radiographic, or physeal-histopathologic differences between these 2 groups. All of the children were markedly obese, and both groups had mild-to-moderate varus deformity and less pronounced radiographic characteristics (Fig 18–2).

The entire physis from the proximal tibia was analyzed histopathologically in 7 knees in 5 patients; findings were essentially identical to those in both patients with the infantile form of tibia vara and in patients with slipped capital femoral epiphyses. These findings, including islands of densely packed chondrocytes with a high degree of hypertrophy, areas of almost acellular cartilage, and abnormal groups of capillaries, suggest a common cause between the 2 disorders. Deformity recurred after surgical correction in boys with juvenile-onset disease. There was no recurrence among girls with juvenile-onset disease or the adolescent-onset group. In-

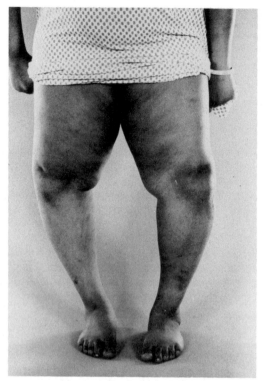

Fig 18–2.—This standing preoperative photograph illustrates a 15-year-old black male with bilateral adolescent-onset tibia vara. The measured genu varum roentgenographically was 10 degrees on the right and 20 degrees on the left. Observe the mild internal tibial torsion as well as the marked obesity. (Courtesy of Thompson GH, Carter JR: *Clin Orthop* 255:24-35, 1990.)

complete correction of the varus deformity was more common in adolescent-onset patients.

The causative mechanism of idiopathic tibia vara appears to involve suppression of varus stress growth and disruption of endochondral ossification. The major differences among the 3 age-onset groups are a result of the age at onset, the amount of remaining growth, and the magnitude of the medial compression forces across the medial side of the knee.

▶ Dr. Norris C. Carroll, Professor of Orthopedic Surgery, Northwestern University Medical School and Head, Division of Orthopedics, Children's Memorial Hospital, comments:

Tibia vara is classified based on the age at onset. In this article the authors have studied juvenile and adolescent Blount's disease. Late-onset Blount's has a relatively slow rate of progression compared with the infantile form of the disease. Patients with late-onset tibia vara usually are obese black males with normal or above-normal height; half of them will have both knees involved, and usually they are seen because of pain, not because of the severity of their deformity. Wedging of the medial portion of the epiphysis and mild posteromedial articular decompression without the marked fragmentation changes seen in the infantile form of the disorder are seen on x-ray views of the proximal tibia.

The cause appears to include varus stress, growth suppression, and disruption of enchondral ossification. Histologic sections of the medial physis demonstrate disorganization and misalignment of the physeal zones. It is important to do a careful preoperative assessment when planning treatment. The patient should have 3-foot standing films of the lower extremity with the limb aligned so that the patella is facing forward. This will allow measurement of the true varus deformity. The alignment of the distal femur and the proximal tibia should be assessed in both the AP and lateral views. There may be a compensatory valgus alignment at the distal femur. In selecting the appropriate treatment the patient's age, the amount of remaining growth, and the severity of the deformity must be considered. With the Ilizarov external fixator it is possible to restore alignment by correcting angulation, translation, and rotation, while, at the same time, lengthening the tibia. Because there is very little growth remaining, the adolescent form of late-onset tibia vara will not recur once it is corrected, but there is a 25% recurrence rate in the juvenile-onset group. For this reason, patients with juvenile-onset tibia vara should undergo magnetic resonance imaging of the proximal tibia to check for evidence of premature closure of the proximal medial tibial physis. If there is a partial closure, a physeal bridge resection should be performed. If the closure is more extensive, an intraepiphyseal osteotomy or physeal excision is required. Treatment must then include management of the leg length discrepancy.—N.C. Carroll, M.D.

Surface Electrical Stimulation Versus Brace in Treatment of Idiopathic Scoliosis
Durham JW, Moskowitz A, Whitney J (Albany Med College)
Spine 15:888–892, 1990   18–5

Brace treatment reportedly is effective in 60% to 84% of cases of scoliosis and in up to 85% of cases if larger curves (greater than 40 degrees) are omitted. Surface electric stimulation with the ScoliTron was evaluated as an alternative in 40 adolescents with idiopathic scoliosis. Stimulation was done nightly for at least 8 hours at a level of at least 70 mamp.

Treatment failed in half of the 30 patients who were available for follow-up. Five patients responded well at first and then failed, and 10 had a good outcome. Nine patients underwent fusion because of a progressing curve and 6 had a brace. The 5 patients with transiently successful results had only slight progression and did not require alternative treatment. The response to stimulation could not be predicted.

The ScoliTron fails considerably more often than bracing in patients with single thoracic curves (table). Electric stimulation is not reliably effective in preventing the progression of idiopathic scoliosis. Bracing remains the treatment of choice.

▶ We have discussed the topic of surface electric stimulation as a method to treat idiopathic scoliosis on several occasions in previous YEAR BOOKS. No one

Scoli Tron Versus Brace Failure Rates

	All patients	Risser 0-1	Single thoracic curves
Scolitron	50%	58%	67%
Brace	16%	26%	20%

(Courtesy of Durham JW, Moskowitz A, Whitney J: *Spine* 15:888–892, 1990.)

likes to undertake the complex surgery that is traditionally required to manage scoliosis. Even the lesser treatments (external bracing or plastic jacketing) are quite cumbersome. Thus the rationale for looking for something that is less invasive and easier to apply. This article was selected because it represents a fairly well done investigation that shows an unacceptably high failure rate for electric stimulation. This editor promises no more articles on electric stimulation for treatment of scoliosis unless someone refutes these data, which appear to show it to be a dismal failure.

All the above is not to say that we have not learned a lot from our orthopedic colleagues about certain aspects of the management of scoliosis. For example, orthopedists are using fibrin sealants to reduce blood loss during major surgery for scoliosis (1). This fibrin sealant is a 2-component system that produces an activated fibrin molecule that can be topically applied by syringe or by aerosol spray and is a remarkable new way to reduce blood loss by application to exposed oozing areas. You may recall from last year's YEAR BOOK a notation that orthopedists were using intraosseous methacrylate cement to stabilize the spines of patients with metastatic cancer to bone. A spinoff of this is the use of "crazy glue" in Europe to close skin lacerations. A report from Guys Hospital in London has shown that cyanoacrylate can be a satisfactory agent to close relatively minor lacerations. You simply approximate the edge of the wound with your fingers and after appropriate cleansing and drying, you then glue the 2 sides together. For lacerations less than 3 cm long, this approach is quite comparable to suturing or "steristripping" the wound (2).

Even higher tech, getting back again to scoliosis, is "digital radiography," which is being used to reduce scoliosis x-ray exposure. If you have not heard about digital radiography, that is because it is relatively new. Radiographic examination remains an essential component in the care of children with scoliosis. A child with scoliosis often is followed with full spinal x-ray examinations every 3 to 6 months until skeletal maturation. Recent reports have documented that the radiation exposure of scoliosis patients is among the highest of any undergoing diagnostic radiography (3). Repeated radiation exposure of relatively young patients has been of much concern to patients and parents and their physicians.

Historically, this radiation concern has been addressed in relatively modest ways. For example, there are new rare earth-film technologies that reduce radiation dose somewhat (4). Additional protection can be provided to the bone marrow by taking films in the anteroposterior position rather than the posteroanterior position and by the use of breast and thyroid shields.

The new technology, however, referred to above, is "digital radiography."

This is a new computerized system of making x-ray examinations in a digital (electronic) format. The system was developed by the Fuji Photo Film Company in Japan and is marketed in the United States by Phillips Medical Systems, Inc. In brief, images are obtained using a special detective plate, which is divided into a grid of pixels (over 2,000 × 2,000). Each pixel can display 1,024 shades of gray. A detective plate is contained in a standard radiographic cassette and is exposed using conventional x-ray machines. The radiation dosage required is a fraction of what is normally needed. The exposure creates a latent image on the plate. The detective plate is read by laser scanner, which releases the latent image in digital format. The image then can be enhanced in a number of ways to get the proper shading—all done by computer. The image can then be visualized on a screen, and an operator can further enhance or decrease the final image by computer adjustments. The final processed image then is automatically printed out on regular x-ray film for viewing on a standard x-ray view box. Unlike photographic film, this system is capable of producing images in which the film density is virtually independent of the radiation dose (5).

It was only a couple of years ago that we in the United States, were concerned about the Japanese having the only licensable technology for producing digital tape players and recorders. American industry fought it tooth and nail. In this instance, our hats are off to Fuji because they have developed what may, in the long run, significantly reduce the risk of cancer resulting from radiation exposure. Fuji, the next time I see one of your blimps flying over Chicago, I will swallow my American pride even though I wish it were a Goodyear up there.—J.A. Stockman, III, M.D.

References

1. Tredwell SJ, et al: *Spine* 15:913, 1990.
2. Caemmerlin P, et al: *N Engl J Med* 321:121, 1990.
3. National Council on Radiation Protection and Measurement: *CPR* 56:App A, 1981.
4. Nash CL, et al: *J Bone Joint Surg* 61:371, 1979.
5. Kling TF, et al: *Spine* 15:880, 1990.

The American College of Rheumatology 1990 Criteria for the Classification of Henoch-Schönlein Purpura
Mills JA, Michel BA, Bloch DA, Calabrese LH, Hunder GG, Arend WP, Edworthy SM, Fauci AS, Leavitt RY, Lie JT, Lightfoot RW Jr, Masi AT, McShane DJ, Stevens MB, Wallace SL, Zvaifler NJ (Massachusetts Gen Hosp, Boston; Rheumaklinik Universitätsspital, Zurich, Switzerland; Stanford Univ; Cleveland Clinic Found; Mayo Clinic, Rochester, Minn; et al)
Arthritis Rheum 33:1114–1121, 1990   18–6

The clinical diagnosis of Henoch-Schönlein Purpura (HSP) is easy, but there are as yet no diagnostic criteria that compare the clinical manifestations of HSP with other forms of systemic arteritis. To address this, clinical data from 85 patients with HSP were compared with clinical data of 722 control patients who had other forms of vasculitis.

Comparison of the clinical, laboratory, and pathological features indicate that palpable purpura showed the best sensitivity and specificity, followed by age at onset of disease (table). Using a traditional format rule of choosing different combinations of criteria to determine which combination best separates the HSP cases from controls, 4 criteria were identified: age ≤20 years at disease onset, palpable purpura, acute abdominal pain, and biopsy showing granulocytes in the walls of the small arterioles or venules. The presence of any 2 of these 4 criteria differentiated HSP from

Comparison of the Sensitivity and Specificity of Potential Variables for Henoch-Schönlein Purpura*

Criterion	No. of patients (n = 85)	No. of controls (n = 722)	Sensitivity (%)	Specificity (%)
History				
1. Age ≤20 at disease onset†‡§	85	722	70.6	90.7
2. Abdominal angina	83	718	37.3	94.0
3. Bowel ischemia	84	716	16.7	95.8
4. Bowel angina (variables 2 or 3)†‡	83	717	51.8	91.6
Physical				
5. Palpable purpura†‡§	85	718	88.2	79.9
6. Monarticular synovitis	85	716	11.8	94.8
7. Oligoarticular synovitis	84	716	39.3	86.7
8. Synovitis (variables 6 or 7)†	84	717	50.0	82.6
Laboratory				
9. Gross hematuria	85	720	17.6	95.3
10. Microhematuria ≥5 RBC/HPF	81	696	38.3	79.2
11. Hematuria (gross hematuria or microhematuria ≥1 RBC/HPF)†	82	695	54.9	59.7
12. Melena	85	718	15.3	94.4
13. Hematochezia	85	716	23.5	94.8
14. Positive stool guaiac	54	473	53.7	82.9
15. GI bleeding (variables 12 or 13 or 14)†	61	477	67.2	78.6
16. Proteinuria	80	681	43.8	70.5
17. Decreased C3 level	46	298	10.9	83.2
Biopsy				
18. Granulocytes in arteriole wall	33	460	36.4	85.4
19. Granulocytes in venule wall	37	431	54.1	83.3
20. Wall granulocytes (variables 18 or 19)†‡	38	428	63.2	75.0
21. Periarteriolar granulocytes	32	459	40.6	87.6
22. Perivenular granulocytes	36	432	58.3	85.2
23. Extraarteriolar granulocytes	33	456	27.3	92.5
24. Extravenular granulocytes	37	432	35.1	89.8
25. Extravascular/perivascular granulocytes (variables 21 or 22 or 23 or 24)†‡	37	430	73.0	74.9

Abbreviations: RBC, red blood cells; *HPF*, high power field; *GI*, gastrointestinal.
*For the variable tested or described values are the number of cases or controls, sensitivity is the proportion of positive cases, and specificity is the proportion of negative controls.
†Criterion is one of the final "short list" of variables (n = 8) (see text).
‡Criterion is used for the traditional format classification.
§Criterion is used for the tree classification.
(Courtesy of Mills JA, Michel BA, Bloch DA, et al: *Arthritis Rheum* 33:1114–1121, 1990.)

other forms of vasculitis, with a sensitivity of 87.1% and a specificity of 87.7%. The same 4 criteria were selected with the tree classification method, and this method had a sensitivity of 89.4% and a specificity of 88.1%.

Palpable purpura and age ≤20 years at disease onset appear to be the best discriminators between HSP and other forms of vasculitis. The 2 additional criteria, presence of granulocytes around small blood vessels and gastrointestinal bleeding, identify HSP in patients over age 20 or in the few patients who have no purpura.

▶ Although the bedside diagnosis of HSP is easily made in most cases, the authors of this article are quite correct in saying that there are no previously established diagnostic criteria that compare the clinical manifestations of HSP with other forms of vasculitis. The most confusing differential diagnosis is usually hypersensitivity vasculitis. The latter is usually the result of a drug reaction. If you followed the suggestions provided in the table, the diagnosis of HSP should jump out at you.

Frankly, I don't think I've ever had much difficulty deciding when someone did or did not have HSP. The symptoms of palpable purpura ± any of the following: urticaria, melena, abdominal pain, arthritis, hematuria/proteinuria, or edema are pretty straightforward.

The syndrome of acute purpura and arthritis in children was first described by Schönlein in 1837. The manifestations of colicky abdominal pain and of nephritis were added by Henoch in 1874. The correct term is "Schönlein-Henoch purpura" (SHP). If any of you can figure out why the names were transposed somewhere back in history, please let me know. I'd be curious to find out why.—J.A. Stockman, III, M.D.

Analysis of a Pediatric Rheumatology Clinic Population

Rosenberg AM (Univ of Saskatchewan, Saskatoon)
J Rheumatol 17:827–830, 1990   18–7

From July 1981 to February 1989 a total of 875 patients was referred for the first time to a pediatric rheumatology clinic serving a population of 290,000, for a mean yearly referral rate of 113 patients. A diagnosis was established in 580 patients (66%). Three hundred thirty-seven (58%) had a rheumatic disease, including juvenile rheumatoid arthritis (JRA) in 156 (46%), spondyloarthropathies in 104 (31%), connective tissue-collagen vascular disease in 62 (18%), and other rheumatic disorders in 15 (5%) (table).

Among the 243 children with nonrheumatic disease, 79 had a mechanical or traumatic cause for musculoskeletal symptoms, 33 had an infection, 15 had a neoplastic disorder, and 71 had a variety of other disorders. In addition, 45 healthy children were evaluated because of a family history of rheumatic diseases or questionable abnormal signs and symptoms. The remaining 295 subjects (34%) had no definite diagnosis.

Three hundred fifty-five of the 875 patients continue to be followed up

Rheumatic Disease Diagnoses		
Disease or Condition	Number of Patients (N=337)	
	Total in Class	Number with Diagnosis
Juvenile Rheumatoid Arthritis	156	
Pauciarticular		97
Polyarticular		42
Systemic		17
Spondyloarthropathies	104	
SEA Syndrome (excluding patients with diagnoses of another spondyloarthropathy)		54
Reactive arthritis		22
Arthritis associated with inflammatory bowel disease		8
Ankylosing spondylitis		7
Reiter's syndrome		6
Psoriatic Arthritis		5
Acne arthropathy		1
Behçet's disease		1
Connective Tissue/ Collagen Vascular Diseases	62	
Henoch-Schönlein purpura		20
Kawasaki's disease		13
Systemic lupus erythematosus		10
Localized/linear scleroderma		7
Dermatomyositis		5
Raynaud's disease		4
Neonatal lupus		1
Polyarteritis		1
Wegener's granulomatosis		1
Other Rheumatic Diseases	15	
Acute rheumatic fever		7
Arthropathy associated with cystic fibrosis		4
Reflex sympathetic dystrophy		1
Sarcoidosis		1

(Courtesy of Rosenberg AM: *J Rheumatol* 17:827–830, 1990.)

and all have or are suspected of having a rheumatic disease, for a point prevalence in a rheumatic disease clinic of 122.4/100,000. The mean annual incidence of JRA is 8/100,000; for the spondyloarthropathies the mean annual incidence is 5/100,000; and for connective tissue-collagen vascular disease the mean annual incidence is 3/100,000.

In addition to diagnosing and caring for children with rheumatic disorders, a pediatric rheumatology clinic serves to identify nonrheumatic conditions with manifestations that mimic a rheumatic disease. The fact that one third of the subjects had no diagnosis reflects the often transient and nonspecific nature of childhood rheumatic diseases.

▶ Dr. Lauren M. Pachman, Professor of Pediatrics, Northwestern University Medical School, and Chief of the Division of Immunology/Rheumatology, Children's Memorial Hospital, comments:

▶ This paper illustrates the critical role that the pediatric rheumatologist serves in identification and care of the child with musculoskeletal complaints. Somewhat sobering is the observation that of the 875 children referred, rheumatic disease was diagnosed in only 58%, while 33% had a mechanical or traumatic disorder. As expected, neoplasia and infection were diagnosed in a large number of children, and the appropriate therapy was instituted. These data reinforce the fact that the pediatric rheumatologist should be acquainted with a wide range of potential factors that are related to musculoskeletal disease, including infection and malignancy. Of interest was the observation that 34% of the children with complaints did not have a definite diagnosis, underscoring the need for careful clinical observation and the development of more specific and informative diagnostic tests for pediatric rheumatic disease.

The analysis of this patient population is potentially of great use in comparison with the experience of others in different geographic and ethnic settings. By having a credible database, this clinic in Saskatchewan, Canada, was able to provide information concerning the relative frequencies and epidemiologic characteristics of childhood rheumatic diseases. The upcoming Pediatric Rheumatology Boards should help further define the information base needed to train physicians who are committed to the diagnosis and care of children with rheumatic disease.—L.M. Pachman, M.D.

Safety and Efficacy of Methotrexate Therapy for Juvenile Rheumatoid Arthritis
Rose CD, Singsen BH, Eichenfield AH, Goldsmith DP, Athreya BH (Univ of Pennsylvania; Thomas Jefferson Univ; Children's Hosp of Philadelphia; Alfred I duPont Inst, Wilmington, Del)
J Pediatr 117:653–659, 1990   18–8

Low oral doses of methotrexate (MTX) are safe and effective in the treatment of refractory rheumatoid arthritis in adults. Its safety and efficacy in children were studied in 14 boys and 15 girls aged 3 to 18 years with juvenile rheumatoid arthritis (JRA). Twenty-five children had previous inadequate therapeutic response. Eight had toxic reactions to 1 or more prior drugs, including gold, D-penicillamine, and hydroxychloroquine, and another 18 showed intolerable toxic effects of corticosteroids or corticosteroid dependency.

The initial dose of MTX averaged 7.1 mg/m^2/week and was given as a single, oral weekly dose or as 3 divided doses given 12 hours apart. Concurrent nonsteroidal anti-inflammatory drugs were continued. Mean duration of MTX treatment was 18.5 months (range, 8 to 39 months).

Treatment with MTX effectively controlled fever and rash in 83% of children with systemic JRA, reduced morning stiffness by 63%, eliminated recalcitrant joint restriction in 48%, reduced the number of swollen joints by 46%, and reduced the swelling indices by 52%. Eight children did not benefit from MTX therapy; 6 had systemic-onset JRA, and all had advanced erosive disease. Toxic effects were limited, consisting of gastrointestinal upset in 2 children and increased levels of serum transaminase in another. No child was withdrawn from the study because of adverse reactions.

Low weekly oral doses of MTX are safe and effective and should be recommended early in the treatment of JRA. Further studies are warranted to define the potential toxic effects of MTX on the lungs and reproductive system, as well as the outcome after discontinuation of MTX therapy.

▶ As sure as you can be that William Tell, Jr, had headaches, you could be as sure that MTX would finally come of age as an agent to treat JRA.

Rheumatologists are the world's experts (said in a very positive sense) in applying the pyramid approach to the management of inflammatory joint disease. Aspirin is usually used first and if that fails, other nonsteroidal anti-inflammatory agents are added (such as naproxen or tolmetin). It takes about 6 to 8 weeks to be sure if any 1 of these therapies is effective. When not effective, up the pyramid the pharmacologic approach goes. Steroids are best reserved only to ameliorate, in a temporizing way, severe inflammation or disability, particularly while waiting for something higher on the pyramid, such as gold, D-penicillamine, or hydroxychloroquine to become effective. The latter group of agents are frequently called slow-acting antirheumatic agents. These, along with cyclophosphamide, chlorambucil, or azathioprine all have significant toxicities. Because of this, MTX is quickly being added to the pyramid as a substitute for most if not all of the other slow-acting medications. This report from Children's Hospital of Philadelphia and the A. I. duPont Institute in Wilmington demonstrated that MTX worked amazingly well in the large majority of children in whom it was tried.

These data suggest that low weekly doses of MTX given orally are safe, efficacious, and should be considered a mainstay of treatment for children in whom trials of nonsteroidal anti-inflammatory agents fail. I have checked around, and it is amazing how quickly this antimetabolite has caught on among pediatric rheumatologists.

Remember that within every silver lining there is a cloud. Methotrexate does have potential side effects. A higher than expected incidence of herpes zoster has been reported in patients with rheumatoid arthritis who were treated with weekly, low-dose MTX (1). Also, many physicians initially prescribe MTX while continuing treatment with nonsteroidal anti-inflammatory agents. Be careful if you do this because an interaction between these 2 classes of drugs has been reported (2). Nonsteroidal anti-inflammatory agents markedly prolong the MTX elimination half-life, increasing its toxicity.

The only other new thing being talked about with respect to the management of JRA is the use of intravenous immunoglobulin. Two reports have described the use of intravenous immunoglobulin, and the results in both were positive (3, 4). But I'm a betting person, and my bet is that intravenous IgG will not catch on as a major player in the management of JRA. It is just too expensive compared with the relatively few dollars it costs for nonsteroidal drugs or for those 2.5-mg tablets of methotrexate.—J.A. Stockman, III, M.D.

References

1. Antonelli MAS, et al: *Am J Med* 90:295, 1991.
2. DuPuis LE, et al: *J Rheumatol* 17:1469, 1990.
3. Jayne DRW, et al: *Lancet* 337:1137, 1991.
4. Silverman ED, et al: *Arthritis Rheum* 33:1015, 1990.

The Toddler's Fracture Revisited
Tenenbein M, Reed MH, Black GB (Children's Hosp, Winnipeg, Man; Univ of Manitoba, Winnipeg)
Am J Emerg Med 8:208–211, 1990   18–9

Toddler's fracture, a subtle, undisplaced oblique fracture of the distal tibia in toddlers, is often unrecognized. Experience was reviewed with 37 cases of toddler's fracture. The 22 boys and 15 girls were aged 12 to 52 months (mean age, 27 months).

There was a history of trauma in all but 2 cases, and the nature of trauma was typically mild (table). Physical findings suggested a fracture in only 26 cases; local warmth was a valuable sign because it was positive in all 6 cases in which it was noted. Radiologic appearances were often subtle; in 5 patients fractures were demonstrated only on subsequent follow-up studies. Characteristically, a faint oblique line that crossed the distal tibial shaft and terminated medially was seen on the anteroposterior and oblique views but was poorly visualized on the lateral view.

Four patients with a history or suspicion of child abuse demonstrated fractures that were radiologically similar to toddler's fractures, but they were midshaft, rather than distal, fractures. All 37 children recovered fully after immobilization.

Because toddler's fracture can be difficult to diagnose, a high degree of suspicion is necessary, particularly in a child aged 1 to 4 years with acute onset of a limp or refusal to bear weight. The findings of a midshaft tibial fracture should raise the suspicion of child abuse.

▶ This report pretty much speaks for itself, and I am having difficulty thinking of anything to add. When you have nothing to add, the best thing to do is to change the subject.

On that note, what percentage of adolescents are nail biters? Is a nail biter a former thumb sucker? Do nail biters bite all 10 fingers equally, or are they

---

Clinical Features of Toddler's Fracture

Mechanism of Injury	
Tripped, or twisted ankle	19
Fell from a height (<4 feet)	15
Other (another child fell on leg)	1
Unknown	2
Duration of Symptoms (Hours)	
<24	20
24–48 H	7
48–72	3
>72	6
Unknown	1
Physical Findings Suggestive of a Fracture	26
Local tenderness	24
Increased temperature	6
Swelling	3
Weight Bearing	
None	27
Partial	6
Not noted	4

(Courtesy of Tenenbein M, Reed MH, Black GB: *Am J Emerg Med* 8:208–211, 1990.)

---

rather selective? Is the intelligence of a nail biter subnormal? Does nail biting stunt your growth? Is it an antecedent for paronychia? Does nail biting stunt the growth of your teeth.

The answers to these and other fascinating questions concerning nail biting may be seen in an excellent review of Leung et al. (1). Forty-five percent of adolescents are nail biters. Nail biting is very frequently a sequela of thumb sucking. Most nail biters bite all 10 fingers nonselectively (no discrimination against "pinkys" here). One of the beneficial effects of nail biting is that it increases nail growth by about 20%. This may be the only theoretical benefit of nail biting because more than 80% of patients requiring treatment for paronychia have it as the result of either nail biting or nail picking. The dental implications of nail biting are pretty straight-forward. All that chumping on your teeth increases the risk of apical root absorption. Additionally, chronic nail biting may produce small fractures along the edges of the incisors.

For the nail biters in the reading audience, the most important issue is whether or not you are of normal intelligence. Well, rest intact tonight knowing that you are. You may not have nails, but you are as smart as your genes allow you to be.

Unlike many other editorial comments, this one shall close with no biting remarks.—J.A. Stockman, III, M.D.

Reference

1. Leung L, et al: *Clin Pediatr* 29:690, 1990.

Location on Chromosome 15 of the Gene Defect Causing Marfan Syndrome

Kainulainen K, Pulkkinen L, Savolainen A, Kaitila I, Peltonen L (Natl Public Health Inst, Helsinki; Kuopio Univ, Kuopio, Finland; Helsinki Univ; Univ of Helsinki)
N Engl J Med 323:935–939, 1990   18–10

Marfan's syndrome is an autosomal dominant connective tissue disorder with extremely variable clinical manifestations. Despite intensive research, the fundamental defect in Marfan's syndrome remains to be defined. By combining genetic data from a linkage analysis of 8 three-generation families with Marfan's syndrome, an international collaborative study constructed a preliminary exclusion map for the likely loci of the defective gene for the syndrome. Five families with Marfan's syndrome were tested for genetic linkage to polymorphic markers on chromosome 15.

The 5 families had positive lod scores for three polymorphic markers (D15S45, D15S29, and D15S25), indicating a significant genetic linkage of Marfan's syndrome to these markers on chromosome 15. The most probable location of the gene for the disease is currently D15S45.

The chromosomal localization of the mutation in Marfan's syndrome is a first step toward the isolation and characterization of the defective gene in the syndrome. Furthermore, the linkage of Marfan's syndrome to chromosome 15 will allow diagnostic testing in families in which cosegregation of these markers with the disease has been confirmed.

Marfan Syndrome: A Diagnostic Dilemma

Viljoen D, Beighton P (Univ of Cape Town, Observatory, South Africa)
Clin Genet 37:417–422, 1990   18–11

Marfan's syndrome is a common and well-known entity, but diagnosis can prove difficult. The records of 66 patients in whom Marfan's syndrome had been diagnosed between 1972 and 1987 were reviewed.

After applying the Pyeritz diagnostic criteria, promulgated in the *International Nosology of Inherited Connective Tissue Disorders* (table), the diagnosis of Marfan's syndrome was confirmed in 33 patients aged 7–68 years. The genealogies of 19 patients (57.5%) were consistent with an autosomal-dominant inheritance, and in 14 patients (14.5%) the disease was apparently sporadic. The musculoskeletal manifestations were consistent with previous reports, but 15.2% of patients required surgery to correct kyphoscoliosis. Dislocation of the lens of the eye was present in only 27.3% of patients. Cardiovascular manifestations were severe in almost one quarter of the patients, and significant respiratory complications occurred in 15.2%. Of the 33 patients in whom the diagnosis of Marfan's syndrome could not be confirmed, 17 had tall stature and a marfanoid habitus but insufficient additional manifestations for firm diagnosis. The other 16 had marfanoid habitus, tall stature, and arachnodactyly but had additional manifestations suggestive of a different syn-

The Pyeritz Criteria for the Diagnosis of Marfan Syndrome

1. Marfan syndrome (15470)
Diagnostic manifestations (Listed in approximate order of decreasing specificity. Major manifestations indicated by an asterisk)

Skeletal
  Anterior chest deformity, especially asymmetric pectus excavatum/carinatum
  Dolichostenomelia not due to scoliosis
  Arachnodactyly
  Vertebral column deformity
    scoliosis
    thoracic lordosis or reduced thoracic kyphosis
  Tall stature, especially compared to unaffected 1° relatives
  High, narrowly arched palate and dental crowding
  Protrusio acetabulae
  Abnormal appendicular joint mobility
    congenital flexion contrctures
    hypermobility
Ocular
  *Ectopia lentis
  Flat cornea
  Elongated globe
  Retinal detachment
  Myopia
Cardiovascular
  *Dilatation of the ascending aorta
  *Aortic dissection
  Aortic regurgitation
  Mitral regurgitation due to mitral valve prolapse
  Calcification of the mitral annulus
  Mitral valve prolapse
  Abdominal aortic aneurysm
  Dysrhythmia
  Endocarditis
Pulmonary
  Spontaneous pneumothorax
  Apical bleb
Skin and integument
  Striae distensae
  Inguinal hernia
  Other hernia (umbilical, diaphragmatic, incisional)
Central nervous system
  *Dural ectasia
    lumbosacral meningocele
  Dilated cisterna magna
  Learning disability (verbal-performance discrepancy)
  Hyperactivity with or without attention deficit disorder

Genetics
  Autosomal dominant inheritance
  25–30% of cases are sporadic; paternal age effect

Requirements for diagnosis
  In the absence of an unequivocally affected 1° relative:
    Involvement of the skeleton and at least 2 other systems; at least one major manifestation
  In the presence of at least one unequivocally affected 1° relative:
    Involvement of at least 2 systems; at least one major manifestation preferred, but this will depend somewhat on the family's phenotype
  Urine amino acid analysis in the absence of pyridoxine supplementation confirms absence of homocystinuria

Conditions most often considered in differential diagnosis
  Homocystinuria
  Familial or isolated mitral valve prolapse syndrome
  Familial or isolated annuloaortic ectasia (Erdheim disease)
  Congenital contractural arachnodactyly
  Stickler syndrome

Comments
  The syndromic status of congenital contractural arachnodactyly is uncertain; most patients so diagnosed likely have the Marfan syndrome.
  The Marfanoid hypermobility syndrome is not a distinct entity.

(From Viljoen D, Beighton P: *Clin Genet* 37:417–422, 1990. Courtesy of Beighton, et al: *Am J Med Genet* 29:581–594, 1988.)

drome. These included blue sclerae, frequent fractures, articular hypermobility, cystic nodular acne, sensorineural hearing loss, and mental retardation.

Outstanding problems in the diagnosis of Marfan's syndrome include accurate categorization of doubtful cases, recognition of possible heterogeneity, and confirmation of independent syndromes in atypical cases. Presently, the Pyeritz criteria provide the best approach to the diagnosis of Marfan's syndrome, but a biomolecular marker may be the final solution to this diagnostic dilemma.

▶ Articles on the Marfan syndrome are included in 2 other chapters of this year's YEAR BOOK (Adolescent Medicine and Heart and Blood Vessels). This may seem like a little bit of overkill. All the controversy in Congress about the ethics of doing genetic studies on President Lincoln's remains using the molecular biologic techniques to determine whether he had a chromosome 15 defect has made this past year the "Year of the Marfan Syndrome." This, together with the emerging knowledge of how serious a problem it is to miss an athlete with the Marfan syndrome makes inclusion of the new information about this disorder mandatory for the YEAR BOOK.

The table provided here on the clinical manifestations of Marfan's syndrome is included so that we look for these physical findings, particularly at the time of school physicals. There is increasing emphasis on physical fitness in the schools, with the majority of states mandating physical education even at the elementary grade level. At the same time, however, most states do not have a policy on fitness testing; less than one quarter of states require fitness testing at the present time. More precisely, 11 states require periodic fitness testing, and 17 simply recommend this practice. To say this differently, it may be up to pediatricians to "take the ball and run with it," making sure that these school programs are adequately supervised and that preparticipation fitness testing is carried out. Without this, a large number of children who should not participate in these programs, including the child with Marfan's syndrome, unfortunately, will be, perhaps to his or her detriment.—J.A. Stockman, III, M.D.

Exercise and Body Composition
Forbes GB (Univ of Rochester, New York)
J Appl Physiol 70:994–997, 1991   18–12

Exercise and/or training programs are believed to augment lean body mass (LBM) and reduce body fat. Although many athletes tend to have a larger LBM than their sedentary peers, the contributions of heredity, training, and nutrition have not been established. Changes in lean weight and fat associated with exercise programs were examined.

Forty-one young adults engaged in various exercise and/or training programs on ad libitum diets were studied. Most of those who gained weight also had an increase in LBM. Most of those who lost weight also lost LBM. Lean body mass change was directly related to weight change, with a regression slope of .500. A literature review confirmed these findings, lending further support to the notion that the magnitude of the change in body composition in exercising persons is affected by body fat content, just as it is for nonexercising individuals.

Changes in LBM in exercising individuals are directly related to changes in weight. The magnitude of body composition change is influenced by body fat content in both exercising and nonexercising persons.

▶ Dr. Gilbert Forbes, author of this study, has been on the trail of changes in body composition related to athletic performance for quite some time. If you ever have an opportunity to visit his laboratory in Rochester, New York, it will represent a fascinating experience for you. He has photos and data on body builders that would amaze you. The transformations these individuals undergo in a somewhat cyclic fashion because the body-building season is not necessarily all year long, shows how adaptable the human body can be to self-directed (destructive) changes in its composition.

In the 1980s anabolic steroids were quite the fashion. In the 1990s, however, what we are seeing is that the typical athlete may very well be "all juiced up with nowhere to go." The "juice" is self-administered recombinant erythropoietin. The "nowhere to go" is the disaster that the athlete can get into by using this drug. The brand name for recombinant erythropoietin is Epogen. The drug is now most commonly called by the term "EPO." It was developed in 1986 by Amgen, a California Biotechnology Company, using new DNA cloning techniques. The Federal Drug Administration approved Epogen for use in 1989 for patients with anemia related to chronic renal failure. The drug was and still is considered a breakthrough for the more than 100,000 individuals who have this problem in the United States. Currently, some 70,000 already receive EPO injections instead of supportive blood transfusions. With EPO, the hemoglobin can be literally "set" to virtually any level depending on the dose of the drug and the frequency of its administration.

For athletes in search of the next performance-enhancing drug, EPO's significance has not been lost. In Europe, it is suspected that patients who legitimately obtain EPO are selling their supplies to local cyclists. It's performance-enhancing capability results from raised oxygen unloading capacity achieved by higher levels of hemoglobin. Currently, the only way to accomplish this is by high-altitude training or blood doping. High-altitude training will probably never be abolished as a training technique because it is a form of physiologic training and is impossible to control. As you might suspect, high-altitude training is fairly expensive and requires some weeks to accomplish. With blood doping, blood is withdrawn weeks to months before a competition, is stored, and is then readministered. Blood doping has been banned by the International and U.S. Olympic Committees, as has been the use of EPO. The problem with EPO is that it is a much more convenient version of high-altitude training or blood doping. All you need is a supplier, a syringe, and a lot of money. Once administered, EPO is absolutely undetectable, so any regulations against its use are unenforceable. There are no published studies showing beneficial effects on exercise training by using EPO, but one unpublished study conducted by Bjorn Akblom of Stockholm's Institute of Gymnastics and Sports did substantiate an 8% improvement in maximal aerobic power among 15 Swedish athletes. This is a 50% improvement over the effects of blood doping. It has been estimated that EPO could trim 30 seconds off a 20-minute running time, enough to turn a pack finisher into a winner.

So what's all the fuss? Although there have not been unequivocally documented deaths linked to EPO, the drug is now under suspicion. Adamson et al. (1) relate some of the potential risks. In 1987, soon after EPO was developed, 5 Dutch pro and amateur racers died suddenly. In 1988, a Belgian and 2 more Dutch riders died. In 1989, 5 more from the Netherlands were gone, and in 1990, there were another 3 Belgians and 2 Dutch. No such cluster of deaths from apparent "coronaries" was ever noted before among these racers. The suspicion is that EPO was the culprit. One can overshoot one's mark and easily achieve hematocrits of 55% to 60%. As a consequence of sweating, hemoconcentration at the end of a long-distance race can raise the hematocrit to 70% or greater. At that point, the fluidity of blood is not dissimilar to that of mud.

The moral here is to keep your eye out for the average athlete who emerges as a superstar in a very short period of time. There is no question about it: EPO is cheating. It may convert a mediocre competitor into a hero, but the outcome could be disastrous for that particular individual. F. Scott Fitzgerald commented in *Early Success* (1937): "Show me a hero and I'll write you a tragedy." He also appropriately added in the *Beautiful and the Damned* (1922): "The victor belongs to the spoils." Do you think that Fitzgerald might have been foreshadowing the use and abuse of EPO?

To read more about the link between athletes and EPO, see the correspondant's report by Les Woodland in *Bicycling* (2).—J.A. Stockman, III, M.D.

References

1. Adamson JW, et al: *N Engl J Med* 324:698, 1991.
2. Woodland L: *Bicycling*, April, 1991, pp 80–81.

Catastrophic Injuries and Fatalities in High School and College Sports, Fall 1982–Spring 1988

Mueller FO, Cantu RC (Univ of North Carolina; Emerson Hosp, Concord, Mass)
Med Sci Sports Exerc 22:737–741, 1990   18–13

Major research on catastrophic injuries in football have made important contributions to that sport. Rule changes, helmet standards, and new coaching techniques have resulted from such projects. Data on catastrophic injuries and fatalities in high school and college sports in 1982–1988 were analyzed. Included were direct and indirect deaths and catastrophic injuries, defined as any injury incurred during participation in high school athletics or a college sponsored sport in which permanent, severe, functional neurologic disability or transient functional neurologic disability was sustained.

There were 271 direct catastrophic injuries in high school and college sports. In high school athletics, there were 218 injuries and fatalities, including 44 deaths, 74 nonfatal injuries, and 100 serious injuries. College athletics were associated with 4 fatalities, 13 nonfatal injuries, and 36 serious injuries. There were 76 indirect injuries at the high school level and 25 at the college level. All injuries were fatal except for 1 indirect injury. Football had the largest number of participants and contributed the greatest numbers of catastrophic injuries. The other sports in which participants were at great risk of catastrophic injury or death were ice hockey, gymnastics, and wrestling.

High school and college catastrophic injuries may never be completely eliminated, but with reliable injury data, they may be reduced dramatically. High school wrestling, gymnastics, and ice hockey should receive close attention in the future.

▶ Because there is an article dealing with sudden cardiac death in young athletes in the Heart and Blood Vessels chapter, there is no need for extensive further commentary on the things that people do to their bodies in the name of sporting activities. This past year or so has seen manuscripts appearing in the literature entitled: "Sudden Cardiac Death in Young Athletes, a Review" (1); "Incidence in Severity of High School Athletic Injuries" (2); "Disc Degeneration in Young Gymnasts" (3); "Sudden Death During Basketball Games" (4); "Sports Injuries in Adolescent's Ballgames: Soccer, Handball, and Basketball" (5); "Skateboard Injuries in Children and Adolescents" (6); "Skateboarding Injuries in Children: A Second Wave" (7); and "Football-Related Spinal Cord Injuries Among High School Players — Louisiana, 1989" (8). These reports speak for themselves with respect to the benefit–risk ratio of certain activities that our teenagers and young adults engage in.

This is the last entry in the Musculoskeletal System chapter. Each year we attempt to bring you up to date with new medical terminology that has to do with complications of certain physical activities. In this past year or so, 4 medical "terms" were introduced or revisited in the medical literature. These are "pallbearer's palsy," "trekker's shoulder," "bowling plexopathy," and "high-impact aerobic deafness."

Trekker's shoulder (9) and pallbearer's palsy (10) are variants of the same condition. Trekker's shoulder is an injury to the upper brachial plexus associated with carrying a heavy backpack. Pallbearer's palsy is a pleasingly sepulchral term that describes a condition caused by a stumble while carrying a coffin. The latter commonly is associated with the development of an Erb's palsy. Bowling plexopathy was recently reported in a 26-year-old man who awoke after an evening of bowling with pain in his neck and shoulder. He had weakness of the right deltoid and biceps muscles, absence of the right bicep reflex, and a reduced brachioradialis reflex. This represented a classic right upper brachial nerve plexopathy that lasted for quite some time (11). Those engaging in high-impact aerobics may very well experience auditory vestibular dysfunction (12).

I have been arguing against all forms of exercise for many years. When it comes to the middle ear problems related to high-impact aerobics, it is easy to see why this message has been largely ignored. It has been falling on deaf ears.

With respect to the various "plexopathies" noted above, it is impossible to avoid the conclusion that any plexopathy associated with exercise is, in fact, not an "opathy" but rather a normal expected physiologic reaction to the "opathy" known as exercise.

My apologies to those of you who are annoyed by these comments against any form of human activity that is not sedentary. You have to understand the YEAR BOOK'S editor's psyche. He is 47. When one is "pushing" 50, that is exercise enough.—J.A. Stockman, III, M.D.

References

1. McCaffrey FM, et al: *Am J Dis Child* 145:177, 1991.
2. Whieldon TJ, et al: *Athletic Training JNATA* 25:344, 1990.
3. Tertti M, et al: *Am J Sports Med* 18:206, 1990.
4. Thomas RJ, et al: *Physician Sports Med* 18:75, 1990.
5. Yde J, et al: *Br J Sports Med* 24:51, 1991.
6. Pendergrast RA: *J Adolesc Health Care* 11:408, 1990.
7. Retsky J, et al: *Am J Dis Child* 145:188, 1991.
8. CDC: *JAMA* 264:1520, 1990.
9. West RJ: *N Engl J Med* 324:62, 1991.
10. Loni NK: *BMJ* 2:808, 1966.
11. Shukla AY, et al: *N Engl J Med* 324:928, 1991.
12. Weintraub MI: *N Engl J Med* 323:1633, 1990.

19 Gastroenterology

The Steatocrit Test as a Guide in the Prevention of Cow's-Milk Enteropathy Following Acute Infectious Enteritis
Iacono G, Carroccio A, Alongi A, Montalto G, Cavataio F, Comparetto L, Balsamo V, Notarbartolo A (Ospedale Pediatrico G. Di Cristina, Palermo; Università di Palermo; Ospedale Civico, Palermo, Italy)
J Pediatr Gastroenterol Nutr 11:48–52, 1990   19–1

Ninety infants with acute enteritis were studied to evaluate the influence of different types of milk on the evolution of the acute phase of the diarrhea. The degree of steatorrhea during the acute phase was evaluated as a possible risk factor for the development of cow's milk enteropathy (CME).

The 90 infants with enteritis were divided into 3 groups and were refed differently after the acute episode. The groups were refed with semielemental formula, milk containing soy proteins and vegetable oils, or cow's milk formula.

The risk of CME development after an episode of acute enteritis is lower in patients with a low level of steatorrhea during the acute enteritis phase. The risk is inversely related to patient age. The simple steatocrit test for monitoring malabsorption is recommended.

Patients less than 2 months of age with severe steatorrhea should be refed with breast milk, semielemental formula, or soy milk for at least 4 weeks to prevent sensitization.

▶ The measurement of fecal fat excretion is an essential test for the diagnosis of many gastrointestinal disorders. Unfortunately, the standard test, which requires a 72-hour stool collection and special equipment for analytic assay, is a bit cumbersome, to say the least. No one likes collecting stool much less keeping it around for 3 days in a pail.

More recently, Phuapradit et al. (1) described the "steatocrit." The steatocrit is sort of the counterpart of the measurement of fat in breast milk better known as the "crematocrit." If you think a child has a malabsorption syndrome like cystic fibrosis or has not yet recovered full absorptive capacity after a case of infectious diarrhea, challenge the child with a fatty meal and check the steatocrit of the stool. It's a wonderful teaching tool on rounds.

The Julia Child recipe for preparation of the steatocrit is as follows:
1. Take .5 g of fresh stool and homogenize it with a mortar with 2.5 mL of water and .06 g fine sand.
2. Take the resulting suspension and draw it into a capillary hematocrit tube.
3. Seal the tube at one end with wax and centrifuge for 15 minutes at 1,300 RPM in a hematocrit centrifuge.

4. Determine the steatocrit, which is the relative length of the fatty layer divided by the sum of the fatty layer plus the solid layer: steatocrit (%) = F ÷ (F + S) × 100.

Any steatocrit value greater than 2% is abnormal (2).—J.A Stockman, III, M.D.

References

1. Phuapradit P, et al: *Arch Dis Child* 56:725, 1981.
2. Iacono G, et al: *J Pediatr Gastroenterol*

A Controlled Trial of Corticosteroids in Children With Corrosive Injury of the Esophagus
Anderson KD, Rouse TM, Randolph JG (Children's Natl Med Ctr, Washington, DC)
N Engl J Med 323:637–640, 1990   19–2

Many accidental ingestions still occur each year despite legislation to control accessibility to caustic materials. Experience over 18 years with 131 children thought to have ingested such materials was evaluated (Fig 19–1). Steroids were given to 31 of 60 children who had serious esophageal injury. All of these children also had burns of the mouth or pharynx. Study patients received prednisolone, 2 mg/kg daily intravenously, until oral intake resumed, and then 2.5 mg of prednisone per kg daily was given orally for 3 weeks before tapering.

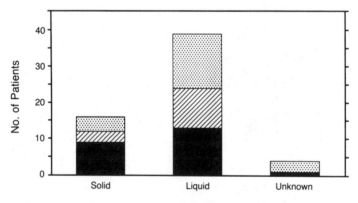

Type of Caustic Agent

Fig 19–1.—Relation of the severity of esophageal injury to the type of caustic agent ingested. *Solid bars* denote first-degree burns, *hatched bars* show second-degree burns, and *stippled bars* represent third-degree burns. The causative agent was known in 55 of 60 children with esophageal injuries. The difference between injuries caused by the ingestion of solids and those caused by the ingestion of liquids was not statistically significant. (Courtesy of Anderson KD, Rouse TM, Randolph JG: *N Engl J Med* 323:637–640, 1990.)

Strictures developed in 10 of the 31 steroid-treated patients and 11 of 29 control patients. Third-degree injuries were similarly frequent in the 2 groups. No patient with a first-degree burn and only 1 with a second-degree burn had an esophageal stricture. Eleven of the 21 patients with stricture required esophageal replacement. The one serious side effect of steroid therapy was a brain abscess in a young child.

The value of steroid treatment in patients with caustic injury of the esophagus remains to be established. Development of stricture in this series was related only to the severity of corrosive injury.

▶ Dr. Lauren D. Holinger, Professor of Otolaryngology, Northwestern University Medical School, and Chief of the Section of Otolaryngology, Children's Memorial Hospital, comments:

▶ This well-written report of an 18-year clinical study reaffirms the need for endoscopy to document the status of the esophagus after infection of corrosive material. The authors point out that the severity of the initial injury is the most important predictor of stricture formation. Interestingly, they found that 7 of 8 untreated patients with moderately severe burns developed strictures, whereas only 1 of 4 patients with moderate burns treated with corticosteroids developed a stricture. However, this trend was not statistically significant; there were not enough cases to prove the benefit of steroids.

Our experience, and that of others (1), suggests that strictures that develop in patients treated with corticosteroids may be easier to manage than those that develop in untreated patients. This concept is also supported by the data of Anderson et al. They found that esophageal replacement was required by almost twice as many patients in the untreated control group (7 patients) as in the steroid-treated group (4 patients). Again, the trend suggested that steroids indeed are helpful, but the number of patients in this crucial category was too small to be statistically significant.

The equivocal results of the study may also be related to the relatively low dosage of prednisolone chosen (2 mg/kg/day). Hawkins et al. (2) recommend twice the initial dose that Anderson et al. use for children: intravenous methylprednisolone, 4 mg/kg/day for 2–4 days. Prednisone, 5 mg/kg/day, is then given orally and is slowly tapered to a relatively low (.5 mg/kg/day) maintenance dose that is continued for approximately 6 weeks until the esophagus heals. Had Anderson et al. chosen a higher initial dose they might have shown a significant steroid benefit. This issue might be addressed in another study.

Unfortunately the authors conclude (on the basis that their study does not show a steroid benefit) that steroids are not helpful. However, the numbers of patients in the study and the dose of steroids given are inadequate to demonstrate the positive effect of steroids in the treatment of corrosive injuries of the esophagus.

Prevention of caustic ingestion remains of paramount importance. Parent education, child-proof packaging, and other legislation that limits the concentration of caustic substances have reduced the incidence of this difficult problem.—L.D. Holinger, M.D.

References

1. Cardona JC, Daly JF: *Ann Otol Rhinol Laryngol* 80:521, 1971.
2. Hawkins DB, et al: *Laryngoscope* 90:98, 1980.

Pediatric HBsAg Chronic Liver Disease and Adult Asymptomatic Carrier Status: Two Stages of the Same Entity
Zancan L, Chiaramonte M, Ferrarese N, Zacchello F (Univ of Padua, Italy)
J Pediatr Gastroenterol Nutr 11:380–384, 1990   19–3

In chronic hepatitis B virus (HBV) infection more than 60% of adults are diagnosed as being asymptomatic chronic carriers with normal levels of transaminase. However, this asymptomatic carrier status is rarely found in children. To determine whether chronic hepatitis in childhood leads to the asymptomatic carrier status in later life, 36 adolescents and young adults with chronic HBV infection for a mean duration of 12.6 years and with histologically proved chronic hepatitis during childhood were reexamined. All patients were screened for tumor by using an α-fetoprotein assay and hepatic ultrasound. Eight patients with cirrhosis underwent esophageal fiberoptic endoscopy.

All patients were in good health, with no clinical or biochemical signs of liver failure (Table 1). Only 2 patients had abnormal levels of transaminase, and both had antibodies to delta virus. All but 1 patient became anti-HBe positive (97%), compared with 11% who were anti-HBe positive at the onset of disease (Table 2). Similarly, none of the patients were HBeAg positive (0%), compared with 72% who were HBeAg positive at the onset of disease. These prevalence rates are similar to those found in adults at the onset of the asymptomatic carrier status. Five patients had HBsAg clearance. None of the patients studied had varices or tumors.

These data suggest that chronic hepatitis in childhood may evolve into the chronic carrier status with no signs of liver disease in adulthood. These findings support the hypothesis that chronic hepatitis and asymptomatic carrier status may be subsequent stages of the HBV infection.

TABLE 1.—Clinical Features

Sex	20 males; 16 females
Mean age	16 yr (range, 10–25)
General condition	Good
Height, weight, and sexual development	Normal
Hepatomegaly	5/36 (17/36)
Hepatosplenomegaly	2/36 (14/36)
Absence of hepatosplenomegaly	29/36 (5/36)
Jaundice	0/36 (0/36)
Ascites	0/36 (0/36)
Esophageal varices	0/36 (0/36)

Note: Data in parentheses refer to onset of disease.
(Courtesy of Zancan L, Chiaramonte M, Ferrarese N, et al: *J Pediatr Gastroenterol Nutr* 11:380–384, 1990.)

TABLE 2.—Biochemical Features

Albumin (g/dl)	5.06 ± 0.4	
	(3.67 ± 0.53)	
γ-Globulin (g/dl)	1.08 ± 0.36	
	(1.49 ± 0.43)	
Bilirubin (mg/dl)	0.67 ± 0.26	
Prothrombin activity (%)	87.0 ± 11.54	
AST (IU/L)	26.5 ± 19.23	
	(119.0 ± 83.26)	
ALT (IU/L)	35.0 ± 37.18	
	(129.9 ± 97.87)	
AFP (ng/ml)	2.78 ± 1.39	
HBsAg	31/36	86% (100%)
anti-HBs	4/36	11% (9%)
anti-HBc	36/36	100% (100%)
HBeAg	0/36	0% (72%)
anti-HBe	35/36	97% (11%)
HBeAg/anti-HBe negative	1/36	3% (17%)
anti-HDV	2/36	6%

Abbreviations: AST, aspartate transaminase; *ALT,* alanine transaminase; *AFP,* α-fe-toprotein.
Note: Data in parentheses refer to onset of disease.
(Courtesy of Zancan L, Chiaramonte M, Ferrarese N, et al: *J Pediatr Gastroenterol Nutr* 11:380–384, 1990.)

▶ If these authors are correct, they have explained a puzzle that has been difficult to understand for some years. Unlike with adults, in children it is rare to find an individual who is a chronic HBV carrier and has normal transaminase levels. Chronic HBV infection in childhood is characterized by a high level of virus replication for many years, corresponding more or less to biochemical signs of liver cell damage and corresponding histologically to various degrees of inflammation. Adults, on the other hand, very frequently become carriers and continue to have normal enzyme levels. What these investigators have documented is that the adult who is an asymptomatic carrier but has normal enzyme levels was once the child who had chronic active hepatitis with evidence by enzyme assay of ongoing liver damage. If you believe these data, the majority of kids ultimately get better and may become adults who are hepatitis B carriers. This does not mean that these individuals are not at risk for hepatocellular carcinoma. They certainly are, and they should be under periodic surveillance with α-fetoprotein determinations to screen for this malignancy.

Population-based surveys for antibodies to hepatitis B indicate that among white Americans, the life-time chance of contracting hepatitis B if one is not vaccinated is less than 5%. The point prevalence of the carrier state for hepatitis B surface antigen (HBsAg) is less than .5%. Like the infection in Asia and Africa, the disease in the United States tends to cluster in certain high-risk groups: parenteral drug abusers, male homosexuals, promiscuous heterosexuals, health care workers, recipients of blood or blood products, babies of certain of the above groups, and, of course, immigrants from areas of the world where hepatitis B is common in the general population, most notably China and Southeast Asia.

Given the enormous variations in the diseases produced within the liver by HBV, how does one evaluate the severity of the disease or advise on prognosis? These issues are becoming important as reports of successful treatments for chronic hepatitis B infection appear. The largest and most comprehensive such report appeared in the *New England Journal of Medicine* (1). A large multicenter trial of the use of interferon-α in 169 patients with chronic hepatitis B was reported. A 4-month course of interferon-α induced remission of disease in 38% of patients. Unfortunately, interferon-α must be given by parenteral injection, is not without side effects, and is ineffective in a significant proportion of patients. When it works, it works extremely well, however. The sticky issue is what criteria should be used to decide which patients with chronic hepatitis B warrant such rigorous therapy.

The answer to the question posed in the preceding paragraph may be the combination of laparoscopy and liver biopsy. It would appear that laparoscopy, in which you actually look at the liver, in conjunction with liver biopsy will replace needle biopsy of the liver alone in the management of children with possible chronic hepatitis. Liver biopsy alone has been shown to be an unreliable means to rule out the presence of cirrhosis because of problems with sampling error. Vajro and associates have reviewed their own experience with laparoscopy in the evaluation of chronic hepatitis in 96 children (2). Among the children in the series found to have cirrhosis, half had gross laparoscopic findings suggestive of this diagnosis but without the standard histologic criteria on needle biopsy.

Hepatitis B can be considered to be a very serious problem for some patients. It is sufficiently serious that the current trend of recommending universal immunization with the hepatitis B vaccine seems to make reasonable sense. I've had mine; have you had yours?—J.A. Stockman, III, M.D.

References

1. Perrillo J, et al: *N Engl J Med* 323:626, 1990.
2. Vajro P, et al: *J Pediatr* 117:392, 1990.

Transplantation of Two Patients With One Liver: Analysis of a Preliminary Experience With 'Split-Liver' Grafting
Emond JC, Whitington PF, Thistlethwaite JR, Cherqui D, Alonso EA, Woodle IS, Vogelbach P, Busse-Henry SM, Zucker AR, Broelsch CE (Univ of Chicago)
Ann Surg 212:14–22, 1990   19–4

The availability of donor organs is a major limitation to the more widespread application of orthotopic liver transplantation (OLT). Although the supply of cadaver donors is adequate for adult patients with advanced liver disease, there is a critical shortage of donors for small children. This discrepancy is attributable to the disparity between the epidemiology of pediatric liver disease affecting primarily infants and small children and that of brain death and organ donation for this age group.

Reduced-size OLD involves the reduction in size of cadaver livers from larger donors to fit into the abdominal cavity of children. Reduced-size OLT has been performed for the past 2 years at this institution. In addition, since July 1988, 18 patients have undergone split-liver transplantation, whereby a second patient was treated with the liver portion that would have been discarded during preparation of a reduced-size graft in children (Fig 19–2)

Among the 18 patients who underwent split-liver OLTs, survival was 67% and graft survival was 50%. In comparison, patient survival for the 34 patients treated with full-sized OLT during the same study period was 84% and graft survival was 76%. Biliary complications occurred in 27% of the patients with split-graft OLT, but in only 4% of the patients who received full-sized grafts. The difference was statistically significant. Primary nonfunction and arterial thrombosis occurred with similar fre-

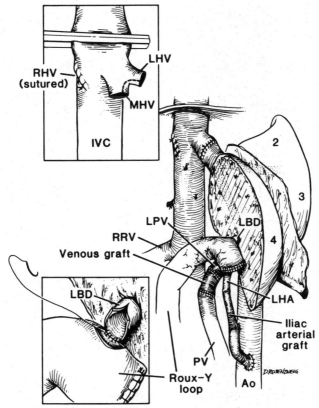

Fig 19–2.—The left lobe graft after revascularization. Note the preservation of the inferior vena cava and the anastomoses of the segmental pedicles using interposition grafts. *Upper square* shows the preparation of the inferior vena cava and hepatic vein using the common trunk of the left and middle hepatic veins for suprahepatic venous anastomosis. *Lower square* shows the anastomosis of the Roux-Y loop on the left hepatic duct, which is enlarged by an anterior spatulation. (Courtesy of Emond JC, Whitington PF, Thistlethwaite JR, et al: *Ann Surg* 212:14–22, 1990.)

quency in split-graft and full-sized OLT. The high incidence of biliary complications after split-graft OLT can most likely be reduced by technical improvements. Split-liver OLT will eventually have a substantial impact on the practice of liver transplantation, because it will make more livers available.

▶ It is difficult to believe that it has been 25 years since the first human liver transplantation was performed. It wasn't done in an adult, either. It was done in a 19-month-old child who had hepatocellular carcinoma. One-year survival rates before 1980 were only 30%; now they are in the 70% to 80%+ range. The National Institutes of Health concluded nearly 10 years ago that liver transplantation should be considered as the definitive therapy for various forms of end-stage liver disease in both adults and children (1).

For children, the primary liver diseases requiring transplantation are roughly divisible into 5 groups: (1) chronic progressive liver disease, with biliary atresia predominating; (2) inborn errors of metabolism, with α_1-antitrypsin deficiency predominating; (3) acute liver failure; (4) a variety of congenital or acquired structural anomalies of the liver; (5) primary hepatic malignancies. Far and away, biliary atresia is the most common indication for liver transplantation in children.

One of the largest series of children's transplants reported recently was from UCLA (2). There, 103 patients have undergone liver transplants since 1984. The 5-year survival rate was 77%, and nearly all of the deaths occurred within 5 months of the transplant, with only 1 death occurring more than 1 year after transplantation.

As may be seen from the above article, livers come from all kinds of donors in all sorts of sizes. They can come from cadavers. A single cadaver can be used to make more than 1 liver for more than 1 recipient. Similarly, if a baby is too small to accept a whole liver from a cadaver or a parent, the liver can be "whittled" down to the child's size. Thus, either intact livers or segments of the liver can be used.

The lingering problem with orthotopic liver transplantation is the risk of secondary malignancy. We are recognizing that a small but significant percentage (about 5%) of patients who undergo liver transplantation will ultimately have a lymphoproliferative disease, usually triggered by the Epstein-Barr virus. To date, half of affected individuals have died. It seems a shame that patients who have gone through so much may live only to fight another battle that they may not win.

The latest data on cost of liver transplantation indicate that the procedure itself runs approximately $100,000, with the average total hospital bill being about $250,000 (3).—J.A. Stockman, III, M.D.

References

1. NIH Consensus Development Conference Statement: *Hepatology* 4:1075, 1984.
2. Busuttil RW, et al: *Ann Surg* 213:248, 1991.
3. Fishbein MH, et al: *Internat Pediatr* 5:9, 1990.

Gallstones in Children: Characterization by Age, Etiology, and Outcome

Reif S, Sloven DG, Lebenthal E (Children's Hosp of Buffalo, Buffalo; St John's Mercy Med Ctr, St Louis; Hahnemann School of Medicine, Philadelphia)
Am J Dis Child 145:105–108, 1991   19–5

Gallstones have been uncommon in children, but are now being diagnosed more frequently. The records of children with gallstones identified at 1 institution over a 10-year period were reviewed to determine the clinical presentation, method of diagnosis, and means of treatment in different age groups.

Fifty patients met study criteria. They ranged in age from prenatal to 20 years (mean age, 12.2 years). Conditions associated with the development of gallstones included hemolytic disease, parenteral nutrition, and adolescent pregnancy (table). Right upper quadrant pain was the most

Conditions Associated With Gallstones
in 50 Children

Associated Conditions	No. of Patients
Hemolysis	18
Sickle cell anemia	11
Spherocytosis	3
Autoimmune	2
Thalassemia major	1
Pyruvate kinase deficiency	1
Parenteral nutrition	8
Adolescent pregnancy	7
Ileal resection	4
Obesity†	3
Sepsis	3
Nectrotizing enterocolitis	2
Spinal cord disease	2
Transverse myelitis	1
Spina bifida	1
Other	
Hemobilia	1
Chronic intestinal pseudo-obstruction	1
Chylous ascites	1
Muscular dystrophy	1
Sarcoidosis	1
Systemic lupus erythematosus	1
Hyperlipidemia	1
Cystic fibrosis	1
Hepatitis type B	1
Dysgammaglobulinemia	1
Prolonged ceftriaxone therapy	1
Idiopathic	10

*Children with gallstones could be categorized into 4 main groups: patients with hemolysis (18), patients with parenteral nutrition (8), adolescent pregnancy (7), and patients with other predisposing factors (7). More than 1 predisposing factor was present in some patients.

†Obesity is defined as weight divided by height, 95th percentile.

(Courtesy of Reif S, Sloven DG, Lebenthal E: *Am J Dis Child* 145:105–108, 1991.)

common symptom in 32 patients. Six of 7 asymptomatic patients were under the age of 5 years, including 1 diagnosed in utero during a routine maternal ultrasound study.

Ultrasonography, used for diagnosis in 48 patients, proved to be accurate, with no false-positive results. Jaundice was noted primarily in those with hemolytic disease. The female predominance seen in adult patients with gallstones was present here only after 15 years of age, suggesting a hormonal influence. Cholecystectomy was performed in 36 patients, but conservative treatment was preferred, for children receiving parenteral nutrition. Complications included pancreatitis in 4 patients, retained duct stone in 1 patient, and recurrence in 1 patient.

It is not certain whether this rise in the rate of gallstones in children is a true increase or is a result of improved diagnostic methods. The variety of symptoms in children should alert the clinician to the possibility of gallstones whenever there are nonspecific abdominal symptoms, particularly in the presence of associated conditions.

Self-Management of Dietary Compliance in Coeliac Disease by Means of ELISA "Home Test" to Detect Gluten
Skerritt JH, Hill AS (CSIRO Wheat Research Unit, Division of Plant Industry, New South Wales, Australia)
Lancet 337:379–382, 1991
19–6

Maintenance of a gluten-free diet for patients with celiac disease may not be simple because of possible gluten contamination, particularly in processed foods. The long-established methods of food protein analysis are slow and can be unreliable when foods are baked or processed. A simple prototype test kit to detect gluten in foods was developed for use at home.

The enzyme-linked immunosorbent assay (ELISA) test kit is based on monoclonal antibodies to heat-stable gluten protein, which cross-react appropriately with barley and rye proteins. The food is extracted with 5 mL of 2 mmol/L hydrochloric acid and 1 drop of the extract and is transferred to an antibody-coated tube. The enzyme-labeled gluten detection antibody is added, and after 3 minutes, the tube is washed. The presence of gluten is detected by addition of a color developer. The reaction is stopped at exactly 2 minutes, whereby the substrate turns blue in the presence of gluten.

The ELISA "home test" kit was compared with a quantitative laboratory kit. The tests showed very good qualitative agreement. The home test kit clearly differentiated foods with trace gluten contents, which are acceptable for a gluten-free diet, from those with a slightly higher but unacceptable gluten content. Forty-seven patients with celiac disease, aged 7 to 76 years, with diverse educational backgrounds, participated in a trial of the prototype kit. Most participants found the method easy to use despite lack of step-by-step diagrams, with an average 93% of tests correctly identifying foods as acceptable or unacceptable. More important, the rate of false-negative results was extremely low. This simple ELISA home test to detect gluten in foods should increase dietary compliance in patients with celiac disease.

▶ The ability to do your own gluten assays on food could revolutionize the management of celiac disease. The test itself can be done faster than you can get an oil change at your local "Jiffy Lube." You can then eat with confidence, knowing that your diet is free of something that could wipe out your small intestinal villi and put you at an increased risk of small bowel lymphoma. The "home test" is truly better than sliced bread, pizza, and even bagels, none of which a patient with celiac disease can eat anyway. Would that there were additional simple assays for things in food that people react to. Recently, in the *New England Journal of Medicine,* there was described an individual who, not being a meat eater, ordered a vegetable burger only to have anaphylaxis develop. The vegetable burger didn't contain any hamburger, but it did contain peanuts, to which the individual was highly allergic. Obviously, vegetable burgers are "nut" all they appear to be. Vive la carnivore!

Back to the topic of celiac disease and what's new in this area. What's new is very impressive. A noninvasive test has long been sought to obviate the need for small bowel biopsies to make the initial diagnosis. Antibodies to gluten, gliadin, reticulin, and endomycium (EMA) have been detected in up to 96% of untreated patients. However, the sensitivity and specificity, particularly for gliadin and reticulin antibodies, have varied so widely from center to center that most physicians do not rely on them at all. The 2 most recently discovered antibodies, EMA and human jejunal antibody (JAB) may, however, be quite useful for diagnosis and for monitoring the efficacy of treatment. The levels of EMA and JAB are elevated when the patient is following a gluten-containing diet and disappear after gluten withdrawal. They are specific for jejunal mucosal atrophy associated with celiac disease. The specificity and sensitivity of EMA and JAB are high. EMA has not been detected in patients with other gastrointestinal diseases and was found in only 1 of 100 blood donors. This donor later was found to have celiac disease!

The clinical application of these antibodies awaits further assessment, but the potential value of serum antibody in raising the suspicion of celiac disease as a screening tool is a goal that may, in fact, be quite achievable. Not only that, but both EMA and JAB can be used to tell whether a child is adhering strictly to his or her diet.

There has been a lot of mystique surrounding celiac disease. The disorder commonly defies diagnosis. Most experts have come to the conclusion that it is much better to use one's common sense when approaching the disorder than to use a highly oriented intellectual sense. To say the latter more simply, follow your celiac plexus rather than your cerebral cortex. I trust my gut reaction over my brain any day of the week.—J.A. Stockman, III, M.D.

Appendicitis in Children: Current Therapeutic Recommendations
Neilson IR, Laberge J-M, Nguyen LT, Moir C, Doody D, Sonnino RE, Youssef S, Guttman FM (The Montreal Children's Hosp; McGill Univ, Montreal)
J Pediatr Surg 25:1113–1116, 1990   19–7

Current controversies in the management of appendicitis in children include skin closure and duration of antibiotic therapy. The results of a prospective protocol followed rigidly in 420 children, aged 1–18 years (mean age, 10.3 years), who underwent emergency appendectomy in a 2-year period were reviewed. The protocol included preoperative triple antibiotic therapy (ampicillin, gentamicin, and clindamycin) that was continued postoperatively for 2 doses in patients with normal or simple acute appendicitis, for at least 3 days for gangrenous appendicitis, and at least 5 days for perforated appendicitis. Antibiotics were also continued if the patient remained febrile or had a white blood cell count greater than 10,000. The operative technique was standardized, saline lavage was performed for diffuse peritonitis, no peritoneal or wound drains were used, and the skin was closed primarily.

Misdiagnosis of appendicitis occurred in 40 (9.5%) patients, including 22 with no other disease to account for the clinical presentation (table). Appendicitis was confirmed in the other 380 patients. The overall infectious complication rate was 1%. There were no infectious complications among the 263 patients with simple acute appendicitis. Among the 117 patients with gangrenous or perforated appendicitis, there were wound infections in 1.7% of patients and intra-abdominal abscesses in 1.7%. Duration of hospital stay was 2.1 days in patients with simple acute appendicitis and 6.9 days in those with complicated appendicitis. In children with appendicitis, a protocol of preoperative triple antibiotics, intraoperative lavage, avoidance of drains, and primary skin closure results in a low incidence of infectious complications and a shorter hospital stay.

Misdiagnosis of Appendicitis in 40 of 420 Patients
Undergoing Appendectomy

No other associated pathology	22
Normal appendix	19
Fecolith	3
Associated pathology	18
Ovarian cyst	4
Salpingitis	5
Enteritis	
Salmonella	1
E coli 0157	1
? Crohn's	1
Pinworms	2
Meckels's diverticulitis	1
Nephroblastoma	1
Polyarteritis nodosa	1
Primary peritonitis	1

(Courtesy of Neilson IR, Laberge J-M, Nguyen LT, et al: *J Pediatr Surg* 25:1113–1116, 1990.)

▶ Dr. John Raffensperger, Professor of Surgery, Northwestern University Medical School, and Surgeon-in-Chief, Children's Memorial Hospital, comments:

▶ The successful treatment of appendicitis in the past 100 years is one of the great, most successful sagas of American medicine and surgery. One hundred years ago appendicitis was a new-found disease, unknown to most physicians. The great Sir William Osler cautioned against an operation but surgeons, such as John B. Murphy of Chicago, lectured endlessly to the profession, describing the symptoms of appendicitis and recommending operation before the appendix perforated. Unfortunately, in many children the diagnosis was delayed. The appendix became perforated, sepsis and shock developed, and the child died. The introduction of intravenous fluids in the 1920s and 1930s further decreased the mortality rate by providing vascular support and nutrition. In the late 1930s sulfa drugs further reduced complications and the mortality rate. By the 1950s the mortality rate from perforated appendicitis with abscess and generalized peritonitis, was reduced to practically zero with the addition of various antibiotic combinations, particularly penicillin and streptomycin.

Despite these antibiotics, however, many children languished in hospitals with residual intra-abdominal abscesses and wound infections. Until 1980, I advocated the use of intra-abdominal drains and packing open the skin wound in these children. At this time I completely agree with Neilson et al. This article describes precisely the method that we use in treating appendicitis at the Children's Memorial Hospital in Chicago.

When the diagnosis is made, the child should be given sufficient fluids and electrolytes to completely restore electrolyte balance and urinary output. During this time a combination of antibiotics, including ampicillin, gentamicin, and clindamycin is given. We then remove the appendix and irrigate the peritoneal cavity, with or without the addition of antibiotics. We then close the entire incision, including the skin. This therapy has essentially eliminated residual intra-abdominal abscesses and has reduced the instance of wound infection, even in children with a perforated appendix, to 1% to 2%.

In appendicitis, as in many other diseases, our current goals of therapy are not just to save the life and prevent complications; we are also concerned about the overall comfort of the patient. Primary closure of the skin improves the cosmetic appearance of the scar and reduces the duration of hospital stay. These same factors also reduce the cost of care. We can truthfully say that with appendicitis, advances in medical technology have allowed a reduction in the cost of care.—J. Raffensperger, M.D.

Polymerase Chain Reaction for Detection of Adenoviruses in Stool Samples

Allard A, Girones R, Juto P, Wadell G (Univ of Umeå, Umeå, Sweden; Univ of Barcelona, Barcelona, Spain)
J Clin Microbiol 28:2659–2667, 1990   19–8

Adenoviruses, especially the enteric types 40 and 41, are believed to be the second major cause of gastroenteritis in young children. Three different polymerase chain reaction (PCR) systems for detecting human adenoviruses were tested.

Several primers were assessed. These included primers specific for the hexon-coding region and enteric adenovirus types 40 and 41. The PCR technique was validated against cell culturing in routine diagnostic procedures and restriction enzyme analysis of viral DNA. The PCR method was used to evaluate 60 diagnostic specimens. Twenty were positive on the basis of cytopathic effects and latex agglutination. Sixteen were identified and typed as adenoviruses by polyacrylamide gel electrophoresis. Polymerase chain reaction was done on all specimens in parallel directly on diluted stool samples and viral DNA was extracted from cells inoculated with the same stool samples. When general hexon primers were used, 51 of the 60 specimens from infected cell cultures were identified by PCR as positive. Only 13 were found positive when PCR was done directly on stool samples. Using selective primers for enteric adenoviruses, 16 cell cultures were shown to exhibit amplification products by PCR. Four were detected in stool samples. Polymerase chain reaction identified none of the specimens when an adenovirus type 40-specific primer pair was used.

Polymerase chain reaction is a fast, sensitive, reliable technique for detecting adenoviruses in diarrheal disease when the amplifications are performed directly on diluted stool-samples. The general primers can be used when fastidious adenovirus infections are suspected.

▶ There is a lengthy discussion of the use of PCR as a diagnostic tool for both viral and bacterial infectious agents in the Infectious Disease and Immunology chapter of this year's YEAR BOOK. If you want to make a diagnosis of adenovirus as a cause of diarrhea in children, you can do it within 4 hours using PCR.

This is the first Gastroenterology chapter in several years of the YEAR BOOK that hasn't had an abstract on *Campylobacter* species (new name *Helicobacter* species). Out of reverence to this fascinating group of bacteria, we will simply ask a question about it and not ignore it in the YEAR BOOK. The question is: Is *Campylobacter jejuni* an airborne infection?

Well, the answer to this question comes in an interesting way. The answer may indeed be yes. Recent outbreaks have been described in which *C. jejuni* infection was associated with bird attacks on milk bottles. There are still parts of the world in which milk is delivered to doorsteps, and individuals have been suspected to have acquired *C. jejuni* infection after birds, presumably infected with the organism, pecked away at the lids of milk bottles.

To establish whether birds such as jackdaws and magpies could act as vectors of milkborne *C. jejuni* infection, Hudson et al. demonstrated *Campylobacter* species in 12 of 123 pecked bottles submitted for laboratory examination between March 18 and July 1, 1990. Furthermore, to confirm that birds may transmit organisms to milk by pecking bottles, these same investigators thought it was important to demonstrate *Campylobacter* species on the birds' beaks. Accordingly, birds were netted and sampled on 4 separate occasions between mid-April and late June of 1990. Thirty-five birds were sampled (a combination of jackdaws, magpies, rooks, and crows), and 63 isolates were obtained from 33 of them. Thirty of these were from the birds's beaks, and 33 of the isolates were from cloacal swabs (no privacy for these birds).

It has been estimated that as few as 500 *C. jejuni* organisms can cause infection, so even minor contamination caused by bacteria washed off beaks may represent a true health hazard (1).—J.A. Stockman, III, M.D.

References

1. Hudson, et al: *Epidemiol Infect,* in press.
2. Lightfoot NF, et al: *Lancet* 337:734, 1991.

Rice-Based Oral Electrolyte Solutions for the Management of Infantile Diarrhea
Pizarro D, Posada G, Sandi L, Moran JR (Hosp Nacional de Niños, San José, Costa Rica; Mead Johnson Research Ctr, Evansville, Ind)
N Engl J Med 324:517–521, 1991   19–9

Treating acute diarrhea in infants with glucose-based solutions results in rehydration but does not decrease the severity of diarrhea. Oral rehydration with rice-based oral electrolyte solutions may both reduce stool output and restore fluid volume. A randomized, double-blind study was done to assess the safety and efficacy of rice-based solutions in the treatment of mild to moderate dehydration in infants with acute diarrhea.

Two rice-based rehydration solutions and a conventional glucose-based solution were tested. Solution A contained rice-syrup solids only; solution B contained rice-syrup solids and casein hydrolysate; and solution C, the glucose-based solution, served as the control. Eighty-six infant boys aged 3–18 months were studied. All were mildly to moderately dehydrated and had been admitted to a children's hospital with acute diarrhea. Fluid intake, fecal and urine output, and absorption and retention of fluid, sodium, and potassium were measured for 48 hours at regular intervals.

Infants given solution A had a significantly lower mean fecal output than infants given solution C during the first 6 hours of treatment. Infants given solution A also had higher fluid absorption during the entire 48 hours of treatment and higher potassium absorption in the first 6 hours, compared with infants given solution C. Solution B had no advantages over solution A.

Rice-based oral electrolyte solutions effectively rehydrate infants with acute diarrhea. In this series they reduce stool output and promoted greater fluid and electrolyte absorption and retention, compared with a glucose-based solution.

▶ Dr. Emanuel Lebenthal, Professor and Chairman, Department of Pediatrics, Hahnemann University School of Medicine, comments:

▶ The main concerns regarding the use of oral rehydration solution (ORS) are its apparent lack of efficacy in reducing diarrheal volume and duration and the lack of acceptability of the ORS by traditional beliefs. These concerns were the impetus for the use of rice-based oral electrolyte solution instead of glucose in ORS.

Rice water, which is the starchy water left after the boiling of rice, has been the traditional treatment for diarrhea in many countries. In the early 1980s, rice water was compared with the standard World Health Organization oral rehydration solution in infants with acute diarrhea. In these studies, there were apparently decreased numbers of stools in infants given rice water. A disadvantage of rice water solutions is their variable carbohydrate and electrolyte compositions, making these solutions a less reliable way to treat dehydration than solutions with a defined composition.

The most important advantage of rice-based solutions over the standard glucose-containing solution may be its effect on stool output and diarrhea duration.

The rice syrup solids (glucose polymers) in the current study included glucose 3.5%, glucose polymers 2–6 units (64.9%), and glucose polymers greater than 7 units (31.6%). The randomized, double-blind study evaluated the safety and efficacy of the rice-based oral electrolyte solution in mild to moderate dehydration caused by acute diarrhea of less than 7 days duration. The rice-based ORS decreased stool output compared with glucose ORS. It has been suggested that the stable, rice-electrolyte, ready-to-use, commercially prepared oral rehydration solution (Ricolyte) is more efficient than the glucose-based solution in promoting fluid and electrolyte absorption during the rehydration phase in infants with acute diarrhea. It is important to emphasize that our laboratory (1) showed that in an animal model short-chain glucose polymers of rice comprising 2–9 units of glucose are hydrolyzed and absorbed in the small intestine faster than isocaloric D glucose.

I believe that a new generation of oral rehydration solutions based on short polymers of glucose will be an important therapeutic modality in acute diarrhea with mild to moderate dehydration.— E. Lebenthal, M.D.

Reference

1. Azad MAK, Lebenthal E: *Pediatr Res* 28:166, 1990.

Azathioprine in the Treatment of Children With Inflammatory Bowel Disease

Verhave M, Winter HS, Grand RJ (Floating Hosp, New England Med Ctr Hosps; Children's Hosp; Tufts Univ; Harvard Med School, Boston)
J Pediatr 117:809–814, 1990   19–10

Inflammatory bowel disease in children and adolescents is often chronic and difficult to control. Encouraged by the beneficial effects of azathioprine and other immunosupressive agents in adult patients with inflammatory bowel disease, 21 patients, aged 3.5–17 years, with inflammatory bowel disease, were treated with azathioprine as an adjunct to their customary regimen. Azathioprine was given initially at a dose of

Response of 21 Patients Treated With Azathioprine

Response	Ulcerative colitis	Crohn disease	Total
Complete	6	6	12
Partial	1	3	4
None	2	3	5

(Courtesy of Verhave M, Winter HS, Grand RJ: *J Pediatr* 117:809–814, 1990.)

.5 mg/kg/day and increased slowly to a dose of 2 mg/kg/day for 10 days. The most common indications for starting azathioprine therapy included relapse during steroid therapy and inability to taper the dosage of steroids. The median follow-up period was 2 years. Response to therapy was evaluated in terms of control of symptoms; weight gain and increased linear growth; improvement of hematocrit, sedimentation rate, and serum level of albumin; and reduction of steroid dose.

Overall, 16 (76%) patients responded to azathioprine therapy. Six of 9 patients with ulcerative colitis and 6 of 12 patients with Crohn's disease had complete responses, and 4 patients had partial response (table). Treatment was unsuccessful in 2 patients with ulcerative colitis and 3 patients with Crohn's disease. The median response time to improvement was 3 months in patients with ulcerative colitis and 4 months in patients with Crohn's disease. Most of the patients who responded to therapy were able to discontinue corticosteroid therapy within 6 months of starting azathioprine treatment, or to reduce their steroid dose. Only minimal side effects to azathioprine were observed. Azathioprine is a valuable adjunctive agent for the treatment of inflammatory bowel disease in children, particularly those with refractory or progressive disease and those with severe steroid side effects. Although short-term side effects are minimal, the long-term effects of this cytotoxic agent remain a concern.

▶ There is an excellent editorial in the same issue of the *Journal of Pediatrics* that this article appeared in. This editorial, by Dr. John Lloyd-Still (1), reviewed all of the data concerning immunosuppressive and other therapies used to treat both Crohn's disease and ulcerative colitis. Although steroids remain the mainstay of the initial management, there are other therapies. For example, metronidazole has been reported to be successful in the treatment of chronic perianal manifestations of Crohn's disease in an uncontrolled series of patients. A Scandinavian trial found that metronidazole was equally effective in comparison with sulfasalazine in the treatment of patients with ileocolitis and colitis (2). Other new therapies include 5-acetylsalicylic acid. This is the active component of sulfasalazine and can be administered topically as well as orally. Studies in the *New England Journal of Medicine* and in *The Lancet* show the value of cyclosporine therapy in the management of both active Crohn's disease and ulcerative colitis in children (3,4). Methotrexate, sodium cromoglycate, sulcralfate, and clonidine are associated with variable, unsubstantiated but potentially promising results. The majority of all these drugs cause significant side effects, including a subsequent risk of malignancy with cyclosporine.

To round out this commentary, a few other things that are new this past year or 2 about inflammatory bowel disease. One fact that appeared recently in the literature was the documentation of a tenfold increase in the familial risk of ulcerative colitis and Crohn's disease, suggesting that both disorders have a genetic cause (5). Another observation was the documentation that children who are younger than 15 years of age and have pancolitis should have an early prophylactic proctocolectomy (6).

Finally, there are now data indicating that regional enteritis (in addition to ulcerative colitis) carries an increased risk of colorectal cancer. Crohn's disease diagnosed before an individual is 30 years of age and involving any part of the colon carries a higher relative risk of malignancy (29.9-fold) than Crohn's disease diagnosed at older ages (less than twofold) (7). It probably will be some time before we learn proper surveillance techniques for the detection of malignancy subsequent to Crohn's disease, but we should begin this type of surveillance soon.—J.A. Stockman, III, M.D.

References

1. Lloyd-Still JD: *J Pediatr* 117:732, 1990.
2. Ursin GB, et al: *Gastroenterology* 83:550, 1982.
3. Brynskov J, et al: *N Engl J Med* 321:845, 1989.
4. Lichtiger S, et al: *Lancet* 336:16, 1990.
5. Orholm M, et al: *N Engl J Med* 324:84, 1991.
6. Ekbom A, et al: *N Engl J Med* 323:1228, 1990.
7. Ekbom A, et al: *Lancet* 326:357, 1990.

Twenty-Five Years' Experience With Hirschsprung's Disease
Foster P, Cowan G, Wrenn EL Jr (Rush-Presbyterian-St Luke's Med Ctr, Chicago; Univ of Tennessee Med School at Memphis; Lebonheur Children's Med Ctr, Memphis)
J Pediatr Surg 25:531–534, 1990   19–11

Congenital megacolon has been cured in thousands of infants and children. Despite recent advances in the treatment of Hirschsprung's disease, however, surgery can result in wound infection, anastomotic leakage, anastomotic strictures, chronic encopresis, and enterocolitis.

Sixty-three patients with biopsy-proved Hirschsprung's disease treated between 1955 and 1980 were reviewed. Fifty-eight had pull-through procedures done by 3 comparably trained pediatric surgeons. All patients were followed up for an average of 8 years from initial diagnosis. Anastomotic strictures occurred most often when the level of aganglionosis was at the sigmoid colon (Fig 19–3). Postoperative encopresis was most likely to occur when the endorectal pull-through procedures were performed before the patient was 10 months old. The incidence of enterocolitis was low with selective use of colostomies or enterostomies done before the pull-through procedure, with a mortality of 0%.

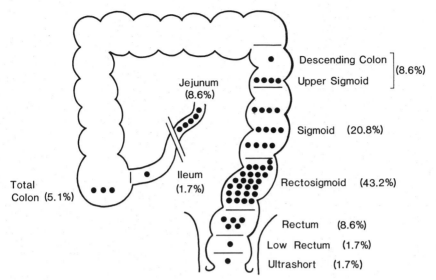

Fig 19–3.—Level of aganglionosis of patients undergoing pull-through procedures. Each *dot* represents 1 patient's most proximal level of aganglionosis. (Courtesy of Foster P, Cowan G, Wrenn EL Jr: *J Pediatr Surg* 25:531–534, 1990.)

When the most proximal level of aganglionosis is the sigmoid colon, clinicians must critically inspect the angulation of mesenteric blood vessels and viability of the splenic flexure pull-through colon segment to prevent ischemia and anastomotic strictures. The endorectal pull-through procedure should be delayed until after the patient is older than 10 months. Babies with Hirschsprung's disease should have a colostomy or enterostomy before a pull-through procedure is performed. Candidates for pull-through without a previous fecal diversion procedure include babies aged 10 months or more who have not had earlier bouts of enterocolitis, who are not low percentile weight, and who do not have signs of severe obstruction.

▶ Dr. Joseph O. Sherman, Professor of Clinical Surgery, Northwestern University Medical School, comments:

▶ Reports on the long-term experience with major surgically correctable birth defects such as the paper by Foster et al. are important to the pediatrician for several reasons. They provide helpful insights into the diagnosis, which is especially important for Hirschsprung's disease because of the diversity of the signs and symptoms these patients can have. An analysis of the postoperative complications and the long-term results helps the pediatrician advise parents about their child's future.

We have reported our results treating 880 patients with the Swenson procedure over a 40-year period (1). The only reliable birth history suggesting the correct diagnosis is the time of passage of the first meconium stool. Only 10% of patients with Hirschsprung's disease will pass meconium within 24 hours of birth. More than 92% of normal babies will pass meconium on the first day of life. Any newborn who has delayed passage of meconium should be watched carefully for other signs and symptoms of Hirschsprung's disease. Another important finding is the presence of an empty rectum on digital examination. This is true for patients with aganglionosis of the rectosigmoid colon or higher. The small number of patients (<10%) with aganglionosis limited to the rectum may have a rectal impaction and concomitant straining. Impaction and straining usually suggest constipation, not Hirschsprung's disease. A barium enema is very helpful in making the diagnosis, but its accuracy is affected by the age of the patient and the length of aganglionic bowel. When given to patients during the first month of life, 24% of barium enemas will be incorrectly reported as normal. The rate of false-negative examinations is reduced to 12% in patients between 1 month and 1 year of age and to 6% in patients more than 1 year of age. False negative examinations are also more common in patients with very short and very long segments of aganglionosis.

One of the most serious postoperative complications is leak of the coloperineal anastomosis. This complication occurs in about 5% of patients and is treated by immediate diversion. One group of patients, those with Down's syndrome, have a much greater incidence of anastomotic leak (13.5%) and should have a diverting ileostomy or colostomy left in place at the time of the pull-through procedure. Another serious complication is enterocolitis. This nonspecific bacterial infection can occur before or after the pull-through procedure and is characterized by fever, vomiting, distension, and an explosive, watery green diarrhea. It can progress rapidly, leading to the patient's death. Nine of our patients (1%) died from this condition after the pull-through procedure. Treatment consists of parenteral antibiotics, rehydration, and vigorous and frequent rectal irrigations with saline solution. Fortunately, most postoperative enterocolitis occurs within the first year after the procedure and is rare later in life.

Our long-term results have been excellent. Almost 40% of our patients have been followed for more than 10 years and more than 90% have normal bowel habits, no soiling, and 1 to 3 bowel movements per day.—J.O. Sherman, M.D.

Reference

1. Sherman JO, et al: *J Pediatr Surg* 24:833, 1989.

The Leadpoint in Intussusception
Ong N-T, Beasley DW (Royal Children's Hosp, Melbourne, Australia)
J Pediatr Surg 25:640–643, 1990   19–12

Childhood intussusception is usually idiopathic. A pathologic lesion at the leadpoint is identified in only a small proportion of patients. Intussusception episodes treated at 1 institution were reviewed retrospectively.

In a 16-year period, 56 patients with a pathologic lesion at the leadpoint of their intussusception were encountered at the Royal Children's Hospital in Melbourne. Meckel's diverticula, small bowel polyps, lym-

Pathologic Lesions at the Leadpoint

	No.
Meckel's diverticulum*	27
Polyps	14
Multiple polyps	3
Peutz-Jegher syndrome†	2
Polyposis coli	1
Ileal carcinoid	2
Malignant	1
Lymphosarcoma	5
Duplication cyst*	4
Postoperative intussusception	4
Aplastic anemia	2

*Early recurrence in 1 patient each.
†Late recurrence once in each patient.
(Courtesy of Ong N-T, Beasley DW: *J Pediatr Surg* 25:640–643, 1990.)

phosarcomas, and duplication cysts were the lesions most frequently seen (table). The only factor distinguishing these patients from those with idiopathic intussusception was the age at which the child was first seen. More than two thirds of those with identifiable lesions were older than 2 years of age when they were first seen. The duration of symptoms was not useful in identifying a pathologic leadpoint. Hydrostatic reduction successfully decreased the leadpoint in 3 of 21 attempts. A policy of initial enema reduction of intussusception was associated with no morbidity or mortality, regardless of patient's age.

In this series, no pathologic lesion could be identified at the leadpoint in more than 90% of children with intussusception. Intussusception caused by a localized pathologic lesion appears to have a different age distribution. The most common specific leadpoint causing intussusception is a Meckel's diverticulum, which can produce intussusception at any age.

Intussusception: Barium or Air?

Palder SB, Ein SH, Stringer DA, Alton D (The Hosp for Sick Children, Toronto)
J Pediatr Surg 26:271–275, 1991   19–13

The use of an air enema instead of a barium enema to reduce intussusception is an attractive idea because it will limit radiation exposure and reduce potential peritoneal contamination should perforation occur. Barium enema use in 100 infants and children with intussusception was compared with use of an air enema in the next 100 consecutive patients.

A barium column was delivered using a Foley catheter placed in the rectum, and the distribution of barium was monitored fluoroscopically. Air reduction was with a pressure-regulated intussusception pump. Air pressure was introduced at 80 mm Hg and increased in increments of 20 mm Hg to 140 mm Hg, if not contraindicated. Air was visualized fluoroscopically within the colon.

Seventy-five percent of episodes were effectively managed by barium enema and 76% by air enema. Ileocolic intussusception was present in about half of the patients who failed to respond in both groups. Perforation occurred during 3 attempted barium reductions and 2 attempted air reductions. Ten patients treated by barium enema and 4 given an air enema had recurrences; two thirds of the recurrences occurred during the same hospitalization.

The air enema is preferable for initial treatment of intussusception in infants and children. It is as effective as the barium enema and reduces radiation exposure.

▶ The preceding 2 abstracts (Abstracts 19–12 and 19–13) must be considered together. There has been significant concern over the use of air insufflation to reduce intussusceptions. This concern has to do with the potential lack of sensitivity in picking up "leadpoint pathology."

The best article that I have read in some time on intussusception was that of Stringer et al. (1) who, since October 1985, have seen 364 children with suspected intussusception. All of these children were examined with air enema. Of these, 152 had intussusception, and reduction was possible in all but 31. These investigators noted that the time for reduction and the time of the x-ray examination were much less than they had seen in their previous experience with barium. Their success rate was slightly higher with air reduction, at almost 80%. Furthermore, the recurrence rate was slightly lower than with barium. Stringer et al. used a selective approach, however. This seems to make sense. They prefer to use a liquid contrast enema in children under the age of 3 months because the differential diagnosis within this age group, particularly in neonates, is much wider than idiopathic intussusception. Between 3 and 6 months of age, pneumatic reduction is used if no obstruction is present on a plain film. In children older than 6 months and younger than 4 years of age, pneumatic reduction is the procedure of choice, if there is no evidence of peritonitis or of severe small bowel obstruction. These investigators rarely used air enemas in children older than 4 years of age because the incidence of significant leadpoint disease is much higher, and they believe that the effectiveness of air enemas in showing subtle abnormalities when a leadpoint is reduced is not clear.

This commentary on pneumatic reduction of intussusception may leave you with an "air of uncertainity" regarding its current status. If your local radiologist doesn't use it, ask him or her to try. They may like it.—J.A. Stockman, III, M.D.

Reference

1. Stringer DA, et al: *Pediatr Radiol* 20:475, 1990.

Use of a Metal Detector to Identify Ingested Metallic Foreign Bodies

Arena L, Baker SR (Bronx Municipal Hosp Ctr, Bronx, NY)
AJR 155:803–804, 1990

19–14

Despite the uneventful course of most ingested foreign bodies, plain radiographs of the chest and abdomen are routinely obtained. Because many foreign bodies contain metal, the accuracy of a metal detector was compared with that of plain radiographs for the detection and localization of ingested metallic objects in 28 patients. All but 1 patient were between the ages of 10 months and 8 years. Except for its smaller size and simpler design, the metal detector used was similar in principle to those used for passenger surveillance in airports.

The metal detector confirmed the presence of a metallic object in 15 patients and the absence of a metallic object in 13 patients. There were no false positive or false negative results. Localization of the objects within the gastrointestinal tract based on anatomical clues agreed with localization determined by radiographs, although differentiation between proximal esophagus and trachea based on anatomical clues may be difficult.

A metal detector reveals the presence of metallic objects by measuring the change in the inductance of a coil placed near a metallic mass. It is sensitive to both magnetic and nonmagnetic material including lead, silver copper, aluminum, and brass. The use of a metal detector is a simple and accurate technique for the localization of an ingested metallic foreign body and avoids routine exposure to ionizing radiations. Because there are no false negative studies, metal detectors can be used as the initial examination in patients with suspected foreign-body ingestion.

▶ Fantastic! The idea that a hand-held metal detector would work to detect metallic foreign-body ingestions has been speculated on for a long time. This report is almost too good to believe, with 100% sensitivity and specificity. The only thing that can throw off the metal detector's accuracy is the metal amalgam in fillings. Small surgical staples will not set off the detector, but coin-sized objects are readily found. Tooth fillings should not be a problem because the intraoral position of a foreign body should be determinable on physical examination by anyone with an IQ greater than 0. The only thing better than a hand-held metal detector (the one used here was a Model 2000, White's Electronics, Inc. Sweet Home operating room instrument) that does not involve radiation would be a super-conducting quantum interference device. The latter instrument, originally designed for the measurement of weak magnetic fields within the human brain, has been successfully adapted by limoniemi et al. (1) for the localization of millimeter-sized magnetic objects within the human body. The use of such an expensive and complex apparatus would be unnecessary for the detection of commonly ingested larger foreign bodies.

So, what do you do the next time somebody comes into your office or into your local emergency room who is suspected of having ingested a coin or other metallic object? You might use a hand-held metal detector, which can examine the entire body in less than 2 minutes. This is a tremendous improvement over plain radiographs and avoids routine exposure to ionizing radiation. Because there was a 0% false negative rate in this one study, this approach can be used as the initial examination in cases of suspected foreign-body ingestions that involve metal. If the patient is asymptomatic, and the metal detector does not find a foreign body, no further evaluation may be necessary. If the clinical suspicion is high, radiographs of the chest and abdomen can be obtained, even in the case of a negative metal-detector examination. If the metal-detector examination is positive, and the ingested object is known to be round or smooth, a second metal-detector examination done in 6 to 7 days would verify whether the object has been evacuated. None of this applies if the swallowed object is sharp or of an unknown shape, in which case a radiograph would be mandatory.

What do you do if you don't have a hand-held metal detector sitting around the office or emergency room? Simple, have the guard at your local airport "frisk" the child. The hand-held devices they use are the ones described in this article.

This is the last commentary in the Gastroenterology chapter, so we close the chapter with a word of advice concerning flatus: "Never break wind in church, otherwise you will wind up sitting in your own phew."—J.A. Stockman, III, M.D.

Reference

1. Iimoniemi J, et al: *IEEE Trans Biomed Eng* 35:561, 1988.

Subject Index

A

Aarskog syndrome, 166
Abscess
  perirectal, in infants and children, 77
Abuse
  sexual, evaluation in anogenital warts, 165
Acne
  fulminans, 131
  vulgaris incidence after infantile acne, 130
Acyclovir
  vs. vidarabine in herpes simplex in
    newborn, 18
Adenopathy
  in oropharyngeal tularemia, CT of, 410
Adenovirus(es)
  enteritis, clinical features, 75
  in stool samples, polymerase chain
    reaction to detect, 473
Adolescence
  anorexia nervosa with bone density
    decrease in girls, 217
  of blacks, sexual activity and problem
    behaviors during, 216
  dieting concerns during, 219
  empyema during, microbiology of, 282
  fetal alcohol syndrome and, 229
  health care expenditure patterns during,
    209
  Marfan syndrome during, psychosocial
    functioning and knowledge, 207
  parenthood and problem behavior, 211
  smoking during pregnancy, 214
  smoking during, risk factors for, 273
  unmarried motherhood during,
    determinants of child rearing vs.
    adoption, 215
  violent death and injury during, 150
  weight concerns during, 219
  xanthoma and inherited
    hyperlipoproteinemia during, 124
Adoption
  vs. child rearing for unmarried
    adolescent mothers, 215
Adrenoleukodystrophy
  X-linked, neurologic and
    neuroradiologic manifestations
    reversed by marrow transplant, 175
Age
  characterization of gallstones, 469
Air
  enema in intussusception, 481
Alcohol
  fetal alcohol syndrome and adolescence,
    229

Allergic
  reactions to milk-contaminated
    "nondairy" products, 113
Allergy
  to insect stings, immunotherapy with
    venom, 122
Alpha$_1$-antitrypsin
  aerosol, in cystic fibrosis, 279
Alpha-fetoprotein
  elevated maternal, absence of need for
    amniocentesis in, 21
Ammoniated
  mercury ointment, as outdated, 130
Amniocentesis
  absence of need in elevated maternal
    alpha-fetoprotein with normal
    ultrasound, 21
Amniotic fluid
  glucose concentration detecting
    intraamniotic infection in preterm
    labor, 17
Amoxicillin
  in otitis media, 403
Anemia
  aplastic, antilymphocyte globulin,
    methylprednisolone and
    cyclosporine in, 337
  of burns in Jehovah's Witness,
    recombinant human erythropoietin
    for, 323
  in HIV infection in children, as
    prognostic factor, 339
  of prematurity, erythropoietin in,
    recombinant human, 322
  sickle cell (see Sickle cell anemia)
Anesthesia
  general vs. local for tonsillectomy, 405
Angioplasty
  balloon, of coarctation in neonates and
    infants, 308
Anogenital
  warts, evaluation for sexual abuse, 165
Anomalies
  brain, congenital, and hypoplastic left
    heart syndrome, 314
Anorexia nervosa
  with bone density decrease in girls
    during adolescence, 217
Antibody(ies)
  antineutrophil cytoplasmic, ocular
    manifestations of, 385
  hepatitis C virus, in hemophilia, 346
Antihistamine
  -decongestant for common cold, 241
Antilymphocyte
  globulin in aplastic anemia, 337

Author Index